36.95

Ron Parton

Background for joint.

1. Does it offer the mass an adequate choice of policy and leaders.

2. Does it reflect accurately the desires of the people and the members of the party.

3. Do the int. organ. of the party sufficiently democratic to provide a channel for actual political participation for the rank & file.

4. Does it assist at arriving at a peaceful settlement or does it exacerbate the differences in a given community.

5. Is the party system an affective instrument for carrying out the judgement of the voters once they have made a choice.

McGraw-Hill Series in Political Science
JOSEPH P. HARRIS, *Consulting Editor*

AMERICAN POLITICS AND THE PARTY SYSTEM

McGRAW-HILL SERIES IN POLITICAL SCIENCE

Joseph P. Harris, CONSULTING EDITOR

✦ ✦ ✦

ADRIAN · Governing Urban America: Structure, Politics, and Administration

BONE · American Politics and the Party System

CHASE · The United Nations in Action

FERGUSON AND McHENRY · The American Federal Government

FERGUSON AND McHENRY · The American System of Government

FERGUSON AND McHENRY · Elements of American Government

FIELD · Governments in Modern Society

FRANK · Cases on the Constitution

GOSNELL, LANCASTER, AND RANKIN · Fundamentals of American National Government

GROSS · The Legislative Struggle

HAAS AND WHITING · Dynamics of International Relations

HARTMANN · Basic Documents of International Relations

HARTMANN · Readings in International Relations

HOLLOWAY · State and Local Government in the United States

LEONARD · Elements of American Foreign Policy

LEONARD · International Organization

MANGONE · A Short History of International Organization

MILLETT · Management in the Public Service

NEUMANN · European and Comparative Government

PIERSON AND GIL · Governments of Latin America

REED · Municipal Management

RIEMER · Problems of American Government

ROCHE AND STEDMAN · The Dynamics of Democratic Government

RODEE, ANDERSON, AND CHRISTOL · Introduction to Political Science

STRAUSZ-HUPÉ AND POSSONY · International Relations

SVARLIEN · An Introduction to the Law of Nations

TURNER · Politics in the United States: Readings in Political Parties and Pressure Groups

VANDENBOSCH AND HOGAN · The United Nations: Background, Organization, Functions, Activities

WALDO · Ideas and Issues in Public Administration: A Book of Readings

WILSON · The American Political Mind

WILSON · Police Administration

AMERICAN POLITICS AND THE PARTY SYSTEM

Hugh A. Bone

PROFESSOR OF AMERICAN GOVERNMENT AND POLITICS
UNIVERSITY OF WASHINGTON

SECOND EDITION

McGRAW-HILL BOOK COMPANY, INC.

New York   Toronto   London

1955

AMERICAN POLITICS AND THE PARTY SYSTEM

Copyright © 1955 by the McGraw-Hill Book Company, Inc.

Library of Congress Catalog Card Number 54–12248

III

Preface

Since the appearance of the first edition of this book, American party and pressure politics have undergone considerable change. Social scientists have continued their researches and have made available new data in many aspects of political behavior. These developments have provided new insights and illustrative data and have made necessary changes in emphasis and in certain analyses and interpretations.

This new edition notes the return, after 20 years, of a Republican administration and the character of that party under Eisenhower. Recent years have seen renewed interest in "ethics in government" and this subject is included as a conclusion to the volume. Political scientists are debating anew party responsibility in Congress, provoked in part by the appearance of the Report of the Committee on Political Parties of the American Political Science Association. Two chapters have been added to take cognizance of this debate and of the character and effectiveness of parties in the government.

The great increase in public relations activities and changes in the distribution of power called for almost a complete rewriting of the section on pressure politics. A new chapter has also been added to this section. More attention is given to the professions as a political interest group. The influences of group interests on the administrative branch and the growth of administrative pluralism receive extended treatment. More attention is paid than in the previous edition to the subjects of sectionalism, suburbanism, urbanism, radio and television, agrarianism, unofficial party organizations, state and regional parties, and the nature and pattern of American politics.

Fresh and current data have been utilized throughout the volume; more than half of the chapters have been completely revised. To keep the volume to a manageable size the materials on party history previous to 1900 are reduced, as is the treatment of some of the older suffrage problems. Tables on election statistics since 1896 are retained, and the selected references at the end of the chapters are brought up to date.

The author acknowledges his great debt to teachers who have made helpful suggestions. To the numerous party leaders and public office-holders with whom he has been privileged to associate likewise go sincere thanks for their candor and their usually refreshing pragmatism. Errors of fact, of course, are the author's responsibility, as are his interpretations and opinions.

HUGH A. BONE

Contents

PART ONE

Basic Factors in American Politics

CHAPTER 1

Politics: The Citizen's Business

Vox Populi may be Vox Dei, but very little attention shows that there has ever been any agreement as to what Vox means or as to what Populous means.

SIR HENRY MAINE

The so-called typical "man in the street," the "John Q. Public," the "John Doe"—be he Yankee, Southerner, or Westerner—seldom theorizes about democracy. When the meaning of "democracy" is asked, the answer will vary from person to person. Yet all will commonly associate democracy with freedom to think, act, and speak without interference from government. Indeed, freedom of one kind or another will probably be the starting point of a discussion of the term. It may then proceed to the general rights accorded persons accused of crime, such as jury trial and freedom from cruel and unusual punishment. Although most citizens are familiar with occasions where money and power have had undue influence in the courts of law and where "third degree" methods have been employed, they nevertheless rightly believe that the American system of justice is superior to the systems found in totalitarian nations.

The American citizen believes his system of government, in spite of its acknowledged shortcomings, affords a greater equality of opportunity than does that of other countries. The American continent was peopled by those who felt it was the "land of opportunity," socially, politically, and economically. James Truslow Adams [1] views "the epic of America" as

. . . the American dream, that dream of a land in which life should be better and richer and fuller for every man, with opportunity for each according to his ability or achievement. It is a difficult dream for the European upper classes to interpret adequately, and too many of ourselves have grown weary and mistrustful of it. It is not a dream of motor cars and high wages merely, but a dream of a social order in which each man and each woman shall be able to attain the fullest stature of which they are innately capable, and be recognized by others for what they are, regardless of the fortuitous circumstances of birth or position.

American democracy has emphasized the importance and dignity of the individual; the state exists to serve the individual. Totalitarianism has

[1] *The Epic of America* (1932), p. 404. By permission of Little, Brown & Company and Atlantic Monthly Press.

3

subordinated the importance of the individual; the individual achieves greatness only in so far as he serves the state.

Before the discussion of democracy with "John Doe" proceeds very far, a comment on "public opinion" usually is forthcoming. In one way or another he sees American government as resting upon "public opinion," the "consent of the governed," the "general will," in contrast to those governments wherein decisions are made by the ruling oligarchy and enforced upon the people all too often without their approval. The man in the street is little interested in definitions of public opinion but somehow regards it as a force that makes itself felt to protect his freedom and his opportunities. He is not too well informed on how this public opinion works, but he has a "hunch" it works remarkable things.

Democracy in the United States stands for many different things. Politically, however, democracy implies equality of opportunity, free and periodic elections, and the participation of all in the control of government. This expression is most effective, however, when persons of similar interests or beliefs have banded together in private-interest groups or political parties. An analysis of the more specialized objectives and methods of such groups and parties comprises the major portion of this volume. Before turning to these subjects, we should give some attention to the meaning of public opinion and to some of the basic factors in American politics.

WHAT IS PUBLIC OPINION?

Although the major sanctions and purposes of public opinion are easy to describe, a universally acceptable definition of the term has yet to be made. The nature of public opinion has provided the subject matter for many highly provocative discourses. But, as Professor Childs notes, "the multiplicity of definitions of public opinion is really due to the effort of students to restrict the meaning of the term to some aspect of public opinion in which they are especially interested." [2]

Until comparatively recently public opinion simply meant the opinion of the people living together in a community. This community might be Hometown, Kalamazoo, Philadelphia, Minnesota, or an even larger area. Since the turn of the present century social scientists have attempted to evolve a "scientific" definition and have drafted concepts of the term which are unnecessarily complicated and technical. For most citizens more heat than light on the subject has been engendered by this search for elongated definitions. Though the student of politics is primarily interested in the dynamics rather than in definitions of public opinion, it is useful to observe a few of the definitions in order to indicate wherein the

[2] Harwood L. Childs, *An Introduction to Public Opinion* (New York: John Wiley & Sons, Inc., 1941), p. 45.

differences occur and to raise questions about the meaning of the term.

"Public" and "Opinion." As A. Lawrence Lowell once pointed out, each of the two words making up the expression "public opinion" is significant and requires that each be examined by itself. "To fulfill the requirement," he notes, "an opinion must be public, and it must be really an opinion." [3] For an opinion to be public, Lowell believes, it is not enough for it to be majority opinion, "but the opinion must be such that while the minority may not share it, they feel bound by conviction, not by fear, to accept it. . . ." [4] This definition would rule out as public opinion those opinions which are shared because of fear or superior force; by this analysis many so-called "opinions" which the ruling class has forced on its subjects in numerous countries are not properly public opinion.

Major disagreements continue over the meaning of the word "public." One social psychologist prefers the use of "group opinion" rather than "public opinion" because "the word public often implies some mystical entity which scarcely exists in reality. There are rather *publics* revolving around objects of interest than any single entity which may be called *the public*." [5] That no single all-inclusive public but a multiplicity of publics exists seems obvious. When conflict arises as to which public is intended, it may be resolved by so designating. Thus the Roanoke public may be said to be favorable to municipal ownership of electrical utilities, the Virginia public favorable to poll taxes, and the United States public opposed to political union with Great Britain, and so on.

Process of Opinion. Another area of discussion concerns the process by which one arrives at an opinion. One group of writers sees public opinion as "the social judgment reached upon a question of general or civic import after conscious, rational public discussion." [6] According to this point of view popular "sentiments," "impressions," and "judgments" are to be distinguished from public opinions. Lowell and others, however, recognize that opinions may be only part rational but nonetheless real opinions, such as religious faiths or secular convictions consciously adopted from someone who is better informed. Careful reasoning does not invariably accompany many fundamental beliefs, such as those of jury trial and free elections, but one cannot say that these convictions are not opinions.

[3] *Public Opinion and Popular Government* (New York: Longmans, Green & Co., Inc., 1913), p. 4.

[4] *Ibid.,* p. 15.

[5] Kimball Young, *Source Book for Social Psychology* (New York: F. S. Crofts & Co., 1927), pp. 722–723.

[6] On this point see the introduction by Clyde L. King in W. Brooke Graves, *Readings in Public Opinion* (New York: Appleton-Century-Crofts, Inc., 1928), pp. 23–28.

Many of these codes of beliefs, however, do not resolve current political issues that call for analysis and personal judgments. The regulation of unions, tariff policies, and the extension of unemployment insurance, for example, cannot be settled by reference to a catechism. For this reason most writers during the past generation have recognized that opinion worthy of the name involves some process of reasoning. Much of this thought may be based on inheritance, feeling, emotion, and inadequate facts, but it is nevertheless partly based upon reflection. As Lowell expresses it, "real public opinion on any subject, not involving a simple question of harmony or contradiction with settled convictions," requires that "the bulk of the people must be in a position to determine of their own knowledge, or by weighing evidence, a substantial part of the facts required for a rational decision." [7]

James Bryce in *Modern Democracies* [8] saw public opinion as

. . . commonly used to denote the aggregate of the views men hold regarding matters that affect or interest the community. Thus understood, it is a congeries of all sorts of discrepant notions, beliefs, fancies, prejudices, aspirations. It is confused, incoherent, amorphous, varying from day to day and week to week. But in the midst of this diversity and confusion every question as it rises into importance is subjected to a process of consolidation and clarification until there emerge and take definite shape certain views, or sets of interconnected views, each held and advocated in common by bodies of citizens. It is to the power exerted by any such view or set of views, when held by an apparent majority of citizens, that we refer when we talk of Public Opinion as approving or disapproving a certain doctrine or proposal, and thereby becoming a guiding or ruling power. . . . Some currents develop more strength than others, because they have behind them larger numbers or more intensity of conviction; and when one is evidently the strongest, it begins to be called Public Opinion *par excellence,* being taken to embody the views supposed to be held by the bulk of the people.

Walter Lippmann has added to this potpourri of concepts the idea of "pictures inside our heads." He wrote: [9]

Those features of the world outside which have to do with the behavior of other human beings, insofar as that behavior crosses ours, is dependent upon us, or is interesting to us, we call roughly public affairs. The picture inside the heads of these human beings, the pictures of themselves, of others, of their needs, purposes, and relationships, are their public opinions. Those pictures which are acted upon by groups of people, or by individuals acting in the name of groups, are Public Opinion with capital letters.

[7] *Op. cit.,* p. 24.

[8] *Modern Democracies*, Vol. I, pp. 153–156. Copyright, 1921, by The Macmillan Company. By permission of The Macmillan Company, publishers.

[9] *Public Opinion*, p. 29. Copyright, 1922, by Walter Lippmann. By permission of The Macmillan Company, publishers.

Further definitions of the terminology could be mentioned but would add little to our discussion. In summary, opinion implies the choice of two or more conflicting views. An opinion or idea often begins as a confused and vague thought, impression, or idea. Gradually it takes shape, both from rational consideration and, perhaps too often, from irrational considerations. Finally, as Bryce says, there is a "consolidation and clarification" with a fairly definite view emerging, which is held by an "effective" but not necessarily numerical majority of citizens; then private opinion has emerged into a public opinion.

Not Necessarily Majority Opinion. The term "public opinion" is bandied about uncritically in public usage. When legislators are deluged with communications on a specific proposition, they often regard the sentiment expressed as "public opinion" and majority opinion at that. In reality, opinions of this type are the opinions of the most vociferous and articulate group or groups. Indeed, on relatively few public issues are there majority opinions in the numerical sense of the term. The definition of public opinion as the opinion of the majority of the electorate is unrealistic, for the majority have given no consideration to many issues. Real public opinion in a democracy must have some rational base and come to be recognized as the most dominant expression of an opinion. Other groups holding dissimilar views acknowledge and acquiesce in the viewpoint of the most effective opinion but at the same time are free to use methods of peaceful persuasion to change it.

Opinions held by the public are not invariably correct and are always subject to change. It is important for the student of politics to understand the nature of public opinion, how it is formed and how it expresses itself. This will include an understanding of the various influences of public opinion as well as its limitations. Finally, a study of the role of opinion will show the dangers of following public opinion on many subjects about which there can necessarily be no informed opinion. The soundness of what may currently be regarded as public opinion on a public issue must always be questioned. Even if the voice of the people is not the voice of God it is a basic and indispensable fact that it controls and changes the course of public policy in a democracy.

POLITICS

Nature of Politics. The person who reflects on the role and significance of public opinion in his political life recognizes the importance of "politics." Politics appears as vital to his political life as public opinion and, like public opinion, means different things to different people. To some, politics is a means of attaining personal or collective goals through social interaction and implies methods and maneuvering, perhaps open and aboveboard or perhaps undercover and in the "smoke-filled room." Harold Lasswell wrote that politics is "the science of who gets what, when, and how" and that the study of politics is the "study of influence and influential." D. W. Brogan sees politics as "the study of the means whereby liberty and authority may be best combined, whereby the dignity of the free man is made compatible with the highest and richest forms of cooperation." [10] From these definitions, politics would not be limited exclusively to the governmental relationships of man but would embrace activities within one's sorority, club, league, trade-union, or other group.

For purposes of this volume our major concern is to view the relationship between the governors and the governed. In this context politics is a struggle for power, the attempt to influence the course of public policy and public decision. It means, as Max Weber has said, "striving to share power or striving to influence the distribution of power, either among states or among groups within a state." [11] Some people want power and influence in order to bring about reform and changes in a governmental program. Others seek power and influence to prevent innovation and to bring about stability or a freezing of the *status quo*. Power is sought by some individuals for its own sake; others may wish to use power to enhance their prestige or economic well-being; still others may be motivated by an overriding desire to promote the good of a special group or of the general will and general welfare. To quote Weber again, "He who is active in politics strives for power either as a means in serving other aims, ideal or egoistic, or as 'power for power's sake,' that is, in order to enjoy the prestige feeling that power gives." [12] Our study of politics, then, is a study of political behavior, political techniques, and relationships within those groups in our society seeking governmental power and influence. From an individual's point of view it concerns an analysis of the methods by which one "throws his political weight around" or why and how he exerts political influence. One of the advantages of a representative democracy is that it affords the citizen many channels or avenues in which to engage in politics—indeed, politics becomes every citizen's business.

Politics and the Ballot. To the voter is accorded the obligation of selecting the members of his national, state, and local lawmaking bodies, the President, his governor, and certain other state administrators. The public officials set the general tone and administration of public policy and exercise highly important political power in their respective jurisdictions.

If the voter has carefully studied the merits of these Federal and state

[10] *The Study of Politics* (New York: Cambridge University Press, 1946), p. 7.
[11] "Politics as a Vocation," in H. H. Gerth and C. W. Mills (eds.), *From Max Weber: Essays in Sociology* (New York: Oxford University Press, 1946), p. 78.
[12] *Ibid.*

candidates and recorded an intelligent judgment, it might be assumed that he has done all that could be expected of him. But his job has scarcely begun. Most voters are then asked to render their choices for a bewildering array of additional county and municipal officers, ranging from county treasurer to the school superintendent. As if these were not enough, the names of candidates for the state and local judiciary are also likely to be on the ballot. The outcome of an election is likely to influence—often profoundly—the distribution of power within the community. For this reason suffrage is an important element in the political arena and it is a wise voter who can anticipate the changes in the power relationship which an election will bring.

In a quarter of the states of the Union the voters are given the authority to "recall" or remove certain public officials before the end of their terms. It is comparatively rare for an officer to be recalled, but potentially the recall may influence the conduct of public men.

Again, if John Doe judiciously performs his task of choosing and removing his rulers, he might be acquitted with honor. But his trial is not yet over. In every state except Delaware state constitutional amendments are submitted to him for ratification and from time to time he may be asked to express his will on the adoption of a revised constitution. In a number of states the voter has the power of "direct legislation" by initiating statutes or by requiring bills passed by the state legislature, city, or county chambers to be referred to a popular vote before becoming law. Voting or shifts of the tax burden, legislative reapportionment, welfare programs, school and highway bonds, new charters, and annexation are but a few of the many typical proposals which may have quite as much influence on shifts of power and influence within the community as an election. Walker's comment is too often overlooked that "interest groups which cannot secure the adoption of their measures through the representative legislative body have made excessive use of direct legislation to secure their ends." [13]

Party Politics. Sometimes the alpha and omega of political activity and power struggles appear to be largely carried on by political parties. The often amorphous and inchoate group which we call a party selects candidates for public office and tries to get them elected. Out of the welter of individual ideas and interests the party formulates some general principles and policies which it hopes will be honored by the persons it nominates and helps to elect. The winning party attempts to maintain public support for its so-called program while the losers endeavor to offer an opposition and to provide an avenue to expression for the discontented.

[13] *The Legislative Process* (New York: The Ronald Press Company, 1948), p. 457.

It is not easy to find a universally acceptable definition of an American political party. Viewed pragmatically, whenever individuals band together for the purpose of nominating and electing persons in order to gain control of the government, the association may be called a "political party." The party may lack cohesion and rarely if ever meet as a group, but its members, regardless of their many differences on public issues, ordinarily loyally support the candidates of the party. Indeed, a party is composed of many diverse groups. There is a party-in-the-government which is composed of public officials who have a party attachment. Sometimes a political party is little more than its professional hangers-on who operate the so-called machine and party headquarters. There are millions of persons who are fairly active Republicans and Democrats who attend some party meetings, hold minor offices, make financial contributions, attempt to win converts, or otherwise regard themselves as party members. This is an amorphous group but nonetheless a real one.[14] Whatever one accepts as a satisfactory definition of parties, politics and parties go together. The organization, functions, behavior, and problems of political parties constitute the largest single section of this book. Parties, however, are not the only political groupings in the political arena; various social and economic interests have organized for purposes of extending their influence.

Interest-group Politics. The large occupational, professional, and citizens associations are growing in importance as institutions for molding and expressing public opinion and millions of persons find them one of their best opportunities for political self-expression. A major distinction between political parties and pressure groups is that the latter do not ordinarily nominate candidates and are more likely to be concerned with the specific policies affecting their group. Membership in the interest group is more clearly defined and the program of the group is narrower. In other words, parties encompass the interests of pressure groups but have had to accommodate these interests and certain other larger party interests as well. Interest groups try to attain status and favor with all branches of the government and usually at all levels of the government.

Senator James A. Reed of Missouri once said, "A lobbyist is anyone who opposes legislation I want. A patriot is anyone who supports me." "Lobbying," like so many other terms, is defined to fit the exigencies of the user. Lobbying consists of the activities and attempts of individuals and groups to influence the minds of legislative and executive officials (and sometimes the courts) in regard to public issues, problems, and policies. Generally it is a form of channelizing group interest for or against

[14] Ralph M. Goldman has used the descriptive phrase "the-party-in-the-electorate" to indicate a type of party life and activity; see *Party Chairmen and Party Faction, 1789–1900* (Ph.D. dissertation, University of Chicago, 1951), Chap. 17.

a public policy. Pressure groups and lobbying are not *ipso facto* sinister forces nor is the interest of a pressure group invariably the antithesis of the interest of the public. Public officials are more and more looking to these interests for guidance in the formulation of policy. Much of our national and local policy is evolved by the sifting and modifications of these group opinions and demands. Part II of this volume deals with political-interest groups and lobbying.

THE PATTERN OF AMERICAN POLITICS

The proliferation of political organization and activity in the United States presents a confusing picture to the person who would understand its pattern of politics. Perhaps it is no exaggeration to say that the pattern of American politics is an absence of a pattern. Variations are the rule rather than the exception. One sees great concentrations of economic power, yet in many respects the real locus of power in our national political parties, great trade-union federations, farm associations, and to some extent business organizations rests in the "locals" in the states and counties. "Decentralization," "atomization," "fragmentation," and similar words are often used to describe party organization and the formulation of public policy.

Decentralization and the seeming lack of pattern and often of rules are attributed to many factors. For one thing, it is almost impossible to describe the infinite variety and number of interests and organizations brought about by the factors of the home, race, occupation, sex, religion, ethnic background, and geography. James Madison was one of the first Americans to realize the importance of "interests," and Alexis de Tocqueville a half century later regarded the complex organization of interests as one of the most important characteristics of American life. The growth of a vast network of national, state, and local associations has continued with little interruption since the beginning of the nation. The melting-pot character of the population and great variations of climate and natural resources have encouraged the growth of diverse groups.

The American constitutional system has likewise provided the base for a diverse associational life. Consider, for example, the influence of federalism and separation of powers. People possess many values which are realized through government. Some of these aspirations must be obtained at the Federal level, some from the states, some from the cities and counties, or perhaps from a local educational, sanitary, or library district. Hence, some interests are best met by local organization; others require a state or national hierarchy. Some interests can be fulfilled by administrative action, others from the courts, and still others require statutory action. A few demands may call for action on the part of all these governmental establishments. In the struggle for influence some groups will try to exert pressure mainly on nonpartisan boards at the state level or on the independent regulatory commissions of the national government.

Bicameralism, the great maze of boards, commissions, quasi-judicial agencies, and so on both complicate and facilitate those seeking assistance and power. For those wishing a legislative remedy there are two houses to convince (except for Nebraska and local governments) and the support of the executive. Many feel frustrated and complain of being given a "runaround" in trying to accomplish their aims. On the other hand, the citizen or group wishing to block a policy finds many channels of access to the government for this purpose. Indeed, the versatility and capacity of the government in meeting demands of citizens, both organized and unorganized, is remarkable. For the citizen the avenues of politics are many and varied.

As E. E. Schattschneider has pointed out, there is a discernible large pattern of politics at the national level,[15] which he calls "a triangular tug of war" between the (1) great pressure groups, (2) local political party leaders and bosses, and (3) President and presidential parties. All attempt to win influence in Congress for their objectives. The presidency itself is, of course, a focal point of politics at the national level, with local party leaders and interest groups trying to curry the favor of and winning support from the Chief Executive.

On the state level the pattern of politics does not necessarily revolve around the comparable three sets of interest groups. In many cases the governor lacks the power and authority of the President and in one-party states the local party leaders have relatively little influence or prestige. Pressure groups usually exert great power and in some states one or two large industries or economic groups dominate the political life. Within a city or local community the distribution of power is often a very fluid matter and defies satisfactory evaluation if not description.

Another important characteristic or part of the organizational pattern of politics is factionalism. Many large associations are able to obtain cohesion and unity on relatively few matters. To understand the factions of an organization is to understand much of its internal and often external politics. Our political parties and large interest groups are frequently composed of a "left wing," "right wing," and "center." Republicans have what has sometimes been called an "Eastern internationalist" wing and a "Middle Western isolationist or nationalist" bloc. Then there are personal factions which group themselves around some leader to try to capture control of the party machine, the "local," or other organization. It is a rare political organization which does not go through the ordeal of sharp factional quarrels.

[15] *Party Government* (New York: Rinehart & Company, Inc., 1942), especially Chap. 9.

For years the national and local governments have been spending from $75 to $100 billion on public activities. These vary from education to foreign aid, from paving sidewalks to maintaining a huge military establishment. There have been taxes and a shifting of tax burdens and public benefits among the citizenry. New public programs are constantly being proposed and discussed at every government level. All these are matters of politics and of real concern to every citizen. Fortunately for the citizen, if he only realizes it, he has a multiplicity of opportunities for political self-expression and innumerable channels for engaging in politics. The organizational and procedural problems and the implications of our organized political life constitute the substance of this volume. Certain underlying themes are bound to recur and to permeate the pages to follow. One of these is that the American system of politics is full of expedients, opportunism, and variations. Another is the great fact of decentralization and factionalism, especially among the parties, and lack of highly disciplined and cohesive political organization. Public policy comes from fragmented sources and the citizen can make himself heard in the deliberation over its development.

DEMOCRACY AND PUBLIC OPINION

Public opinions influence government throughout the year, not merely on election day. The outcome of elections is determined by the forces of public opinion building up on many issues. These issues are seldom sharply focused in the campaign, and because of the multiplicity of issues and personalities, elections constitute only a rough means of expressing public opinion on any particular issue. Elections are the final sanction on who shall rule and in some cases on policy expressed in a referendum proposition, but in many instances it is impossible to make any definite interpretation of the public will in an election with respect to issues. It becomes necessary, therefore, to study the growth and molding of public opinion and its influence upon government between elections. Lobbying and interest-group politics and political parties offer avenues for the expression of opinions. But it is public discussion which brings about public opinion, and discussion, written and oral, is at the heart of politics in a free society.

Public Discussion. Public opinion is largely dependent upon and expresses itself through freedom of speech, press, and assembly. That discussion and talk about public affairs are basic to the democratic way of life is axiomatic. People are expected to keep informed on the issues of the day. As James Madison once wrote, "A free, virtuous, and enlightened nation must know well the great causes and principles upon which its happiness depends."

Public discussion may assume organized or unorganized forms. Among the former is the debate which enables the listener to hear two or more sides of a question presented in or organized in an argumentative way. Many of the affirmative propositions of high-school and intercollegiate debate questions have dealt with some of the nation's foremost problems. Somewhat less formal debate and discussion is found in the large number of radio forums.

Less formal, of course, is discussion on the street corner, in the lodge, in the subway, and over the "cracker barrel." Although spontaneous and often highly prejudiced, these interchanges of ideas probably play a larger part in the molding of public opinion than objective, organized presentation of issues. Letters to the editors of newspapers and *vox populi* radio programs also offer an opportunity for criticizing the conduct of government and pointing out the way to betterment.

However desirable, public discussion is not always accurate and fair in presenting what is represented as the facts, nor always limited to the presentation of constructive suggestions. Indeed, much comment is destructive in character, an unwarranted criticism of a proposed action or existing policy without at the same time advocating a better one. Such criticism may serve the useful purpose of keeping bad things from being done and an unhappy situation from growing worse. But destructive criticism is limited in usefulness because it often fails to take notice of all the facts and may be charged with emotion and hate. Constructive criticism directed toward a better solution of a problem or more efficient administration of a public function is a healthier type of discussion. Regardless of whether criticism is fundamentally destructive or constructive, the more facts at the disposal of the listener or speaker, the more enlightened is likely to be the opinion.

Public opinion implies not only differences as to public laws and activities but also freedom to criticize those who conduct the government. Personal criticism sometimes takes the form of heated and vitriolic vituperation, which does not serve a worthwhile purpose. Wisely used, criticism directed at the performance of official duties is extremely useful. American history has seen a few gag laws and sedition acts to forbid publications and speeches designed to bring into disrepute the constituted agents of government. One of the most recent illustrations of a law of this type was passed in Minnesota in 1925. This statute provided for the abatement, as a public nuisance, of a "malicious, scandalous, and defamatory newspaper or magazine." After enactment of this law, a Minneapolis publisher wrote articles accusing a chief of police of gross neglect of duty, of illicit relations with gangsters, and of graft. The mayor was accused of inefficiency and dereliction. Other officials came in for similar criticism. The county attorney forbade the further publication of this "malicious, scandalous, and defamatory newspaper." The case was finally appealed to the United States Supreme Court, where a majority held the Minnesota law to be unconstitutional. The case is notable for our purposes because it stresses the importance of leaving the press free to criticize public officials. The point is well taken that a more serious evil would result from suppression of criticism. A few sentences deserve citation here: [16]

The fact that for approximately one hundred and fifty years there has been almost an entire absence of attempts to impose previous restraints upon publications relating to the malfeasance of public officers is significant of the deep seated conviction that such restraints would violate Constitutional right. Public officers, whose character and conduct remain open to debate and free discussion in the press, find their remedies for false accusations in actions under libel laws providing for redress and punishment, and not in proceedings to restrain the publication of newspapers and periodicals. . . .

While reckless assaults upon public men, and efforts to bring obloquy upon those who are endeavoring faithfully to discharge official duties, exert a baleful influence and deserve the severest condemnation in the public opinion, it cannot be said that this abuse is greater, and it is believed to be less than that which characterized the period in which our institutions took shape. Meanwhile, the administration of government has become more complex, the opportunities for malfeasance and corruption have multiplied, crime has grown to most serious proportions, and the danger of its protection by unfaithful officials and of the impairment of the fundamental security of life and property by criminal alliances and official neglect, emphasizes the primary need of a vigilant and courageous press, especially in great cities. The fact that the liberty of the press may be used by miscreant purveyors of scandal does not make any the less necessary the immunity of the press from previous restraint in dealing with official misconduct. . . .

Charges of reprehensible conduct, and in particular of official malfeasance, unquestionably create a public scandal, but the theory of the constitutional guaranty is that even a more serious public evil would be caused by authority to prevent publication. . . .

Limitations on Freedom of Expression. In time of war public discussion is subject to some censorship and restriction, especially where matters printed and discussed involve information, military and otherwise, vital to the national security. Although the record in the United States was unenviable in World War I, a generally admirable climate of free expression prevailed during World War II. The number of interest groups actually multiplied, congressional investigations of the war effort proceeded, and radio commentators were essentially unfettered in their criticism of the administration's foreign and domestic policies. While some other democratic nations declared a moratorium on elections, in the United States political campaigns proceeded as usual. Some of our

[16] *Near v. Minnesota*, 283 U.S. 697.

best studies of public opinion and propaganda have resulted from war-time experience.

But what of the limitations placed on freedom of speech, press, and assembly in peacetime? The political climate and degree of tension and feeling of security in the community have an important bearing on the amount of latitude and tolerance of public discussion of unpopular views in time of peace. The folkways and mores of a community often place obstacles in the way of free speech even when there is no war in progress. Left-wing candidates for public office frequently are unable to rent rooms for meetings and self-styled vigilantes have broken up gatherings of un-popular groups by strong-arm methods. The so-called "isolationists," which included many prominent people before the bombing of Pearl Harbor, were often able to hold a public meeting only under extraordinary difficulties. After World War II those holding socialist views and advocates of world federalism ran into difficulties in some communities where certain groups were opposed to any public discussion of such ideas. It might be noted that after every war the nation has gone through some degree of witch-hunting.

After 1945, the zeal with which several congressional and state legis-lative committees attacked alleged Communist sympathizers led to some stifling and placing of restraints on freedom of expression by those advo-cating social, economic, and political reforms. President Truman issued a loyalty order in 1947 for the purpose of weeding out persons in the Federal service who belonged to Communist, fascist, or subversive "front" organizations. This led to a large-scale investigation of the loyalty of Federal employees, and a relatively small number were discharged after hearings. Some congressmen were dissatisfied with the work of the Loyalty Board and took over the function of trying to find disloyal employees. As a result of these activities the nation suddenly became "loyalty con-scious" and some groups carried heresy-hunting to extremes. Both Presi-dents Truman and Eisenhower made public statements warning against excesses in such investigations which have the effect of discouraging the discussion of controversial questions.

Judge Learned Hand warned of the menace of suspicion and fear in these widely quoted words: [17]

Risk for risk, for myself I had rather take my chance that some traitors will escape detection than spread abroad a spirit of general suspicion and distrust, which accepts rumor and gossip in place of undismayed and unintimidated inquiry. . . .

I believe that a community is already in the process of dissolution where each man begins to eye his neighbor as a possible enemy, where nonconformity with the accepted creed, political as well as religious, is a mark of disaffection; where

[17] *The New York Times,* Oct. 25, 1952.

denunciation, without specification or backing, takes the place of evidence; where orthodoxy chokes freedom of dissent; where faith in the eventual supremacy of reason has become so timid that we dare not enter our convictions in the open lists to win or lose.

The outer limits of freedom of discussion are ever changing, but there is much to be said for broadening rather than restricting discussion devoted to changing the personnel and policies of government. It is an indispensable requisite to government by the consent of the governed to give the pleaders for stability and the pleaders for change a chance to debate in the open market place of ideas; it is also a desirable safety valve.

Perhaps the best if not the only way by which democracy can satisfactorily be distinguished from other forms of government is that it rests on the rule of opinion, which allows all the people to determine who shall govern them and by implication to what ends. This is done by permitting the free expression of opinion on the policies of government, followed by acceptance of the verdict of the polls. In order to have the rule of opinion, the existence and free expression of opposing opinions are necessary. Democracy no longer exists when a single creed or dogma crushes with violence other faiths. Democracy is always concerned with the free discussion of political issues and ideas, with the freedom to resort to constitutional means for expressing the changing currents of opinion, either individually or through a group. Though numerous oligarchic, one-party states profess to be democratic they but confuse terms, for they fail to operate on the fundamental postulate of democracy—the free organization of rival opinions. Politics in its finest sense cannot become every citizen's business unless the citizen is free to express opinions and to hear those of others, to associate, to organize, and to petition. The crucial test of freedom of speech is whether it is extended to minorities holding unpopular views.

SELECTED REFERENCES

See the end of the following chapter.

CHAPTER 2

Basic Factors in American Politics

I often think it's comical—
Fal, lal, la!
How Nature always does contrive—
Fal, lal, la!
That every boy and every gal
That's born into the world alive
Is either a little Liberal
Or else a little Conservative!
—GILBERT AND SULLIVAN, "Iolanthe"

One of the most intriguing questions to the student of politics is the origin and development of a person's political loyalties, beliefs, and opinions. What causes one to become a Republican, a Democrat, or a Socialist? What is the basis of one's belief in the protective tariff or in free trade, in world federalism or in nationalism, in *laissez faire,* public regulation, or in socialization? Is belief in social equality, white supremacy, or restricted housing covenants a reasoned response or an uncritical, emotional one? To what extent is the home, the school, the church, the section, a radio commentator, a club member, and so on responsible for the political opinions of an individual?

It is not easy for a person to isolate and discover the part played by the home, church, school, communications mediums, and other opinion-forming institutions in the molding of opinions upon which a great deal of one's political behavior may be based. One cannot hope to evaluate the relative importance of each of these in his own or in his community's life. Nevertheless, a recognition of the role, potential or actual, of these in the formation and development of public attitudes is necessary in gaining an insight into basic factors in American politics. In this and in the succeeding chapter a survey is made of these primary institutions which seek to mold and influence political opinions.

THE FAMILY

Despite the alleged decline of the influence of the home, it remains one of the basic educational units in society. The child is "taught" conformity

18

in his home and receives the fundamental values of his family. His basic attitudes toward his neighbors, individualism, competition, brotherly love are, in effect, "given" him in the home. Says F. C. Irion: [1]

> By the time most children enter school they think in categories which carry almost incurable prejudice. The pleasantly polite words their teachers use have little effect, since the students will think in the familiar family-used words even though they may write the school-approved expressions in order to pass examinations. The casual way in which families indoctrinate their children with distrust and fear through the use of hate-fear words is the significant factor.

Attitudes toward politicians in general or some in particular, toward other economic groups, social classes, religions, races, and nationalities often are inculcated at an early age and profoundly affect viewpoints of the growing citizen. "Black Republican" and "Damn Yankee," "crackpot," "Wallstreeter," "Red," and the uncomplimentary terminology applied to racial and religious stock are often carelessly and casually used in family circles in a way which may lead to a hate-fear-despise reaction.

Within the family the child sometimes learns to accept rumor and the "they say" of his parents as the basis of evidence and belief. The newspapers, radio and television programs which come into the home likewise may profoundly affect the political conditioning of all members of the family. Undoubtedly one of the greatest contributions of the home to the young citizen is the inheritance of party affiliation. Party faith appears quite largely an inherited matter. Some polls of students have noted that three-fourths of them belong to the same party as their parents. This is not necessarily an accurate indication of the family influence, for the children are subject to the same group, sectional, and other pressures as their parents. In observing home influences, of course, one finds numerous contrary instances where a child reacts negatively to the indoctrination carried on in the home and goes to the other extreme.

Finally, the family is likely to be the origin of first political interests, the place where the youngster first hears of government and politics. A study of 2,500 students in one of our large universities attempted to ascertain the origin of political attitudes and interests. By use of an initial check sheet, a follow-up questionnaire, and interviews with a select cross section, the study tried to determine where or how students first became conscious of government. The results are shown in Table 1. Notwithstanding the margins of error which may occur, it seems obvious that the majority of these students obtained their first contact with and concepts of public affairs in the home. A great many students admitted that

[1] *Public Opinion and Propaganda* (New York: Thomas Y. Crowell Company, 1950), p. 242.

Table 1. Origin of Political Interests

Item	Number *	Per cent
Discussion at home..............	1,456	58.8
Public school..................	723	29.2
An election....................	377	15.2
Newspaper or political literature..	232	9.4
Teacher.......................	138	5.6
Friend or relative in politics......	128	5.2
A political leader...............	39	1.5
Church........................	21	0.8
Lawyer........................	18	0.7
Radio broadcast................	16	0.6
Minister......................	7	0.3

* In some instances students checked two sources; in these cases both are recorded in the table.

SOURCE: Hugh Alvin Bone, Jr., *The Effect of College Training on Student Political Attitudes* (unpublished doctoral dissertation, Northwestern University, 1937), p. 67.

this political awakening was narrow and prejudiced. The following remark of one senior is typical of many responses: [2]

My father, being an ardent partisan of one of our major parties, decided that I should understand what a great party his was. As a result I got quite a biased form of opinion as far as the national government was concerned. I am still biased in this respect and with the exception of the functions of a governing body, I probably will always be a partisan of the party ordained by my father.

That the home still has considerable influence in molding initial public attitudes and on their development may be assumed; yet this fact is often forgotten. America has seen many outstanding political families such as the Adamses and Lodges of New England and the La Follettes of Wisconsin. Diaries and biographies of these families show that the home influence was responsible for arousing an interest in politics as a career. In thousands of other families the civic and political activities of one or both parents likewise have helped promote an interest in public affairs on the part of the young people. The opposite may also be the case. Where public and civic problems are never mentioned in the home, and perhaps there is no voting by the elders, any stimulation the child and youth is to receive in these matters must come from the schools, the press, discussion with friends, or other sources.

[2] Hugh Alvin Bone, Jr., *The Effect of College Training on Student Political Attitudes* (unpublished doctoral dissertation, Northwestern University, 1937), p. 60.

If party loyalties and attitudes toward public policies are transmitted by the family, then the better informed the family, the greater the opportunity for the newer generations to take a wholesome interest in the life of the community and of the nation. The transmitting of the ideals of democracy and citizenship is as much a function of the home as the inculcation of personal honesty and morality. As Professor MacIver points out [3]

The family is bound up with all the great crises and transitions in life. . . . It is the primary agent in the molding of the life habits and the life attitudes of human beings. It is the center of the most impressive celebrations and rituals, those associated with marriage, with death, and with the initiation of the child into the beliefs and ways of the community. It is brought continuously together, where old and young must learn to make ever changing adjustments to their ever changing roles in the life cycle.

THE CHURCH

Church Interest in Public Policies. In contrast to many other nations, separation of state and church in the United States is taken for granted. Officially, the church often professes to be nonpartisan and above the hurly-burly of economic and political life. Yet the church has made its influence felt in the enactment and enforcement of laws since its inception, and organized religion in America is taking an increasing interest in politics and economics for a number of reasons. For one thing, religion concerns itself to a considerable extent with standards of human behavior, and it attempts to reach the young as well as the old in order to inculcate basic creeds and opinions. As the state took over education, the church inevitably had an interest in the subject matter and instruction, especially as they affected religious tenets. Difference of opinion over the support and uses of parochial and private education is a case in point, and so is the teaching of evolution in the public schools. Similarly, legislation that might tax church property or interfere with the free exercise of religion became a matter of interest to the church.

The church enjoys the prestige of an influence for good in the community and in the nation. Accordingly, other organizations seek its aid in furthering what are deemed to be worthy causes. For example, the National Association of Manufacturers and the Congress of Industrial Organizations prepare special programs for the churches. The fact that pressure groups solicit help from religious institutions is a recognition that the churches are believed to be influential in molding public opinion and that it is desirable to have the sanction of church opinion for their objectives.

[3] *The Web of Government*, p. 23. Copyright, 1947, by Robert M. MacIver. By permission of The Macmillan Company, publishers.

Religion and Political Attitudes. Whether religion is of the same large importance in forming basic political attitudes as the family offers an interesting matter for debate. Irrespective of denominationalism, religion tends to have an ameliorative influence on economic and political institutions and on the persons operating them. It has taught the golden rule or variations of it, kindliness, brotherly love, humility, and charity. The church has bred ethics and faith and the intensity to which its members practice them may profoundly affect the economic and political life of the community. The influence may also be conditioned by the degree to which the individual sees the relationship between his religious tenets and politics and acts accordingly. Organized religions also denounce materialism, exploitation, and dishonesty in both public and private life. A large volume of literature appears on the relationships of religion to the manner of earning a living and the historical development of the church and capitalism.[4]

Several of the social concerns of present-day American churches will be considered later.[5] A few may be mentioned here to illustrate matters upon which the church may influence the outlook of its members. In 1936 the Catholic Church began a particularly militant crusade against communism. Vatican authorities noted that "thousands of speeches, lectures, and debates are given daily in all corners of the world by Catholic priests and laymen," and the Pope asked the "episcopacy and the clergy to bring his words to the notice of the masses and members of the Catholic Action to spread them by means of lectures and other propaganda."[6] As far back as 1891 the papal encyclical Rerum Novarum set forth the responsibilities of employers and employees who believed in Christianity, and the Church has had much to say in favor of the labor movement.

Many Protestant churches have likewise taken strong positions on national and international concerns. Several have conditioned their members toward passive resistance, conscientious objection to the Selective Service law or to combatant service in the Armed Forces, prohibition of intoxicating liquors, internationalism, and to certain social and humanitarian legislation. Most Protestant churches have been outspoken in opposition to the appointment of an ambassador to the Vatican.

In 1953 a great many clergy and prominent church laymen became deeply concerned when certain congressional committees announced that they planned to investigate communism in the churches. There were fur-

[4] See especially Max Weber, *The Protestant Ethic and the Spirit of Capitalism* (London: George Allen & Unwin Ltd., 1939); R. H. Tawney, *Religion and the Rise of Capitalism* (New York: Harcourt, Brace and Company, Inc., 1947); F. H. Knight and T. W. Merriam, *The Economic Order and Religion* (New York: Harper & Brothers, 1945).

[5] See Chap. 8.

[6] *The New York Times*, Dec. 14 and 20, 1936.

ther repercussions when a staff member of Sen. Joseph McCarthy's investigating committee published an article asserting that a number of the clergy were engaged in a Communist conspiracy. The article resulted in a sharp statement of criticism by President Eisenhower, followed by the resignation of the staff member. Several clergymen appeared before the House Committee on Un-American Activities, denouncing its methods of procedure and also the suggestion of its chairman to investigate the clergy. A few of the clergy, however, supported the committee. These incidents particularly highlighted the role of the clergy and some church associations in politics.

The Jews have quite naturally interested themselves in the plight of European Jews, statelessness, and the admission of displaced persons into the United States. A "national home" for the Jews in Palestine, and more recently the affairs of the new state of Israel, are matters about which young Jewish boys and girls hear at an early age. The National Conference of Christians and Jews has tried to promote interracial and interreligious tolerance and to combat social and economic discrimination. For this reason one often finds discussion of antidiscrimination legislation in both Christian churches and Jewish synagogues.

Politicians often speak of the "Jewish vote," the "Catholic vote," and to a lesser extent the "Protestant vote." This assumes a voting cohesion to which there appear to be as many exceptions as there are rules. The "balanced ticket" of some cities will often fail to win a majority of voters who presumably have a member of their own faith on the ballot. Clergy and prominent laymen who have counseled their congregations to vote for "our candidate" find their advice more than occasionally disregarded. Farm, labor, and business leaders frequently make the same voting pleas only to learn that they cannot necessarily deliver huge voting majorities. The church is unlikely to be the origin of one's party affiliation, but it does affect the character, opinions, and lives of its members in ways which directly or indirectly influence politics. Christian ethics, though not invariably honored in practice, still provide a cornerstone and a yardstick for judging civilization and the social order.

THE SCHOOL

"Education for democracy" has come to be an accepted slogan and objective. Education as distinct from propaganda places greater reliance on truth, facts, and the objective attitude. Education transmits the heritage of customs and ideas and attempts to gain acceptance of these. New beliefs emerge from time to time and the educational process likewise tries to get the members of a group or society to accept them. Education becomes a weapon of the home, the church, the organization, the communications agencies, and the government. Much that passes for "education" is prejudice. But the need for education, regardless of its content, is accepted and recognized; and individuals, associations, and governments in the United States spend billions of dollars a year for that purpose.

The school is singled out by society as the institution for educating the younger members and to a lesser extent the older persons in the community. In fact, education is regarded by many as obtainable only in the school. This is because of the school's formalized function of instruction and its position as the organized transmitter of group tradition. We have noted that much informal education comes from the home and the church. To these should be added the role of the press, radio, television, motion pictures, clubs, and other associations. In the actual molding of political attitudes and interests these agencies may be of as much, or even greater, importance as the school. The home and the church have had a great deal to say before the child arrives at school and he sees his community much as his parents do. Many students find teachings in the schools at variance with those of other institutions; some schools recognize and attempt to undo what seem to be incorrect assumptions and opinions emanating from other agencies in the community. Other schools merely reflect the prevailing ideas of the community. Colleges and universities are more advanced in analysis and ideas than elementary or secondary schools. Institutions of higher learning also rely more heavily upon the impact of analysis and research. The controversy over progressive as opposed to traditional education, as well as a lengthy analysis of school education, must be omitted here in order to review the basic factors of political education in the schools.

Curriculum. History forms an important part of the elementary- and secondary-school curriculums. The other social sciences, especially political science, economics, and sociology, have been slow to appear; they are commonly incorporated into American history courses or as current events. The curriculum of some of the larger high schools, however, includes Problems of Democracy, Economics, and Civics courses. The lack of emphasis on specially trained teachers in government is shown by the fact that in most states a college degree with a major in political science does not qualify one for teaching in the public schools.

The content of social-science courses in the secondary schools shows great variations. Most social-studies classes do cover the structure, organization, and operation of the national and state governments. Some emphasis is placed on the duties of citizenship, the Bill of Rights, and the Constitution. Beyond this it is difficult to generalize on the subject matter taught. Many subjects are omitted or receive insufficient treatment, such as current governmental policies, industrial and labor relations, pressure politics, property and vested interests, public administration, local government, and an understanding of the governments and politics of other nations. A knowledge of the fundamentals of one's own economic and constitutional system is necessary, and many schools are supplying this. Yet the real core is often missed when little or no appreciation is gained of the forces operating this system. Public-opinion polls show an amazing area of ignorance on the nature, purpose, and control of industrial strife, foreign policies, congressional activities, and the like.

Six of every seven future citizens end their formal education at the high-school level. If understanding is an element in developing good citizenship and healthy democratic attitudes, adequate information on the ethical as well as the legal aspects of our political system is needed and should be provided on the secondary level. It is generally recognized that political education at this point is inadequate and in need of vitalization. However, there are several obstacles in the way of adding any great amount of political education to the curriculum.

In the first place, there is great competition for the student's time at school. Teachers are under pressure from parents and interested outsiders to give the students more science, more mathematics, more physical education, more music appreciation, and so on. The curriculum is highly diversified and more time can be given to one subject only at the cost of less emphasis on others. Closely related to this is the fact that in nearly every community there are influential persons who feel that the high school should not deal frankly—perhaps not at all—with labor relations, public health, race, war, social security, and other problems of modern civilization. It becomes "safer" for the school to concentrate on "fundamentals" such as reading, arithmetic, and science, rather than to invade contemporary social science.

Instruction and Materials. What of the teachers? As noted before, many of them are inadequately trained in social science. Those capable of presenting a realistic and objective approach to government and economics find themselves circumscribed in many cases by community attitudes. Howard K. Beale has provided a voluminous and illuminating study of this subject.[7] He comes to the conclusion that teachers generally must teach the viewpoints which are accepted by the locality and avoid those points of view which clash with the controlling interests in the community. In 1936, he concluded:[8]

In the realm of politics, teachers are restricted in classroom discussion, in participation in party activity, and in adherence to tenets of unpopular political groups. A general feeling exists among teachers and their constituents that politics should be kept out of the classroom. "Warnings" to avoid political

[7] *Are American Teachers Free?* (New York: Charles Scribner's Sons, 1936) and *A History of Freedom of Teaching in American Schools* (New York: Charles Scribner's Sons, 1941).

[8] *Ibid.,* p. 79.

questions are frequently issued unofficially. Some communities go so far as to taboo subjects upon which either party has taken a stand, such as the tariff, the League of Nations, or local party issues.

In Los Angeles certain groups and some of the press were successful in persuading the public schools to drop some publications issued by the United Nations Educational, Scientific, and Cultural Organization (UNESCO) from the curricula because among other reasons the materials were regarded as "un-American." A similar attempt to remove UNESCO publications from the school libraries in Marin County, California, was thwarted when citizens rallied against it.[9] However, the board of education permitted Karl Marx's work to be discussed in a class in Marin Junior College with a proviso that the discussion should be recorded and monitored! President Eisenhower at Dartmouth College took cognizance of situations like this and said: [10]

Don't join the book burners. . . . Don't be afraid to go in your library and read every book as long as any document does not offend your own ideas of decency. That should be the only censorship.
How will we defeat communism unless we know what it is? What it teaches— why does it have such an appeal for men? . . .

Some of the community concern about discussion of national and international issues arises from a lack of understanding of the purpose of discussion. The object is not to inform the student of the "correct attitude" of a special problem, but rather to use it as a case study illustrative of an objective approach, the application of verifiable data and fact, and in the use of logic. "Academic freedom" is an ill-defined term, depending upon one's comprehension of it; the degree of it in a given community is bound to be a moot point.[11] In terms of an intelligent electorate a strong case can be made for a responsible and free discussion of public questions. These questions can be discussed within the calm of a classroom in a more detached fashion than is likely to be the case elsewhere. If the significant problems of the day are avoided at school, the high-school graduate will soon obtain ideas on them from sources far less objective and often in an atmosphere kindled with emotion.

[9] See "The Defenders of Public Schools Score a Victory in Marin County," *Frontier,* August, 1953, p. 20.
[10] *The New York Times,* June 15, 1953.
[11] For example, most boards of education no longer will knowingly permit the retention of a teacher who is a member of the Communist party or a member of an organization deemed subversive. In many communities activity within the Republican and Democratic parties is not welcomed. Other concepts of academic freedom are concerned only with the activity of the teacher in the classroom, not with his private life.

The effectiveness of the school in training for citizenship is dependent not only on the quality of the teachers, the curriculum, and on community attitudes, but also on the books and materials used. Teachers and school librarians have often found that they are not invariably free to use the texts, references, and materials they wish. After World War II some radio news commentators, patriotic, veterans, and other groups were successful in having some school systems drop certain United Nations materials. In addition to the afore-mentioned organizations, the American Federation of Labor, public-utilities groups, and peace societies are among the more important associations which have conducted surveys of textbooks to see if they present proper "American" attitudes.[12] There are many cases where American history texts were taken out of schools because they were objectionable in one way or another.

School a Basic Foundation. After taking full cognizance of these limitations of the school in molding attitudes, we must recognize that its role is important, vital, and generally of wholesome influence. Many community views which are inculcated through the school are desirable. The teaching of obedience to the law and respect for representative government are quite universally accepted aims of the classroom. Millions of young Americans do receive basic knowledge of their political and economic institutions which helps to equip them for responsible citizenship. During the school years, many students come in contact with radio programs, magazines, and papers dealing with public affairs and form reading and other habits invaluable for political participation in later life. As is true with the home, the school is a great potential for developing political interests.

Also to be remembered is the fact that the school is a community center. To it are brought programs of interest to adults as well, and its influence transcends merely that of instruction to the younger generation. The dominant role of the school was shown in a study of civic education in eight modern countries, including the United States. In summarizing the conclusions of those investigations, Professor Merriam pointed out that in all cases the school system was the basic factor in the development of civic interest and loyalty. In modern times, Merriam says, the school tends "to take the place of force and fear in the earlier regime and of religion, the family, the army, in the later."[13] It is truly a basic foundation for the development of civic attitudes and interests.

[12] A highly illuminating work on this subject has been done by Bessie L. Pierce, *Civic Attitudes in American School Textbooks* (Chicago: University of Chicago Press, 1930).

[13] Charles E. Merriam, *The Making of Citizens* (Chicago: University of Chicago Press, 1931), Chaps. 7–8.

STUDENT GOVERNMENT

For years the National Self-Government Committee has been stressing the potentialities of student self-government in the schools. This often-overlooked device offers real potentialities as a laboratory in government. There are a few cases where the student officers in the high school make a firsthand study of their municipality and on a given day take over and operate the city. A carefully guided system of student government is a valuable "colt's pasture" for future civic leaders.

The average college campus has many attributes and problems of a regular community. It is surprising that relatively few universities have recognized the potentialities of student government as a training ground in self-government and civic leadership. Student government, in the first place, can provide a knowledge of the nominating process, election systems, balloting, campaigning, parliamentary law, the management of finances, and many other phases of civic life.

A look at campus politics in many if not most universities presents a discouraging picture. At a number of schools the governing groups are given no responsibility and the holding of office is an empty honor. The record also shows frequent examples of political lethargy on the part of the student body and failure on the part of the leaders to perform their functions. Perhaps the greatest mark against the system has been the low level to which some of them have sunk. Campus politicians in some instances have resorted to unsavory practices such as double-dealing, misappropriation and dishonest use of funds, ballot-box stuffing, boss rule, and favoritism. A study of the morale of undergraduates by the Institute of Social and Religious Research included a survey of campus politics and elections in 23 universities. According to this study,[14]

Elections to positions of prominence in campus activities are frequently the occasion of internal political rivalry and of dubious methods. In the interviews the inquirers heard many expressions of opinion as to the undesirable characteristics of campus politics. . . . No department of political science was found by the inquirers to be stressing the importance of campus politics as a training ground for future citizenship.

There are illustrations of highly successful high-school and college student self-government systems. Examples of faculty-student cooperation resulting in constructive political activity are the Universities of Cincinnati and Toledo. The department of political science and the student body at the latter institution carried on a successful municipal campaign to obtain an enabling act, and finally a city-manager form of government

[14] *Undergraduates* (1928), pp. 99, 102; see also Chap. 23, "Student Government."

for Toledo.[15] At the same institution a charter convention is held each year and the deliberations are devoted to working out amendments to improve the Toledo city charter. More and more colleges today are sponsoring model United Nations organizations, legislative assemblies, and national nominating conventions.

COLLEGE TRAINING AND POLITICS

The effect of college training on social and political attitudes and interests is unknown but presumedly is important. An increasing number of leaders in the field of government, industry, and the professions are college graduates, and the conditioning they receive in the university lays a foundation for leadership in the community and in their profession. College should provide training in the forming of opinions and in logic. There is no other agency which directs itself more toward this end than the educational institution and therein lies its peculiar importance as compared with political parties, the press, the home, and other opinion-expressing agencies.

Most institutions of higher learning today are equipped to give a well-rounded program in the social sciences. Unfortunately, the student's program is too crowded with prescribed courses and electives in his own field to take full advantage of the offerings in social science. Even with an abundance of government courses, Sir Ernest Simon, onetime Lord Mayor of Manchester and president of the English Association for Education in Citizenship,[16] observed the lack of useful consequences of American political-science instruction by noting the

. . . incomparable and almost innumerable college courses in government on the one side and the failure of the young men and women who took these courses to participate in politics after graduation. . . . In England [he noted] we have very few courses in government but many of our best young people are nevertheless much interested in politics. Here you have magnificent courses in government but very little active interest in politics.

The alleged lack of interest in politics on the part of college students has provoked much discussion and many suggestions. One approach has been to provide better courses in political and social science and to offer inducements for students to take them. Numerous medical, agricultural, and professional colleges are now including time in students' programs for work in social science. On many campuses some courses in social

[15] See Nita Cavaris, "We Helped Put Across the City Manager Plan," in *The Youth Leadership Survey,* published by National Youth Council (undated).

[16] Recorded in a memorandum from Dean Arthur T. Vanderbilt of New York University to the Advisory Panel on Methods of Encouraging Political Participation of the American Political Science Association, 1947.

science (other than history) are required. The political-science clubs, workshop-in-politics projects, and extracurricular activities have had considerable impact on the student body and even on the local community.

Another development is illustrated by the activities of the Citizenship Clearing House, located on the campus of New York University, and its various state affiliates. This organization is designed to prepare college men and women for actual participation in party politics.[17] Its program attempts to bring the problem to the attention of college teachers, presidents, trustees, and party and civic leaders and has set up a special training program for young teachers. In many colleges students in political-science courses are encouraged or assigned to participate actively in election campaigns by doing precinct work, ringing doorbells, and engaging in other activities, all of which give firsthand insight into political campaigning. Some discover that actual practice differs from published accounts and their own preconceptions of political behavior. One of the principal merits of such experiences is the interest which they arouse in students, many of whom later become active members of the party of their choice. Notwithstanding recognized merits of this program, there are some groups in the community and within the colleges who remain unconvinced that this is a proper activity or function of a university education. At the same time the colleges may become a greater factor on the political scene if there is increased student interest and participation in politics.

GEOGRAPHY AND POLITICS

Soil, climate, topography, and natural resources affect the way persons earn their living and their mode of living as well. In turn, occupation conditions outlook and attitude. When a group is engaged in the same essential occupational pursuits in a given area, there is a tendency to develop certain customs and folkways. Many of these traditions continue to prevail even after the methods of living become widely diversified. As one grows up in a certain community he tends to accept local customs, which consciously or unconsciously influence his thinking.

Since the seventeenth century sectionalism and geographical environment have played an important role in North American history and politics. In the United States each of the great sections has a history of its own and has acquired certain distinct political and economic characteristics. During the nineteenth century rivalries and jealousies arose

---

[17] The inspiration for the project was provided by Arthur T. Vanderbilt, Chief Justice of the Supreme Court of New Jersey, who believes much more could be done "to encourage college students to prepare for participation in politics on a self-respecting basis." The Citizenship Clearing House has published a comprehensive survey of the problem by Thomas H. Reed and Doris D. Reed, *Preparing College Men and Women for Politics* (1952).

between the different sections over such vital questions as slavery, the tariff, disposition of Western lands, currency, and the nature of the Union. These were not resolved without bitter debate, compromise, and even bloodshed; some of these issues carried over to the twentieth century. Since the beginning of our national government, the Congress, the President, and even the Federal judiciary have been confronted with the great task of accommodating the interests of the sections.

The word "sectionalism" is applied to areas or groups of states which appear to hold certain views or aspirations at variance with or not held by other groups of states. It is often used to denote similar differences within the boundaries of a given state, such as northern and southern California, eastern and western Tennessee. Even within a city geographical sections take on certain characteristics. Our first concern is to note the attributes of sectionalism in the first and broadest of these categories.

Sectionalism is in part psychological, a feeling that people in one's own area possess interests, ideals, mannerisms, dialects, social traits, and attributes in common. The patriotisms brought about by the Civil War have lingered on and have been consciously perpetuated. In the days before easy communication and transportation, isolation from other areas developed an attachment to locale; vestiges of this remained in modified form after modern modes of communication brought in the outside world. Many Easterners still regard themselves as something of a different breed from a Southerner or a Middle Westerner.

Sectionalism varies in degree and according to time. A. N. Holcombe's various studies of sectionalism and its influence on party politics show how the parties at different times have been formed from a combination of different sectional interests and that contemporary politics is much less sectional than nineteenth-century politics.[18]

Even within a section itself there are constantly divisive forces which result in a regrouping of alliances within the area and place cohesion of a section in a fluid condition. In 1952 the South was supposedly united in support of state ownership of the submerged oil lands off the coasts of several Southern states; at least this appeared the "correct" position for the South in terms of its "states' rights" leanings. Yet the major rival bill, which would retain Federal title to these lands, was sponsored by Senator Lister Hill of Alabama. Secretary of the Interior Douglas McKay and Senator Wayne Morse, both of Oregon, took sharply opposite views on this tidelands oil and other problems on the development of natural resources.

[18] See especially *The Political Parties of Today* (New York: Harper & Brothers, 1924); *The New Party Politics* (New York: W. W. Norton & Company, Inc., 1933) and "The Changing Outlook for a Realignment of Parties," *Public Opinion Quarterly*, Vol. 10 (1947), pp. 455–469.

Economic interest has been the major basis of sectionalism in the United States. Both agricultural and industrial raw materials have often been located in a different section from their processing and manufacturing. "States' rights" and "sectionalism" are often the war cries which mask the real contending economic interests. But sectionalism has also been nurtured by social traits, isolation due to competitive transportation, rivers, rainfall, and ethnic background.

Several factors are causing the old sectionalism to break down. Among these are the rise of industrialism, improved means of transportation, the migration and redistribution of population during war years, the spread of labor unionism, the increasingly higher standard of living and level of education. All of these help to erase regional cleavages, to dispel the feeling of sectionalism, and to modify provincial outlooks. Sections may help to pull class interests together, but likewise, class interests cut across and soften sectionalism. Income levels may change political outlook. As the South becomes industrialized, it may change its views on the tariff and its attachment to the Democratic label.

Population distribution during the last generation has been especially marked by a continuation of its westward movement and also by the mushroom growth of eight to ten states, most of which are on the outside edge of the United States. Largest recent gainers in population have been California, Oregon, Washington, Texas, Florida, North Carolina, Maryland, New Jersey, and Michigan. All of these except Michigan are littoral states. A few other rapid-growing states such as Arizona and New Mexico are likewise a long distance from the population center of the nation. At the same time the eight states losing the most in relative population position form a solid bloc of geographically center states—Nebraska, Kansas, Oklahoma, Iowa, Missouri, Illinois, Indiana, and Kentucky. Thus the population is being stretched from the center to the periphery, and more particularly to the coastal areas from the center. The congressional reapportionment based on the 1950 census portrays this distribution.[19] As the outer and seaboard areas gain in numerical strength in Congress, there will be a flow of power in their direction. However, political power is not evidenced simply in terms of seats in Congress but also by seniority in committee assignments. Seniority at present highly favors the South when the Democrats are in control and the Middle West when Congress has Republican majorities.

[19] On this and other reapportionments consult *Law and Contemporary Problems* Vol. 17 (Spring, 1952); the entire issue is devoted to congressional and state reapportionment problems. California, Washington, Texas, Florida, Maryland, Virginia, and Michigan gained congressional seats on the basis of the 1950 reapportionment.

SECTIONALISM TODAY

In spite of the fact that the old sectionalism is being eroded by some vital new forces in politics, the section and the locale are still prominent factors in the formation of initial political attitudes and also in their development. Party allegiance is often a matter of inertia, the line of least resistance and prejudice. Those who take only a passive interest in politics are inclined, therefore, to accept the prevailing "socially correct" party and to subscribe to the so-called "policies" of the dominant party of the area. If one grows up in Maine, New Hampshire, or Vermont, it is easiest to embrace the Republican label. In the South the Democratic party is the acceptable one. Elsewhere the sectional influence on nominal party politics is less apparent. But the influence of neighborhood in a metropolitan region, or section within a given state, may affect party registration.

Public-opinion polls recognize the utility of dividing the nation into at least a half dozen areas for purposes of sampling the country's opinion on political candidates and issues, and the results frequently show considerable differences between the areas. Some of these differences, beliefs, biases, and interests may be noted here.[20]

The East and Middle West. In his studies of sectionalism W. P. Webb has lumped the East and the Middle West together as "the North." [21] He points out that the North has one-fifth of the total land area of the United States, with almost three-fifths of the population, while the West has half of the territory with one-seventh of the population. The South has approximately one-fourth of the territory and one-fourth of the nation's population. Of greater significance is the ownership of from 80 to 90 per cent of the nation's wealth by the North; and its share of banking, insurance, and sale of nationally advertised merchandise is far out of proportion to its population. All of this is true in spite of the fact that the South and the West provide the great wealth of resources such as gold, silver, oil, coal, lumber, and agricultural products. It is small wonder that the Northern interest in public policies affecting banking, finance, and manufacturing should be keen regardless of occupation.

East of the Mississippi River and north of the Ohio River is to be found the greatest concentration of wage earners. Likewise, one finds in these areas the largest melting pot population and numbers of immigrants from Europe. The greatest battles between labor and capital have been

20 For other aspects of sectionalism including congressional voting see Chap. 12. Only the four broad sectional categories of the East, Middle West, South, and Far West are used here. The distinctions are largely delineated by the Ohio River, Mason and Dixon's line extended, and the state of Colorado.

21 *Divided We Stand* (Austin, Tex.: Acorn Press, 1944).

fought in this area and problems of racial accommodation have been many.

Notwithstanding the similarities between the present-day East and the Middle West, there are likewise political and economic differences between the two sections. The East is usually regarded as a "business civilization" with a distinct industrial and commercial outlook. The major communications industries are located there and maritime commerce is much greater even though the Great Lakes serve parts of the Middle West. Hard-money doctrines, the protective tariff, and governmental aids to business remain as popular public policies. Here some of the loudest voices are raised against governmental interference and for inflationary monetary policies.

Although the Middle West has often aligned itself with the protective tariff supporters in the East, it has frequently been at variance with the latter's sound-money doctrines. The Middle West has only a few great melting pot cities, and has been slow to show an interest in foreign affairs and quick to distrust Europe, especially the British. This has made the area something of a bastion of isolationism against the internationalism of the East. Since 1940 the *Chicago Tribune,* aided by many prominent leaders in the area, has vigorously articulated a doctrine of nationalism. This nationalism is considerably different from that of Clay, Jackson, and Lincoln, and from the "new nationalism" envisaged in Theodore Roosevelt's foreign policy. This group has accused Eastern Republicans of "stealing" the Republican National Conventions and of sellouts to the British. It has proclaimed states' rights and something of an "Asia first" line. In Republican National Conventions this sectionalism has been quite intense.

The principal sectional agricultural interests in the Middle West are the great corn belt, stretching from Ohio westward through Nebraska, and a winter wheat belt, running south of this. Summer wheat is found in abundance in the area and individual states in the section claim the record for the production of such diverse crops as hay, soybeans, popcorn, hogs, oats, and rye. Almost 90 per cent of Illinois' total land is in farms, making it an agricultural leader among the states with a cash income of nearly $2 billion in 1950. Dairying, truck-garden produce, livestock, fruits, and vegetables are also major enterprises in the region. Although favoring Federal aid for transportation and regulation of some of the practices of big corporations, the Middle Western farmer inveighs against governmental paternalism and is proud of his individualism and self-reliance.

The South. In the South one finds the greatest expression of sectionalism. Agriculture has always been and still is the principal occupation of this area, the main products being cotton, tobacco, sugar cane, and citrus fruits. In recent years, however, industrialization on a large scale has taken place in many Southern states, vitally changing the economy and the attitude on national issues. Traditions in the South resulting from its cotton economy and the issues of the Civil War have been perpetuated over a wide area, even though the economic and social institutions have undergone considerable change. Sharecropping, however, has remained as one of the most significant economic institutions in the South.

Unlike that of the East and Middle West, the population of the South is more homogeneous and more nearly native American. The South has maintained a friendship for Great Britain which is not shared by many groups and areas to the north. In foreign policy the South has strongly supported England, with intervention on her side when necessary.

Three basic and fundamental traditions, exclusive of the attachment to the Democratic party, have prevailed in the South and profoundly influence its thinking—the low tariff, states' rights, and white supremacy. The first is a carry-over from the cotton economy and a belief in free trade. The South has fought the high protective tariff since the beginning of the Republic because it has wanted a foreign market for its goods and low prices for the finished goods it must buy. This also accounts, in part, for the friendship with her good customer England. Since World War II some Southern state agricultural officials have expressed dissatisfaction with the low-tariff attitudes of the South; the growing industrialization of the area may also eventually result in a revision of its position on free trade.

Fearful of Northern dominance of its social and economic life, the South has clung to states' rights when confronted with the possibility of Federal interference or regulation in such fields as elections, law enforcement, and welfare. Filibustering in the Senate has provided a last line of defense when the South feels its institutions or prerogatives are in danger.

The race problem overshadows and conditions many social, political, and economic attitudes. Sometimes referred to as the "doctrine of white supremacy," [22] the traditional race relationships far transcend merely social equality. Many sincere white citizens fear that the abandonment of segregation will lead to racial tension and violence. It is similarly felt that changing the political and economic *status quo* will also have the effect of stirring racial strife. There is a strong feeling that the individual communities and states must be left free to handle the racial problem

[22] Many Southerners, including the 1948 States' Rights presidential nominee Governor J. Strom Thurmond, regard the term "white supremacy" as biased and inaccurate. They believe the issue should be discussed in the broader terms of states' rights and racial relationships.

in their own way; Federal intervention in these matters is resented and resisted. This viewpoint has led large numbers to accept laws restricting suffrage and political participation, and political machines in the area are only too happy to have a smaller, more easily managed electorate.

Political scientists Heard, Key, and Shannon have given us some excellent insight into the political sectionalism of the South.[23] In one way or another the South tries to inculcate the impression that Southerners should stand together in national politics. This Southern cohesion often shows up on roll calls in Congress—particularly on the race issue. As Key has pointed out, the backbone of Southern solidarity consists of the whites of the black belt.[24] They set the general tone and others follow. In 1948 the revolt against President Truman was led by persons from the areas where there was the largest concentration of Negro population, and the greatest voting defection from the Democratic party that year came from those areas. Moreover, relatively fewer Negroes vote in those areas where the largest number of them live.

Race is not the only factor in Southern politics. Democratic factionalism is often between the richer lowlands and the less productive highlands, or what is sometimes called the "politics of the hills." Political power is held by conservative groups which have often made alliances with industrial interests of the North and West. Despite the vigorous efforts of the major labor unions to organize workers in the South, labor in most sections remains relatively weak and unorganized.

The Far West. There has always been a Western frontier in American history. First it was the east side of the Appalachian Mountains. Then it pushed across into the "old Northwest," which was recognized for settlement in the Ordinance of 1787. Interestingly, the Ohio area is now commonly referred to by Pacific Coast radio commentators as "the East." Then the wave of migration spilled into the Great Plains, the Rockies and Southwest, and finally into California and the Oregon Territory. Hawaii and Alaska beckoned additional settlers. The eleven Western states and the two territories now have a population in excess of 20 million.

The freshness of the political and economic democracy of the Western frontier and the impact of the West on the nation's national character have been described by Frederick Jackson Turner and other historians. The ruggedness and lustiness of the nineteenth-century mining, ranching,

---

[23] Alexander Heard, *A Two Party South?* (Chapel Hill, N.C.: The University of North Carolina Press, 1952); V. O. Key, Jr., *Southern Politics* (New York: Alfred A. Knopf, Inc., 1949); J. B. Shannon, *Toward a New Politics in the South* (Knoxville, Tenn.: University of Tennessee Press, 1949).

[24] *Op. cit.,* pp. 5 ff.

and farming frontiers have left their mark on the West but the influence of tradition is much less marked on political attitudes than in the East and the South. Politicians appeal to the sectionalism of the West but it seems to have less effect than in many other areas. From a political standpoint the West has been the scene of experimentation with economic and political reform. Some of this was motivated out of a sheer optimism and a spirit of independence and partly as an attempt to protect itself from Eastern dominance and corruption. The initiative and referendum, recall of public officers, broadened manhood suffrage, woman suffrage, and direct primaries, to mention the more important, were nurtured in the West. Economically, railroad regulation, the free coinage of silver, greenback currency, and Populism were Western cries during the last century. The present generation has witnessed demands for public power, pension schemes for the aged, including the Townsend movement, "Thirty Dollars Every Thursday," wide-open primaries, and extensive economic reforms such as Upton Sinclair's "End Poverty in California" in 1934, and the Non-Partisan League of North Dakota. The West's flirtation with easy-money doctrines has horrified Eastern bankers and the "silver bloc" remains a formidable influence in Congress.

Although the Far West has become well known through the novel and motion picture, few studies have been made of its politics, politicians, political psychology, and attitudes.[25] Its economic interests are more diversified than those of the South and the area as a whole appears less closely knit than any other section. Huge agricultural lands are given over to grazing, cattle raising, timber, ranching, and to fruit orchards. Some of the nation's finest wheat and cotton are grown respectively in Washington and California. These agricultural interests are well organized and well mechanized. The extractive industries flourish in the area, particularly copper, oil, and precious metals.

During World War II the West was heavily industrialized and the impact of the war was probably greater on the Pacific Coast than on any other region. The Coast and Southwestern states have been the beneficiaries of regional developments including the irrigation of new farm land, electric power, and reclamation. Big industry and huge defense enterprises, including atomic energy, have mushroomed along the coast. The editor of *Western Industry* sees the United States on the verge of a shift of economic and financial power from the East and Middle West to the Far West and Southwest.[26] This may be premature but it is

---

[25] Some interesting state-by-state accounts will be found in the election sections of the *Western Political Quarterly*, March, 1949, 1951, and 1953; and in T. C. Donnelly (ed.), *Rocky Mountain Politics* (Albuquerque, N.M.: The University of New Mexico Press, 1940).

[26] See *The Christian Science Monitor*, Oct. 28, 1950.

illustrative of Western optimism, and statistics of production in the area bear out its claim of the large role it plays in the nation's economy.

With even greater enthusiasm than the East and Middle West, the Far West has approved Federal aid and promotion of transportation, commerce, industry, and agriculture. As the area has become industrialized, labor unions have grown rapidly and there is an intensification and proliferation of associations. Suffrage qualifications and comparatively lax primary laws encourage political participation and the crossing of party lines. The area has seen rather sharp shifts of political opinion between the Republican and Democratic parties and there are lively contests between the two. In presidential elections the eleven Western states have a remarkable record for following the national trend.

"Inside U.S.A." We are told of the intense Texas "nationalism," the "European outlook" of New York, and the "wide-open" towns of Nevada. Kentucky is said to be the "land of fair women and fast horses" and Oregon the "land of man-sized men and happy homes." In a half-facetious vein Henry Adams once said "Only Bostonians can understand Bostonians and thoroughly sympathize with the inconsequences of the Boston mind," and Carl Becker in *If the Prospect Pleases* remarked: "To understand why people say 'Dear old Kansas!' is to understand that Kansas is no mere geographical expression, but a state of mind, a religion, and a philosophy in one." Such statements as these attribute traits to localities and possess some substance but are incorrect if applied indiscriminately to the political and economic viewpoints. It is easy to overgeneralize the habit patterns of a section. To say the Northwest, for example, is radical is to overlook the greater conservatism in Oregon than in Washington. To speak of California as a state of extreme economic panaceas is to miss the strong conservative forces of the Associated Farmers, the utilities, and oil interests. Water is one of the great issues in the West but at the same time is a barrier to a closely knit regional-interest unit, for the struggle to attain or retain water is an intrasectional one. Although the South has provided the prototype illustration of sectionalism and of a one-party area, it delivered a sizable Republican vote in 1948 and 1952. There is a vigorous progressive movement in the South which is often obscured by the greater attention given to conservatism. As V. O. Key, Jr., phrased it, the political distance between Alabama and Virginia should be measured in "light-years." Similarly, great divergencies are easily found elsewhere.

Political sectionalism arises when the dominant interests of one section sponsor national policies which appear to offer a threat to the policies of the predominant interest or interests of another. The latter try to mold opinion for the section by appeals to tradition, history, and geography. In the growth and development of the United States each section has made contributions, both cultural and economic, and each area is proud of its traditions and history.

URBANISM AND SUBURBANISM

Population Distribution. Every recent decennial census continues to show three striking facts which are of profound importance to politics: (1) intense mobility, (2) increase in the urban population, and (3) shifts from the central city to the suburban regions. Wars, depressions, and booming new industries have encouraged widespread movement of the nation's population. Between 1940 and 1947, 70 million people changed homes; 13 million changed counties within the state, 7½ million moved to noncontiguous states and 5 million moved into an adjacent state.[27] This fluidity and mobility is bound to break down sectionalism and bring about some changes in party registration. Many Republicans have moved South and vice versa.

Thomas Jefferson feared that increased urbanization would result in mob politics. If one looks alone at statistics, Jefferson's worst fears have materialized. The first census in 1790 showed only 5 per cent of the population living in towns of over 2,500. By 1920 urban dwellers were in the majority and in 1950 the nation was 64 per cent urban. More people also are living in larger cities; about 3 out of every 10 persons live in the 106 cities which have a population of over 100,000. About half of the nation's population is living within 140 metropolitan centers. The greatest concentration of urban areas is found along the Atlantic seaboard. Of the ten most urban states (New Jersey, New York, Massachusetts, Rhode Island, California, Connecticut, Illinois, Michigan, Pennsylvania, and Ohio, in order) six are on the Eastern seaboard.

One of the most interesting populational developments is the growth of "suburbia." Indeed, the 1950 census contained surprises for many chambers of commerce which found the population of the master city less than estimated and the surrounding metropolitan areas considerably larger than anticipated. In many large urban counties today one-third of the inhabitants are found outside the city limits. Politically the important question mark is what political values those living outside the city have and will develop. It is obvious that suburbanites are considerably more Republican than Democratic. For example, the city of Chicago gave 58.6 per cent of its votes to Truman, while Cook County, which includes Chicago, gave only 54.5. Truman carried the city of San Diego but Dewey carried the county. This difference in voting behavior between the central city and its suburbs was pretty generally pronounced. It has

27 Newton Edwards, "Population Changes in the United States," *The Annals of the American Academy of Political and Social Science,* Vol. 265 (1949), pp. 80–91.

been popular to say that one moves to the city and becomes a Democrat, then moves to the suburbs and becomes a Republican. Even though this is an oversimplification, it is a process through which a great many voters have gone. The relationship between the central city and its satellites forms the basis of a great deal of politics in the states and counties. The governance of the suburban areas affords one of the greatest challenges to the politician. Annexation, restricted covenants, support for schools, sewers, libraries, and transportation are but a few of the controversies arising out of suburbia.

Metropolitan Politics. In terms of influence on basic political attitudes, the neighborhood locale is probably greater than the section or region. On the community level the rural-urban background commonly defies sectional loyalties. Using metropolitan to embrace both urban and suburban areas, some of the major influences on local and national politics may be noted.

The rural-urban division is at the heart of the most heated and difficult problems facing most of the state legislatures. Among the divisions usually appearing are those dealing with daylight-saving time, allocation of state tax revenues to local governments, distribution of highway funds between rural and urban roads, special legislation fixing the organization and functions of towns and cities, types of taxes available to local governments and the extent of debt limitations, and state legislative reapportionment. Local rural and urban politicians often whip up considerable animosity between the two areas and rural legislators often try to play one metropolitan area against another. Provincial viewpoints exist in both town and country, and each often has a misconception of the other which manifests itself particularly in state legislatures.

In terms of party politics, it has often been stated that the Republicans have their major strength in rural America outside the South, while the Democrats have both town and country in the South and the urban areas in the North. Samuel Eldersveld has shown that the metropolitan areas between 1932 and 1948 were responsible in delivering to Democratic presidential nominees from 106 to 212 electoral votes and these urban pluralities gave them victory in three of the five elections.[28] In 1952 the sizable loss of votes in these areas by Adlai Stevenson undoubtedly helped Dwight Eisenhower to amass large state pluralities. Even in this landslide Stevenson still carried a great many of the large cities outside the West [29]

[28] "The Influence of Metropolitan Party Pluralities in Presidential Elections since 1920," *The American Political Science Review*, Vol. 43 (1949), pp. 1189–1206.

[29] Perhaps showing less attachment to the Democratic label, Stevenson failed to carry more than one or two cities over 50,000 population in the entire West. Urban dwellers in the Western cities gravitated in large numbers to Eisenhower. See Hugh A. Bone, "Western Politics and the 1952 Elections," *Western Political Quarterly*, Vol. 6 (March, 1953), p. 96.

but his pluralities were much less than those of Truman and Roosevelt and suburbia was of great help to Eisenhower. Democratic candidates for the House of Representatives outside the South likewise do much better in urban areas, and Republicans have a virtual monopoly on seats from the rural districts.[30] In mixed rural-metropolitan districts the favoritism for one or the other party is much less pronounced.

Within the confines of metropolitan areas one finds neighborhoods where matters of party faith are strong, with sharp differences between the East Side and the West Side; the river district and the "heights," the "skid row" and the "silk-stocking" district. Immigrants and newcomers into these areas often embrace the prevailing party and register accordingly. Ethnic politics result from the heterogeneous mixtures of nationalities, religions, and races. The urbanite has more or less accepted the principle of the "balanced ticket" of religions and nationalities and the minority appeals which so often disgust his rural brethren. Millions of Americans swallowed up in urban life have little or no understanding of rural America and the rural dweller has many perverted notions of the city.

Industrialism in the cities has brought with it class politics. Labor unions first attained their strongest influence in Eastern cities and subsequently spread to other areas. Unionization among farm workers has been much slower than among industrial employees. The resident of the modern city is likely to come into contact with left-wing and reformist theories and to witness fomentation of strife between classes and groups. Class conflict and class consciousness appear considerably less in the rural than in the urban areas. Housing, collective bargaining, wage-and-hour laws, fair-employment practices, social-security measures, and consumer protection comprise the class politics of today. While radicalism and reform once sprang from the soil, from the frontier, from the plains of Kansas and Nebraska, and from impoverished farm areas, it now springs from the large cities. Should farm prices again become thoroughly depressed, radicalism would again spring from the soil, as well as from the depressed lower incomes in the cities. Industrialism in the cities has brought in class politics but it has also brought a higher standard of living to the lower classes and has reduced somewhat the sharp class politics. Urban classes also have diluted sectionalism.

In view of the wide differences in school training, within families and churches, and within a given area, it is hazardous to attribute beliefs to whole sections, states, or communities. But it is likewise incorrect to dismiss as inconsequential the effect of locale on millions of citizens in terms of nominal party faith, voting habits, and attitudes toward the

[30] On this point see A. N. Holcombe, "The Changing Outlook for a Realignment of Parties," *Public Opinion Quarterly,* Vol. 10 (1947), pp. 455–469.

government and the economy in general. These primary institutions and geography provide the setting for, and raw materials of, American politics. As we shall see later, political leaders quite generally reflect their environment and are ever conscious of the underlying biases, prejudices, aspirations, and emotions of their state, of their city or community, and, if they hold that grass-roots job of precinct captain, of their election district.

SELECTED REFERENCES

Literature on the role, significance, and foundations of public opinion is voluminous. Much useful background as well as detailed references will be found in the numerous texts on public opinion. An annotated and classified bibliography of over 2,500 titles will be found in Bruce L. Smith, Harold D. Lasswell, and Ralph D. Casey, *Propaganda, Communication, and Public Opinion: A Comprehensive Reference Guide* (1946) and the earlier work of the same authors, *Propaganda and Promotional Activities, An Annotated Bibliography* (1935). Equally indispensable to the researcher in this field is the *Public Opinion Quarterly*, which contains up-to-date references as well as specialized articles on a wide range of subjects. Students of public opinion should also be familiar with Walter Lippmann, *Public Opinion* (1922) and *Phantom Public* (1927); A. Lawrence Lowell, *Public Opinion and Popular Government* (1913) and *Public Opinion in War and Peace* (1923); Graham Wallas, *Human Nature in Politics* (1921); Peter Odegard, *The American Public Mind* (1930); Edward L. Bernays, *Crystallizing Public Opinion* (1934); G. W. Allport and L. Postman, *The Psychology of Rumor* (1947); and Hadley Cantril, *The Psychology of Social Movements* (1941).

On the home and church see Ernest L. Mowrer, *The Family: Its Organization and Disorganizations* (1932); E. R. Groves and G. H. Groves, *The Contemporary American Family* (1947); Alvin W. Johnson, *The Legal Status of Church-State Relationships in the United States* (1934); F. H. Knight and T. W. Merriam, *The Economic Order and Religion* (1945); L. E. Ebersole, *Church Lobbying in the Nation's Capital* (1951); G. C. Treacy, *God in Society* (1944). The publications of the denominations are usually available at their national offices and should be consulted for direct materials.

On the schools the series of books in the Studies in Civic Education published in the 1930's by the University of Chicago Press should be consulted, especially Charles E. Merriam, *The Making of Citizens* (1931) and Bessie L. Pierce, *Civic Attitudes in American School Books* (1930). The numerous volumes arising from an investigation of social studies in the schools by the American Historical Association are rich in materials on the role of schools. Especially pertinent works of this series (published by Charles Scribner's Sons) are. Charles E. Merriam, *Civic Education in the United States* (1934); Merle Curti, *The Social Ideas of American Educators* (1935); George S. Counts, *The Social Foundations of Education* (1935); Howard K. Beale, *Are American Teachers Free?* (1936). See also Robert R. Raup, *Education and Organized Interests in America* (1936); Newton Edwards and Herman Rickey, *The School in the American Social Order* (1947) and *General Education in a Free Society* (1945). On college training for citizenship see the symposium published by the University of Oklahoma Press, *Higher Education and Society* (1936), and Robert L. Kelly, *The American Colleges and the Social Order* (1940).

A few of the useful works on sectionalism include Frederick Jackson Turner, *The Significance of Sections in American History* (1920); W. P. Webb, *Divided We Stand* (1944); W. T. Couch (ed.), *Culture in the South* (1935), Jonathan A. Daniels, *A Southerner Discovers the South;* H. W. Odum and H. E. Moore, *American Regionalism* (1938); Thomas C. Donnelly (ed.), *Rocky Mountain Politics* (1940); A. G. Mezerik,

The Revolt of the South and West (1946); J. B. Shannon, *Toward a New Politics in the South* (1949); Alexander Heard, *A Two Party South?* (1952); V. O. Key, Jr., *Southern Politics* (1949).

On the popular level John Gunther, *Inside U.S.A.* (1947), gives some interesting and keen observations of community, state, and sectional viewpoints; the volume contains many useful references. formulators of attitudes

1. Family   2. Church
         (a) interest (1) use of funds
         (b) Take position on national concerns
3. School (Edn. is weapon — for democracy)
      a. curriculum
      b. Inst. & materials
4. Student government.
5. College interests are lacking in politics.
6. Geography and politics (sectionalism influences politics)
      (a) (sect. is people with views & aspirations in common
      (b) What is sectionalism today
              1. East & middle west   3. Far West
              2. South   4.

7. Urbanism and Suburbanism
      (a) Pop. distribution
      (b) metropolitan politics

CHAPTER 3

Mass Communications and Politics

I am but a comparatively young journalist, but I have seen cabinets upset, Ministers driven into retirement, laws repealed, great social reforms initiated, Bills transformed, estimates remodeled, programmes modified, Acts passed, generals nominated, governors appointed, armies sent hither and thither, war proclaimed and war averted, by the agency of the newspapers.

—W. T. STEAD (in England in 1886)

The earliest foundations of public opinion remain the home, the locale, the school, and the church. But later in life the individual's political views, tastes, and interests are profoundly affected by the great inventions in the field of communications. Although the degree to which the press, radio, television, and motion pictures affect an individual cannot be accurately determined, the student of political processes can ill afford to overlook their role in a free society. How these instruments influencing public opinion and politics are controlled, and for what ends, are of perennial interest to the observer of public affairs.

THE NEWSPAPER

The oldest of the mass communications media is the press. Before the motion picture and radio were improved for widespread public use, the American daily newspaper had a circulation running into the millions and was perhaps the most important opinion-molding and opinion-reflecting agency. Total circulation of daily newspapers in 1954 was 54,473,000 and 46,948,000 for Sunday editions. When the unknown but fairly large circulation of foreign-language newspapers and some 11,500 weekly papers is added, it is obvious that the newspaper has a tremendous potential in the realm of political education.

Commercial Aspects. The modern newspaper is at once a commercial and a public-service enterprise. Advertisers are often accused of controlling the news and editorial content of papers, causing editors to slant news with strong pro-business and antilabor biases. The press under these circumstances becomes a *views*paper rather than a *news*paper. There are some cases on record where advertisers put pressure on publishers to "kill" a story or to present it in a distorted manner.[1] Generally,

[1] For a useful discussion on why and how news is suppressed see George L. Bird and Frederic E. Merwin, *The Newspaper and Society* (New York: Prentice-Hall, Inc.,

however, publishers contend that they are not influenced by advertisers with reference to the presentation of the news, and in many cases editors have printed news accounts which are offensive to certain advertisers.

It would seem fairer to the modern publisher to state the influence of the commercial aspects of the press another way. Publishers must make money or the newspaper goes out of business. They are under constant pressure to increase or to maintain circulation, and hence items which will attract or hold readers are of major importance. Of greater concern is the avoidance of issues which will cause readers to change to rival papers. This often leads papers to shun a specific position on local and state as well as national policies and personalities. Further, policies resulting in a decrease in circulation cannot long be continued. The importance of reader censorship, therefore, must not be underestimated. This may result in the abandonment of a certain political crusade which was popular with a minority group. Large newspapers may at times defy the wrath of both readers and advertisers to crusade for causes not supported by either group. The *Chicago Tribune,* for example, has often hammered away for lost causes and yet has suffered no substantial decline in circulation. Its distortion of some news is common knowledge among many if not a majority of its readers. Other attractive features of the paper, therefore, "sell" it in spite of its slanted presentation of political news.[2]

If newspapers did not need the financial support of advertisers, would they carry on more vigorous political crusades and present fairer treatment of labor news and of minorities? Unfortunately, an affirmative answer is difficult of conclusive proof because of a lack of experiment. One important example, however, was the New York newspaper *PM* in its early years. Founded in 1939 and backed by Marshall Field,[3] the paper began as a crusading daily without advertising. By 1945 its circulation had reached 225,000, with many mail subscriptions from all over the country. The circulation, however, failed to increase as rapidly as many expected. From the beginning *PM* was one of the most controversial papers in the nation, with ardent enthusiasts on the one hand and bitter critics on the other. That it wrote without restraint was denied by neither its friends nor its enemies, and it printed much in line with its slogan "News You Can't Get Elsewhere." It exposed certain sharp businesses, engaged in muckraking, and featured much news on antitrust suits which even liberal papers carrying advertising omitted or gave little prominence.

1942), Chaps. 5–6. See also Oswald Garrison Villard, *The Disappearing Daily* (New York: Alfred A. Knopf, Inc., 1944), Chap. 1.

[2] See Villard, *loc. cit.*

[3] See Marshall Field, *Freedom Is More than a Word* (1945). *PM* published a comprehensive history of itself as a supplement to its June 18, 1946, issue.

At the same time, many who were sympathetic with its objectives felt that accuracy and trustworthiness were too often sacrificed in the interest of supporting certain causes. It suspended publication in 1949 because it was financially unsuccessful.

Decline in Number of Newspapers. Many newspaper owners have been unable to keep their papers going and the number of daily papers has been steadily declining. In 1915 there were 2,500 daily and 16,323 weekly newspapers. By 1954 this had declined to 1,785 and 8,549 respectively. Although most of the larger American cities still have two or more daily papers, Villard reported that in 1944 there were "1,103 towns and cities with only one newspaper, and in 159 large towns having more than one daily there is complete ownership of the local press by one man or one group." [4] Raymond B. Nixon noted that in 1945 there were 10 states where there was not a single city with a competing newspaper and 22 states without Sunday newspaper competition.[5]

As many dailies have disappeared, ownership has become more concentrated. This is because of mergers, consolidations, and the buying of "chains" of papers. One company dominates 3,000 weeklies and more than a quarter of the daily circulation is absentee owned. Fourteen companies owning 18 papers control nearly a quarter of the circulation.[6]

The decline in the number of newspapers is hardly to be welcomed but at the same time has not necessarily resulted in cutting off sources of news for the reading public. For one thing, the circulation of the remaining newspapers has increased. Moreover, many large city dailies have increased their mail and delivery circulation to suburban and rural areas. The smaller newspapers may obtain the outpourings of the giant news-gathering associations such as the Associated Press, International News Service, and United Press. This makes for standardization so that the reader in Georgia and in Idaho may read identical accounts of non-local news events, the same editorials and "boiler plate" features, the same columnists, and perhaps see the same political cartoons. On national and international matters, therefore, large numbers of newspapers present to their readers the same facts, slants, and coverages. On local affairs, however, various good government associations have been forced into publishing small sheets dealing with matters of real importance in the community. Newspapers and magazines published by labor, business, and other organizations now reach millions of persons and probably exert considerable influence on the membership in laying down the group "line."

[4] *Op. cit.*, p. 3.
[5] "Concentration and Absenteeism in Daily Newspaper Ownership," *Journalism Quarterly*, Vol. 22 (1945), pp. 98–99.
[6] *Ibid.*

COLUMNISTS, NEWSLETTERS, AND NEWS MAGAZINES

In earlier times Americans followed the personal views of their favorite editor with interest. Today many rural readers still follow the country editor, for he is quite often active and influential in politics and public affairs. This remnant of "personal" journalism is unknown to millions of urban readers because the writer of editorials in the dailies is for the most part anonymous. As the editorial page lost its appeal, many readers turned to the columnists. Column writing has become a lucrative profession, some urban dailies boasting as many as a half dozen or more. Some columnists specialize in international affairs, others in city or national concerns. A number are uninhibited and write on all phases of politics. To some extent the stock in trade of all columnists is political gossip, "inside dope," and some prognostication.

Columnists are more widely read than editorials and in general serve a useful purpose. They provide a much-needed analytical and interpretative commentary on the news. Columns often carry supplementary material necessary for reaching an enlightened judgment. Some columnists are widely quoted, have their materials inserted in the *Congressional Record,* and often distributed in reprint form. This suggests that certain of the public respect their views. The political column can give the reader information that the editor cannot obtain from his own resources and also give the reader another viewpoint than that of the editorial page.

The columns have their weaknesses. Some of the writers are neither well trained nor particularly balanced in judgment. They become crusaders for particular views, men, and interests. Some columnists sometimes appear to be out to "get" certain public men and resort to abuse and distortion to gain their ends. Readers may tend to accept the opinions of the columnist as their own, especially if they read only one column and accept its views uncritically. Not every newspaper carries a balanced diet of commentary and its several columnists are all of similar political faith. Where this exists the reader, perhaps unknowingly, is hardly in a position to arrive at an informed judgment. Syndicated columns also are no substitute for a newspaper's own leadership of local opinion.

A curious development in American journalism which some believe has considerable influence on business and professional people is the newsletter. It is put up in the form of a forecaster's bulletin, mailed confidentially to subscribers who are willing to pay from $18 to $50 a year for "inside," "advance" news on what the government will do next. The harassed businessman will probably obtain little more from a newsletter than he would from regularly reading a paper such as *The New York Times* but the letter is a great timesaver. The most widely circulated of these letters is issued by Willard Kiplinger and is known as the

Washington Letter. Subscribers to this weekly letter number over 50,000. The service includes numerous other letters on labor, agriculture, and taxes.

"They offer," says Dixon Wecter, "a grandstand seat at the passing show of Washington. Here are excitement, color and rumor—the last sometimes flushed from the Potomac brakes only to be shot on the rise as a canard. The tone of urgency is heightened by underlining and by printing words in solid capitals. Omission of the definite article creates the air of a messenger's breathlessness, posting with hot news from the capital." [7] His study of the Kiplinger and other newsletters leads him to conclude that much valuable information on laws and Federal controls is given but that many forecasts miss the mark. Though these letters profess to be scientific and nonpartisan, partisan slants and wishful thinking creep into them. Much of the time the letters tell the readers what they want to hear or merely ratify existing viewpoints of the clientele.

Millions of persons subscribe to the mass-circulation news magazines. Here they receive, usually in capsule form, news and commentary embellished with pictures, diagrams, and charts. Undoubtedly many are drawn to these magazines because of their readability and these publications provide an undetermined but probably large number of persons with their impressions of politicians and public policies.

THE POLITICAL CARTOON

Early in the nineteenth century political caricatures appeared in Europe and soon found their way to America. The first use made of them in the United States was in 1832. For a graphic weapon opponents of President Jackson turned to a caricature picturing him as King Andrew. The caricatures were in the form of lithograph sheets displayed in shop-windows and nailed or posted on walls and fences. A famous one of his successor, Van Buren, portrayed the latter as an infant in the arms of General Jackson receiving sustenance from a spoon held by "Old Hickory." These lithographs were often coarse and highly exaggerated. They reached a high pitch in caricaturing the angular President Lincoln.

Lithograph-sheet caricature passed out of existence when the illustrated newspapers began to publish weekly cartoons. Best known of the early political cartoonists was Thomas Nast (1840–1902), who first drew cartoons that were serious in purpose at the time of the Civil War. His series of some fifty exposing the Tweed Ring during the 1870's stand as an epoch in themselves. The symbol he chose of the Tammany tiger to

[7] For a useful history and analysis of the newsletter see Wecter, "How Much News in the News Letter?" *Atlantic Monthly*, Vol. 175 (1945), p. 45.

depict the plunderings of that machine prompted Boss Tweed to mutter that someone ought to "stop them damned pictures." But nobody did, and Nast soon created the Republican elephant and Democratic donkey, which have become timeless political symbols.

The popularity of Nast's cartoons led newspapers to seek more and more of them, but it was not until the 1884 campaign of Cleveland that daily cartoons began to appear in newspapers.[8] Today practically all large metropolitan dailies have one or more cartoonists on the staff. Both large and small papers are served by syndicated cartoons. Some newspapers carry one or more cartoons on political and related subjects every day. The treatment is usually strongly satirical, partisan, and an oversimplification.

Symbolism is used to get the observer to associate bad or good causes with certain individuals and groups. Bureaucrats are depicted with sour countenances and are "snooping" into other people's business. Communists are shown as long-haired, bewhiskered bomb throwers. Some hostile newspapers used the same theme for New Dealers. College professors, the "brain trust," suffragettes, internationalists, bankers, and political bosses are among those frequently caricatured in an uncomplimentary fashion. The Stalin pipe, the Churchill cigar, and the Roosevelt cigarette holder became daily cartoons during the war, just as the Japanese war lords and Nazi leaders were depicted as savages.

Following a negative tradition, most political cartoons attack rather than support a person or cause. Newspapers seem to believe that readers prefer to have fun or sarcastic barbs leveled at opponents rather than see stressed the virtues of their own cause. On the positive side, however, some political cartoons have sought support for persons and causes through the use of Uncle Sam, the Statue of Liberty, the Bible, the Constitution, great documents, the flag, and the famous "little guy," John Q. Public.

The tabloid, news picture, and cartoon have made today a day of pictures. Cartoons tell a story and are an editorial in themselves; they supersede the editorial page as a molder of political thought. Often they are used in conjunction with a leading editorial. The effect of cartoons cannot be measured accurately but many observers felt that hostile cartoons were a powerful influence in keeping the United States out of the League of Nations. Many also believe that the uncomplimentary portrayal of labor leaders and bureaucrats has made numerous readers

[8] See Isabel S. Johnson, "Cartoons," *Public Opinion Quarterly,* Vol. 1 (1937), p. 44. Two excellent books of predominantly political cartoons are Herbert Block, *The Herblock Book: Text and Cartoons* (Boston: The Beacon Press, 1952) and D. R. Fitzpatrick, *As I Saw It* (New York: Simon and Schuster, Inc., 1953).

suspicious of unions and of the executive branch of the government. Cartoons are more and more finding their way into campaign literature and in the publications of private-interest groups.

THE HYDE PARK "TREE GROWER"

Courtesy of the Chicago Tribune.

THE PRESS AND PUBLIC OPINION

How influential is the press in public affairs or in deciding the outcome of an election? Former Secretary of the Interior Harold L. Ickes and many others have insisted that the newspapers have little or no effect on the outcome of an election. The election and the reelection of Franklin D. Roosevelt are given as evidence to support this contention. In 1932 only 41 per cent of the dailies which took sides in the election supported

Mr. Roosevelt, and in succeeding elections the percentage favoring him was considerably smaller. In many cities, including Chicago, where he was under especially severe attack by the large dailies, he was reelected by large margins. Publishers nevertheless insist that the newspaper is influential in determining the outcome of an election and that the case of Franklin Roosevelt was without precedent, i.e., that previously the press had usually been on the winning side and that it could not hope to overcome the popularity of any leader in time of crisis or war. The publishers' contention overlooks the fact that Roosevelt reached the public through the medium of radio.

The assumption that the press always is on the winning side in presidential elections has been effectively disproved by Dean Mott's study.[9] In a survey of the 34 presidential campaigns in which there were actual contests from 1796 to 1944, it was found that 17 nominees were elected without the help of the majority of the newspapers, while 17 had the majority on their side. Including the three elections since the study, the press through the 1952 election had been on the winning side 18 times and on the losing side 19 times.

Mayors and governors are often elected without substantial newspaper support, but evidence can be mustered to show that the majority of the press has about as often been on the winning side. For minor political contests, and especially where one newspaper dominates the area, press support is very often a decisive factor in the winner's victory.

The 1952 campaign saw overwhelming editorial support for Eisenhower (see Table 2). In nine states not a single daily newspaper supported

Table 2. Editorial Support in Daily Newspapers, 1952

Candidate	Number of papers	Per cent of papers	Per cent of circulation
Eisenhower....	933	67.34	80.24
Stevenson.....	202	14.52	10.88
Independent...	250	18.14	8.88

SOURCE: *Editor and Publisher*, Nov. 1, 1952.

Stevenson and in several states not more than one paper endorsed him. Only in Georgia, Kentucky, and North Carolina did more papers support Stevenson than Eisenhower. A poll of the American Press Institute showed

[9] Frank Luther Mott, "Newspapers in Presidential Campaigns," *Public Opinion Quarterly*, Vol. 8 (1944), pp. 348–367.

75 per cent of 617 weeklies favoring Eisenhower and 20 per cent endorsing Stevenson. This situation led Governor Stevenson to deliver a speech on the "one-party press," in which he deplored the one-sided character of party endorsement.[10] Since the press has been generally friendly to the Republican party, its endorsement of Eisenhower was no more surprising than its similar opposition to Roosevelt and Truman.

A more serious charge was raised by numerous journalists that most newspapers were playing up the Republican nominee and ignoring the Democratic candidate. Some called for an investigation of the newspapers because of alleged unfair coverage of the Democratic campaign. One of *The Christian Science Monitor's* most objective reporters wrote: "Stevenson is not getting an even break in the news columns of newspapers. . . . My own daily observations lead to the conclusion that much of the daily press is committing a serious offense against its readers and against the canons of responsible journalism, in showing marked one-sidedness in covering the news of this campaign and in slanting much of the news it does cover." [11] Evidence is easily found by reference to specific papers to support this contention. One can also point to many papers supporting Eisenhower which were commendably reporting the Democratic campaign. Charges and countercharges of this kind occur in every campaign. Fairness in the news columns cannot be legislated. The integrity of the publisher and protests of the readers provide the greatest safeguard against biased reporting of campaigns.

The newspaper's influence cannot be judged in terms of winning an election. Many editors believe it is the function of the press to give political news and to interpret it. The next question arises: Does the press mold, lead, or follow public opinion and is it influential in this respect? Again conclusive evidence is wanting. However, a study conducted by Bernard Berelson on the relationship of newspapers and public issues in 1940 found that the press is influential both in converting its readers and in reinforcing their ideas but that it reinforces more than it converts.[12] It was found that the more frequently an argument or issue appeared in print, the more it was recognized by readers and the more it was discussed. On this basis it seems fair to assume that if news of a labor strike is repeated more often in the press than, for instance, an antitrust suit, then the strike is likely to become more familiar to readers. This is another illustration of the familiar device of repetition. Berelson produces evidence to show that repetition leads to recognition and that recognition causes the undecided reader in more cases than not to make up his mind

10 Portland, Ore., Sept. 8, 1952.

11 Roscoe Drummond in the issue of Oct. 10, 1952.

12 "The Effects of Print on Public Opinion," in Douglas Waples (ed.), *Print, Radio, and Film in a Democracy* (Chicago: University of Chicago Press, 1942), pp. 41–65.

in favor of the argument.[13] Hence the press is not likely to change an ardent free trader into a high protectionist, but a person who has no convictions on the subject may come to accept protectionism if his newspaper constantly features protectionist arguments. He concludes: "People come across arguments which the mediums of communication emphasize; they also tend to see the arguments they want to see and other arguments whose statement is appealing. Mainly, people accept the arguments which support their own general position; they also tend to accept the arguments which they see in the public communications and those whose statement is persuasive." [14]

A real challenge to the newspaper is the overcoming of its rapid, single-dimensional handling of the news which results in printing "objectively" news stories but which leave the reader without understanding and meaning of the news. Newspapers tell the reader who, what, and where but do not explain why. The same space is given to accusation and charge, however false, as to rebuttal. Truth is often more complex and more difficult to explain than the charge or contention. Loyalty cases have featured the headlines for many years but the papers felt they could not hold back publication until proof or modification was produced. Some editors were candid enough to admit that they knew the charges were false at the time they were made, but felt compelled to print them in the interest of providing the news at once. The giving of background, perspective, and content of events is one of the great problems facing the conscientious operator of all communications media.

The American press has been under investigation on many occasions and many recommendations have appeared for its improvement.[15] Actually, the American Society of Newspaper Editors at its first annual meeting in 1923 adopted "canons of journalism" which, if scrupulously observed, would blunt charges against certain newspapers. The editors codified their aspirations under these captions: "Responsibility, independence, sincerity, truthfulness, accuracy, impartiality, fair play, decency, and freedom of the press."

AMERICAN RADIO TODAY

General Character. The management and control of radio broadcasting has followed three general patterns in the world. In totalitarian countries the ruling cliques seized all channels and, under strict monopoly of the government, used them to preach ideology, to attack democratic theories, and in general to broadcast materials to perpetuate the party in power.

[13] *Ibid.*, p. 57.

[14] *Ibid.*, p. 63.

[15] See, for example, Commission on Freedom of the Press, *A Free and Responsible Press*, published by *Fortune* (New York) in 1947.

Radio in these countries has had tremendous influence on public opinion for it has controlled news at the source. In many European democracies radio broadcasting is also a government monopoly but is kept out of partisan politics through operation by a proprietary corporation and the cost of broadcasting is largely borne through licensing fees on radio sets.

American radio broadcasting has been developed almost exclusively by private enterprise. Partisan broadcasts, especially during campaigns, must be paid for either by the candidate, his party, or a sponsoring group. Since radio stations are for the most part owned by a business organization, American radio is characterized by a commercial compulsion with major emphasis upon features, humor, entertainment, and amusement, and on programs which will draw sizable audiences and result in increased sales for the sponsor. Comedian Henry Morgan once described this in what he called "Morgan's law": "As the intellectual content of a program decreases, the number of listeners increases; as intellectual content goes up, listenership goes down. Radio needs a vast audience for maximum profit and what it broadcasts is therefore the lowest common denominator of the multitude." [16]

The emphasis on the commercial has led sponsors of broadcasts to avoid driving listeners from the loud-speaker. In turn this may result in shunning programs which deal with economic and political questions, especially if they are controversial. The daytime serials, for example, refrain from touching vital political and economic issues. Lazarsfeld observed that [17]

. . . in forty-five serials carefully followed up for three weeks, not one character was found who came from the laboring class. Inasmuch as they are upper-class characters, they are used to lend glamour to the middle-class settings rather than play a role of their own. All problems are of an individualistic nature. It is not social forces but the virtues and vices of the central characters that move the events along. People lose jobs not for economic reasons but because their fellow men lie or are envious. A simple black or white technique avoids any insoluble conflicts.

Many other radio dramas likewise fail to deal realistically with controversial problems and so avoid loss of listeners or complaints.

Several observations made about newspapers apply equally to the radio. Just as many readers are content to rely on the headlines and possibly the first paragraph of a news item, so have listeners come to accept the "flash" and brief summaries appearing "on the hour" on radio stations. Radio has gone in for condensation and has carried "on the trend from

---

[16] Quoted in N. J. Powell, *The Anatomy of Public Opinion* (New York: Prentice-Hall, Inc., 1951), p. 363.

[17] In Waples, *op. cit.*, p. 67.

detailed information—suited to the interest of a small, well-educated minority—to the barest essentials of current news—designed for the larger masses of people, who are not interested in the details." [18] Radio commentators, like newspaper columnists, are legion. Again listeners tend to follow those who confirm their fears, prejudices, and wishes and to tune out those with whom they disagree.

Problems of Political Education. There is no definitive study which shows the number of persons who rely upon radio for their major source of news and political commentary. Judging by the number of news broadcasts and commentators, it may be presumed to be considerable. Several problems have arisen in connection with the reconciliation of avoidance of controversy on the one hand and the presentation of information which the listener needs for a political judgment on the other. An informed judgment is not likely to be one which results from hearing only one side. Some sponsors keep a commentator on the air because they like his views; others because the views are at least inoffensive to them; still others are unconcerned with the broadcaster's views so long as he has a large audience. In the last-mentioned case the advertiser may be led to drop a reporter because of the volume of protest mail.

Beginning in 1946, the nation began to swing to the right in its thinking. This was soon reflected on the radio. Commentators friendly to labor and to the Fair Deal lost their sponsors and word went out in the trade that they were "hot" or "too controversial." Some were carried for a time on a sustained basis, i.e., without a sponsor and at the expense of the station, but many were dropped. Those who specialized in straight news could usually get a sponsor, but those who brought in editorial and interpretive comment were under considerable pressure, even though the line between the two is not always easy to draw. There were some within the radio industry who advanced the view that all political commentary should be carried by stations and networks on a sustained basis as a public service.

Subject to moral consideration and libel laws, public policy has decreed that there shall be freedom of speech over the air. Because of financial and other factors, this principle has resulted in controversy. There are many cases on record where stations have refused programs on labor unions, consumer cooperatives, and spokesmen for unpopular political and economic doctrines on the ground that they were "too controversial" or "could not be fitted in the schedule." Charges of partiality in the granting of time on the air have been made by labor unions and other groups. After a monitoring of programs it was found that labor received an overwhelming number of "unfavorable" comments by sponsored news-

[18] *Ibid.,* p. 71.

casters.[19] In most instances persons disagreeing with a commentator were unable to reply because the newscasters were regularly sponsored and their remarks on labor were only incidental. In part to counterbalance the alleged unfriendly tone of some commentators, the American Federation of Labor and the Congress of Industrial Organizations sponsor their own commentators.

The financial aspects of broadcasting automatically restrict minorities in the use of the air waves, especially if they must pay for the time. A full network may cost as much as $20,000 an hour. The superior financial resources of the two major parties enable them to put their campaign pleas on the air for hours and hours; minor parties are unable to afford more than a few minutes. In local campaigns there is often sharp discrepancy between the campaign funds of even two major party candidates.[20]

For many years the party out of power has protested the granting of free time to the President for his public addresses between elections, on the ground that he is giving a "political" talk and should pay for it. Time for replies has sometimes been given but the minority party has then protested that the hour assigned for rebuttal was not so good as the one given the Chief Executive. Equalization of access to the air waves for diverse views remains one of the sharpest issues in the use of radio for political education.

TELEVISION

America entered a new era of electronic mass communication with the advent of television, frequency-modulated broadcasting, and facsimile broadcasting. The last-mentioned is only at the threshold of commercial development and it is so expensive that it will be some time before it can compete with sound broadcasting and become "the newspaper in the home."

Although television was first used in 1941, it has come into its own very recently. In 1950 there were only about 4 million television receivers; in 1954 there were about 400 stations and 31 million sets. Television has the attribute of being more vivid and real than radio and by adding the extra sense of sight can make potentially a greater impact. A Department of Commerce report commented that "television has the visual impact of newspapers and magazines, the oral persuasion and personal immediacy of radio." One communications expert, in urging educational television, remarked: "If television can make wrestling fans, it can also make citizens who are informed on public affairs." [21]

[19] See summary by L. A. Sussman, "How Radio Treated Labor in the Elections," *Common Sense*, Vol. 14 (March, 1945), pp. 34 ff.

[20] The use of radio in campaigns is covered in Chap. 21. Radio and television are used very little in local elections except in large cities.

[21] Wilbur Schramm, *Variety*, Feb. 22, 1950.

Television was not widely used in campaigns until 1952, though in the mid-term election of 1950 it was estimated that 25 per cent of the total broadcast budget went to this medium. The telecasting of the 1952 national conventions, which reached mass audiences, had a tremendous advertising build-up. A year earlier the Senate Crime Investigating Committee had its hearings televised. In some communities business was almost at a standstill while customers stayed home to watch the proceedings, which were more exciting than a "whodunit" novel. Policemen, underworld characters, gamblers, mayors and officials paraded before the cameras in an unprecedented show. His appearances on these telecasts as chairman of the committee built Senator Estes Kefauver overnight into a leading contender for the Democratic presidential nomination.

The Republican convention met first, and, according to the ratings, had much the larger audience than its Democratic counterpart two weeks later. Many people found one convention enough. Undoubtedly the telecasting of the Republican convention excited great electoral interest. Here the real-life struggle between the Taft and Eisenhower forces was portrayed—the battles in the credentials committee, then on the floor, the keynote address, the demonstrations, and so on. Attention was focused on amusing personal incidents and not a few speakers at the convention were selected on the basis of photogenic and telegenic qualities.

Television has come in for much of the same criticism as radio, such as overcommercialism, inferior programs, and emphasis on shows of violence. In view of the expensiveness of the medium it seems doubtful if it will carry, at least for some time, the large number of public-interest and news programs on a sustaining basis. The emphasis on pure "entertainment" aspects appears somewhat greater than in radio, though in time this may be changed.

The round-table or panel discussion offers real potentialities for enlightened discussion; potentialities which as yet are not fully realized. A study of two-panel or public-forum programs showed that entertainment rather than education appeared to be the goal. It concluded: [22]

The participants are not concerned with seeking a mutually satisfactory solution to a common problem; nor does the moderator of either program encourage such cooperative thinking. . . .

The primary source of entertainment on such a program stems from the element of conflict involved; . . . everybody likes a good fight, especially when a woman is one of the combatants. It is the heated argument, the personal accusations, the name-calling, and clever retort which give the program its "punch." Both moderators agree that fan mail doubles after a rousing wrangle. They therefore play up and promote conflict when possible [and] invite speakers whom they know to be quick-tempered, vitriolic, or bombastic.

[22] Frank Washburn, "The Television Panel as a Vehicle of Political Persuasion," *Western Speech,* Vol. 16 (1952), pp. 246–247.

In terms of politics and political education television's costliness high-lights, at least at the moment, the serious problem of access to the use of facilities. During the 1952 campaign a 30-minute coast-to-coast televi-sion network cost about $75,000. This was prohibitive to candidates of minor parties and even the Democratic party was hard pressed at times to obtain money for telecasts. For local candidates, those having the funds were able to buy time, those of lesser resources were unable to make much use of the medium. One study showed that not more than a fifth to a fourth of the campaign shows were carried free by either radio or tele-vision.[23] In many if not most cases radio and television shows reinforced each other; i.e., the same party bought time on both and also had news-paper support. Where this happens one party is not able to use effectively one medium as a counterbalance to another.

To some extent this same situation operates between campaigns where political commentators with unorthodox views are unable to get sponsors, and minorities likewise cannot afford to purchase time to present their views. Professor Levin has stated the problem in these terms: [24]

Prohibitive political time rates, and not planned discrimination by radio execu-tives, seems largely to blame for minimizing expression of unpopular, non-conformist views. The net effect is little different from a concerted plot; and what can even a willing FCC do in such a case?

Surely the inadequate discussion of U.S. policy in Korea, prisoner exchange issues, the seating of Red China in the UN, etc., must be considered in this context. For the groups most vitally concerned with presenting "the other side"— and questioning existing U.S. policies—are today often the least wealthy political minorities, unable to buy needed TV time.

MOTION PICTURES

Development. There are many persons living who can still remember seeing the first important story in film, "The Great Train Robbery," when it appeared in 1903. The first full-length talking picture, "The Jazz Singer," did not appear until 1928. Today the motion-picture industry has a $2 billion capital investment and is one of the largest enterprises in the United States. Several television operators have expressed the belief that Hollywood is "finished" because movie attendance took a drastic decline after television set ownership began to run into seven and eight figures. One study found television cutting into movie attendance by 72 per cent.[25] Television likewise has had an impact on the numbers of persons listening to the radio. The belief that television will result in the demise of the commercial motion picture and radio seems highly

---

[23] Conducted by R. M. Mall of WLWC (TV), Columbus, Ohio; cited in Harvey Levin, "TV in the Campaign," *Frontier*, Vol. 4 (April, 1953), p. 9.

[24] *Ibid.*

[25] See *Variety*, Mar. 1, 1950, July 6, 1949; *Fortune*, March, 1949, pp. 12–13.

premature. Millions of persons still attend theaters each week and American motion pictures continue to do a thriving business in foreign countries. Millions of foreigners receive their impressions of the United States from films. The influence of the movies upon styles, humor, dress, speech, and morals has been widely recognized. The effect upon political attitudes and interests is less obvious and more subtle.

As in the case of the press, radio, and television, many authoritarian governments have taken over or have controlled motion-picture production for purposes of propaganda. The Soviet Union has made great use of the film for ideological purposes. It has several pictures on "American plots" to take over Eastern European countries. Following Lenin's dictum that "the cinema can and must be Soviet Russia's greatest cultural weapon," the government has seen to it that the movies stress the great achievements of the Soviet Union, its superiority over capitalism, and documentaries on the Five-year Plan. Numerous American movies, however, such as "The Iron Curtain" and "The Conspirator" have followed an anti-Soviet Union theme and related themes relevant to the cold war. These are the exception rather than the rule because American films are multiple purpose; indeed, the trade is in general agreement that these pictures are not great money-makers. Hollywood producers have been known to tone down pictures to meet the objections of the State Department. But the industry in this country has been free to develop without fear of government interference and competition. The industry has imposed its own code on producers and has largely "policed" itself through the office of the Motion Picture Producers and Distributors of America. Producers try not to offend any important group in the community and the industry selects its "villains" with great care.

Character and Influence. The production, distribution, and exhibition of full-length feature films is a money-making enterprise and this means that the pictures produced must attract the largest numbers possible. If one asks the industry what the people want of the movies, the unanimous answer is entertainment. Many will go further and say that propaganda, education, and controversy are disliked and hence to be avoided. One authority says: [26]

Exhibitors will tell you that audiences don't want controversy. That, too, may be true; but again the source is suspect. For the exhibitor as an individual is not eager to have his opinion changed. If you ask him to define controversial materials, he will say that it is anything counter to the prevailing view of the local community. . . . It is the exhibitor who snips controversy out of the newsreel. An enterprising company may go out of its way to present popular and unpopular views, only to have the theater manager black out what he doesn't want to see.

[26] Waples, *op. cit.,* pp. 82–83.

It is said that if politics and propaganda made money, then producers would make political and propaganda films. If education brought high salaries to producers and distributors and large box-office receipts, then producers would make educational pictures and exhibitors would show them. Many educators object to this view and insist that both film and radio producers underestimate the interests and intelligence of the public. Those who see the potentialities of the movies as an educator believe the theatergoer would respond to pictures which portray public issues and problems. They point out, for example, the success of "Wilson" and "Tennessee Johnson" in terms of money. Both pictures portrayed the battle between the President and Congress. "All the King's Men," a prize-winning, money-making movie, told the story of the rise and fall of a political leader who bore resemblance to Huey Long. Robert Sherwood's "Abe Lincoln in Illinois" was a thoroughly successful play, but as a picture it was a financial failure. For every political film which is successful, exhibitors will report that there are many which fail.

Several conclusions emerge from a study of full-length feature pictures which impart a "message" or which attempt to depict social and political problems. The more successful ones, financially speaking, are of biographical nature or strongly tinged with human interest. This is not to belittle them, since politics is filled with biography and human interest. However, accuracy is often sacrificed for dramatic effect. Oversimplification is used in place of a faithful and comprehensive portrayal. Some of our best political pictures have come from novels but with the more controversial parts modified.

After surveying the various studies on the influence of films, N. J. Powell [27] believes it has been demonstrated that "noncommercial films can appreciably increase the informational level of the audience. Commercial films tend to find an attitudinal bar in the minds of the audience, the members of which expect no education in the motion pictures." Films can shift attitudes but this shift is unpredictable on the basis of current research; and films sometimes strengthen attitudes opposite to those intended. Motion pictures are probably least influential in affecting the attitudes which are most remote from the major purpose of the picture. Finally, Powell believes that the claims that "motion pictures are a potent device for achieving good will and peace in modern society are unsupportable."

Newsreels and Documentary Films. By far the greatest amount of education by film is imparted through the newsreels, shorts, and documentaries. Here the audience is given propaganda and education in smaller doses, and producers have seemed a little less worried about making

[27] *Op. cit.,* p. 341.

money from them. Some of the most dramatic aspects of our democracy are touched upon by the newsreels, such as nominating conventions, campaigns, presidential addresses, meetings of the United Nations, and labor strikes. Their brevity, however, is a serious limitation because the audience gets no well-rounded conception of the importance of the item.

The United States government had two excursions into the making of documentary films. The first of these began during the 1930's as an educational program to awaken the people to the need for conserving the human and natural resources of the country and for a measure of national planning. Beginning in 1936 four full-length films were produced within as many years: "The River," "The Plow That Broke the Plains," "The Fight for Life," and "Power and the Land." The first was produced to show the efforts of the government to halt ruinous erosion and the havoc wrought by the overflow of the Mississippi and its tributaries. In the second the Resettlement Administration told of the dust storms and measures designed to combat their effects, while "The Fight for Life" portrayed childbirth mortality in the slums. As a project of the Rural Electrification Administration, "Power and the Land" dealt with the coming of electricity to rural homes. Each picture received praise from the critics, but, with the exception of "The Plow," was given a limited showing in commercial theaters. The experiment came to an abrupt end in 1940 when critics in Congress found that no specific funds or authority had been granted to engage in the production of these films. Irrespective of the merits of the pictures, it is obvious that Congress and many constituents view with misgiving the entry of the government into the business of producing motion pictures. Legislators fear the adverse effects which result from showing pictures of unsavory conditions within their sections.

Congressional criticism is avoided so long as "controversial" subjects are omitted. For example, a picture showing the areas blighted by the boll weevil and measures taken to fight the menace are acceptable. Pictures showing the plight of the sharecropper, however, are not considered a proper subject for a government film, especially if a specific program of rehabilitation is included. Because of this point of view, the government has been limited in its activities to use the film as a means of influencing public opinion and rallying support for causes on which there is a sharp difference of opinion.

MASS MEDIA AND MONOPOLY

The effects of government monopoly of or complete control over the great agencies of communication in authoritarian nations are alone enough to dramatize the importance of keeping them free from the dominance of a ruling clique. Western democracies have been sensitive to this problem and opposition parties are constantly on the alert against legislative or executive control which might interfere with the free expression of ideas. In the United States the mass media are for the most part privately owned, though they operate professedly in the public interest. The party in power enjoys certain advantages over the opposition. It is the party in power which makes the greater portion of the news and the press, radio, and television receive much of their news from incumbent boards, departments, and the press conferences of officeholders. At the same time the opposition expects to have its views widely disseminated.

With few exceptions the government has not been associated with monopoly controls over the press and broadcasting facilities in the United States. A great many bills have been introduced in Congress to provide for certain types of regulation over the production of motion pictures, especially with a view toward deleting "Communist propaganda." These, however, have had little serious chance to be adopted. Congressional committees have investigated the industry, and state and local boards have at times censored portions of certain movies. These activities have led some figures in Hollywood to charge that the government has intimidated the industry and discouraged it from making controversial films.

For the most part, the alleged dangers of monopoly in the communications industries have come not from the government but from the owners themselves. Smaller operators of newspapers, broadcasting stations, and motion-picture producers have at times called upon the government to help assist in the creation of a social climate wherein the various interest groups may have reasonable access to these instruments, not only in order to make a living but to use them to express criticism, set forth policies, and for the edification of themselves and their special clienteles. Morris Ernst and others feel that more government control of these media is necessary because "concentrated power" has destroyed free enterprise in the field.[28]

A few common examples of this concentration of control within communications are the block booking of films by theater producers and the fact that the great majority of television stations are owned by radio stations. In 1954 newspapers owned a majority or minority share of about one-third of all television stations. The majority of TV stations are owned by radio stations and over half the radio stations in turn are owned or controlled by newspapers.[29] A congressional committee reported in 1950

[28] See *The First Freedom* (New York: The Macmillan Company, 1946), on the contention that ownership by a few score owners is endangering the American democracy; see also Nixon, *op. cit.*, pp. 97–114.

[29] In 1944 a congressional committee found that about 57 per cent of the stations were owned or controlled by newspapers. See *Economic Concentration and World War II*, 79th Cong., 2d Sess., S. Doc. 26, 1948, p. 275. Some private sources hold that only from 30 to 40 per cent of the stations are majority-owned by newspapers. See also *Television Age*, April, 1954.

that 243 of the 687 commercial FM stations were either owned outright or in part by newspapers.[30] Recently chain daily newspaper circulation has been about 55 per cent of the total.

In an attempt to mitigate potential monopoly by the newspapers over radio facilities, the Federal Communications Commission refuses to permit the same person to own more than one station in the same vicinity. The attempts to enforce the antitrust legislation have probably had some effect in deterring monopolistic practices but the results have by no means been conspicuous.

The larger economic groups use the communications media to enhance and maintain their positions. The various publics rely to a considerable extent upon the press, movies, radio, and television for sources of information and even judgments of public events. In turn the media are dependent upon the man in the street for support and they give him what he wants or at least what he tolerates. When unorganized groups become aware that the media are not adequately serving them, they protest, and may even organize in order to try to change the situation. The larger organized groups print papers of their own, purchase broadcasting time or sometimes buy a radio station, and some put out their own films. To an increasing degree groups are using the communications industries as power outlets, and the press and radio in particular are creatures of the public they influence. The more financially powerful groups, however, usually have greater access to the opinion-molding, opinion-expressing mass media; the less well-to-do groups and the unorganized publics at times appear to have unequal access. Educational television, FM, and the carrying of political commentary on a sustained instead of sponsored basis offer some promise as methods of providing the citizen with the chance to consider the range of views along the political spectrum.

There are many newspapers which display a high degree of public responsibility by providing comprehensive and objective treatment of news. Notwithstanding this, the newspaper business is big business and necessarily identified with the business point of view. Outside the South, newspapers are overwhelmingly Republican in their party sympathies and many communities are served by only one paper. This situation has challenged many to write of its dangers and possible remedies. In 1943 a Commission on Freedom of the Press, headed by Robert M. Hutchins, was appointed to launch a large-scale investigation into the mass communications media both as to present state and future prospects. The Commission's report was filed in 1947 and merits reading by students of public opinion.[31]

[30] See *General Interim Report of House Select Committee on Lobbying Activities,* 81st Cong., 2d Sess., H. Rept. 3138, 1950, pp. 26 ff.

[31] Published by the University of Chicago Press.

Among the Commission's recommendations were greater use by the government itself of the media to inform its citizens of facts and policies and the fostering of more competition through use of antitrust laws. It recommended repealing laws which might be used to prohibit public expression of revolutionary ideas and an independent agency to appraise and report annually upon the performance of the press. Greater mutual criticism among the carriers of information was recommended. The public itself can share in improvement by demanding higher quality performance. These proposals provoked controversy but nonetheless provided some constructive suggestions for consideration. In conclusion the report stated the realities of the matter when it noted: "The outside forces of law and public opinion can in various ways check bad aspects of press performance, but good press performance can come only from human beings who operate the instrumentalities of communications."

SELECTED REFERENCES

The dynamic field of communication has produced a plethora of materials. The radio, television, and theater pages of metropolitan newspapers, notably *The New York Times,* contain much worthwhile information on current developments, and periodicals such as *Harper's Magazine, Atlantic Monthly, Fortune, Frontier, Hollywood Quarterly, The New Republic, The Nation, Public Opinion Quarterly, Journalism Quarterly, Variety,* and *Broadcasting-Telecasting* carry many articles of value.

On the newspapers consult the readings edited by George L. Bird and Frederic E. Merwin, *The Press and Society* (1951); an extensive bibliography is also found in this volume. Other useful works include John E. Allen, *The Modern Newspaper* (1940); F. L. Mott, *American Journalism* (1941); George Seldes, *Lords of the Press* (1938) and *Freedom of the Press* (1935); C. B. Gosnell and R. B. Nixon, *Public Opinion and the Press* (1933); Alfred M. Lee, *The Daily Newspaper in America* (1937); Oswald Garrison Villard, *The Disappearing Daily* (1944); Douglas Waples (ed.), *Print, Radio, and Film in a Democracy* (1942); Stanley Walker, *City Editor* (1934); Quincy Howe, *The News and How to Understand It* (1940); Harold L. Ickes, *America's House of Lords* (1939) and *Freedom of the Press Today* (1941); Charles Fisher, *The Columnists* (1944).

The general and special reports of the Commission on Freedom of the Press under the chairmanship of Robert M. Hutchins provide many searching questions on the operation, control, and influence of the communications media. All are published by the University of Chicago Press. Those published in 1947 include the concluding report, *A Free and Responsible Press;* Ruth A. Inglis, *Freedom of the Movies;* Llewellyn White and Robert D. Leigh, *Peoples Speaking to Peoples* (international communication); and Llewellyn White, *The American Radio.*

Other volumes on radio and television include Hadley Cantril and Gordon Allport, *The Psychology of Radio* (1935); Thomas B. Grandin, *The Political Use of Radio* (1939); Harold N. Graves, *War on the Short Wave* (1941); Robert J. Landry, *Who, What, Why Is Radio?* (1942); Thomas P. Robinson, *Radio Networks and the Federal Government* (1943); Cornelia B. Rose, *National Policy for Radio Broadcasting* (1940); Maurice Gorham, *Television—Medium of the Future* (1949); "Radio: The Fifth Estate," *The Annals of the American Academy of Political and Social Science,* Vol. 177 (1935); C. A. Siepmann, *Radio, Television, and Society* (1950). For a highly useful annotated bibliography on radio see Oscar Rose, *Radio Broadcasting and Television* (1947).

Materials on the social implications of the films are less abundant and largely confined to periodicals. A bibliography on censorship is found in L. T. Beman, *Selected Articles on Censorship of the Theatre and Motion Pictures* (1931). See also John E. Harley, *Worldwide Influences of the Cinema: A Study of Official Censorship* and *International Cultural Aspects of Motion Pictures* (1941); Margaret F. Thorp, *America at the Movies* (1939); Leo C. Rosten, *Hollywood, the Movie Colony, the Movie Makers* (1941); "The Motion Picture Industry," *The Annals of the American Academy of Political and Social Science,* Vol. 254 (1947); Paul Rotha, *The Documentary Film* (1939).

1. Newspaper :
    a. Commercial aspects & public service enterprise.
    b. Decline in number makes for standardization.
2. Columnists, news letters & news magazines (widely read)
3. Cartoons (tell a story & editorial in themselves.

Radio : 1. Private are legion
        2. Too much commercial
        3. Finances limit freedom of speech.

Television : 1. criticisms (a) overcommercialized, inferior
               programs (c) shows of violence
             2. Round table is a potential development.

motion pictures:
    1. do money making so it caters to masses.
    2 Newsreels are limited in usage,

PART TWO

Political Interest Groups

CHAPTER 4

The Politics of Business

> A zeal for different opinions concerning religion, concerning government, and many other points, as well of speculation as of practice; an attachment to different leaders ambitiously contending for pre-eminence and power; or to persons of other descriptions whose fortunes have been interesting to the human passions, have, in turn, divided mankind into parties, inflamed them with mutual animosity, and rendered them much more disposed to vex and oppress each other than to cooperate for their common good. . . . But the most common and durable source of factions has been the various and unequal distribution of property.
>
> —JAMES MADISON, *The Federalist*, No. 10

Our founding fathers were keenly aware of the importance, utility, and dangers of "factions" and "interests" in the political life. James Madison expanded considerably on the theme which he stated in the quotation above. He recognized both the economic and noneconomic interests which "grow up of necessity in civilized nations." The former he saw as including a landed interest, a manufacturing interest, a mercantile interest, and a moneyed interest. He and others of his time saw the role of government as essentially that of reconciling these interests within the state. In 165 years of the American experiment in government is seen the validity of his insight in writing: "The regulation of these various and interfering interests forms the principal task of modern legislation, and involves the spirit of party and faction in the necessary and ordinary operations of the government."

A generation after the adoption of the Constitution, Andrew Jackson was declaring war on the banking interests, and Roger B. Taney was inveighing: "It was obvious to my mind . . . that a great moneyed corporation possessing a fearful power for good or for evil, had entered into the field of politics and deliberately preparing its plans to obtain, by means of its money, an irresistible political influence in the affairs of the nation so as to enable it to control the measures of the Government." The ever-growing vitality and influence of pressure groups seem to have made them as certain as death and taxes. Even in time of war there has been no moratorium on pressure politics. As a matter of record, the great contenders for power appear to increase their organizational activities during wars and during the inevitable periods of maladjustment follow-

69

ing them. After the cessation of hostilities in 1945, Congress and the Chief Executive were bombarded with communications, and public buildings teemed with spokesmen of interests desiring relief from a continuation of wartime measures and for policies which would help them enhance their power.

No one has undertaken the titanic task of fully identifying and describing the organization and techniques of the thousands of interest groups in the nation. The U.S. Department of Commerce attempted in 1949 to catalogue national associations and to estimate local affiliates or chapters. Combining national and local groups, it was estimated that there were 16,000 businessmen's associations, 70,000 labor unions, 100,000 women's organizations, and 15,000 civic and professional groups.[1] Four times a year the *Congressional Record* carries a list of lobbyists who have registered under the Federal Regulation of Lobbying Act. These lists are extraordinarily interesting and give some idea of the range and diversity of political interest groups. The Department of Commerce's study gave some information on 4,000 national organizations and indicated the number of groups in the categories shown in Table 3.

Table 3. Numbers of National Organizations, 1949

Type of organization	Number
Manufacturers	800
Distributors	300
Transportation, finance, insurance	400
Other national business associations	300
Professional and semiprofessional	500
Labor unions	200
Women's	100
Sports and recreation	100
Veterans and military	60
Commodity exchanges	60
Farmers	55
Negroes	50
Public officials	50
Fraternal	25
All other fields	1,000
Total	4,000

SOURCE: U.S. Department of Commerce.

Fortunately there are many excellent works available on specific groups and on the significance of their activities to the public and to government. Newspapers and periodicals are filled with accounts of organized groups and offer a rich source of information. The organizations themselves are

[1] *National Associations of the United States* (Washington, D.C.: Government Printing Office, 1949).

usually prolific publishers and their materials provide excellent basic data for the student of interest-group politics. The more one understands of the aims and activities of the pressure interests, the greater becomes his insight into the real extralegal aspects of the political system. Here we can only identify the more influential of these groups, note their aims, and describe the methods they use to try to accomplish their objectives.

In the literature of politics "interest group" and "pressure group" are often used synonymously and interchangeably. There are some who have attempted a distinction. The *Encyclopaedia of the Social Sciences* distinguishes "interest" according to objectives and "pressure" according to techniques used. David Truman sees an interest group as a "shared-attitude group that makes certain claims upon other groups in the society" and "when it makes its claims through or upon any of the institutions of government, it becomes a political interest group." [2] Our main concern is with those groups which have the intention to make demands on the government. Every group is an interest group or a group with an interest, but not every group attempts to influence public policy.

In order to facilitate the study of political interest groups, several different types of classification have been attempted. One designation is according to the geographical area in which they operate, such as national, regional, state, county, neighborhood, and so on. Another classifies according to aims, techniques, or the responses they seek to elicit. Still another type of classification separates groups according to public or unselfish objectives and private or selfish aims. None of these categories is without its limitation because local groups are constantly "going national" and are in a federation this year and out the next.

In classifying groups it must not be overlooked that they are constantly changing and that their relationships with other groups are undergoing change. At times parent-teacher associations are intensely active in applying political pressure, then for months they may be concerned merely with the internal problems of a school and engage in no pressures on the board of education or city council. New groups are constantly being created and countergroups are formed to meet these "adversaries." Classification may also lead one to ascribe an interest and a cohesion to certain groups which do not exist or which are exaggerated.

For purposes of brief treatment and simplicity a functional classification of political interest groups is used here. This classification is likewise subject to the same limitations just noted. Functional groupings include (1) commerce, business, and industry; (2) labor; (3) agrarian; (4) the pro-

---

[2] *The Governmental Process* (New York: Alfred A. Knopf, Inc., 1951), p. 37. Mary E. Dillon, "Pressure Groups," *The American Political Science Review,* Vol. 36 (1942), pp. 471–481, sees the method of propaganda as a distinguishing characteristic of the pressure group.

fessions; (5) foreign policy; (6) patriotic; (7) veterans; (8) religious and ethnic; (9) consumers; (10) citizens' associations; and (11) government. Consideration will be given to the groups under these headings, with emphasis largely on the relationship of these interests to government and politics.

BUSINESS AND THE AMERICAN ECONOMY

General Character. One does not have to be a Marxist to recognize that business is and must be in politics. The operators of commerce and industry have in our society been the largest owners of property and wealth, which makes them *ipso facto* interested in public policies that will protect and enhance their interests. From the earliest days of the nation the voice of businessmen has been influential in the councils of government. In his famous study, *Economic Interpretation of the Constitution,* Charles A. Beard depicted the influence of persons with large holdings in money, public securities, manufacturing, trade, and shipping in the drafting and adoption of the Constitution. The period from Jackson to Lincoln was marked by the struggle between the planter aristocracy of the South and the business interests of the North and East, with the latter gaining unquestioned ascendancy following the Civil War. The establishment of the national banking system in 1863, the raising of the tariff, the application of the due-process clause of the Fourteenth Amendment to curb state regulation, and the tendency of the Supreme Court decisions to protect business interests were evidences of the growing influence of industrial and business interests in government.

During the last century agriculture has declined and the relative importance and influence of business has grown. A hundred years ago less than a third of the population was employed in commerce, manufacturing, and mining; today well over half are gainfully employed in these pursuits. Less than one-tenth of the national income today comes from agriculture and over a third from manufacturing. One American corporation, General Motors, now has annual sales of over $7 billion. The income produced by the various segments of the economy is shown in Table 4.

Business activity and industrial production have grown enormously in the United States, not only because of vast natural resources, but also because of technological innovation and an increase in output per man hour. Between 1929 and 1950, population increased 20 per cent but agricultural production increased 45 per cent and industrial production went up 75 per cent.

The extremely rapid growth of business activity is but one striking characteristic of the American economy. Another is the consolidation and concentration of business ownership into a relatively few enormously rich, multiplant corporations. Large-scale management or big business

Table 4. Origin of National Income, 1930–1952

(In millions of dollars)

Segment of economy	1930	1940	1952
Agriculture, forestry, fisheries.....	$ 6,022	$ 6,599	$ 19,296
Mining........................	1,665	1,903	5,984
Contract construction...........	3,088	2,593	14,812
Manufacturing..................	18,270	22,368	90,647
Wholesale and retail trade.......	11,998	13,748	50,771
Finance and real estate..........	10,693	8,489	24,977
Transportation.................	5,513	4,915	15,525
Communications and utilities.....	2,787	3,039	8,937
Services.......................	9,019	8,637	26,038
Government and its enterprises....	5,336	8,796	34,033
All industries..................	$75,003	$81,347	$291,629

SOURCE: U.S. Department of Commerce, *Survey of Current Business* (July issues give income for preceding year).

has come to dominate the picture. During World War II the 100 largest companies held 67 per cent of all war contracts in terms of dollar values. A study of economic concentration for the year 1947 by the Federal Trade Commission showed that (1) the 113 largest manufacturing corporations each had assets in excess of $100 million and (2) these corporations owned nearly one-half (46 per cent) of all net capital assets used in manufacturing.[3] Among manufacturers, 1,500 companies had a net worth of $37 billion and a net income of well over $6 billion in 1948.

As might be expected, there has developed a considerable unevenness in the distribution of income. In 1935, 82 per cent of the families and individuals had an income of less than $2,000 annually. The war, inflation, and high taxes have helped to level up incomes and by 1952, 27 per cent of the families had less than a $2,000 yearly income, and the median family income was $3,025.[4]

The American economy continues to show a high degree of concentration in business ownership, with a resulting condition of oligopoly (fewness of sellers) and monopolistic pricing behavior in many lines of manufacturing. According to a Federal Trade Commission study made after World War II, three companies in each line produced all of the alumi-

[3] Federal Trade Commission, *The Concentration of Productive Facilities, 1947* (1949), p. 4.

[4] U.S. Census estimates.

num, and over three-fourths of the cigarettes and copper smelting, and over two-thirds of the distilled liquors, motor vehicles, tires, and agricultural machinery.[5] Cement, cans, iron ore, steel, zinc, and plumbing equipment companies, to mention only a few others, showed a similar concentration. Even at the end of the war a Senate committee report declared: "No less than 33 per cent of the total value of all manufactured products was produced under conditions where the four largest producers of each individual product accounted for over 75 per cent of the total United States output." [6]

Trade Association Movement. One of the most striking characteristics of the American economy is the number and importance of trade associations. The U.S. Department of Commerce has defined a trade association as a "nonprofit, cooperative, voluntarily-joined organization of business competitors designed to assist members and industry in dealing with mutual business problems such as research, practices, ethics, standardization, statistics, trade promotion, relations with government, and the public."

The beginnings of the trade association movement were found in early America but it was not until the Civil War that regional and national organizations were formed to represent business before Congress and the state legislatures and to advance the commercial interests of the particular group. Among the first trade associations was the United States Brewers' Association (1862). Its formation offers an interesting case study on how and why many organizations come into existence. Allegedly, the purpose of the brewers was to help the North win the war by patriotically offering to sacrifice their interests for that of the Union. But it is an interesting coincidence that the association came into being immediately after Congress levied a tax of $1 per barrel on beer. Within a year and after continued conferences with government officials, the brewers saw the tax reduced to 60 cents per barrel and after the war further downward revisions were effected. The National Association of Cotton Manufacturers was formed eight years prior to this, and national associations of wool manufacturers and fire underwriters came into existence in 1864 and 1866 respectively.

Other trades soon came to appreciate the value of national organization; the Bureau of Foreign and Domestic Commerce estimates that some 50 national associations representing business were in existence by 1875. This figure was doubled by 1900 and skyrocketed to 1,000 in 1920 and to 2,500 by 1935; this is all the more remarkable because no "individual" corporations are included in the tabulation. The Department of Commerce in 1949 listed about 16,600 national and local associations. The

[5] *Op. cit.,* p. 21.

[6] *Economic Concentration and World War II,* 79th Cong., 2d Sess., S. Doc. 206, p. 55.

number of national trade associations rose from 500 in 1900 to over 2,000 in 1950. A majority of the national groups had a membership of less than 200 firms, but 210 associations had a staff of at least 15.

Trade associations arose in response to many different needs and disturbances. A major cause was the desire of business interests to replace competition with "cooperation" in pricing. Modification or control of competition is one of the purposes of trade associations. Technological changes, sharp price and market fluctuations also led to a desire for "stability." [7] During World War I, and especially during the depression of the 1930's, the government itself encouraged trade associations at the request of business interests. Trade associations are attractive to industrialists because they offer the possibility of "self-regulation of industry" as opposed to prospective government regulation. Trade associations, like other political organizations, have sought services from the government and also the aid of government in protecting it from rivals. This has taken the form of seeking legislation or regulation that would help to control their rivals or, conversely, of fighting legislation and administrative orders which would place their own members at a disadvantage. Perhaps the most important fact about the purposes of trade associations is that, in order to fulfill their objectives, they feel compelled to engage in political activity on the various national, regional, state, and local levels. As such, these associations are at the very core of the politics of business.

THE RANKS OF BUSINESS

General Character. The term "businessman" does not admit so easy a definition on careful analysis as it does at first glance. Owners and owner-managers of business enterprises have long been so recognized. But what of the many presidents, directors, and managers in large corporations who exercise "control" with very little or no stock ownership in the companies which they manage? This group, commonly referred to as "management," is now generally recognized as constituting entrepreneurship. Historically, foremen and overseers have been regarded as a part of the business group, but the drive to unionize supervisory employees and the extension of the Wagner Act to include them by the National Labor Relations Board raised a question of their status. This question was resolved, at least for the moment, by the Labor-Management Rela-

[7] G. W. Stocking and M. W. Watkins, *Monopoly and Free Enterprise* (New York: The Twentieth Century Fund, Inc., 1951), note that the trade association movement "reflects a lack of confidence in genuinely free enterprise, a fear of destructive consequences of uninhibited price warfare. It is based on a belief that the welfare of individual companies may be bought at the expense of the industry and that 'rugged individualism' may prove self-defeating" (p. 234).

tions Act of 1947, which denied collective-bargaining rights to supervisory workers.

Another occupational group, running into the hundreds of thousands, has also been regarded as "business," namely, agents and salesmen of insurance and real estate who derive income either from commissions or from a fixed salary. Their psychology and outlook have invariably been identified with the entrepreneur, and the companies themselves have fostered this attitude among their agents.

There is doubt as to where certain professional groups belong, such as architects, engineers, teachers, dentists, pharmacists, and physicians. In terms of point of view, they have largely associated themselves with the propertied class. The decision of the United States Supreme Court, which found medicine a trade within the terms of the Sherman Antitrust Act, lends even more substance to the contention that the practice of medicine has strong commercial aspects.

More and more the word "management" instead of "business" or "capitalist" is being used to describe those who share the business outlook. When speaking of industrial relations, it is common to refer to the "spokesmen for management" and the "spokesmen for labor." However general these terms, they are useful in describing differences around the bargaining table. It is estimated that there are five million businessmen in the nation. They derive their income as managers, officials, and proprietors.

Business Ranks Not Unified. While all business groups are in general agreement on the preservation of private enterprise, there are many dissimilarities of interest. Like labor, all management groups are not found in the same organization and this has often kept business from presenting a united front on policies. This was dramatized, for example, on the important issue of continued government control over prices after World War II. The National Association of Manufacturers came out for a complete and categorical abolition of all price controls by June, 1946. The Chamber of Commerce of the United States, over the protest of some of its local organizational members, later came out for a more cautious program of lifting price controls but favored the retention of rent controls. The Committee for Economic Development, formed during the war by businessmen styling themselves as "progressive," favored the gradual elimination of price control, beginning with those having the least effect upon the cost of living, looking to complete termination in the spring of 1947. The CED's programs are not invariably received with enthusiasm by either the NAM or the Chamber. On rent controls business groupings also found themselves opposed. The National Association of Real Estate Boards and National Home Owners and Property Association pressured Congress for a lifting of all restrictions, while a number of small business tenants together with consumers vigorously fought for the retention of rent ceilings.[8]

On taxation, collective bargaining, minimum wages, international monetary and tariff policies, fair-trade practices, and monetary and fiscal policies, to mention only a few, the business community has often seen marked internal differences of opinion. At its 1953 annual meeting the United States Chamber of Commerce adopted the most liberal foreign trade policies in its history by calling for the repeal of the Buy American Act, encouragement of increased imports, and the assertion that broad national interests in the matter of tariffs must be put ahead of the welfare of a single industry. On the same day spokesmen for ten industries appeared before a congressional committee demanding the strengthening of the tariff in the interests of greater protection.[9] Among the associations appealing for protection were those representing chemical manufacturing, fishing, wool growers, wood screw, rope, trunks, leather goods, mushroom growers and processors, and flint glass workers. Owners of large chain stores have registered opposition to proposed laws sponsored by independents, such as the Robinson-Patman Act and state "fair-trade" legislation. Some business groups have joined with organized labor and consumers to fight against sales taxes advocated by other business interests.

Small business has at times had its quarrels with bankers and big business.[10] It has encountered difficulty in forming a federation for purposes of presenting its interests to the nation's lawmakers. The House of Representatives Committee on Small Business says: [11]

It is an accepted fact that small business is the only important segment of the economy which is still unorganized on a national basis. It is true that there are numerous organizations, claiming many thousands of members, which address the Congress and the Executive Branch with respect to the alleged problems of small business, but the total number of small businessmen belonging to such organizations is but a handful compared with the three million small firms now in existence in this country.

The National Federation of Small Business, the Smaller Businesses of America, Inc., the Conference of American Small Business, and the National Tax Equality Association all purport to speak for the small busi-

[8] See "Rents and the Real Estate Lobby," *Fortune*, June, 1947.

[9] For an account of these pro- and anti-high tariff demands see *The New York Times*, Apr. 30, 1953.

[10] For a description of the structure and problems of small business see *First Annual Report of the Small Business Administration*, Jan. 31, 1954. This agency was created by Congress in 1953.

[11] *Report of the Activities of the House Committee on Small Business*, 79th Cong., Vol. 11, No. 26, July, 1946, p. 2.

nessman. These organizations are unable to obtain enough money for the general purpose of representing their constituents, although they may raise funds for a special purpose. Illustrative of this is the fight of the Conference and Tax Equality organizations against cooperative businesses. Both seek legislation detrimental to cooperatives and have collected ample funds for a large-scale lobbying program. The cooperatives in turn are organized to protect their interests and to further an educational program. The struggle between cooperative enterprises and other business enterprises is increasing in Congress, in the state legislatures, and within the domain of business itself.

The House Small Business Committee is convinced that several so-called small business organizations are not bona fide representatives of such interests. It was charged by the committee that several groups take money from big business and are "fronts" for it, and that they fail to espouse distinctly small business proposals and are of "anti-labor-union variety" and definitely include "big business as a beneficiary." Small, medium, and large businesses are not natural enemies or the antithesis of each other. At the same time, they are not unified on all economic or public policies.

Additional illustrations of the lack of cohesion and common agreement would only labor the point; it is clear that there is no single authoritative spokesman for finance, commerce, manufacturing, and trade. Each has its own organization, which speaks out when its estate seems threatened. For example, the American Bankers' Association may register a sharp viewpoint on foreign and domestic loans, while the National Retail Dry Goods Association and National Small Business Association may remain silent. When in Washington, D.C., it is an education to peruse the directory of offices in the Munsey or National Press Buildings or the dozen packed pages in the telephone directory listing special-interest organizations. Among the business groups one sees the American Association of Railroads, American Road Builders Association, National Apple Dryers Association, National Association of Bedding Manufacturers, and the Tobacco Merchants of America. Out of the welter of groups we may review the composition and activities of the two largest groups which hold themselves as spokesmen for business, commerce, and industry, the Chamber of Commerce of the United States and the National Association of Manufacturers.

CHAMBER OF COMMERCE OF THE UNITED STATES

"What is good for business is good for the country" runs the slogan of the Chamber of Commerce of the United States. This organization, formed in 1912, seeks to integrate the opinions of the thousands of local chambers so as to speak authoritatively for American business. There are 8,000 Chambers of Commerce throughout the world working for improved trade relations and expanded trade between nations and for public policies that will foster these objectives.[12] Local chambers are influential in promoting community projects designed to aid business and in stating viewpoints on measures before city councils.

The national Chamber, with its constituent state and local bodies, is an example of geographical organization. These "organization" members are entitled, in national meetings, to one vote for each 25 members or less, and one additional vote for each 250 members in excess of 25. The larger the local organization, the greater its voting power and financial responsibility to the national office. An individual and associate membership in the Chamber entitles one to receive the publications of the organizations and have access, without a vote, to the floor of the meetings. All voting, however, is by state and local chapters, and for all practical purposes the national Chamber is composed of organizations rather than individual members. The Chamber represents an estimated 1,600,000 businessmen throughout the country. Active direction of the affairs of the Chamber is in the hands of a board of directors, numbering 45, who are chosen at the annual meeting.[13]

The Chamber endeavors to be the spokesman for business and uses a unique "referendum" system to ascertain the views of American business on national issues. Whenever a question is considered to be sufficiently important to call for a referendum, it is placed in the hands of a special committee for study and report.[14] The committee prepares and presents a report to the board of directors, which decides if a referendum shall go out to the membership. If submitted, the committee's report becomes the affirmative statement and negative arguments are prepared by the research department in the form of objections to the committee's statement. The two statements are printed in parallel columns, together with a ballot, and mailed to all organization members, state or local chambers of commerce. Each member then has 45 days to study the proposition and to cast its vote. Voting is according to the size of the member, with a maximum of 10 votes allowed to any one member. The policies adopted by majority vote become known as the official position of the national Chamber on the subject.

[12] See *8,000 Chambers of Commerce Throughout the World* (Washington, D.C.: Chamber of Commerce of the U.S., 1940). The most useful work on the origin and development of the Chamber is Harwood L. Childs, *Labor and Capital in National Politics* (Columbus, Ohio: The Ohio State University Press, 1930).

[13] See *By-laws of Chamber of Commerce of the United States*. The national office is in Washington, D.C.

[14] Consult the Chamber's pamphlet *The Referendum System and Methods of Voting* (undated), obtainable from the national office.

A number of criticisms might be made of the Chamber's referendum technique. The affirmative report is easier to read and to understand. Local organization members often give inadequate study and debate to the questions and authorize the secretary or president to cast the ballot, even though the national organization discourages this practice and urges full discussion at a meeting. Also there are times when not more than half of the local organization members take the trouble to vote. Trade associations can also vote, although with their scattered membership they must rely upon a mail referendum, which has the disadvantage of no discussion.

In spite of these shortcomings, the referendum is a useful instrument both as an educational device and as a method of crystallizing and articulating the views of a large segment of business on national questions. It seems safe to assume that on the general question the referendum represents a fair reflection affirmatively or negatively of American business even though its percentage points are inaccurate or incomplete. The hands of the Chamber's legislative agents are strengthened by the results of the poll if they can point to a referendum on the subject.

The Chamber's publications are voluminous, and about 200 different ones are available on such diverse subjects as railroad consolidation, civil aviation, agricultural parity, building codes, city planning, taxation, foreign commerce, industrial health programs, life insurance, natural resources, and employer-employee relations.[15] In recent years the organization has sponsored a radio network program. The Chamber also publishes two widely distributed periodicals, *Nation's Business,* issued monthly, and *Business Action,* a weekly. The latter is designed as a weekly report from the national organization, and subscriptions may be had only by its members. In its six to eight pages, news of meetings, organizational activities, policies, and the position of the Chamber on legislation are presented in attractive fashion. A large portion of *Business Action* is devoted to brief feature articles dealing with such relevant topics as profit sharing, world finance, production problems, budget balancing, interest rates, public and private ownership, marketing and agricultural problems, tax relief, economic planning, labor relations, transportation, patents, employment services, government corporations, and education. During sessions of Congress the Chamber issues a legislative and an administrative daily.

NATIONAL ASSOCIATION OF MANUFACTURERS

The NAM arose out of the dislocations of the panic of 1893 with organization being formalized two years later. Its immediate objective

---

[15] See *List of Publications of the Chamber of Commerce of the United States* (1954).

was to promote trade expansion, an objective still retained.[16] Within a few years after its creation, the NAM became involved in labor questions. This was partly due at least to the rapid increase in the membership of the American Federation of Labor and its demands for better wages and hours and for a closed shop. Here was something that could get manufacturers excited enough to pay membership fees and to create state and local groups, as well as the national organization, to act. The NAM and its locals adopted an aggressive open-shop policy and fostered organizations designed to arouse the public against the "dangers of unionism." Its campaign against the closed shop was militant and it has continued to the present to give direct or indirect sanction in state legislatures for so-called "right-to-work" or anticlosed-shop legislation. Numerous of the NAM's publications continue to be critical of some of the activities of organized labor, particularly the CIO.

The professed objects of the NAM as stated in its bylaws [17] differ from the Chamber of Commerce only in detail, but on the whole are more clearly stated, especially as to the influencing of public opinion. These include "the protection of the individual liberty and rights of employer and employee, the dissemination of information among the public with respect to the principles of individual liberty and the ownership of property, the support of legislation in furtherance of these principles and opposition to legislation in derogation thereof."

Active membership in the NAM is limited to any individual, firm, or corporation engaged in manufacturing and approved by the board of directors. The directors are chosen on a state basis, with each state having 25 active members and paying $50 or more in dues entitled to one director; 100 memberships permit two directors, and 200 memberships give a state three directors. Provisions for additional directors are also made, and as many as 150 persons are sometimes found on the board. Notwithstanding geographical representation, 125 corporations of the about 18,000 member-manufacturers, constituting less than 5 per cent of the total membership, hold about two-thirds of the positions on the board.[18] Like many other groups, certain counsels, presidents, or persons holding positions in the hierarchy become highly influential in the affairs

[16] Among the useful accounts on the development, governance, and program of the NAM are A. G. Taylor, "The National Association of Manufacturers," *University of Illinois Studies in the Social Sciences*, Vol. 15 (1927) and *Labor Policies of the National Association of Manufacturers* (1928); A. S. Cleveland, "N.A.M. Spokesman for Industry," *Harvard Business Review*, Vol. 26 (1948), pp. 353–371; Richard W. Gable, "NAM: Influential Lobby or Kiss of Death?" *Journal of Politics*, Vol. 15 (1953), pp. 254–273. *Fortune*, July, 1948, also carries some interesting items on the NAM.

[17] The bylaws and other publications of the NAM may be obtained from its national office in New York.

[18] See Cleveland, *op. cit.*

of the Association, notably James A. Emery, Ira Mosher, and Noel Sargent, and often become its official spokesmen.

Policies are determined in several ways. The paid staff in the national office has much to do with formulating objectives and policies. The referendum device is used, but much less frequently than by the Chamber of Commerce. The annual meeting of the NAM, called the Congress of American Industry, adopts broad policies, leaving specific statements on legislation to the discretion of the board of directors. The standing committees of the Association operate as a year-round working congress to help the organization live up to its "mission," which is seen as the "authoritative expression of American industrial thinking."

Interest groups which are confined to persons engaged in similar business and with the same problems are able to be more specific and hard hitting in their policies; the NAM and Chamber of Commerce offer an illustration of this. The former is composed of manufacturers and is fairly cohesive and unified in its approach to issues. By contrast, the Chamber has a broader base and more heterogeneous membership, making it more difficult to weld a community of interest.

The NAM relies heavily upon publications to influence public opinion. Members are kept informed on legislation and labor relations through the weekly *NAM News*. Addresses by its officers are printed in attractive format and mailed to members and civic associations. The research staff produces pamphlets, sometimes of considerable length, on a variety of subjects, always with a strong emphasis upon private enterprise and ownership and upon freedom in the choice of economic activity and endeavor. In addition, elaborate materials in social science are prepared for schools and colleges. Instructors are sent check sheets with lists of pamphlets and posters available in classroom quantities, which will be sent, with few exceptions, free of charge. Manuals and guides for teachers are also obtainable, as are specially prepared motion pictures. Out of its three million annual budget approximately one million dollars per year is spent on educational activities.[19] When the occasion demands, extra sources are tapped for carrying on special crusades. In the spring of 1946 the NAM spent upward of $400,000 in an effort to defeat the extension of price control. Full-page advertisements in newspapers blamed the lack of consumers' and producers' goods on price control and promised an abundance of products if price controls were lifted. Other materials outlining the position on this policy were prepared for libraries, churches, schools, radio stations, and civic organizations, and

[19] Not all the informational activities are reflected in the educational budget. The NAM's subsidiary, the National Industrial Information Committee, has an annual outlay of about $1½ million for "public information."

speakers were sent out to carry the message to the public and to the nation's legislators.

LEGISLATIVE OBJECTIVES OF BUSINESS

Fiscal Policies. Legislative aims of interest groups must and do usually undergo some change and modification each year. Attention has been drawn to the lack of a united opinion on many matters within the industrial and commercial world itself. On governmental fiscal policies, however, commerce and industry show a high degree of cohesion. For over a decade they have urged a balanced budget and an end to deficit financing, except, of course, during the war. Business is fearful of the inflationary dangers of a growing public debt, and the wide use of bank credit to cover the deficit causes anxiety. The mounting Federal debt is seen as requiring higher taxes to cover interest charges and to provide funds for amortizing the debt; this in turn would tend to diminish future productive capacity and to lower the standard of living. There is added concern lest the dollar be devaluated, which would result in disastrous consequences, such as have occurred in some European nations. Business, therefore, favors a reduction of Federal expenditures, and it has cooperated with congressional committees seeking ways and means of promoting governmental economy. When at long last, however, Federal expenditures in 1947 began to lag behind revenues, the NAM expressed much greater enthusiasm for a substantial tax reduction than for applying the surplus to reduce the national debt. It opposed the President's anti-inflation program as "regimentation" and declared against increased wages because of their "inflationary" character. In 1953, when the Eisenhower Administration was pressing hard for a balanced budget, many spokesmen for business received coolly the Administration's proposals to delay tax cuts. A poll was taken among 3,000 delegates at the annual NAM convention that year and only 25 per cent of them were recorded as believing that a tax reduction should wait until after the Federal budget was balanced.

Organized business stands firmly for reduction of governmental expenditures. Conventions of trade associations, national or local, denounce governmental "extravagance" and call for reduced appropriations except possibly for public-works programs in their respective local areas. The Federal regulatory commissions such as the FTC, ICC, SEC, and FPC are often targets for reduced appropriations. Amusement and resort owners lobby in the states for increased items for the promotion of tourist trade. Reduction of personal income taxes is also high on the priority of business groups. Although some retail trade groups have lobbied against sales taxes, business, when confronted with the need for additional public revenue, has generally not opposed a sales tax. Here it often finds itself in opposition to organized labor, which has bitterly fought the tax as shifting the burden unduly upon the backs of the consumer.

Labor and Welfare. Business associations generally show cohesion on labor matters. This comes as a result of fear that labor unions will become extremely powerful and will be able to put over expensive public programs which business will have to bear in whole or in part. Business is united on "management's right to manage" and has insisted that certain items not be the subject of bargaining, including the determination of products to be manufactured and services rendered, financial policies, prices, inventories, and job content. Management has opposed the unionization of foremen and supervisory personnel on the ground that it interferes with management functions and would promote cleavages in management organization, disrupt grievance machinery, and impair productive organization.

Almost before the Wagner Act was in effect, a demand was made by business that amendments be made defining and controlling the activities and responsibilities so that both labor and management would have "equal status under law." After many years of careful groundwork and extensive publicity, the Chamber of Commerce and the NAM got behind the drive of several congressmen to curtail the power of organized labor. Immediately after the congressional elections of 1946, a concerted drive was made to obtain a similar bill. In supporting a regulatory labor law the NAM launched a big newspaper advertising program under the caption, "Americans Won't Stand for Monopolies," attacking many current labor practices as monopolistic. In this drive the NAM took a specific stand against industry-wide collective bargaining, the closed shop, the union shop, secondary boycotts, jurisdictional strikes, featherbedding, and a host of other practices. Tidbits such as the following appeared in their advertising:

All three employees at a small paint plant in California refused to join a union. So the union put an outside picket at the plant—and union truck drivers refused to deliver supplies. The factory closed down until the workers paid $75 initiation fee. High prices and scarcity of goods were also traced to that "form of union monopoly—secondary boycott."

After twelve years, organized business won its battle with the enactment of the Taft-Hartley bill in 1947, which went even beyond the Case labor bill.[20] Although organized labor accused the NAM of writing the bill, there is little evidence that it did so. However, virtually every provision, save that of permitting a union shop under certain conditions, met the legislative objects of both the Chamber and the NAM. The passage of

[20] The provisions of the Labor-Management Relations Act of 1947 (popularly called the Taft-Hartley Act) are given in the following chapter.

the bill saw the fulfillment of the program of "industrial harmony" and "equality of bargaining power" of organized business in America. It is worth observing that only a very few businessmen raised their voices against any provisions of the Act. On few issues has business, at least outwardly, been as united as on the Taft-Hartley law. On few issues also have the forces of big business on the one hand and big labor on the other been so divided. Among the current objectives of business is to keep the Act substantially intact.

On two matters of industrial relations labor and management find themselves in agreement. Both favor the extension and use of governmental conciliation services and both are opposed to compulsory arbitration. Officially the two usually agree that reliance upon government to solve labor-management problems is unsound, though both at times have called for government interference when expediency seemed to dictate. The backing of the Taft-Hartley bill by business, however, was an abandonment of the belief that government should stay out of labor disputes.

In 1931 the national Chamber of Commerce overwhelmingly committed itself to the principles of voluntary reserves for unemployment, old age, sickness, and accident and hence to the opposition of legislation requiring or establishing such reserves. The enactment of the Social Security Act four years later provided for unemployment compensation and old-age annuities through compulsory taxation on industry. This Act has met with such general public acceptance that organized business has not attempted to secure its repeal. The few objections raised usually center about the depressing effect of the supporting tax on specific businesses. For example, those businesses with high labor costs or operating under a small margin of profit insist that the tax rests too heavily on them. The Act itself called for gradually increasing the pay-roll tax from 1 to 3 per cent to support old-age insurance, and the business organizations have opposed this increase. The present position of business is to oppose any further extension of the social-security program and to adjust the financial aspects to the actuarial experience gained since 1935. Industry is as much opposed to a national compulsory health-insurance program as is the American Medical Association and holds that improvement of public health is a local function. Individual employers are urged to adopt their own systems of sickness compensation and health insurance.

Private Enterprise and Protectionism. On the subject of public ownership and freedom from governmental competition with private enterprise, business has enjoyed a unity of purpose. Taking cognizance of the great expansion of public businesses during the war, the national Chamber of Commerce asserts: [21]

---

[21] "Policy Declarations, 34th Annual Meeting, 1946," p. 19.

The government now should withdraw with all possible dispatch from those manufacturing, merchandising, and other business operations which it felt impelled to undertake during the war emergency. Where government agencies control products for sale or distribution, they should use the established channels of private trade, which provide practical and economical distribution.

The water- and electric-power lobbies joined organized business in opposing the extension of the river authority projects patterned after the Tennessee Valley Authority. A Chamber of Commerce referendum opposed additional TVA's as "creating a super-government, inimical to free enterprise, destructive of state rights, and socialistic." [22] States' rights is a slogan of business groups because it is felt they can get more concessions from the state governments. The oil and many other interests spent large sums of money on behalf of the Federal law which turned full title over the offshore submerged lands to the states. The passage of the bill in 1953 was hailed by these interests as a great victory for private enterprise and a blow against "socialism." Federal conservation officials are under constant pressure to lease Federal lands to timber and other interests.

In his travels *Inside U.S.A.*, John Gunther found private-utilities organizations exerting formidable pressure in every section of the nation against Federal river valley development programs, municipal ownership of utilities, and other public businesses. As evidence of the importance of these groups, it might be noted that in 1952 the National Association of Electric Companies reported an expenditure far greater than any other single lobbying organization which registered under the national lobbying law. These and other businesses are fearful that if the tent door is opened for public ownership of power, it will soon be thrown wider to other enterprises.

Many segments of American industry grew up with the doctrine of protectionism, and the protective tariff issue has loomed large in politics since the time of President Washington. Organized business has generally supported the idea of a "realistic" tariff policy, which is interpreted as protection against "unfair competition" from abroad. What is "unfair" competition is not clearly defined and many enterprises regard any policy that would admit foreign goods into the United States in competition with their products as inimical to the "American system." On specific tariffs business may not be united. Some industries approved certain of the reciprocal trade treaties because they provided a better market abroad

[22] *Congressional Record,* June 18, 1946 (daily edition), p. 7175. A large section of this issue is given over to a review of propaganda by power lobbies and the Flood Control Act of 1944, and to the extension of the TVA idea; see especially pp. 7173–7190. See also the Chamber's pamphlet *The Continuing Cost of the TVA* (1954).

for their goods, while others were vociferous in denouncing the treaties where competing goods came in at lower rates. The intriguing story of how different groups sought special rates and combined in logrolling fashion to push over the Hawley-Smoot Tariff has been told by Prof. E. E. Schattschneider [23] in one of the best of the studies of pressure politics. As is pointed out, tariff politics is a "story of dubious economic policy turned into a political success" with "reciprocal noninterference" leaving each industry free to seek its own duties but acquiescing in the results of benefits granted to other businesses.

Official spokesmen for industry endorse antimonopoly and antitrust measures, but a great many businesses still strive to limit competition. Hence business associations are unable to go beyond generalities and avoid naming "monopolistic" trade practices of certain industries which are detrimental to the public interest. Indeed, this subject provides some of the most bitter internal quarrels among various types of businesses.

Government-Business Relationships. By way of summary, business since the advent of the New Deal has reluctantly and tacitly accepted the necessity for positive government. But, as Professor Thomas P. Jenkin [24] points out in his study of this reaction:

Much of this acceptance was defined in terms of the emergency conditions that obtained, and much of the approval was not at the same time approval of the bases upon which the New Deal chose to rest its case. . . . The acceptance of the program by business groups, for instance, has been partial and has contained many elements. Confronted with a *fait accompli* many of the business spokesmen found it expedient to shift their immediate point of view to accord with political facts. This did not compromise their future right to object or to aid in alteration of governmental policies.

The Chamber of Commerce of the United States had a large part in drafting the National Industrial Recovery Act (1933–1935). This is not an inconsistency since the Act relaxed the antitrust laws and relied heavily on the principle of self-regulation of industry. Businesses themselves were asked to formulate their own "codes of competition" and therefore to help both in the determination of policy and in administration. Many of the codes drafted remained in effect voluntarily after the NRA was voided by the Supreme Court.

The Eisenhower Administration was officially proclaimed by some of its Cabinet officers as a "businessman's administration." High-level policy positions were given to prominent executives and businessmen gravitated

[23] *Politics, Pressures, and the Tariff* (New York: Prentice-Hall, Inc., 1935).
[24] *Reactions of Major Groups to Positive Government in the United States, 1930–1940* (Berkeley, Calif.: University of California Press, 1945), p. 398. For an analysis of business' views of government see M. H. Bernstein, "Political Ideas of Selected American Business Journals," *Public Opinion Quarterly*, Vol. 17 (1953), pp. 258–267.

to lesser government posts and to advisory committees. Business groups hailed the efforts to get the government out of certain businesses and welfare programs and on the whole felt they had a healthier atmosphere in which to conduct private enterprise, and that for the present at least government-business relationships would be friendlier.

TECHNIQUES OF BUSINESS ORGANIZATIONS

Public Relations. The techniques used by any group to assert its demands are conditioned by its size, solidarity, financial resources, leadership, and type of organization. There are certain practices in which nearly all engage, but very often certain groups employ, at least to a larger degree, some techniques used infrequently by others. Where labor and farmer associations, for example, are able to mobilize millions of votes and hence can be effective through mass voting, business alone cannot deliver millions of votes nor necessarily make strong threats of reprisal at the polls. Business relies upon its superior financial resources. It can subsidize the political campaigns of its friends and hire the best legal talent to plead its case before the courts, the legislatures, and the administrative agencies. In the states business groups sometimes pride themselves on their ability to employ the best brains to represent them. The cases for business before public agencies are well prepared, urbanely presented, and possess a *savoir-faire* lacking in presentations by other groups.

Looking at the political area broadly, use of public relations is probably the most important technique of business. With the press, radio, television, and motion pictures in the hands of private enterprise, industry, trade, and finance are able to bring their messages directly and subtly to millions of independent voters. Corporations sponsor symphonies and other radio programs and often stress American enterprise, initiative, and "competition" in advertising themes. Similarly, pro-management radio and television newscasters, favorable editorials in the press, and friendly newspaper columnists build up much "good will" for commerce and industry through the channels of communication. Business elicits and usually receives the general approbation of white-collar and professional groups and emphasizes the "middle-class" values which all have in common. Charles E. Wilson, former head of General Motors Corporation, told a congressional investigating committee that "what is good for General Motors is good for the country." Although there were some criticisms of this comment, millions of Americans in and out of industry in general subscribe to this view, or at least that what is good for business is good for the country. The fact that this opinion is widely held is a tribute in part to the public-relations programs of business. However true it may have been that business once took the view that "the public be damned," today it hires the best public-relations experts to curry favorable public sentiment for it and often to curry public disfavor for governmental regulation.

Business associations are spending large sums of money to develop a friendly relationship with students, school administrators, and college professors. Many colleges are beneficiaries of research funds provided by businesses. Numerous professors are invited to attend summer seminars or to accept internships in large industrial concerns, and the former have profited by learning how large corporations are facing and solving problems. Graduate scholarships for students are a part of the program.

An infinite variety of motion pictures, charts, pamphlets, reports, and materials on business are made available in quantities to schoolteachers, and speakers' bureaus are ever ready to supply classroom lectures without cost. In one large city all schools are dismissed one day each year while every teacher becomes the guest of a business corporation and is given a specially conducted tour and indoctrination on the operation of the plants. Business associations have publicly endorsed larger salaries for teachers, though some individual managers working privately as members of taxpayers' associations have opposed increased appropriations for the public schools on the ground that it meant increased taxes.

Businesses "affected with a public interest," or public utilities, have been especially active in the field of public relations. Because their rates, services, and operations come under considerable control of public-regulatory agencies, the utilities resort to "institutional" advertising. This is aimed at developing public attitudes that the telephone, gas, electric, or other company is being well managed, that its rates are just and reasonable, and the services excellent.

Power through Combination. Economist R. A. Brady has advanced the thesis that with the rise of manufacturing and corporate power, the owners of property or businessmen, consciously or intuitively, are engaged in weaving parallel webs of control all over the world.[25] He saw evidence of this in the cartelization movement in Germany, in the syndicalism and corporatism in Mussolini's Italy, the state-encouraged, patriarchally governed family enterprises in prewar Japan, and the activities of the Federation of British Industries, and the National Association of Manufacturers in the United States. The system of power is based upon the pyramiding of a "peak" association which fixes the lines of the trade associations and subordinate peak associations. In all countries this system is monopoly-oriented and centralized with a view toward trying to consolidate, coordinate, integrate, and expand the power of business, and to dominate government by "control over the thinking processes of the

[25] *Business as a System of Power* (New York: Columbia University Press, 1943).

mass of the people who dwell at the base of the social pyramid." [26] In this system small business appears to be losing out and has attempted, as a matter of survival, to employ the powers of government to defend itself from business monopolies.

The Brady thesis has been widely debated; it is also recognized as being at least partly an oversimplification. At the same time, it has served the purpose of directing attention to an important tendency and technique—the concentration and centralization of power through price-fixing arrangements, interlocking directorates, trade associations, personal ties, banking and legal affiliations, holding companies, and subsidiaries. It also shows how business relies on cooperation and combination to achieve its ends. A few examples may be noted.

Business associations frequently ally themselves with the conservative wing of professional and civic societies to fight proposals that appear to endanger the *status quo*. The mutual interchange of addressographs of business and professional organizations is by no means rare. The reception room of a doctor or dentist often has copies of *Nation's Business* and pamphlets issued by the NAM and business groups. In some corporation reception rooms one finds literature against compulsory health insurance and the "socialization of medicine." Each group to some extent is using the prestige of the other. The "cooperation" of organizations on certain mutual interests is one of the perennial techniques of interest groups.

In fighting unions some employers resort to the device of enlisting the aid of prominent persons and more particularly patriotic and citizens' committees. The last-mentioned are used for the purpose of issuing statements that plants will be moved from the community unless the employees reject certain, if not all, unions. The National Labor Relations Board outlawed this practice in 1946, but the enlisting of groups for other programs still goes on. For example, business received much help from the Committee for Constitutional Government in its crusade against many policies of Presidents Roosevelt and Truman. Indeed, some persons raised the question as to whether the Committee was not in reality a political arm of business rather than a self-styled, patriotic organization crusading for the "principles of constitutional liberty."

It is a characteristic of American political life for political parties and interest groups to conduct hard-hitting campaigns through auxiliary or "front" organizations. This enables certain intemperate activities—often of factional character—to be carried on which would be embarrassing to the more respectable sponsoring association. Extremists who are impatient with the program of the latter may find an outlet for their frustrations

[26] *Ibid.*, p. 320.

in the peripheral or front groups. These front groups, moreover, often conduct a political program which is not within the purview of the objectives of the established association. Also it may be possible to obtain additional or better financing through a separate group. Subsidiary groups may be viewed as a part of the public-relations program.

The use of front organizations to promote the interests of business or certain specific businesses is a common occurrence and many nonbusiness people are brought into the cause. Taxpayers and "civic development" leagues in many local communities are often little more than groups representing right-wing business interests who wish to reduce taxes or shift the incidence of taxation or fight for the reduction of local expenditures. The National Economic Council, the National Industrial Conference Board, and the Foundation for Economic Education are prolific publishers and provide many educational services for business. The Committee for Economic Development was formed around 1944 to provide research and other services for businessmen whose views are nearer the center or left of center.

Business resorts to lobbying, as do the other political interest groups. In Chapter 9 a review will be made of the stock lobbying techniques and the devices used to influence public policy. It may be mentioned, however, that the large number of legislators and administrators who were erstwhile businessmen has assured commerce and industry access to the channels of government. Gerrymandering and the rotten borough system of apportioning of representatives in the state legislatures have given a conservative cast to those bodies and hence have usually favored business. It is not unusual to find business on the side of those opposing redistricting which would increase the representation of urban areas.

Businessmen and their organizations suffered many recriminations as a result of the depression of the early 1930's. But business leaders today are a far cry from the "robber barons," even though some political, labor, and other leaders continue to wave the "bloody shirt" of "Wall Street" and make big business synonymous with exploitation and corruption. Business has done much to clean its own house and to discountenance shady practices. The president of the Chamber of Commerce of the United States told his associates in 1950 that they must assume some responsibility for corruption in government. "It is just as culpable," he said, "to buy government influence as it is to sell it. If there were no businessmen willing to hand out home freezers, mink coats, and costly vacations, there would be fewer public officials ready to take them."

Many business groups are displaying statesmanship in understanding the public interest in such actions as supporting the continuance of certain business taxes in order to keep the budget from becoming too unbalanced. The Chamber of Commerce has become increasingly forthright in stating that international trade can be maintained only if the nation accepts a tariff policy which will facilitate trade. The Committee for Economic Development has championed numerous progressive policies. Business organizations regard it as a part of their function, as do other political interest groups, to lay down a propaganda line for their membership. The only justified criticism of this practice for all groups should be when facts are misrepresented or when an organization is unable to see its true interests in the context of the public interest.

SELECTED REFERENCES

From the abundant references on the general organization and objectives of the commercial and industrial interests the following citations are of particular value to the students of pressure groups: Harwood L. Childs, *Labor and Capital in National Politics* (1930); E. E. Schattschneider, *Politics, Pressures, and the Tariff* (1935); E. P. Herring, *Group Representation before Congress* (1929); Carl D. Thompson, *Confessions of the Power Trust* (1932); E. Gruening, *The Public Pays: A Study of Power Propaganda* (1931); Kenneth Crawford, *The Pressure Boys* (1939); Miriam Beard, *A History of the Business Man* (1938); Ray F. Harvey, *The Politics of This War* (1943); Stuart Chase, *Democracy under Pressure* (1945); Marshall Dimock, *Business and Government* (1953); Merle Fainsod and Lincoln Gordon, *Government and the American Economy* (1949); G. A. Steiner, *Government's Role in Economic Life* (1953); J. K. Galbraith, *American Capitalism: The Concept of Countervailing Power* (1952); Earl Latham, *The Group Basis of Politics: A Study of Basing Point Legislation* (1952); C. C. Rohlfing, et al., *Business and Government* (1949).

On big business and monopoly consult the publications of two select committees of the United States Senate, the Senate Temporary National Economic Committee, particularly Monographs 21, 26, and 27; and the Senate Small Business Committee, especially *Economic Concentration and World War II* (1946). See also Arthur R. Burns, *The Decline of Competition* (1936); R. A. Brady, *Business as a System of Power* (1943); David Lilienthal, *Big Business* (1953); R. A. Gordon, *Business Leadership in the Large Corporation* (1945); David Lynch, *The Concentration of Economic Power* (1946); G. W. Stocking and M. W. Watkins, *Monopoly and Free Enterprise* (1951).

The publications and trade journals of trade associations, the Chambers of Commerce, the National Association of Manufacturers, and local business groups contain informative materials on policies and objectives of business.

1. Interest groups or of every interests, and, etc

2. Business and the american economy.
   a. Large business has shrinkled trade movement.
   b. Business ranks aren't unified.

3. Groups.
   c. Chamber of commerce of U.S.
   d. Natl. association of Manufacturers.

, Leg. objectives of business;

CHAPTER 5

Organized Labor

It is to his union that the worker naturally looks for protection of his wages, hours, and working conditions. It follows as day follows night that political governmental measures having an impact on those same wages, hours, and working conditions must also be approached by the worker through his union.
—PHILIP MURRAY

Today considerably more than half of the American people are regarded as "laborers." In turn, over half of them do not belong to a labor union. In 1953 it was estimated that 16 million persons had union membership. Of these around 8 million belonged to American Federation of Labor affiliates; at least 4 million had membership in the Congress of Industrial Organizations; and the remainder belonged to unions outside these two. Numerically, at least, the workers are potentially the most powerful occupational group. Yet seldom if ever can it be said that they are the strongest and most cohesive power in America.

The rise of organized labor is a long story and a complicated one filled with conspicuous successes and heartbreaking failures. Its history is bound up with the industrial revolution, depressions, urbanization, technological changes, industrial warfare with management, radical social movements, and radical changes in the occupational composition of the nation. The rise and fall of membership in labor unions resembles a barometer. In the history of labor organization is found an illustration of practically every principle and facet of group life—of success and failure because of adherence to principle or to expediency, of changes wrought by the upset of economic and political equilibrium, of changes made necessary by the interaction with business and other groups. As a result, labor's tactics have had to be highly adaptable, and when they were not, failure usually resulted. A major barrier to a strong, class-conscious labor movement has been the fact that the American worker has traditionally regarded his status as temporary and looked forward to the time when he would own and manage his own business.

RISE OF UNIONISM AND LABOR POLITICS

Slow Growth. Though trade-unionism did not reach impressive proportions until the present century, it had its beginnings during the administration of President Washington.[1] The real beginning of a "labor movement" in the sense of worker unity as opposed to the mere interest of a single trade came about in 1829 under the guidance of Thomas Skidmore. A Committee of Fifty New York mechanics proposed that labor go into politics by nominating candidates for the state legislature. The proposal was opposed by several groups, notably the Owenite and Cook factions. Because of the lack of the unified support of the labor movement and the inexperience of its leaders in the art of politics, this early movement to establish a workingman's party quickly collapsed. Soaring prices and lagging wages following the Civil War led to the formation of the National Labor Union in 1866, which supported Greenbackism.

In 1872 the Union in a political convention nominated a candidate for President to run on a Greenback platform. Its candidate, David Davis, withdrew after the Democrats designated Horace Greeley. With the party a failure, the NLU disintegrated and labor's first attempt to engage in political activity on a national scale received another setback. However, this participation in politics resulted in forcing the major parties to accept some of labor's demands, such as the eight-hour day on government public works, the Chinese Exclusion Act, and the Bland-Allison Act of 1878.

The Knights of Labor, formed in 1869, began as a secret organization; a decade later it revoked its secrecy and adopted an educational and intellectual appeal, but soon it found itself enmeshed in politics. It drafted a social program with strong political implications, including direct legislation, compulsory schooling, income taxes, retention of greenbacks, public ownership of railroads and telegraphs, the eight-hour day, equal rights for women, safety and health laws. The Knights, whose membership reached a peak of 700,000, lobbied in the state capitals and aligned itself nationally with the Greenbackers, then the Populists, and finally with the Bryan Democrats. The failure through political action to achieve these broad vistas of social reform showed the difficulties of purely wage-earner political action and confirmed the viewpoint of a substantial number of workers who held job interest paramount, namely, that efforts should be channelized in the direction of forming an exclusively economic organization of labor.[2]

While these moves to federate were under way, locals of various trades

[1] On the development of labor unions see Selig Perlman, *History of Trade Unionism in the United States* (New York: The Macmillan Company, 1922) and *A Theory of the Labor Movement* (New York: The Macmillan Company, 1928); Philip Foner, *History of the Labor Movement in the United States* (New York: International Publishers Co., Inc., 1947); and H. A. Millis and R. E. Montgomery, *Organized Labor* (New York: McGraw-Hill Book Company, Inc., 1945).

[2] The fact that many of the earlier attempts of organized labor to enter politics resulted in a split-up of labor organizations explains the steadfast policy of Samuel

were attempting nationwide organization with the typographical workers, hat finishers, cigar makers, and iron machinists, completing this job before the Civil War. The powerful railroad brotherhoods arose during the war, and after that conflict, the carpenters, bricklayers, and other groups of craftsmen organized nationals. During the following three years nine new national unions appeared.

Cleavages. On the eve of the formation of the Federation of Organized Trades and Labor Unions (1881), later (1886) named the American Federation of Labor, three more or less distinct schools of thought regarding the form and objectives of a national labor union were in evidence, the ideas of which are still found in one form or another today. The skilled workers desired combination for the attainment of trade-union, not "uplift" or socialistic, objectives. A second group desired social reforms that would enable wage earners to rise out of their class and restore equality of opportunity and continual interest in the social program as once championed by the NLU. A final group, composed largely of immigrants, sought the establishment of an organization built upon class-conscious socialism.

Many skilled craftsmen were attracted to the idealism of the Knights but disliked the all-inclusive membership with authority located in mixed assemblies whose decisions often ran counter to their particular interests. Out of the conflict of interest between the skilled and semi- or unskilled wage earners grew the American Federation of Labor. This organization allowed complete autonomy, with each organized craft retaining its own constitution, rules, and procedures for dealing with employers. The AFL enjoyed a steady growth to 350,000 in 1899 and to about 1,675,000 in 1904, with a series of ups and downs in membership until the depression came in 1929.

While many socialists were in the AFL unions, there were many advocates of doctrinaire purity who felt that the AFL was a betrayal of the workers' real interests and of the class struggle. The AFL, therefore, constantly had to contend with socialist-laborites who sought membership and control of various unions for the purpose of endorsing collective ownership and engaging in independent political action. To carry out a direct actionist movement the Industrial Workers of the World was launched in 1905, composed predominantly of Western miners and hitherto unorganized migratory workers of the wheat fields and lumber camps. Its membership probably never exceeded 60,000 and it was constantly torn with internal dissension over both dogma and tactics. The antiwar stand of the IWW, the imprisonment of many of its leaders by the government on charges of sedition, and the vigilante organizations

---

Gompers, as the first leader of the American Federation of Labor, to eschew identification with any political party.

formed to combat it brought a virtual end to the IWW as an effective economic force by 1919.

During the 1920's, the Communist party and the Trade Union Unity League kept the left-wing movement from complete collapse. The majority of labor during this time was satisfied with the more conventional methods and procedures. The AFL executive council did depart from custom to endorse Robert M. La Follette for the presidency, but many national leaders opposed this stand. For unionism itself it was a dark decade, with collective membership declining from approximately 5 million in 1920 to 3,400,000 in 1930; during the same period the AFL suffered a loss from over 4 million to 3 million. Much of this was due to a vigorous antiunion movement and to declining employment. The "return to normalcy" following the great wave of strikes in 1919 led managers' associations and even the National Grange to unite in a program styled as the "American Plan" to rescue workers from "the shackles of organization to their own detriment." In effect, this was a drive for the open shop and was bulwarked by labor spies, strikebreakers, and blacklisting. The passage of the Norris-La Guardia Act in 1932 outlawing court injunctions against peaceful activities of the unions and yellow-dog contracts helped to arrest declining unionism somewhat, but the depression continued to hurt union membership. By 1933 there were only about 2,975,000 members.

Organized Labor under the New Deal. With inauguration of the New Deal, organized labor took a new lease on life, and, operating in a highly friendly climate, unions grew until their membership had reached approximately 15 million in 1947. The National Industrial Recovery and the National Labor Relations Acts contributed much to the growth of labor unions. The NRA provided for the establishment of codes of fair competition which were to include maximum-hour and minimum-wage provisions. Labor was given advisory status in the preparation of these codes. The vital part of the act for unionism was Sec. 7 (a), which required each code to contain provisions for collective bargaining and freedom from employer coercion in organization. Before the courts invalidated the NRA, membership in the AFL alone increased over 40 per cent. The Railway Labor Act amendments in 1934 also assisted the growth of the railroad brotherhoods.

By the time the NRA was invalidated in May, 1935, collective bargaining between management and labor had become widely accepted. Three months later Congress passed the National Labor Relations Act (popularly known as the Wagner Act), which guaranteed the right of labor to organize and to bargain collectively, free from interference and restraint by employers. The Act was upheld by the Supreme Court in April, 1937.[3]

---

[3] *National Labor Relations Board v. Jones and Laughlin Steel Corp.*, 301 U.S. 419.

In terms of the labor movement since 1935, it is difficult to exaggerate the importance of the Wagner Act. The broad powers given to the National Labor Relations Board to enforce and interpret the Act greatly strengthened unionization, and the Supreme Court in the main backed the Board's decisions. The latter's rulings in effect liquidated company unions and outlawed the once-effective antiunion techniques of employers. Many states followed the lead of Congress by passing "little Wagner acts," thus assuring protection to unions of employees engaged in intrastate commerce. Following the NRA and NLRA, Congress gave much additional aid to labor through the Social Security, Walsh-Healey, and Fair Labor Standard and Full Employment Acts. The remarkable change in labor's position both at the bargaining table with management and in the counsels of government within about a decade is one of the most amazing chapters in American history.

During World War II, labor was taken into partnership by the government and management on a scale hitherto unknown in war or in peace. A labor representative, Sidney Hillman, was appointed an associate director of the Office of Production Management. The presidents of the CIO, AFL, and Railway groups served on the national Management-Labor Policy Committee. Labor was invited to participate in government administration by becoming a coequal on the tripartite National War Labor Board. Unions participated in negotiating master agreements in the shipbuilding industries and aided in drawing up basic wage and other standards in various industries. Indeed, labor was represented in one way or another in nearly all the war agencies and councils. In several thousand plants labor-management committees were created which, in practice, gave workers a share in the process of planning and organizing production.

A final illustration of labor's status under Democratic administrations is the fact that in the closing days of the Truman Administration more than 70 AFL and CIO people were on union leave serving in domestic government posts. In addition, there were 60 union people serving in overseas labor offices, mostly in the Mutual Security Agency.

Labor Today. Both the AFL and CIO endorsed Stevenson for President in 1952 and lost out. Hard on the heels of this defeat, their two long-time leaders, William Green and Philip Murray, died. As a gesture of unity, President Eisenhower appointed Martin Durkin, an AFL leader, as Secretary of Labor. However, the Labor Department had been stripped of many of its former functions and Durkin seemed to wield little influence in the Cabinet. More than this, labor publications complained that advisory committees and "revaluation" committees in the administrative branch were being filled with business representatives and that labor was having less voice in the councils of government. Further, the new Congress seemed to be in no hurry to amend the Taft-Hartley Act and labor membership appeared to be on a plateau with some fears that it might go into a slow decline. Secretary Durkin resigned after seven months because the Eisenhower Administration failed to do anything about the Taft-Hartley Act during the first session of its Congress. To labor leaders at least, 1953 marked the end of an era; actually labor's influence in Congress had declined earlier.

Union membership reached a peak in 1946 and remained stationary thereafter even though the labor force of the nation increased. This condition of saturation was due in part to the fact that most of the new worlds had been "conquered" and the unorganized sectors such as the South and some of the Rocky Mountain areas were difficult to conquer. Unionism had established itself in the manufacturing, transportation, and construction industries, and it was difficult to make progress in agriculture, domestic service, and in small businesses. Moreover, after such a meteoric rise in membership, the accomplishment of a large number of national legislative objectives, and a somewhat more conservative temper of the nation, unionism needed some time to consolidate and the movement was bound to lose some momentum.

To a considerable extent the labor unions had realized their role of providing a vehicle for immigrant and ethnic groups to attain status. For years leaders, who retired or were decreased by 1953, such as Philip Murray, Sidney Hillman, Matthew Woll, Allan Haywood, and Dan Tobin had been immigrants themselves. The Germans, Irish, Jews, Poles, and other immigrants joined unions which were led by men like themselves who wanted status, self-improvement, economic betterment, and security. As there were fewer immigrants, so the number of unionists and their leaders who were foreign born declined. Many of the newer leaders were less militant, at least in organizing drives.

Labor does not have an orderly way of training and bringing up new leaders who can take over the tremendous problems of operating huge unions so as to give the organization managerial continuity and competence such as is enjoyed by business corporations. Several students of labor feel that its own organizational structure is not equal to the job it is trying to do. The leaders, moreover, were concerned with the inflation taking place after the war and had to spend long hours at the economic bargaining table.

THE VOICES OF ORGANIZED LABOR

The bulk of organized labor today is found in national and international unions. Like local chambers of commerce and trade associations, the unions recognize the value of federation; the AFL in fact was formed in part to cope with the federating tendencies of employers' associations.

Today most unions are affiliated with either the AFL or the CIO. Important exceptions are some of the railroad brotherhoods, which have their own federations, and a few unions of public employees such as the post-office clerks and telephone and other utility workers, especially in the field of transportation.

American Federation of Labor. According to Article II of its constitution, the objectives of the AFL are (1) to encourage the formation of trade-unions and the closer federation of them through the organization of central trade and labor unions in every city, and the further combination into state and territorial organizations "to secure legislation in the interest of the working masses"; (2) to establish and promote national and international trade-unions, based upon strict autonomy of each trade; (3) to aid and assist each other, encourage the sale of union-label goods, and influence public opinion in favor of organized labor; and (4) to aid and encourage the labor press of America.

The sovereign legislative body of the AFL is the annual convention, which generally meets in October for about two weeks. International unions are represented in the convention roughly according to size of membership; each union having less than 4,000 members is entitled to 1 delegate; 2 delegates are permitted for from 4,000 to 8,000 members, 3 delegates for from 8,000 to 16,000 members, 4 for 16,000 or more, 5 for 32,000, and so on (see Article IV of the constitution). Each city central, state federation, and directly affiliated federal union is entitled to 1 delegate. In convention meetings the international delegate is permitted to cast one vote for every 100 members or a major fraction thereof. As Professor Childs [4] points out in his study of the operations of the AFL, this schedule

. . . gives the larger unions an absolutely larger representation but the smaller unions a proportionally larger number of delegates. . . . In view of the fact that no restriction is placed upon the total number of delegates from national or international unions, it is possible for a few of the larger unions to dominate the meeting, the more so for the reason that the voting strength of the unions is adjusted more in accordance with the size of the membership.

It is at the convention that resolutions, principles, and programs of action are debated and adopted, and a wide variety of proposals are submitted for ratification by over a dozen convention committees. Individual members also have the freedom to introduce resolutions. Many of the subjects coming before the convention are first screened by the executive council, enabling those not requiring immediate action or

[4] Harwood L. Childs, *Labor and Capital in National Politics* (Columbus, Ohio: The Ohio State University Press, 1930), p. 127; see also Lewis Lorwin, *The American Federation of Labor* (Washington, D.C.: Brookings Institution, 1933).

those which can be taken care of by the staff to be disposed of in a more efficient manner. Executive council members also serve on many of the convention committees, which promotes a further method of facilitating the disposition of resolutions. An executive council is designated to carry out the decisions of the convention.[5]

The president and secretary-treasurer devote full time to Federation matters and the presidency is a highly responsible and powerful position. When Emerson said that "an institution is the lengthened shadow of one man," he coined a phrase of which the AFL provides an illustration. Except for one year, Samuel Gompers served as its president from its beginning to 1924. Gompers became to the tradesmen what Weaver was to the Populists, Debs to the Socialists, and later Fishbein to the medical profession and Lewis to the miners. In the popular mind Gompers and the AFL were synonymous. William Green took over the Gompers' mantle and served 28 years until his death in 1952. George Meany became the new head and likewise became its recognized spokesman, especially on legislative and international policies. The philosophies and tactics of Gompers and Green made a permanent imprint on the thinking of organized labor, particularly the AFL. Both were regular callers at the White House and few Presidents acted on labor matters without consulting them. There are few if any federated groups where personal leadership has meant more than in the AFL. In their long histories no president of the National Association of Manufacturers or the Chamber of Commerce of the United States ever became identified with the voice of organized business over so long a period of time as did Gompers and Green, speaking for organized labor.

Similar to other large interest groups, the AFL has built up a press and public-relations program of its own. It felt it was receiving unfair treatment at the hands of many radio commentators and so it hired its own network commentator who reports the news five nights a week. The organization has begun a weekly television program. The *AFL News-Reporter* comes out as an eight-page weekly and the monthly *American Federationist* is found on newsstands. Pamphlets on a large variety of subjects are issued and many locals publish journals of their own.

Congress of Industrial Organizations. From the beginning of the labor movement, a sharp difference of opinion has existed over industrial versus craft unionism and the extent to which unions should be conterminous

---

[5] Composed of the president, secretary-treasurer, and 15 vice-presidents elected annually, the council also acts for the convention during the interim between the yearly meetings. It has even suspended or revoked charters of unions found guilty of promoting dual unionism, subject, of course, to an appeal by the disciplined unions to the next convention.

with the industries involved. As the "aristocrat" of labor, the AFL was dominated by the large skilled-trades unions, even though there were industrial unions such as the miners within the organization. The NRA focused attention on the difficulties of organizing the mass-production industries along craft lines because millions of workers were outside the skilled trades in which unions had been formed. When an attempt was made to organize the mass-production industries, a bitter conflict arose with the skilled-trades unions claiming jurisdiction and resulting in the inability of the AFL to undertake a campaign to organize these industries.

In a tense and dramatic situation in the 1935 AFL convention an industrial union resolution was defeated 18,024 to 10,933. The heads of eight disgruntled unions then formed a committee to aid the organization of workers "in mass-production and other industries upon an industrial basis," and the AFL executive council suspended them for this action.

Nevertheless, the committee kept up its work and in 1938 the Congress of Industrial Organizations was formed. To the CIO were brought many prominent unions and union leaders, including John L. Lewis of the United Mine Workers as president, Sidney Hillman and David Dubinsky from the clothing workers' unions, and representatives of the typographers and textile unions. Internal quarrels led Dubinsky and his International Ladies' Garment Workers' Union to go back to the AFL in 1940, and the United Mine Workers to leave the CIO in 1942 and to reaffiliate with the AFL in 1946, then to withdraw a year later. Differences between John L. Lewis and President Roosevelt led Lewis to support Willkie in 1940 and to resign as president of the CIO after Roosevelt's reelection. Philip Murray was elected president of the CIO and continued to serve until his death in 1952. After some struggle for power, Walter Reuther, the head of the United Automobile Workers, became president.

The structure of the CIO is similar to that of the AFL, with supreme authority resting in the annual convention and an executive board. The latter is a body of 46 representing all CIO unions. A formula based largely on size of the union is used to determine the number of delegates each union has in the annual convention. Each local industrial and industrial union council is entitled to one delegate. Every national, international, and local industrial union, and each organizing committee is entitled to one vote for each member and each industrial union council has one vote. "Industrial union councils" are organized on a geographical basis and are composed of locals of national and international unions and organizing committees.[6]

The CIO consists of two big unions, the United Automobile Workers

[6] A useful description of the CIO regional organizational structure is found in the *CIO News*, June 1, 1953, p. 3.

and the United Steelworkers, each of which have more than one-fourth of the total membership. These two constituents have the greatest power on the executive board because each representative votes in proportion to the membership of his union. By centralization of working arrangements, many jurisdictional disputes and much factionalism have been reduced. With Murray out as its leader, the future of factionalism is bound up with the need for cooperation between President Reuther and David J. McDonald, the new leader of the steelworkers.

The objects of the CIO as set forth in Article II of its constitution differ only in detail from the AFL. The CIO has managed to maintain an enthusiastic and able research staff in its national headquarters in Washington and has turned out a volume of pamphlets on themes varying from housing to the church and labor. A weekly newspaper, the *CIO News,* costs subscribers a very small sum and contains union and governmental items of interest to labor. The *Economic Outlook,* published monthly, interprets various problems confronting labor, particularly those arising from government action.

The differences between the AFL and CIO are not so apparent as they were in the 1930's. On three matters, however, there is a difference in emphasis. The idea of craft unions or "horizontal" unions remains strong with the AFL, while the CIO's emphasis is on "vertical" combination or company-wide and industry-wide organization. The two attempt both types of organization today but the underlying concerns and successes show this tendency. A second characteristic, growing in part out of this, is the somewhat greater control by the top hierarchy in the national and regional CIO leadership, whereas the locals and internationals in the AFL pride themselves on considerable autonomy. Again, this is but a matter of degree. Finally, the CIO leadership has been somewhat more aggressive because it was the youngster and the insurgent of the movement. The AFL leadership has remained somewhat more in the hands of the Old Guard.

Membership Issues and Schisms. In addition to the AFL and CIO there are numerous independent unions and powerful unions within the larger federations. The railroad brotherhoods represent the oldest of the confederations and enjoy a high degree of cohesiveness, though some are affiliated with the AFL and others the CIO. Spokesman for the brotherhoods is the Railway Labor Executives' Association, which claims to represent 1½ million workers in 20 unions. Dave Beck leads the powerful International Brotherhood of Teamsters (AFL), which boasts 1 million membership. The U.S. Department of Labor reported in 1953 that of the 215 unions, 109 were affiliated with the AFL, 33 with the CIO, and 73 were independent. Perhaps best known of the last-mentioned is the United Mine Workers, which has been led for over a quarter of a century by John L. Lewis. Over 39 unions reported a membership of over 100,000, and almost seven of eight union members belonged either to the AFL or CIO.

Sharp rivalries have taken place between the various labor unions in the drive for members and for recognition as the collective bargaining representative. The public has at times been inconvenienced by jurisdictional strikes. From the standpoint of the government, the fact that labor speaks with many voices, and not a single one, has had profound significance. Major political parties, especially in state and local politics, have tended to play one federation against another. It is common to see an "AFL bill" and a "CIO bill" on the same subject introduced in state legislatures. The latter is often more sweeping. For example, the AFL has been more willing to settle for a disability insurance law in the states while the CIO has held out for compulsory health insurance. During World War II there was no one voice which could speak officially for all of labor and President Roosevelt found he had to deal with several union heads instead of one. On tripartite boards and on labor panels care had to be taken to make certain that both an AFL and CIO man were included. Governors of states have likewise at times found the task of governing more difficult by reason of schisms within the ranks of labor. Some governors have successfully courted one federation and received enough electoral strength so that they could afford to ignore the demands of the other big labor group.

The cleavage between the CIO and AFL has sometimes manifested itself in state and local campaigns. In Detroit, New York City, and in California the two unions have backed different candidates. On quite frequent occasions the two groups' respective political arms have refused to work together in election activities. Since 1950, however, the two have attempted with some success to pool their political strength on a permanent basis and Reuther and Meany have taken steps to cement certain political ties.

Management has at times played one union against another in the hope of keeping organized labor divided, although many business firms have been plagued by jurisdictional strife. Notwithstanding this, collective bargaining between business and labor, irrespective of divisions within labor, continues to be marked by labor drives for union security, guaranteed annual wages, wage-price formulas, premiums, welfare funds and fringe benefits, and industry-wide collective bargaining. Labor has already extended its influence into advertising methods, sales policies, plant organization and coordination, the purchase of materials, and many other areas formerly regarded as within the prerogative of management.

Labor unions have run into numerous membership problems, particularly the question of admittance of Negroes, women, and Communists. The railroad brotherhoods for a time explicitly confined their membership to white persons. In the AFL, restrictive policies were not set by the national organization, leaving the matter to constituent unions. From its beginning the CIO vigorously combatted discrimination. With the help of the courts and union leadership, membership is no longer discriminative and racial groups have been able to attain considerable political influence through the channels of their union.

Women have won their battle for union membership slowly, especially among the craft unions. Although there appear to be about 3 million women members, over 80 per cent of them are in 45 unions and over half of the unions report no women members. This is not exclusively a discriminatory practice, however, as there are many lines of work in which there are virtually no women.

On the question of political beliefs, the unions have had their trials and tribulations, especially as to Communist infiltration. The AFL constitution forbade any local whose organization was "officered or controlled by Communists" from having any representation in the federation; the CIO was originally silent on political beliefs. For a time one of the distinguishing characteristics between the two groups was their attitude toward Communists. The CIO leadership originally attempted to work with the Communists in the belief that it could control them but the AFL leaders did not share this view. Since World War II both groups have taken a sharp stand against communism in their ranks. The CIO expelled several unions commanded by left-wing, pro-Communist leaders, notably the electrical and farm equipment organizations. The non-Communist affidavit required by the Taft-Hartley law helped to identify Communist influence.

Friends of labor and Presidents of the United States have tried to bring about amalgamation or unity within the ranks of unions. The issues of craft unions, attitude toward communism, and membership problems no longer seem to have the divisive character they once did. But labor unions have built up bureaucracies and vested interests which make mergers difficult. None of the labor groupings represents an integrated organization; all are loose confederations of economic interests, which are not necessarily in full sympathy with one another. In spite of this, substantial uniformity exists as to public policy from labor's point of view. Labor is united, regardless of labels, on the social-welfare objectives for its individual members.

THE LEGISLATIVE PROGRAM OF LABOR

Early Program. The attitude of organized labor toward a positive program of legislation to further its social-welfare objectives has shown a phenomenal change since 1930. The long-time leadership of Samuel Gompers (and of William Green in his earlier terms) was essentially negative or defensive with regard to labor legislation. Gompers regarded it as a duty of government to provide services for labor, and he fought diligently for the creation of the Department of Labor and for measures designed to promote collective bargaining and unionism. By means of free collective bargaining, Gompers believed labor could obtain contracts providing for higher wages, shorter hours, and improved working conditions. Legislation was favored to protect women and children in industry, to provide workmen's compensation, and related objectives, but national laws providing social security and regulation of hours and wages were not favored and were even regarded as paternalism. During the depression of the early 1920's, labor made no demands for a Federal public-works program or for wage-hour or social-security legislation. Nevertheless, by 1930 the AFL laid claim to having placed 200 laws on the statute books, demonstrating the scope of the legislative program.

Six months after the stock market crash of 1929, William Green departed from orthodoxy to endorse a public-works program during economic depression, but still saw the proper regulatory function of government as applying only to the employment of women and children, employer's liability and factory expansion, and the promotion of health and education. In 1930 Green said, "Unemployment insurance is unfair, discriminatory, and unscientific."[7] This statement, which represented the general labor viewpoint of the time, is all the more remarkable against which to review the demands on government by labor in 1933 and today. The Social Security, Walsh-Healey, Fair Labor Standards, and Full Employment Acts are a far cry from Green's 1930 position. These became proper objects for lobbying, and it was assumed that these gains were possible through government alone. Simultaneously, labor remained consistent in its demand for social-welfare services. Labor now looks increasingly to the state and national governments for social insurance, wage-hour legislation, and the guaranteeing of collective bargaining.

Current Objectives. Labor's legislative program calls in the first place for the extension of benefits now guaranteed by Federal legislation. This includes the perennial demand for higher minimum-wage levels, the extension of unemployment compensation both as to maximum amount of weekly benefits and in the number of weeks which such benefits will be given. The unions are pressing for additional programs for maternal, child health, and public health, and aid to disabled and physically handicapped workers. Beginning in 1938, the CIO has demanded a national health program based upon the principle of compulsory health insurance.

[7] D. H. Joseph, "Employment Insurance," *American Federationist,* January, 1933, pp. 37–38.

A little later the AFL joined the CIO in lobbying for the passage of the Wagner-Murray-Dingell bill for compulsory sickness insurance.

Following the general line of attack, William Green delivered lengthy testimony before congressional committees denouncing the opponents of national health insurance and the American Medical Association in particular. President Truman and several of his Cabinet secretaries endorsed a national health-insurance plan and the President sent Congress messages and prepared bills on the subject. President Eisenhower and his Cabinet, however, opposed these measures. Meanwhile, labor has sought to obtain health coverage plans at the bargaining table and from the states. Even though national health insurance is not an immediate prospect, it remains on labor's agenda and is potentially one of the great legislative battles of the future.

After World War II, labor threw vigorous support behind the Murray-Patman Full Employment bill, but Congress emasculated the measure by enacting it in a form devoid of committing the government to maintain full employment. Although the unions are unhappy over this weakening of the Act, they are pleased over the fact that it became public policy to support the idea of economic analysis. In terms of employment, an unrealized objective is the attainment of Federal fair-employment-practices legislation. Several states, however, have enacted laws which are designed to combat discrimination in hiring.

Labor is one of the stanch supporters of Federal aid to education for children's school lunches. It vigorously opposed the measure giving title to offshore oil lands to the states as a "give-away" program and favored Federal ownership with royalties going to the states to aid public education. Other aid programs which have received labor's endorsement included roads, rivers and harbors, and housing.

Other Federal legislation for which labor has lobbied includes increased salary and retirement for Federal employees, maintenance of government control over atomic energy, crop insurance and subsidies to farmers, and the enactment of "stand-by" or emergency price and rent controls.

It is in the field of public finance that organized labor has quite generally found itself in sharp opposition to the position of the business community. Both are publicly on record as favoring a balanced budget but do not agree on means. Labor has in general supported high-expenditure programs and has favored keeping high tax rates in order to bring the budget into balance. Labor has always objected to policies that would place a greater burden on persons of smaller incomes. The application of the income tax to those in the lower brackets met with labor's opposition, as has the sales tax. Conversely, excess profits, corporation income taxes, together with progressively higher personal income-tax rates on those in the upper income brackets, are favored. Legislative committees are accustomed to hearing charges of "soaking the poor" or "soaking the rich" from labor and business respectively.

In the last quarter century organized labor has turned to the Federal government for positive aid in furthering the welfare and condition of the working classes. It has received far more from Washington than from state capitals. Indeed, it has had to fight what it has sometimes called the "reactionary farmer-lawyer-merchant-dominated state legislatures." In many states, however, labor has done well and has exercised real influence. But labor's main arena of politics has been the great stakes involved in national legislation. One of labor's newest goals is the security of a guaranteed annual wage. It seems doubtful that any general legislation on the subject is feasible, but it is being carefully studied by labor's economists. Labor, like business, has not been monolithic in outlook in legislative matters. In spite of the fact that some union spokesmen speak against a high protective tariff and in favor of the reciprocal trade treaties, workers in the watch, shoe, and canned fish industry want protection from foreign competition. Although most union journals are for the extension of public power, the electrical workers are often found supporting management in its battle against public ownership of utilities. Contrary to popular opinion, labor and management work together in many legislative struggles.

The Taft-Hartley Act. Organized labor's long list of successes was interrupted by its inability to defeat the Labor-Management Relations Act of 1947, popularly known as the Taft-Hartley Act. The strength labor developed under the National Labor Relations Act, the accentuation of its lobbying and election activities, together with widespread work stoppages immediately after World War II, led to demands for a national labor policy which would curb some of labor's power. Republican leaders announced after the mid-term election of 1946 that they would press for legislation of this type. With the Republican majorities winning in both houses and with the help of Southern Democrats, the omnibus bill was not only carried but was passed over the President's veto.

The new labor law is one of the most sweeping ever passed. Concisely, the Act abolishes the closed shop but permits a union shop if the majority of eligible workers vote for it, and the coercion of employees to join unions is forbidden. Secondary boycotts and jurisdictional strikes are made unfair labor practices. In an effort to end featherbedding, the Act holds it an unfair labor practice for a union to require an employer to pay money "in the nature of an exaction" for services not rendered. The Norris-La Guardia Act of 1932 is modified to the extent of allowing both workers and employers to ask the NLRB to petition for injunctions in all unfair-labor-practice cases. Industry-wide bargaining is limited in that the

NLRB is required to supervise elections by employees of each individual employer on the basis of the latter's last offer, thus opening the way in the coal industry, for example, for a multiplicity of "final offers" which may in some cases be accepted and in others not. A 60-day cooling-off period before striking is to be inserted in each contract, and employees summarily lose their rights under the Act if they violate this regulation. In cases of a strike or contemplated strike threatening the national health or safety, there is also a delay with the final step in the form of a report by the President to Congress for action. The national government is projected far into the field of industrial disputes. Bargaining rights are denied to supervisory workers, government employees, and workers in nonprofit hospitals. Unions are required to file considerable information about their officers, elections, and finances. Many other restrictions are placed on union control of welfare funds and the checkoff of union dues. It should be noted that the Act did not strike at labor benefits but rather at union structure and organization.

Virtually all these provisions were fought by spokesmen for organized labor as well as any amendment or change in the Wagner Act. Radio network programs, the purchase of full-page advertisements in metropolitan dailies, and even skywriting was used to denounce the "slave-labor" bill. But President Truman's veto, a short filibuster by pro-labor senators, plus labor's campaign were of no avail.

The Act was a stunning legislative defeat for labor unions but it did not result in "enslaving" labor. It gave to union leadership a new battle cry—"repeal Taft-Hartley"—and caused some reorientation of legislative sights toward that end. Although President Truman championed repeal, he was never able to muster anywhere near the needed majorities in Congress. With the Eisenhower Administration pledged to retain the Act, many labor leaders have changed their demands from outright repeal to amendments.[8] It seems that, for the moment at least, labor unions will have to live with the major provisions of the Taft-Hartley law in force.

POLITICAL TACTICS

Areas of Labor Politics. From this review of the rise of labor it is clear that labor has always been in politics in the broadest sense and that its role is on the increase both in scope and intensity. The politics of labor is channelized in five directions: (1) intraunion politics and interunion jurisdictional disputes; (2) public relations; (3) lobbying activities; (4) election activities; and (5) labor political parties. The first four of these are also

---

[8] Discussion of the amendments recommended by the CIO will be found in the *CIO News,* Feb. 9 and 16, 1953. Amendments offered by the Eisenhower Administration failed to pass in Congress in 1954.

characteristic of many if not most political associations. Only brief mention will be made of the first three as they relate to labor unions.

Labor, perhaps more than most groups, must keep up a constant drive for membership and for loyalty of all members, because mass support is so essential for successful collective bargaining, strikes, and in elections. A campaign is continuously waged to stress the advantages of unionism. The federations and the larger unions may spend over a million dollars a year on organizing drives. Considerable money and effort have gone into drives to organize the workers in the South ("Operation Dixie").

Within the unions themselves there is a struggle for power and for control of the group. Here the discord between ideologies, personalities, and leadership in union interests, policies, and tactics, and attitudes toward management come into play. Many unions, notably the United Automobile Workers, are democratically governed and their meetings and conventions are characterized by heated debates and caucusing not unlike political conventions. Most unions, however, are not so democratically controlled. Within labor itself there is room for shades of opinion, and these differences often seem of more importance than the strong forces that bind them together.

In the preceding chapter it was noted that a major tactic of organized business is public relations. Labor unions have suffered from bad public relations. For years their leaders ignored the field or were too busy with matters seemingly of more immediate importance. Few persons skilled in public relations were found in the hierarchy. The organizations are now paying more attention to courting good will among the public. This is shown in the increasing number of pamphlets and materials put out for school children and the general public. For many of these the unions make nominal charges. Labor does not yet make available nearly as many journals and materials for the schools and the public as business. It has few fellowships, internships, schools, and so on.[9] Only a few labor organizations have a speakers' bureau and radio and television programs designed to build good will and understanding of its viewpoint. Its speakers and publications show a vast improvement over bygone days but they still generally lack the finesse and *savoir-faire* of business' public relations.

Labor's lobbying techniques are quite similar to those of other groups and its leaders spend much time in such enterprises. Its activities in this connection are being more and more bolstered by direct or veiled threats of reprisals at the polls. Lobbying and election activities are very closely tied together.

[9] The CIO conducts a dozen or more "summer schools" each year to prepare those attending for union work and to help them become better informed on legislative issues, community relations, and political activity. These schools, however, are for union members and are not designed specifically for the public or for public relations.

Labor in Elections. Throughout its history the AFL has followed the dictum of "defeating its enemies and electing its friends." Word is soon passed along the line as to which nominees are friendly or unfriendly. With the exception of the 1924 and 1952 elections, the AFL has not endorsed presidential candidates but gives space to both national parties in *The American Federationist.* A number of locals in the AFL, however, have made presidential endorsements. The CIO has generally officially approved Democratic presidential candidates.

During congressional elections many union papers carry the voting record of individual candidates on labor matters under the headings of "voted right" and "voted wrong." The railroad labor paper, *Labor,* goes further and publishes the names of all congressional candidates who are approved by the Railway Labor Executives' Association. These are usually incumbents who have an outstanding pro-labor voting record and whose reelection seems particularly desirable. Failure to be included on this list signifies that the record was undistinguished or unacceptable. State governors, legislators, mayors, and city councilmen also have their records combed before endorsement is given.

In addition to official and unofficial endorsement of candidates by labor leaders, labor has resorted from time to time to the creation of special organizations other than political parties, whose exclusive purpose is to work for the election of certain candidates. The Nonpartisan League of North Dakota and Minnesota, formed in 1915, worked through Republican primaries to secure nominees favorable to its legislative program and later ran candidates of its own. In 1922 the Conference for Progressive Political Action was formed by the railway unions to intensify political activity without at the same time becoming an independent labor party.[10] One of the initial objectives was to secure the nomination and election of progressives for Congress wherever this would not result in splitting the vote to the advantage of the conservative candidates. Following this, bitter internal dissension arose over transforming the organization into a national political party to work with the Socialist, Workers, and Farmer-Labor parties. Finally the CPPA endorsed "Fighting Bob" La Follette for President in 1924, postponing a decision on the formation of a new national party till after the elections. La Follette's popular vote impressed neither the AFL nor the railroad unions, and the final result was a disintegration of both the CPPA and the third-party movement.

Again in 1936, a political organization, Labor's Nonpartisan League, was formed to implement trade-union political activities. John L. Lewis, its organizer, led the League to make a considerable financial and elec-

[10] A useful summary of labor's political activities during this period will be found in Henry David, "Labor and Political Action after World War I: 1919–1924," *Labor and Nation,* Vol. 1 (February-March, 1946), pp. 27–33.

toral contribution to the reelection of Franklin D. Roosevelt. When soon afterwards strained relations developed between Lewis and President Roosevelt, the influence of the League declined. William Green and his followers refused to go along with the League, and it never became more than a CIO adjunct. When Lewis left the CIO, the League collapsed, but CIO leaders had had a taste of this form of political action, and shortly a new and virile organization arose which both psychologically and politically has become a powerful group on the national political scene—the Political Action Committee.

Political Action Groups. The CIO-PAC excursion into "nonparty, non-partisan" politics began in 1943 under the leadership of Sidney Hillman. Among the motives for what the CIO calls "labor's political arm" was a desire to create an organization that would protect labor after the war against soaring prices and from legislative action designed to take away the gains won by unions before and during the war. Leaders of the CIO also felt that the public and the soldiers were receiving a slanted and unfavorable picture of labor's contribution to the war effort through widespread newspaper publicity on strikes. In the judgment of the executive board of the CIO, a national organization was needed to fight political apathy among the workers and the potential antipathy of the public reminiscent of 1919 to 1924.

The PAC first trained its guns on the 1944 election with a drive to get out a large vote, on the theory that the greater the vote, the greater the victory for progressives. First it was agreed that millions must be registered and a spirited campaign was carried on with the help of groups like the League of Women Voters to educate the public on the purpose of and necessity for registration. When the doorbell ringers from PAC went out to work they sang:

> Let's go out and ring doorbells and get the neighbors to vote,
> Is your Congressman stalling, is he getting your goat?
> Let's go out and ring doorbells and get the neighbors to vote,
> It's neighbor meeting with neighbor that made America jell,
> So when we're out ringing doorbells, we're ringing the Liberty Bell!

Following the registration, the PAC concentrated on the primaries. Here it was pointed out that it mattered little if, in the November elections, the voter had only a choice between two unprogressive "tweedle-dee" and "tweedledum" nominees. Literature on the primaries was widely distributed and the doorbell-ringing corps again went into action; this undoubtedly helped to swell the numbers at the primaries. The PAC educational campaign on registration and nomination was a success and about $375,000 was spent for these purposes. Most of this money was raised by union contributions.

To carry out its functions the PAC created a vast organization with a national office in New York and 14 regional offices embracing all 48 states. The purpose of the regional offices was to coordinate the activities of unions willing to participate. Each union was asked to form its own political action committee, whereupon the national office sent pamphlets, posters, radio scripts, slogans, songs, clipsheets, stickers, buttons, and organization and canvassers' manuals, together with the voting record of the local congressman seeking reelection.[11] The publications are easy to understand and, with simple phraseology, cartoons, and graphics, educate the reader in the dynamics of political action. These manuals, each running about 45 pages, were thorough in their discussion of techniques for specific audiences—*Radio Handbook, Speakers' Manual,* and *A Woman's Guide to Political Action.* Altogether, 85 million pieces of literature of all sorts were printed and distributed in 1944 alone, and there has been little letup in the plethora of publications since then.

The CIO-PAC was at first denounced by the American Federation of Labor as "the strongest antilabor force in America" and locals were urged to shun cooperation with the group. Nonetheless, some locals assisted the PAC, especially in registration activities. In 1947 the Washington State Federation of Labor, which had one of the largest per population memberships in the nation, formed an "educational and political league" resembling the CIO-PAC. In the same year and under the impetus of its failure to defeat the Taft-Hartley law, the American Federation of Labor created Labor's League for Political Education.[12] This group, like the CIO-PAC, is at once a political committee and a pressure group. Between and during elections both groups hold mass meetings and conferences with public officials, lobby, and publish pamphlets on a wide variety of subjects. Both profess to be nonpartisan and to work within the framework of the two-party system.

Even though both unions continue to operate separate political leagues, the two have worked very closely together in some communities and are usually found endorsing the same candidates and taking the same position on legislation. The CIO-PAC has been somewhat more active in work at the precinct level. This statement from the bylaws of a state league typifies the purposes of both the PAC and the LLPE: [13]

[11] Full reprints of many of these publications, as well as interesting details of the PAC, are found in Joseph Gaer, *The First Round: The Story of the CIO Political Action Committee* (New York: Duell, Sloan & Pearce, Inc., 1944).

[12] The group was first called Labor's Educational and Political League. For organizational details see *The New York Times,* Dec. 6 and 7, 1947. The railroad brotherhoods formed their political league at the same time; see *ibid.,* Dec. 8, 1947.

[13] Taken from Arts. III–IV of the bylaws of Labor's Educational and Political League, Washington State Federation of Labor.

It shall be the purpose of the League by means of dissemination of information concerning national and state issues and candidates for public office, by use of education and the ballot, and other democratic and lawful means, to bring about the election to public office of public-spirited citizens who will protect and promote the interest and welfare of workers and the general public. . . . It may cooperate with organizations representing farmers, veterans, workers and other citizen groups, whose aims and objects are compatible and in harmony with those of the League.

Both groups work with other political groups on candidates and issues. The CIO-PAC has cooperated to a high degree with the Americans for Democratic Action and the Farmers' Union.

Appraisal of the Political Action Committees. Labor's newest political arms are by no means revolutionary, for labor has been in politics for over a century. However, PAC's early effectiveness in its program of registering voters, the adoption of a well-rounded program for national security and prosperity, the scope of its organization from precinct to national headquarters, and its propaganda techniques placed labor in politics on a scale without precedent in the United States. Businessmen, farmers, officeholders, and many others are unable to view its rise with equanimity. Although the comparative infancy of both the PAC and LLPE and the absence of objective studies of their operations make evaluation difficult, some attention to their results may be briefly noted.[14]

It is impossible to know on a national scale whether the endorsements by the political leagues and activities on behalf of those candidates are a net liability or asset. In many American election districts labor-endorsed candidates failed to win. In 1946, in California Republicans made an effective issue of the CIO-supported candidates for Congress, labeling them "package" nominees. In this election only 73 PAC-endorsed candidates out of 318 in House contests won. With the support of both federations' political arms, Adlai Stevenson was unable to poll as large a vote as expected. Yet in 1948 and 1950, labor-endorsed candidates fared reasonably well. In the 1948 election the LLPE saw 172 of its "friends" elected to Congress and 106 of its "enemies" retired. It can hardly be proved one way or another that a man would or would not have been elected without the activities of the labor political committees on his behalf. At least one thing is clear: labor groups cannot consistently deliver a "labor vote."

If one turns to the registration campaigns, labor's activities here have received approbation and undoubtedly have helped to enlarge the rolls

[14] Labor newspapers often carry a "box score" on their successes following elections. One of the few illuminating studies conducted by officers of the CIO is *The Effectiveness of CIO-PAC in New Jersey in 1950* (Newark, N.J.: New Jersey State CIO Council, 1951).

of eligible voters. In New Jersey convincing evidence is available to show that the CIO did a relatively better job in 1950 in registering its members than the general public. "Not counting family members, PAC conservatively registered 12,000 CIO members during September, 1950, in four key counties." [15] In that election the organization had 800 PAC blockworkers in seven counties and in addition mobilized 35 students to work on election day. Various citizen groups have worked with both the LLPE and PAC in registration.

Within the ranks of labor and among labor's sincerest friends some misgivings are apparent. Those from the old school feel, as did Gompers, that activities of this sort are harmful to the cause of organized labor because of the tendency to identify unions with the Democratic party. Several AFL leaders, although privately for Stevenson for President, opposed official endorsement and campaigning in his behalf. Many felt that their position with Eisenhower and the Republicans was weakened because of this. National authorities of both great federations deny any intention of a permanent alliance with the Democratic party and can name several Republican candidates who have received labor's endorsement.

LABOR POLITICAL PARTIES

Organized labor's tactics have mainly been the use of the strike, boycott, union label, lobbying, the mass vote, and related electoral activities within the two-party system. A number of union members who have always regarded these tactics as inadequate have called for the creation of an independent labor party, with labor running its own candidates. A few believed the bid to labor by the Socialists and Communists should be accepted but the rank and file membership has shown little tendency to gravitate to the left-wing parties. The success of labor parties abroad, especially in England, has tended to keep some discussion alive for either national or state (or both) labor parties in the United States.

For the most part, the national union leaders have opposed a third party for the practical reason that they felt it had little chance of success. Lack of strong leadership and potential candidates within the ranks, the existence of internal dissension, and the unwillingness to carry on for years as a minor party have been stumbling blocks. Third parties face difficult financial problems and stringent election laws. The public also has opposed parties constructed along class lines and labor parties would have to have the votes of nonunion people to win. In spite of these obstacles, there have been several attempts to launch labor-based regional and state parties.

Attempts following World War I. The Labor party of Cook County, Ill., was launched in 1919, with a program of anti-imperialism, labor par-

[15] *Ibid.*, p. 13.

ticipation in the peace conference, and the democratization of industry.[16] This evolved into the Labor party of Illinois, and the AFL and independent union delegates from neighboring states met to extend the scope of the party. In spite of a denunciation of this practice by Samuel Gompers, the group went ahead to adopt a platform calling for an extension of public ownership, loans to farmers, and protection of the rights of labor. It nominated Perley Christensen for the presidency in 1920 under the label of Farmer-Labor, and he polled 265,000 votes, while local candidates received 600,000 votes in the 19 states where the party appeared on the ballot. After 1924, the national organization collapsed but the Farmer-Labor party continued as a force in the Dakotas, Minnesota, and surrounding areas. The Farmer-Labor party gained its strongest hold in Minnesota, where it was successful in electing governors and senators and running first or second in most elections until 1936, although it failed to control the Minnesota legislature, largely because of the nonpartisan election method.[17]

American Labor Party. The most recent excursion into a third party began in New York in 1936 with the formation of the American Labor party. Created out of trade-unions, a group of Old Guard Socialists, and Labor's Nonpartisan League (a Democratic auxiliary), the ALP soon became a real factor in New York politics. In reality, it was established to work for the reelection of President Roosevelt, since the Democratic organization (Tammany Hall) in New York City showed little enthusiasm for the President. Also the new party was used to attract voters who disliked to vote for New Deal candidates under the Democratic label.[18] At its inception the ALP was composed of 250 trade-unions, the largest being the International Ladies' Garment Workers' Union. All its first state officers were union officials. Operating as a state-wide party it has at times endorsed Republican and Democratic candidates but more often and lately has run its own nominees. It gave President Roosevelt his margin of victory in New York state in 1940 and 1944, and duplicated the same feat one or more times for Governor Lehman and Mayor La Guardia. It siphoned off enough votes from Truman in 1948 to give the state to the Republicans. It has been successful in electing a few state legislators, congressmen, and city councilmen. Three-fourths of its voting strength comes from New York City.

[16] On labor parties during this period see David, *loc. cit.*

[17] See Arthur Naftalin, "The Failure of the Farmer-Labor Party to Capture Control of the Minnesota Legislature," *The American Political Science Review*, Vol. 38 (1944), pp. 71–78, and J. R. Starr, "Labor and Farmer Groups in the Three-party System," *Southwestern Social Science Quarterly*, Vol. 17 (1936), pp. 7–19.

[18] On the origin and development of the ALP see Louis Waldman, *Labor Lawyer* (1944), and Hugh A. Bone, "Political Parties in New York City," *The American Political Science Review*, Vol. 40 (1946), pp. 272–282.

From the beginning the ALP has been beset with internal quarrels and factional strife, most of them being concerned with the party's attitude toward working with Communists and admitting Communist unions en bloc into the party. The right wing consistently opposed plans for inviting Communists into the councils of the ALP, fearing it would alienate sympathetic middle-class progressives and professional people. Finally in 1944, when the left wing captured control of the party, the right wing bolted and formed a state party of its own under the label of Liberal.[19] Both parties supported the Roosevelt-Truman ticket, but in local elections the Liberals refused to endorse local nominees of the ALP.

After the split, the ALP became almost exclusively a party of trade-unions and received most of its support from CIO affiliates, working closely with the CIO-PAC. The Liberal party was bolstered by a large number of AFL unions, but on the whole was more heterogeneous in character, including Republican and Democratic liberals who were disgruntled with the major-party leadership, and a sizable number of progressives and independents.

The ALP suffered a further split in 1948 over the third-party candidacy of Henry Wallace. Even before Mr. Wallace's announcement, the CIO and PAC leaders indicated that they would support President Truman for reelection. The strong left wing of the ALP won the endorsement of the party for Wallace early in 1948. State CIO leaders denounced the Wallace movement and, led by the Amalgamated Clothing Workers, withdrew a large bloc of unions from party membership.[20] Following this, President Truman and the Democrats strengthened their ties with the Liberal party and the non-Communist unions.

After 1948, only the left-wing union support remained and thereafter the ALP was no longer able to deliver its 400,000 votes. More and more it ran its own candidates instead of endorsing those of other parties. In 1952 it supported the Progressive party candidate but delivered only 63,000 votes for him. In 1954 it failed to poll the necessary votes to maintain its legal status as a political party. The Liberal party, meanwhile, supported Stevenson and became a balancing if not pivotal force. Yet its successes have been in forcing the major parties into innumerable alliances and in vetoing the nomination of certain hopefuls in the old-line parties. The Liberal party has strong trade-union backing but is not precisely a labor party. It speaks for New Deal and Fair Deal liberalism, while the ALP has more and more followed a pro-Communist line.

[19] See *The New York Times,* May 20 and 21, 1944. David Dubinsky and his International Ladies' Garment Workers' Union were initially the most important element in the Liberal party.

[20] See *The New York Times,* Jan. 11, 1948.

Table 5. Labor Party Strength in New York
(Figures in round numbers)

Presidential

1940

Republican (Willkie)	Democratic (Roosevelt)	American Labor (Roosevelt)	
3,027,000	2,834,000	417,000	

1944

Republican (Dewey)	Democratic (Roosevelt)	American Labor (Roosevelt)	Liberal (Roosevelt)
2,988,000	2,479,000	496,000	329,000

1948

Republican (Dewey)	Democratic (Truman)	American Labor (Wallace)	Liberal (Truman)
2,841,000	2,558,000	509,000	222,000

1952

Republican (Eisenhower)	Democratic (Stevenson)	American Labor (Hallinan)	Liberal (Stevenson)
3,934,000	2,676,000	63,000	394,000

Gubernatorial

1938

Republican (Dewey)	Democratic (Lehman)	American Labor (Lehman)	
2,302,000	1,971,000	420,000	

1942

Republican (Dewey)	Democratic (Bennett)	American Labor (Alfange)	
2,148,000	1,501,000	403,000	

1946

Republican (Dewey)	Democratic (Mead)	American Labor (Mead)	Liberal (Mead)
2,814,000	1,538,000	425,000	176,000

1950

Republican (Dewey)	Democratic (Lynch)	American Labor (McManus)	Liberal (Lynch)
2,812,000	1,985,000	209,000	262,000

1954

Republican (Ives)	Democratic (Harriman)	American Labor (McManus)	Liberal (Harriman)
2,549,000	2,296,000	46,000	264,000

Labor and the Democratic Party. Some Republicans have had the support of labor's political committees but the great majority of their endorsements have gone to Democratic candidates. In many areas of the
nation there is a close identification between labor and the Democratic
party because labor has had the major wherewithal to finance the campaigns of the Democrats. A Democratic hopeful in such instances is
reluctant even to enter a primary unless he receives approval from labor
with promises of support and financial aid.

Labor unions often wish to enjoy the advantages of party strength without the liabilities attendant to forming a labor party. Fay Calkins found
some interesting alternative relationships between the CIO and the Democrats.[21] For example, in Winnebago County, Ill., which contains the
third largest city, Rockford, the PAC decided it should influence the
Democratic party from within as a medium for promoting its legislative
objectives. It tried, successfully, to elect precinct captains and to effect
alliances thereby to elect a county chairman. The CIO entered the Democratic party in Michigan, was able to send a majority to the state convention, and to determine the composition of the Democratic state executive.

For the most part the CIO has not tried to take over the Democratic
organization, and where it has tried to do so, was often not successful.
In the Ferguson-Taft senatorial race in 1950, the PAC did not enter the
Democratic party or primaries but was simply content to supplement
Ferguson's campaign by organizing CIO members in his behalf. In the
same year in an Ohio congressional district the PAC operated successfully
as a balance-of-power voting bloc which would be offered to whichever
candidate came closest to its demands. In a state senatorial district in
Chicago the PAC decided to challenge the Democratic machine on a state
senatorial nomination. It built an independent organization among CIO
workers but its lack of funds plus the experience of the party's workers
was too much for the PAC and its candidate was decisively defeated. The
PAC, moreover, failed to obtain AFL support. These illustrations indicate
the diverse methods of action open to an interest group in trying to influence a political party.

Organized labor is in politics to stay. Its politics remain essentially
opportunistic in approach and its national leaders consider it wisdom to
work through the two-party system except in the peculiar situation in
New York City where it benefits at times by having its own organization
to some extent. Ideologically, the Communists no longer attract many
of its leaders. Many labor leaders, however, still champion the foreign
and domestic programs of the former Democratic administrations, while

21 *The CIO and the Democratic Party* (Chicago: University of Chicago Press, 1952).

professing to be "nonpartisan." The much-talked-of organic unity of labor still seems far away but some progress is being made in cooperation with lobbying and campaign endeavors. It will take time to see whether the "no-raiding" agreement between the AFL and CIO which began in 1954 will be successful.

Criticisms of Labor's Tactics. Labor, like most other organizations, has received criticism from friend and foe for some of its activities. It has shown ineptness and weakness at the local level, which is the training ground for future leaders at the state and national levels. Too often its candidates for local offices have not been attractive or particularly well qualified and have made poor public impressions. In such cases it would have been better to have withheld endorsements than to back mediocrity. The ratings of having voted "right" or "wrong" on certain measures do not invariably show enlightened self-interest, although on most of them the vote appears properly interpreted from labor's point of view.

Some of labor's publications contain erroneous comments and are given to dogmatic, unreasoning, and extreme statements. Wildcat and jurisdictional strikes, racketeering and gangsterism have made bad impressions which have hurt honestly and competently run unions. The wisdom of an inflexible approach to legislation displayed by some leaders is doubtful. All of these are important aspects of public relations which labor statesmanship must overcome if labor is to have wide nonlabor support for its candidates and policies. Labor's own newspapers, publications, radio commentators, and speakers would profit by a more restrained and objective approach. Considerable progress in this direction, however, has been made.

Organized labor leaders, similar to many in other groups, often neglect to lift their sights beyond the internal problems and objectives of their unions. This calls for revaluation of program, tactics, and relationship with the world outside the organization. It calls for a fresh approach, reorientation, efforts to develop new leadership with new ideas, and the reconciliation of power and responsibility in the hierarchy. Statements adopted at recent labor conventions reveal more and more concern for these matters. The decade of the 1950's is for labor a period of reorientation and for learning how to handle the organizational arrangements of a sprawling domain.

SELECTED REFERENCES

For background on the AFL and CIO consult Harwood L. Childs, *Labor and Capital in National Politics* (1930); Lewis L. Lorwin, *The American Federation of Labor* (1933); Benjamin Stolberg, *The Story of the CIO* (1938).

General references on labor unionism include H. E. Millis and R. E. Montgomery, *Organized Labor* (1945); Louis Waldman, *Labor Lawyer* (1944); Benjamin Stolberg. *Tailor's Progress* (1938); Selig Perlman, *History of Trade Unionism in the U.S.* (1922);

Florence Peterson, *American Labor Unions* (1945); Thomas P. Jenkin, *Reactions of Major Groups to Positive Government in the U.S., 1930–1940* (1945); Samuel Gompers, *Seventy Years of Life and Labor: An Autobiography* (1925); G. H. Soule, *Sidney Hillman: Labor Statesman* (1939); Cecil Carnes, *John L. Lewis: Leader of Labor* (1936); C. Wright Mills, *The New Men of Power* (1948); Herbert Harris, *American Labor* (1939), *Labor's Civil War* (1940); James Wechsler, *Labor Baron* (1944); Philip Foner, *History of the Labor Movement in the United States* (1947); Aaron Levenstein, *Labor Today and Tomorrow* (1946).

On labor's political activities and parties see Joseph Gaer, *The First Round: The Story of the CIO Political Action Committee* (1944); Nathan Fine, *Labor and Farmer Parties, 1828–1928* (1928); Stuart Rice, *Farmers and Workers in American Politics* (1924); Fay Calkins, *The CIO and the Democratic Party* (1952); and Mathew Josephson, *Sidney Hillman* (1952).

CHAPTER 6

The Agrarian Interests

The great cities rest upon our broad and fertile prairies. Burn down your cities and leave our farms and your cities will spring up again as if by magic; but destroy our farms, and grass will grow in the streets of every city in the country.

—WILLIAM JENNINGS BRYAN, "The Cross of Gold"

Big business and big labor are joined by big agriculture in attempts to influence public opinion and in making demands upon government. Each uses some of the techniques of the other but each in turn has developed certain tactics and strategies based upon the peculiar advantages of its position. Business relies upon public relations and the fact that the communications media are favorable to its viewpoint, while labor recognizes the potentiality of its mass vote. Agriculture likewise has a larger vote than business but not so large as that of labor. It too uses public relations but, as will be seen shortly, has other sources of strength. Farm groups have great strength at the local community level and enjoy certain attitudinal and psychological advantages. "Cultivators of the earth," said Thomas Jefferson, "are the most valuable citizens. They are the most vigorous, the most independent, the most virtuous." During these many years, Jefferson's association of the cultivators with virtue, individualism, and independence has in one form or another persisted. Farmers are seen as the "backbone of America" and the personification of good moral and stable character and epitomize the simple, good life. The city man is expected to yearn for a "home in the country" (or perhaps more aptly in the suburbs) and to exert some effort to make contact with the soil on or before retirement. The millions who prefer to live in cities nonetheless proclaim the spiritual values of those living next to the soil.

CHARACTER OF AMERICAN AGRICULTURE

History books have not let the reader forget that the population and endeavors of the United States were once predominantly agricultural. For over a half century farm population has continued its sharp decline. The two great wars brought about an accelerated migration from the farm to the city. In 1940 the census classed 5,144,000 as farmers and farm managers and this dropped to 4,308,000 in the 1950 census. Even today rural people account for about 40 per cent of the nation's population.

121

A decline has taken place in the number of farm laborers as well as among farm owners. The deployment in the total labor force of the nation between 1930 and 1950 and covering the period of a major depression and large-scale war is shown in Table 6. Agriculture was the only field showing a sharp drop during the period, a decline of over two million. Persons engaged in mining, transportation, communications, and utilities dipped in numbers between the period but in general leveled off and remained constant in 1950. Manufacturing added six million to its

Table 6. Number of Persons Engaged in Production by Industry
(In thousands)

Industry	1930	1940	1950
Agriculture................	8,804	7,918	6,884
Mining....................	956	965	966
Contract construction........	2,183	1,941	3,558
Manufacturing..............	9,423	11,012	15,108
Wholesale, retail trade.......	7,437	8,646	11,225
Finance and insurance........	1,551	1,628	2,047
Transportation.............	2,795	2,252	2,893
Communities and utilities.....	1,034	902	1,277
Services...................	6,214	6,555	7,571
Government................	3,328	6,267	7,301
All industries..............	43,725	48,088	58,835

SOURCE: *Survey of Current Business*, 1951.

force, and trade, contract construction, and services made impressive gains. Government employees more than doubled in numbers and during the war rose to over 17 million (including military personnel). All these figures show that millions of workers and managers have changed positions and job mobility is one of the greatest characteristics of the American economy.

There are some six million farms in the United States with an average in 1950 of 215.3 acres to a farm. This average represents an increase in size of 42 per cent over 1920 and underlines the basic change in American agriculture from individualistic farming practices toward larger and more highly industrialized farming or "factories in the fields." "Between 1910 and 1940 the number of farms of 1,000 acres or more increased from 50,135 to 100,531; acreage involved increased in number from 167,000,000 acres to 364,000,000 acres. Simultaneously, smaller farms were decreasing in numbers. In fact, the number of farms between 20 and 260 acres in size decreased by 694,781 during this same period." [1] In some regions of Iowa and Kansas the owner of a 400-acre farm is referred to as a "small farmer."

The structure of agriculture may be shown another way. About half of the farms are small to medium family farms which produce commodities commercially. Another 30 per cent are part-time, country-estate types which carry on some farming as a side line. About 2 per cent are huge farms operated as industrialized enterprises rather than as family farms. Numerous small farm operators carry on a second occupation during the course of the year. The character of American farming shows an undetermined but large number of persons called farmers but who are no longer devoting all their efforts to farming as a way of life. Clearly, the agrarian interest is no longer one of the small dirt farmer. There is a differentiation between the commercial farmer and the family farmer; the former particularly is a businessman and feels at home in a chamber of commerce meeting and with those who keep accounts and meet payrolls.

Although the number of farm owners and farm workers has declined, the vast technological changes, methods of overcoming pestilence, and improved farming methods have brought a vast increase in the productivity of the farm worker. In 1947, the United States was the largest wheat producer and exporter in the world and its farmers received the highest wheat prices on record. The American wheat farmer exported 400 million bushels as compared with a combined export of all other nations amounting to 360 million bushels. [2]

The National Resources Committee noted that in 1787 it took the surplus food of 19 farmers to feed one city person but by 1937 the same number of farmers produced enough to feed 56 nonfarm people and, for good measure, ten living abroad. [3] The structure of agriculture again shows itself in production. A House of Representatives Committee on Agriculture found that about half of all farm products are produced by the top 10 per cent of farms. [4]

There is a striking disparity of income within the agricultural community itself and between agriculture and certain other pursuits. Illustrative of the latter are the figures of annual earnings of employees in all industries which averaged $3,253 in 1951. By contrast, agricultural and fishing workers averaged $1,489. In the same years income for other workers

[1] Carey McWilliams, *Small Farm and Big Farm* (New York: Public Affairs Committee, 1945), p. 4. A useful over-all view of American agriculture is found in H. G. Halcrow, *Agricultural Policy of the United States* (New York: Prentice-Hall, Inc., 1953).

[2] See *The New York Times*, Jan. 19, 1948.

[3] See *Technological Trends and National Policy* (1937), Part 3, Sec. 1.

[4] Hearings on *Long-range Agricultural Policy*, 80th Cong., 1st Sess., 1948, Part 1, p. 108.

showed: $4,044 in transportation; $3,611 in manufacturing; and $2,342 in the service industries. Hourly earnings in the construction industry in 1950 were about $2.00, in factories around $1.50 but only $0.75 on farms.[5]

Among the farmers themselves, about 80 per cent of the national farm income is earned by only one-third of the farms and the least prosperous third received only 4 per cent of the total farm income, many averaging less than $500 per farm.[6] Over 50 per cent of all farm families and individuals not living in families had money incomes below $2,000 in 1948 and 2.2 per cent had an income exceeding $10,000; among urban folk figures were 28 and 2.7 per cent respectively.[7]

Negro farm families are a special problem in rural poverty for 80 per cent of them receive less than $2,000 annually, as compared with 44 per cent of the white families. Although tenant farming has been on the decrease since 1935, approximately 30 per cent of all farms are still tenant-operated. Tenant farmers are usually in the lower income groups.

These characteristics of the American agricultural economy make for deep-seated cleavages and for many voices purporting to speak for agriculture. The politics of agriculture is complicated by long-range and short-range problems, technical changes, mechanization, dietary changes, transportation and communication, climatic changes, industrialization and absenteeism on the farms, and the overcoming of rural poverty as exemplified by inadequate housing, lack of educational opportunities and health facilities. Despite its handicaps, agriculture maintains an influence on American society greater than might be expected in terms of its numerical strength.

THE VOICES OF AGRICULTURE

Commodity Groups. Because farming interests, similar to those of industry and labor, are beset with internal cleavages, their associations, objectives, and movements are likewise complex and interdependent. The term "farmer" now includes the growers of grain, cotton and wool producers, livestock breeders, dairy interests, rice producers, and growers of vegetables, sugar, and fruits. These interests are organized into great commodity associations resembling trade associations, such as the American Dairy Association, American National Livestock Association, Texas and Southwestern Cattle Raisers Association, National Beet Growers Association, and the California Walnut Growers Association. Each arose in

[5] Income figures are obtainable from *Survey of Current Business* and from the Bureau of Agricultural Economics.

[6] Many useful figures on farm income and assets are summarized in "The Farmer Goes to Town," *Fortune,* October, 1947.

[7] From Joint Committee on the Economic Report, *Low-income Families and Economic Stability,* 81st Cong., 2d Sess., S. Doc. 146, 1950.

response to particular conditions and many today have become powerful lobbyists at various or all levels of government. Some of these commodity groups are referred to in unfavorable terms by public officials as the "potato bloc," "cotton bloc," "beet lobby," "meat bloc," and even the "beekeepers' lobby."

Some groups have put "co-operative" in their titles, such as the National Co-Operative Milk Producers Federation. Cooperatives, however, are not necessarily commodity associations even though commodity groups may be at the base of the group. The National Council of Farmer Cooperatives fosters, aids, and represents cooperatives and claims a membership of thousands of affiliates. The U.S. Department of Agriculture has estimated that more than half the nation's farmers patronize cooperatives in some phase of their operations, and these may be in the form of producers', marketers', or buyers' associations. Cooperatives have strong backing of rural legislators who have fought the battle to retain certain favorable tax laws for these enterprises.

The tobacco grower in South Carolina may not appear to have much in common with the potato grower in Idaho or the citrus grower in Arizona, and this has helped to promote strength in the commodity associations. In time it became clear to farmers that the special commodity groups could not adequately represent the common interests of agriculture and speak effectively for it before Congress and the Department of Agriculture. Moreover, there was need for broader organizations to promote unity, develop broad legislative programs, and to represent the farmers in numerous peripheral matters. Three national associations arose in response to these needs—the National Grange or Patrons of Husbandry, founded in 1867; the Farmers' Educational and Cooperative Union (popularly called the Farmers' Union), founded in 1902; and the American Farm Bureau Federation, launched in 1920. Some profess to see commodity dominance even in these general-purpose organizations and associate dairying with the Grange, wheat with the Union, and cotton and corn with the Farm Bureau. Nevertheless, these three national groups treat the whole range of agricultural policy and hold themselves as spokesmen for more than one agricultural interest.[8]

The Grange. The Grange is the oldest general farm organization in the world and the only farmers' fraternal organization of this kind. It

[8] Among the general treatments of farmers' organizations are Wesley C. McCune, *The Farm Bloc* (New York: Doubleday & Company, Inc., 1943); M. R. Benedict, *Farm Policies of the United States* (New York: The Twentieth Century Fund, Inc., 1953); Charles M. Hardin, *The Politics of Agriculture* (Glencoe, Ill.: Free Press, 1952). For a keen analysis of the American Farm Bureau Federation and an extensive bibliography of this and other farm groups see Grant McConnell, *The Decline of Agrarian Democracy* (Berkeley, Calif.: University of California Press, 1953).

was founded as a secret society on the pattern of the Masonic order for the purposes of enhancing the social and intellectual life of the farmer.[9] In spite of suspicion about it, its membership rose to over a million within a few years, then declined to 100,000, only to rise again, and has now leveled off at 860,000 members in 37 states. Its 4,000 grange halls are valued at $45,000,000 and there are over 7,200 local granges. The organization has an elaborate ritual, with titled officers, and characterizes itself as a fraternal society, completely nonpartisan in politics. The Declaration of Purposes of the National Grange admonishes the locals: "No Grange, if true to its obligations, can discuss political or religious questions, nor call political conventions, nor nominate candidates, nor even discuss their merits in its meeting."

The organization is centralized with typical lines of hierarchy. Subordinate granges elect delegates to the Pomona (county) grange, and these in turn elect delegates to the state grange, and pyramid finally to the top organization, with voting carried out on a state basis. In addition, there is a juvenile organization for children between the ages of five and fourteen. Many Presidents of the United States have been members of the organization, as are a large number of governors and legislators. A large portion of the Grange membership is centered in the North and East, with approximately one-fourth located in New York and Pennsylvania. In many communities it is an outstanding influence. In New York, says Belle Zeller, "the Grange stands next to the church and the school as the most important spiritual force in the community." [10] In Washington state it is the most important farm association and has been one of the leaders in support of direct legislation, the blanket primary, and public power.

In spite of its profession of being nonpolitical, the Grange reached the height of membership and importance when it became involved with the protest against abuses by the railroads in the early 1870's. Agrarian discontent was not only against high freight rates and high taxes and subsidies to the railroads but also against grain elevators and middlemen. The Grange was instrumental in several states in obtaining regulatory legislation. Inadequate though this legislation was, it provided a background of agitation for eventual national railroad legislation and the development of inland waterways. It likewise relieved some farm distress through

[9] On the history and techniques of the Grange see Solon J. Buck, *The Granger Movement* (Cambridge, Mass.: Harvard University Press, 1913) and *The Agrarian Crusade* (New Haven, Conn.: Yale University Press, 1920). For an illuminating account of a state grange and its relationship to national and state politics see H. A. Crawford, *The Washington State Grange* (Portland, Oreg.: Binfords & Mort, 1940). For an official history see C. M. Gardiner, *The Grange: Friend of the Farmer* (Washington, D.C.: National Grange, 1949).

[10] See *Pressure Politics in New York* (New York: Prentice-Hall, Inc., 1937), pp. 91–99, for influence of the Grange in that state.

the operation of cooperative enterprises and by operating insurance companies of its own. A vehicle for protests against monopoly, corporate abuses, and graft in government was also provided by the Grange. After attaining its objectives in the field of railroad, public-utilities, and grain-elevator legislation, the organization declined in political influence. However, the group threw its influence behind land-grant colleges, the Extension Service, pure-food and drug laws, conservation plans, and postal savings banks.

On its own admission, "the Grange has been a stalwart champion of the dairy interests." In all legislative battles over imitation butter the Grange has joined other farm groups in proposing restrictions, heavy taxes, and outright bans on colored oleomargarine. The story of the fight against margarine is one of the most amazing in the annals of modern politics.[11] The mounting cost of butter after World War II led many groups to seek repeal of Federal and state tax laws on margarine and the dairy interests lost the struggle to keep the Federal tax on margarine. A few states still prohibit the sale of colored margarine and a great many state and governmental agencies are forbidden by law from using margarine in welfare and other public institutions.

On domestic legislation the Grange's position is usually regarded as conservative, with emphasis on state and local as opposed to national initiative.[12] Yet its program in the fields of education and health calls for much publicly supported activity and recognizes need for Federal aid where the local governments need it. Although the Grange opposes the closed shop, featherbedding, and jurisdictional strikes, it has taken a moderate if not friendly view toward labor unions in recent years. The right of labor to organize on an industry-wide basis and to a "parity wage formula for wage contracts" is recognized. On taxes the Grange opposes a Federal sales tax and increases in corporate income and capital gains taxes but has declared for a timber severance tax and objects to the proposed amendment which would place a 25 per cent limit on Federal income taxes.

For over a quarter of a century one of the farmer's great bugaboos has been that of surpluses. "Parity" with commerce and industry remains a goal of the Grange. At present it favors "parity adjustments when necessary to establish an equitable price" and has worked out an elaborate formula to achieve it.[13] In principle it honors "flexible price supports . . . through the use of nonrecourse loans and purchases to help stabilize

---

[11] See McCune, *op cit.*, Chap. VII, and W. T. Mickle, "Margarine Legislation," *Journal of Farm Economics*, Vol. 23 (1941), pp. 567–583.

[12] See the pamphlet *Summary of Legislative Policies and Programs of the National Grange for 1953*, published by its national office, Washington, D.C.

[13] *Ibid.*, p. 7.

farm parity income; to meet needed emergency adjustments; to discourage continued production of surpluses beyond any reasonable demand; and to help keep margins of profit to producers balanced between all farm products." [14]

Failure of the Grange to take a stand in favor of "easy money" led many farmers to look to the Greenback and Populist parties for leadership in seeking paper money or bimetallism to relieve debt. The gap left by the Grange in expressing agrarian discontent in the late 1870's was soon filled by the Farmers' Alliance which, after a meteoric membership rise to nearly two million in 1890, became absorbed by the Populist party in 1892. Although it avoids electoral endorsement and the sponsorship of nominees of its own, the Grange remains a formidable force for representing more or less of the center as opposed to the right and left in agricultural thinking.

National Farmers' Union. As the spiritual successor to the Farmers' Alliance, the Union was formed in Texas among low-income farmers. The group opposed the credit mortgage system and gambling in farm products, and was especially interested in cooperative buying and selling. It operates the highly successful Farmers' Union Grain Terminal Association. During the Wilson Administration the Union spread into the Middle West and Northeast. Today it has units in perhaps three-fourths of the states. Although its membership, estimated at 200,000 families, is much smaller than either the Grange or Farm Bureau, the Union has achieved prominence through its leader James G. Patton and its championship of policies is often at variance with other farm organizations. The Union's major strength has been from the Great Plains south from the Dakotas, an area with a deficiency of rainfall.[15] Partly because of this and its origin, the Union has attained at times the "radical" label and has provided a vehicle for the expression of left-wing agrarian politics.

Because the Union has its center of gravity in the small and often marginal farmer, as contrasted with the more prosperous farmers and those engaged in commercialized agriculture, it seeks a guaranteed return for the farmer equal to his cost of production. For this reason it concentrates attention upon developing an agricultural program for low-income farmers. It calls upon Federal agencies to "localize and humanize" themselves in order to make them "more responsive to the needs of the people." [16] To achieve this objective an elaborate plan of rural county agricultural committees is proposed, composed of farmers freely elected. To each com-

---

[14] *Ibid.*, p. 5.

[15] The Union's headquarters are in Denver, farther west than the other national groups.

[16] For the text of the Union's program see *Congressional Record*, Mar. 20, 1946 (daily edition), pp. A1611–1613.

mittee is to be submitted annually a farm plan for the area. In addition, members of the county committee will choose a national price committee to negotiate with the Federal government and to help establish "support" prices fair to the producer and the consumer.

Another objective of all farm plans is "to place all farms ultimately on an economic-size, family-farm basis" and to provide all farmers with an opportunity for "full-time, year-round, remunerative employment." This employment is to be obtained through a continuous "nationwide, con-servation-works program, including soil, forest, timber farming, and water conservation, which shall offer socially productive work to those farmers who are unemployed." On all such work the statutory minimum wage for industry labor is to apply.

A further aspect of the Union's program, which is resisted by commer-cialized farmers, is the advocacy of government acquisition of large farms for "subdivision into economic family-farm units and resale to family farmers, and of 'too-small' farm units for resale in order to complete eco-nomic-size family farms." The Union would avoid, however, the drastic redistribution-of-land policies used in many other countries in favor of long-range and gradual purchase of large estates as they come to the mar-ket. Meanwhile, the national government is asked to step up its farm ownership, loan, and rural rehabilitation policies to enact legislation to improve rental contracts and land-tenure policies. Laws providing tech-nical aids to low-income farmers and minimum-wage legislation for farm labor comparable to industry are also advocated. It has supported legisla-tion to help tenant farmers and the school-lunch program. Almost alone among the agricultural associations, the Union fought for the early pro-gram of the Farm Security Administration in its efforts to aid the low-income farmers.

Another distinguishing feature of the Union is its cooperation with organized labor on legislative matters. Patton has often been invited to speak before labor unions and the two groups frequently show a strong identity in their legislative programs. This has increased the fears of the Grange, the Farm Bureau, and commodity groups that the Union has left-wing proclivities which threaten to upset the status of cooperative farming and cheap farm labor.

American Farm Bureau Federation. The Federation is only a genera-tion old but has become what many Washington observers concede to be "the capital's most potent lobby." [17] It is a tribute to its smooth, com-paratively quiet working organization that it achieves this recognition while avoiding the sensational headlines given in the press to the activities of organized business. It has 1,500,000 member families in 47 states

[17] See "The Farm Bureau," *Fortune*, June, 1944.

(Rhode Island excepted) and over 17,000 local and 2,400 county farm bureaus.

The organization grew out of the Smith-Lever and Smith-Hughes Acts, World War I, and the county-agent system started early in the century. Through the first-mentioned Act, passed in 1914, the county agent was made the basis of a federally aided system of extension education and has worked closely with the Department of Agriculture and the state agricultural colleges. The county agent soon became,[18]

. . . at one and the same time, a national, state, and local official. This highly interesting administrative expedient combined centralized supervision of standards with a form of decentralized administration which ensured actual personal contacts with farmers in practically every agricultural county in the country.

During World War I the county-agent system was rapidly expanded through funds to increase food production. State extension forces simultaneously began organizing county farm bureaus as instruments through which county agents could deal with local farm problems. By 1918 there were nearly 800 county farm bureaus, and state federations of the county bureaus were making headway. With the states and counties organized it was only a step to forming a national organization to correlate the work of these bureaus, to advise representatives of the public agricultural institutions on methods of improving production, marketing, and distribution, and finally to cooperate with national authorities in the determination of nationwide policies.

The farm bureaus in effect are built into the Extension Service and other Federal programs and serve as an informal liaison between the government and the farmers by helping the county agents to reach the farmers. "The state extension forces," says Kile, "were quick to realize that a state federation of the county farm bureaus would provide a powerful influence in securing liberal appropriations from the legislatures for furthering extension work." [19] An Extension Service official has cogently remarked: "The county agent has been the John the Baptist of the Farm Bureau movement. The agents have done many things to commend themselves to public esteem, but nothing probably greater than the unselfish devotion they have given to their brother, the county Farm

[18] Reprinted from *Government and the American Economy*, p. 111, by Merle Fainsod and Lincoln Gordon, by permission of W. W. Norton & Company, Inc. Copyright 1941, 1948 by the publishers. See also Gladys Baker, *The County Agent* (Chicago: University of Chicago Press, 1939). Early in the history of the county-agent system it was the rule for the county farm bureaus to pay part of the agent's salary, and this accounts for the close tie, which has remained to this day.

[19] O. M. Kile, *The Farm Bureau Movement* (New York: The Macmillan Company, 1921), p. 111. See also his *The Farm Bureau through These Decades* (Baltimore: Waverly Press, 1948).

Bureau." [20] The president of the AFBF returned the compliment by saying, "The county agent is the keystone of the Federation." In many respects the Bureau is unique for it is, in a sense, a private lobby supported and sponsored by the government it seeks to influence. The local farm bureaus are the official or unofficial sponsors of the Extension Service in their area and farmers generally identify the two together.

The Federation is sometimes referred to as a corn-hog-cotton coalition because six states—Illinois, Indiana, Iowa, Alabama, Arizona, and Mississippi—provide half its membership. About half also comes from the Middle West. At the same time, the AFBF is well organized in almost every state and in the great majority of states is the dominant voice. Few organizations can claim more accomplishments than the Federation. At the end of its first 25 years, it pointed with pride to 100 major legislative and administrative achievements.[21] Hardin has noted that on an agricultural matter "it is not too much to say that unless AFBF actively supports it the chances of its success are slight." [22]

On general objectives the AFBF used to be placed between the Grange and the Farmers' Union. But the Federation has continued to move toward the right and has frequently taken a position more conservative than that of the Grange. It sided with business, as opposed to the Grange and the Union, on state ownership of the submerged offshore lands and has taken a strong states' right stand on many other matters. Its 1952 resolutions stated:

The Federal government should primarily occupy the role of a fact finder and impartial judge. When it must operate a program it should do so on the basis of clearly defined laws—not on administrative orders alone; . . . if a township, county or state can best handle a problem, it should be permitted to do so. When a single state cannot handle a problem, every effort should be made to solve it on the basis of two or more states working together, perhaps by conference or compact.

The Federation continues to support the Taft-Hartley law and, if anything, would strengthen it.[23] The Federation's positions on a great many national policies parallel that of organized business. Concisely, the Federation has come to speak for the more prosperous farmers and it speaks eloquently and effectively.

In the early days of the New Deal the Federation's president Ed

[20] Arthur Moore, "Earl Smith: Farmers' Boss," *Atlantic Monthly*, Vol. 175 (1945), p. 83.

[21] See AFBF, *Accomplishments 1919–1944*, and *Farm Bureau Achievements, 1952*.

[22] "Political Influence and Agricultural Research," *The American Political Science Review*, Vol. 41 (1947), pp. 668–686.

[23] See its digest of 1953 policies, *Forward from Here*, and the *1953 Policies of the American Farm Bureau Federation*, obtainable from its national office in Chicago.

O'Neal [24] was a regular caller at the White House and the Federation was a stanch supporter of the Roosevelt program for the expansion of farm credit, rural electrification, conservation measures, production controls, rigid price supports, commodity loans, and improvement of educational and rural health services. It was an important part of the farmer-labor alliance forged by the President.

During Mr. Roosevelt's third term there was a sharp cooling off between the Federation and the New Deal. The group became concerned over the growing power of organized labor and the CIO's cooperation with the Farmers' Union and its drive to organize Southern workers. The Federation then joined business in its demand for antistrike and regulatory legislation. The AFBF trained its guns on the Farm Security Administration and charged that the FSA was in the hands of radical leaders "who have joined hands with the radical labor leaders of the nation to sell agriculture down the river in order to gain their own selfish bureaucratic ends." [25] Fear was expressed that the CIO and Farmers' Union would put over "state land socialism" and duplicate the Extension Service. Although the AFBF denounces government controls, it has approved such highly regulatory measures as the McNary-Haugen bill, the AAA, and the Soil Conservation and Domestic Allotment Act. The Federation, however, was never pleased with price-control legislation or with Federal subsidies to farmers and fought for drastic revision of these laws in 1946 so as to exempt agricultural products from price ceilings.

This Januslike position is shown also in regard to public ownership. The Federation specifically endorsed the New Deal programs of ownership and management of electric-power plants, especially the Tennessee Valley Authority, the Rural Electrification Administration, and Federal entry in the credit market and marketing assistance. On the other hand, grave concern was expressed in 1945 about the government's land-acquisition policies. In that year the annual resolutions said:

We oppose any further acquisition of privately owned lands by any governmental agency without the consent of the appropriate state except where such lands are needed for general public works or general public welfare, such as dams, irrigation, flood control, power, and navigation. Lands except aforementioned and commercial timber lands now owned by the government, should be returned to the States, or should be returned by the Federal government to private ownership.

Subsequently, the Federation has come out for local development of water resources. "Irrigation districts," it holds, "should be permitted to run

[24] O'Neal retired in 1948 and Allan B. Kline, an Iowa farmer, became president. Charles B. Schuman, an Illinois stock raiser, succeeded Kline in 1955.

[25] See McCune, *op. cit.,* p. 176. Chap. 10 of this work gives much information on the AFBF's cooperation with large Southern planters in opposing the organization of farm workers.

projects and repay project costs. State governments or interstate agencies should be encouraged to take over full responsibility for running federally owned projects."

McConnell's study of the AFBF emphasizes that the organization is founded on one stratum or a group of strata of farmers. It is an entity in itself which has effectively maintained its own power while limiting the effectiveness of other farm groups, and indeed it enjoys a condition of power which excludes "so large a part of the farm population from the benefits of the political process." He says: [26]

We could view the rise of a structure of power in agriculture with equanimity if there were alternative structures open to those for whom it has no part or place. The pluralism of American society is one of its greatest political virtues. Yet for this to continue as virtue presupposes that the means of power shall not be made the property of the few. This presumption has failed in agriculture. . . . The great paradox of modern farm organization in America is that an intensified social stratification has occurred within agriculture, the source of much of our equalitarian democracy. . . . Agrarian democracy is gone from our scene.

U.S. Department of Agriculture. The agrarian interest is not only expressed through private associations; powerful voices are raised in its behalf by various public agencies. We have just seen that the Extension Service and the American Farm Bureau Federation have become common-law partners. There is a strong tie of social and common interest between the two. Both are for decentralized administration and were unfriendly toward the Farm Security Administration. Both often find themselves in common opposition to the Soil Conservation Service. The National Farmers' Union has charged that the Extension Service has aided the Federation in membership drives and the Grange has likewise been critical of the Federation-Extension tie-up. Thus far proposals for a divorce between Extension and the AFBF have not been adopted.[27]

A newer agency, the Soil Conservation Service, received status and considerable powers in 1935. Its function is to fight soil erosion and handle land management. In operation it works through some 2,300 soil-conservation districts and is devoted to the proposition of treating every acre according to its "land-use capabilities." The program is quite technical and professional conservationists tend to dominate the organization. In practice the SCS is a highly centralized and line agency operating directly from Washington to the farmer and bypassing the state colleges of agriculture. As a general practice, it has tried to keep from being too

[26] *Op. cit.*, p. 181.

[27] Hardin, in *The Politics of Agriculture*, has described the internal cleavages and interest-group tie-ups within the U.S. Department of Agriculture.

thoroughly coordinated with the rest of the Department of Agriculture and has fought decentralization to the states. On the issue of centralization it is in opposition to the Extension Service.

The descendant of the Agricultural Adjustment Administration, the Production and Marketing Administration, has become another important voice of the farmer. It handles the regulatory programs such as marketing quotas and is charged with achieving parity for the farmer. Soil conservation and parity payments, acreage allotments, and marketing quotas are administered by PMA as a part of a package. The field-unit organization rests in farmer-elected county and community committees. PMA has been dedicated to high-level support prices, an issue which has split the AFBF.

The PMA and SCS offer a contrast. The PMA is a farmer-administered program based on payments to encourage individual farm practices; the farmer-committeemen are paid on a per diem basis. The SCS, on the other hand, emphasizes a technical, "scientific" conservation-planning program.

Hardin [28] finds that the PMA has virtually become a farm organization in itself:

The PMA incorporates its own farm organization in its committee system; . . . the PMA is so large and powerful that any organization other than the Farm Bureau would have to accept the role of the junior partner in a permanent alliance. . . . More fundamentally and more consistently than most agencies, it has apparently challenged the authority of the Secretary of Agriculture. At the same time it has proved to be the most formidable antagonist of the powerful American Farm Bureau Federation.

In 1946 the Farmers Home Administration succeeded the Farm Security Administration and brought a change in emphasis. The FSA had concentrated on relief for victims of rural poverty and was in many respects the champion of the migratory workers and low-income farmers. With the approach of full employment and the rise of farm income, the successor FHA concentrated on loans to farmers who were unable to secure credit elsewhere on reasonable terms. Should a depression occur, the agency would probably become important in handling rural relief. The Farmers' Union has strongly endorsed the FSA and FHA.

The Association of Land-grant Colleges and Universities (formed in 1887) is made up of the officials of educational institutions who are the beneficiaries of numerous Federal laws. State colleges of agriculture receive considerable money from the national government in order to further agricultural research and education. Colleges of agriculture have found themselves engaged in politics in attempting to oppose "encroach-

[28] *Ibid.*, pp. 130–131.

ment" by the Federal government and in championing decentralization of public programs for agriculture. Their position has usually placed them in close sympathy and cooperation with the farm bureaus and the Extension Service and the colleges would like to have Federal policy for research and education devolved into their hands. In turn, the farm bureaus support the colleges of agriculture. The Association has been identified with the U.S. Department of Agriculture and has provided a large number of officials for the latter.

WHAT THE FARMER WANTS

Notwithstanding the cleavages and different ideologies within the farming community and the expression of these in the Department of Agriculture, farm organizations are often found banded together in support of certain programs before Congress and the state legislatures. The list of legislative objectives of organized agriculture is lengthy and has tended to broaden. It now includes foreign policy pronouncements such as support for the United Nations and its specialized food and welfare organizations. These represent a considerable departure from the alleged "isolationism" of the farmers.

The politics of agriculture is inextricably woven with the politics of transportation and communication and the struggle to overcome physical isolation. Farm organizations were in the vanguard of the drives first for state, then Federal, regulation of the railroads, water, and motor carriers. This included not only matters of routes and service but regulation of freight rates. The farmer has lobbied at every level of government for improved roads and marketing facilities. The American Farm Bureau noted that in 1953 nearly 60 per cent of the farm homes were still without telephones and urged government loans to help get phones into rural areas. Long ago the farmers won their battle for rural free delivery of mail. In the realm of farm betterment the farm groups have lobbied effectively and 90 per cent of American farms are now electrified. Today the Farm Credit Administration will loan money at low interest rates on an infinite variety of the farmer's needs, from home repairs to the purchase of machinery, and extend general credit from short to long periods. Numerous resettlement and farm health programs have been made available for certain groups. Relief from natural disasters such as blights and weather has been rather well taken care of through crop insurance and other measures.

In the field of taxation the farmers have attempted to shift the burden from tangible to intangible property on the local level. Spokesmen for agricultural groups argue for personal income taxes as the major source of Federal revenue, taxation of income from all government bonds, and the elimination of "hidden taxes." Agriculture has generally joined labor in opposing a Federal sales tax. It has opposed taxation of cooperatives and has argued that the government should provide a favorable climate for such private organizations because of their potential help in improving the farmer's life.

The ever-present large surpluses result in driving farm prices down, making it difficult for the farmer to buy the necessary products of commerce and industry. When this happens, he seeks an "equity" between industrial and agricultural prices. For a number of years this has centered around the concept of "parity" between the two prices.[29] As a Washington wit expressed it, the new version of scripture by which the farmer lives is "faith, hope, and parity, and the greatest of these is parity."

Bolstered by the American Farm Bureau, the farm bloc pushed through the McNary-Haugen bill in 1926 and 1927 to dispose of surpluses abroad, only to witness a frustration by presidential veto. During the Hoover Administration it was successful in obtaining passage of the Agricultural Marketing Act, which created the Federal Farm Board to encourage cooperative marketing associations and thereby dispose of surpluses. To stabilize prices the Board bought up huge surpluses in an effort to head off tumbling farm prices. The job was too big and the Board went out of existence, warning that stable prices could be maintained only if production is held to demand.

Turning to a new theory, the Agricultural Adjustment Act, passed in 1933, attempted to reduce acreage. When this was declared unconstitutional, a new program under the guise of soil conservation was enacted to achieve reduced acreage on overly abundant crops and to restrict the amount marketed in order to guarantee adequate prices for the goods sold. A crop-insurance program was also instituted to insure the farmers' losses against unavoidable hazards. Beginning in 1939, $225 million was appropriated for parity payments and by 1942, upward of $650 million was spent for parity benefits.

World War II, with its price-control law, brought another great achievement for parity and for the farm bloc in the form of a new parity formula to compensate the farmers for mounting industrial progress. After long parliamentary fencing and through the use of riders and logrolling, the farmers' legislators were able to get through what many opponents called "superparity." Under this formula four yardsticks were set up, with the provision that no price would be set below the tallest of the yardsticks. From 1942 on, increases in farm prices took place though ostensibly price control was in effect. Prices rose rapidly after the war and parity rose from 75 per cent in 1940 to 131 per cent in 1946. In the legislative session of 1946 the farm bloc won elimination of most controls on farm products

[29] See John D. Black, *Parity, Parity, Parity* (Cambridge, Mass.: Harvard Committee on Research in the Social Sciences, 1942).

and the boosting of ceiling prices on meats. The ratio between prices which the farmer paid and those which he received kept at reasonable parity thereafter.

The Republican Eightieth Congress in 1948 passed the Aiken Act, which provided for the continuance of the price-support system for 19 commodities but on the basis of a sliding scale ranging from 60 to 90 per cent of parity. In the 1948 election President Truman advocated straight 90 per cent support and the farm states gave him a large vote. The Truman Administration was successful in getting the 90 per cent parity program extended through 1954. No legislative action came from Secretary of Agriculture Brannan's plan to let farm prices meet their "natural levels" by means of supply and demand, thus giving the consumer the benefit of declines in the commodity market. The Brannan plan proposed to protect the farmer by a direct subsidy payment representing the difference between the prices received and parity prices. Big farm groups denounced this as "socialized agriculture" and Republicans made a party issue of it. Among the farmers, only the Farmers' Union backed the Brannan plan.

When Eisenhower's Secretary of Agriculture, Ezra T. Benson, announced for "free enterprise in farm prices," there were likewise outcries from organized agriculture and the new secretary found himself pressured into buying commodities to keep up prices.[30] Spokesmen for agriculture denounce supports and subsidies but are likewise unenthusiastic about permitting the free play of supply and demand to set prices. In effect, nearly all farm leaders are wedded to the concept of parity though they may endorse only "flexible" or "variable" support instead of high, inflexible supports. "Farm price supports," said the American Farm Bureau Federation, "are a necessary protection against unreasonable price declines. Price-support laws should be for the farmers what minimum-wage laws are for labor." Occasionally a group such as cattle raisers may forego price supports and even declare against them, but the general purpose organizations approve in principle the position of the Federation. The Farmers' Union, unlike the Grange and the Federation, has refused to accept the principle of flexible price supports and calls for support at 100 per cent of parity. Significantly, farmers voted for controls and rigid support prices by a vote of 7 to 1 in the agricultural referendum taken in the summer of 1953.

[30] During the campaign Eisenhower had come out in favor of supports at 90 per cent parity.

POLITICAL TACTICS OF AGRICULTURE

Legislative Representation. Despite the backwardness and naïveté with which farmers are often caricatured, the farm organizations have learned well the game of pressure politics. They have used with impressive success the familiar lobbying techniques and express gratitude to representatives who voted "right" and do not forget those who voted "wrong."

Even in the face of a decline in farm population, the agricultural interests maintain a disproportionately large share of representation in the legislatures. In the state legislatures it is not uncommon to find 20 or 25 per cent farmers by profession and there are always a considerable number in Congress. However, the farmers do not have more of their numbers in the legislature than does business. Farmer and business state legislators often vote together and give a conservative cast to the state assemblies. It is through gerrymandering and the rotten borough system, however, that the farmers have often been able to maintain a disproportionate share of representation and to protect themselves far beyond the numerical importance of rural people.

Geographical representation gave the rural area of the United States an early dominance and over the years the farming areas have tried to protect this position while the urban areas attempted to whittle it away. The inconsistency of many state constitutions has helped to maintain discrepancies in representation. It is often prescribed that one or both branches of the legislature shall be based upon population, except that no county shall have more than one representative or that each county shall be entitled to at least one representative. Either way, some urban areas are bound to be underrepresented and some rural areas overrepresented. The ten largest metropolitan centers are all underrepresented. Baltimore and St. Louis have only about half the number to which they would be entitled if population were the criterion, Detroit and Los Angeles less than half, and Chicago and New York are short by one-fourth. Although the legislators from the so-called "rotten borough" or thinly populated districts are very frequently not farmers, many if not most show a strong affinity for farm viewpoint. Often a "silent" gerrymander takes place whereby the state legislatures refuse to reapportion even though charged to do so by the state constitution. The preservation of overrepresentation of the more sparsely settled regions remains an important, even if unacknowledged, tactic of the rural and farming interests.

The Farm Bloc. For over a quarter of a century agriculture has been effective in keeping together the farm bloc, an informal organization and coalition of senators and representatives of both parties. Blocs have long been present in legislatures. Vice President Dawes once referred to sponsors of the Sheppard-Towner Act as the "baby bloc," and the silver, labor, and other blocs are familiar today. The farm bloc differs in some respects from these. Its bipartisan membership is easily identified and well known and sometimes meets and confers as a group with outside interests seeking legislation.[31] The farm bloc's achievements are more obvious and over a period of time there has been less division in its ranks than in other blocs. Agriculture committee rooms of the House and Senate are the scene of formal preparation of farm programs and for meetings between farm spokesmen and congressmen. Meetings also take place through informal luncheons and social affairs.

Not to be overlooked is the U.S. Department of Agriculture, which is sometimes regarded as the physical center of gravity of the farm bloc. It is here that the all-important matters of personnel and the problems and techniques of administration are threshed out. Perhaps more than any other department, the Department of Agriculture serves as a pleader for its constituents and as a superservice agency. Agricultural organizations seek "friendly" personnel to carry out legislative enactments and, with aid from Capitol Hill, carefully scrutinize appointments to important posts in the Department.

Party and Electoral Activities. Like labor, the farmers have not relied solely on lobbying and pressure tactics to influence government but have experimented with party and election activity as well. During the nineteenth century a sizable number of farmers joined with the Greenback-Labor party to put up candidates of their own. The high-water mark for the party was 1878, when over one million votes were cast for its candidates, resulting in the election of 15 members to Congress, including James B. Weaver of Iowa, who became its presidential nominee in 1880. Illustrative of the agrarian base of the Greenback party was the fact that approximately two-thirds of its votes came from the Middle West. In 1892 the discontented agricultural and labor forces fused into the People's or Populist party to cast over one million votes for Weaver; major strength emanated from Colorado, Kansas, Idaho, Nevada, and Oregon.[32] After the failure of Bryan to win in 1896 even with Populist support, the agrarian party collapsed, though it continued to run candidates for Congress until 1911.

During the present century the farmers have been unable to organize an effective national party. Two regional parties, however, had some local

[31] McCune, *op. cit.,* discusses both the personalities and techniques of the farm bloc. The agricultural bloc had real successes in wresting leadership from the parties in the early 1920's; see Arthur Capper, *The Agricultural Bloc* (New York: Harcourt, Brace and Company, Inc., 1922). A more recent account of some aspects is found in the *Congressional Quarterly* report, *The Farm Bloc,* Vol. 11, No. 20, May 15, 1953.

[32] See John D. Hicks, *The Populist Revolt* (Minneapolis: University of Minnesota Press, 1931).

success—the Non-Partisan League of North Dakota and the Farmer-Laborites. The latter represented a joint attempt of workers and farmers to forge a third party.[33] Unlike earlier farm movements, the Non-Partisan League, organized by Arthur C. Townley in North Dakota in 1915, was not born during a time of depressed agriculture. Resentment against middlemen and interference with and domination of marketing processes by railroad and financial interests provided the immediate reason for its formation. As a Socialist, Townley employed the idea of his own party and of the trade-unions of raising money by means of dues from the memberships. The funds were used to train an army of organizers and for publishing a paper, *The Non-Partisan Leader*. Under Townley's centralized direction the League spread to a dozen nearby states and claimed a membership of about 200,000 by the end of World War I.

The tactics of the League were those of political action and infiltration rather than third-party politics. League nominees were placed in the Republican primaries of North Dakota and were successful in capturing not only state offices but the Republican State Committee as well. By 1918 the Republican party, platform, and state government were completely taken over, and a program of state ownership of granaries, mills, and elevators, together with a graduated income tax, a Bank of North Dakota, and regulation of freight rates, was pushed through. Conservative elements, horrified at the increased tax rate to finance state enterprises and viewing the program as the harbinger of socialism in America, formed an Independent Voters Association to fight the League. The Association received important aid when Eastern bankers refused to accept $6 million worth of bonds to finance state institutions. Capitalizing on this and other dissatisfactions, the Association in 1921 led a movement which resulted in the recall of the Non-Partisan League's Governor Lynn Frasier and several other officials. Aided by the depression, Leaguer William Langer captured the governorship in 1932 and League control was again momentarily complete, but its influence soon declined. Langer was removed by the Supreme Court of North Dakota in 1934 for filing an affidavit of prejudice against a judge but was elected governor again in 1937. In 1940, 1946, and 1952 he was elected as a Republican (with League endorsement) to the United States Senate. The League's influence in North Dakota has greatly diminished since 1940.

In the immediate future there seems little prospect of a revival either of national or of regional agrarian political parties. Prior to World War II farmers flocked in large numbers to the New Deal and the Democratic party. Dissatisfaction over wartime restrictions led many to turn to the Republican party and pressure politics rather than to an alliance with organized labor or third-party movements. The Minnesota Farmer-Labor

[33] The Farmer-Labor parties were also considered in Chap. 5.

party formed an alliance with the Democratic party in that state. Certain progressives have urged the formation of a farmer-labor political party. From the analysis of the agrarian interests and of the views of spokesmen of leading farm organizations, the suggestion appears to have little hope of adoption because agricultural leaders seem to find a larger community of interest with business than with labor.[34]

Farm organizations are usually nominally nonpartisan in elections and none of them have developed political arms comparable to the CIO's PAC or the AFL's LLPE. But agricultural journals carry appeals to register and to vote. Some have carried voting records of candidates on farm issues in very pointed ways so as to be tantamount to giving or withholding endorsement. Farmers have only seldom formed special agricultural political committees during campaigns in order to rally the farm electorate. On referendum propositions farm organizations have actually financed some campaigns, especially those dealing with farm policies, daylight-saving time, and oleomargarine.

In summary, certain contrasts between the political tactics and techniques of agriculture and those of labor and business are fairly apparent. Farm organizations rarely openly and militantly oppose a legislative candidate as does labor. Nor do they pour money into campaigns and engage in expensive propaganda publications and public relations to the extent of business groups. It is seldom that farm groups have to oppose a candidate because nominees from rural or semirural districts are most solicitous of farm interests. If an incumbent fails to go down the line with the interests of agriculture, he is almost certain to face stiff opposition and his opponent will expose his voting record. Word is quietly passed to members of farm organizations and their families and to friends "in town," and without much fanfare an impressive vote can be mobilized for or against a candidate. The political techniques of business and labor sometimes come under sharp criticism but farmer groups and activities are seldom publicly denounced because they are less obvious and blatant.

The overrepresentation of rural areas, especially in the state legislatures, has protected the agrarian interests. Business interest groups in large cities have often opposed reapportionment which would result in awarding representation to the cities in accordance with population. They join with the farmers to defeat this type of reapportionment. The battle for reapportionment is much more a fight between rural and urban areas; it is often a contest between labor and capital, conservatives and liberals. In the legislatures farmer-representatives frequently find themselves in the enviable position of having both business and labor bidding

[34] Stuart A. Rice, *Farmers and Workers in American Politics* (New York: Columbia University Press, 1924), noted that farmer and labor legislators showed little inclination to support each other's positions on legislation.

for their support and the farmer is reasonably certain, by shrewd bargaining, to protect his domain.

SELECTED REFERENCES

Useful historical works on agrarian politics include Solon J. Buck, *The Granger Movement* (1913; 1933) and *The Agrarian Crusade* (1920); John D. Hicks, *The Populist Revolt* (1931); Arthur Capper, *The Agricultural Bloc* (1922); O. M. Kile, *The American Farm Bureau Movement* (1921) and *The Farm Bureau through Three Decades* (1948); Stuart A. Rice, *Farmers and Workers in American Politics* (1924); A. A. Bruce, *The Non-Partisan League* (1921); Anne Rochester, *The Populist Movement in the United States* (1944); and W. B. Bizzell, *The Green Rising* (1926).

A critical examination of the present agricultural bloc will be found in Wesley Mc-Cune, *The Farm Bloc* (1943), and articles on the American Farm Bureau Federation in *Fortune*, June, 1944, and in *Commonweal*, Dec. 17, 1943, are worth consulting. See also J. G. Patton, "Some Problems of Postwar Agriculture," in *Third Series of Conferences, Institute on Postwar Reconstruction*, Series III, No. II (May, 1944); John D. Black, *Parity, Parity, Parity* (1942); Carey McWilliams, *Small Farm and Big Farm*, Public Affairs Pamphlet No. 100 (1945); Murray Benedict, *Farm People and the Land after the War*, Planning Pamphlets No. 28 (1943); Arthur Moore, *The Farmer and the Rest of Us* (1946); D. C. Blaisdell, *Government and Agriculture* (1940); S. M. Rosen, *Political Process* (1935), Chap. 7; M. R. Benedict, *Farm Policies of the United States 1790–1950* (1953).

Especially analytical treatment of the politics of agriculture will be found in C. M. Hardin, *The Politics of Agriculture* (1952) and Grant McConnell, *The Decline of Agrarian Democracy* (1953).

1. Voice of agriculture:
   (a) Grange:
   (b) national farmer's union:
   (c) Farm bureau
   (d) U.S. dept. of agriculture:

CHAPTER 7

The Professions and the Bureaucracy

Physicians, who a few short centuries ago occupied the position of barbers, are now very differently placed. Aided by association with both prestige and the achievements of science, "men in white" enjoy a respect that gives them influence disproportionate to their numbers in the population. . . . Some other professional groups—those of churchmen and lawyers, for instance— also derive advantages from the high status of their members, although it may not be quite so exalted.

—DAVID TRUMAN

If one has difficulty in identifying the interests of business, labor, and agriculture, it affords only a little relief to observe somewhat greater cleavage in the professions. Because the concept of a "professional" is broadening, it is becoming less easy to distinguish him. Professional boxers and other athletes have come to refer to their occupation as a "profession." The pharmacist may also own and operate a drugstore which vends articles ranging from newspapers to swimming caps. He is at once a professional who fills prescriptions and a businessman. Beauticians and barbers have also become recognized by law in some states as "professionals." How then can one distinguish a professional from others? Does he have an interest which can be promoted by association with other like-minded persons?

NATURE OF PROFESSIONS

For years a professional was one who procured prolonged and often expensive education in preparation for practicing his calling, such as medicine, law, teaching, or engineering. But many actors, beauticians, and athletes lack lengthy specialized scholastic training. Another standard was that the professional lived by practicing his talents and giving services, as contrasted with making or repairing things, dealing in goods or harvesting crops. Again there were cases where the rule did not hold, especially where the service rendered was in the nature of a highly skilled repair job. The 1950 census listed almost five million persons as "professional, technical, and kindred workers"; yet only one and a half million are engaged in the practice of medicine, law, and teaching. Others in the category included airplane pilots, clergymen, surveyors, accountants, dietitians, and a host of others.

143

Professions are sometimes distinguished by having sacrificed high income for prestige, status, and a comparatively independent life. Incomes of professionals, however, show very wide diversity. In 1951 average net incomes were: physicians $12,518; dentists $7,743; lawyers $9,375; and public-school principals and teachers $3,126.[1] The figure for teachers and school supervisors, however, is on a 10-month basis and some of them supplement their incomes during the vacation months. Within each profession there are great variations. Lawyers attached to a business concern as counsel generally do better than those on their own. The salary of a dentist in Washington state is two and a half times that of a college professor. In 1949, mean net income of a physician in Maine was $8,419, in Washington state, $13,041.

Over the years the determination of a professional became to some extent a matter for the state legislature to decide through a system of licensure. This was in response to the so-called "professionals" themselves, who sought legal sanction for the practicing of their talents. Licensing has grown from both admirable and selfish motives. Law, medicine, and education were particularly concerned with "elevating the profession," raising standards, requiring increasingly higher qualifications for practice, and with keeping incompetents out of the profession. At the same time they were interested for economic reasons in restricting the number of practitioners. "Too many" lawyers and doctors would drive down fees. One of the most effective ways of meeting the situation was to control entrants into the field. This could be done by raising the entrance requirements in law or medical schools and getting the faculty to "make it tough" on those pursuing such specialized education. In effect, this would limit the number of graduates and potential practitioners. In addition to raising entrance requirements, the professional associations brought pressure to bear—often successfully—to set up a system of examination before a license would be issued. What is more, the examinations have become increasingly difficult.

The success of doctors and lawyers led many other groups to seek the help of the state in policing their occupation and by indirection to restrict the number of new entrants. Among these are barbers and beauticians, insurance agents, morticians, real-estate agents, plumbers, accountants,

---

[1] *The Survey of Current Business* periodically carries articles showing figures on incomes of occupational groups. The figures above were obtained from this periodical and from the U.S. Office of Education. For a general description of the professionals see H. F. Gosnell and M. J. Schmitt, "Professional Associations," *The Annals of the American Academy of Political and Social Science,* Vol. 179 (1935), pp. 25–33. Gosnell and Schmitt regard a profession as "a vocation founded upon extensive and specialized intellectual training which enables a particular service to be rendered" (p. 25).

and architects. Physicians may not countenance these people as professionals but the latter enjoy the fruits of this important intervention by the state to "protect the profession." Again, obtaining a license may not be *ipso facto* the badge of a professional. A public-school teacher must obtain a license in order to teach but most college professors can teach without a license, although the college may require them to have a Ph.D. degree as a mark of competence. The professional musician requires no state license to play but he must stand in the good graces of the musicians' local in order to receive compensation for his playing. Notwithstanding their failure to hold a license, the professor and musician nonetheless may lay just claim to being in the professions.

To the present time at least, the professional societies have been distinguished from the general-purpose groups representing business, labor, and agriculture in having narrower political and legislative objectives. Professional associations are reluctant to take positions on peripheral matters not directly related to the purposes of the professional societies themselves. A great many associations avoid any semblance of becoming a political interest group and discussions of and resolutions on public affairs have no place in their annual conventions. At the same time, one of the most important developments of the present era is the great increase in the political interests and activities of those who make their living in the professions.

There are several reasons for this change. For some time the doctor, musician, and teacher remained as individual enterprisers, advancing themselves through education, by means of endowed talent, and by becoming skillful practitioners of their arts. Under this system, however, thousands failed to receive the financial and other rewards that they believed they merited, and the insecurity of the depression of the 1930's found them disconsolate, discontented, and searching for new means of improving their lot. Annual meetings of the professional societies were the occasion for heated debate over courses of action, legislative or otherwise, for "saving the profession." Proposed programs for health insurance prompted the medical societies to step up their activities and inflation, especially after 1945, led teachers to organize to bring pressure on the appropriating authorities. The disturbing of the comparative peace and equilibrium of the group helped to bring professionals into politics. The destructive qualities of atomic energy led many scientists to take positions on questions of public management and control of the atom. The activities of congressional investigating committees after World War II were responsible for stirring many professional groups into action in the political arena, especially teachers, writers, public employees, and even the clergy. Professionals have looked around for weapons, other than licensing and examination, to protect and enhance their position and to fight off what appeared to be threats to their profession. Some of the tactics and interests of various professional groups may be reviewed.

MUSICIANS AND WRITERS

The musicians under the leadership of James Caesar Petrillo followed the tactic, seldom used in the professions, of unionization. It seems doubtful if any group is as completely organized as the musicians, for there appear to be more members of the locals of the American Federation of Musicians than the census recognizes as professional musicians! [2] This is due in part to bringing technicians into the Union, but even so, virtually no person can play music professionally unless he belongs to the Union. On many occasions musicians' locals have demonstrated their power by virtually crippling radio stations and concert plans. At the same time, the Union has greatly improved the wages, hours, and working conditions of musicians and music appears as one profession where unionization provided the power needed to gain a better deal for its members.

No significant attempt was made to organize the white-collar workers on newspapers until 1933, when columnist Heywood Broun and others threw their influence behind a news writers' union which became the American Newspaper Guild (now CIO). The NRA codes also set minimum wages for those full-time workers engaged in the gathering and editing of news. These paved the way for news writers and others to get their battle under way for job security and better wages. Publishers were extraordinarily antagonistic to the Guild, denouncing the whole idea as incompatible with if not dangerous to freedom of the press and an interference with the prerogatives of the publisher. The battle has continued to the present but the Guild has held on and more than half of the daily newspaper circulation today has a contract with the Guild.

These successes gave encouragement to the growing body of writers in the radio, motion-picture, and television field and many of them likewise joined unions. The problem has been a multiplicity of independent unions which many of the leaders have decried as resulting in "dual unionism" and factionalism. Four of these are The Authors League of America, the Screen Writers Guild, the Radio Writers Guild, and the Television Writers Group. The first two are the parent groups which spoke in 1953 for 6,000 writers working in all media and who regard the radio and television organizations as essentially upstarts. Actors and entertainers likewise belong in large numbers to unions.

The unions representing the musicians, writers, and entertainers have been reasonably successful in securing by bargaining the economic better-

[2] On the rise and accomplishments of the union see Victor Riesel, "Petrillo of the Musicians Union," *American Mercury*, Vol. 63 (1946), p. 57.

ment of their members. In general, their activities have been confined to these goals and they have comparatively few legislative objectives. They are nonetheless important in disciplining their members and carrying on guild functions. The Newspaper Guild is not particularly concerned with such broad questions as ethics in journalism, or even journalism as a profession, but concentrates on materialistic goals. Some union leaders have attempted to get the groups of professionals to adopt the broad programs of the AFL and CIO but this is generally resented by the rank-and-file members who do not wish to see the organizations used for the attainment of political goals other than those very directly connected with the welfare of the membership.

THE LEGAL PROFESSION

As an occupational group, there is none which is more overrepresented in government than the lawyers. They are found in large numbers in every branch of government and some observers bemoan the fact that "the legislatures are in bondage to the lawyers." Many persons aspiring to a career in politics regard a law education, if not practice, as a prerequisite to running for public office. It will remain a moot point, however, whether the numerous lawyer-legislators and lawyer-administrators are more susceptible to appeals from the bar associations than from other groups. But the tremendous representation of lawyers in the counsels of government assures a sympathetic hearing for the views of the bar groups.

The major concern and also the major successes of the bar associations are the promotion of professional standards and the repression of those who are engaging in the unauthorized practice of law. These are accomplished by requiring higher standards for admission to the bar and the withholding of approval from law schools unless they meet certain requirements. As in several other professions, the control of examinations and of licensing boards themselves provides an important means for limiting entrants and elevating standards.

Among the public-policy matters on which bar associations attempt to influence government are court organization and procedure, the appointment and election of judges and in turn their appointment of lesser court officials, administrative courts, and criminal legislation. The American Bar Association has furthered research into legal problems and has promoted small claims and other special courts. It is always on the alert to support measures which will increase the need for legal services of lawyers in the administrative branch. As a strong devotee of judicial review, the lawyers pushed the Administrative Procedures Act of 1946. Original proponents of this measure wanted judicial review of all administrative orders. In its final form the Act does not provide for this but does broaden court review. Bar associations also often pass upon the qualifications of candidates for judicial office.[3]

Fortune, after studying the structure and leadership of the American bar, called it "one of the most conservative of all institutions."[4] The magazine conducted a poll among lawyers on the question of whether the government had carried regulation of business too far. The results showed that 63 per cent of the lawyers felt regulation had been carried too far, as against 37 per cent of the general population holding that view. Answers to other questions showed the views of the legal profession likewise much more conservative than those of the general public. There is some schism in the ranks, as evidenced by the creation of the National Lawyers Guild, founded by a number of liberal New Deal and labor lawyers. The Guild has only a small proportion of the nation's 170,000 lawyers. Its legislative program resembles that of organized labor.

THE POLITICS OF HEALTH

Health Costs and Associations. In the 1930's, the Committee on the Costs of Medical Care discovered that the people of the United States spent annually more than $3½ billion for medical services and commodities.[5] Over a half billion dollars in wages were lost due to illness and an estimated $6 billion in preventable mortality. At the same time, hospitals had a capital investment of $3 billion, and the education and facilities of medical practitioners constituted an additional investment of $3 billion, and more than one million persons derived their living from the medical industry. A current survey would undoubtedly show a marked increase in these figures. As such, medicine represents one of the largest industries in the nation. In spite of the tremendous outlay, complaints persist on the high cost of medical care, the inadequate distribution of medical services, and the lack of adequate medical care among a sizable proportion of the population. Labor and, to a lesser extent, farm and consumers' organizations have lined up with proponents of a public medical-care program.

The great battles over public education took place in the nineteenth century, while the government's role in improving the health of the

[3] See E. M. Martin, *The Role of the Bar in Electing the Bench* (Chicago: University of Chicago Press, 1936). The history and activities of bar groups receive coverage in M. L. Rutherford, *The Influence of the American Bar Association on Public Opinion and Legislation* (Chicago: Foundation Press, 1937), and in F. P. DeLancey, *The Licensing of Professions in West Virginia* (Chicago: Foundation Press, 1938).

[4] "The U.S. Bar," May, 1949. The article is one of the best recent statements on the legal profession. In the same magazine see also "Lawyers and Lobbyists," February, 1952.

[5] The Committee's publications cover a wide area and were published in a series in the early 1930's by the University of Chicago Press.

people is being fought during this century both in the United States and abroad. Hundreds of books and pamphlets on the history of health insurance and other programs are available on the subject; only the current political aspects can be summarized here.

Besides the well-known American Medical Association and American Public Health Association, one finds the American College of Surgeons, American Dental Association, American Pharmaceutical Association, American Academy of Pediatrics, National Organization for Public Nursing, American Optometric Association, to mention only a very few, all organized for the purpose of professionalizing certain aspects of the industry and to speak officially for the interests involved. The physicians and surgeons have their private war with the chiropractors, osteopaths, natural healers, and groups that they regard as quacks or near-quacks.[6] In fighting the unorthodox healers, local medical societies have successfully persuaded the states to pass licensure laws and to create examining boards to license physicians. In several states these activities have resulted in denying licenses to osteopaths and chiropractors. Members of the medical profession are also invariably consulted on if not in charge of the administration of these laws. Public-health and medical doctors frequently disagree on state health programs.

Medical groups have particular power and strength in the states and counties and exert pressure on health measures as well as on Federal and state pure-food and drug legislation. The New Jersey Medical Society was found to be very influential in this area of legislation and able to "block such bills as it does not like, and it can secure the passage of measures it approves." [7] To the extent that these groups have lobbied to provide an increasingly higher standard of medical care and professional education and have attempted to protect the public from nostrums and dangerous self-medication, they have rendered an important public service.

The overwhelming majority of the nation's 180,000 medical doctors belong to the American Medical Association, one of the oldest associations, which was created in 1846. At one time its national representation followed a more or less functional pattern, but it is now based on geographical units, the county and state medical societies. These local societies are powerful groups and physicians are likely to find it difficult to practice and to take their patients to hospitals unless they keep within the good graces of the county organization.

The major policy-making body of the AMA is its 185-member House of Delegates. In the main, these delegates represent the older, more

6 See Louis Reed, *The Healing Cults* (Chicago: University of Chicago Press, 1932).

7 D. D. McKean, *Pressures on the Legislature of New Jersey* (New York: Columbia University Press, 1938), p. 71.

conservative, and wealthier members of the profession and specialists from the urbanized areas.[8] The House of Delegates is generally quick to resist innovations and proposed changes. One reporter covering the 1953 convention wrote that " 'socialistic' and 'social' seem to be synonyms to the House of Delegates. Typical of the A.M.A.'s fastidious sense of public relations was a resolution, passed by the House of Delegates, which branded the federal regulation that provides free diagnostic services for crippled children as 'socialistic.' " [9]

In 1938 Senator Robert Wagner introduced a measure to establish a national health-insurance program based in principle on the Social Security Act provisions for unemployment and old age. This measure remained before Congress, but the serious business of hearings was not begun until 1945, after President Truman urged in a special message a national compulsory health-insurance program.[10]

At once the foremost and most articulate of the opponents of the program was the American Medical Association. The AMA and its powerful constituent bodies, the state and county medical societies, for years had fought every state and local, as well as national, bill designed to set up a state-administered health program and have denied many of the complaints that the present economic arrangements for the distribution of medical care are inadequate. The AMA expelled some of its members who flirted with unorthodox schemes of compulsory or voluntary health-insurance plans and sought to deny hospital privileges to physicians who agreed to participate in plans of this type.[11] The United States Supreme Court, however, found this practice a violation of the Sherman Antitrust Act, and proponents of group practice and prepaid health systems won an important victory. After having lost the case against voluntary group practice schemes and, with the threat of compulsory health insurance a reality, the AMA lessened its hostility to voluntary health plans and urged the county medical societies to study plans for wider distribution of medical care. Such plans might envisage prepayment arrangements but at all times would be physician-controlled. The AMA and its locals have often succeeded in leading the physicians to extend their value judgments from things medical into the realm of medical politics and economics. The line has been shifted often, from vigorous opposition to the Federal maternal and child-health program

[8] The basic work on the AMA is Oliver Garceau, *The Political Life of the American Medical Association* (Cambridge, Mass.: Harvard University Press, 1941).

[9] *Life*, June 22, 1953, p. 32.

[10] Text in *The New York Times*, Nov. 20, 1945.

[11] See Oliver Garceau, "Organized Medicine Enforces Its 'Party Line,' " *Public Opinion Quarterly*, Vol. 4 (1940), pp. 408–428. One of the best, concise discussions of the problem of "cohesion and rebellion" within the AMA is found in David Truman, *The Governmental Process* (New York: Alfred A. Knopf, Inc., 1951), pp. 167–177.

to support of it, from denunciation of all experimentation with prepaid medical plans to favoring voluntary plans under the control of medical societies. On at least two proposals the AMA has shown a high degree of consistency. As already noted, one of these is vehement opposition to publicly administered health-insurance plans; the other is support for a Federal department of health in the Cabinet. When the Eisenhower Administration created the new Department of Education, Health, and Welfare, it did not fulfill the AMA's concept of a health department but the organization was grateful for the President's opposition to a national health-insurance program.

In spite of the conservative position of the official spokesmen and the House of Delegates of the AMA, there are substantial minorities within the profession and disagreement between the county medical societies is frequently pronounced. Several insurgent groups, notably the Committee of Physicians for the Improvement of Medical Care, are fighting the attitude of the AMA on medical economics and have officially endorsed prepayment plans and compulsory health insurance. Many of the younger doctors incline to regard group practice under either public or private authority as a desirable method of improving medical service and a better solution to the present economic arrangements both for the practitioner and for the patient.

Doctors in Politics. Most of the political activity of physicians has centered around the battle against proposed health-insurance programs at any level of government. It fought Governor Earl Warren's proposals for health insurance in California with the same vehemence with which it attacked President Truman's national health program. The campaign of organized medicine has been along three fronts. First, it attempts to promote solidarity within the profession and to fight those within the ranks who oppose the official position of the AMA. Some of the methods used were just noted. Second, the AMA conducted a public-relations program on an extraordinarily broad front. Third, several physicians' groups were organized into political committees for the purpose of campaigning in elections.

The public-relations program of the American Medical Association was for many years largely in the hands of the editor of the *Journal of the American Medical Association,* Dr. Morris Fishbein. Fishbein and the AMA were almost synonymous in the public mind and he was regarded by the press as the organization's official spokesman. After he was eased out of his position, essentially the same program was continued. Health insurance was denounced as "un-American," "regimentation," and because it would interfere with sacrosanct physician-patient relationships. The *Journal* carried stern warnings to doctors and popular magazines found in their waiting rooms carried the message to the general public.

Illustrative of reception room literature was a comic book entitled *The Sad Case of Waitingroom Willie,* depicting the sordid trials of a patient under a program of "compulsory Federal medicine." Reprints of speeches against health insurance by prominent leaders adorned the tables, along with copies of John T. Flynn's *The Road to Socialism* and pamphlets under such titles as *The Achilles Heel of American Medicine* and *Can Politics Cure Appendicitis?* Numerous doctors enclosed anti-health-insurance materials with bills sent to patients. Many doctors readily brought up the subject with their patients.

Several auxiliary arms were created by the AMA to carry on the public-relations program, notably the Coordinating Committee of the National Education Campaign and the National Physicians' Committee. These groups worked with business and patriotic organizations, often inter-changing addressographs for purposes of sending out literature. One especially crude effort was the distribution of a copy of *Dan Gilbert's Washington Letter* to all members of the AMA and to Protestant ministers. It began:

DEAR CHRISTIAN AMERICAN:

As a father, my right to choose our family physician is as sacred as my right to choose the church which my children attend. It is part of the "police state" system for politicians to step in and to seek to "regulate" or dictate the relation-ship between my family and our physician. . . .

As a minister of the Gospel, I am preaching against this monster of Anti-Christ —political medicine. I am urging Christian believers everywhere to work and pray that our beloved land may be delivered from the blight of this monstrosity of Bolshevik bureaucracy. I am urging my fellow-ministers to give the facts on this subject to their congregations on the first or second Sunday of January to the end that the church people of America may pray and work for the preserva-tion of our free and righteous way of life.

The *Louisville Times* reported that the AMA teamed up with the American Legion in obtaining the services of the latter in opposing President Truman's proposal. In return for this assistance, the AMA refrained from opposing expansion of veterans' hospitalization. "The AMA was worried about the Truman plan and felt that they had to have the Legion's support to beat it. They made a deal and so the AMA withheld its criticism of the Veterans Administration." [12] Some officials of the AMA denied the story but other officials said the actions of the AMA bore out the charges. The technique of logrolling and joint agreements between interest groups is an established one and the AMA's cooperation with other groups is no more than one of many illustrations of interest-group politics.

[12] Associated Press item, Apr. 8, 1953, as carried in the *Seattle Times* of the same date; see also *The New York Times*, Feb. 6, 1949.

In order to carry out its crusade against the Truman health plan each doctor was assessed $25, though some refused to pay. In the two weeks during October, 1950, the National Education Campaign conducted a $1,100,000 public-relations program to parallel the congressional election of that year. The program was entitled "Message of Freedom" and was budgeted as follows: $560,000 for full-page newspaper advertisements in 11,000 newspapers in 48 states; $300,000 for spot announcements on practically every radio station in the nation; and $250,000 for advertising in national magazines.[13] As a part of the program there was considerable tie-in advertising support from dry goods associations, railroads, power companies, drugstores, hospitals, and hospitalization plans. An advertising kit with posters was sent to 25,000 firms telling why they should participate in displaying the anti-health-insurance materials. Within a period of a few weeks over 6 million pieces of literature were distributed.

According to figures filed with the Clerk of the House of Representatives in compliance with the Federal lobbying law, nine medical societies, including the AMA, spent $370,000 in the first three months of 1950 to influence Congress.[14] Medical groups were one of the largest, if not the largest, spenders per capita on lobbying and public relations in 1950. Their expenditures for this purpose were continued after the Eisenhower victory, though they were reduced sharply from the high levels during the Truman Administration. The medical groups are in essentially the same position as certain trade associations. They lack the mass vote so they utilize their financial resources to win the good will of the public for their political objectives.

Election Activities. One of the most important developments within the profession in recent years is the creation of political committees to aid candidates for public office; these more or less resemble a "Doctors' PAC." In Nebraska in 1950, one such committee was generally credited with the defeat of Representative E. D. O'Sullivan. A "Second District Healing Arts Committee," composed of close to 1,900 doctors, dentists, nurses, technicians, drug services, optometrists, and chiropodists, sent out over 65,000 letters in the district and worked in aggressive fashion to elect O'Sullivan's Republican opponent.[15] Campaign literature was also enclosed in bills to patients.

During the same campaign, doctors and nurses registered patients in hospitals and worked for the election of Senator Robert A. Taft in Ohio,

[13] See figures in *Editor and Publisher*, Aug. 26, 1950, and *Congressional Record*, Dec. 19, 1950 (daily edition), pp. A8259–A8262.

[14] See reports appearing in the *Congressional Record*, Aug. 3, 1950.

[15] Congressman O'Sullivan read extensive materials into the *Congressional Record* on the organization and operation of this group; see especially issues of Dec. 13, 14, 19, and 20, 1950.

and were active in opposing Senator Scott Lucas in Illinois. There is no record on the number of congressional candidates who received support or opposition from medical political committees that year, but it appears to be considerable. An important characteristic of the electoral activities is their almost invariable identification with the Republican party. Even where a Democrat specifically denounced compulsory health insurance, as did Congressman O'Sullivan, the medical groups nonetheless opposed him on general grounds.

In several states, notably California, physicians are most active in forming political committees to aid and to oppose candidates for Congress and the state legislatures. These committees write to doctors and dentists seeking support of the committees' positions on nominees. The request is usually made that the doctors send letters, prepared by the political committees, to their patients, urging them to vote for certain nominees because they will support sound legislation affecting the health and welfare of the patient's family and children. There is no documentary evidence of the number of doctors who responded to the requests. Several physicians themselves have questioned the propriety of these activities, particularly the writing of letters of this type to patients. Other questions were raised over the fact that the candidates endorsed were invariably conservative Republicans and that endorsement was apparently not even considered for Democrats who opposed compulsory health plans and who had a good voting record on health bills.

Numerous physicians have entered the arena of presidential politics. Oregon physicians were especially active against Harold Stassen in the presidential primary of May, 1948, because they believed him less "safe" than Governor Dewey. Every delegate to the Republican National Convention received a printed circular from the Oregon Physicians Fighting Political Medicine, on a letterhead containing the names of the past presidents of the medical societies, urging that he cast his vote for Dewey in order to forestall "socialized medicine" in America. "Governor Dewey," it said, "is the only leading Republican presidential aspirant who does not carry with him a partial compromise with socialized medicine." In 1952, the National Professional Committee for Eisenhower and Nixon was led by Dr. E. L. Henderson, who resigned from heading the AMA's National Education Campaign to take over the political work.[16]

From this brief review it is obvious that doctors are in politics to a larger degree than is commonly realized. After Eisenhower's election, the four-year campaign against compulsory health insurance was called off but the public-relations program continues in order that the public may not forget the AMA's objections to publicly sponsored programs of health

16 See *The New York Times,* Sept. 23, 1952.

insurance. On the local level there are the ever-present issues of public care for the medically indigent, sickness compensation proposals, and fluoridation of water, to mention only a few, which local medical leaders carefully watch. Many dental, druggists', and nurses' groups make sporadic forays into politics on these issues, but they usually follow the leadership of the county medical society.

PUBLIC EDUCATION

The Politics of Education. It is sometimes argued that politics can and should be kept out of education but this has overlooked the realities of the forces concerned with public education. There is an annual public expenditure for public elementary and secondary education of about $6 billion. In this expenditure are opportunities for contracts for school buildings, equipment, fuel, textbooks and supplies, and certain influences are bound to be felt in expenditures for these items. As the institution for inculcating attitudes and for passing on the heritage, the schools, as noted several times before, are under pressure from interests concerned with the curriculum and with the materials used. As if these are not enough to place the schools in the position of becoming targets for pressure, the popular election of school boards makes the boards' officials keenly sensitive to political considerations. Where board members are appointed, as in many large cities, the appointment is usually made by a political officer such as the mayor, or by the governor for the state colleges. These officers in turn are popularly elected and are often influenced in the selection of board members by powerful interests.

The politics of education are involved and do not lend themselves easily to brief treatment. Current issues of education which bring government and various political interest groups into education are (1) adequate financial support at a time when other services such as welfare and highways are providing stiff competition for the tax dollar; (2) approaching equality of educational opportunity within a given state and between states; (3) some public support for parochial schools such as purchase of equipment and transporting pupils to nonpublic schools; (4) attracting and keeping promising men and women in the teaching profession; and (5) community-school relationships.

Unlike most other professions, teaching is largely dependent upon public moneys and teachers are placed in the position of seeking appropriations. Since 1940, hundreds of thousands of teachers deserted the profession for more lucrative posts and teacher groups began a drive to secure higher salaries, laws providing for automatic increments and better retirement programs. By 1954 the average annual salary had reached $3,725, but in view of mounting inflation during the period the increase was unimpressive compared to many other professions. The National Educa-

tion Association recommended minimum-salary scales for teachers ranging from $3,500 to $8,200.

In their effort to secure financial support for themselves and for the
schools, teachers often find themselves in opposition to taxpaying groups
who are resisting increases in property taxes, special assessments or bond
issues designed to raise additional money for the schools. Public-school
teachers are also in competition with the state colleges of agriculture,
state universities, and junior colleges for the tax dollar. While the higher,
secondary, and elementary educational institutions have interests in common, they all become competitors for state support and may be found
as rivals in the halls of the state legislatures.

In addition to improving their financial status, teachers are concerned
with several other problems, such as promotions, tenure, raising standards, and unified administration of education. Several of these can be
modified by law, so teacher groups are often found lobbying for these
objectives. The teaching profession has also been deeply concerned about
matters of prestige, morale, academic freedom, and loyalty oaths.[17] Legislative investigations and so-called "witch-hunts" by private groups in the
community have had, according to some educators, deleterious influences
on morale. Teachers have usually not objected to the taking of such loyalty oaths as are prescribed for public employees and civil servants but
they have fought the taking of special oaths which other public officials
are not required to take.

Teacher Associations. Teachers have utilized two different types of
groups to present their cases to the public and to government agencies.
One channel is the teachers' union. Generally, unionization of teachers
has been frowned on by teachers themselves and their professional associations. Most teachers appear to prefer action through their own professional groups rather than "forming an alliance with labor." Gradually,
however, teachers' unions have built up some membership, usually in
independent locals in the larger cities. In a few instances teachers have
gone on strike. These work stoppages usually resulted in the board of
education or the city council bettering the financial status of the teachers.
It also made the authorities so incensed that they passed measures inflict-
ing heavy penalties for striking, including demotion if not loss of job.
There are some local teachers' associations which have resembled a union
in operation and have employed their own lobbyists and developed a
legislative program.

Generally, the teaching profession has realized its greatest strength
when it has cooperated with and helped to stimulate other groups in
the cause of better education. Two groups whose help is particularly necessary are the school administrators and the parents. School administra-

[17] See also pp. 23–27.

tors in turn solicit the help of members of the board of education and local public officials in going to the state capital to seek increased aid for public education. It is not unusual for teachers to receive help from labor unions and farm associations in such matters as equalization of school financing. In 1897 the National Congress of Parents and Teachers was organized for the purpose of coordinating and unifying the work of local parent-teacher associations. The Congress has a branch in each state and has a joint committee with the National Education Association to advance common objectives of the programs of both organizations. In 1953 the organization boasted a membership of 7,219,165 in 38,000 local units. School administrators and teachers provided 550,000 of this number.[18]

In several states legislators and the press have complained of the great pressure exerted by the "teachers' lobby." This is a misnomer and would better be called the "educational forces" or the "school lobby," for it is the combined effort of teachers, parents, and school directors, and not just the former which has made itself felt so effectively in many states. For example, the national PTA Congress prides itself on these accomplishments: [19]

Encouraged other groups, by its own example, to stand up and be counted whenever and wherever issues involving the welfare of children are at stake.

Built a backlog of public opinion so strongly in favor of our school programs that state legislatures, boards of education, and other community agencies have appropriated more funds for teachers' salaries and for improved school equipment.

Supplied the voting power and citizenship education needed to turn the tide when issues affecting the welfare of our schools and of our children have been at stake.

Spearheaded cooperative campaigns with other service and civic groups to secure tax measures that have raised school standards in hundreds of school districts.

A strong emotional appeal which the PTA groups use is centered around "giving the kids a break." Appeals for funds are made on the grounds of overcrowding, "firetrap" schoolhouses, good citizenship, better equipment, and so on. PTA meetings sometimes are given over to strategy for political action. Children take home materials appealing to parents for votes or for letters to public officials. In some communities children have been mobilized to ring doorbells and hand out literature on "saving kindergartens" or "saving the schools." More than one state representative has felt the fury of school groups, either at the polls or in his office,

[18] The Congress has published voluminous materials on the schools and PTA groups; see especially its 250-page *Parent-Teacher Manual, 1950–1953.*

[19] See leaflet *7,219,165 Volunteers,* pp. 14–15.

when he voted against an educational program. The press reported one legislator complaining, "I can't vote against the teachers' lobby without being damned as against children and motherhood!"

In spite of their numerical strength, teachers are, nationally speaking, loosely and inadequately organized compared to doctors and lawyers. Only a half of them belong to the NEA. A major reason for this is that education remains essentially a state and local function and the arena of educational politics is primarily at the community level. Through the columns of the *N.E.A. Journal* and its annual conventions, the NEA continues its fight for Federal aid to education, use of revenues from off-shore land leases for education, and for an expanded U.S. Office of Education. It has fought politically corrupt school boards and pressures on the schools.

Institutions of higher learning likewise have their politics on the local level, except for colleges of agriculture whose authorities maintain close relationships with the U.S. Department of Agriculture. Each discipline has its own professional group such as the American Political Science Association and the American Chemical Society but these are almost never engaged in pressure politics. The American Association of University Professors investigates alleged breaches of academic freedom and probably has had a mitigating influence in some colleges where the authorities would dislike the publicity attendant to an investigation. An increasing number of college professors appear to be engaged in politics in one form or another but these activities are through political rather than professional groups.

PROFESSIONS IN POLITICS: SUMMARY

Politically, the role of the professional societies is less effective than that of business, labor, and agriculture. For one thing, the associations have limited the scope of their activities to matters more immediately related to the profession; theirs has been a guild function. Teachers, physicians, lawyers, and artists, for example, often remark that engaging in politics, party or otherwise, may harm their practice or prestige. Many dislike to take a position placing themselves at variance with existing customs or with a major community interest such as business or labor. Not a few leaders feel that by concentrating their attention on problems of direct concern to the profession, they will be able to speak with greater authority on them, a case of speaking with power and influence on a few things, rather than running the risk of making enemies by broadening the program to include peripheral matters.

There is evidence, however, that the "ivory tower" is being left on more and more occasions for the forum and legislative committee room. Control of atomic energy is a subject on which views of the scientist are sought and Congress even asked the advice of political scientists on how to reform itself. Legislators recognize that any health-insurance program is apt to be ineffective without the support and cooperation of the medical profession, though they have been less aware of the value of properly trained teachers to public education. More than ever before, the talents of professional men and women were commanded and used by the government during World War II and many were used in a broad capacity. There is a marked increase in political participation by the professional societies. The professional today is finding that as in business, labor, and agriculture, some knowledge of *Realpolitik* and power politics is becoming necessary for survival in the professions.

The professional, as compared to business, labor, and agriculture, is a small minority. Each profession, cognizant of the fact that it does not possess in itself a potentially large voting bloc, has looked around for weapons of power and influence. Law, medicine, and education in particular have attempted to exploit their prestige to help their cause. They have enjoyed a "respectability" and status in the community by virtue of education and special skills. To some extent the spokesmen for these professions and the individual practitioner himself attempt to transfer the authority of the expert knowledge in their specialties to the area of practical politics. This has been truer of the lawyer and doctor than of the teacher, but the last-mentioned has at times used this tactic. A medical man is an expert when he reads a cardiogram, gives views on the antihistamines, or on the amount of time necessary to train new physicians. But is the doctor equally as competent in passing judgment on the organizational arrangements for the payment of medical care, on taxation, or on how to administer medical care to those on relief? Are a corporation lawyer's views on foreign policy necessarily more entitled to respect than those of a union leader or a kindergarten teacher? At what point does the professional expert become no more than a layman whose views are no longer expert but simply those of an interested citizen? So long as segments of the public regard the professional as an expert in political matters outside his own field, the professional is able to exploit his prestige.

BUREAUCRACY AS AN INTEREST GROUP

Government is operated by persons who have desires and interests and who function through myriads of groups often called collectively "the administration" or "the bureaucracy." Each group or agency has its own interests and relationships with others. It is a part of the over-all general team of the executive and also a team unto itself. Most, but by no means all, public employees regard themselves as professionals. Yet their interests and organizations have certain differences from those considered in the preceding pages. Some of the problems of public employees together with the nature of administration may be treated at this point. The relationship between interest groups and the administration is considered in Chapter 9.

Character of Employment. In 1954 there were seven million civilian public employees, of which about 2,230,000 were Federal employees. If these millions were welded together into a single class, they could become one of the most powerful forces in the nation. In the popular mind the "bureaucrats" are often credited with a unity of purpose and voting cohesion which they do not possess.

Government employees differ sharply in status, function, and in the ways in which they were recruited. At the top, the President, governor and mayor, and their immediate advisors form a political echelon in themselves and their relationship with the legislature and the public differs from that of others in the executive branch. Many employees have very little contact with the public and the legislature while others spend much time in such a capacity. Some persons hold their jobs by virtue of special skills and technical competence and their work is highly professional in character. In some cases these jobs are held under civil service regulations, in many others they are not. Numerous positions are now filled only by civil service regulations. In 1951, 87.5 per cent of all Federal civil employees held appointments under the regulations of the Civil Service Commission. A considerable number of these were helped by veterans' preferences. A good-sized army of employees is made up of persons who have demonstrated their party loyalty or who did not obtain their jobs under civil service laws. According to the National Civil Service League, only half the states had a state-wide merit system in 1953. Of 1,347 cities over 10,000 population, only 814 had civil service laws and not more than a handful of counties had any central personnel system.

The American public servant has both hazards and securities which are not characteristic of his counterpart in private business or the professions. He is given certain legal protections in his position. Notwithstanding these, he is not always assured the opportunity of pursuing a career in the government service. For this reason he tries to maintain contact with groups in his field composed of persons in private as well as public employment. He has seen his job "abolished" when a new party comes to power. Beginning in 1947, the Federal employee found himself screened and investigated, first by the executive, then by congressional committees. Since that time the loyalty program has been a highly controversial subject.[20] In 1953 several newspaper correspondents noted that morale among Federal workers both at home and abroad was the lowest

[20] See *Loyalty in a Democracy* (New York: Public Affairs Committee, 1952).

it had been in many years because of "excesses of congressional investigations."

The Politics of Administration. Administration is concerned with fostering, promoting, aiding, and regulating the activities of private groups. It is also concerned with policy and program formulation. These activities are bound to involve politics. Administration is expected to be in the public interest, and administrative officials find themselves in the hapless position of being charged with serving particular interests on the one hand and the public interest on the other. Bureaucracy is forced into being a pressure group and in turn is the recipient of counter-pressures. It is small wonder that the bureaucrats are in a cross fire much of the time.

Bureaucrats have little influence or power except as they are identified with clienteles or interest groups. Although the executive agencies are accused of "power politics" and "empire building," a more realistic criticism would be their close alliance with and frequent subservience to outside pressure groups. Lumbermen and grazing interests have great influence with the Forest Service and agricultural associations dominate many of the agricultural bureaus. Relatively few government departments wield great power in their own right over legislatures. A danger of bureaucracy, and one seldom mentioned by legislators, exists when bureaus in league with outside interests—and with individual legislators— are able to obtain favors and pork-barrel expenditures so as to be beyond the pale of executive and legislative control.

Administration and Legislation. The public and the legislature have come to expect the President and the governors to present a legislative program. In fact, their standing as chief executives is measured to a considerable degree by their effectiveness as legislative leaders. Reelection campaigns are broadly based on the specific policies of the executive. The executives in turn must look to the departments and agencies concerned for expert assistance in preparing programs and bills for submission to the legislature. If it is a farm program, the President looks to the Secretary of Agriculture for concrete recommendations. If it is a highway bill, the governor will look to the highway department to conduct the necessary studies and investigations, to hold conferences, and perhaps make the necessary compromises to secure support for the passage of the program.

The national reclamation program was largely developed in the Bureau of Reclamation and received both help and pressure from the National Reclamation Association. In the fields of social welfare, public education, and public health almost all recommendations come from within the bureaucracy. In the three most costly functions of state government— education, highways, and welfare—attitudes, leadership, and programs are sparked by the professional. For the legislature it has become a question of how much of what the bureaucrats insist we need can we afford.

Though the two are necessarily intertwined, the role of the Chief Executive differs from that of the department and agency heads in their relations with the legislature and the public. Administrators are invariably interested in improving the laws they are called upon to enforce, together with obtaining adequate appropriations for the job. Their contacts with interest groups and firsthand experience with the laws themselves provide a basis upon which to request amendments to strengthen provisions of existing laws. The technical knowledge possessed by administrators makes them valuable agents for planning and for originating legislation which the President and public opinion seem to demand. Concisely, the functions of government departments in legislation are (1) the preparation either in outline or in detail of bills which deal with a program, established or contemplated, relating to the department; (2) the rendering of expert advice to the legislature; (3) the presentation of testimony and the use of lobbying devices to influence the passage (or defeat) of a bill.

Initiation of legislation by the President's official and unofficial advisers and by members of the administrative departments and agencies has assumed increasing importance. In the early days of the New Deal President Roosevelt utilized the services of several aides whom he called a "brain trust," to prepare key legislative measures, in consultation with the departments affected and with members of Congress. Says Professor Witte: [21]

A large part of the energies of many of the ablest persons in the administrative agencies of government have gone into the consideration and preparation of legislative bills to be presented to Congress. . . . Bitter battles have been fought within the bureaucracy over such prenatal legislation, which have centered in gaining the support of the department head and ultimately of the President for the position taken by a particular group.

So regular became the practice of executive preparation of bills that even a congressman of the majority party, Monroney of Oklahoma, sardonically commented, "There is a criticism attaching to the Gore Bill —a blight that I am afraid may kill it, according to the popular conception on Capitol Hill, and that is that the Gore Bill originated in Congress." [22]

In summary, bureaucracy becomes an interest group because it formulates a program, tries to rally support for it in and out of government,

[21] E. E. Witte, "Administrative Agencies and Statute Law-making," *Public Administration Review,* Vol. 2 (1942), p. 117.

[22] *Congressional Record,* 77th Cong., 1st Sess., p. 9392.

and, having secured a program, is faced with maintaining and defending it. Administrative agencies must seek appropriations and other legislation in carrying out these objectives. They have the further interest of maintaining the support and confidence of their clienteles and special publics. Sometimes an agency is able to mobilize pressures that neither the executive branch nor Congress can control. The Corps of Engineers, assisted by local groups interested in promoting civil works projects, has frequently been able to do this. The legislation which a department or agency is likely to seek will fall into one of two broad categories. First, those measures which are a part of the Chief Executive's legislative program; only the more important bills get the active support of the governor or the President. Second, the numerous measures which the department seeks on its own. A competent department head sees, probably more clearly than anyone else, the need for new legislation, new policies, new programs, and modifications and corrections in the existing one. Because of this, the administrator will regard the active promotion of needed legislation as one of the most important functions of his office. Apart from the legislation which he initiates, if he is well regarded, the legislative committees will turn to him for advice on bills relating to the work of his department.

Methods of Influence. In terms of influencing legislation, the techniques of the bureaucracy differ only in detail and emphasis from those of private interests. Administrative officials are customarily requested by the legislature to testify on both administration-sponsored bills and those submitted by other groups. A reading of the list of witnesses appearing before congressional committees commonly shows half or more of them to be spokesmen of the executive establishments. Because municipal ordinances deal in a great measure with administrative problems, the city manager is almost invariably present at council meetings and conferences to provide information and advice.

A united front for executive proposals on the part of the departments and agencies does not invariably follow. On the Army-Navy unification proposal, for example, President Truman spoke out harshly against "lobbying" by many Navy officials opposing his plan. He called together the naval high command to prevent further opposition to the proposal and enjoined all active officers from further public discussion of the plan except when called upon by appropriate committees.[23] When executive reorganization proposals are before Congress, bureaus, boards, and commissions are often found trying to get congressmen to fight for exemptions of their respective agencies, the action of which partly explains the failure to achieve any great measure of administrative reorganization.

[23] *The New York Times,* Apr. 4, 1946. For an illuminating account of armed services politics see William H. Neblett, *Pentagon Politics* (New York: Pageant Press, 1953).

A Federal law forbids the use of an agency appropriation directly or indirectly to pay for any service intended to "influence a member of Congress to favor or oppose any legislation or appropriation." Congressmen perennially accuse certain administrators of violations of this statute. A special committee investigating the National Labor Relations Board charged that a secretary of the Board tried to induce friends in the labor movement to testify against proposed changes in the National Labor Relations Act, and the committee sought an opinion of the Attorney General on the matter.[24] At the same time it produced evidence showing that certain officials of the Board sought to obtain other witnesses who would oppose still other amendments. The Attorney General refused to give an opinion on the ground that Congress should more carefully define what is permissible conduct for administrative officials.

The practice of having "friends" in the form of private groups to testify for the agency is a common one and seemingly inevitable when a strong identity of interest exists between organized pressures and a government unit serving those groups, such as the departments of Agriculture, Commerce, and Labor, and the independent regulatory agencies. Sometimes the regulatory agencies, like the Interstate Commerce Commission and the Federal Communications Commission, find themselves the object of an "undermining" attempt on the part of the parties-in-interest being regulated and seek congressional backing for their program to protect the public interest. The result is competition between the private parties and the government agency for congressional favor.

A practice paying dividends for the agencies is to cultivate the "good will" of legislative committee chairmen and their members. Personal friendship between department and committee heads makes possible much less wrangling on the floors of the legislature or in formal hearings. Differences are ironed out informally before bills are introduced or reported out. In many states a committee endorsement is tantamount to passage, so that when a labor committee favorably recommends a labor department bill, little opposition is likely on the floor of the legislature.

Direct lobbying by administrative groups is somewhat more restricted than similar activities by private associations. The spending of agency funds for a barrage of telegrams or for social events is prohibited. But through publicity and public relations, administrators can indirectly influence legislation. Issuance of press releases, pamphlets, charts, periodicals, and films informs the public, helps to promote good will, and to build understanding and sympathy for the program. The favorable publicity and public relations of J. Edgar Hoover and the Federal Bureau of Investigation have resulted in widespread public approval of the agency

[24] *Ibid.*, Feb. 1 and Mar. 17, 1940.

and in its ability to obtain from Congress almost anything it asks. The U.S. Department of Agriculture has had effective public relations with its clientele.[25]

Because of criticisms of administrative publicity, Congress passed a statute in 1913 prohibiting spending for "publicity agents" unless an appropriation was specifically designated for such a purpose. A few years later another law forbade spending any appropriations for purposes of influencing legislation except on the request of a congressman or through official channels. Several Republican congressmen warned the Eisenhower Administration that they would investigate publicity activities which appeared to violate these laws. The subjects on which it appears legitimate for the government to issue releases and bulletins are a perennial matter of debate.

Conclusion. Bureaucracy as an interest group is here to stay and the public must understand this fact and live with it. The organization, methods, and activities of the bureaucracy should and do come under surveillance and criticism. Individual staffs and units are not only guilty of seeking excessive power and authority but are guilty of myopia and parochialism. The more serious of these charges is the latter and the fact that bureaucrats are often lacking in enough aggression in terms of initiative and in trying new methods of achieving their tasks. What is perhaps needed most is a positive approach whereby administrators might perform their functions with more competence and enlightened self-interest. The attraction of promising men and women into the public service with the high ideals of promoting the general welfare affords one of the best assurances of a responsible bureaucracy.

Bureaucratic attitudes reflect "protective self-interest" primarily to those who disagree with the program they propose or with the way in which they are performing their functions. For the most part, the legislature and the political leader, as well as public groups, look to the professional administrator to (1) define public needs in his field; (2) propose effective methods for meeting them; (3) determine appropriations essential for results; and (4) evaluate the strength and shortcomings of the programs. The professional administrator is often a person of considerable personal stature and prestige. When he speaks, he speaks for his professional group and often for supporting groups among the public.

[25] One study shows, however, that only a fraction of government publicity appears designed to influence legislation. See Dick Fitzpatrick, "Measuring Government Publicity: Volume of Press Releases," *Journalism Quarterly,* Vol. 26 (1949), pp. 45–50. On this subject see also James L. McCamy, *Government Publicity* (Chicago: University of Chicago Press, 1939).

PUBLIC EMPLOYEE ORGANIZATIONS

The personal and social interests of public employees are not greatly unlike those of persons employed by private organizations—job security, wages, hours, working conditions, and morale. To further their interests, the millions of public employees have begun to emulate the practices followed in private industry and the professions. This has led to the rise of unions and attempts at collective bargaining and of professional associations.[26]

Public Employee Unions. Machinists, printers, plumbers, and workmen employed by the government generally join locals of the AFL or CIO or independent groups operated along union lines. Postal employees began organization in 1889, but until the Lloyd-La Follette Act of 1912 was passed legalizing unions of Federal employees, unionization developed slowly. Early unions were along craft lines, but unions of the industrial type subsequently arose. Most postal unions are affiliated with the AFL and claim the majority of organized workers in the national government. Three unions bidding for the employee's allegiance are the Government and Civic Employees Organizing Committee (CIO), the American Federation of Government Employees (AFL), and the National Federation of Federal Employees (independent).

In the larger city governments policemen, firemen, and transit workers are fairly well organized. The employees engaged in public safety use their unions and leagues to gain public support and sympathy for higher salaries and relief for their families in case of permanently disabling injury or death of the employee. In many cities the unions of policemen and firemen are politically powerful. The largest AFL union in the local field is, in fact, the International Association of Fire Fighters. Athletic contests, picnics, and outings are a part of the public safety group's program to raise money, to promote morale, and to gain prestige for the service.

In the Federal government wage rates for "blue-collar" workers are set at competitive rates for like employment in the same labor area. This is done by wage boards and is often a question of negotiation with union representatives. In effect, the point of view of these workers is presented by the union representatives. Among blue-collar workers there is often a good deal of informal consultation and clearance with union representatives on standards in positions.

---

[26] See the monograph of the Civil Service Assembly of the United States and Canada, *Employee Relations in the Public Service* (1942), and Sterling Spero, *Government as Employer* (Brooklyn, N.Y.: Remsen, 1948). Typical questions arising in negotiations between government supervisors and union representatives are adequacy of lighting and ventilation, rest periods, washroom facilities, attitudes concerning sick and annual leave, lunchroom facilities, and arbitrary supervisory behavior.

It is widely believed that public employees should not be permitted to use the strike as a technique of bargaining or to enhance their welfare. This denial of the right to strike is based on the assumption that the sovereign functions of the state and protection of the people would be jeopardized. Several of the large organizations of public employees have no-strike clauses in their constitutions, and Presidents, governors, and mayors have generally asserted that civil servants may not strike against the government.[27] The Taft-Hartley law forbids strikes among government workers and imposes as a penalty the loss of a job.

In the classified service, salaries, hours, vacations, promotions, and retirement are fixed by law and rarely are the result of collective bargaining with executive officers. Public-employee unions customarily lobby before the legislative body for higher salaries and improvements of working conditions, often with conspicuous success. It should be noted that they have limited objectives and have not displayed any great degree of identification with the labor movement. These organizations present the employees' viewpoint to Congress and to the state legislatures on matters pertaining to the public service and employ lobbyists similarly to private groups. The Federal civil service unions have as major objectives the promotion of an *esprit de corps,* the improvement of working conditions, and the extension and protection of the merit system.

Professional Associations. A great many professional, semiprofessional, and technical workers in government have organized outside the labor movement in professional groups. The U.S. Department of Commerce has estimated that there are about 75 national organizations composed entirely or mainly of government officials. Most of these are officials and high-status personnel, as is indicated by their titles, such as attorney general, city manager, health officer, chief of police, and city-planning officer. There are professional organizations in personnel, finance, welfare, and so on, which strive to develop professional standards. Some of the organizations are primarily concerned with the advancement of the Federal or local civil service as a career system. In pursuit of this they publish journals, run training conferences, and work for legislation designed to promote a high-grade civil service.

On the local level there are hundreds of state and local associations of public employees, from tax assessors to mayors. Leagues of cities, county supervisors' associations, and similar groups are less concerned with, if at all, the promotion of civil service. A major purpose has been to secure special legislation from the legislature and to kill legislation

[27] David Ziskind, *One Thousand Strikes of Government Employees* (New York: Columbia University Press, 1940), points out that strikes have usually risen in the absence of recognized unions rather than where they exist.

injurious to their unit of government. In their fight to protect their interest they have become formidable pressure groups.

Professional employees in government are often active in professional societies with which members of the profession generally affiliate, such as the American Bar Association, Society for the Advancement of Management, American Economic Association, and engineering societies. Often these associations formally or informally set professional standards for membership and expect a standard of treatment to members of the profession. This has a real effect upon employment of these professional groups in government. For example, Federal attorneys are not subject to competitive examination. State education associations influence, if not set, the standards of public-school teachers.

Political Activities. When the Federal civil service was established, it seemed desirable to protect classified employees from political pressure; at the same time it was decided to restrain them from voluntary partisan activities. Administrative and executive officers and employees (except the President) were prohibited from soliciting or receiving contributions from other officers or employees for a political purpose. This did not free the employee from pressure from nonofficeholders—except that he could not be approached at his place of employment—an obviously large loophole in the law.

While this law afforded some relief to employees under the merit system, it excluded the thousands of officers and employees, as well as recipients of relief from the Federal government, who were not within the classified civil service. Moreover, these people were free to engage in partisan political activity. Abuses arising from these exemptions led to the passage of the Hatch Acts (1939–1940).[28] Concisely, it was declared unlawful in the 1939 law for any person employed in the executive branch of the government, except for certain policy-determining officials, to (1) take any active part in a political campaign; (2) use his official authority to affect the nomination or election of candidates for a Federal office; (3) promise a public job or benefit as a reward for a political activity; (4) solicit or receive any political contributions from persons benefiting from Federal relief programs. The following year the provisions of the law were extended to cover state and local employees who are engaged in activities financed wholly or in part by Federal funds. Numerous municipalities also have laws restricting political activities of their employees.

The result of these laws in practice is to permit a public employee to

[28] 53 STAT. 1147 and 54 STAT. 767. An extended treatment of the financial aspects of the acts is found in Chap. 23. For an analysis of the limitations of Federal employees see L. V. Howard, "Federal Restrictions on the Political Activity of Government Employees," *The American Political Science Review*, Vol. 35 (1941), pp. 470–489.

vote and to attend political rallies and party meetings provided that he takes no active part and does not hold an office in his party or political club.[29] He may express political views privately but may not campaign in any way or serve as a delegate to a nominating convention or run for office on a partisan ballot. The Civil Service Commission has declared that employee organizations may not support or oppose congressional candidates even through representatives of these organizations who are not in the public service. An employee may make a financial contribution to a party provided it is not made through any person employed by the United States. In practice, unclassified employees are not so severely restricted as those under the Civil Service Act. The former may express political views publicly, even though they may not campaign. Classified employees who violate the Act are removed from office by the Civil Service Commission, while unclassified workers are simply reported by the Commission to their agencies, which are supposed to make the removals.

These laws have limited the activities of those employed in the executive branch of the Federal service and have denied them the rights accorded to other citizens. They have protected the public interest, however, from some of the "pernicious political activities" which have too often been associated with partisan influence within and on the bureaucracy. They have also protected classified Federal employees from being forced to make political contributions and to campaign—a protection, incidentally, which does not exist among all state employees.

Noncivil Service Employees. Despite these laws, the administration still participates in elections and to a very considerable extent. The President and his Cabinet secretaries, as well as other high officials, deliver speeches during campaigns and make financial contributions to political committees which support their program. The Postmaster General and national chairman of the party in power are commonly one and the same person. Naturally these officials point out to special-interest groups the desirability of retaining popular programs with the implication that a change of parties would endanger some of the services being rendered by their agencies and the administration in general. Public employees and their families are aware that certain elections may vitally affect their positions and hence are on hand to vote and, where it can be done privately, to encourage their friends to come to the polls.

A large number of employees on the state and local levels who are not under the civil service system take an active part in elections. It is not uncommon to see public employees around campaign headquarters aiding in secretarial work, assisting in speech writing, gathering materials, and the like. Although this is not necessarily a happy spectacle it is

[29] Federal employees may not belong to Communist or pro-Communist, fascist, or other organizations declared subversive by the Attorney General.

understandable, for the jobs of most of these persons are likely to depend upon the outcome of the election. It is not surprising also to find public employees active in political parties, for many received their positions at the hands of the party and are expected to continue their party work after appointment. In many cities the rank and file of party workers of the party in office hold minor jobs in the city or county.

In all states the governor and other state-wide nominees of the party in power look to departmental and bureau chiefs for material to be used in the campaign, especially on such vital subjects as public roads, health, education, and the promotion of the interests of business, labor, and agriculture. The reservoir of good will that the executive agencies build up with particular constituencies is useful during the campaign, and the party organization does not overlook its potential. State agricultural agents have valuable personal contacts with farm groups, which may help the party in power to get its points across to the rural electorate. It is probably correct to assume that election activities of public employees are proportionately wider spread in the states, counties, and cities than in the Federal service, for in the former there are a much smaller number who come under the merit system.

SELECTED REFERENCES

The bylaws, annual resolutions, and publications offer the best source material for the professional associations, together with such books as Howard K. Beale, *Are American Teachers Free?* (1936); Newton Edwards and Herman Ridey, *The School in the Social Order* (1943); M. L. Rutherford, *The Influence of the American Bar Association on Public Opinion and Legislature* (1937); F. P. DeLancy, *The Licensing of Professions in West Virginia* (1938); E. P. Martin, *The Role of the Bar in Electing the Bench in Chicago* (1936); "Professional Associations," *The Annals of the American Academy of Political and Social Science*, Vol. 179 (1935). For a list of works on education and politics see the selected references at the end of Chap. 2.

On the pressure politics of health insurance and organized medical groups see J. A. Kingsbury, *Health in Handcuffs* (1939); James Rorty, *American Medicine Mobilizes* (1939); Oliver Garceau, *The Political Life of the American Medical Association* (1941); H. D. Simpson, *Compulsory Health Insurance in the United States* (1943); M. A. Bealle, *Medical Mussolini* (1938); John L. Spivak, *The Medical Trust Unmasked* (1929); *Hearings on a Bill to Provide for a National Health Program*, Report of the Senate Committee on Education and Labor, 79th Cong., 2d Sess., 1946. The publications of the professional and pro-public medical care groups include much propaganda on the subject. A great deal of the most informative literature on the political aspects of health is found in periodicals.

The periodic reports of administrative agencies, congressional hearings, and the *Congressional Record* are rich sources of data on the activities of administrative agencies. Certain additional aspects of administration are considered in the following two chapters. A wealth of material in administration and public-employment problems will be found in the periodicals *Public Administration Review, Public Personnel Review, Public Management,* and the *Industrial and Labor Relations Review.* See also the various textbooks in public administration and public personnel.

Useful books on the subject include Sterling Spero, *Government as Employer* (1948); C. H. Rhyne, *Labor Unions and Municipal Employee Law* (1946); J. M. Gaus, *Reflections on Public Administration* (1947); P. H. Appleby, *Policy and Administration* (1949); E. P. Herring, *Public Administration and the Public Interest* (1936); J. L. McCamy, *Government Publicity* (1939); M. R. Godine, *The Labor Problem in the Public Service* (1951); and the numerous publications of the Civil Service Assembly of the United States and Canada. See also "Bureaucracy and Democratic Government," *The Annals of the American Academy of Political and Social Science,* March, 1954.

1. Have narrower pol. + legislative interests:

2. musicians and writers (minimized under Petrillo

3. Legal professionale very numerous.
   (one of the most conservative of all groups)

4. Public Health A.M.A

5. Public education
   (guild functions are these groups)

6. Bureaucracy

CHAPTER 8

Other Interests

> As soon as several of the inhabitants of the United States have taken up an opinion or a feeling which they wish to promote in the world, they look out for mutual assistance; and as soon as they have found one another, they combine. From that moment they are no longer isolated men, but a power seen from afar, whose actions serve for an example and whose language is listened to.
>
> —ALEXIS DE TOCQUEVILLE

Although receiving the most attention, business, labor, agriculture, and the professions are by no means the only interests effectively organized to influence public policy. Others are represented by hundreds of associations, all with permanent representatives in Washington, and varying in name from the Indian Rights League to the People's Lobby. Numerous of these are spurious, ineffective, and formed for the purpose of personal or financial enhancement of the directors and are little more than small-time rackets preying upon the gullible. Others provide an avenue of expression for fanatics and crusaders. A great many others, however, offer a channel for bringing together persons with specialized interests only secondarily served through the occupational associations.

It is difficult to keep track of or even catalogue the miscellaneous interests which have organizations. Many of them are semipermanent but regroup under another label. Certain other political interest groups are formed on a temporary basis to precipitate a definite action and then go out of existence after they have accomplished their objective. One such group, the Citizens Committee to Repeal Chinese Exclusion, acted as a catalyst to stimulate repeal among other groups and to coordinate their activities. The group was small but effective and was successful, as Riggs [1] points out, in releasing "forces which already existed but were largely inoperative or not specifically directed." Some of the more permanent interests which have found expressions in pressure group activity will receive brief attention here.

---

[1] On this group see F. W. Riggs, *Pressures on Congress* (New York: King's Crown Press, 1950). This is an exceptionally good study illustrating the catalyst character of a temporary organization.

FOREIGN POLICY ASSOCIATIONS

With the United States as a major power, high taxation to support defense expenditures, and a sizable number of men in the armed services, foreign policy has become a lively subject for debate. Nearly all the larger multipurpose interest groups adopt annual resolutions on foreign policy, print information on foreign affairs, and send their spokesmen to testify before legislative committees on the subject. Agriculture, business, and labor associations can hardly ignore foreign policy because it is so often interwoven with domestic policies in which the occupations are concerned.

The question of peace has provided the basis for organized activity on the part of specially constituted groups which operate under descript and nondescript titles. In the 1930's "patriotic" and "pacifist" societies were commonly regarded as the antithesis of each other, with the former stressing large armaments and military training and the latter urging disarmament and appropriations for "schools instead of battleships."

An interesting phenomenon of 1940 and 1941 was the rise of numerous groups seeking to crystallize public opinion for or against participation in World War II, with both sides claiming memberships running into seven figures.[2] Washington has seldom witnessed more vigorous debate and dramatic demonstrations than occurred when these groups converged on the capital. Propaganda publications by the ton, replete with name calling, deluged Congress and the public. Special appeals were directed to induce housewives, labor, business, agriculture, Negroes, youth, churchgoers, and others to join the cause. Other activities included picketing the White House, hanging of congressmen in effigy, parades, and the conducting of "wakes" on the grounds of the Capitol.

Professor Masland saw the extent of prewar pressure-group activity as "proof that foreign policy is democratically controlled. If it had been otherwise, their promoters would not have devoted such tireless energy to the direct stimulation of public opinion. They would have concentrated on more devious approaches to the seats of authority."[3] While the proposition "that foreign policy is democratically controlled" is debatable, the activities of foreign policy societies testify to the healthy state of interest of the people in international affairs and policies and a willingness on the part of a large number of them to work for what they considered, rightly or wrongly, was to the nation's best interest. The

[2] On the pro- and anti-interventionist groups see T. S. Cole, *America First: The Battle against American Intervention, 1940–1941* (Madison, Wis.: University of Wisconsin Press, 1953), and Walter Johnson, *The Battle against Isolation* (Chicago: University of Chicago Press, 1944).

[3] John W. Masland, "Pressure Groups and Foreign Policy," *Public Opinion Quarterly*, Vol. 5 (1942), p. 122.

importance of the pre-Pearl Harbor committees is also shown in their ability to bring together diverse elements on a vital national issue.

The bombing of Pearl Harbor brought the dissolution of the temporary antiwar committees. With the United States committed to international cooperation, societies based on narrow nationalism no longer attract any significant number, but associations dedicated to preserving the peace are of vital importance. Oldest of these are the American Peace Society and the National Council for the Prevention of War. The latter engages in pressure politics to a considerable extent. Its purpose is to promote the establishment of international good will and to arouse and formulate opinion on the subject. Besides lobbying, it acts as a clearinghouse for other peace action societies and concentrates on issuing and making available material to educational, civic, and church organizations.

Many new foreign policy associations have appeared since 1945 and many old ones have regrouped.[4] These associations, however, continue to fall into two broad categories, those which support programs of international cooperation and those critical of them. The League of Nations Association gave way to the American Association for the United Nations. The latter has concerned itself with strengthening the UN and fending off attacks against the organization. Particularly in 1950 the nation became aware of a vigorous anti-UN program in the United States. It operated under the slogan "Get the United States out of the United Nations and the United Nations out of the United States." The movement appeared well financed and issued scurrilous materials. Persons attempting to defend the UN in public addresses found themselves subjected to organized heckling, "planted questions," direct personal attacks, and dramatic walkouts during their speeches. Among the most firmly implanted suspicions was that the United States is threatened with loss of its identity in a world government which will evolve out of the UN and that the UN headquarters is Communist-dominated, with American representatives participating in plots to destroy the sovereignty of the Western democracies.[5] In order to mobilize the weight of the millions of members of women's clubs against this, and to try to cultivate patience, tolerance, and sympathetic understanding of the UN, an affiliated group known as the Women United for the United Nations was formed in 1953.

Nongovernmental organizations may be and are consulted by the United Nations, particularly the Economic and Social Council. The Council recognizes that these groups possess technical and other knowledge which is of real value to the Council. Organizations, set up in

---

[4] The Foreign Policy Association has published a useful directory of these: *U.S. Citizens in World Affairs* (1953).

[5] For certain aspects of the anti-UN movement see *The New York Times*, Apr. 5, 1953.

special categories, are placed on a register for consultation; the UN has thus recognized the representative character of international interest groups.[6]

Several groups, while not hostile to the UN, believed it did not go far enough, and they organized to promulgate their views. One of these became the Atlantic Union Committee, which supports the strengthening of the North Atlantic Treaty Organization and advocates a union of sponsors of the Atlantic Charter as a realistic method of maintaining peace. A substantial number of citizens have become reconciled to a Western bloc for the purpose of opposing the extension of communism. The Committee on the Present Danger, which numbers several college presidents in its organization, is likewise devoted to a mutual security program and has taken particular interest in military manpower.

After the end of the war, a new movement for some form of world federation or world government developed. In 1947 a number of these organizations merged into the United World Federalists, with a platform calling for a world government with powers adequate to prevent war. The organization numbers among its members prominent scientists, journalists, educators, and politicians. The World Federalists would avoid "supergovernment" by following the principle of federalism, giving the international authority only limited powers to deal with international tensions. Activities of the World Federalists are directed toward mobilizing public opinion through the press and radio for its program, the establishment of local chapters in communities and on college campuses, and the drawing up of world government referendums to be placed on the ballots in the states. The World Federalists soon drew the fire of patriotic and ultranationalist societies as subversive and devoted to giving up American sovereignty. With the UN under attack and a reaction against the internationalists during the Korean War, the World Federalists failed to continue its earlier momentum.

There are scores of organizations and institutes devoted to the study of foreign affairs. Scholars and public officials have come to rely on the Foreign Policy Association for information. Its publications are refreshingly objective compared to the more emotional ones so often issued by other peace, patriotic, and foreign policy interest groups.

The nation is divided over foreign policy and in its attitude toward participation in international organizations. It is only natural, therefore, that there have sprung up sentiments and organizations representing "Asia-firsters" and "Europe-firsters," Zionists and pro-Arab supporters, idealists and cynics. Even the American Bar Association is split over

[6] See Lyman C. White, *International Non-governmental Organizations* (New Brunswick, N.J.: Rutgers University Press, 1951); also the UN reference, *Everyman's United Nations* (1952).

certain legal aspects of the UN and disagreed on the Bricker Amendment, which would have circumscribed to some extent the President's conduct of foreign policy and strengthened Senate control over executive agreements.

ORGANIZED PATRIOTISM

Samuel Johnson saw patriotism as "the last refuge of a scoundrel," and many sins and abridgments of human liberties have been committed in the name of patriotism. So-called "patriotic" societies are in abundance in the United States. They take many forms from sincere advocates of jingoism, supernationalism, and superpatriotism, to racketeering under clandestine robes and nomenclature. A strong nativist tinge underlies the program of a number of these organizations, such as the Ku Klux Klan, the Paul Reveres, the American Vigilant Intelligence Federation, and the Silver Shirts. All these groups have generalized and ill-defined objectives of promoting patriotism with a capital *P* by "combating radicalism," fostering "Americanism," fighting "bureaucracy," and the perpetuation of "civilization and Christianity." In his study of anti-Semitism in the United States, Strong [7] found 121 organizations in existence, including the above. A sizable number operated under self-styled patriotic titles with an amazing array of interlocking directorates. Activities are carried on in more or less secret fashion by means of printed propaganda with occasional resort to public pageantry. Although the mortality rate is high in these organizations, they regroup and bound back with great resiliency. Many of them are under investigation by Congress and the Department of Justice.

Another group of organizations operates essentially as a political committee under the label of a patriotic organization. Perhaps best known of the politico-patriotic societies is the Committee for Constitutional Government, formerly the National Committee to Uphold Constitutional Government, founded in 1937 by publisher Frank Gannett, to defeat the proposal for reorganization of the Supreme Court. From this it trained its guns on the executive reorganization measure in 1938 by sending thousands of telegrams to Congress, alleging that the bill was a "threat to our form of government." When testifying before a congressional committee, Mr. Gannett admitted that in the first seven years of existence his Committee "distributed more than 80,000,000 pieces of literature, including pamphlets, leaflets, and books." [8] Under the spotlight of inves-

---

[7] Donald Strong, *Organized Anti-Semitism in America* (Washington, D.C.: Public Affairs Press, 1941).

[8] Hearings before the House Committee to Investigate Campaign Expenditures, 78th Cong., 2d Sess., Part 7. This hearing, comprising 176 pages of testimony on the Committee, is a highly illuminating illustration of the mixture of patriotism and political objectives.

tigation, the Committee was found to urge the election of the "right congressmen" and a drastic limitation on personal income taxes and to oppose the third term of the presidency, so-called "socialization of insurance," and the CIO Political Action Committee. Several hundreds of thousands of dollars were spent for the promotion of these objectives and on political activities. Yet the Committee insists it is nonpolitical and therefore beyond the pale of the Federal Corrupt Practices Act.

"Saving the Constitution" also led the Committee to work with auxiliaries of the American Medical Association to defeat health-insurance proposals. Letters were sent to members of the AMA warning of the dangers of "political medicine" and asking, "Can politics cure appendicitis?" [9] No better illustration exists of the use of patriotic symbolism to crusade for a partisan political and class interest than in the program and pressure activities of the Committee for Constitutional Government.

Finally, there are numerous ancestral societies,[10] best known of which are the Daughters of the American Revolution and the Sons of the American Revolution, which attempt to perpetuate the glorious episodes in American history, especially military exploits and the drafting of the Constitution and the Declaration of Independence. These follow a traditional concept of patriotism, including nationalism, "adequate national defense," fighting "subversive" doctrines, and a general suspicion of aliens. These and other groups have taken a highly critical if not hostile view toward the United Nations, foreign aid, and have favored the Bricker Amendment.

An enlightened patriotism is a welcome part of the program of every interest group, but a danger exists when so-called "patriotism" becomes the *raison d'être* of an organization, for many associations of this type pervert revered principles to serve the purposes, financial or otherwise, of the professional patriot, a class or political interest, or a dubious if not un-American concept of Americanism. Because of "Americanization" and military preparedness programs of veterans' organizations, they are sometimes classed as patriotic societies.

VETERANS

Political Interests. After every war there are those who express fear of and those who express hope for the political power of veterans. Heads of veterans' organizations often talk of their potential as a balance of power. The "veterans' vote," like the "farm" or "labor" or "Catholic"

---

[9] The interesting story of the tie-up between the patriotic and the medical societies for the purpose of defeating a national medical care program is told in John A. Kingsbury, *Health in Handcuffs* (New York: Modern Age, Inc., 1939).

[10] The American Coalition, formed in 1925, purports to speak for three million persons in its constituent societies, mainly ancestral associations.

vote, is a chimera pursued by office seekers. After the Civil War the vote of the Grand Army of the Republic came close to being a bloc vote for the Republican party. When the Democratic President Grover Cleveland vetoed pension and other bills favored by the G.A.R., the Republicans tightened their hold on the G.A.R. vote by showing what happens "when you vote for a Democrat." [11] Veterans of subsequent wars, however, have not identified themselves so solidly with any one party. After World War II there were many GI candidates, and slates of nominees in local elections and office seekers today make public fact of their veteran's membership. Veterans met defeat as many times as success in nominating conventions and primaries in 1946 when special pleas were made to vote for veterans.

Reasons why the veterans' appeal alone did not mean electoral success are easy to understand. The Selective Service law drew from all sections of the population and one could hardly expect the men to be of the same class or to have a close identity of a number of interests. Most Americans soon lose their sense of being a veteran when they settle back in their business and social backgrounds, the more so as the memory of their military service begins to dim and the pressures of family, occupational, and civic life exert themselves. A strictly veterans' political party or a "GI-PAC" would soon run into conflicts with the wide variety of personal interests of the membership. Moreover, there is the absence of any sizable number of overriding, dominant issues around which a political party might be formed. The fraternal ties of common experiences and reminiscences of the past provide a strong bond for a social and philanthropic organization but hardly for sustained and concerted political action.

It is always a matter of speculation on the extent to which there is or ought to be a veterans' interest separate and distinct from an occupational or the general public interest. Veterans' organizations, however, with considerable success have found a few matters of primary concern for pressure politics on a national scale, namely, pensions and bonuses, hospitalization, rehabilitation programs, postwar educational opportunities, preferences in the civil service, and other benefits. Upward of $10 billion were appropriated by August, 1946, for purposes of benefiting veterans and their families. Annual Federal expenditures since that time have run from about $5 to $8 billion for veterans' programs.[12]

Notwithstanding the citizen army and broad cross section in the armed services, there has been an enduring veterans' interest centered primarily around pensions, bonuses of land or money, or so-called "adjusted com-

[11] An excellent work on this organization is Mary R. Dearing, *Veterans in Politics: The Story of the G.A.R.* (Baton Rouge, La.: Louisiana State University Press, 1952).

[12] A useful summary table on laws benefiting veterans is found in the *Congressional Record,* Aug. 12, 1946 (daily edition), pp. A5200–5202.

pensation." The first pension system seems to go back to 1691 and provided help for wounded veterans of King William's War.[13] Gradually, pensions not connected with disability and for veterans' widows came to be paid. Veterans' groups have been able to muster enough support on Capitol Hill to override the vetoes of pension bills by numerous Republican and Democratic Presidents. The veterans of World War II have succeeded in obtaining bonuses in a large number of states.

Over the years the legislative interests have broadened to take in proposals not directly related to veterans' benefits. The American Legion reported that in one session of Congress Legion representatives gave testimony in 40 different congressional hearings, reviewed over 400 bills which "concern American Legion mandates," and that 110 of the bills directly concerning the organization were enacted.[14] These measures included such diversified ones as Federal aid to education, increased postal rates, conscientious objectors, hospital construction, displaced persons, and embargoes on Communist China. Virtually all veterans' organizations have taken a position in favor of large defense expenditures and universal military training or selective service, and some form of veterans' preference in the civil service.

Veterans of all wars number about 17,240,000, with about one-fourth belonging to veterans' organizations. Memberships of the five major associations in 1953 were: American Legion, 2,765,000; Veterans of Foreign Wars, 1,200,000; Disabled American Veterans, 185,000; American Veterans of World War II (Amvets), 90,000; and American Veterans Committee (AVC), 10,000.[15] In addition, there are divisional associations including organizations for the blind, holders of the Purple Heart, and for Catholics, Jews, Negroes, Greek-, Polish-, and Italian-Americans. All shades of political and economic color from conservative to socialist are represented, the last-mentioned being reflected by a small group calling itself the Veterans League of America. As a rule these organizations have operated on two bases: one to obtain maximum benefits for veterans; the other to endeavor to speak for the bulk of veterans on matters of public policy. So far no one organization has been able to speak for the greater mass of those serving their country in the Armed Forces, and each new war has seen the rise of new associations.

---

[13] Some interesting historical facts on the development of pension and other veterans' legislation may be found in Talcott Powell, *Tattered Banners* (New York: Harcourt, Brace and Company, Inc., 1933); and Dixon Wecter, *When Johnny Comes Marching Home* (Boston: Houghton Mifflin Company, 1944).

[14] See *Reports of the American Legion* (1951), pp. 115–134.

[15] This is a decline of over one million members for all groups combined over the immediate postwar figure; for the latter figures see *The New York Times,* Aug. 11, 1946.

Older Veterans' Groups. Oldest of the larger existing organizations is the Veterans of Foreign Wars, founded after the Spanish-American War as an elite group whose members had seen foreign service. Unlike most other groups, women veterans are not admitted. In general, the VFW follows a more conservative line in public policy and argues that overseas veterans deserve higher remuneration and bonuses than those who "sat out the war" in the United States. It joined with liberal forces in 1946, however, to urge continuance of price control. The VFW works closely with the American Legion in legislative matters, and the two have already issued joint statements endorsing compulsory military training, opposing immigration, and opening the door to foreign refugees. Both are conducting a militant fight against communism and support the activities of the House Committee on Un-American Activities.

The Disabled American Veterans have given no great concern to legislative matters except those which particularly apply to their exclusive membership. Their objectives of adequate hospitalization and rehabilitation programs meet with general approval.

By far the best-established organization financially, politically, and numerically is the American Legion.[16] Organized in 1919 in Paris by a group of officers, the Legion enjoyed the approval of the War Department and for years was the major power behind the Veterans Administration. The Women's Auxiliary of the Legion provides an excellent arm by which the parent organization may extend its influence into community affairs.

The influence of the Legion was and still is considerable on the public schools; the National Education Association, as evidence of this, has curried its favor. During the depression of the 1930's, the Legion, to its credit, fought for adequate appropriations for public schools. In spite of its worthy philanthropic and fraternal enterprises in the local community, the Legion has been a storm center in political matters. Millions of dollars were expended during the 1930's on its program of "Americanization," which consisted in part in investigating school textbooks, offering prizes for essays on Americanism, and conducting a vigorous crusade against the Communists and "subversive elements." Non-Communist liberals, pacifists, socialists, and school administrators often found themselves in trouble with local Legion posts, and school librarians on occasions had their magazines critically scrutinized. On several other matters the Legion aroused the enmity of sizable groups. One of these, the prohibition forces, objected to the type of fight waged by the organization

16 The Legion is one of the most written-about organizations in the nation. Major works include William Gellerman, *The American Legion as Educator* (New York: Columbia University Press, 1938); Marcus Duffield, *King Legion* (New York: Cape and Smith, 1931); R. S. Jones, *A History of the American Legion* (Indianapolis: The Bobbs-Merrill Company, Inc., 1946); Justin Gray, *The Inside Story of the Legion* (New York: Boni & Gaer, 1948).

against the Eighteenth Amendment. On the bonus issue, which finally culminated in a "march on Washington," President Hoover and a large segment of Congress were at variance with the demands of the Legion. There were many persons within the Legion itself who objected to the position of its national officers on these questions and who firmly believed the organization should keep out of politics.

The Legion's constitution declares that the organization shall be "absolutely non-political." But this has not kept the group leadership from gravitating toward a politically conservative ideology. Commanders of the Legion have quite often been bankers, businessmen, small merchants, independent farmers, and professionals, and several who have studied the organization and its policies find it friendly to big business, the upper middle class, and at times close to antilabor, especially in the local posts.[17] In following an essentially conservative pattern it has, for example, been critical of public-housing programs, while other veterans' groups lobbied for them. The Legion's anti-Communist program has led it into support of congressional investigations of the State Department, and the demand that all American Communists be tried as traitors and that the American Communist party be outlawed by constitutional amendment. In general, the Legion's literature announces itself opposed to radicalism.

World War II Groups. Of the two major associations emerging from World War II, the American Veterans Committee (AVC) and the American Veterans of World War II (Amvets), the latter has gained the larger membership.[18] Both groups have been faced with serious membership and organizational problems. Except for support of veterans' programs and civil liberties, the Amvets' political interests are not yet following a pattern, though some hope it will become the "Legion of World War II." On one matter, however, the Amvets have shown themselves as a pioneer, namely, that of "peace." One of its leaders noted that after World War I there were plenty of measures sponsored by veterans' groups to end wars, but "in the race to procure legislation looking to benefits and a bonus, the peace program was sidetracked, and there it stayed until war came."[19] The Legion, for example, became an uncompromising foe of the League of Nations and the World Court, as well as of other proposals for international cooperation and disarmament. It remains to be seen if the suggestion of an Amvet leader for a Security Council of War Veterans "to aid in the establishment and maintenance of peace" bears fruit.

[17] See especially Duffield, *op. cit.;* and Gellerman, *op. cit.*

[18] For bylaws and principles of the Amvets see the *Congressional Record,* Feb. 12, 1953 (daily edition), pp. A645–650.

[19] See letter in *The New York Times,* Aug. 13, 1946.

The AVC, in spite of its relatively small numbers, has received a lion's share of publicity since its formation in 1943. This is due not only to the several prominent figures in its membership but also to its sharp break with the conventional procedures and principles of other veterans' organizations. Under its slogan "Citizens First, Veterans Second," the AVC uses none of the semimilitary procedures characteristic of veterans' groups and refers to its local units as chapters instead of posts. It shocked some to see it oppose a bonus and to emphasize that jobs, full-employment measures, and social security were more important to help the veteran's integration into the community than a program of rehabilitation and bonuses. International control of atomic energy and unification of the Armed Forces are also in the AVC's platform.

The militant liberal program and activities of the AVC have led certain conservative interests to try, as they do with many other groups with similar objectives, to pin the Communist badge on it. Among the activities which were criticized were the AVC's public demonstrations for the continuance of price control, and earmarking for defeat certain "reactionary" congressmen. In program there are similarities between the AVC and the more progressive labor unions, including, for example, the guaranteed annual wage.

Considering the wide differences in background from the American Legion to the AVC, the next few decades will witness an interesting contest for power to influence the Defense Department, the Veterans Administration, Congress, and community life in the thousands of villages and cities in the nation. It remains to be seen whether and to what extent the Amvets and AVC can make inroads into the entrenched position of the Legion and the VFW. The Legion and VFW decided to assure their groups by making a drive for membership among World War II veterans. In the main this has succeeded and many young veterans followed in their fathers' footsteps and joined the Legion or VFW because they were respected and established in the community.

The Veterans Administration is to the veterans and their organizations what the Department of Agriculture is to the farmers. It has fought the veterans' battles in and out of government. At times the schisms in the ranks of the veterans' organizations have been felt in the VA. A Legion commander once called for the removal of General Bradley as head of the VA but the other veterans' groups rallied to his defense and he was not removed.

RELIGIOUS AND ETHNIC GROUPS

Religion and Politics. The separation of church and state and the popular assumption that politics and religion should not mix have obscured the fact from many Americans that there is a formidable "church lobby" both in Washington and in the states. In 1930 very few religious groups had an office in the nation's capital. Nowadays nearly every major denomination has a Washington representative.[20] These representatives are not highly paid and seldom draft legislation but they attempt to alert congressmen to the position of their churches on public matters. The National Council of Churches of Christ in the U.S.A. consists of 30 Protestant and Orthodox groups representing 35 million members. There are in addition numerous individual church groups such as the Council for Social Action of the Congregational Christian Churches, the Baptist Committee on Public Affairs, and the National Lutheran Council. An active temperance bloc is spearheaded by the Methodist Board of Temperance and supported by the Woman's Christian Temperance Union and the National Temperance League.

The Catholic viewpoint is represented through the National Catholic Welfare Conference and the National Conference of Catholic Charities. Locally, the Knights of Columbus, the Legion of Decency, and certain Catholic men's and women's councils have influenced some policies in the community.

Among the important Jewish organizations are the National Jewish Welfare Board, American Zionist Council, American Jewish Committee, and various B'nai B'rith associations. With the formation of the new nation, Israel, the Zionist groups saw the culmination of a half century of hard work, organization, and propaganda both in America and abroad. At one time there were some thirty national groups in the United States engaged in political activity. Many of these remained intact to influence American policy toward Israel.

Church interest in governmental policy stems from many sources. There is first of all the philanthropic side of the churches and their advocacy of a humanitarian society. Most if not all Christian denominations teach the doctrines of personal salvation, faith and good works, the golden rule, the free and voluntary fellowship of man, the dignity of the individual, and freedom to seek the truth. The church is therefore concerned with the type of society whereby its adherents may pursue these tenets. Legislation may help to provide some aspects of the good life both by restraining those who would interfere with it and by positive action. In answer to a question of a congressman with reference to the

[20] On the various church organizations operating in Washington see Luke E. Ebersole, *Church Lobbying in the Nation's Capital* (New York: The Macmillan Company, 1951). Zionist and Jewish groups are listed in *The Palestine Yearbook,* Vol. 2 (1946), pp. 545–575. Some other aspects of the church as a basic factor in politics are covered in Chap. 2.

church seeking government action, Monsignor John O'Grady,[21] secretary
of the National Conference of Catholic Charities, replied in part:

If I believe in Christian charity, I am supposed to help people who do not
have sufficient food. . . . I am supposed to provide clothing for them; I am
supposed to provide shelter for them. Yes, I think that is my sacred obligation.
And it is my sacred obligation to go out and struggle and try to find it for them,
and to prevail on the Government. . . .

But when we reach the point where we cannot handle it ourselves, then, we
have to go out and talk to citizens, and say, "This is now a responsibility of
the people as a whole, and Government ought to take care of this great need
which we cannot, through our best efforts, take care of. The Government is
merely the organ of the citizenry as a whole, and we must finally appeal to the
Government."

Numerous ministers have for many years preached the social gospel,
which has more or less pointed in the direction of supporting social
legislation.

Humanitarian reasons are not the only ones which have led the
churches to try to influence government. Many churches own and operate
businesses for investment purposes. Some states have attempted to bring
employees of income-producing operations of religious and non-profit-
making organizations under the protection of unemployment insurance
and wage-hours laws. The vigor with which religious and philanthropic
groups assailed these proposals usually led to their defeat. Congressional
investigations have sometimes pointed the finger at church auxiliaries
as supporting "front" causes and this has led the auxiliaries to fight back.
Individual clergymen frequently attempt to influence their parishioners
to vote for members of their faith or for certain candidates.[22]

If one is to judge by the "social-action" programs adopted by churches
and the auxiliaries, the public matters upon which their spokesmen speak
and their ministers preach, the churches in the United States have a
most ambitious legislative program. On many proposals, however, the
various denominations are unable to present a united front and, as a
matter of fact, may be in opposition. Protestants advocating Federal aid
to education, strict temperance laws, and the withholding of an American
ambassador at the Vatican are generally opposed by the Catholic hierarchy and differences have been manifest between the two groups over
assistance to Franco's Spain and direct or indirect state support for
parochial schools.[23] Christian Scientists have taken positions at variance

21 Hearings before the House Committee on Banking and Currency, 80th Cong., 2d
Sess., p. 588 (hearings were on housing legislation).

22 See Madge M. McKinney, "Religion and Elections," *Public Opinion Quarterly,*
Vol. 8 (1944), pp. 110–114.

23 In 1948 some prominent Protestants formed an organization known as Protestants
and Other Americans United for Separation of Church and State.

with other religious groups on putting fluorine in drinking water and on public-health programs. The Protestant churches are usually identified with the "peace," pacifist, and antigambling groups, and Catholics with opposition to legalizing birth control and sterilization.

At the same time, conferences of Catholics, Jews, and Protestants have worked together on many public matters, notably racial relations, anti-discrimination, and civil rights laws, against communism, for displaced persons legislation, cooperation in world organizations, foreign aid, health, fair-labor standards, and social-security laws. Most churches oppose peacetime compulsory military training. On these matters the participation of churches appears to be on the increase.

The methods of church lobbies are not particularly spectacular or unorthodox. They resemble those of other groups in trying to keep their membership informed of governmental actions and proposals. Legislators and administrators do not want to be accused of being antireligious and church groups may capitalize on this in approaching public officials. By implication at least, spokesmen for the church groups carry the force of representing a moral group and a moral cause. "But the churches," says Ebersole, "have moved far beyond mere opposition to 'liquor, war and sin.' They are not relying upon impulsive campaigns and special cause lobbies for representation before government. The trend is to form agencies which have the assigned function of representing their respective denominational and interdenominational church bodies before the Federal government." [24]

Melting-pot Groups. The large number of foreign-born and first-generation immigrants has brought an indeterminate but large number of ethnic associations into existence in the United States. Many of the German, Irish, Polish, Italian, and other nationalist organizations are devoted to social and fraternal matters and only secondarily if ever to political action, except to endorse on occasion nominees of their own ranks in an election. Nationalistic and linguistic groups commonly seek another objective, that of fostering friendship, sympathy, and understanding of their homeland. This is done through radio or printed propaganda and the use of the motion picture and of music designed to create favorable public opinion for the nation. Since 1940, the United States has witnessed an increasing number of societies designated as "friends" of China, of the Soviet Union, of Israel, and of those European nations which seek financial or other aid as well as moral support for their peoples and governments. Since the end of World War II, considerable discussion has appeared on the "China lobby," which has campaigned for increased aid to Nationalist China. Many Americans, however, helped to finance

24 *Op. cit.,* pp. 176–177.

these activities and the organization was by no means limited to Chinese·Americans.[25]

Immigrant groups are usually concentrated in certain areas, especially in the large cities. Here they may become highly influential in local politics. The Scandinavians operate some of the most successful cooperatives in Wisconsin and Minnesota and have even brought about the compulsory teaching of Rochdale principles in certain public schools. Germans, Irish, and Italians became foes of the Eighteenth Amendment, and the Germans showed a lack of enthusiasm for the granting of woman suffrage. One study of isolationism from 1933 to 1950 found that "with important exceptions, heavily Germanic population areas tended to be more isolationist than neighboring areas of different national origins; . . . the most isolationist areas of California, Oregon, Wisconsin, and Minnesota were relatively heavily populated with persons of Germanic origins." [26] In the cities the Irish have entered politics and commonly show a political influence far more important than their proportionate numbers.

Lobbying objectives of the ethnic societies are usually limited to a few matters, including immigration policies, displaced persons, the status of aliens, and foreign policy toward the homeland. The location of the United Nations in New York is leading a number of the ethnic societies to concentrate upon this body, thus opening up a new area of activity.

Linguistic, ethnic, and religious groups, though not particularly important as pressure groups, are strongly catered to by political parties at election time. Intolerance is denounced before groups that feel the sting of discrimination. Demagogic politicians appeal for Irish and German votes by denouncing the British or their policies. It is perhaps ironical that, although constituting the largest stock in the country, the Anglo-Saxons are the least organized ethnic group.

In many ways the political party has been the channel through which the various immigrant groups have sought realization of their aspirations for status and for economic betterment. The parties have taken the nationalities into their organization and many party leaders have come from these groups. The "balanced ticket" has placed representatives of leading ethnic groups on the ballot and recognition of the national groups is made through patronage appointments which allot a certain number of jobs to the dominant minorities. The party has helped the immigrant to assimilate and to achieve status and in turn has hoped to receive his

[25] The so-called "China lobby" is quite amorphous in character; see *The Reporter*, Apr. 15 and 29, 1952.

[26] R. H. Smuckler, "The Region of Isolation," *The American Political Science Review*, Vol. 67 (1953), pp. 400–401. There were some areas, however, of heavily German stock which were nonisolationist.

vote. Many but by no means all of the nationalistic groups have achieved much through the Democratic party and this explains in part its success at the polls in the very large cities.[27]

Racial Groups. The American Indian and the Oriental have their small and essentially ineffective groups which make their problems known to the various state and national governments. By far the greatest racial problem is the Negro, both because he numbers a tenth of the population and because close to three-fourths of his members are concentrated in one section of the nation, the South. His interests have resembled those of all low-income groups—better wages, houses, health, and education. By joining labor unions he has built up some bargaining strength and has achieved considerable economic advancement in this way. At the same time, he has been faced with dilemmas in attempting to build political influence because of segregation practices and the difficulty of voting in some areas.[28]

Negroes themselves disagree on the question of militantly seeking to abolish restrictions on Negro political rights and "Jim Crowism." The followers of Booker T. Washington feel that too vigorous insistence upon suffrage and other political privileges will only stir up strife and benefit the Negro but little. In the review of his progress from servitude to leadership of his people in *Up from Slavery* (1901), Washington concluded:

I believe it is the duty of the Negro as the greater part of the race is already doing to deport himself modestly in regard to political claims, depending upon the slow but sure influences that proceed from the possession of property, intelligence, and high character for the full recognition of his political rights. I think that the according of full exercise of political rights is going to be a matter of natural, slow growth, not an overnight gourd vine affair.

This school of thought holds that suffrage will eventually be granted when the Negro becomes educated and improves his economic status. Booker T. Washington did not oppose suffrage for the Negro and in fact urged him to vote whenever and wherever he could. But he supported educational and property tests for the "protection of the ballot," such tests to apply equally to both races.

In 1909 the National Association for the Advancement of Colored People was founded and now numbers a half million members. It has little patience with lack of militance. The NAACP takes the position that without political power and the right to vote Negroes have little hope of obtaining from city councils and legislative bodies better schools, health

---

[27] On this and related matters see Samuel Lubbell, *The Future of American Politics* (New York: Harper & Brothers, 1952); F. J. Brown and J. S. Roucek, *One America* (New York: Prentice-Hall, Inc., 1945).

[28] Negro suffrage and the role of the Negro in politics are covered in Chap. 23.

services, housing facilities, and other things necessary for their improvement. Concisely, the organization advocates a militant struggle for the
civil rights to which the Negro is entitled by law. Added to its earlier
objectives of fighting against lynching, peonage, debt slavery, and disfranchisement in the South, the NAACP's major objectives include the
seeking of greater justice for Negroes in the courts, equitable distribution
of funds for public education, abolition of segregation, "equal pay for
equal work," and antidiscrimination laws for the race. Through pressure
politics the organization has won many legal battles and has stanchly
worked for Federal and state antilynching, anti-poll-tax, and antidiscrimination laws.[29] Few organizations enjoy a greater advantage of single-
ness of purpose, and caution is often abandoned for a hard-hitting program carried through both intellectual and emotional appeals.

One of the most important victories of the NAACP was won in 1954
when the United States Supreme Court outlawed segregation in the public schools—a decision called the most important in the field of race relations since the Dred Scott case. In many ways the organization realizes
that its fight is barely begun. It recognizes that many suits will have to
be brought in order to secure effective implementation of the decision.
The decision, moreover, is the opening wedge for attacks on the "separate-
but-equal-accommodations" doctrine which applies to many other aspects
of life. The carrying out of the antisegregation decrees is bound to involve certain changes in emphasis in Southern politics.

About the same time the NAACP was formed, the National Urban
League was also created. Although the two work together, their approach
is somewhat different. The League through its journal *Opportunity* seeks
better employment opportunities for Negroes. Through its dozens of local
leagues, which usually take the title of the geographical area of operation,
such as the Cleveland Urban League, it works with employers to erase
job discrimination and in general to improve the Negroes' social and economic status. Both Negro organizations open their membership to white
persons and the latter in turn have helped to finance the groups.

CONSUMERS AND "PROGRESSIVES"

When confronted with the demand for consumer representation in the
counsels of the NRA, Administrator Hugh Johnson replied negatively,
saying that everyone is a consumer, that there is no such thing as a "consumer interest." This attitude suggests in part the difficulty of bringing

[29] Representative Adam Clayton Powell, Jr. has summarized the newer approach of
the Negro for equality in *Marching Blacks* (New York: The Dial Press, Inc., 1945).
One of the best works on antidiscrimination politics is Louis Kesselman, *The Social
Politics of FEPC: A Study in Reform Pressure Movements* (Chapel Hill, N.C.: University of North Carolina Press, 1948).

together this sprawling interest and the absence of the equivalent of a CIO or NAM for the consumer. In the popular sense there is, however, a consumer interest, an interest basic to the low- and middle-income classes—the seeking of one's money's worth. It is an interest in low-cost housing, in lower prices, in properly branded and measured food and drugs, together with protection against adulteration and dangerous concoctions or substitutes. The consumer fights against "let the buyer beware," and for "let the seller beware," not only in food and drugs but in all other items and in stocks and bonds. In spite of this real interest, only a few organizations exist, notably the National Consumers' League, Consumers' Union, Consumers' Research, National Association of Consumers, and the League of Women Shoppers, for the purpose of bringing together a program and membership dedicated to these worthy purposes.

Despite this fact, the torch is carried for the consumer by dozens of the larger pressure groups through the development of policies designed to give protection to the buyer-member. Farm organizations vigorously champion the cause for their constituency. Some labor organizations are more and more concentrating on legislation designed to make the workers' dollars go farther through lower prices, grade labeling, and an increase in the amount of low- and medium-priced garments. What little support has come for adequate food and drug legislation is from these ranks and the few consumer societies.

The cooperative movement is strongly rooted in consumer interest and its growth is steady and persistent. In rural areas the agricultural organizations generally back the movement wholeheartedly. In cities, the labor unions, women's clubs, and civic associations commonly provide the nucleus for consumer cooperative stores. The formation of health cooperatives and group plans augurs the development of a new area of consumer activities. The lobbying of the cooperatives has consisted, with reasonable success, in obtaining legislation protecting them from the onslaught of vested interests which see a potential threat to their domain. It may be safely predicted that the general consumer and cooperative movement will grow and within the foreseeable future become a formidable force. Potentially this may change the character and emphasis of pressure politics.

There are invariably manifestations of "organized progressivism" and "liberalism." Progressivism and liberalism in this sense have meant the demand for state intervention to protect the consumer, the less privileged, and the promotion of a public-welfare and social-security program. Progressives attempt to operate through political parties; the progressive wing in both the major parties is in a struggle for control. Still others have felt the need for a permanent interest group which will work in the parties, lobby, and in general mobilize those of progressive and liberal persuasion. Best known of the latter is the Americans for Democratic Action, formed in 1947 by a group of non-Communist liberals.

In the general policy statement at its organizing conference the ADA stated:

> Our objective is to raise again the banner of progressivism in America, the only banner under which the free peoples of the world can be rallied against totalitarianism.
>
> It is our conviction that bread and freedom are ultimately interdependent. . . .
>
> By economic security we mean freedom from want and a fair distribution of the fruits of labor. More concretely we mean the guarantee of full and steady production and employment; the protection of labor's right to organize democratically and bargain collectively; fair levels of income and security for the farmer; protection of the people's inheritance in natural resources against waste and monopolistic exploitation; and a system of minimum wages and social insurance broad enough to maintain adequate standards of nutrition, education, medical care, and housing.

Many former New Dealers and several Democratic congressmen joined the ADA. The organization became an important force in the 1948 Democratic National Convention and spearheaded the successful drive for a vigorous civil rights plank. During the last few years of the Truman Administration it gave support to most of the President's program and supported Governor Stevenson for President in 1952. The ADA not only takes positions on legislative questions but commonly gives endorsements to and campaigns for political candidates.

INTEREST GROUPS AND LOCAL POLITICS

There is a tendency for the citizen and the student of politics to direct major attention to the great national panorama and to neglect careful observation of those groups operating in his neighborhood and town. Up to this point we have been preoccupied mainly with identifying the major interests which are organized on a national basis. Yet with very few exceptions the great national groups are coordinators and stimulators of action on the part of the local constituent societies. The locals have a life apart from the national and the national headquarters has a life apart from the locals. Constituent societies may take their cue from the national organization but find it necessary to modify, add, or drop certain objectives and techniques in order to be realistic and effective in their local communities. Certain county medical societies have been at variance with the American Medical Association, as have local American Legion posts with their national hierarchy. The mere study of the programs, strategies, and techniques of the national office is not invariably an accurate picture of the political behavior of all of its locals.

Perhaps the best illustration, and too often overlooked, of strictly local political interest groups is the hundreds of voters' leagues, citizens' associations, taxpayers' leagues, and community clubs. The major concern of many of them is to promote better government, lower taxes, civic responsibility, and education of the voter. Though differing little from private-interest associations in technique and in methods of exerting pressure, the civic societies generally have different ends, primarily the seeking of community betterment and the public interest rather than purely private objects. Greater emphasis is placed upon political reform by citizens' associations. Working for a county or city-manager plan, administrative reorganization, fighting corrupt political machines, and improvement of public personnel are common objectives of that group. At times there are organizations with a selfish motive which masquerade under the respectable label of "good government" or "taxpayers' leagues" while actually seeking special privileges or private favors.

It is easier to identify the types of citizens' associations than to define them, because their purposes and emphases show considerable variation.[30] Outstanding among the civic associations is the League of Women Voters, which has national, state, and local affiliates. Its members have no pecuniary or sentimental interests to protect, and the organization is remarkable in that it promotes the interest of its members in civic questions, is concerned with the promotion of good government, and conducts study groups on a large number of public issues, both national and local. Sincere and independent lawmakers express high regard for the League's educational program and for the issues it has championed and opposed. During elections the League is active in promoting voter registration, issuing data on candidates and referendums, and in sponsoring public forums for candidates. The American Association of University Women and the General Federation of Women's Clubs also take an interest in public affairs and express themselves officially on many issues; their programs, however, are concerned with social and philanthropic matters and not exclusively with government.

Another group of associations, operating as leagues or city clubs, is interested in good government and is especially tax-conscious. These groups often publish reports on candidates and make studies of current political and public issues of interest to the community. Taxpayers' leagues may be placed in a narrower category, since their interest is limited mostly to problems affecting the tax rate. Bureaus of municipal re-

---

[30] *The National Municipal Review* carries many illuminating articles on the achievements of civic organizations. The National Municipal League acts as a national headquarters for all such groups through the Federation of Citizens' Organizations. The president of the League, Richard L. Childs, has written an informative book on the activities of various civic groups, *Civic Victories* (New York: Harper & Brothers, 1950).

search, located in the larger American cities, are generally supported by large taxpayers.[31] While they are concerned with efficiency and economy and the improvement of the administration of municipal government, they also reflect the desire of their sponsors to bring about economies and keep the tax rate down.

There are a number of organizations which sponsor candidates and closely resemble municipal political parties, such as the Cincinnati Charter Committee and the Fusionists in New York. In many communities organizations of this type are active only at election time and are often effective in the absence of any competing political organization, especially where the political parties have withdrawn from nonpartisan elections.

Other organizations which have an incidental interest in and participate in local issues are various service clubs, local chambers of commerce, and institutes and associations engaged in adult education and citizenship training. These groups usually avoid any political action in elections. Finally, mention may be made of two nationally organized societies concentrating on a single political reform—the National Civil Service League,[32] and the Proportional Representation League.

Public opinion as expressed through citizens' associations cannot be said to be continually successful in terms of achievement. Time and time again good-government leagues have failed in their missions. Reasons for their lack of success are legion. The forces of opposition have been strong, well financed, and effectively organized; they include the so-called "politicians" commanding all or most of the party organization. Frequently selfish economic interests are on the same side, either openly or secretly. The civic association is apt to labor under the handicap of inadequate finances, lack of dynamic leadership, improper organization, and failure to coordinate and marshal the energies of reform and public-spirited groups in the community. Because of the dissimilarity in objectives, it is not easy to get proper coordination and support for a united front of civic groups on proposals and candidates. Civic interest dies out quickly and leaders of civic movements are the first to admit the difficulty of maintaining a sustained enthusiasm in the face of setbacks.

In spite of the many failures of citizens' movements, their ineffectiveness is too often overemphasized. The instances are numerous where increased efficiency in government has resulted from the tireless activities of good-government leagues. The Citizens' Union of New York and the

31 On these bureaus see N. N. Gill, *Municipal Research Bureaus* (Washington, D.C.: Public Affairs Press, 1944).

32 The League was formed in 1881. See Frank M. Stewart, *The National Civil Service Reform League: History, Activities, and Problems* (Austin, Tex.: University of Texas Press, 1929). The League conducted a crusade for the extension of the merit system and today seeks an expansion of the classified service where the system is adopted.

Municipal Voters' League of Chicago were formed prior to the present century and have had a long record of success. The former has a special legislative committee of civic leaders to analyze all measures introduced in the state legislature and makes known to legislative committees, through its agent, the organization's position. Biennially the Citizen's Union publishes the *Voters' Directory*, containing a map of all election districts in New York City, with biographies of each candidate running for every state, municipal, and national office. Nominees are rated as "unqualified," "qualified," "recommended," or "endorsed." This pamphlet is extremely helpful to the new and independent voters in a city of bewildering political complexity. Many other cities have leagues which engage in similar activities.

Certainly the least that can be credited to citizens' associations is that they offer to thousands, perhaps millions, of persons a chance to become familiar with neighborhood, village, and municipal problems and have provided the first clarion call for political reform. Their most effective role is that of a critic. As driving and liberalizing forces in the body politic and as a potential antidote to private-interest groups they are to be encouraged. Communities without vigorous citizens' associations are usually lacking in civic interest if not badly governed.

INTERESTS WITHOUT END

The miscellaneous private-interest groupings by no means end here. Students of the politics of interests might go on indefinitely in finding curious organizations and alignments, mostly of fleeting, but some of permanent, character. Depressions bring organized expression for new or old economic panaceas, and the single taxers plug away at their cause in good times and bad. It is scarcely a decade since pension movements exemplified by the Townsend Movement and "Thirty Dollars Every Thursday" made the front pages.[33] Fraternal societies, men's and women's clubs, and youth organizations are omnipresent. Young people's and women's auxiliaries of farm, labor, and other associations have become commonplace and all are becoming concerned with "who gets what, when, and how."

Books on pressure politics a generation ago devoted much attention to pro- and antiprohibition associations. At the time of the passage of the Eighteenth Amendment, the Anti-Saloon League was regarded as one of the most effective national pressure groups.[34] The temperance cause is furthered today by certain church groups and the Woman's Christian

[33] See A. Holtzman, "Analysis of Old-age Politics in the United States," *Journal of Gerontology*, Vol. 9 (1954), pp. 56–66.

[34] See Peter Odegard, *Pressure Politics: The Story of the Anti-Saloon League* (New York: Columbia University Press, 1928).

Temperance Union. Major attention is given to pressing for "dry-by-local-option" laws and to educational programs dealing with the deleterious effect of alcoholic beverages. These societies also fight any liberalization of state liquor laws.

Antivivisectionists are organized to seek measures restricting the use of animals for purposes of experimentation in medical schools. The Hearst newspapers have aided this crusade and a New York state legislator complained that the antivivisectionists were as "pestiferous and stubborn as any group representing a large economic interest." State legislatures also feel the pressures of pro- and antibirth control societies and of a host of reformist groups.

Over a century ago Alexis de Tocqueville included a chapter in *Democracy in America* entitled "Of the Use Which the Americans Make of Public Associations in Civil Life." [35] He wrote:

Americans, of all ages, all conditions, and all dispositions, constantly form associations. They have not only commercial and manufacturing companies, in which all take part, but associations of a thousand other kinds, religious, moral, serious, futile, general or restricted, enormous or diminutive. The Americans make associations to give entertainments, to found seminaries, to build inns, to construct churches, to diffuse books, to send missionaries to Antipodes; in this manner they found hospitals, prisons, and schools. If it is proposed to inculcate some truth or to foster some feeling by the encouragement of a great example, they form a society. Wherever at the head of some new undertaking you see the government in France, or a new man of rank in England, in the United States you will be sure to find an association.

The ensuing decades of American history provide mountains of evidence on the validity of this shrewd observation. Of one thing the individual can be certain: if he decides which of his concerns is paramount, he will find an organization somewhere to champion it. As an old adage has it, "You pays your money and you takes your choice."

SELECTED REFERENCES

A few of the useful works on melting-pot, racial, and moralist groups are Donald Strong, *Organized Anti-Semitism in America* (1941); Emerson H. Loucks, *The Ku Klux Klan in Pennsylvania: A Study in Nativism* (1936); C. J. Culp, *The German-Americans in Politics* (1939); R. L. Jack, *History of the National Association for the Advancement of Colored People* (1943); N. F. Nowlin, *The Negro in American National Politics* (1931); Peter H. Odegard, *Pressure Politics: The Story of the Anti-Saloon League* (1928); F. J. Brown and J. S. Roucek, *One America* (1945); J. H. Franklin, *From Slavery to Freedom* (1947); H. L. Moon, *Balance of Power: The Negro Vote* (1948); T. C. Kesselman, *The Social Politics of the FEPC: A Study in Reform Pressure Movements* (1948); E. L. Tatum, *The Changed Political Thought of the Negro* (1951).

35 Vol. 2, p. 106. By permission of Phillips Bradley, editor, and Alfred A. Knopf, Inc., publishers.

Some of the books on veterans' groups are Marcus Duffield, *King Legion* (1931); William Gellerman, *The American Legion as Educator* (1938); Dorothy Culp, *The American Legion: A Study in Pressure Politics* (Ph.D. dissertation, University of Chicago, 1939); R. A. Jones, *A History of the American Legion* (1946); Justin Gray, *The Inside Story of the American Legion* (1948); M. R. Dearing, *Veterans in Politics: The Story of the G.A.R.* (1952).

Periodical literature on peace, pacifist, and foreign policy movements is abundant. Among the better references are Merle E. Curti, *Peace or War; The American Struggle, 1636–1936* (1936); Mary H. Jones, *Swords into Ploughshares* (1937); Walter A. Linn, *False Prophets of Peace* (1939); Mary A. Matthews, *The Peace Movement* (1940); Harold Lavine and James Wechsler, *War Propaganda and the United States* (1940); Walter Johnson, *The Battle against Isolation* (1944); T. S. Cole, *America First: The Battle against Intervention, 1940–1941* (1953).

The hearings and reports of the United States House of Representatives Committee on Un-American Activities from 1938 to date contain many interesting aspects on so-called "fascist" and "Communist" organizations.

Churches publish much information on their political interests and political action programs. One of the best all-round analyses is L. E. Ebersole, *Church Lobbying in the Nation's Capital* (1951); an earlier work is Stanley High, *The Church in Politics* (1930) ; see also "Organized Religion in the United States," *The Annals of the American Academy of Political and Social Science*, March, 1948.

CHAPTER 9

Influencing Government

To say that private men have nothing to do with government is to say that private men have nothing to do with their own happiness or misery; that people ought not to concern themselves whether they be naked or clothed, fed or starved, deceived or instructed, protected or destroyed.

—CATO

To a constantly increasing extent American politics is the politics of organized groups. Individuals more and more organize into groups, and the power and influence of all sorts of associations in the United States and the ineffectiveness of unorganized interest are little short of astonishing. Group bargaining for economic, political, or social power and influence is on the increase. In this process individuals are shifting from one group to another; new associations are born while old ones expire or regroup. Organizations assuming greater political significance are those possessing a higher degree of cohesiveness, internal discipline, and financial resources. The preceding chapters have indicated the organization, objectives, and operation of the more important interest groups seeking legislative ends. Several of the tactics and methods peculiar to certain groups have been noted. At this point it may be helpful to give a general summary of the ways by which political interest organizations try to press their demands on the agencies of government and why the associations are able to exert the influence they do.

The process by which public policy in the United States is developed is diffused. Interest groups, political parties, legislators, administrators, and judges all participate in formulating programs. This sometimes makes for a complicated, confused, and unneat picture. But this fragmentation gives organized interests highly diverse opportunities to influence policy. They can and do bring their cases to the political parties, the legislatures, the executives, and sometimes to the courts. The decentralization incident to federalism results in many policies being evolved on the state and local as well as the national levels and increases the channels through which influence may be directed. If an interest group fails to obtain its demands from the government, it can in many states sponsor an initiative or constitutional amendment or demand a referendum to realize them. The decentralized and atomized way by which policy is developed and administered and the comparatively weak party organiza-

196

tion in Congress account in part for the influence of private-interest groups on government.

The techniques of lobbyists show infinite variation and ingeniousness. The direction of their energies undergoes modification with changed conditions; at one time expediency dictates that major efforts be directed toward a committee chairman, at other times toward a department head, the Chief Executive, party chairman, or a bureaucrat. A list of major techniques and methods of interest would start with the mobilization of the membership and by a process, democratic or not, of having an "official" policy of the organization adopted. From this, agents for the group will resort to (1) stimulating grass-roots pressure on the various branches of the government; (2) meeting with legislators and administrators; (3) making use of legislative committees; (4) logrolling and effecting alliances with and mutual assistance of other groups; (5) influencing the election of friends and enemies; (6) seeking the intervention of the courts if possible. Some detailed attention may be given to these techniques.

ACCESS TO THE LEGISLATURE

Some writers have noted that a bill must go through 22 steps in order to become a law. Potentially this offers 22 stages at which opponents have the opportunity to defeat or to emasculate the proposal. There are ways outside the halls of the legislature by which interested parties attempt to influence the course of a bill. One of these is popularly known as the "plush-horse" or social lobby. Washington and the various state capitals are highly social places, and providing dinners, stag parties, cocktail parties, and other forms of social entertainment affords the opportunity for both legislator and agent to meet. It remains a moot point whether there is a line between social activity for its own sake and entertainment designed to influence the lawmaker's opinion. Social lobbying is used less than formerly but it has by no means disappeared. Crawford [1] reports how the motion-picture industry provided a special car for senators to travel to the Kentucky Derby, all expenses paid, as guests of the industry. Investigations from time to time turn up lavish parties where prominent lawmakers and administrators are guests of a group known to have legislative objectives. But parties are much less frequently attended than in the past and many hostesses and lobbyists complain that legislators shun these social affairs.

Much was made in earlier chapters of the growing realization on the part of the interest groups of the value of winning the support of public opinion for certain pieces of legislation. The use of the press, radio, television, and even the film, and the hiring of public-relations experts to

[1] Kenneth Crawford, *The Pressure Boys* (New York: Julian Messner, Inc., Publishers, 1939), Chap. 6.

secure public support or disapproval for legislation form one of the outstanding developments of this century. Similarly, the forming of a committee with a high-sounding title is a part of the technique of getting public support. As Joseph G. ("Uncle Joe") Cannon, Speaker of the House from 1903 to 1911, shrewdly observed:

The way to secure legislation and escape all suspicion of ulterior motive is to form an association and proclaim its object as moral. The next step is to organize a committee of highly respectable men and women to act as figureheads and have the actual work done by paid agents who profess great interest in their work but whose real interest is in their salaries.

Grass-roots Pressure. One of the comparatively new forms of bringing pressure upon legislators is "pressing the button" which brings forth an avalanche of letters, cards, wires, and phone calls from the faithful back home. Rank-and-file members are given the names and addresses of committee heads, key lawmakers, or other officials, together with instructions or a prepared communication pleading the cause. This is to give the appearance of a grass-roots request or protest. Collecting signatures on petitions and sending them en masse to the same officials is a variation of the same idea. Of this high-pressure barrage of communications Congressman Robert Luce commented, "The old-time lobbyist is gone, but the new brand, though more respectable, has perhaps a more damaging effect by working on the timidity of lawmakers rather than on their cupidity." Since Mr. Luce's observation, the public utilities, labor unions, and other groups have pushed these devices almost beyond the point of effectiveness. These simulated popular uprisings no longer deceive the discriminating public official.

A highly effective technique, which usually escapes public attention because it is done without undue commotion, is the applying of pressure through friends and associates of the congressman in his own district. This is easily done where the national organization has branch offices that can approach persons of influence back home and persuade them to see the lawmaker. The technique of the railroad lobby, for example, as developed by the officials of the Association of American Railroads, relies not so much on mass appeal as on prominent persons in the legislator's district. A letter from its onetime vice-president to the general counsel said in part: [2]

All of us have long recognized that the only effective way to influence congressional action is to convince the influential men in each congressional district that the public interest and the interest of the railroads coincide.

[2] *Congressional Record,* May 8, 1947 (daily edition), pp. A2294–A2295. For a comprehensive and interesting study of the railroad and transportation lobby and its tac-

I have the impression that most of the congressmen, particularly those living in the smaller states and in rural districts, depend for support upon a comparatively few men in each county in their respective districts. If we could reach the men upon whom a congressman depends for advice and assistance in his political campaign, we could go far toward having the problem solved.

I have visualized a type of organization with which we could assemble here in Washington information as to who are the influential men in each congressional district. . . .

We could then be in a position to suggest to railroad officers, local attorneys, railroad security owners, and others with whom they might discuss these matters, so that our influence would be felt. . . . We could call upon a hundred of his influential constituents in his congressional district and persuade those persons to write or wire him their really sincere convictions on the question.

This "influential man" theory of the railroads has many manifestations. Sometimes those approached are the donors to a congressman's campaign fund. Often they are the prominent party officials who are influential with the men who sit in the legislature.

The threat of defeating his reelection is always a potential weapon to hold over the head of the legislator. At a conference of commanders and adjutants a lobbyist for a veterans' organization [3] with remarkable candor said:

We're strong, but a lot of the new [Congress] men don't know it yet. It's necessary to impress them. That's where you fellas come in. . . . Find out for me the attitude of your new Congressman, don't just wire me that "He's all right." I want to know if he's all right where *we*'re concerned. If you're not sure about him, tell me and I'll have a talk with him. If you hear from me after I see him, I expect you to put the fear of God in him. *From back home.* That's where he gets his votes.

I'm a realist about legislation and I know he's worried about . . . his votes. And if he doesn't like Washington society, his wife does. After you've put the heat on a man I always know, because he always comes to me and complains about it.

Legislative Contacts. A traditional but nevertheless effective method of influencing legislation consists in securing interviews with legislators, executives, and administrators in their offices or in more socially amenable surroundings. Even better may be a meeting with a state or county delegation in Congress or the state legislature respectively. Sometimes these meetings cut across state lines and embrace a conference with the "silver," "farm," "cotton," or other lawmakers. Personal friendships with legisla-

---

tics see John G. Shott, *The Railroad Monopoly* (Washington: Public Affairs Institute, 1950).

[3] Bill Mauldin, "Poppa Knows Best," *Atlantic Monthly*, Vol. 179 (1947), p. 31. This article presents a critical analysis of the American Legion lobby.

tors and administrators are sought and are always of value. For this reason former legislators are valuable persons to have on the organization
payroll.

In looking at interest group–legislator relationships many persons overlook the fact that many representatives and senators are "joiners" and
members of groups which have legislative objectives. In the Eightieth
Congress, 195 representatives and 44 senators were members of the American Legion, which also claimed the membership of the President, five
Cabinet secretaries, three Supreme Court justices, and the Attorney General. Although similar statistics are not available for membership in other
groups, a brief reading of biographies of legislators will indicate that a
large number have group affiliations.

Legislators are not necessarily neutral persons, weighing the merits of
issues which come before them, and many of them are actively identified
with the lobby groups that appear before the legislature. This is not to
maintain, however, that lawmakers consider it their duty to give prior
consideration to the demands of the organizations of which they are members. But lobbyists work through the members of the legislature who are
closely associated with their group. The fact that many political groups
have persons sitting in the legislature means that potentially, at least,
their demands will have the opportunity to be heard and will receive a
sympathetic understanding. Many state governors have decried the "legislator-lobbyist" character of some of those who sit in the assembly. Numerous state lawmakers are counsels for groups; still others look forward to
future positions of this type in their postlegislative careers.

Because of the crucial importance of the committee stage in the legislative process, the greatest effort is expended here. Attempts are made
to influence the composition of the committees in order to secure a committee friendly to proposals sponsored by the group. For many years the
dairy interests successfully resisted efforts to lift the restrictions on the
sale of colored margarine by getting such measures referred to the agricultural committees which were usually dominated by men friendly to
the dairy farmer.

Groups which are able to put their case before the chairman of the
committee and gain his support have accomplished a most important
step, for the chairman has enormous power over a bill. It is he who normally assigns time to witnesses during the public hearings, conducts the
hearings, and often plays a major role in the line of questioning. He
holds great power in the executive sessions of the committee and may
have considerable influence on amending or rewriting the measure and
reporting a bill out for consideration.

Perhaps the most indispensable of lobbying techniques is the cultiva-
tion of personal friendships with legislators so that the organization has

friends in court who can introduce its representatives to fellow legislators and committee chairmen, and who are potential introducers of bills and amendments. The privilege of sending franked or post-free mail which is enjoyed by public officials may be helpful to the group. An official of the Committee for Constitutional Government admitted that 10 million pieces of its literature were franked in less than four years, saving the group $300,000 in postage.[4]

Special investigating committees often have the backing of certain interest groups and the opposition of others. The Buchanan Committee of the House of Representatives in 1949 and 1950 exposed activities of opponents of public housing and brought upon itself the wrath of the real-estate interests and the approbation of labor unions. Political organizations are quick to publish materials in their journals from investigating bodies which reflect unfavorably on an opposing interest group. Members are urged by their leaders to telegraph support for continuance or discontinuance of an investigating committee on the basis of evaluation of the committee's usefulness to the group's cause. Many conservatively oriented organizations have pressured Congress to continue the House Committee on Un-American Activities while liberals have called for its abolition.

Alliances and Combinations. In each legislative stage, from the initial drafting of a bill until it is signed or vetoed by the Chief Executive, interest groups seek to enlist the support of other groups and to form a united front. The railroad industry makes use of civic organizations and more particularly chambers of commerce, boards of trade, shippers, and business luncheon clubs.[5] The Association of American Railroads prepared bills and secured the help of chambers of commerce in getting them introduced. In one of the best studies of alliances, Schattschneider has shown how the high-tariff forces worked for one another to put over the high-protectionist program of the Hawley-Smoot bill.[6] In the battle over Federal maternal health legislation, the welding together of 30 groups into a "baby bloc" helped very much to secure its passage. Farmer and business groups in alliance likewise helped to kill price control.

The Employment Act of 1946 was given great support by a broad alliance including labor unions, the National Association for the Advancement of Colored People, the American Veterans Committee, the Farmers Union, and the Lawyers Guild. The process of accommodation and working together is shown over and over again in rivers and harbors improvements, where legislators from different areas support each other's projects.

[4] *The New York Times,* June 29, 1950.
[5] On this technique see Shott, *op. cit.,* Chap. 8.
[6] *Politics, Pressures, and the Tariff* (New York: Prentice-Hall, Inc., 1935).

Although this is called "logrolling," it is a process of accommodating and equating group demands.

The billboard lobby offers a case in alliances on the state level. It is present in every state but seldom operates as a single organization. Rather, it is a network of companies, trade organizations, and prominent individual executives and frequently lines up with brewers and oil companies. One legislator in a study of the outdoor-advertising lobby points out that the "industry's overlords may use one group to spearhead their drive in a certain state and a completely differing outfit in a neighboring state." [7] In carrying on its work, the billboard lobby was found creating "dummy highway property organizations and bogus farmers' and workers' leagues capable of flooding legislators with thousands of letters of protest from these groups."

THE INFLUENCE OF LOBBYISTS

Expenditures. When interest groups decide to take their case to the government, representation is made by officials of the organization or by hired professional lobbyists who are persons of ability and intelligence with the know-how of winning friends and influencing people. Adaptable and gifted with the social graces, the lobbyists can move in any circle required. The fraternity of professionals is often composed of former legislators and public officials who hire themselves out to one or more organizations. A story persists that one individual received a retainer of $75,000 annually on behalf of the Anti-Saloon League, and after the adoption of the Eighteenth Amendment, was employed by antiprohibition forces for a similar fee. One wonders if this story is as apocryphal as it sounds, for Senator George Norris reported the career of one enterprising newspaperman, turned lobbyist and public-relations expert, as simultaneously "getting $500 a month from the Standard Oil Company of New Jersey, $500 a month from the Standard Oil Company of Indiana, $700 a month from the Atlantic Refining Company, $400 a month from the Freeport Sulphur Company, and $500 a month from the General Electric Company." [8] The professional lobbyist soon becomes a fixture and is easily identified as often working both sides of the street for mercenary purposes. It would seem, therefore, that the opinions of the sincere advocates and members of a pressure interest would be more highly respected by the public official, though this does not necessarily apply to editorial and publication work. Fabulous salaries for lobbyists [9] appear

[7] See Thomas C. Desmond, "The Billboard Lobby," *American Mercury*, Vol. 65 (1947), p. 347. This article by a New York state senator is one of the most candid accounts of the power and tactics of the billboard lobby.

[8] *Congressional Record*, Vol. 60, Part 2, pp. 1877–1878.

[9] A Washington employee of the NAM received $18,000, and an agent of the St. Lawrence Project Conference, $36,000. Many receive handsome salaries as heads of

to be the exception rather than the rule, but talented publicists can command a fair price for their services for groups whose budgets for public relations run high. Many Washington newspapermen believe the salary and expense accounts as reported are absurdly low. The Buchanan Committee, which studied lobbying from 1946 to 1950, found several lobbyists on a "contingent fee" basis. One lobbyist received a $10,000 annual salary, $15,000 for expenses, and was to receive an additional $25,000 whenever a bill was passed to repeal the cabaret tax.[10]

Some fair-sized sums of money are spent, probably an average of $8 million annually, by those registered as attempting to influence Congress. In the first six months of 1947, the American Federation of Labor spent $819,000 in an effort to defeat the Taft-Hartley bill. In the first six months of 1948 the National Physicians Committee for the Extension of Medical Services spent $240,000 in its campaign against national health insurance and the Committee for Constitutional Government spent a similar sum on its objectives.[11] Among the other large spenders were the Citizens Committee on Displaced Persons, the electric companies, the margarine manufacturers, and real-estate associations. Not all of these amounts are expended directly in Washington; some include sums for public relations and are not separated from legislative expenses.

Some huge sums of money are spent on the state level, as evidenced in the testimony of Arthur Samish, liquor lobbyist in California. When placed on trial, he testified that the California Brewers Institute "placed up to $150,000 in a political fund to influence legislation . . . and that the liquor interests spent $750,000 in an advertising campaign to confuse voters on the local option referendum the last time the issue came before the voters." [12] The extent to which there is a correlation between the

---

organizations but indicate that only a fraction of their time is given to lobbying. The president of the National Association of Electric Companies receives $65,000 annually, but only one-fourth of his time is credited as spent on attempting to influence legislation. Two lobbyists hired by the Long Beach, Calif., Harbor Commission received collectively $65,000 a year to lobby for giving state title to the submerged coastal lands (*The New York Times*, Dec. 18, 1952). The House Select Committee on Lobbying Activities, 81st Congress, published a dozen hearings and reports on lobbying. On identification of lobbying organizations and their agents see the two documents of the committee published in 1950: *Lobby Index, 1946–1949*, and W. B. Graves, *Administration of the Lobby Registration Provision of the Legislative Reorganization Act of 1946*. See also Karl Schriftgiesser, *The Lobbyists* (Boston: Little, Brown & Company, 1951). The *Congressional Quarterly Weekly Reports* contain materials on newly registered lobbyists.

[10] See Part 3, *Contingent Fee Lobbying*, of the hearings of the House Select Committee on Lobbying Activities, May 18, 1950.

[11] See Graves, *op. cit.*, pp. 22–23.

[12] *The Christian Science Monitor*, Nov. 27, 1953. In the State of New York lobbyists filed expenses of $233,000 in the 1953 legislative session; see *The New York Times*, May 22, 1953.

amount spent for influence and the results obtained is indeterminable. But the fact remains that the huge financial outlays by some groups are bound to give them certain advantages in publicity if nothing else over organizations of small monetary means.

Influence. The influence of private groups in legislative matters remains a moot point and evidence may be cited for any viewpoint. On one occasion President William Green of the American Federation of Labor requested Congressman Cannon to vote for a food subsidy bill. Cannon was reported as saying, "I have always followed Mr. Green on labor bills. But this is not a labor bill. This is a farm bill. On this bill I follow the farm leaders." [13] Not all legislators are so candid but they "highly regard" the viewpoint of an interest organization on a bill especially pertaining to its economic or social segment. It is significant that many speeches on the floor of Congress against continuation of price control in 1946 showed a strong undertone of the NAM's arguments and, public-opinion polls and labor pressures notwithstanding, Congress continued price control in a form little more than a shadow of its former self.

Stuart Chase [14] relates this story of journalist Richard L. Neuberger, shortly after the latter was elected to the Oregon legislature:

He was waited on by a group of earnest women who wanted a law passed to restrain billboards on highways. The bill made sense to Mr. Neuberger and he endorsed it. . . . It was clearly in the public interest.

Poor innocent! The advertisers' lobby began to teach him the facts of life. Here were no fine questions of public safety and order, but a vested interest threatened with pecuniary loss. The next thing Mr. Neuberger knew, the lobby had got the Signpainters' Union to denounce the measure and call him an "enemy of labor." This is a fearsome charge to levy against any legislator. Then came a torrent of letters from "widows and orphans" who would starve if rents from the beneficent billboard companies were cut off. Then telegrams rained in, and editorials in the papers.

The legislature ran to cover, and the bill was quashed. Mr. Neuberger believes that a large majority of the citizens of Oregon would support it, but citizens are not organized, and the lobby gets there fustest with the mostest.

This story can be duplicated with different issues in the experience of any number of seasoned as well as neophyte legislators.

If one is to believe the claims of the groups themselves when seeking new members, virtually all major pieces of legislation are put through by pressure tactics. The Chamber of Commerce of the United States points with pride to the "achievement" in putting through the Budget and Accounting Act and a sizable Bureau of Foreign and Domestic Commerce.

---

[13] See editorial, *New York Herald Tribune,* Nov. 25, 1943.

[14] *Democracy under Pressure* (New York: The Twentieth Century Fund, Inc., 1945), pp. 21–22; see also Desmond, *op. cit.*

The American Legion in its recruitment program underlines the securing of the bonus and the Veterans Administration. In length of legislative achievements claimed, the American Farm Bureau Federation probably earns first prize.

However, a number of the asserted legislative successes of associations belong in the category in which Mark Twain once placed reports of his death—as highly exaggerated. Relatively few of the thousands of laws and executive orders, or the defeat of others, are traceable to the singular efforts of one organization, especially if the policy is of any widespread public importance. Passage or defeat is more likely to be the result of a combination of groups than of a single organization. Professional associations, the League of Women Voters, and veterans' groups may work with one of the large organized occupational federations on one bill and join with another federation in opposition on still another.

The claims of effectiveness and influence of pressure organizations are publicly and irately denied by any number of public servants. Our history is fortunately full of instances of men who have maintained a long and honorable record of independence and adherence to deep-seated principles; of men who have gone along with interest groups when they championed measures seemingly in the greater interest and have fought them when they appeared actuated from narrow, selfish motives. Certainly most of the nation's lawmakers are sincere, conscientious, and hard working and as a rule seldom bow to the demands of a specific organization, especially if the demands are out of harmony with the known will of the majority of constituents. If a combination of pressure groups, however, seems to represent the will of a majority of their constituents, then the legislators feel compelled to give serious consideration to the demand, for political as well as other reasons. This suggests the need for protecting the public official from harassment by selfish associations, at the same time giving him information on the real objectives and the composition of the association making demands.

Some of the more honest leaders and publicity agents will candidly admit off the record a lack of influence on certain policies about which they made sound and fury. They will go further to confess that some of the verbal battles and torrents of words were motivated in part by a desire to impress their own membership with how hard they were working to promote the organization's desires. One trade association agent baldly admitted, "Sometimes we have to raise a little hell, kick up some dust, and exaggerate some things in order to keep the organization going. The members like to see us in fights once in a while, you know." [15] In rival unions, for example, the Amalgamated Clothing Workers and the Inter-

[15] Told to the author during an interview.

national Ladies' Garment Workers, the rank and file have expected their respective heads to have quarrels with one another. Part of the science of raising money, both in private organizations and in political parties, includes sensational emphasis, exaggerated claims, playing up fears, and the crying of "wolf."

LOBBYING LAWS

The rise of new organizations during the New Deal and the accelerated tempo of pressure politics during and after World War II revived public consciousness of the problem. Curiously, it was not these activities so much as their combination with other fortuitous circumstances which resulted in the enactment of a general lobbying law. In 1935 and 1936 the lobbyists for the public-utility holding companies and the ship-builders and operators were required to register. The activities of foreign agents a short time later (1938) came under regulation through the For-eign Agents Registration Act. Much attention was given during World War II to the need for a long overdue thorough reorganization of Con-gress itself. The Joint Committee on the Organization of Congress recom-mended the registration of organized groups and their agents. Finally in August, 1946, the Legislative Reorganization Act was passed. Unno-ticed by many in the numerous provisions of this act was Title III, desig-nated as the Regulation of Lobbying Act.[16] After 157 years, the national government finally in an unobtrusive fashion recognized by legal sanction the existence of the lobby and took steps to provide identification of those engaged in it! It marked the first step toward providing compre-hensive data on the persons and forces seeking to influence legislation.

Under the law every person, partnership, committee, association, cor-poration, or other "group of persons" soliciting or receiving contributions to be used *principally to aid* in the passage or defeat of any legislation in Congress must register with the Clerk of the House of Representatives and the Secretary of the Senate. A statement is to be filed including (1) all contributions received, (2) the names and addresses of all persons mak-ing a contribution of $500 or over, (3) all expenditures made by the or-ganization or person, and (4) the name and address of every person to whom the expenditure is made together with the date. Receipted bills for every expenditure exceeding $10 are to be retained for two years from the date of filing, and receipts for contributions over $500 are also to be preserved. Statements are to be filed quarterly, with a cumulative report for the calendar year. Records filed are open to the public; some

16 Public Law 601, Chap. 753, 79th Cong., 2d Sess. On the provisions, interpretations, and weaknesses of the law see Belle Zeller, "The Federal Regulation of Lobbying Act," *The American Political Science Review*, Vol. 42 (1948), pp. 239–271; see also Schrift-giesser, *op. cit.*

of the data are published four times a year in the *Congressional Record*. Persons merely appearing before a committee of Congress on behalf of or in opposition to legislation, public officials acting in an official capacity, newspaper owners and employees acting in the regular course of business, and party committees are exempt from the provisions of the Act.

Today 35 states regulate lobbying in one way or another; the remainder merely rely on general laws or corrupt-practices legislation.[17] In 25 states the registration of legislative agents and counsels employed in such capacity for compensation is obligatory. Among the information required is the name and address of the agent, by whom employed, date and duration of employment, and special legislative objects. Only 17 states require the filing of statements of expenses incurred in the promotion of legislation. Appearance on the floor of the legislature and bribery are usually prohibited. Concisely, the major objects of miscalled "antilobbying" laws are to disclose the identity of agents and their employers, together with the measures they are sponsoring or opposing, to do away with bribery, and to make available to the public a knowledge of expenditures incurred. The laws established the principle that the public has a right to know the identity of paid lobbyists.

Many of the purposes of lobby regulation go unfulfilled. Enforcement is not strict in most states and there seems little demand for conscientious administration. Many persons fail to file their expense accounts. On certain occasions data gathered under state laws find their way into the press if there is real news value involved but there is always a question of just what the data mean and show. The Federal law, however, provides more up-to-date information and the data sometimes appear in the newspapers.

The Federal law contains many ambiguities and contradictions. One is the application only to those whose purpose is *principally to aid* in the passage or defeat of legislation. This exempts many powerful organizations or their agents from making full disclosures. It is difficult to separate the legislative from the nonlegislative budgets of most organizations. The registered lobbyists are usually subordinate staff members and the Justice Department has told associations that their registration alone does not constitute complete compliance with the law. The National Association of Manufacturers challenged the constitutionality of the lobbying law and contended that, even if constitutional, its provisions did not apply to the NAM because it was not an organization whose "principal pur-

[17] On state laws see Belle Zeller, "State Regulation of Lobbying," in *The Book of the States, 1948–49*, pp. 124–130; and *State Regulation of Lobbying* (Chicago: Council of State Governments, 1951, mimeographed).

pose" was to influence Federal legislation. A lower Federal court decided in 1952 that Secs. 303–307 were invalid because they were too vague "to constitute an ascertainable standard of guilt" as required by due process.[18] The court held that these sections did not adequately describe the grounds for prosecution. The United States Supreme Court in 1954 upheld the constitutionality of the key registration section of the law but declined to rule on its penalty provisions. In this decision the Court took the view that the registration section applies only to persons who solicit, collect, or receive money or other things of value for purposes of influencing legislation. Other litigation, now in the courts, may serve to clarify the applicability and penalty sections.

INTEREST GROUPS AND ADMINISTRATION

Administration and Policy Determination. Very gradually the general public is coming to see that notwithstanding what is often narrowly construed in theory as separation of powers, the administrative branch of the government does far more than faithfully execute the laws. The President and the governors are leaders of their parties and possess methods of influencing the lawmakers. Access to the popularly elected executives therefore provides at least indirect access to the legislature.

Interest groups are vitally concerned with administration because administrators are engaged in the process of making decisions. Congress lays down broad policies and programs, leaving to the administrators the function of interpreting and implementing them by means of decisions and policies. The independent regulatory commissions enjoy an independent status and Congress passes to them a quasi-legislative function. Congress tells the Federal Communications Commission to see that American radio broadcasting operates in the "public interest, convenience, and necessity." To the FCC is given the job of examining applications for new licenses and renewal of old ones in light of the public convenience, interest, and necessity. This has called for making many unpopular decisions with certain interests and minorities, such as quiz programs essentially based on lotteries, rulings on permitting Communists and agnostics access to the air waves, acceptance of liquor advertising, and allocation of time for campaign speeches. It becomes the function of the Interstate Commerce Commission not only to see that rates are just and reasonable but in effect to develop a transportation policy.

Often the legislative mandate from Congress is vague and undefined. For example, the Federal Trade Commission was called upon by statute to eliminate "unfair methods of competition." There was no degree of

---

[18] 103 F. Supp. 510. For a summary analysis of this litigation see the NAM law department memorandum of Jan. 28, 1953.

unanimity in Congress as to what this meant. Over the years the FTC has had to develop its policy in a context of interests which wanted to protect the *status quo* in trade practices or which wanted the elimination of certain of their competitors' practices. The FTC and FCC often find themselves in a defensive position both in and out of Congress.

It is sometimes suggested that the legislative process is one of crystalliz-ing a policy into a legal standard which can be applied and that the administrative process is the application of public policy. However true this may be, it must be added that the end product coming out of the legislature is to a considerable extent the values imposed by interest groups. The legislature makes compromises in the demands of the inter-ests and in so doing may make the law imprecise if not contradictory. This often leaves policy questions to be decided and clarified by the ad-ministrative agencies.

There are two major types of administrative action—coercive and non-coercive. The former involves the use of compulsory powers, imposing restrictions, and requiring licenses. Naturally the affected interests try to influence the use and degree of coercion. The obtaining of permits in order to engage in certain activity such as burning fires, outdoor wiring, and Sunday closings has often gone by default through lack of enforce-ment.

In recent years the noncoercive functions have vastly increased in scope. Public education, veterans' services, street repair, welfare, fire protection, and social-security services, to mention only a few, affect millions of per-sons organized and unorganized. Pressures by citizens' associations have resulted in increased appropriations for parks, better streets, changed bus schedules, and increased police protection. The Veterans Administration is created to serve a special group and for the most part is engaged in dispensing services and benefits. The U.S. Department of Agriculture has huge sums to appropriate for noncoercive as well as for regulatory purposes. The "welfare state" is at heart an issue of how far and in what ways the government will serve various interests within the society.

Relationships. After a law is passed, a chain of intimate relationships is developed between the administering agency and interest groups. The methods of access to administration vary from highly informal ones to those carrying legal sanction. The relationships are often more or less opportunistic and fluid but they remain continuous so long as the au-thority administers a law of interest to the group. Contact between the bureaucracy and the group becomes semipermanent in contrast with the often fleeting relationship between the private organization and the con-gressman. The major methods by which groups gain access to the policy determination process in the administration are (1) conferences and meet-ings, (2) advisory committees, (3) furnishing of administrative personnel,

(4) delegation and devolution of authority to interest groups, (5) lay participation in law enforcement.[19]

Scores of conferences between representatives of private groups and of the government take place every year. Some are regularly scheduled events, others are called as the occasion demands. These grow out of the recognition of the representative function of administration and the need for mutual understanding between interest groups and agencies in executing laws. In turn, the interest groups quite generally invite public officials to attend their annual conventions and to participate in round-table discussions. The head of the Veterans Administration and the Secretaries of Agriculture, Commerce, and Labor are almost invariably invited to the annual conventions of the American Legion, American Farm Bureau Federation, Chamber of Commerce, and the Congress of Industrial Organizations respectively.

The value of the conferences, educational campaigns, and demonstrations lies in their two-way influence. Public officials become familiar with the desires and wishes for action from those persons and groups directly affected. Round-table techniques help to focus attention on the differences, on the areas of agreement, and on the possibilities of compromise on the different points of view. In the conference room the government's attitude toward a problem, information on the feasibility of certain types of action, and the need for support from the interest groups are presented in a more or less informal face-to-face manner.

Methods of Formalized Recognition. One of the most important ways by which interest groups gain access to administrative agencies is through advisory committees. Many if not most Federal agencies provide in their procedures for such committees; in some cases the law itself provides for their creation. These committees are composed of spokesmen or representatives from the various parties-in-interest and have virtually built themselves into the government. The Forest Service consults with advisory boards representing local, state, farm, and livestock associations. State governments have numerous advisory bodies which enjoy legal or quasilegal status. City-planning commissions are frequently supplemented by advisory committees composed of realty interests and racial minorities, as well as of the large occupational interests.

Some of the most significant experiments with advisory committees have occurred during wartime and in emergencies. Price control, war

19 Among the numerous works dealing with relationships between interest groups and administration are Avery Leiserson, "Interest Groups in Administration," in Fritz Marx (ed.), *Elements of Public Administration* (New York: Prentice-Hall, Inc., 1946), Chap. 14, *Administrative Regulation: A Study in Representation of Interests* (Chicago: University of Chicago Press, 1942); C. H. Monsees, *Industry-Government Cooperation: A Study of the Participation of Advisory Committees in Public Administration* (Washington, D.C.: Public Affairs Press, 1944).

mobilization and reconversion bodies included representatives of labor, management, consumers, and other groups. The Office of War Mobilization and Reconversion provided for an advisory board of 12 members, three each from agriculture, business, labor, and the general public.

The advisory committee and group consultation system has implications and problems too involved for extended treatment here. It may be noted that these committees offer the groups whose spokesmen are selected as members a chance to present their viewpoint directly to administrators. To groups not having a representative on the committee there is some denial of access which, theoretically at least, raises a question of fair play and also as to who is entitled to representation. For the administration, advisory committees provide a means of obtaining technical knowledge possessed by certain groups. They can serve something of the same purpose as a legislative committee hearing by helping to identify those forces which appear favorable as well as those opposed to a proposed administrative policy decision. They can, says Truman, "minimize both by modification of the projected policy and by placing groups under some obligation to defend or at least not to oppose policies that they have had some share in setting. Finally, under skillful leadership the advisory committee can be a means of inducing the represented groups to run interference for the agency both in the legislature and with the remainder of its public." [20]

Just as interest groups attempt to influence the personnel on legislative committees and their staffs, so they attempt to influence certain appointments in executive agencies. At times they formally or informally furnish the personnel for certain agencies. In the field of agriculture, farm groups have provided members for local committees and even the county agents. Tripartite boards have been extensively used in industrial disputes where labor and management furnish members for their representation on boards, as exemplified in the National War Labor Board. In state administrations there are many boards and commissions composed in part of representatives of private groups.

Another type of formalized recognition of group interests is that of devolving upon a group the responsibility for administering or carrying out a function of government. A striking illustration is provided in the National Industrial Recovery Act, which devolved upon trade associations or similar groups the power to make codes of fair competition. Codes were made by public authority only when the interest groups were unable to agree. The delegation of rule-making power in this case was relatively short-lived because the Act was declared unconstitutional. But somewhat similar powers were given to organized groups in the Bituminous Coal Acts and in the Taylor Grazing Act.

[20] *The Governmental Process*, p. 459.

On the state level the occupational licensing boards are most frequently cited as instances where a group has sought and received legal sanction for operating more or less of a guild system. In general, this means a compulsory licensing statute to be administered by an independent board composed of officials nominated by the association. Further, the board may enforce a code of ethics and lay down rules which will protect practitioners from certain types of competition and "keep up the standards" of the profession. State medical licensing boards are almost wholly composed of medical doctors who are in good standing in their medical societies. Because the function of licensing is not invariably performed by representatives of the profession itself, the professional association may attempt to influence the governor in his appointments to the board and in some instances the executive must appoint the association's nominees. Whatever the arrangement, the authority of the state is outwardly preserved but power is exercised to a degree by the private association.

ADMINISTRATION AS REPRESENTATION

The representation of interests in administration, which is sometimes called "administrative pluralism," is a fairly new development.[21] Oregon was among the first states to provide for representation on administrative boards and by the 1920's the practice became reasonably well established.[22] Since that time, group representation on or before administrative bodies has been on the increase both nationally and locally due in part to the vast increase in government services and the crises incident to depression and war. More and more groups demanded, and many of them received, the "legal" right to advise the government on policies concerning their affairs.

A simple but commonly overlooked fact is the part played by pressure politics in the very origin of administrative agencies. The American Fish Cultural Association, concerned over the diminishing food fish supply, was responsible for bringing into existence a commission that eventually became the Bureau of Fisheries. Bicycle riders brought in the Bureau of Public Roads, ornithologists had a hand in the Fish and Wildlife Service, and women's groups lobbied for the Children's Bureau. It is perhaps only a slight exaggeration to say that the departments of Agriculture, Commerce, and Labor sprang from and became the institutionalized

[21] See Alfred de Grazia, *Public and Republic: Political Representation in America* (New York: Alfred A. Knopf, Inc., 1951); M. P. Follett, *The New State* (New York: Longmans, Green & Co., Inc., 1918); E. P. Herring, *Public Administration and the Public Interest* (New York: McGraw-Hill Book Company, Inc., 1936); and Leiserson, *op. cit.*

[22] See J. D. Barnett, "Representation of Interests in Administration," *National Municipal Review*, Vol. 12 (1923), pp. 347–349.

expression of the respective organized occupational interests. There are relatively few boards, commissions, and bureaus today that have not resulted from the agitation of some special-interest group.

For many interest groups, contacts with the government are more frequently maintained with the administrative officers than with members of the legislature. A congressman, for example, is only sporadically interested in the problems of foreign trade, while the Bureau of Foreign and Domestic Commerce is concerned with them daily. It is only natural for an exporter to take his problems in the first instance to the Bureau rather than to Congress. This relieves Congress from constant harassment from important and influential economic groups. As private associations become satisfactorily represented in an administration, many of their demands are met and result in somewhat less pressure on Congress.

The interest groups often find it more advantageous to deal with a single or a few administrators and agencies than with individual congressmen and congressional committees. For one thing, the agencies are staffed with experts who can supply professional advice and perform specialized functions. Trained personnel is quick to perceive problems and to know if existing remedies are available; if the remedies are unavailable, then the interest group and the agency may be able to agree on some form of legislation that can be taken to Congress. In this respect the administration agency is an intermediary between the congressman and his constituents, and this procedure is in many cases more wholesome for securing needed laws than the path of legislative lobbying and pressure politics.

Private associations come to feel they have a vested right and a vested interest in certain administrative agencies, especially those serving large and powerful clients such as the Veterans Administration and the Department of Agriculture. The American Legion had a battle with the new Veterans' Administrator after World War II, General Omar Bradley, because they felt he was not giving the proper amount of deference to their viewpoint. The Legion officials even summoned him to its national headquarters in Indianapolis to account for some of his policies; he did not go but invited them to see him in Washington. On another occasion he was booed while addressing the national Legion convention. The American Farm Bureau Federation gave the cold shoulder to Secretary of Agriculture Brannan at some of its meetings.

After certain groups have made contacts with agencies in a way to give themselves satisfactory access, influence, and representation, they often oppose executive reorganization which would affect "their" agency. The Army Corps of Engineers and the Bureau of Reclamation in the Interior Department have built up allies in Congress and with interest groups and have provided formidable resistance to reorganization and to an integrated valley authority in the Columbia River Basin.[23] Leiserson noted that a bill providing for a change in the name of the Department of the Interior to one which would designate it as an agency clearly concerned with conservation and resource development was attacked "and successfully cornered, by the Department of Agriculture and the lumber interests as a move to gain control of the United States Forest Service on behalf of the Western cattlemen and grazers." [24]

The existing methods, arrangements, and philosophies of interest-group representation in administration give rise to many serious questions which can only be enumerated here. There is the problem of every agency to keep the "public interest" in mind. It is not easy to define the public interest where the agency's major function is to provide services for a particular segment of society. Political representation on administrative boards raises the question of whether a representative of a special-interest group is ultimately responsible to his organized group or to the public. If the group claims a "right" to name its own member, is this sound administration in the public interest? Finally, should private-interest representation go beyond that of "advice"? In general, administrative–interest group relationships are the result of opportunism, expediency, and pressure rather than of reflection and philosophy.

INTEREST GROUPS AND THE COURTS

In reviewing the ways by which interests seek to realize their aspirations from the institution of government, passing mention should be made of attempts to seek the aid of the judiciary. The courts, like the other two branches of government, have the power to make decisions which profoundly affect the distribution of power of private groups. This function of the judiciary comes through its power of judicial review, the interpretation of statutes, executive orders, treaties, and of the Constitution itself. The judge in addition can exercise considerable discretion in the issuing of injunctions, awarding of money damages, and in property settlements.

The case of the Negro illustrates the importance of the courts. In a few Northern states Negro organizations have obtained antidiscrimination and fair-employment-practices legislation. From the President they obtained certain executive orders in defense contracts which amounted to the same thing but filibustering in the Senate promises to defeat a

---

[23] See especially Charles McKinley, *Uncle Sam in the Pacific Northwest* (Berkeley, Calif.: University of California Press, 1952); Arthur Maass, *Muddy Waters* (Cambridge, Mass.: Harvard University Press, 1951). Other examples are cited in Avery Leiserson, "Political Limitations on Executive Reorganization," *The American Political Science Review,* Vol. 41 (1947), pp. 68–84.

[24] *Ibid.,* p. 73.

Federal law on the subject. On suffrage matters and on segregation Negroes have had no great success with the Southern legislatures. Again, the Senate is likely to defeat Federal bills to abolish suffrage restrictions and the President can do little to admit Negroes to Democratic primaries or to abolish suffrage restrictions. Having found frustration for various reasons in seeking legislative and administrative relief, the National Association for the Advancement of Colored People has turned to the courts and has obtained from them numerous decisions which are helping to fulfill the objectives of the organization. Indeed, the NAACP is spending considerable time and money to bring cases before the courts and this method has become a primary activity of the organization.

Utilities groups and labor unions, when defeated in efforts to prevent the Public Utility Holding Company and Taft-Hartley measures respectively from becoming law, challenged their constitutionality in the courts. A long list of *amici curiae* appeared in connection with such diverse measures as the Federal Maternity and Infancy Act and the first Agricultural Adjustment Act. Poultry dealers were successful in challenging the National Recovery Act, while stockholders were unsuccessful in their efforts to have the Tennessee Valley Authority invalidated.

Interpretation and clarification of laws is no less important. Consider, for example, three important interpretations of the Sherman Antitrust Act. The United States Supreme Court applied the "rule of reason," holding that only "unreasonable" restraints of trade were illegal. It declared that the activities of certain medical societies in dealing with group health doctors and plans constituted a violation of the Act. In another interpretation, basing-point pricing systems were prohibited. Where any agency of government has the power to make such decisions, even though the legislature may, through amendment, modify or override the decision, interest groups are bound to follow its decisions and often seek its aid. Moreover, they are bound to watch appointments to the bench. Negro, business, and labor groups have from time to time protested presidential appointments to the Federal courts and have made recommendations in state and local judicial elections.

In conclusion, recourse to the judiciary is likely to be used when there is defeat or dissatisfaction at the hands of the legislature and executive. Much but not all of the time the court is the last resort. Direct involvement of an individual or of an organized group in litigation is a long and expensive process. Many if not most groups find it quicker and less costly to get their cases before the legislature and the executive than before the courts. Nevertheless, the judiciary is a part of the political process. An interest group wishing to defeat a proposal tries to kill it in one house of the legislature. Failing this, it tries to influence the administration of the law and perhaps then to challenge the law or its enforcement in one way or another before the courts. If defeated in the judiciary, then the lobbyists begin all over again, working for amendment or repeal and influencing the personnel charged with the law's application.

SELECTED REFERENCES

See the end of the following chapter.

1. Access to the legislature.
   a. Grass roots pressure.
   b. Legislative contacts (at home)
   c. Alliances and combinations.

2. Influence of lobbyists : (interests in gov.)
   a. Expenditures $1 million annually.
   b. influence

3. Lobbying laws
   a. Reg. with clerk of the House & Sec. of Senate
   b. States (35) regulate laws.
   c. Fed laws contain many ambiguities

4. Laws.
   a. on administration instead of legislation
   b. Judicial review and the courts:
      (interpret and clarify laws.

CHAPTER 10

Function and Management of Group Interests

Reason, justice, and equity never had weight enough on the face of the earth to govern the councils of men. It is interest alone which does it, and it is interest alone which can be trusted. . . . Therefore the interests within doors should be a mathematical representation of the interests without doors.

—GABRIEL MIRABEAU

A citizen possesses ultimate power in the United States by being able to vote the operators of his government in or out of power. Yet the actual exercise of influence over government depends to a considerable extent on the outcome of the competition of "private governments" or powerful interests which are trying to influence public policy. More and more the individual has power and influence as the organization to which he belongs has power and influence. Back of the power of the organization lies the function of aiding or opposing the legislator or other elected official. Money, publicity, and votes to varying degrees are the weapons of pressure groups. All have their legitimate uses. But there is as much reason for curbs on the excessive use of power by private authorities as there is by public authorities. In this concluding chapter on interest groups we shall note the legitimate uses and function of interest-group activity in the arena of government, the undesirable aspect, and the problem of control and management in the public interest.

INTEREST GROUPS: SOME SUMMARY ASPECTS

Pattern of Organization. Notwithstanding great differences in detail, *nucleus* the organization and techniques of the major interest groups follow a fairly distinct pattern. A small nucleus formulates a set of purposes and appeals to widen the membership. Often the group is formed around a person of magnetic attraction who enjoys the confidence of the members and exerts a powerful force in welding and keeping together the diverse elements in the association. Aggressive leadership helps to increase the morale of the groups as it matures. Organizations having a Walter Reuther, a James Patton, or a John L. Lewis enjoy the advantage of sustained vigorous leadership. Conversely, personalized identity carries the liability of the enemies which a strong personality invariably makes. That business and the American Legion, for example, have succeeded

without the prolonged leadership of any one person indicates that personal direction for long periods of time, however advantageous, is not
indispensable to effectiveness.

Organization of the membership is perfected by the drafting of bylaws
or a constitution. These documents provide the rules for governance
and for periodic conventions and specify in a general manner the group
objectives and the methods of formulating policy. Gradually a folklore
is built around the objectives of the group, which becomes the gospel
and myth by which it lives, if not its *raison d'être*. Purposes are high
sounding and public-spirited in tone, though the gap between *alleged*
and *real* purposes is often wide. Stated ends and slogans follow patriotic
and revered symbols, with the American Medical Association laboring
for "private practice" and "freedom of choice of physician," while the
American Legion fosters "Americanism." The American Federation of
Labor marches into battle behind "the American standard of living," the
Chamber of Commerce of the United States preserves "free enterprise,"
and the National Association of Manufacturers promotes "the American
system." American publishers maintain "free speech and a free press,"
the investors' lobby fights for "widows and orphans," the National Committee to Uphold Constitutional Government "saves the Constitution,"
the CIO-PAC knows "a large vote is a good vote," agricultural blocs bring
"parity for the farmer," and America First promotes "America first." It
would be an ingrate indeed who opposed these objectives, since they all
seem worthy enough. Who would dare to propose "America second"?
As against sin, all are opposed to things "un-American." Yet opposing
forces call each other socialistic, reactionary, or bureaucratic. Nor are
they likely to agree with the boast of the People's Lobby that it is the
only lobby working for all the people when it advocates a greater degree
of public ownership and control of the economy. All profess to operate
for the public interest.

Public Relations. On this organizational and ideological background
are built the action techniques which follow a general pattern. At the
outset is self-preservation, which includes the answering of attacks and
the maintenance and extension of membership. Public-relations units are
created for this purpose, and regular journals and publications are prepared for members, prospective members, and the general public. *Nation's
Business, Nation's Agriculture,* the *Economic Outlook,* and so on, find
their way into members' homes and into libraries. The broad front of
publicity extends as well to news releases, to radio and television scripts,
sometimes to motion pictures, and to thousands of pieces of literature
distributed gratis or for nominal sums.

Public relations and publicity have become increasingly important in
the power and influence of private groups in what Edward L. Bernays

has so aptly called the "engineering of public consent." This engineering is more and more being placed in the hands of public-relations experts and advertising men, with the belief that ideas can be sold in much the same manner as products. The California advertising firm of Whitaker and Baxter conducted the American Medical Association's multimillion-dollar campaign against national health insurance, which was invariably called "socialized medicine." Public-relations experts are being called into politics to prepare scripts, slogans, and devices and numerous private interests are hiring political commentators and writers who are expected to slant to some degree the interpretation of events to favor the views of their employers.

While much publicity is geared toward the public in order to get the public to engineer its own "consent" for the group's views, a great bulk of private interest-group propaganda is directed to the membership of the organization itself. The purpose is to establish a "party line," faithfulness, and loyalty to the cause. Members who feel the "crusade" keenly will applaud the efforts of their leaders in "the good fight," bring pressure on the government, and solicit the help of their friends and families. Publicity helps to bolster sagging morale and to reinforce the myths of the group. Large corporations and organizations now employ highly qualified expert staffs, whose business is to keep their members informed and to explain complex issues in simple, understandable terms. As a matter of fact, the publicity directed toward the government, the general public, and the membership has become a major part of the work of the officials of interest groups.

This trend contains certain liabilities if not dangers. So-called "admen" may regard their job as essentially amoral and not be concerned with whether the idea they are called upon to sell is good or bad, public-spirited or antisocial. Emphasis may rest too much on oversimplification and catch phrases. One manager of a political advertising firm was quoted as saying: "You can interest voters if you put on a fight. No matter what the fight, *fight for something*. You may wonder if that is the only technique in campaigning. It isn't the only one. There are two. The average American also likes to be entertained. . . . He likes movies and he likes fireworks and parades. So if you can't fight, put on a show!" [1]

Prof. William L. Miller poses a point in these words: [2]

A public-relations man in politics may say he is only doing better what politicians have always done. But though the "old-style" politician often did oversimplify and sloganize and appeal to fear and greed, he does not seem to have

[1] Quoted in William L. Miller, "Can Government Be 'Merchandised'?" *The Reporter,* Oct. 27, 1953, p. 12. This is a penetrating and critical article on the use of advertising men in political campaigns.

[2] *Ibid.*

done this quite so systematically or so effectively as the modern advertisers in politics. He did not have the dominating control of the sources of opinion that the modern national "mass media" advertiser can enjoy. And he had a restraining set of pressures on him to which some of the political advertising men do not seem to be subject; at least he had to pay some attention to the facts. His campaigns may have lacked moxie, but he had to deal with the interests of his constituents, which were real and which were independent of his manipulation.

One public-relations man countered with the remark: "It's because the public relations profession, and its allied professions, know something about presenting abstract ideas, in attractive form, to masses of people who are too occupied with their daily lives to think analytically on their account, that the average man today is in a position to know more about the trend of human affairs than ever in history." [3]

Democratic Control. The increased use of advertising and public-relations techniques by organized interests calls for careful study and a pondering of its implications. It becomes important to know if the membership and the public are being given all the facts and if they are being victimized and misled by slogans. This raises the question of the democratic basis and governance of the group and of the extent to which the officials of the association actually represent the desires and interests of the majority of their members. When their spokesmen speak to administrators, legislators, and to the press, do they voice the views and aspirations of the membership? Is the organization democratically governed? Large groups generally tend toward control by leaders who are rather easily able to perpetuate themselves in power through what Robert Michels termed the "iron law of oligarchy." [4] The tendency is one of "one-party" government and, even though factionalism exists, it is difficult for the opposition to organize effectively and regularly.

An interesting deviation is that of the International Typographical Union (AFL). The Union established a referendum system of electing international officers biennially in 1898 and there have been seven times in which the incumbent officers were defeated.[5] Over 500 referendums have been taken on union policies. Members have the right to organize permanent or temporary political parties and to publish attacks on the incumbent administration in *The Typographical Journal*. In nearly every election there is a rival slate, sometimes more than one. Generally, however, the ITU operates under a two-party system, each with its own press. Says Lipsit: [6]

3 *Ibid.,* p. 13.

4 *Political Parties* (Glencoe, Ill.: The Free Press, 1949).

5 See Seymour M. Lipsit, *Democracy in Private Government: A Case Study of the International Typographical Union*, Reprint 42 (Berkeley, Calif.: Institute of Industrial Relations, University of California, 1952).

6 *Ibid.,* p. 49.

The tendencies towards "bureaucratic conservatism" that arise within the leadership of most organizations have been checked by the existence of the permanent opposition group, which stands ready to capitalize on any fault of the administration and play up every demand which seems to have support among the members. Each party, when in opposition, has been too strong to be crushed or denied its opposition rights without destroying the union.

The problems of democratic structures and procedures of private associations provide the subject matter for several chapters. We can do no more here than to point out their importance and to state that the ITU system of an institutionalized opposition merits careful study. The use of referendums such as used by the Chamber of Commerce, the strike votes taken by some unions, the annual convention and periodic elections are potential instruments of democratic control. As these are perfected, the government will benefit by the activities of private associations when they attempt to influence the decisions of government.

THE LOBBY: FUNCTIONS AND USES

Lobbying refers to those aspects of organized interest-group activity which bring claims directly to bear on public officials. Originally, lobbying was associated only with trying to influence the legislature. In the preceding chapter it was noted that a lobbyist's activity is also directed toward administrative agencies and even the courts. Using "lobby" in its broadest connotation, we may first look at the useful and essential role which it plays.

Reasons for the Lobby. The lobby is a much-maligned institution.[7] Popular assumption has it that the "invisible government" is invariably bad. Perhaps ignorance of the nature and functions of pressure groups and the vaguely defined term itself account for this reaction. Pressure groups are in part the result of our system of representation. Lawmakers are chosen on a geographical basis, but technology has changed the meaning of geography. The voter's basic interest does not lie in his election district or even in his state; it lies in his social, fraternal, and business relationships. Yet the state constitutions and that of the nation make no provision for occupational or group representation and election laws are not geared, except partially perhaps in a few systems of proportional representation, to bring about the election of representatives of organized minorities. In a society of diverse pursuits, spokesmen for special interests should have a place in government. Through the extralegal channels of pressure politics, then, the interest groups strive to compensate for the absence of formal recognition in the structure of our govern-

---

[7] See Mary E. Dillon, "Pressure Groups," *The American Political Science Review*, Vol. 36 (1946), pp. 471–481. on distinctions between "pressure groups" and "lobbies."

ment. It may be said that pressure politics is America's answer to the problem of occupational representation.

The absence of an over-all economic planning agency working in direct contact with major economic interests also leads to the diffusion of group expression in the direction of scores of administrative agencies, legislative committees, and individual lawmakers. In England the cabinet, serving as the government, integrates the political and economic program, whereas in the United States the presidential system operates under separation of powers and without centralization of the functions for total planning. On the Continent, group interests are represented in a great multiplicity of political parties.[8] The heterogeneous composition of American parties makes them an opportunistic and less effective channel for group expression. The organized interests, therefore, though getting favorable planks in party platforms, expend most of their efforts in going directly to the persons, agencies, and committees which offer the greatest opportunity for meeting specific demands.

The multiplication of organized groups with political objectives is not an American phenomenon, nor is it of recent origin. Madison, Calhoun, Jackson, and many others spoke of the political role of groups, factions, and minorities. Notwithstanding different party systems in Britain and France, the parties have neither displaced nor kept organized expressions of interest from developing. The increased complexity and specialization of society have heightened conflict and controversy. Organizations spring from and give voice to the aspirations, struggles, frustrations, and fears of segments of society.

Group Representation. To begin with, the lobby has become the organized expression of minority economic and social interests growing out of the peculiar nature of the American representative system. Interest groups themselves are a natural outgrowth of a free society, and the lobby is the vehicle by which these interests are carried to those in political authority. The useful services which group representation renders are the providing of information, the proposing of innovations, and the checking of those in authority.

Because of the increasing complexity of the economic order, no lawmaker can hope to understand thoroughly the problems of agriculture, business, commerce, foreign trade, labor, and transportation, not to mention the hundreds of problems related to them. The hours spent performing "errand-boy" services for constituents leave the legislator no great amount of time for study and reflection concerning issues. Yet he is called upon to vote and sometimes to draft policies in many fields while being an expert in only a few. Of equal importance are the probable effects of proposed national policies on certain groups. Here the spokes-

[8] The British and European party systems are described in Chap. 13.

man for the groups can provide the policy maker with useful opinions, facts, and information, however biased. Very frequently the persons directly affected can render a useful judgment on practical application, especially on details. Many government officials have found that interest groups are the only sources of data on some of the situations with which they must deal.

The information which the staff of an organization gathers from the government and elsewhere is transmitted to its membership and helps the individual member to crystallize and to formulate his own thinking and ideas about public affairs. Private associations clarify and crystallize the sentiments of their constituents. The individual, preoccupied with matters of livelihood, is seldom in a position to approach his representatives directly and regularly on economic matters. This function is performed for him by his organization. His needs and desires, moreover, are probably more clearly and persuasively presented by a skilled spokesman for his group. The individual in this case profits by the strength of collective bargaining.

A person may not realize that some of his needs can be taken care of by the government, but it is the business of the experts in his organization to know where to go and the best techniques for presenting these needs. In meeting with public officials, the spokesman for his group is performing a service for the member, just as his plumber or physician perform other types of services for him. The interest-group interaction is twofold— it takes the group's or member's problems to the government and it brings back from the government a service, advice, an interpretation, or perhaps the news that nothing can be done under existing law or practice.

The association generally goes beyond simply calling the attention of the public and the government to the problems of the constituency. It presents proposals for remedial action. These may call for legislation, for a court or administrative order, or for the creation of a new agency within the government. Proposals often result in stimulating debate and act as a catalyst in setting other forces in motion. Different groups at one time or another called for separate Federal departments of health, education, and welfare. Ultimate response consisted in the creation of a Cabinet office including all three. This did not result in meeting the zealous separatist demands but for the moment elevated each interest into a Cabinet status. The creative function, both actual and potential, is most important and one which gives zest to the political process. Government is a reflection of the claims of successful interest groups.

Government, however, also reflects interests that are held by vast segments of the unorganized populace. Good roads are not the exclusive result of a high-powered automobile owners' or truckers' lobby nor civil liberties of the American Civil Liberties Union. The millions of highway users are essentially unorganized, and the billions spent for armaments are not the result of a munitions maker's campaign contributions or propaganda. Government recognizes great public interests of this type without being pressured. But even here there are interests which are organized and which call attention in dramatic fashion to the need for a new six-lane through way, a larger air force, or merchant marine, or the dangers to civil liberties of present or proposed actions. Pressure groups help to focus attention on the dereliction of public authorities and to compel public action. These activities have an important and on the whole salutary impact on the government.

In summary, we may speak of the legitimate functions of interest groups as including (1) the formulation of a group policy and the presentation of that policy to public officials, (2) the providing of information on specialized matters to lawmakers, administrators, constituents, and the general public, and (3) protective and "watchdog" services for their constituencies by exercising surveillance over public policies and administration.

CRITICISMS OF PRESSURE POLITICS

Pressure groups are under constant attack as being evil, dangerous, and subversive of the public interest. Careful students of American politics, though recognizing the useful role of groups just presented, are nonetheless not fully complacent over the power possessed by private associations. Pressure groups come under attack on the grounds that they (1) tend to put the private interest ahead of the public interest, (2) lack democratic governance, (3) result in inequal influence on the government and the public, (4) control the thinking of their membership, and (5) use unethical and corrupt methods to press their claims.

The essence of pressure politics where most organized minorities are concerned consists in the shaping of public law and public action for private advantage. With our society becoming increasingly complex and interdependent, the activities of powerfully organized minorities assume large importance because of their ability to slow down, modify, or speed up the general tempo of economic and social life with resulting injustice to innocent, unorganized millions. America has become increasingly conscious of political, diplomatic, and economic bottlenecks. Where private associations are possessed with the power to create or to break bottlenecks, they are affected with a public interest and their responsibility becomes one of the highest order.

To the extent that group policies are evolved by considering the larger as well as the narrower interest, or in an enlightened self-interest, they are a valuable expression of group sentiment. Where the association is motivated by purely personal aggrandizement when it resorts to dubious and dishonest methods to achieve objectives, it may be called unworthy and pernicious. Bribery, influence peddling, and blackmail are not un-known methods used by less scrupulous groups, even though there are laws which attempt to curb their use. Admittedly, the line between "good" and "bad" lobbies is at times thin, but it becomes the function of the general public and its officials to attempt to make such a judgment.

Unless policies of an organization are expressive of the will of the membership, their presentation by the leadership lacks clear sanction. There is considerable evidence that some policies are put forth by leaders without discussion or the sanction of the membership and the latter were not presented with the alternatives or implications of the steps which the leadership advocates. Public officials and the general public will place more credence in views expressed by the officials of an organiza-tion if they feel the views have the understanding and the support of the rank-and-file membership.

Closely related to the criticism that the leaders sometimes do not reflect the wishes of the membership is the charge that they dictate to the members. In this case the hierarchy, which is the actual minority, exerts influence over the individual member in a way to determine his thinking on the group objectives. As the "price of belonging," the indi-vidual accepts the values, attitudes, and prejudices of the group which to a considerable extent are those of the leadership. Methods are used to promote internal cohesion and fight insurgency but at the same time may result in discouraging criticism of the leadership and its program.

The ability, financial or otherwise, of some numerically small groups to gain easy access if not control over the communications media and to reach the public with propaganda techniques is of profound social sig-nificance. Small, cohesive, well-disciplined groups are able to exert an influence far out of proportion to their numbers. At one time this may be a handful of tugboat operators who can paralyze a great port, another time photographers who can stop publication of newspapers, or on still another occasion a big business which may build a monopoly, create scarcity, and fix prices. Veterans, pensioners, physicians, and many others at times have secured expensive legislation or special privileges which appear to have served their private interests much more than the public good.

The activities of group interests may be divisive where democracy is interested in national unity and the common welfare. Certain large interests in society in the nature of things are not or cannot be adequately represented. Conservation of the natural resources and the preservation and extension of parks, for example, are clearly in the national interest. Well-organized private groups press for policies which will permit them to exploit resources, to obtain water-front land which might be a public beach, a park, and so on. It is difficult to organize effectively the public interest on these and many other matters. Some have suggested that the public welfare can be promoted by vigorous organizations of consumers, white-collar workers, and consumer cooperatives, all of which would combat the monopolies built up by organized business, labor, and agriculture. The charge that different pressure groups are of unequal influence is easy to make, but a remedy is not so easy to find. Even if desirable, it would be difficult to create a system whereby all groups could be equally represented at all times in all the major divisions of government.

THE MANAGEMENT OF GROUP PRESSURES

In theory it has become the function of democratic government to break up or modify the monopoly of any group where tactics and objectives threaten the national interest. It is said with some merit that big government is needed to control big business, big labor, and big agriculture. How the conflicts between interests shall be harmonized and the common welfare protected from the excesses of power concentrated in and irresponsibly used by private groups is one of the great tasks of democracy. Lobbying laws do not cope with the situation leading to pressure politics. Numerous formal and informal ways are being tried here and abroad to accommodate the public demands of group interests. Among the mitigating devices operating or being proposed are (1) natural accommodation and counterbalancing, (2) special statutory or administrative regulation, (3) functional representation, and (4) accommodation by political parties.

Counterbalancing Factors. In the process of exerting organized pressure, pressure stimulates counterpressures. Pressure groups beget pressure groups and help to modify to some extent the influence of each other. While the multiplication of organizations is not a happy prospect, the *laissez faire* of pressures helps to provide a balance between rival interests. In numerous cases, however, no important counterforce is built up. Veterans' groups, for example, have often obtained bonuses and other programs because there is no effective opposition to their demands.

Galbraith sees a new restraint on private power, a restraint nurtured by "the same process of concentration which impaired or destroyed competition." This new power he calls "countervailing." [9] As concentration of the industrial enterprise in fewer and fewer hands developed, it created not only strong sellers but strong buyers who act as a countervailing power. The buyers or customers are on the other side of the market and act as a check on the producer or seller. Buyers exercise pressures on the seller as well as vice versa. Says Galbraith: [10]

[9] *American Capitalism: The Concept of Countervailing Power* (Boston: Houghton Mifflin Company, 1952), Chap. 9.
[10] *Ibid.,* p. 126.

At the end of virtually every channel by which consumers' goods reach the public there is, in practice, a layer of powerful buyers. In the food market there are the great food chains; in clothing there are the department stores, the chain department stores and the department store buying organizations; in appliances there are Sears, Roebuck, and Montgomery Ward. . . . The drug and cosmetic manufacturer has to seek part of his market through the large drug chains and the department stores; a vast miscellany of consumers' goods pass to the public through Woolworth's, Kresge's and the other variety chains.

This principle of the countervailing force does not prevail universally, for some producers have not had to face such forces or they have been able to secure themselves from the exercise of countervailing power. The oil and automobile industries, for example, have integrated their distribution down to the consumer level because the small and relatively powerless dealers are dependent. The residential building industry likewise has successfully resisted countervailing power since the myriad of housebuilders have not been able to organize effectively for buying. Building supplies are not generally sold directly to builder but through jobbers and retailers.

To the student of politics the presence of countervailing forces is of real significance. These forces help to distribute private economic power among different segments of the economy and to act as a check on those producers who no longer have great competition among themselves. It helps to decentralize certain decisions and to keep business from having completely unified ranks. Different business organizations of sellers, jobbers, and buyers make demands upon the courts, the legislatures, the Federal Trade Commission, and antitrust units to protect them from the power of rival business associations or to seek advantageous rulings. Countervailing power is in a sense collective bargaining, and it can be developed only if there are ample opportunity, capacity, and freedom to organize. Groups have frequently sought the assistance of government in organizing and the government itself has at times actively tried to organize trade associations and has aided and abetted cooperatives, labor unions, and farmers' associations.

Stated another way, a function of government is to provide a climate where useful countervailing forces may be built up, especially where original forces are powerful and may exercise their influence in an antisocial way. By keeping the channels of organization and activity open, the government assists the build-up of countergroups. At times it is not enough simply to provide an environment for the free play of forces. Where one force is weak but where it appears that the public welfare would be served by making it stronger, it has become the task of government to promote the development of the weaker force. When and how the government should assume this affirmative role is one of the great issues of the times. It underlies the arguments between so-called liberals and conservatives, socialists and nonsocialists, New Dealers and anti-New Dealers, and between the various wings of the two great political parties. In addition to the negative role of trying to keep a fertile soil for the development of the distribution of power and the affirmative role of actively assisting it, the government has the third role of arbiter between the original and countervailing powers which is usually performed by the judicial and quasi-judicial agencies.

The safeguards in the heterogeneity of individual and group interests and in the fact that it is seldom that any one group can completely dominate an individual must not be overlooked. In the maze of pressures and counterpressures the individual finds conflict in his loyalties and in defining his own larger interest. A wheat farmer wants reduced taxes on property and supposedly economy in government. As a parent and family head he desires good schools for his children, rural electrification, and roads which will give his family easy access to schools, shopping centers, and recreation, all of which cost public money. Ideologically, as an individualist he opposes government subsidies and controls but feels he must accept price supports and marketing quotas because he sees no other more acceptable way of achieving parity prices. This is a comparatively simple illustration of certain conflicts facing the individual. He will find taxpayers' leagues, community improvement associations, parent-teacher groups, and the Farm Bureau seeking his membership. One calls for lower taxes while the other champions certain increases in public appropriations. He may, and probably does, belong to more than one organization, a situation which David Truman calls "overlapping membership." [11] This overlapping membership raises problems of cohesion for the group and may have a modifying and tempering influence on it. Multiple memberships may lead groups to compromise or accommodation when threatened with loss of members as a result of a proposed policy.

Regulation of Operation. Natural accommodation has not always satisfied segments of the public and the government has acquiesced in some of the demands for public regulation of the internal as well as the external operation and activity of certain private groups. The operation of banks, railroads and common carriers, insurance companies, stock exchanges, and public utilities is under fairly strict governmental surveillance. The number of businesses "affected with a public interest" has lengthened markedly.

A recent illustration of a public attempt to bring a private group under regulation is the Taft-Hartley Act. This law goes far beyond bringing certain aspects of labor-management relations and strikes under Federal control. The internal operation of the unions is partially regulated. In

[11] *The Governmental Process* (New York: Alfred A. Knopf, Inc., 1951), Chaps. 6–7.

order to curb some of the power of union leaders, the law permits an individual worker to take his grievances to his employer without intervention of the bargaining agent, so long as adjustment does not conflict with the terms of the collective bargaining contract in effect.

It remains a debatable point whether the Taft-Hartley Act has made unions more democratic in operation and more responsible to the public. The legislation did not bring an end to strikes any more than speculation has been cured by regulating the stock and grain exchanges or monopoly been abolished by the Sherman Antitrust Act. Laws of this type are piecemeal in approach and constitute no solution for the broader problems of pressures by various interests. They do represent an attempt, nonetheless, to bring certain activities of some groups, formerly thought to be purely private matters, under public control and observation.

Functional Representation. There are those who believe that a more formal recognition of the social and economic interests is desirable, with institutions and methods for reconciling them in the interests of the common welfare. One proposal which has been advanced, and in some places tried, is functional or social-vocational representation. In essence, this would provide for representation of individuals as members of legally-recognized socioeconomic units rather than as inhabitants of a specified territory.[12] Enormous practical difficulties stand in the way of basing the legislative branch on functional rather than territorial representation, including questions of what groups shall be represented and in what numbers.

More within the realm of possibility, however, is the creation of an economic council to serve as an advisory council to the legislature or executive or both. Several European nations have constitutional provisions for these councils. The new French constitution creates an economic council to which the National Assembly will refer proposed laws before the Assembly discusses them. Sweden has a planning commission whose breadth of membership embraces members of the Riksdag and representatives of employers' associations, trade-unions, the cooperative movement, and women's organizations.

Functional representation is unlikely to be adopted in the United States, since Americans are not addicted to such a revolutionary change or to the corporative state. It is debatable whether this form of representation would decrease the power of special-interest groups. Legislative bodies constituted along these lines might likewise accentuate and magnify minority interests and hamper the effectiveness of legislatures.

---

12 See Fritz Nova, *Functional Representation* (Dubuque, Iowa: W. C. Brown Company, 1950); Herman Finer, *Representative Government and the Parliament of Industry* (London: George Allen & Unwin, Ltd., 1923); and Mary P. Follett, *The New State* (New York: Longmans, Green & Co., Inc., 1918).

Accommodation through Political Parties. Abuses of private power might better be curbed by the formulation of government policies and legislation by responsible officers who must consider the general public interest. In many democratic nations this function is performed by the cabinet. A complete reorganization of the government in the United States would be required in order to bring about a cabinet system. A sharp change in the political system exemplified by the cabinet system is hardly foreseeable in the United States, but greater concentration of responsibility for legislative planning is possible.

As noted before, some students of government believe that strong national political parties offer the most promising antidote for overpowerful private organizations. According to this view, organized groups are unable to obtain undue power where there are strong national parties because excessive interest-group power arises when there is no representation of the national interest. Schattschneider maintains that "at all points the problem of the management of pressure is a problem of the political parties." [13] In the European multiparty systems the many interests can operate directly through a party. In Great Britain the national parties in Parliament formulate a program which they can defend to the nation and the parties accommodate interest-group demands in the national interest.

The character of American parties, it is sometimes argued, has kept our parties from effectively compromising group demands. Yet American parties, at election time and to some extent in Congress, are constantly engaged in trying to adjust and modify the diverse interests and demands of political groups. The degree of success in doing this varies from time to time. There have been times when the party leadership showed a high sense of obligation for formulating and executing policies and for saying "no" to pressure groups whose programs were questionable in terms of the national interest. At other times the parties were slow to formulate programs and pressure groups, at least on the surface, appeared dominant. The creation of policy committees in Congress, the political strength of state governors, and the attention given by party officials to policies and to party discipline are reminders that the parties themselves are aware of the importance, potentialities, and responsibility of parties for making policy.

The subject of social control of the power and influence of organized minorities is one deserving of considerably greater thought than it has received. Stronger national parties, functional representation, and regulation by law have recognizable merit but contain liabilities and would raise

[13] *Party Government* (New York: Rinehart & Company, Inc., 1942), p. 205; see also J. M. Burns, *Congress on Trial* (New York: Harper & Brothers, 1949).

new problems. The fact that there have been experiments of one kind or another with each of them and that they have exponents in and out of government testifies that a laissez-faire attitude toward the behavior of organized interests does not exist. The diffused and complicated pattern of American politics suggests that none of these, or stringent lobbying laws, is likely to be adopted with all of its trappings. Controls over interests and the public management of group interests are likely to continue on an opportunistic and decentralized basis.

In taking leave of political interest groups, it may be well to point out again that the alternative to them may be a monolithic party and state where the contests for power, except for the ruling group, are not permitted or are so highly circumscribed as to make contests meaningless. Organized groups are a necessary part of any large, free society. The legislative struggle is largely a struggle between these contesting forces, with all sorts of combinations and common fronts. Perhaps the most hopeful remedies are in helping the unorganized sectors to organize and in the strengthening of official party leadership in the government.

SELECTED REFERENCES

The volumes cited for the several preceding chapters on pressure groups have application to these summary chapters. Those especially pertinent are Number 10 of *The Federalist*; *The Annals of the American Academy of Political and Social Science,* May, 1935; January, 1939; and the supplement on lobbying to Vol. 144, 1929; E. P. Herring, *Group Representation in Congress* (1929); Stuart Chase, *Democracy under Pressure* (1945); Donald Blaisdell, *Economic Power and Political Pressures,* Monograph 26, Temporary National Economic Committee (1941); Belle Zeller, *Pressure Politics in New York* (1937); Dayton McKean, *Pressures on the Legislature of New Jersey* (1938); E. B. Logan et al., *The American Political Scene* (1936), Chap. 6.

Additional works dealing with the broader and philosophical aspects of group interests and government are E. P. Herring, *Public Administration and the Public Interest* (1936); David Truman, *The Governmental Process* (1951); J. M. Burns, *Congress on Trial* (1949); Fritz Nova, *Functional Representation* (1950); M. P. Follett, *The New State* (1918); E. E. Schattschneider, *Party Government* (1942); Alfred de Grazia, *Public and Republic: Political Representation in America* (1951).

Specific materials on lobbying and its regulation include the hearings and reports of the House Select Committee on Lobbying Activities, 81st Congress, especially the *Lobby Index, 1946–1949;* and W. B. Graves, *Administration of the Lobby Registration Provision of the Legislative Reorganization Act of 1946.* The *Congressional Quarterly Weekly Reports* and the growing body of periodical literature on lobbying are most informative. Two especially useful articles are those of Belle Zeller, "The Federal Regulation of Lobbying Act," *The American Political Science Review,* Vol. 42 (1948), pp. 239–271; and R. E. Lane, "Notes on the Theory of Lobbying," *ibid.,* Vol. 43 (1949), pp. 153–161. Provisions of state laws have been compiled by the Council of State Government under the heading of *State Regulation of Lobbying* (1951). Stephen K. Bailey has provided a recent interesting case study in legislator-lobbyist relationships in *Congress Makes a Law* (1950), as has F. W. Riggs in *Pressures on Congress: A Study of the Repeal of Chinese Exclusion* (1950). See also Karl Schriftgiesser, *The Lobbyists* (1951). The various textbooks on the legislative process include extensive treatment of lobbying; see Harvey Walker, *The Legislative Process* (1948); W. F. Willoughby, *Principles of Legislative Organization and Administration* (1934); Bertram Gross, *The Legislative Struggle* (1953) and George Galloway, *The Legislative Process in Congress* (1953).

[handwritten marginal notes:]

factions:
Calhoun;
Madison;
Jackson
Washington

1. *Functions of interest groups:*
   a. Formulation of group policy and the presentation of this policy to elected public officials.
   b. Providing of information on specified matters
   c. Protective and "watchdog" services for their constituencies by exercising surveillance over public policies

PART THREE

Development and Nature of Political Parties

CHAPTER 11

Modern Party Politics

American politics was originally rustic politics. The national parties were founded upon alliances between sectional interests, and the sectional interests were at first mostly agrarian interests. . . . The passing of the frontier and the growth of urban industry have shaken the foundations of the old party system in national politics. . . . The character of the new party politics will be determined chiefly by the interests and attitudes of the urban population. It will be less rustic than the old and more urbane. There will be less sectional politics and more class politics.

—Arthur N. Holcombe

Political parties as they are known today are probably no more than 300 years old, dating from seventeenth-century England. Regular two-party contests for the presidency began in the United States in 1832, although there were struggles between the Federalists and Jeffersonian Republicans in several elections prior to that time. Contemporary party battles are better understood by a knowledge of the historic contests between the national parties and of the main currents of political thought which sought expression through them. In this chapter the background and present character of party alignments and issues will be sketched; the following chapter will consider the general nature of the American party system.[1]

Modern party cleavages, organization, and techniques have evolved slowly. The many periods of party struggles each made their imprint on the modern parties and the parties are still contending over some of the issues discussed in the Constitutional Convention. For example, Alexander Hamilton saw the wealth and security of the nation bound up with "the prosperity of its manufactures" and favored a tariff, a national banking system, and assumption of debts by the national government. He felt the Federal government should be strengthened so that it could "triumph altogether over the state governments." He feared the "turbulent

[1] Many fine books are available on party history and on the parties themselves. The best general work is W. E. Binkley, *American Political Parties* (New York: Alfred A. Knopf, Inc., 1943). T. W. Couzens, *Politics and Political Organizations in America* (New York: The Macmillan Company, 1942), pp. 81–289, gives a comprehensive chronological history including complete voting statistics and the composition of the various Congresses. See the Selected References at the end of this chapter.

and changing" masses and would give them only a minimum share in the control of government. The rich and the well born, he believed, should be given the larger, "distinct, permanent share in the government."

Thomas Jefferson voiced opposition to many of these ideas. He felt the farmers were the most valuable citizens and dreamed of an agrarian America. He upheld states' rights, strict construction of the Constitution, majority rule, frequent rotation in office, and the right of revolution. "It is necessary," he wrote, "to introduce people into every department of government as far as they are capable of exercising it." [2] Hamiltonian and Jeffersonian disciples are found in each major party today. In these early formative years other great debates took place, as they do today, over public expenditures, intervention and neutrality, and the extension of suffrage. The country has adopted and rejected some of the policies of the Federalists and the Anti-Federalists or Jeffersonian Republicans.

DEMOCRATS AND WHIGS

Between Jefferson and Lincoln, economic power was entrenched in the East but political power was growing in the West. Jefferson's equalitarian and leveling theories found many sympathizers in the West. New political organizations and techniques were being developed. In terms of the development of modern party practices, the years from 1828 to 1850 were more important than any other comparable period of time. In fact, relatively little has been added to the basic mechanics and organization of party politics since the Democratic-Whig era.

Among these developments were the creation of the national convention for the purpose of nominating candidates for the presidency and vice presidency and the broad general rules for governing the convention were established. Party platforms were drafted at each convention. The national committees were established near the end of the period and local organization was rapidly extended. Patronage was widely used to help build party organization. The potentialities of the presidency were recognized by the Jacksonians and President Jackson saw the office as "a tribune of the people." Jobs were used as a method of party control, for strengthening the hand of the President in dealing with Congress, and in suppressing factionalism.

Suffrage was radically broadened and longer ballots and rotation in office encouraged many to be potential officeholders. Showmanship, demagoguery, personal vituperation, gaudy parades, and propaganda were increasingly used in political campaigns. Class consciousness was ap-

[2] There are many excellent biographies of Hamilton and Jefferson. Basic political ideas of the two men are summarized in J. M. Jacobson, *The Development of American Political Thought* (New York: Appleton-Century-Crofts, Inc., 1932).

pealed to in a greater degree than ever before. Claude Bowers notes that
1832 "marked the beginning of the active participation of powerful corporations, witnessed the adoption of the methods of intimidation and of
coercion, of systematic propaganda, of the subsidization of disreputable
newspapers." [3] The initial drive for woman suffrage got under way in 1848
as adult males were successful in eliminating property qualifications in
the Eastern states. Politics became more of the business of every citizen
instead of the few.

Finally, the two-party system became firmly established during the era.
Never again was there to be an era of "good feeling," when no opposing
party challenged the rights of the "ins" to control the personnel and
policies of the government. Every two years in peace and in war the minority party has waged a campaign, regardless of the absence of basic
differences. If issues were lacking, the ability and personality of the White
House incumbent or of the party's opponent became the campaign cry
of the opposition party. That the Whig party with its highly heterogeneous composition could hold together for 20 years is a remarkable demonstration of the binding force of negativism, protest, and the hope for
patronage.

FROM LINCOLN TO MC KINLEY

American party history has been characterized by relatively long periods of control by one party. It is rare that control of the presidency shifts
to a party for four-year periods only. The Democrats were dominant from
Jackson to Lincoln, although they lost the presidency twice. The Republicans were dominant from 1860 to 1912, except for the election of Grover
Cleveland. The Wilsonian Democrats lasted only eight years and Republican rule was reestablished until 1932, when the Democrats took over
for 20 years. The periods of dominance resulted from forging voting alliances capable of lasting several years.

The Civil War and the accession to power of the newly formed Republican party resulted in a realignment which saw the Democrats successful
in winning the presidency only 4 out of 18 times between 1860 and 1932;
the cleavages, moreover, are still partially in evidence. The Democrats
emerged with the "Solid South," a bloc which they have been able to
rely upon rather generally since that time. Capitalists, financiers, transportation magnates, and large manufacturers gravitated to the Republican party when it restored the national banking system, fostered the
promotion of business, and supported the high protective tariff. Creditors
and bondholders stayed with the party which offered a bulwark against
the easy-money, radical, debt-ridden agrarianism, and the free-silver Populists. Union veterans applauded the generous pensions granted by the

[3] *The Party Battles of the Jackson Period* (Boston: Houghton Mifflin Company, 1922),
p. 368.

Republicans and the newly enfranchised Negroes expressed gratitude by supporting the party of the Emancipator. The Republican Homestead Act was liked by many Western farmers and native and immigrant alike were in a position to take advantage of the land boom in the West. With popular programs of this type the Republicans were able to appeal to many beneficiaries.

But the Republican party failed to satisfy many elements after the Civil War. A large number of farmers were uninterested in homesteading, but wanted freedom from debt and high interest rates. Many laborers saw inflation reducing their wages and wanted relief from long hours, debts, and unsatisfactory working conditions. Strikes were accompanied by violence, often due to the employment of strikebreakers by corporations. Farm leaders began to urge farmers to "raise less corn and more hell." Farm foreclosures were coming thick and fast and farmers became peeved at the Supreme Court for voiding the income tax. Interpretations of the Court of the "due-process" clause which seemed to favor corporations, and the corruption in government led muckrakers to say that the nation had a government "of the people, by the rascals, for the rich."

The mounting discontent gravitated in part to the Democrats but did not find their presidential nominees before 1896 to be particularly sympathetic to their pleas. Some supported the Greenback party and urged a farmer-labor third party. This culminated in a People's party, popularly known as the Populists. Its candidate James B. Weaver frightened the major parties by polling over a million votes and carrying four states in 1892. Weaver's greatest strength was west of Iowa, where he had financial support from the silver interests. The Populist revolt set the stage for the great battle over bimetallism in 1896.

Both major parties had a silver wing, but the Republicans succeeded in nominating William McKinley, a gold-standard supporter. William Jennings Bryan captured the Democratic nomination and ran on a bi-metal plank. Since Bryan had stolen their thunder on silver, the Populists elected to support him rather than to split the vote.

The campaign of 1896 was one of the most colorful in American history. Tons of literature were distributed. McKinley, as "the advance agent of prosperity," waged a "front porch" campaign from his home in Canton, Ohio. Business and commercial interests heavily subsidized his campaign to prevent the "anarchist" Bryan from being elected. Over $7 million was collected for the Republican coffers, largely from frightened capitalists. Bryan received liberal help from the silver miners but only about one million dollars was raised. He stumped the country from one end to the other as the "defender of the poor and the protector of the oppressed" and identified his campaign as an economic crusade in "the cause of humanity."

Table 7. Presidential Election Statistics, 1896–1912

Year	Candidate	Party	Popular vote	Electoral vote
1896	William McKinley	Republican	7,111,607	271
	William J. Bryan	Democrat & Populist	6,509,052	176
	Joshua Levering	Prohibition	141,676	
	John M. Palmer	National Democrat	134,645	
	Charles Matchett	Socialist Labor	36,454	
	Charles Bentley	National Prohibition	13,968	
1900	William McKinley	Republican	7,219,530	292
	William J. Bryan	Democrat	6,358,071	155
	James Wooley	Prohibition	209,157	
	Eugene V. Debs	Socialist	94,864	
	Wharton Barker	Populist	50,232	
	Joseph Maloney	Socialist Labor	32,432	
	Seth Ellis	Union-Reform	5,698	
1904	Theodore Roosevelt	Republican	7,628,834	336
	Alton B. Parker	Democrat	5,084,491	140
	Eugene V. Debs	Socialist	402,890	
	Silas Swallow	Prohibition	259,257	
	Thomas Watson	Populist	114,753	
	Charles Corregan	Socialist Labor	33,724	
1908	William H. Taft	Republican	7,679,906	321
	William J. Bryan	Democrat	6,409,106	162
	Eugene V. Debs	Socialist	420,890	
	Eugene Chafin	Prohibition	252,683	
	Thomas Hisgen	Independence	83,652	
	Thomas Watson	Populist	29,084	
	August Gilhaus	Socialist Labor	13,999	
1912	Woodrow Wilson	Democrat	6,286,019	435
	Theodore Roosevelt	Progressive	4,126,020	88
	William H. Taft	Republican	3,483,922	8
	Eugene V. Debs	Socialist	901,873	
	Eugene Chafin	Prohibition	208,923	
	Arthur Reimer	Socialist Labor	29,179	

Besides the unprecedented financing, the campaign was notable for its emotional appeals of "mass against class" and its sectional sentiment. The outcome of the election also reflected these appeals. The East and North Central States voted unanimously for McKinley, while the Solid South and most of the Western silver mining states cast their lot for Bryan.

The Democratic-Populist strategy of class appeals to workers and farmers showed that control of the party was in different hands than under Cleveland, who had been able to carry a sizable Eastern commercial vote. Although Bryan was a "common man," he was not successful in carrying Eastern wage earners with him. The Republicans were able to unite most business interests through promise of seeking new foreign markets, preserving sound money, and continuing the protective tariff. They were able to sell the workers on these programs too with the promise that these meant employment and greater security. The ideas, moreover, sounded plausible to workers unemployed as a result of the recession of the panic of 1893. Furthermore, McKinley had dealt fairly with organized labor and industrial laborers believed his slogan of "a full dinner pail" would pay better dividends than the Populist Bryan's assault on financial capitalism.

As the nation turned the page to the present century it was confronted with seven major issues, largely economic in nature, many of them dating from 1876. These were destined to be great issues on the floors of legislative assemblies, in the smoke-filled hotel rooms of party caucuses, on the floors of the national conventions, in campaign literature, and in the speeches of men who would be rulers. As in the preceding century, much of the discussion also centered around how to take a position on the problems so as to avoid alienating large ethnic and economic interests. Succinctly, these twentieth-century problems have centered around:

1. Foreign policy; isolation or intervention in world affairs
2. International trade, finance, and tariff policies
3. Social legislation; labor policies and social security
4. Regulation of business; "trust busting," fair trade practices
5. Public enterprise; banking, credit, electricity, and railroads
6. Regulation of the liquor traffic
7. Farm relief and the control of agricultural surpluses

During the first decade of the twentieth century many of these issues were ignored by the major parties. The Prohibition and Socialist Labor parties, now entrenched as permanent minor parties, kept up a steady barrage of protests demanding Federal or state remedies for what they considered the more serious ills. One of these, the regulation of liquor, was settled one way in 1918 and another in 1933. Collective bargaining, minimum wages, the maximum work week, social insurance, public ownership, and regulation of business, agriculture, and labor are still without a completely definitive solution and will continue, as in the past, to divide parties and men. Pressure politics and party politics have become bound up to a large extent with the politics of social security. The coming in rapid order of the automobile, airplane, radio, and television brought new and vital methods for the control of public opinion and made possible easy communication between the sections. As never before, the masses could be reached without difficulty by public men both in and out of office. Mass bombing and the splitting of the atom revolutionized the concept of international security and have made the twentieth-century debates on foreign policy the most important in the nation's history. Of these things are twentieth-century politics made.

Although Bryan and McKinley ran again in 1900, the former did no better. Bimetallism was settled in 1896, and the majority of the voters did not respond to Bryan's issue of "imperialism" brought on by the Spanish-American War. But other populist cries against economic monopoly and political corruption continued as a new progressive leadership arose from agrarians, socialists, intellectuals, humanitarians, and organized labor. Although the socialists joined in voices of protest, the wellspring of the movement came from those believing in private enterprise and reform within the framework of capitalism. Actually, the movement had no one plan or reform. It was a series of many reforms directed by many leaders in many directions, and often contradictory. But great economic and political reforms took place which had lasting effects on the life of the nation. The movement cut across party lines and to some extent class lines.

Economically, the old socialist-populist cries for a graduated income tax, shorter working hours, and public regulation of certain segments of the economy such as transportation became public policy. The Clayton Antitrust and Federal Trade Commission Acts, the Federal Reserve banking system, railway regulation, farm loan and grain speculation acts, food and drug inspection legislation, and the creation of a separate labor department were some of the other answers which the government provided to the protests of humanitarians and reformers.

The era was most fertile in terms of political reforms, reforms which had a lasting impact on political parties. Corporations were forbidden to contribute to political campaigns. The selection process was further removed from the party leaders through the rapid extension of direct primary laws in the states, and presidential primaries for the choice of delegates to national conventions. Popular control was extended through the introduction of the initiative, referendum, and the recall. Prominent leaders of both political parties endorsed direct election of senators, and the amendment was adopted in 1913. These progressive schemes were running counter to the short-ballot movement which was making headway in some cities. The voter's burden was added to by primary elections and ballot propositions and campaign costs went up accordingly.

President Wilson made considerable progress in extending the Federal merit system. On the local level, the replacement of weak mayoral systems by commission and city-manager plans and the extension of nonpartisan elections in municipalities deprived the parties of a certain amount of patronage. These measures, however, failed to kill off corrupt bosses and machines as much as their advocates had hoped. Longer ballots were confusing to voters and political machines could mobilize their followers to take advantage of the confusion. Clearly, the political reforms of the progressive movement failed to go deep enough to bring about any radical reorganization of the parties or the electoral system.

The expansion of popular participation was especially marked during this era. Large numbers of nonpartisan political clubs were created by church, labor and women's groups, and the latter succeeded in pressuring President Wilson and Congress into supporting the woman suffrage amendment. The amendment resulted in women being placed on party committees and assuming a formal place in the councils of the party.

The most significant party battle of the period was in 1912, when Theodore Roosevelt made a formidable third-party bid for the presidency. The bitter campaign between the Bull Moose leader and President Taft enabled Wilson to be elected and returned the Democrats to power for eight years. The foundation of Wilson's strength was stronger than that of Cleveland but it did not bring about a significant realignment of party forces. Wilson's concept of a strong President helped him to keep control over his party and to push through, with the aid of the Democratic caucus in Congress, a progressive program.

REPUBLICAN HEGEMONY

The last two years of Wilson's regime were marked by sharp Republican-Democratic differences over foreign policy. Wilson had alienated powerful Republican leaders and, with Republican control over Congress beginning in 1919, his program for peace settlements was blocked. This failure to secure bipartisan support for foreign policy prompted Presidents Roosevelt and Truman in the 1940's to try to remove foreign policy from the arena of party politics.

With partisan politics back in the saddle in 1920, the Republicans were able to capitalize on weariness with wartime controls and to return to power by huge majorities. During the 1920's the Democrats could do little more than hold the Solid South, and they even lost some Southern states in 1928. Scandals broke out during the Harding Administration and this looked like a favorable omen for the Democrats. Vice President Coolidge, however, was able to remain disassociated from this corruption. The Democrats also killed their own chances in 1924 when they became embroiled in one of their bitterest fights in the national convention over the Klan issue, McAdoo versus Smith, and the Prohibition and Catholic issues. It took the delegates 103 ballots to nominate. They ended by turning their backs on progressivism and nominating a conservative, John W.

Davis. Many of the old-line progressives rallied around the third-party ticket of Senator Robert M. La Follette of Wisconsin. But the voters responded to the "Keep Cool with Coolidge" appeals and preferred to

Table 8. Presidential Election Statistics, 1916–1928

Year	Candidate	Party	Popular vote	Electoral vote
1916	Woodrow Wilson	Democrat	9,129,606	277
	Charles E. Hughes	Republican	8,538,221	254
	Allan Benson	Socialist	585,113	
	J. Frank Hanly	Prohibition	220,506	
	Charles E. Hughes	Progressive	43,319	
	Arthur Reimer	Socialist Labor	13,403	
1920	Warren G. Harding	Republican	16,189,925	404
	James M. Cox	Democrat	9,147,353	127
	Eugene V. Debs	Socialist	915,302	
	Perley Christensen	Farmer-Labor	265,411	
	Aaron Watkins	Prohibition	189,408	
	James E. Ferguson	American	47,689	
	William Cox	Socialist Labor	31,175	
	Robert Macauley	Single Tax	5,837	
1924	Calvin Coolidge	Republican	15,718,211	382
	John W. Davis	Democrat	8,385,586	136
	Robert M. La Follette	Progressive, Socialist & Farmer-Labor	4,832,614	13
	Herman Faris	Prohibition	57,551	
	Frank Johns	Socialist Labor	39,400	
	William Z. Foster	Communist	36,386	
	Gilbert O. Nations	American	24,430	
1928	Herbert Hoover	Republican	21,431,501	444
	Alfred E. Smith	Democrat	15,016,443	87
	Norman Thomas	Socialist	267,964	
	William Z. Foster	Communist	48,666	
	Verne L. Reynolds	Socialist Labor	21,603	
	William F. Varney	Prohibition	20,106	
	Frank Webb	Farmer-Labor	6,390	

stay with the conservative wing of the Republican party. There was a moratorium on progressive legislation but at the same time the legislation put through by Roosevelt, Taft, and Wilson remained on the books.

The contest between Herbert Hoover and Governor Alfred E. Smith in 1928 brought to the fore the split character of the Democratic party.

The Protestant, "dry," rural wing had been pitted against the Catholic, "wet," urban elements in the national conventions of 1924 and 1928. Smith represented the latter group and the fact that Senator Joseph Robinson, a Protestant and a dry from Arkansas, was named as his running mate failed to unite the Democrats and they were able to carry only six of the Southern states, Rhode Island, and Massachusetts. The nation was not quite ready to repeal national prohibition and Hoover undoubtedly gained by his support of the Eighteenth Amendment.

The election was significant in a number of other respects. Smith demonstrated considerable strength in the large cities of the nation, a factor which was to become very important to the Democrats in subsequent elections. The selection of a Catholic nominee provided an underlying religious issue which had formerly gone untested in presidential campaigns. Radio was used extensively for the first time. The third overwhelming defeat in a row led some to predict the complete demise of the Democratic party. No one then could have foreseen the phenomenal realignment which would sweep the Democratic party back into power in 1932.

Republican rule was brought to an end primarily because of a sharp recession resulting in a large volume of unemployment, decline of farm prices and increase of farm foreclosures, and the bankruptcy of many businesses. Almost every segment of the economy suffered and Democratic publicity capitalized on the "Hoover depression." Hoover's renomination drove many progressives out of his party and they supported the Democratic nominee, Governor Franklin D. Roosevelt, instead of starting another Bull Moose party. There had been, in fact, a Senate Democratic-Progressive-Republican coalition which often found itself in opposition to President Hoover. Roosevelt carried 42 out of 48 states and 57.4 per cent of the popular vote. More than a million voters, however, were dissatisfied with both Roosevelt and Hoover and cast their votes for minor-party candidates. Roosevelt's victory also resulted in tremendous Democratic majorities in both houses of Congress.

THE NEW DEAL

Rooseveltian Policies and Techniques. The regimes of Roosevelt and Truman constitute an era not simply because they represented 20 years of unbroken Democratic occupancy of the White House. The New Deal-Fair Deal period brought unprecedented Federal action in new fields as well as great extension in old ones. Although Roosevelt and Truman were strikingly different personalities and each used quite different methods, the programs and party alignments remained essentially intact under both men except for certain defections in Truman's later days. The New Deal era, as had the Progressive era, shifted some power and influence away from the business and financial community to other segments in the economy.

President Roosevelt ushered in an age of positive government where, in the words of the President, "new instruments of public power" were to be built up and placed "in the hands of a people's government." This power was "to assist the development of an economic declaration of rights, an economic constitutional order." In his second inaugural address Mr. Roosevelt said: "Nearly all of us recognize that as intricacies of human relationships increase, so the power to govern them must also increase—power to stop evil; power to do good. The essential democracy of our nation and the safety of our people depend not on the absence of power, but upon lodging it with those whom the people can change or continue at stated intervals through an honest and free system of elections." Concisely, the government was to control that power possessed by private groups in order to make "private office a public trust."

Another basic policy of profound significance was the bringing about of a gradual reversal of American foreign policy from nonintervention to active participation in international affairs, especially the aiding of those nations fighting the Axis powers. This was achieved in the face of organized hostility to aiding the Allies and the reluctance on the part of Republican congressional leaders to intervention prior to Pearl Harbor. After involvement, Roosevelt led his party and the nation in dedicating the United States to cooperation in international organization and world leadership.

These broad policies were brought into effect by means of thousands of laws and executive orders, by unprecedented Federal expenditures, and through a huge increase in the executive establishment. They required the mobilization of public opinion on a grand scale, the support of the masses associated with powerful organized minorities, and vigorous party leadership. Like Andrew Jackson and Theodore Roosevelt, Franklin Roosevelt assumed personal leadership of his party and the government; few Presidents were so gifted in the techniques of dynamic leadership or in the ability to lead public opinion. Many of his actions and methods were tradition-shattering and spectacular and resulted in strengthening and maintaining a hold on some segments of the population while at the same time incurring an abiding hatred and enmity from other groups.

Recent political history may be viewed in terms of the struggle to achieve economic security for the individual and his family and national security for the United States in the world. The politics of the New Deal became the politics of security to a greater extent than in any other period of our history. Within four years after the inauguration of Roosevelt a Federal public-works and job-security program, a Federal-state system of old-age pensions, unemployment compensation, and various health and welfare services were established. Credit was extended to homeowners, farmers, and business.[4] Investors and consumers were given a larger degree of protection and the underprivileged were helped by public power projects. An underlying concept of the New Deal, as enunciated in its earlier days, was that the people had been made less secure because they were "regimented into the service of the privileged few." By curbing these few, the Rooseveltian philosophy held, greater freedom, liberty, and security for the average man would result.

This social pioneering, the President stressed, would bolster, not weaken, private initiative and enterprise and help to promote competition. The role of the Federal government became to regulate private economic forces, set up a social-security system, place several economic enterprises under public ownership, and extend public services to private individuals and groups.

To a considerable extent the New Deal was not a carefully thought-out, consistent social program. It was based upon opportunism and expediency with certain immediate successes and the smoothing out of difficulties for the moment. Roosevelt was more a master of politics than of economics, and the New Deal, like the Progressive movement, contained contradictory features. Nevertheless, the Roosevelt regime left a permanent imprint on the economic and political life of the nation.

The President became not only the Chief Executive but the "Chief Legislator." New ideas, proposals, and policies emanated from the White House so rapidly from 1933 to 1936 that Congress could scarcely keep up with them. Executive initiative of legislation became the rule, while hostile groups dubbed Congress the President's "rubber stamp" and Congress itself often protested the loss of initiative to the President. The New Deal became epitomized in the person of the President and he mustered public confidence by the use of "fireside chats" over the radio, and dramatic personal appearances.

The success of Franklin Roosevelt's party leadership also lay in his ability to muster great support from private-interest groups, especially farm and labor organizations, who in turn brought pressure to bear on reluctant Democrats. Until 1938, many Democratic lawmakers felt that their reelection would depend in a large measure upon their record and support of the New Deal program.

Political Alignment and Support. Though high-sounding in purpose, the general program and methods of the New Deal were bound to—and did—alienate vested interests and many groups. The New Deal program

[4] Credit to business was started by President Hoover through the Reconstruction Finance Corporation and continued under the New Deal. Similarly, farm credit programs were in existence but were expanded during the Roosevelt Administration.

likewise endeared itself to millions of individuals and many organized groups. Few people felt neutral about the President or his program. To many "that man in the White House" became the horned devil incarnate, while to others he was the patron saint of social justice. In effect, the President and his program brought about a substantial realignment of group interests and political parties. This revolution in party life and division was comparable to that of Jackson in 1828 and the birth of the Republican party. The revolution of 1932 in party strength was all the more remarkable because of the three previous disastrous defeats of the Democratic party. Moreover, the strength of the alignment enabled the Democrats to break the two-term tradition and produce consistently sizable Democratic congressional majorities.

The victories of Roosevelt were on a somewhat different basis from those of Wilson. Roosevelt's agrarian support from the West and North was stronger, and he had to rely less on Southern conservatives. Wilson's support, moreover, had much less of a class basis. Granted that Roosevelt's initial victory was in the form of a mounting protest against the party in power, Roosevelt's reelection in 1936 and 1940 rested largely in the strong support given by (1) lower income groups and those on relief, (2) organized labor, and (3) farmers. The American Institute of Public Opinion reported that Mr. Roosevelt received 84 per cent of the relief vote in 1936 and 80 per cent in 1940 and about the same support from union members and only a little less from lower income groups.[5]

Between the two extremes of relief and upper income the gap was wide, indicative of the cleavage in political sentiment between the "haves" and "have-nots." The upper groups were repelled by the reforms and policies, while the lower groups were attracted, illustrating the epigram: "Reforms come from below. No man with four aces howls for a new deal." The same alignments were shown in the occupations, with about 47 per cent of businessmen voting for the President in 1936 and much less in 1940. The professional class gave slightly greater support than the business community, but the polls show that a majority voted against him. The medical profession was especially critical of the President, out of concern for what it believed was his tendency to favor "socialized medicine." Second only to those on relief, organized labor formed a strong pro-Roosevelt bloc. Labor legislation, especially the Social Security, National Labor Relations, Walsh-Healey, and the Fair Labor Standards Acts (Wages and Hours law) kept organized labor in the Democratic column.

During the first half of the Roosevelt Administration spokesmen for organized agricultural groups went along with the New Deal, but many

[5] Figures in this section on cleavages of political opinion are from the Gallup poll as cited in William A. Lydgate, *What America Thinks* (New York: Thomas Y. Crowell Company, 1944), Chap. 9.

of the more conservative and prosperous farmers gradually turned against the program. The Farmers' Union, as spokesman for many of the lower income farmers, remained loyal. Unfortunately no definite breakdown has been made of the voting behavior between the large and small farm owners or between owners and laborers. Roosevelt, however, carried the farm vote nationally both in 1936 and 1940, though he lost the vote of many Middle Western farmers in the latter year. Were it not for the carrying of the farm vote of the rural South, his farm majority would have been much less.

The rural-urban cleavage became especially marked under the New Deal. Roosevelt carried the ten largest cities in the nation in 1936, and nine out of ten in 1940. In the latter election, says Lydgate,[6]

voters in the cities of more than 500,000 population voted for the New Deal by 61 per cent, while Midwest farmers voted against it by 55 per cent. In the middle of 1944, the city voters continued to be pro-Roosevelt by 3 to 2, whereas Midwest farmers were anti-Roosevelt by nearly 2 to 1. The clash of political opinion between city and farm is found in virtually every state outside of the solidly Democratic South.

In many instances the large city vote saved the state for Roosevelt. Downstate Illinois, for example, went 53 per cent for Willkie in 1940, but Roosevelt's 55 per cent vote in Cook County carried the state for him.[7] In 1940 and 1944, the President lost upstate New York by 500,000, but had respective advantages in New York City of about 750,000 and 775,000. This kept the state in the Democratic column. Although the President received little help from Tammany Hall in New York City, he had the vigorous aid of other political machines, notably Chicago, Jersey City, Memphis, and Kansas City. The urban machines were able to muster this vote for the President, however, because of class and various minority sympathies for him in the cities.

Another interesting cleavage in political opinion was reflected in age groups. Among young voters of the age group twenty-one to twenty-nine, Roosevelt continually polled over 60 per cent. The middle-aged shifted from favoring him in the beginning to about 50–50 in 1944, with voters over fifty years of age, though also initially for him, turning against him by 1940. Undoubtedly the dramatization of government by Roosevelt, plus his program to aid youth, and emphasis upon job security had strong appeal for the younger voters.

[6] *Ibid.,* p. 113.

[7] The vote of every county in each state during the Roosevelt regime is found in E. E. Robinson, *They Voted for Roosevelt* (Stanford, Calif.: Stanford University Press, 1947), pp. 58–182. By studying the results of the vote in urban and rural counties, an excellent picture of geographical changes may be had.

Ethnic, religious, and racial cleavages were also in evidence in the New Deal elections though, with the exception of the racial groups, there were few radical changes from pre-1932 days. The ethnic groups in the large cities have generally been Democratic and remained so under the New Deal. The President had the support of several religious minorities. He carried approximately 81 per cent of the Catholic vote in 1936 and 68 per cent in 1940.[8] In 1940, poll takers reported that 87 per cent of the Jewish respondents were going to vote for the President. While he carried the Protestant vote in 1936, he lost it in 1940.

No satisfactory poll has been taken of the Negro vote as a whole. However, it is known that Roosevelt made sizable inroads into the traditional Republican vote of Negroes. One study of a select number of Negro wards in Chicago showed the Negro Democratic vote rising from 23.4 per cent in 1932 to 48.9 in 1936 and 52.0 in 1940.[9] The Republican tradition among the well-to-do Negroes in the area was strong, but the vote shift to the Democrats among the underprivileged, industrialized, and unionized Negroes was most pronounced. A similar shift in major party allegiance between 1930 and 1940 was found among Detroit Negroes.[10] The shift in allegiance of a segment of the Negro vote from the Republican to the Democratic party in national elections must be regarded as a most important development; whether the shift will be permanent remains a political question mark.

In summary, the Democratic party under Roosevelt was able at the crucial time of election to hold together the conservative forces within the party as represented by the South, the major Democratic urban political machines, organized labor and agriculture, and various minority groups. It was a tribute to the personal qualities of his leadership that Roosevelt was able to hold the diverse elements together until the major legislation was enacted. The breakup in this alignment, however, was imminent even in 1940, but the party was held together in a large measure because of the war. At the time of Roosevelt's death, disintegration of the coalition was becoming increasingly evident and manifested itself soon after the end of the war.

PARTY BATTLES UNDER THE NEW DEAL

President Roosevelt and Vice President Garner were renominated by acclamation in 1936 in Philadelphia. The Democrats entered the cam-

---

[8] Figures in this paragraph are taken from Harold F. Gosnell, *Grass Roots Politics* (Washington, D.C.: Public Affairs Press, 1942), pp. 3–4.

[9] See Harold F. Gosnell, "The Negro Vote in Northern Cities," *National Municipal Review*, Vol. 30 (1941), pp. 264–267.

[10] See Edward H. Litchfield, "A Case Study of Negro Political Behavior in Detroit," *Public Opinion Quarterly*, Vol. 5 (1941), pp. 267–274.

paign hopefully and with a well-knit organization under the direction
of National Chairman James A. Farley. Leading contenders in the Republican presidential primaries were Senator William E. Borah of Idaho,
Frank Knox, publisher of the *Chicago Daily News,* and Governor Alfred
Landon of Kansas. Landon gathered a commanding lead and, through
the careful engineering of the convention by his manager John D.
Hamilton, was nominated by acclamation. Knox was chosen as his running mate. Governor Landon had been built up a year in advance as a
"practical liberal" who had balanced the budget of his state.

Because of the popularity of the Administration's domestic policies
with millions of voters, the Republicans did not take issue with the
major New Deal legislative measures. Republican strategy, therefore,
was to charge that Roosevelt had been inefficient in administering the
laws and to promise better administration and a balanced budget. States'
rights and grass-roots beliefs were championed by the opposition orators,
though little attempt was made to explain what Federal functions would
be returned to the states under a Republican regime. In addition, the
Republicans attempted to show that the Roosevelt Administration en-
dangered American political and financial institutions. The Republican
campaign did not strike fire and Roosevelt carried every state except
Maine and Vermont (see Tables 9, 10). Democratic majorities in both
houses of Congress were also overwhelming.

After his inauguration for his second term in 1937, President Roosevelt
turned his attention immediately to the threat that the major features
of his New Deal program would be held unconstitutional by the Supreme
Court. The NRA program, which had been the major effort to restore
prosperity, had been declared unconstitutional, and the farm control
and subsidy program—the AAA—had also been set aside by the Court.
Cases were pending before the Court testing the constitutionality of the
TVA Act, the Social Security Act, the Wagner Act, and other important
New Deal legislation. The President felt that some means must be found
to prevent the Court from nullifying his program.[11] The members of the
Supreme Court were all appointees from previous administrations, and
the Court was criticized for being "out of step" with the political change
overwhelmingly voted by the people. Several important New Deal measures were held unconstitutional by 5 to 4 votes.

As a part of a judicial reorganization bill, Roosevelt proposed the
addition of a justice to the Supreme Court for each judge over seventy
years of age who had not retired. Keen excitement was aroused through-

[11] Several other Presidents, including Jackson, Lincoln, and Theodore Roosevelt,
had altercations with the courts and the Progressive party platform of 1924 had called
for the election of Federal judges and provisions for overriding judicial vetoes of
legislation declared unconstitutional.

Table 9. Presidential Election Statistics, 1932–1952

Year	Candidate	Party	Popular vote	Number of states carried	Electoral vote
1932	Franklin D. Roosevelt	Democrat	22,809,638	42	272
	Herbert Hoover	Republican	15,758,901	6	59
	Norman Thomas	Socialist	885,314		
	William Foster	Communist	102,991		
	William Upshaw	Prohibition	81,869		
	William Harvey	Liberty	53,425		
	Verne Reynolds	Socialist Labor	33,275		
	Jacob Coxey	Farmer-Labor	7,294		
1936	Franklin D. Roosevelt	Democrat	27,478,945	46	523
	Alfred M. Landon	Republican	16,674,665	2	8
	William Lemke	Union	882,479		
	Norman Thomas	Socialist	187,720		
	Earl Browder	Communist	80,159		
	D. Leigh Colvin	Prohibition	37,487		
1940	Franklin D. Roosevelt	Democrat	26,890,401	38	449
	Wendell L. Willkie	Republican	22,321,018	10	82
	Norman Thomas	Socialist	116,796		
	Roger Babson	Prohibition	57,812		
	Earl Browder	Communist	48,610		
	John Aiken	Socialist Labor	14,881		
1944	Franklin D. Roosevelt	Democrat	25,602,505	36	432
	Thomas E. Dewey	Republican	22,006,278	12	99
	Norman Thomas	Socialist	80,518		
	Claude Watson	Prohibition	74,758		
	Edward Teichert	Socialist Labor	45,336		
1948	Harry S. Truman	Democrat	24,105,695	28	303
	Thomas E. Dewey	Republican	21,969,170	16	189
	J. Strom Thurmond	States' Rights Democratic	1,169,021	4	39
	Henry A. Wallace	Progressive	1,156,103		
	Norman Thomas	Socialist	139,009		
	Claude Watson	Prohibition	103,216		
	Edward Teichert	Socialist Labor	29,061		
	Farrell Dobbs	Socialist Workers	13,613		
1952	Dwight D Eisenhower	Republican	33,824,351	39	442
	Adlai Stevenson	Democrat	27,314,987	9	89
	Vincent Hallinan	Progressive	133,608		
	Stuart Hamblen	Prohibition	72,768		
	Eric Haas	Socialist Labor	29,333		
	Darlington Hoopes	Socialist	18,322		
	Douglas MacArthur	Christian Nationalist	16,949		
	Farrell Dobbs	Socialist Workers	8,956		

Table 10. Party Divisions in Congress, 1933–1957

Session	House			Senate		
	Democrat	Republican	Other	Democrat	Republican	Other
1933–1935	313	117	5	60	35	1
1935–1937	322	103	10	69	25	2
1937–1939	333	89	13	75	18	3
1939–1941	262	169	4	69	23	4
1941–1943	267	162	6	66	28	2
1943–1945	222	209	4	57	38	1
1945–1947	242	190	3	56	38	2
1947–1949	188	245	2	45	51	0
1949–1951	263	171	1	54	42	0
1951–1953	234	199	2	49	47	0
1953–1955	212	221	2	47	48	1
1955–1957	232	203	0	48	47	1

out the country over this specific proposal for what opponents called "packing the Court" and an effort to overthrow the constitutional division of powers. The proposal to add judges was soundly defeated in the Senate in July, 1937, and with its defeat Roosevelt's prestige greatly declined. In a sense, however, the President lost the battle but won the war, because the Court, in effect, reformed itself. Thereafter the Supreme Court upheld the validity of practically all New Deal legislation and validated large numbers of administrative orders emanating from various agencies such as the National Labor Relations Board. This was due in part to a switch in votes of one or two justices. As one scholar remarked, "A switch in time saved nine."

The defeat of the President's "court-packing" bill gave heart to those hoping for an anti-Roosevelt revolt. The next opportunity afforded itself when the President requested power to reorganize and effect improvements in the management of the Executive branch. Opponents of the President's social program dubbed the measure a "dictator bill" and a vigorous campaign resulted in the House of Representatives killing the bill by recommitting it. Further, the President was rebuffed on several appointments requiring senatorial confirmation and barely staved off defeat when his choice for Senate majority leader, Alben Barkley, won over Pat Harrison by only one vote.

Roosevelt hoped the Democratic primaries in 1938 would result in nominating persons more faithful to the New Deal. He said in a radio address (June 24) that he was not taking part as President in the primaries, but that, "as head of the Democratic party, however, charged with the responsibility of carrying out the definitely liberal declaration of principles set forth in the 1936 Democratic platform, I feel that I have every right to speak in those few instances where there may be a clear issue between candidates for a Democratic nomination involving principles or involving a clear misuse of my own name." In a transcontinental tour he bestowed his blessings on Senators Buckley of Ohio, Barkley of Kentucky, Caraway of Arkansas, and Thomas of Oklahoma, all of whom were renominated. In New York he openly denounced the Democratic chairman of the Rules Committee, Representative John O'Connor, and called for the nomination of James Fay. Fay's nomination was probably the most significant primary victory for the President. In several other states, notably the South, incumbents whose reelection was opposed by the President as the leader of his party were reelected by decisive votes.[12]

The action of President Roosevelt in coming out openly in opposition to a number of Democratic members of Congress who were running for reelection was strongly criticized at the time and was referred to by persons opposed to it as an attempt to "purge" those who did not go along with the President's program. Capitalizing upon the "purge," the Court issue, and the "dictator bill," the Republicans staged an impressive revival in 1938 by gaining 87 seats in Congress and a net gain of 12 governorships in the states. Governor Herbert Lehman of New York barely beat the popular young District Attorney Thomas E. Dewey. The Republicans, including Mr. Dewey, looked forward hopefully to the 1940 election.

The Third Term. There was no paucity of potential Republican nominees in 1940. Besides former President Herbert Hoover, there were the "big three" favorite sons, Senators Arthur W. Vandenberg of Michigan, Robert A. Taft of Ohio, and Governor Thomas E. Dewey of New York. The last-mentioned made a 25,000-mile tour of the states on a preconvention campaign and demonstrated marked vote-getting possibilities in several presidential preferential primaries. Taft and Vandenberg entered a few primaries but largely concentrated on building up strength in the states which choose delegates by the convention method.

Dark horses were also plentiful, led by Wendell Willkie, president of the Commonwealth and Southern Utility Corporation, who had grown in strength after a *New York Times* columnist called attention to him in February, 1939. Though entering no primaries, he kept before the

---

[12] An illuminating account of Roosevelt's activity in the South is given by J. B. Shannon, "Presidential Politics in the South," *Journal of Politics,* Vol. 1 (1939), pp. 146–170; 278–300.

public through magazine articles and radio broadcasts. As late as May, 1940, he admitted he would like to run for the office but said, "I am not electioneering. I have not spent a nickel and do not intend to spend a nickel in connection with this talk." His friends and admirers, however, were spending more than nickels in his behalf. All over the country "Win with Willkie" clubs sprang up. Many public-utility publicity directors assisted in the build-up, and by the opening of the convention in Philadelphia on June 24, Willkie constituted a major threat to the favorite sons. Telegrams and letters deluged the delegates from the grass roots demanding his nomination.

Willkie's vote grew substantially on each ballot to the consistent stamping of feet and roar from the galleries, "We want Willkie." On the 6th ballot he had a commanding majority. Willkie's phenomenal nomination without the support of the organization politicians was explained in a dozen different ways, from a "bought" nomination to a spontaneous demand on the part of the rank and file. There is little evidence of any purchase of delegate votes. Certainly, pressure politics, excellent publicity, boring from within, and popular appeal with those delegates who were taken to meet him in his downtown suite in Philadelphia largely account for the unorthodox nomination of a man who had been a Democrat until 1938.

To balance the ticket, Charles L. McNary of Oregon, Senate minority floor leader, was chosen. McNary was believed to have an appeal for the farm and Western voters to balance the Willkie appeal to the urban East. The vice presidential nominee favored the Administration's public-power program and had voted for the Wheeler silver purchase bill in 1934, thus offsetting Willkie's fight against the Tennessee Valley Authority and his hard-money leanings. Furthermore, McNary had generally held to a noninterventionist position in foreign policy. Only a few times has a party chosen two men so apparently antithetical in policy as its 1940 nominees.

At the Democratic convention Chairman Alben Barkley told the delegates he had long known the President did not desire to run again and then read a statement from him leaving all the delegates free to vote as they wished. The tent door was open and the "draft Roosevelt" movement commenced, supported by Mayors Kelly of Chicago and Hague of Jersey City. Mr. Farley, still Democratic national chairman, was publicly against a third term and headed off a stampede to nominate the President by acclamation. After the nominating speeches the President was overwhelmingly chosen, and the delegates looked forward to a free and open fight for the vice presidential nomination. However, they soon found themselves pressured into accepting Roosevelt's choice, Secretary of Agriculture Henry A. Wallace. In spite of much grumbling, a sizable majority acquiesced and gave it to Mr. Wallace on the first ballot.

In his acceptance address Mr. Willkie approved many of the New Deal policies and gave his support to a selective service law, aid to the Allies, and in general approved of the Administration's stand on matters of foreign policy. He charged the Administration with fostering a "defeatist" philosophy and scarcity economics in domestic affairs, bungling administration, and promised his efforts to build a strong, united America. He attempted to make his movement a nonpartisan crusade, and many of the Old Guard Republicans were riled by Willkie's practice of relying on himself to a large extent rather than on the organization. Mr. Roosevelt, in accepting the nomination, said that he would "not have the time or inclination to engage in purely political debate," but that he reserved the right "to call the attention of the nation to deliberate and unwitting falsifications of fact." This opened the way for him to deliver a few political speeches during the last two weeks of the campaign.[13]

Since Mr. Farley was publicly against the third term, he resigned as Democratic national chairman after the convention. However, Mr. Farley remained as New York state chairman and at the eleventh hour urged all Democrats to vote a straight Democratic ticket. The split between the President and Mr. Farley was serious. It apparently went further than mere disagreement over a third term. Charles Michelson, former Democratic publicity director, explains the rift in terms of Farley's ambition to be nominated.[14] The President, according to Michelson, told Farley that just as the religious issue tended to hurt Alfred Smith's candidacy in 1928, the same prejudice would cost the Democrats the election if Farley ran in 1940. Others have generally explained the breach in terms of Farley's belief in a two-term tradition and the President's insistence upon naming Henry Wallace as his running mate.

The third Roosevelt victory was impressive, although its landslide proportions in terms of 1936 were reduced. Mr. Roosevelt was able to break the two-term tradition and overcome opposition of the isolationists, parts of the South, and farming communities because he remained personally popular and had put over a program which benefited millions of voters. The President had demonstrated his ability to carry the enormous burdens of office without a physical breakdown and had been ahead of Congress in foreseeing the critical situation abroad. The widely held belief that Roosevelt was the best-qualified man to lead the country

[13] For issues stressed in the 1940 campaign see Hugh A. Bone, *Smear Politics: An Analysis of 1940 Campaign Literature* (Washington, D.C.: Public Affairs Press, 1941).

[14] See *The Ghost Talks* (New York: G. P. Putnam's Sons, 1944). Chairman Edward J. Flynn, *You're the Boss* (New York: The Viking Press, Inc., 1947), Chap. 12, gives essentially the same explanation of the Roosevelt-Farley break.

during the war period was most important in his overcoming the third-term tradition.[15]

War and the Fourth Election. As a gesture toward "an adjournment of politics," the President appointed many prominent Republicans to important positions in the defense agencies. Mr. Willkie, one week after the election, pledged himself and his party to a "loyal opposition." Many other Republicans publicly supported this stand. The minority floor leaders in the Senate and the House, however, refused to commit themselves. Other Republican groups openly took issue with Mr. Willkie and refused to accept his pledge of nonpartisanship in foreign policy. Many Republican state conventions came close to officially adopting resolutions condemning his "interventionist" views, and the publicity director of the Republican National Committee declared: "The two words do not stand together. They do not make sense. There cannot be a loyal opposition." In 1941, several prominent Republicans petitioned Congress to "put a stop to step-by-step projection of the United States into undeclared war." The bombing of Pearl Harbor, however, brought pledges of national unity from all political parties. But this adjournment of politics was short-lived.

The Republican National Committee, meeting in April, 1942, was called upon to decide which of two paths the party should follow. Mr. Willkie's group urged the party to take an unequivocal stand to pledge itself to active international cooperation after the war. The other faction had a lively recollection of how public opinion swung "back to normalcy" and isolationism after World War I; accordingly, they were unenthusiastic about committing themselves to postwar collaboration. Mr. Willkie's tenets were adopted under a "compromise" plank. Somewhat later Senator Vandenberg and Governor Dewey accepted and worked for a "bipartisan foreign policy," a practice which was adopted and constituted a highly important development in American politics.

Following the Republican upsurge in the 1942 election, the Administration's political fortunes continued to decline. Farmers grew restive

[15] The Republican-controlled 80th Congress in 1947 submitted a constitutional amendment which would forbid a President to serve more than two terms. Most Democratic state legislatures refused to ratify it and most Republican ones quickly endorsed it. In 1950, Republicans captured many state governments and swelled the list of ratifying states. Meanwhile, several Southern legislatures decided this amendment would serve as a moral deterrent to President Truman seeking another term and several of them ratified it. By February, 1951, the Twenty-second Amendment had been ratified by the requisite 36 states. How this amendment will influence presidential leadership during a President's second term is yet to be demonstrated but it seems bound to affect the last two years of a President serving his second term and to encourage hopefuls to begin their preconvention strategy without regard to the President's plans.

over the price-control program. Labor strikes, particularly the one called by the United Mine Workers of America, brought sharp criticism that the party in power was impeding the war effort by "coddling labor." Labor leaders, on the other hand, expressed a desire to change the "Little Steel" wage formula, charging that it no longer gave the workers the pay increases due to them to keep pace with the rising cost of living. Rationing was stiffened and brought additional cries of protest. These reflected themselves in increased Republican victories in special elections and made Republican leaders more outspoken in their criticisms of the Administration's war program. Quarrels broke out between various factions of the Democratic party. President Roosevelt, following his 1940 practice, remained silent. In the face of this, no boom for any other Democratic nominee had been developed. The Democratic National Committee, after calling for the convention to meet in Chicago on July 19, resorted to the almost unprecedented action of calling for President Roosevelt to run for a fourth term and continue "as the great world leader." Several Southern groups announced that they would not go along with a fourth nomination, but the much-heralded Southern revolt failed to obtain any serious proportions in the convention.

The Republicans had their factional quarrels in 1943 and 1944 over foreign policy. A Republican Nationalist Revival Committee was formed to counteract the "internationalism" of the Willkie wing. Abandoning the old term "isolationist," the group adopted "nationalism," a term frequently appearing in American politics. A century ago the nationalism of Henry Clay, Andrew Jackson, and Abraham Lincoln supported a strong national government, internal improvements, and Federal assistance to business and agriculture. Theodore Roosevelt's "new nationalism" envisaged a strong foreign policy. Yet the nationalism of the Republican Nationalist Revival Committee was in general the opposite in principle. Fundamentally, it was states' rights and in opposition to a strong central government even in time of war. Its greatest support came from the old ultraisolationist movement and was strongly sectional in character. Spearheading the movement was (and still is) the *Chicago Tribune*.

Wendell Willkie hoped for a renomination but his sharp setback in the Wisconsin presidential primaries caused him to withdraw. Many Republican delegates and newspapers then rushed to the bandwagon of Governor Thomas E. Dewey. He had remained essentially aloof from the preconvention struggles which were taking place between Governor Harold Stassen and Senator John Bricker of Ohio. But Dewey's supporters were working effectively and the governor was nominated on the first ballot with only one dissenting vote after Bricker and Stassen withdrew. Willkie's supporters soon found themselves out of the party's councils and Willkie died before he was able to state publicly whether he favored Dewey or Roosevelt.

Southern Democrats had made known that they would not accept the renomination of Wallace. The question arose as to whether the President would insist, as he had in 1940, on having Wallace as a running mate. Mr. Roosevelt was caught on the horns of a dilemma. If he put on pressure for Wallace, he would alienate further many Southern delegates and the conservative wing of the party. If he left Wallace to fend for himself, he would mollify some of the conservatives and anti-fourth-term groups but distress the liberal elements.

Before the convention opened, President Roosevelt sent a letter to the permanent chairman of the meeting, saying that if he were a delegate to the convention he would vote for the renomination of Wallace. He stated, however, that he did not wish "to appear in any way as dictating to the convention," and by his faint praise of Wallace it was evident that President Roosevelt would not insist on his renomination. Before the nominations started, Chairman Robert E. Hannegan let it be known that Mr. Roosevelt had also put his blessing on Senator Harry S. Truman and Associate Justice William O. Douglas, and that he had a letter to that effect. Since the letter was dated after Mr. Roosevelt's earlier endorsement of Wallace, the Truman forces claimed that it meant that the President changed his mind. The real motive of the President's letter, however, was not made public; the more objective observers felt that his second letter was not a repudiation of Wallace but merely a statement of preference in the event that the Vice President failed of renomination. Wallace led on the first ballot but failed to obtain a majority. On the second ballot there was a bandwagon rush as delegates abandoned their favorite sons for Truman.

The 1944 campaign resembled that of 1940 in many respects. Seasoned observers were reasonably certain from the start that the nation would reelect the President and public-opinion polls gave substance to this, though it appeared that the contest would be closer than any of the preceding campaigns. While not making foreign policy an issue, Governor Dewey told the electorate that young vigorous hands were needed to write a lasting peace and to take America down the path of prosperity in the postwar years. The New Dealers, he said, "were tired and quarrelsome" and could not hope to perform the job well.

Democratic leaders answered this by emphasizing that it was dangerous to change leadership in the midst of the war and that the President's long experience as Commander in Chief and world leader was needed to prosecute the war to speed total victory. The isolationist voting record of many Republicans was stressed in an effort to show that they promised little in the way of formulating a realistic peace. The President, as in

1940, did no active campaigning until October, when it seemed advisable for him to leave the White House and appear in public. A major reason for this was a whispering campaign about the President's physical fitness and the opposition's emphasis on tiredness. When the ballots were counted, the President carried 36 states. Mr. Dewey had cut into Roosevelt's popular vote margin but carried only two more states than had Wendell Willkie.

After his inauguration on Jan. 20, 1945, the President went to Yalta for another conference with Marshal Stalin and Prime Minister Churchill. Upon his return, he reported to Congress in person on the agreements reached there. Then with considerable dispatch he pushed the convening of delegates of the United Nations at San Francisco for the purpose of drafting an international peace organization. The President himself planned to open the meeting with an address. At this fateful hour, and less than two weeks before the scheduled opening of the San Francisco conference, a shocked nation was told on April 12 that the President had died while resting at his Warm Springs, Ga., home. For the third time in its history the United States was to lose the service of its wartime leader in the building of the peace.

THE FIRST TRUMAN ADMINISTRATION

An anxious nation was suddenly to be led by a comparatively colorless, plain, and not too well-known Missouri senator at one of the most crucial times. The new President vigorously plunged into his gigantic task with a dramatic appearance before Congress and a radio address to the nation, pledging the continuance of his predecessor's policies. He announced his intention of working cordially with Congress to prosecute the war to total victory and to continue Mr. Roosevelt's peace plans. The rapidly moving events of the first four months of his regime ending with V-J Day provided a happy political "honeymoon," while public-opinion polls showed a skyrocketing popularity for the new Chief Executive.

Truman's Cabinet reflected a general trend to more conservative appointments. The New Deal became the "Fair Deal," which was a continuation and expansion of the former's major objectives. Business interests were alienated when Truman insisted on the renewal of price control and when he vetoed a greatly watered-down version of it. He asked for a renewal of the Fair Employment Practices Committee and universal military training and opposed the early return of the United States Employment Service to the states. He proposed a comprehensive housing program, Federal health insurance, a full-employment measure, unification of the armed services, increase of minimum wages and unemployment compensation, and the Missouri Valley Authority. On practically every one of these Congress turned down the President or enacted measures far short of his wishes. On major foreign policies, however, Congress followed the President. Southern Democrats hoped for a retreat from Rooseveltian policies of fair-employment practices, the anti-poll-tax bill, and centralization. When Truman retained these objectives, he found himself denounced as vociferously as Roosevelt had been.

Ordinarily, high wages, production, and prosperity favor the party in power and the economists' charts for the period reflected a very high level of employment and prosperity. This advantage for the Democrats, however, was dissipated by popular unrest about strikes, the slowness of reconversion in some lines, and shortages, especially meat and foods. Congress passed an utterly emasculated price control law which had permitted skyrocketing prices in many lines. In early October, 1946, long queues in front of meat shops were a common spectacle and the mounting discontent with this inconvenience forced Mr. Truman to remove meat ceilings entirely three weeks before the congressional election. In this situation the Republicans found one of the most potent political weapons and astutely exploited it to the hilt—the politics of protest. A New England businessman coined a slogan which was immediately adopted by the Republicans on a national scale, "Had enough? Vote Republican!" This symbolized to millions of voters a method of ending wartime controls, war weariness, and "sweeping clean" the backwash of the war.

Public-opinion polls predicted a landslide for the Republicans in the congressional election, a prediction entirely fulfilled. The party registered a net gain of 13 senators and 57 in the House, providing a comfortable majority, especially in view of the dissension between the Southern and Northern Democrats in Congress. Several popular Democratic governors were also swept from office and the Republican party emerged with a majority of the governorships.

The press regarded the election of 1946 as the "official end of the New Deal." In terms of labor and social-security legislation this proved to be partially correct. As a matter of fact, the war years had resulted in a moratorium on social legislation and the progressivism of the New Deal was really arrested long before the death of Mr. Roosevelt. In terms of foreign policy, however, New Deal policies were continued and Truman was able to muster majorities in Congress for his measures to rehabilitate the Western nations and to attempt to stop the spread of communism into Western and Southern Europe.

RENEWAL OF THE FAIR DEAL

The 1948 Election. The national conventions of 1948 provided few surprises, even though Dewey was not nominated until the third ballot and Truman failed to receive a unanimous ballot but was easily renominated on the first ballot (Truman received 947½ votes to 263 for

Senator Richard B. Russell). Dewey's managers had begun to plan immediately after his defeat in 1944 for his renomination. The governor's
impressive reelection in New York in 1946 and his ability to maintain
silence on controversial domestic policies paved the way for his designation again as a compromise candidate. Senator Robert A. Taft, a
leading contender, was forced to vote upon national legislation which
alienated some groups and his coauthorship of the Taft-Hartley Act had
offended organized labor. Former Governor Harold E. Stassen toured the
nation seeking delegates. Stassen built up an enthusiastic following among
the young Republicans but incurred the enmity of the Old Guard because of his unconventional practices. For example, he violated political
dictum by entering the presidential primaries in Senator Taft's home
state of Ohio. In the Republican convention there was a considerable
lack of enthusiasm for Dewey but opponents were unable to agree on
an alternative. Taft delegates were inclined to take Dewey before Stassen,
and Stassen delegates seemed to prefer Dewey to Taft. Governor Earl
Warren of California, for whom there was great sentiment, was nominated for Vice President.

President Truman's decline in popularity and quarrels with Congress
led a strong anti-Truman movement to develop within the party in the
spring of 1948. Many leaders hoped the President would take himself
out of the race, but Truman let it be known that he expected to be
nominated and elected. A number of Democrats called for the nomination
of General Dwight D. Eisenhower. The General had caught the popular
imagination and public-opinion polls maintained that he could be elected
President either as a Republican or Democrat. His name was first entered
in the Republican primaries of New Hampshire, much to the consterna-
tion of the Dewey forces. At this juncture Eisenhower, in a strongly
worded letter, took himself out of the race for President, saying in part
that the separation of the military from the civilian was a wise policy.
This stymied the boom for him among Republicans, but many Democratic politicians, sensing a Truman defeat, pushed the Eisenhower
candidacy until the General took himself unequivocally out of the realm
of political availability.

Shortly after the Democratic convention, disgruntled Southern Democrats ("Dixiecrats") met and nominated Governor J. Strom Thurmond
of South Carolina and Governor Fielding L. Wright of Mississippi for
President and Vice President respectively. This group adopted a states'
rights platform and pledged itself to carry on the fight even outside the
South.

Former Vice President Henry Wallace let it be known early in 1948
that he would run for President against Truman and the so-called
"bipartisan" foreign policy. His cause was backed by the Progressive

Citizens of America, several left-wing labor leaders, and the Communists. In a remarkable national convention characterized by an extraordinary amount of music, "revivalism," and the absence of professional politicians, Wallace was nominated with Senator Glen Taylor of Idaho as his running mate. The Wallace movement was pledged against selective service, the Marshall Plan, and for greater cooperation with the Soviet Union.

The outcome of the election provided one of the greatest surprises in American political history. Public-opinion polls, newspaper straw votes, and the press predicted a Dewey victory ranging from a comfortable margin to landslide proportions. Democratic managers privately doubted Mr. Truman's reelection and Democrats running for state and congressional offices were generally reconciled to this and concentrated on their own campaigns. Presumably the political tide was also strongly in favor of the Republicans.

President Truman himself put on a vigorous "give-'em-hell" campaign and appeared serious in his expressions of confidence that he would win in the face of what seemed to be hopeless odds. He denounced the Eightieth Congress, a theme from which he made little deviation throughout the campaign, and called Congress into session to act on high prices and social legislation, but it failed, as might be expected, to respond. The President also offered an attractive social program to ethnic groups, laborers, and consumers. By contrast, Dewey and Warren avoided specific commitments, attacked the "wobbling" and "confused" Truman Administration, and preached "unity" and efficient government.

For the first time since 1916 voters were unable to know the outcome of the election until the following morning. As the Republicans had figured, Truman lost several states to the States' Righters—Alabama, Louisiana, Mississippi, and South Carolina. Electors for Mr. Truman were not even on the Alabama ballot. Also the votes cast for the Independent Progressive party led by Wallace cost Truman New York and Maryland. The President lost heavily in the East, where Roosevelt had been strong, but he managed to salvage Rhode Island and Massachusetts. What the Republicans had not counted on was that Truman would carry much of the Middle West and California. Mr. Truman became one of the very few Presidents to win without New York. It was a great personal triumph for the President on his own; no longer was he the mere caretaker of the Roosevelt regime. He had beaten the Wallace group, the Dixiecrats, and some prominent local Democratic bosses, notably Boss Ed Crump of Tennessee, who had formally endorsed States' Righter Thurmond and opposed the pro-Truman candidate for United States senator, Estes Kefauver.

The 1948 election was notable for the large number of nonvoters and also for those who made up their minds late in the campaign—the latter fact helped to mar the accuracy of the public-opinion polls. But among those who voted, Truman reforged the alliances and combinations which the Democrats had had under Roosevelt but which appeared to have been lost by the Republican victories in 1946. In one study of voting behavior it was found that Negroes voted almost 2 to 1 for Truman, as did the Catholics.[16] Laborers voted about 3 to 1 for Truman and, like Roosevelt, the President received a majority of the votes cast by those under thirty-five years of age and who had less than a college education. There was a high percentage of nonvoters among farmers, but those who voted went almost 2 to 1 for Truman. The President also carried practically all of the nation's biggest cities. Dewey kept the traditional vote of the professional and managerial classes, college people, and those living in the smaller towns and cities. The Democrats likewise won both houses of Congress by comfortable margins and were able to retain control in the 1950 elections.

The defeat for the Republicans was a bitter pill, for everything appeared "in the bag" for them. Western Republicans grumbled about "Eastern" control of their party. The election marked the end of a ten-year attempt of Governor Dewey to become President and he found himself very unpopular among the conservatives in his party. Yet the Republicans were not too discouraged since their defeat was not so overwhelming as in previous presidential elections, and they had done reasonably well in state elections.

Prelude to a Republican Comeback. President Truman's second term was a combination of stalemate and of electrifying events which contributed much to the United States' leadership in the world, but which paved the way for the end of 20 years of Democratic control of the executive and all but two years in Congress. The stalemate was caused by the President's inability to maintain unity within his own party in Congress for much of his domestic program. Congressional investigating committees began to reveal alliances between crime and politics in some American cities and eventually turned up cases within the Federal government of influence-peddling, tax-fixing, the acceptance of gratuities and commissions for government contracts and favors. These were widely publicized and even though no Cabinet officers or especially high officials were implicated, the issue of "corruption in government" was exploited by the opposition party, anti-Truman Democrats, and newspapers.

As relations worsened with the Soviet Union, and as the latter was winning political and sometimes indirect military victories in Europe

[16] See Angus Campbell and R. L. Kahn, *The People Elect a President* (Ann Arbor, Mich.: University of Michigan Survey Research Center, 1952), Chap. 3; see also Table 11 below.

and Asia, the nation became concerned over the Communist menace. As early as 1947 President Truman had inaugurated a loyalty program designed to cover Federal employees. As with corruption, congressional investigating committees were making daily headlines on the Communist menace in the country and turned up some Federal employees who were either Communists or had been onetime sympathizers. This issue, like corruption, undermined confidence in the Truman Administration.

In the summer of 1950 the President took steps through the United Nations to resist the aggression of the North Koreans and their Chinese Communist friends. This action involved American Armed Forces in what was soon known as the Korean War. The President's action was widely applauded and Congress responded with the legislation and appropriations necessary to carry out the operation. No quick military victory was forthcoming and the opposition began to dub the action as "Truman's War." Sharp disagreement broke out over objectives of uniting North and South Korea and bombing bases in Communist China. Those favoring an extension of the war criticized the "stalemate" in Korea and charged the Administration with "appeasing Red China." The removal of General Douglas MacArthur from command in Korea and the General's rousing welcome when he returned to the United States added to the unpopularity of the Truman regime.

THE TURN TO EISENHOWER

1952 Nominations and Election.[17] During Truman's regime, public-opinion polls continued to show that the majority of voters, irrespective of which party ticket he might run on, favored General Eisenhower for the next President. The General, meanwhile, served for a short time as president of Columbia University, then returned to uniform to perform a European assignment. Republican leaders beat a steady path to Europe to convince the General that he must accept the nomination in order "to save the country."

Eisenhower finally permitted his name to be entered in the first presidential primary, which was held in New Hampshire. He indicated he would make no speeches for delegates and stayed in Europe until very shortly before the opening of the Republican convention. In the mean-

[17] Considerable additional treatment of the 1952 conventions and campaign is found in Chaps. 18 and 19 respectively. See also V. P. De Santes, "The Presidential Election of 1952," *The Review of Politics,* Vol. 15 (1953), pp. 131–150. For a definitive account of the preconvention campaigns and the conventions themselves see the five-volume report of the American Political Science Association, *Presidential Nominating Politics in 1952* (Baltimore: Johns Hopkins Press, 1954). A useful account of aspects of the election is that of A. Campbell, G. Gurin, and W. Miller, *The Voter Decides* (Evanston, Ill.: Row, Peterson & Company, 1954).

time, his backers were skillfully managing his campaign and a large network of "Citizens for Eisenhower" clubs spread over the nation.

Former Governor Harold Stassen entered in several primaries as did Governor Earl Warren of California, and General MacArthur had some highly vociferous followers. The only real threat to the Eisenhower nomination came from the spirited and vigorous campaign of Senator Robert A. Taft. He stumped the country, appeared on radio and television, and had wide support among county chairmen and of the conservative wing of the party. The Taft forces concentrated especially on states where delegates to the national convention were chosen in state conventions. While he did very well in these states, the contest between the Eisenhower and Taft factions was so bitter that the two groups in some states sent rival delegations with each charging "fraud." It appeared that the nomination might well be settled in the credentials committee of the convention.

Even though it was recognized that the convention in Chicago would be a bitter and exciting affair, most experienced observers were willing to predict an Eisenhower nomination on the eve of the convention. The General had shown remarkable popularity in nearly every presidential primary, including huge numbers of write-in votes where his name was not on the ballot. He took no positions on controversial measures, which Senator Taft had been forced to do, and his backers claimed him to be liberal or conservative as it suited their needs. Taft supporters coined the phrase "I like Ike but what's Ike like?" to dramatize the issue of Eisenhower's silence on public issues, but they had little success. Meanwhile, the Eisenhower forces successfully used the slogan "Taft can't win." It was reported in the press that many delegates preferred Taft because he was a "regular," an experienced politician, and deserved the nomination, but they were fearful he could not win. At least two other factors helped the Eisenhower cause. One was the great support which he had in the newspapers. The other was that the Republican governors with few exceptions were working vigorously for Eisenhower. Governor Thomas E. Dewey was in the vanguard of the supporters and he and several other governors of big states were able to deliver huge blocks of votes on roll calls which aided the Eisenhower cause. The governors had even gone so far as to state that the Republican party would be morally compromised if it failed to seat the Eisenhower delegates from some Southern states. When the Eisenhower forces won the battle to seat their delegates from Georgia, it was reasonably certain that this demonstration of strength would result in his nomination on the first ballot.[18]

[18] For debate and votes on the contest over the report of the credentials committee on Georgia see *Proceedings of the Twenty-fifth Republican National Convention, 1952*, pp. 164–185. After the recorded switches to Eisenhower, the General was nominated

Governors and other Eisenhower supporters met in a "smoke-filled room" to decide upon the Vice Presidential nominee and gave it to Senator Richard Nixon of California. Nixon had won some prominence in investigating subversives and was acceptable to the Taft wing, and it was believed he would be helpful in carrying the West.

The Democrats were set for a wide-open convention after Truman withdrew as a nominee prior to the convention. Senator Estes Kefauver of Tennessee entered many Democratic presidential primaries and had but little opposition. A remarkable number of votes were cast for him and he became a leading contender. Senator Richard B. Russell of Georgia had much support in the South and a few other favorite sons had scattered support. The South was in an angry mood after the convention adopted a "loyalty pledge" whereby delegates were obligated to see that the nominee of the national convention would be placed on the ballot under the regular Democratic label.

Neither Russell nor Kefauver was able to command widespread national support. Russell was a sectional candidate and Kefauver's liberalism had offended some Southern delegates and many Northern Democratic machines were unenthusiastic about him. Governor Adlai Stevenson of Illinois had been boomed by friends for the nomination but he consistently discouraged efforts on his behalf even after the convention had opened. However, when he delivered a brilliant welcoming speech to the convention in Chicago, there was much enthusiasm for him. It was felt that he could unite the Truman and anti-Truman wings and he had proved himself an able vote-getter and governor. He finally acquiesced and accepted the nomination in what much of the press called one of the few genuine "drafts" in history.[19] To placate the South, Senator John Sparkman of Alabama was added to the ticket. Sparkman had a generally liberal record in Congress and he and Stevenson were acceptable to labor.

Polls at the beginning of the campaign showed a 2 to 1 vote for Eisenhower over Stevenson. The latter had no organization to start with and was not well known. The Governor's outstanding campaign speeches over radio and television won many votes for him. But the handicaps under which he ran were too much to overcome, for there appeared to be among the electorate a deep-seated desire to respond to the Republican slogan "It's time for a change" and promises to "clean up the mess in Washington" and terminate the Korean War. When the votes were counted, Eisenhower had carried 39 states and had a popular vote margin

on the first ballot with 845 votes (280 were for Taft, 77 for Warren, and 4 for MacArthur).

[19] The vote for Stevenson on the third and final ballot was 617½; for Kefauver 275½; for Russell 261; and 74 votes scattered for others.

of 6,600,000. Stevenson carried only Alabama, Arkansas, Georgia, Kentucky, Mississippi, Louisiana, North Carolina, South Carolina, and West Virginia.

Republican Party under Eisenhower. The election was notable for setting an all-time record of ballots cast in a presidential election—62 million. Eisenhower received 55.1 per cent of the total vote, a plurality, however, which had been exceeded by Harding, Coolidge, and F. D. Roosevelt in his first two elections. It was a tremendous victory for Eisenhower the man rather than Eisenhower the Republican. The Republicans barely carried the House and Senate, which was remarkable in view of Eisenhower's margin. The General ran ahead of the state Republican ticket in all except six states. For the first time in well over a half century the nation chose a professional soldier as its leader. Eisenhower, moreover, had had no experience in party politics, none in elective public office, and his services in the Executive branch had been in uniform. The issues of a "military man" and "inexperience," which some opponents used, apparently left the electorate unimpressed. In fact, Samuel Lubell in interviews with voters found Eisenhower's strongest asset was his "lack of past political partisanship." [20] In Lubell's judgment the "tide of revulsion against Trumanism" was so strong that "probably any Republican candidate could have won," but Eisenhower made the difference "between what might have been a narrow Republican squeeze and the landslide that occurred."

The extent to which Eisenhower was successful in bringing about a fundamental realignment of party strength is not easy to ascertain and to some extent will not be fully known until after the 1956 and 1960 elections.[21] He captured many Southern states due in part to reaction against Truman's civil rights program and Stevenson's support of it and the Governor's opposition to giving title to the submerged coastal lands to the states. Many supporting Eisenhower in the South insisted that they did so as Democrats and that they would remain Democrats. It is questionable, therefore, whether the Republicans can count on the South and whether, in the absence of successful candidates for state and local offices, a real two-party system is an immediate prospect. One study of voting behavior conducted by the University of Michigan Survey Research Center confirms the general impression of political observers that Eisenhower siphoned votes from virtually every class which had formerly been in the "Democratic coalition" (see Table 11). Young voters who had formerly gone Democratic cast a majority of their two-party vote for Eisenhower and farm voters went close to 2 to 1 for him. Many in

[20] See "Who Elected Eisenhower?" *Saturday Evening Post,* Jan. 10, 1953.

[21] On the Eisenhower alignment see Louis Harris, *Is There a Republican Majority? Political Trends: 1952–1956* (New York: Harper & Brothers, 1954).

Table 11. Voting Behavior of Certain Groups in the 1948 and 1952
Presidential Elections

(In per cent)

A. Occupations and Income

	Professional and managerial		Farmers		Union members		Unskilled workers		Low income *		High income *	
	1948	1952	1948	1952	1948	1952	1948	1952	1948	1952	1948	1952
Democrat..................	15	27	25	24	56	42	33	40	28	22	29	28
Republican.................	57	60	13	42	13	33	12	19	16	31	46	57
Not voting or voted other......	28	13	60	34	31	25	55	41	56	47	25	15

B. Other Groups

	Age 21–34		College		Grade school		Catholic		Negro		Male		Female	
	1948	1952	1948	1952	1948	1952	1948	1952	1948	1952	1948	1952	1948	1952
Democrat.......	32	31	17	24	35	30	49	43	19	26	36	34	29	28
Republican	18	37	55	65	16	31	25	41	10	6	28	45	26	41
Not voting or voted other...	50	32	28	11	49	39	26	16	70	68	36	21	45	31

* Low income regarded as $0–$1,999 in both elections; high income for 1948 was $4,000 and over; for 1952, $5,000 and over.
SOURCE: Figures are based on a study conducted by the University of Michigan Survey Research Center. The sample included 662 cases in 1948 and about 1,600 in 1952. These and other figures may be found in "Political Issues and the Vote: November, 1952," *The American Political Science Review*, Vol. 47 (1953), pp. 359–385, prepared by Angus Campbell, Gerald Gurin, and Warren Miller.

the low-income group switched to Eisenhower perhaps partly because of the high cost of living. Those with a grade-school education who formerly swelled the Democratic vote were about evenly divided between Eisenhower and Stevenson.

On the other hand, Stevenson retained a majority of labor union members, Catholics, and Negroes. Although nonvoting was high among Negroes, those who voted went better than 4 to 1 for the Democratic nominee. Eisenhower made inroads in the big city vote but Stevenson carried 10 of the nation's 12 largest cities. Of the 35 cities over 300,000, however, Eisenhower won in 17, where Dewey had carried only four. There were Republican percentage gains in 1952 over 1948 in all of these except Philadelphia.

The election of 1952 and the Eisenhower Administration symbolized that the nation had moved to the right and had become more conservative in its thinking. The President's Cabinet was drawn in the main from the business community. Where Roosevelt drew upon "brain trusters" and Truman upon the professional politicians, Eisenhower selected highly successful businessmen and a few attorneys. Several Cabinet secretaries publicly stated that "this is a businessman's administration." Journalists and educators noted a general "anti-intellectualism" in the nation and many educators and schools found themselves under investigation and attack. The Eisenhower Administration proclaimed its intention to decentralize controls over the economic order, to encourage private power projects, and to emphasize states' rights and diminution of Federal control and activity. Taxes on excess profits were allowed to expire and reductions in the personal income and business taxes went into effect on schedule in 1954. Coverage under the Social Security Act was also extended. In the main, however, the first two years of the Eisenhower Administration were not marked by a large volume of legislation. It was a period of leveling off and many important legislative decisions were postponed by the expedient of simply extending present laws pending further study.

During his first year President Eisenhower was content to let considerable initiative go to Congress under the leadership of Senator Taft. Taft became mortally ill before the end of the 1953 session and was replaced by Senator William Knowland of California. The President sent Congress a fairly comprehensive legislative program in 1954 but the lawmakers were slow to act on it. Congress appeared in the mood of some indecision on legislation and to do what it could to enhance its position. The Bricker Amendment was pressed by members of the President's own party and, although it was defeated, Republican senators voted nearly 2 to 1 for it. The Amendment stipulated that no treaty or nontreaty presidential executive agreement could become effective as internal law without the approval of both houses of Congress. Congressional investigations were also used to make direct and indirect attacks on the executive establishment without directly attacking the President himself. The President made every effort to avoid clashes with Congress and to cooperate with it. Although many newspapers which endorsed Eisenhower were disturbed by the growing congressional ascendancy and criticized him for vacillating legislative leadership, his popularity remained high with the general public.

In approaching the 1954 congressional elections, the Republicans realized that their bare majorities in Congress left no big cushion to absorb a more or less normal loss for the party in power in the midterm contest. In fighting to retain control of Congress the Republicans emphasized tax reductions, the termination of the Korean War, and the high level of business activity. Both President Eisenhower and Vice

President Nixon campaigned vigorously but were unable to save enough seats to keep Republican control. In the House the Republicans elected 203, next to the smallest number in any mid-term since 1938, and lost the Senate by only one seat. As in 1952, the Republican nominees for Congress were unable to muster strength anywhere near that of the President and his popularity was not transferred in any large degree to other Republicans. The election again raised speculation, as it did in 1952, as to whether the party had become one which could elect a President but lacked the capacity to provide him with an effective legislative majority. The Republicans also lost 8 governorships and the Democrats gained seats in all but three of the 38 state and territorial legislatures where elections were held. Although Democratic gains were impressive, they were far short of a landslide.

Another aftermath of the election was the so-called "censure" of Republican Senator Joseph R. McCarthy of Wisconsin and his public break with President Eisenhower. Republican ranks in the Senate were evenly split on this issue with Floor Leader William Knowland, President Pro Tem Styles Bridges, and Conference Chairman Eugene Millikin supporting McCarthy and Policy Committee Chairman Homer Ferguson and Majority Whip Leverett Saltonstall voting to condemn him. During the debate on the question Mr. Knowland sharply criticized aspects of the Eisenhower-Dulles foreign policy and called upon the Democrats to review it. This further highlighted the deep Republican split over foreign policy, particularly on Far Eastern matters.

A New Party Cycle? The Republican revival set off speculation that the nation had entered a new conservative era comparable to the 1870's or 1920's. In terms of percentage of the popular vote, however, the Republican victories in 1946 and 1952 were much below those of 1896 and 1920. The cycle idea has often appealed to prophets, astrologers, and to the party out of power. Defeated candidates console themselves that no one could "beat the trend." In a two-party system there is bound to be a swing in control between the parties. But the swings in the United States have been of sharply uneven duration. Louis Bean, for example, has noted the ebb and flow of political tides in the House of Representatives.[22] He found peaks and troughs of popularity but noted the "cycles" are "of uneven duration." Business depressions and wars may interrupt or reverse political tides, but Bean finds that there are instances where improvement in business was accompanied by a further loss of seats of the party in power. Prosperity often appears to aid the party in power, but very high levels of employment and business failed to save the Democrats in 1952.

22 *How to Predict Elections* (New York: Alfred A. Knopf, Inc., 1948) and *The Mid-term Battle* (Washington: Cantillon Books, 1950).

Historically, the pendulum has swung from progressive to reaction or to a plateau and back to progressive, though again without precise regularity or for equal periods of time. Arthur M. Schlesinger sees cycles of predominantly this character and that they largely ignore party labels.[23] Long-range trends may be due to progressive-conservative tendencies but do not result in correlation with equal periods of Republican and Democratic rule. The Republicans have always had a progressive wing but they have rarely controlled the party when it was in power. Progressives controlled the Democratic party under Wilson, Roosevelt, and Truman but have not continually been able to nominate their candidate for President.

Before the cycle theory can be used to explain changes in party control, much more must be known about voting behavior. The absence of objective public-opinion polls, voter surveys, and the like prior to 1935 leaves much analysis of party changes and cleavages previous to the New Deal in the realm of surmise, speculation, and assumption. Studies of public perception of parties, issues, and candidates in recent and future elections will be helpful in testing hypotheses about party trends. For example, some suggest that farmers believe that the Republicans can manage a period of inflation better than the Democrats, but that the latter will respond more rapidly and effectively to a deflationary situation. Until more data are available, however, we will have to be content with recognizing that shifts of power appear to be caused by variegated factors such as prosperity, depression, political protest, wars, and attractive leadership. Among the newer influences or trends in the future will be the political activities of organized labor, the power to purchase publicity through the mass communications media, and the international situation.

Perhaps the most important point to be made is that a party's rule ends when its support deteriorates to the point where enough voters are attracted to the opposition party to enable it to win the presidency. The challenge to the student of party politics is to learn the reasons for the loss of strength and the causes of the factionalism leading to the breakup of the majority party.

SELECTED REFERENCES

The political aspects of the New Deal era and the party battles of the period are not available in any one volume, but the following are valuable in this connection: Frances Perkins, *The Roosevelt I Knew* (1946); A. M. Schlesinger, *New Deal in Action, 1933–39* (1940); J. T. Flynn, *Country Squire in the White House* (1940); G. M. Johnson, *Roosevelt: Dictator or Democrat* (1941); Raymond Moley, *After Seven Years* (1939); Frank Kingdon, *That Man in the White House* (1944); Charles Michelson, *The Ghost Talks* (1944); Alfred M. Landon, *America at the Crossroads* (1936); James A. Farley, *Behind the Ballots* (1938), and *The Roosevelt Story* (1948); and E. E. Robinson, *They*

[23] "Tides of American Politics," *Yale Review,* Vol. 29 (1940), pp. 217–230.

Voted for Roosevelt (1947). For selected addresses of the President from 1932 to 1945 see B. D. Zevin (ed.), *Nothing to Fear* (1946). Other useful works are Eleanor Roosevelt, *This I Remember* (1949); John Gunther, *Roosevelt in Retrospect* (1950); Herbert Hoover, *The Memoirs of Herbert Hoover* (1952); R. E. Sherwood, *Roosevelt and Hopkins* (1948); L. B. Wehle, *Hidden Threads of History: Wilson Through Roosevelt* (1953); William Hillman, *Mr. President* (1952); W. P. Helm, *Harry Truman: A Political Biography* (1947). On campaigns see also T. M. Black, *Democratic Party Publicity in the 1940 Campaign* (1941); Hugh A. Bone, *Smear Politics: An Analysis of 1940 Campaign Literature* (1941); R. V. Peel and T. C. Donnelly, *The 1932 Campaign: An Analysis* (1935); H. F. Gosnell, *Champion Campaigner: Franklin D. Roosevelt* (1952). Some very useful information and statistics on party battles from 1936 to 1952 are provided in *The Political Almanac* for 1948 and 1952 by George Gallup.

See also C. W. Stein, *The Third Term: Its Rise and Collapse in American Politics* (1943); and Louis Harris, *Is There a Republican Majority? Political Trends, 1952–1956* (1954).

A good short summary of party history to 1952 will be found in *Current History* (Vol. 23), October, 1952.

CHAPTER 12

The Nature of the American Two-party System

Considered nationally, political parties in the United States may be described as loose alliances to win the stakes of power embodied in the presidency. The centripetalism generated by this office more than any other factor discouraged the development of the multiplicity of parties anticipated by the founders of the Constitution.

—ARTHUR W. MACMAHON

In terms of American experience, a political party consists of a group of persons banded together to capture control of the government through elective processes in order to further a set of interests. There is an important distinction between interest or pressure groups and political parties. Both seek power but parties seek to exercise it in the legal sense of the term. Interest groups are interested in influencing constituents and government but, unlike parties, they do not put forth a slate of candidates who, if successful, will take over the government and exercise power in accordance with the fundamental law of the state. In terms of interest in public policy, in organization and objectives certain interest groups may resemble a political party, but they still lack the distinguishing feature of proposing a set of candidates for public office. Pressure groups do not seek to exercise legal power or to assume legal responsibility for public policy but rather seek results. Parties of necessity seek power and results. They are forced in one degree or another to assume responsibility and to be answerable to the voters in an election.

The men who made the Federal Constitution did not debate the question of political parties in the convention and they included no mention whatever of them in that document. But parties were not unknown. Many of the drafters were fearful of factions. Madison in *The Federalist,* No. 10, discussed the dangers of a faction which he defined as "a majority or minority of the whole, who are united and actuated by some common impulse of passion, or of interest adverse to the rights of other citizens, or to the permanent and aggregate interests of the community." He recognized that factions could not be eradicated without eradicating liberty, so he proposed that they be controlled and, he argued, the government envisaged by the Constitution would help to accomplish this. President Washington in his Farewell Address still warned of "the

273

baneful effects of the spirit of party," a view held by many of the founding fathers. But the very form of government, as we shall see, made parties all the more necessary if the government is to function successfully.

It is widely believed that political parties arise inevitably and are essential to democratic government. They provide a channel through which citizens can influence the course of public policy and are a great force in furnishing the personnel and operation of the government. Local governments often function without affiliates of the national parties but there are still groups which perform the functions of proposing candidates, conducting elections, and help to keep the government running. It is difficult to imagine how the national government could operate effectively without parties capable of doing these things. Parties, moreover, present policies to the electorate and give the voters an opportunity to assign responsibility for the conduct of government.

Parties do not operate in a vacuum but in a social environment. There is a "climate of politics," a "temper of the times" within which the party must move and have its being. To be insensitive to the changing climate of politics or to the results of the great historic processes and issues is, for a major political party, to invite defeat. The party must recognize and live with things as they are and perhaps do some things it does not wish to do. It can espouse some reform and change but it cannot get too far away from the ties, events, ideas, and norms which collectively form the way of life of the community.

Parties must also function within a certain political framework even while they may be trying to change the outward forms of the framework. In the United States, for example, they are called upon to operate within a Federal, separation of powers, presidential system, while in Britain parties live under a unitary government and parliamentary system. The structure of government as well as the social environment in turn modify and influence party organization, leadership, and activity. Although the purposes of political parties are essentially the same in all free societies, the character and emphasis of their activities show much variation from nation to nation. Foreign observers and the more candid Americans admit confusion and perplexity over the apparent contradictions and seemingly utter lack of rules governing American parties.

In this chapter the constitutional and other influences on the major parties and the resulting character of the parties will be examined. In the next chapter an examination will be made of the contrasts between the two great parties and the minor parties and the parties under other systems of government.

PARTIES UNDER THE CONSTITUTION

Federalism and Separation of Powers. In a Federal system the local governments perform many exclusive as well as concurrent functions. This means there will be contestants for power on the state and local levels with the need for political parties of some sort entirely aside from the great national contests. The personnel for the local governments is quite generally selected at different times from that of the national government and the party organizations are continually preparing for some election which is never more than one or two years away.

The Federal system tends to mean 48 different parties and provides the opportunity for 48 independent associations built upon alliances to local group interests. In effect, federalism accentuates the familiar pattern of American politics of atomized, decentralized power. Senators and representatives are the products of the many state parties and their reelection will to varying extents depend upon the strength of their state parties and their own relationships to those parties. It is apparent that there will be real difficulty in achieving principle, homogeneity and discipline, especially on the national level. It becomes easier nationally to operate under a politics of personalities than under a politics of issues.

Separation of powers influences the party system and at the same time requires greater organization and effort. In the English parliamentary system the electorate selects the members of the legislature, some of the latter becoming cabinet officers and one of them prime minister. The party controlling the House of Commons controls the administration. In the American presidential system only the legislature and quadrennially the President are elected. The nation's top administrators are appointed from outside the legislature. It has happened numerous times in American history, moreover, that the majority of Congress and the President are of different political faiths and some degree of stalemate has occurred. This serves to emphasize the important task of parties under a separation of powers system—the attempt to control both branches of the government in order to avoid potential deadlock. Stated another way, parties have the function of trying to integrate the program of the legislative and executive branches by furnishing personnel which, at least in label, is of the same political faith. Parties, by seeking control of both houses, can also help in the integration of the work of bicameral bodies.

Legal Bases. Although neither the Federal nor early state constitutions recognized parties, the provisions for electing the members of Congress, the indirect election of the President, and the election of state officials paved the way for parties to arise outside specific constitutional sanction. It was almost a hundred years after the Constitution was adopted, however, before the states decided to embark upon the regulation of parties. The first legislation was aimed to prevent abuses, fraud, and manipulation of conventions and primaries by party machines. Corrupt-practices laws and laws governing primaries are now found in practically all the states.

The membership of election boards and many governmental commissions and agencies is required by law to be bipartisan, exemplary of further recognition of the existence of political parties. The statute creating the Federal Trade Commission, for example, prescribes that "not more than three of the commissioners shall be members of the same political party." Certain protection from parties is given to civil servants, and under the Hatch Act these employees are prohibited from engaging in political activities. In several states party organization is partially prescribed by law and parties are usually given the sanction of preparing their own rules for government of the party within these limitations. Despite this abandonment of a laissez-faire attitude toward the parties by the state legislatures, a great deal of party activity still remains unregulated.

Congress proposed three constitutional amendments which were adopted and have resulted in broadening party activities. These were the lifting of restrictions on Negro suffrage and woman suffrage, and the direct election of senators. The new amendment limiting a President to two terms may influence his party leadership, especially during the latter part of his second term. Statutory control of parties by Congress has been applied only to corrupt practices. Congress has under consideration proposals for a direct system for the nomination of the President.

The Federal courts in recent years have opened the way for additional statutory control by reversing earlier decisions which held that parties were essentially private associations and not official agencies. In 1944 in *Smith v. Allwright* [1] the Supreme Court held that a state permitting parties to conduct primaries makes the party action a state one. When South Carolina a few years later repealed all its primary laws and attempted to exclude Negroes from the Democratic party, a Circuit Court of Appeals ruled that it was a fundamental error to assume that "a political party is a mere private aggregation of individuals like a country club and that the primary is a mere piece of party machinery. The party may, indeed, have been a mere aggregation of individuals in the early days of the Republic, but with the passage of years, political parties have become in effect state institutions, governmental agencies through which sovereign power is exercised by the people." [2] By refusing an appeal of the case the Supreme Court in effect upheld this statement of the public character of parties.

[1] 321 U.S. 649 (1944).
[2] *Rice v. Elmore*, 165 F. 2d 387, 389 (1947).

Two-party System. Perhaps a more conspicuous feature than the general extraconstitutional character of the American party system nationally is its biparty nature. Its uniqueness becomes more obvious by observing that with a few exceptions [3] the multiparty system is prevalent in practically all other free governments. By contrast, in the United States the gap in size between the two major parties and the minor parties is so wide as to reduce the latter to relative unimportance as far as securing control of the national or a state government is concerned. Minor parties boasting any immediate strength are usually short-lived.

Why does the United States follow the two-party system? Some explain the two-party cleavage as the result of custom and psychology. Initially two parties emerged and the system was so entrenched by the time the first third party arose that the populace was accustomed to only two parties. Americans, it is pointed out, like to vote for a winner and view voting for a minor-party nominee as throwing their vote away. Further, minor parties are often radical and in many quarters considered not quite "respectable."

The high cost of launching and operating a successful party on a national scale makes the undertaking today almost impossible. In the present era millions of dollars are spent biennially by each of the two major parties. Moreover, many services are donated to the party by rank-and-file workers who will be rewarded with jobs if their party wins the election. Only in rare instances can minor parties hope to offer incentives of this type.

Important as these psychological and pecuniary factors are today, they fail to indicate the intensely practical reason for only two parties—*the election system*.[4] Our system of representation is based largely upon a geographical district, with one person elected from each district. The figures in Table 12 show how, in a state sending six representatives to the House of Representatives, the single-member district not only completely defeats minor party nominees but works a hardship on the lesser of the major parties as well. In this case the Democrats captured all six congressional seats, while the Republicans and the third party, although collectively polling about 49 per cent of the votes, would receive no seats. If the six nominees had been chosen from the state at large on a system of proportional representation, the Republican party would have elected at least one and probably two men and the minor party would have had

[3] Much of the time Great Britain and the Commonwealth nations have had for all practical purposes a two-party system.

[4] One of the best works on the reasons for and the significance of the two-party system is E. E. Schattschneider, *Party Government* (New York: Rinehart & Company, Inc., 1942). The respective virtues of the two-party and multiparty system are considered in the following chapter.

Table 12. Single-member District Results

District	Republican	Democrat	Minor party
1	23,000	31,000	15,000
2	45,000	91,000	20,000
3	23,000	38,000	15,000
4	37,200	37,500	16,000
5	20,500	46,500	15,000
6	44,000	46,000	15,000
	192,700	290,000	96,000

SOURCE: The Republican and Democrat columns represent in round numbers the ballots cast in the 1938 Maryland general election. A sample minor party is included to show how it would fare under the system.

a sporting chance to obtain one seat. Concisely, the total popular vote for each party under the present system of election is not accurately translated into representation. In this instance the Democrats have received more representation than they deserved and the other two parties less. A slight shift geographically to the Republican side in districts four and six would have made a significant difference in representation.

Minor groups under the single-member-district plan have a much greater opportunity for electoral success if they merge with one of the major parties. Where three or more candidates are to be chosen from a district and the plurality system [5] prevails, minor parties likewise find it impossible to elect any nominees even if proportionally entitled to do so. Public-opinion polls point out time and again in elections how a very slight shift from a fraction of 1 per cent to 3 or 4 per cent can change the whole outcome of an election under the geographical—single-member —plurality system of election.

By the same logic, the electoral college system as now operated under the general ticket, "winner-take-all" block in each state fosters a two-party system for it has the same effect as a single-member district, even though the states differ in the number of votes to which they are entitled. One of the arguments posed against changing the electoral college system is that it will encourage or facilitate multiple parties. The Lodge-Gossett proposal would substitute for the present system a split-state electoral

[5] A plurality is the excess of votes cast for any one candidate over the other candidates for the same office in an election where there are three or more candidates for the same office.

vote and provide that a 40 per cent plurality of the electoral vote shall be sufficient to elect a President. Under the system a state's electoral vote would be divided in proportion to the popular vote. Both these features, opponents fear, would encourage a multiparty system. Supporters argue that the nation is too strongly committed to two parties for this to happen and that, on the contrary, this would help to build up a second party, the Republicans in the South, and aid the Democrats in several Northern states which rather consistently go Republican.

Ruth C. Silva has applied the Lodge formula to elections beginning in 1880 and concluded that the plan would have redounded to the advantage of the Democrats and handicapped the Republicans, perhaps seriously, in contending for the presidency.[6] This is due primarily to the fact that the Republicans would usually have to gain a margin of approximately 75 electoral votes in the North, which would require the piling up of a huge number of popular votes in that area, while the Democrats could neutralize this Northern margin by polling relatively few popular votes in the South.

The Mundt-Coudert plan would also abolish the general ticket system and provide for the election of one elector in each congressional district with the remainder of a state's allotment selected at large. This plan, according to Miss Silva, might enable Republicans to win the presidency without carrying the larger metropolitan areas if districts continued to be gerrymandered in favor of the Republicans. However, appeals which might win Southern votes might alienate enough ethnic and racial votes in the North, with the net result of a loss of electoral strength. The careful analysis of proposals for changing the general-ticket system reveals a real concern over (1) what it might do to the present party alignments and (2) the effect on the two-party system as facilitated by the present system.

To repeat, the two-party system has been fostered by the combination of interests seeking the presidency. As Professor Macmahon noted, "the centripetalism" generated by the presidency "more than any other factor discouraged the development of the multiplicity of parties anticipated by the founders of the Constitution." [7]

One-party Areas. Although the presidential system and electoral arrangements have nurtured a two-party as opposed to a multiple-party

---

[6] See "The Lodge-Gossett Resolution: A Critical Analysis," *The American Political Science Review,* Vol. 45 (1950), pp. 86–99, and "Reform of the Electoral System," *The Review of Politics,* Vol. 14 (1952), pp. 396–407. For useful recent summary of proposals see "The Question of Changing the Electoral System," *The Congressional Digest,* August-September, 1953.

[7] See his statement on political parties in the *Encyclopaedia of the Social Sciences,* Vol. II, pp. 595–601.

system, the result is not universally a biparty contest. In New York City, and at times elsewhere, a strong third party has appeared. But more often there is the phenomenon of the existence of only one party. In about one-fourth of the states there is no second party in terms of the existence of a party organization which regularly holds primaries or conventions and runs candidates for congressional, state, county, and municipal offices.[8] There are other states where the second of the two parties goes through the formality of conducting campaigns but with little hope of success. In Maine Democratic candidates for Congress are likely to average 25 to 35 per cent of the vote and many of them fare little better in Nebraska. The two-party system in congressional elections in these areas thus becomes more nominal than actual.

In studying the two-party vote covering the House elections from 1942 through 1950, Moos found "105 marginal districts" or districts where the Republican slice of the two-party vote ranged from 45 to 55 per cent.[9] These districts were scattered throughout 29 different states. Northern New England and the lower South were the only sections not having any marginal districts. These figures together with a glance at voting strength state by state will show numerous one-party congressional districts within what is normally a two-party state in national and state-wide elections. Certainly half, and probably considerably more, of the nation's congressional districts are regarded as "safe." Moos found that from 1938 to 1950, 291 districts were consistently Democratic or Republican, and an earlier study covering congressional voting under Wilson, Harding, and Coolidge showed that about 150 seats returned Democratic congressmen irrespective of the political tides.[10]

Within a state are likely to be areas where one party completely dominates and where the second party alternates between running only token opposition or no candidates at all for the state legislature. Sometimes one-party state legislative districts are the result of gerrymandering so that each party has certain "safe" districts. One-partyism on other occasions is the result of a rural-urban cleavage with the Republicans dominating the former and Democrats the latter. This geographical differentiation in party strength makes for the paradox of a one-party system at the county or local level but for a highly competitive two-party struggle

[8] Austin Ranney and Willmoore Kendall have worked out a classification of "party systems" in the United States whereby they place 12 states in the category of having "a modified one-party system" and 10 states designated as having "a one-party system," the latter all being in the South; see "The American Party Systems," *The American Political Science Review*, Vol. 48 (1954), pp. 483–485.

[9] Malcolm Moos, *Politics, Presidents, and Coattails* (Baltimore: Johns Hopkins Press, 1952), Chap. 3.

[10] P. D. Hasbrouck, *Party Government in the House of Representatives* (New York: The Macmillan Company, 1927), pp. 172 ff.

in state-wide and national contests. The dominance of one party may also be due to custom and tradition or to the fact that it has successfully occupied the middle ground in politics, that the opposition is forced to run a candidate too far to the left or the right to win.

Custom and tradition as well as necessity (or lack of it) play a part in one-partyism and concentration of party strength. Historical accident tied the Southern voters to the Democrats so strongly in national affairs that it discouraged the development of Republican state and county organizations except in the border states.[11] Many Southerners see no need for a second party because the Democratic primary has served them satisfactorily in state affairs. In many local areas one of the parties has been in control so long that it is the socially respectable one and the minority regards expending time, money, and energy as a futile gesture. Homogeneity of ethnic background, common economic endeavor, and sometimes religion draw persons together into the same political as well as social outlook and a common party becomes their vehicle for political self-expression in good times and in bad. Party competition in such instances appears unnecessary and meaningless. Single-party domination is sometimes the result of a revered popular leader who becomes a fixture and an institution. Whatever the explanation, American experience demonstrates that the constitutional and electoral arrangements do not invariably result in a two-party system at all levels of government.

The consequences of uniparty dominance vary from area to area. Sometimes it results in a high degree of political apathy and low voter turnout. It lends itself to control by professionals who can take advantage of the comparatively small amount of political participation and the lack of competition. At the same time, the voter is not presented with alternative choices. If he becomes disgusted and wishes to "throw the rascals out," his only opportunity is to function within the one party in the hope of building up a rival faction. Factionalism is bound to break out within the party because the winning faction is assured power without having to meet an opposition-party candidate. It would be difficult to prove that there is invariably more factionalism in a one-party than in a two-party system, for intraparty struggles for control characterize both. But in a one-party division with no effective opportunity for operation through a rival party, the stakes of factionalism become extraordinarily high. The aspirant for public office is faced with the fairly definite but single channel to office, namely, the winning of his party's primary or selection by the party's convention. In a one-party system the nominating process is the important one in terms of democratic choices.

State and Local Parties. State and local party organization appeared first and the real strength and power of parties remains at this level.

[11] See V. O. Key, Jr., *Southern Politics* (New York: Alfred A. Knopf, Inc., 1949).

It was not until 1848 that the Democrats created a national committee. As a new party, the Republicans saw the need for a national organization in their first national election and created a national committee in 1856. In the present century both parties have made an effort to strengthen their national party organizations. At the same time, the state organizations function more or less autonomously as parties in and of themselves and a strong and popular state party does not mean *ipso facto* strong support for the party's candidate for President or even for congressman, though custom dictates that party workers should work for "straight-ticket" voting.

There is no end of illustrations of strong local combinations unable for one reason or another to deliver the vote for national candidates. Republicans remained in control of Philadelphia while Pennsylvania voted for Democratic nominees for President. The Republican national victories in the 1920's failed to dislodge Democratic control of New York City. In 1952, Eisenhower was strong nationally, polling 55.1 per cent of the two-party vote, but his party's candidates for Congress had less strength in the state parties and were able to eke out but a 50.2 per cent popular vote victory and barely won control of the House of Representatives. Conversely, while Stevenson was polling 27,315,000 votes, Democratic candidates for the House were polling 28,178,000 votes. In 1948 Truman likewise ran behind the Democratic congressional vote. The difference, however, can be explained partly by the fact that there was no state Republican party in many parts of the South and no Republicans ran for Congress. But even in the Northern states Democratic congressional candidates as a whole showed considerable strength.

The state of Washington in 1952 provided incongruous results in the form of electoral differentiation between national and state candidates. Eisenhower carried the state by about 107,000 but the Democratic candidate for the United States Senate polled almost as many votes as Eisenhower and swamped his opponent by 135,000 votes. The Democratic candidate for congressman-at-large also won but the Republicans made a clean sweep of all representatives elected by districts and carried the governorship and several state offices. But the Democrats managed to carry some state offices and obtain a creditable though a minority of the representation in the state legislature. Anomalies of this type are present in many states in almost every general election.

It is not unusual to find congressional, senatorial, and state candidates opening their own campaign headquarters and running their own show with little or no demands on either the state or national party organization. Each candidate often seeks out his own support and finances. Friendly relations may be retained with the regular party organizations but reliance is made primarily on one's own friends, cliques, and groups.[12]

A final illustration of the curious pattern of party politics was shown in the 1952 Democratic National Convention with the quarrel over the so-called "loyalty oath." As adopted, the oath obligated all state Democratic organizations to expend every effort to see that the nominees chosen at the convention would appear on the state ballots under the regular Democratic labels. Numerous Southern delegations violently opposed the oath and threatened to bolt. After the convention, the Democratic Governor of Texas, who decided to support Eisenhower, expressed regret at the Texas Democratic convention that there was no legal way from keeping Stevenson and Sparkman from running as Democratic candidates. Presumably the Governor believed Eisenhower and Nixon should have been run as Democrats and, according to the press, the state convention would have voted for this if it had been legal. Speaker Sam Rayburn and Senator Lyndon Johnson, however, resisted this move and supported Stevenson throughout. This is another illustration of where there may be rivalry between the Federal and state officeholders.

The differentiation in party strength in the state legislatures, in Congress, and in other offices is due to highly diverse causes ascertainable only by studying the politics of a given state. Gerrymandering or the rotten borough system may keep a party underrepresented in the state legislatures. Party decentralization and split-ticket voting resulting in a seemingly incongruous pattern may be due to the fact that major issues fail to develop in state and local contests and even in congressional races. Sometimes the opposite is true where issues develop in a local contest which have no relevance whatsoever to national issues. Most municipal and many state elections are held at different times than that for the President and Congress. Local issues, then, can be developed independently of national ones and lead many persons to vote for candidates of a different party from those supported for national offices. There are some instances where Republican politicians moved to change the date of local elections from presidential years because the enormous popularity of Roosevelt appeared to favor Democratic candidates for state and local offices. The isolation of national, state, and local elections for reasons of political expediency, however, far antedated present-day politics and from the point of view of easing the task of the voter, there is much to recommend it.

PARTY MEMBERSHIP

Heterogeneous Character. A striking characteristic of the two-party system is the loose party membership and lack of an exact formula for

[12] Other aspects of the highly independent character of American campaign practices will be found in Chap. 19.

determining who are Republicans and who are Democrats. Party managers do not wish to have too strict rules for membership for it may discourage workers and voters; too exclusive a membership runs the risk of alienating potential doorbell ringers, precinct captains, financial donors, and voters.

Since political desires and grievances are channelized through one of two parties, those parties of necessity tend to become broadly composed of persons from all walks of life and of all shades of economic and political opinion. Conservatives, liberals, nationalists and internationalists, states' rightists and advocates of greater Federal control, and so on, are found in the ranks of both parties. In diagram form party alignment becomes a vertical rather than a horizontal line, with both parties being supported by housewives, workers, teachers, and virtually all groups to some degree. Doctors may be active politically but do not place a slate of nominees before the voters. Medical men are found in both parties. Men of large wealth ar.d men of small means are in both party ranks. Similarly, farmers, lawyers, laborers are distributed throughout both parties. True, in a given era such as under the New Deal, more businessmen were in the Republican ranks and other occupational interests went with the Democrats, yet the majority of farmers and a sizable proportion of organized labor were found supporting Calvin Coolidge and the Republican cause. John L. Lewis, leader of the United Mine Workers, stumped for Coolidge in 1924, for Roosevelt in 1936, and for Willkie in 1940, and tacitly supported Dewey.

Labor and agrarian groups in the nineteenth century attempted, with little success, to create their own political parties. In the present century the various Marxian parties, directing their appeals mainly to the proletariat, have won little favor. Americans have not embraced in large numbers the parties based upon occupational groupings. The farmer, the worker, and the business and professional man have felt that their protests can be best expressed by remaining with one of the two old-line parties.

In Europe, particularly Italy, Switzerland, Belgium, and Bavaria, Catholic political parties are more or less commonplace. In America no party has arisen around the nucleus of a religious denomination. Members of all churches are found in both major parties. Any attempt on the part of a church to organize a party on a local or national scale would meet with general public disapproval. Religion, however, is a factor in politics from time to time. Mormonism enters into Utah politics and the "Baptist bloc" has been influential in the upper South. The Methodists were strong supporters of many Republican nominees during the 1920's, when prohibition was a bitter issue. But none of these religious groups nominally affiliated itself with either of the parties.

Similarly, racial and nationalist groups do not form their own parties. Negroes, Germans, and Italians are in the ranks of both political parties. Both party machines make strong drives in cities to capture the votes of these groups; like religious groups they constitute an important part of the political equation. Studies show, however, that none of these groups can be counted upon to deliver votes consistently en bloc for one of the major parties.

There are no universally accepted criteria with respect to membership in a party. One becomes a Republican by registering as one in those states which have a closed primary; in over a quarter of the states there are no such tests for affiliation. In some states one swears at registration that he will support the party's nominee at the next general election. One may become a Republican by attending meetings, caucuses, or social functions. He may become a Republican by doing none of the above but by simply proclaiming himself to be one. The ambiguity and vagueness of membership was stated by Senator William Borah in 1923: "Any man who can carry a Republican primary is a Republican. He might believe in free trade, in unconditional membership in the League of Nations, in states' rights, and in every policy that the Democratic party ever advocated; yet, if he carried his Republican primary, he would be a Republican."

In conclusion, it is difficult if not impossible to determine the actual membership of a party because no clear distinction exists between loyal party membership and mere voting affiliation. Affiliation consists of an attitude rather than a formal act. Voters do not apply for membership, pay dues, or carry a membership card except in the small Marxist parties, though there are certain party clubs which have these requirements. Even in those states which require party enrollment in order to vote in the primary, there is no way to compel voters to refrain from supporting candidates of the opposite party. In a revealing study of party membership Professor Berdahl noted: "In Pennsylvania, long the bulwark of the Republican party, the Republicans have maintained their lead in enrolled membership throughout the New Deal, although losing the principal offices in 1934, 1936, and 1940. In 1934 about 90,000 and in 1936 nearly 300,000 more Republicans voted the Democratic ticket than were enrolled members of the Democratic party." [13]

Large Independent Voter Class. These voting statistics in Pennsylvania illustrate another attribute of the American voter—his high degree of independence.[14] Within a score of years the Democratic vote fluctuated-

[13] "Party Membership in the United States," *The American Political Science Review,* Vol. 36 (1942), pp. 14–50, 241–262.

[14] Estimates of reputable polling agencies have placed the number from 25 to 40 per cent of the voters. Gallup placed the figure at 15 million in 1952. Two interesting

from only 19 per cent in 1924 to 58 per cent in 1936 and back to 52 per cent in 1944. Equally striking statistics of voter independence could be cited for a number of other states. In California the Democratic party has had a million more enrolled voters than the Republicans, but the latter win most of the contests. Many businessmen voted for socialist mayors in Bridgeport and Milwaukee. Obviously, large numbers of persons accept the party label in name only and feel free to leave the party in a general election. Moreover, in one-party states members of the minority party often enroll in the majority party in order to vote in the primary election, which is recognized as the really decisive election.

A further reflection of the small regard for strong party loyalty is shown by the large bloc of voters who consistently refuse to enroll as party members and participate in the primaries, voting only in the final elections. These voters generally vote for the "best candidate" for a given office, irrespective of party label. In the strictest sense of the word they are the "independents." The comparatively small primary vote, however, cannot be explained purely in terms of independence; the absence of a party contest, failure to appreciate the significance of the primary, and too many elections in some states account as well for the small turnout.

In recent years there seems to be a decline of party affiliation, with millions of independent voters scratching their ticket and oscillating between the two major parties. The shift from one party to the other and back generally follows a pattern of the ebb and flow of business conditions and prosperity. These voters feel no strong affiliation with either political party and take considerable pride in the fact that they are "independent." They are often annoyed by being forced under the primary system to designate one party or the other as their favorite and to confine their choices in the primary to that party, with which they have little sense of affiliation or loyalty.

Viewed another way, the composition of a party in time of election consists broadly of four groups, the professional politicians and office-holders at the center, the strong partisans and consistent party supporters next, then the mild sympathizers near the periphery, and finally the independents, who come into the party for one particular election. Campaign managers are not greatly concerned with the first two groups, who will "stand when hitched," since both parties nationally are fairly equal in the number of "dependable" partisans. On election day in the pivotal areas the regulars and real partisans of the two parties about cancel each

studies of voting behavior by self-identified independents will be found in S. J. Elders-veld, "The Independent Vote: Measurement, Characteristics, and Implications for Party Strategy," *The American Political Science Review*, Vol. 46 (1952), pp. 732–753, and P. K. Hastings, "The Independent Voter in 1952: A Study of Pittsfield, Massachusetts," *ibid.*, Vol. 47 (1953), pp. 805–810.

other. In the final analysis, the independents and party sympathizers comprise the balance of power needed to elect the President and in many states the state-wide officers. The independence of millions of American voters of party labels is one of the most important characteristics of American political life.

Party a Multiple Personality. In view of the nebulous, informal nature of party membership, one may conclude that an American major party is a dual if not triple personality. Goldman has suggested the term of "party-in-the-electorate" as one personality.[15] This is the group of partisans who consider themselves loyal followers of the faith and who can be depended upon to support the party in elections. Another group is composed of the hundreds of party officials who give time, effort, and money to run the organization and campaigns. This group becomes the party machine. Still a third group, sometimes indistinct from the second, are the party's public officeholders who hold the responsibility for the party's record in government and on whose shoulders will rest success or defeat at the polls. Thus, when one speaks of the "Republicans," he may be referring to Republican legislatures and executives, to the party machine, or possibly to those millions who stood for the party by loyally voting for Landon, Willkie, Dewey, and Eisenhower. Party is popularly and legitimately used in all of these senses, though it is helpful to clarify on a given occasion which group making up the party is being referred to.[16]

Notwithstanding the many obvious examples which can be cited to show the lack of a sense of loyalty between different divisions of the party and the disassociation in the minds of many voters between presidential, congressional, state, and local nominees of the same party, it should not be concluded that there is no evidence of similarity in voting pattern. During the Roosevelt era the Democrats were able to control a majority of the governorships. Beginning with the Republican congressional comeback in 1946, Republican candidates for governor and other state offices likewise began to win victories. The Eisenhower victory increased the Republican governors to 30 and the Democrats retained only those of Michigan, Ohio, and Rhode Island outside of the Border and Southern states. There is no instance in modern party history, moreover, where a successful candidate for President has failed to carry a majority of his own party into Congress.

Huntington has developed an interesting hypothesis based upon a study of the popular vote for congressmen in 1946 and the voting record

---

[15] See R. M. Goldman, *Party Chairmen and Party Faction: 1789–1900* (Ph.D. dissertation, University of Chicago, 1951), Chap. 17.

[16] Chaps. 14 and 25 respectively consider party leadership in the party and in the government.

in Congress during the immediately succeeding years of those elected. He found that "one party tends to adjust itself to represent one interest and the other party accommodates itself to the other interest; one becomes the party of labor and the lower class and the other the party of business and the upper class." As the nation becomes more urbanized, he believes, "the Democratic party will not seriously attempt to win the banker and businessman vote and the Republican party will make little effort to secure the support of labor union members and the unemployed. The parties will strive to win not by converting their opponents but by effectively mobilizing their own supporters, not by extending their appeal but by intensifying it." [17] This hypothesis deserves testing over a long period of time. At the moment one can only say that there is evidence that at certain times in certain areas party labels and party memberships are meaningful differentiations.

SECTIONALISM AND THE PARTIES

The influence of sectionalism, urbanism, and geography on political outlook and certain aspects of sectionalism in the nineteenth century were noted earlier.[18] Cleavages along territorial lines still continue to influence the character of the organization and activities of the major American parties. Presidents keep an eye on geography in making Cabinet appointments and the press of an area is quick to note if its section has been slighted. Congress itself recognizes sectional interests by giving as wide a geographical representation as possible on its committees. The major parties are making increased use of regional associations.

Each major party has a hard core of voters in presidential elections, and often in state elections, on which it can depend. In the 14 presidential elections beginning in 1900, Alabama, Arkansas, South Carolina, Georgia, Louisiana, North Carolina, Texas, and Virginia either have a perfect record or have failed no more than once or twice to give their electoral votes to the Democratic nominee. In almost every Democratic National Convention some issue arises and is heatedly debated between the Northern and Southern Democrats. Several times since 1900, the Democrats went to the South for a vice presidential nominee, while the Republicans did not feel impelled even once to do so. Because of the seniority system, the hard-core South is able to obtain a lion's share of the committee chairmanships in Congress and to influence to a considerable degree the support a Northern Democratic President will receive for his proposals. In the Eighty-second Congress, Southern and Border

[17] "A Revised Theory of American Party Politics," *The American Political Science Review,* Vol. 44 (1950), p. 676.

[18] See pp. 30–42.

State congressmen became chairmen of 12 of the 19 House committees and 9 of the 15 Senate committees.

The Republican party also has its sectional hard-core support though it is much less marked than the Democrats'. Vermont has not once deviated from its rock-ribbed Republicanism in presidential elections since the Civil War and Maine left the fold only once. New Hampshire, however, has been much less loyal to Republican presidential nominees. Pennsylvania, Michigan, Iowa, Indiana, South Dakota, and Minnesota have shown a strong Republican bias. The Republicans have had fairly good support in the Middle West for their congressional candidates and seniority has favored that section. In the Eighty-third Congress, 13 of the House and 8 of the Senate chairmanships were in the hands of Middle Western representatives. In the 11 Western states only one senator, and no representatives, inherited a chairmanship in 1953. These states show less consistent attachment to any one party than the other sections.

The populous states gain influence in the national conventions, the electoral college, and in the House of Representatives. But the increasing numerical superiority of the more rapidly growing areas is offset by the older regions retaining the same representation in the Senate, their seniority in committee assignments, and, to some extent, gerrymandering. Farrelly and Hinderaker, after noting the relationship between apportionment and the influence of seniority, suggest that in the House of Representatives "congressional seniority will tend to be lowest in states which increase most rapidly in population, but will be highest in states with the most stable population." [19]

Numerous Republican National Convention battles are fundamentally Eastern–Middle Western cleavages. Speaking generally, the East represents the internationalist and somewhat liberal wing of the party while the Middle West has a corps of strong vocal nationalists who were much sharper in their criticism of the Roosevelt-Truman New Deal. In the 1920's, however, much of the progressivism of the Republicans stemmed from senators from the Middle and Far Western states.

The Republican party is not national in scope and can hardly hope to be so long as the one-party system exists in the South. By contrast, the Democrats are capable of electing congressmen from every state of the Union and have been able to carry, at some time, every one except Vermont for President. The sectional basis was shown even in the Republican year of 1952. In the 11 Southern states Eisenhower received only 300,000 votes less than Stevenson—but only six Republican candidates were elected to the House compared to 100 Democrats.

[19] "Congressional Reapportionment and Political Power," *Law and Contemporary Problems*, Vol. 17 (1952), p. 354.

The two major parties each receive certain sectional support but neither can hope to win the presidency or Congress by simply being a one-section party. Perhaps each party can win nationally while losing all of an entire section, as the Republicans have demonstrated that they can be victorious without the South. But their support was firmly grounded in all other sections so that the party never won with only Eastern or Western support. Successful parties must build their strength on a broad sectional base and the major parties perform the useful function of balancing, accommodating, and compromising the excesses of sectionalism.

Nevertheless, the section is still a factor in the formulation of many public policies and on a number of issues sectional cleavage appears greater than party loyalty. On agricultural, labor, states' rights, and occasionally foreign policies sectional bias has been apparent. Contrary to popular opinion, the sectional alignment on international cooperation and foreign policy before Pearl Harbor did not resolve itself simply into the "isolationist" Middle West and "interventionist" East. The record of Middle Western Democrats was quite as international as the Democrats from the Coastal states. Except for the South, which was solidly for preparedness and aid-to-the-Allies measures, party differences on foreign policy were greater than sectional differences. In general, however, the Northeast and the South have been more favorable to a positive foreign policy than has the remainder of the nation.

In recent years the votes cast on the measures designed to regulate and curb labor unions have shown fairly positive sectional alliances. While the Roosevelt Administration strongly opposed measures of this type, the Southern Democrats assumed leadership to press for their enactment. Every Democratic vote cast in the Senate for the Taft-Hartley bill came from the South. In the battles over farm policies sectional differences are also evident. The bipartisan farm bloc goes into action, especially in the Middle West and South, and party loyalties are badly dissipated on roll calls.

States' rights questions provide sectional divergencies with the South showing the greatest solidarity on these matters. It is able to muster all the way from a three-fourths to virtually unanimous opposition to Federal anti-poll-tax, antilynching, and fair-employment-practices bills.[20] Its senators resort to filibustering when necessary and, assisted by some Republicans in the North, have successfully blocked efforts to invoke closure. Organized labor fought a losing battle against giving title to the offshore

[20] Southern cohesion in Congress is limited primarily to proposals where there is directly or indirectly a racial question involved. Key, *op. cit.*, Chaps. 16–17, found that on only nine out of 598 roll calls in the Senate did the Southern bloc present a united front against the rest of the country and seven of these were on racial issues.

oil lands to the states and had the support of President Truman, Governor Stevenson, and the Northern Democrats. In the Senate vote, however, Southerners provided 19 of the 21 Democratic votes for the bill. The differences over public policies on labor and agriculture are perhaps as much conflicts between industrial and rural areas as they are between the sections.

FACTIONALISM

From the foregoing description of the constitutional and nonconstitutional factors influencing the character of American major parties, factionalism, as might be expected, is one of the most important by-products. Factionalism is found at one time or another in most political interest groups, but is most pronounced and persistent in political parties. There are several major types and causes of factions.

First of all there is a factionalism more or less inherent in the constitutional framework of division of powers between the national government and the states and in the separation of powers in both levels of government. The state is the all-important unit of the electoral process and a member of Congress in the final analysis owes his power and election to the people of his own district and not to such an amorphous group as a national party. Although the President is leader of his party, a member of Congress of the President's party may refuse to support his program and still retain his seat in Congress provided he keeps in good standing with his state and county organizations. The President, on the other hand, has a national constituency and his strength is built on great combinations. He must have a great sense of responsibility for the national point of view. The press often speaks of "presidential or Eisenhower Republicans" and "congressional Republicans" and predecessor Democrats sometimes showed the same dichotomy. These references to a presidential party face to face with a congressional party represent a type of factionalism often developing within a party. Governors and their members in the state legislature frequently are engaged in the same kind of factionalism.

Many interest groups call for national action while many others want decentralization and "states' rights." National forces are apt to cluster around the President hoping he will by patronage, prestige, and other methods push their programs through Congress. Opposing forces find the state and local party organizations potentially strong agencies to oppose centralization. Thus the national presidential party may wish to champion certain policies but with the national party being built on state and local organizations, the latter is in a position to defeat or at least to modify and obtain concessions in a national program.

Factionalism within parties at all levels of the organization may have an ideological basis. Both national parties have a "right wing" and a "left wing" and some call themselves the "center" or "middle-of-the-roaders." Groups advocating or opposing social, economic, and political reforms within the party are variously designated as radicals, liberals or progressives, conservatives, reactionaries, and standpatters. The middle-of-the-roaders and professional politicians (who try to remain aloof from ideological controversies) take over the job of conciliating and placating the wings and factions in order to promote unity during a campaign. A rural-urban or upstate-downstate struggle often marks state committee meetings and conventions. This contest, like the sectional contests between the North, South, East, and West, is at least in part ideological and the result of some differences over policy. It is not easy, however, to tell to what extent geography is used as the rationalization and where the difference is due to principle.

A common type of factionalism is due to psychology and the desire for power and authority within the party. Personality clashes among leaders are often the deep-seated reason for internecine warfare. Those out of power struggle to unseat those in control. Where one group has ruled for a long time and has naturally made some enemies, it may be dubbed the "Old Guard." To defeat them the "Young Turks" cluster around some person who is willing to challenge the "ins." Factionalism may be caused by little more than dissatisfaction with the way patronage is being handled.

PUBLIC POLICY AND THE TWO-PARTY SYSTEM

In the United States little actual disagreement exists between the Republicans and Democrats over the preservation of the constitutional government as outlined in the Constitution and devotion to a capitalistic economic system. These fundamentals are thoroughly rooted in American life and the sameness in attitude of the two major parties toward them seems highly desirable. If division were too marked over these basic principles, the transition of control from one party to another might result in violent revolution; the Bolshevik revolution (1919), the Hitler Third Reich (1933), and the Spanish Civil War (1935) provide illustrations. All involved such sharp differences that violence and bloodshed accompanied the consolidation of these regimes. The bitter disagreement over the nature of the Union in 1860, followed by the War between the States, offers a case of what has happened in our own nation.

With this general consensus over fundamentals, the mixed party membership, and the resultant factionalism, it may be wondered to what extent the two major parties represent genuine differences over issues of foreign policy, states' rights, and the regulation of business, labor, and agriculture. Is not the implication in terms of public policy that there will be little party cohesion and that a President must obtain his majorities by obtaining support from both sides of the aisle? Can party loyalty be expected on legislative matters? Is an official party position on public policy desirable or obtainable? These questions have intrigued students of party government for a long time and much has appeared in print on the subject. Significantly, there is disagreement among scholars and practitioners both as to the degree of party loyalty on policy matters and what, if anything, should be done about it.

Roll Call Votes. A popular method of judging party cleavages and loyalties is an analysis of congressional roll calls on controversial policies. One such study from World War I to the Hoover Administration found interparty differences often much less than those within the party.[21] In the Senate, sectional solidarity was much greater than party solidarity and farm-bloc Middle Western senators tended to vote in a unit on agricultural legislation regardless of party. For several years the *Congressional Quarterly* has regularly prepared party records on roll calls with numerous votes pointing to a similar conclusion.

Tables 13 and 14 show the party divisions by percentages on several important national and foreign measures. Any interpretation of roll call votes is difficult because on many bills there is a high degree of absenteeism. Often the important vote is on a motion to "recommit," which usually has as its purpose the defeat of the measure. When recommitment is defeated, many of the opponents of a bill will vote for it on final passage, realizing the cause is lost and that they might as well get credit with certain constituents for its passage. This is especially true of foreign aid and various domestic appropriation bills. Roll call records tell *how* Republicans and Democrats voted but not necessarily *why* they voted as they did. If one approaches the record cautiously and with these factors in mind, the voting statistics yield some interesting data on the nature of party cleavages.

A study of roll-call votes and of rival-party candidates when they have been alternately in Congress is, however, capable of yielding almost any hypothesis about differentiation over public policy. One can find dozens of roll calls where the parties appear to differ but little and critics of the loose-party system cite these as evidence that the two parties are simply different labels for two precisely similar (and empty) bottles. Other roll calls yield evidence of considerable difference between two parties. Many votes in Congress are cast by persons coming from a one-party district and where party designation is meaningless. There are, on the other hand, a number of districts where the party label is meaningful and where substantial, demonstrated differences exist between the Republican and Democratic parties. It becomes a question of where one draws the

---

[21] See Donald Hecock, *Social and Economic Interests Revealed by Political and Geographical Cohesion in Congress* (M.A. thesis, The Ohio State University, 1931).

Table 13. Party Voting on National Legislation

Measure	House of Representatives				Senate			
	% yea		% nay		% yea		% nay	
	Dem.	Rep.	Dem.	Rep.	Dem.	Rep.	Dem.	Rep.
First AAA (1933).........	88	33	8	62	80	40	8	43
TVA (1933)..............	91	15	1	76	N	N	N	N
Guffey Coal Act (1935)....	54	15	27	71	N	N	N	N
Social Security Act (1935)..	90	75	4	17	87	56	1	20
National Labor Relations Act (1935).............	N	N	N	N	71	48	6	32
Soil Conservation Act (1936)................	71	22	13	48	N	N	N	N
National Housing Act (1937)................	72	27	11	55	73	37	11	50
Wage-Hour law (1938).....	78	52	17	46	66	13	19	87
Farm-bloc amendment (1942)................	39	61	44	33	48	52	46	45
Case labor bill (1945)......	40	70	38	6	N	N	N	N
Farm parity price amendment (1946)...........	N	N	N	N	39	63	45	32
Restricted price-control extension (1946)..........	28	55	47	26	66	24	7	50
Income-tax reduction (1947)................	19	74	52	4	13	83	58	4
Taft-Hartley bill (1947)....	55	88	35	5	38	73	33	4
Income-tax reduction (1948)................	45	83	34	4	60	95	24	0
Override tax veto (1948)...	44	90	44	7	60	98	22	0
National Housing Act (1949)................	73	20	21	87	N	N	N	N
Oleo Tax repeal (1950).....	75	39	10	47	69	52	11	33
Natural gas amendment (1950)................	37	46	44	33	52	38	30	52
Tidelands oil bill (1953)....	46	83	42	8	45	71	53	18

SOURCE: Figures are taken from various compilations appearing in *The New York Times* and the *Congressional Quarterly* and computed into percentages by the author. Paired votes are not included.

line on the degree which one regards as evidence of "party difference." Julius Turner finds a great deal of party cohesion by comparing the vote distribution in one party with that of the other on a single issue.[22]

Nearly all these attempts at constructing an index of loyalty have been criticized as lacking meaning, being unrealistic, or failing to show if there is any real control by the party over its members in Congress. But what is "loyalty"? Loyalty to the position of the President? To the party platform? Voting with the majority of one's party? If 52 per cent of the Democrats vote one way and 48 per cent the other, is the former the true index of loyalty and the latter to be regarded as disloyalty or insurgency? The 48 per cent might well be closer to the party's historical position than the 52 per cent. Questions like this led Lowell to give 90 per cent as the index of a party vote. In making a study in 1901 of party influence on legislation he wrote: "A party vote of any party is arbitrarily defined as one in which more than nine-tenths of those of its members who voted were on the same side of the question; a nonparty vote as one in which one-tenth or more of the members are found on each side, that is, a vote where at least one-tenth of the voting members of the party split off from the rest." [23] If this standard were applied, very few party votes were cast for or against recent measures by either Republicans or Democrats. Even if this percentage were lowered to 75 per cent, the number of party votes cast would not be impressive for either group.

Domestic Policies. To cite a few instances: One-third of the Senate Republicans voted for the National Industrial Recovery Act, while the Democrats were able to muster over 90 per cent for the bill. In the House a slight majority of the Republicans voted for NRA, while again the Democrats enjoyed less than a 10 per cent dissent. The Republicans were somewhat less split on the Tennessee Valley Authority but nevertheless were considerably divided on the issue, while the Democrats polled an almost unanimous vote in both houses for it. On other measures affecting business, the majority of the Republicans were in opposition, particularly on the Public Utility Holding Company Act, the law regulating the bituminous coal industry, and the Securities and Exchange Act. Nevertheless, it was not unusual to find up to 40 per cent of the Republicans voting with the Democratic majority in one or the other house. On these measures there were upward of one-third of the Democrats in one of the two houses who failed to vote with a majority of their party.

The picture of labor legislation during the first half of the New Deal is somewhat different. Substantial majorities of both parties voted for

[22] *Party and Constituency: Pressures on Congress* (Baltimore: Johns Hopkins Press, 1951).

[23] "The Influence of Party upon Legislation," *Annual Report of the American Historical Association,* Vol. 1 (1901), p. 323.

the Social Security and National Labor Relations Acts, and in the House vote on the Fair Labor Standards Act. Only two Senate Republicans, however, could go along with the last-mentioned Act, and their majorities on the other two bills were less than those of the Democrats. On emergency relief measures, however, the majority of Republicans were in consistent opposition.

Beginning about 1939 the Democrats began to have less unanimity on social legislation because of the opposition of Southern Democrats. Time after time they joined with Republicans in an effort to defeat the President's proposals. Among other things, the coalition resulted in discontinuing the Civilian Conservation Corps, passing the Smith-Connally antistrike bill over President Roosevelt's veto, and defeating the proposal for a Federal ballot for soldiers. President Truman soon found himself defeated by the same coalition in his proposal to continue the Fair Employment Practice Committee, the retention of employment services by the Federal government, and price control in 1946. The dissension among the Democrats after the war provided an example of Dooley's comment, "Th' Dimmycratic party ain't on speakin' terms with itsilf." On the whole, the Republicans enjoyed greater unity than the Democrats. However, when the Republicans regained control over Congress in 1947 and again in 1953, deep cleavages in the party over taxation, expenditures, the tariff, and labor were soon apparent.

National Defense and Foreign Policy. From 1935 to Pearl Harbor there was marked cleavage between the two major parties on questions of foreign policy. In the former year President Roosevelt made a strenuous effort to obtain Senate confirmation of a treaty providing for American adherence to the Permanent Court of International Justice. Despite his efforts, the resolution failed by seven votes to secure the necessary two-thirds for passage. The partisan character was shown by 43 Democratic and 9 Republican affirmative votes, and 20 and 14 negative votes respectively. However, the Democratic senators clearly provided the margin of defeat.

An examination of basic roll calls from the beginning of World War II to Pearl Harbor reveals a similar picture. Republican members of Congress showed a considerably greater tendency to vote against revision of the neutrality laws, measures to aid the Allies, and the conscription and disposition of a peacetime army. The Democratic majorities were alone large enough in many cases to assure enactment of these policies. Throughout the New Deal a sharp alignment existed over the tariff, with the Republicans in a few instances casting no votes whatsoever for the reciprocal trade agreements program.

During World War II Republicans supported presidential requests for military needs, usually without a dissenting vote. President Roosevelt and Secretary of State Cordell Hull made efforts during the war to bring about unity for postwar policies, a program continued by President Tru-

Table 14. Party Votes on Foreign Policy Roll Calls

Measure	House of Representatives				Senate			
	% yea		% nay		% yea		% nay	
	Dem.	Rep.	Dem.	Rep.	Dem.	Rep.	Dem.	Rep.
Fortification of Guam (1939)................	58	9	24	82	N	N	N	N
Mandatory arms embargo (1939)................	23	89	63	4	17	52	65	39
Revision of neutrality laws (1939)................	85	11	11	83	78	35	17	65
Selective service (1940)....	81	31	13	66	72	35	25	43
3-year trade agreement extension (1940)..........	80	2	8	87	59	0	22	87
Arm merchant ships (1941)	83	24	8	70	N	N	N	N
Lend-lease passage (1941)..	88	15	9	71	75	34	20	59
Revision of Neutrality Act (1941)................	71	14	20	85	66	21	23	72
Limit armed forces to Western Hemisphere (1941)...	N	N	N	N	18	86	74	59
Ship seizure (1941)........	79	31	7	62	74	34	6	51
Extend selective service 18 months (1941)..........	68	13	24	82	57	48	11	45
British loan (1946)........	59	29	2	24	52	45	27	47
Bretton Woods agreement (1946)................	86	72	0	9	73	48	4	35
Truman Doctrine (1947)...	85	52	7	38	71	69	16	31
European Recovery Program (1948)............	79	68	6	25	84	60	9	25
Selective service (1948)....	72	56	16	36	93	72	4	15
Korean aid (1950).........	70	25	16	58	N	N	N	N
Override veto of Immigration Act (1952)..........	46	85	38	12	51	68	37	17
Mutual Security Act (1952)	71	39	9	45	80	53	2	19
Bricker amendment (1954)	N	N	N	N	27	61	64	36

man and his secretaries of state. Bipartisan delegations were sent to many international conferences in an effort to avoid the kind of sharp differences between the two parties which existed after World War I. Numerous Republicans in Congress worked to bring about greater support within their own party for the Administration's foreign policy.

Contrasted with the state of affairs from 1918 to 1920, these efforts brought considerable improvement in harmony between the parties. The United Nations Charter treaty was approved in the Senate by 89 to 2. Republican majorities, though much smaller, were given to Greek-Turkish aid (Truman Doctrine) and the subsequent foreign-assistance programs. Republicans generally applauded the President's intervention in the Korean War in 1950. In Congress Republicans sought to reduce but not abolish appropriations for foreign aid and many of them displayed a favorable attitude toward giving help to Franco's Spain. Responsible leaders of both parties have publicly endorsed a "bipartisan foreign policy," a term variously defined. Some aspects of the Korean War were made a campaign issue by Republicans in 1952. Eisenhower made no substantial changes in foreign policy during his first year in office, although there were some changes in emphasis.

Conclusion. Out of the confused picture of party loyalty and public policy a few things seem apparent. On comparatively few policies has either party cast a "party vote." Presidents have needed the help of votes from the minority party for enactment of numerous public policies. Nevertheless, majorities of various sizes in each party found themselves in opposition to each other on most of the major legislation concerning business, labor, agriculture, and social reform. In terms of over-all results, party labels during the New Deal era came to stand for something, though the difference is not to be exaggerated.

Heterogeneous party membership and the large independent vote are not the only factors accounting for a frequent lack of meaning of the two-party labels in foreign and domestic policy. Local considerations and a philosophy of responsibility to local constituencies interfere with the welding of party cleavages on a national scale. Another of these influences is that of group representation manifesting itself in the large occupational pressure groups. Workers from a heavily industrialized area look to their congressman, regardless of his label, to support pro-labor measures, and this is also the case with other interests. The farm bloc is essentially bipartisan on agricultural policies. The rural-urban conflict in some states upsets party lines or may prevent parties from taking a stand on controversial proposals. All these factors result in the slowing down of the formation of a party vote and leaders must work for a majority vote composed of members from both parties.

SELECTED REFERENCES

The character of American major parties and politics may be drawn from the whole gamut of literature on parties, so it is impossible to give here a list of even major works.

Both old and new textbooks on parties present the respective interpretations of scholars as to the nature of the American party system, interpretations which enjoy no unanimity of opinion. Each writer has made his contribution to the subject and has thereby enriched the understanding of American parties. For the convenience of the student some of the more useful texts are listed here: H. R. Bruce, *American Parties and Elections* (1936); D. D. McKean, *Party and Pressure Politics* (1949); C. E. Merriam and H. F. Gosnell, *The American Party System* (1949); C. W. McKenzie, *Party Government in the United States* (1938); R. C. Brooks, *Political Parties and Electoral Problems* (1933); T. W. Couzens, *Politics and Political Organizations in America* (1942); P. H. Odegard and E. Allen Helms, *American Politics* (1947); V. O. Key, Jr., *Politics, Parties, and Pressure Groups* (1952); E. M. Sait, *American Parties and Elections* (1942); H. M. Penniman, *Sait's American Parties and Elections* (1952); E. E. Schattschneider, *Party Government* (1942); E. P. Herring, *The Politics of Democracy* (1940); J. Macy, *Party Organization and Machinery* (1912); W. M. Sloane, *Party Government in the United States of America* (1914); J. A. Woodburn, *Political Parties and Party Problems* (1924).

Extensive references on certain aspects of parties will be found at the end of each chapter.

Burke said a political party is " a body of men united for promoting, by their joint endeavors some particular principle in which They are all engaged.

CHAPTER 13

Minor and European Parties

One of my reasons for undertaking the rather arduous task of running six times for President as a candidate of a small minority party was my persistent hope that we could make the party a nucleus, a rallying point, a spearhead . . . for a much larger new party on the electoral field. . . . Responsible parties in other English-speaking countries and in Scandinavian lands have presented clear-cut programs without evoking the specter of revolutionary violence.

—NORMAN THOMAS

According to Burke's well-known formula, a political party is "a body of men united for promoting, by their joint endeavors, the national interest upon some particular principle in which they are all agreed." From the description of the two-party system as it operates in the United States, it is obvious that American major parties do not fit this definition. The basic motivation of each major party is to capture control of the government, and the contest between the two parties is a struggle for power rather than a contest between rival principles. Each major party is a combination of interests which attempts to achieve unity at elections and on personnel, elective and appointive, and to a much less extent on issues and policies.

The minor parties in the United States as well as the European party systems are more illustrative of the Burke definition than are the major parties. It is desirable for the student of politics to have some knowledge of the character and operation of these parties and parties abroad, for they illustrate the formalization of some of the great competing principles in the world today, including clericalism, communism, socialism, monarchism, and the doctrines of the economic rightists.

To many persons, moreover, the two major parties are the only ones which have ever counted in the United States, and minor parties are regarded as not quite socially respectable, if not outright subversive. Such points of view and actions reveal a narrow and limited understanding of the role of minor parties. While the two-party system has served the nation fairly well, it is not necessarily the alpha and omega of all politics. Indeed, on numerous occasions the minor parties were responsible for forcing the major parties to present solutions and policies which saved the two-party system and staved off serious internal national dissension. One historian believes minor parties "have played perhaps quite as important a role as either of the major parties in making the nation what it is today." [1]

ROLE OF MINOR PARTIES

Voting Strength. The 1952 election was a black day for minor parties because their voting strength was at an all-time low. In 1948 the minor parties polled well over 5 per cent of the vote. Collectively, all minor party presidential nominees polled 2,610,000 votes compared to 290,000 in 1952, or less than .05 per cent of the vote. [2]

Reasons for the great decline in the popularity of minor-party candidates for this election are many. There was an absence of overriding economic discontent, and a high level of prosperity, with resulting faith in capitalism. Many 1948 minor-party leaders had deserted or withdrawn and their parties were torn asunder by sectarianism. Many former minor-party voters apparently felt that the major parties were championing civil rights and other programs of interest to them as minorities. Eisenhower and Stevenson, moreover, appeared to offer satisfactory choices. The cold war and hatred of the Communists undoubtedly hurt the extreme left-wing parties. The low state of minor parties in 1952 should not obscure the fact that at times they have been of real substance and influence and that their contribution is greater than generally realized.

In a convincing study of third parties, Professor Hicks relates that in presidential elections "in possibly half a dozen instances, the third party has snatched victory from one major party and given it to another." [3] In 1844 the Anti-slavery ticket polled over 62,000 popular votes, while the Democratic candidate James K. Polk won over his Whig opponent, Henry Clay, by a popular plurality of 38,000. Thanks to a large Anti-slavery vote in New York, Polk barely beat Clay in that state and with it won the election. If the Democratic candidate Winfield Hancock had received the votes given to the Greenbacker James B. Weaver in 1880, the former would have received a comfortable popular majority.

[1] John D. Hicks, "The Third Party Tradition in American Politics," *Mississippi Valley Historical Review,* Vol. 20 (1933), p. 4. A cursory review of minor parties is presented by W. B. Hesseltine, *The Rise and Fall of Third Parties: From Anti-Masonry to Wallace* (Washington, D.C.: Public Affairs Press, 1948); see also Nathan Fine, *Labor and Farmer Parties in the United States, 1828–1928* (New York: Rand School, 1928); T. H. Greer, *American Social Reform Groups* (New York: Prentice-Hall, Inc., 1949); E. F. Goldman, *Rendezvous with Destiny* (New York: Alfred A. Knopf, Inc., 1952), and R. J. Alexander, "Splinter Groups in American Radical Politics," *Social Research,* Vol. 20 (1953), pp. 282–310.

[2] Votes for minor-party presidential candidates from 1896 to 1952 are included in the tables in Chap. 11 giving voting statistics of all political parties. C. A. M. Ewing, *Presidential Elections* (Norman, Okla.: University of Oklahoma Press, 1940), gives an analysis of minor-party voting in presidential elections.

[3] *Op. cit.,* p. 26.

In several succeeding elections the combined votes of minor parties, if added to the losing major-party nominee, would have resulted in popular victory for the latter. Five times in our history—1892, 1912, 1920, 1924, and 1948—a single minor-party presidential nominee polled over a million votes, and in 1860 two "splinter" nominees together polled more than the Democrat Stephen Douglas. In one congressional election in 1914, the Socialists and Progressives each polled over 1½ million votes, and the latter elected 18 members to Congress. This does not mean that the final national electoral verdict would have been altered in each instance, because of the anomaly of the electoral college system. It does show, however, that on numerous occasions major parties have been concerned about the degree of defection to minor parties. Minor parties tend to be presidential parties and seldom run many candidates for Congress. As shown in Table 15, their vote for the candidates to the House remains unimpressive.

Table 15. Minor-party Vote for United States Representatives

Party	1944	1946	1948	1950	1952
American Labor...	499,575	418,992	512,148	225,368	94,946
Communist.......	†	3,408	775	†	†
Independent......	90,625	74,962	29,419	119,634	111,780
Liberal...........	181,928	118,010	220,107	279,168	413,859
Progressive.......	108,068	†	362,514	127,715	5,773
Prohibition.......	35,782	47,653	32,648	34,761	38,664
Socialist.........	28,291	38,052	20,473	4,626	4,892
Socialist Labor....	340	779	48	†	177
Others..........	19,961	71,621	6,238	15,086	162,600

† No candidates on ballot.

Source: Full recapitulation by states will be found in the statistics of these elections published by the Government Printing Office.

For some time New York City has operated under a multiple party system. The Liberal party has elected a president of the city council, chosen in a city-wide vote, and both the Liberal and Labor parties have elected councilmen and state legislators. Without the help of these two parties (and in municipal elections the Fusionist elements), it seems doubtful if Mayor La Guardia would have been reelected in 1941 or if President Roosevelt would have carried New York in 1944.[4]

Minor parties have occasionally captured coveted executive positions in states and cities, though usually thwarted by failure to control the

[4] Voting statistics on the American Labor and Liberal parties in gubernatorial and presidential elections are given on p. 117.

legislature. Governors of Minnesota, North Dakota, and Wisconsin have come from the ranks of third parties. Daniel Hoan, a Socialist, was mayor of Milwaukee for a quarter of a century and Jasper McLevy, a less doctrinaire Socialist, has had a phenomenal record of repeated reelections as mayor of Bridgeport, Conn.

Champions of Discontent and New Issues. The importance of lesser parties lies in a realm other than serious contenders for political power. They offer spectacular criticisms of the party in power, which often the major opposition party fails to provide, and they champion public issues which both old-line parties consider "too hot to handle." Generally united on principles and with little chance for election, and free from the fear of alienating certain blocs of voters, the campaigns and programs of minor parties are generally more specific and hard hitting. The issues of slavery were most squarely met by the minor parties prior to 1860. The agrarian parties of the nineteenth century dramatically portrayed the needs of Western farmers and criticized Eastern monied interests in a vein which no Republican or Democratic nominee (until William Jennings Bryan) dared to do. To the chagrin of many Old Guard Democrats, Bryan was nominated by both the Populist and the Democratic parties in 1896. Major parties were fearful of championing easy money, Greenbackism, and public ownership prior to 1896, and Bryan's free-silver stand drove many gold Democrats out of the party in that election. Since their creation, the socialist parties have usually been ahead of the major parties in demanding widespread social ownership of the utilities and the expansion of social-welfare services.

Although their protests are vociferous, third parties have not contented themselves merely to be against existing public policies. A characteristic of minor parties has been adoption of counterprograms, some carefully thought out, some economically dubious. New issues and new programs generally emanate from small parties. To mention but a few, railroad regulation, the graduated income tax, control of banking, work relief, Federal youth programs, unemployment insurance, old-age pensions, postal savings, direct primaries, and popular election of senators were first advocated by the Populist, Socialist, or Progressive Party. As these programs became "respectable" and demonstrated vote-getting possibilities they were taken over by one or both major parties and enacted into law. This very fact accounts for the lack of permanence of so many minor parties; for after the minor-party policies gain acceptance, they are taken over by the major parties, and the minor party loses its support and membership. Many proposals of third parties, however, never gain support and are relegated to the limbo of defeated issues, and minority party followers, often hopeful of quick success after repeated and disastrous defeats, forsake the fold.

The activities and organization of these various minor groups serve more as crusading or educational movements than as effective havens for the politically homeless and the politically ambitious. Their clubs, campaigns, literature, and zealous insistence upon the protection of the rights of minorities provide, however, a useful political education for many citizens of the country. The hundreds of thousands of voters who have supported minor parties in the past seldom saw immediate triumph but they paved the way for the eventual adoption of a great many far-reaching national policies today.

TYPES OF MINOR PARTIES

Although differences between minor parties are easily seen, it is less easy to place the parties in clearly defined categories. Broadly speaking, the nationally organized minor groups seem to fall within the two classes of splinter and ideological or issue parties. Illustrative of the first group were the Liberal Republicans of 1872, the Progressive or Bull Moosers of 1912, the La Follette Progressives of 1924, the States Rights' or Dixie-crats and the Wallace Progressives of 1948. With the exception of the last-mentioned, these parties endured only one election and quickly disintegrated with most of their followers returning to the parent party at the next election. The Marxist parties are ideological in character and were not specific fragments of the larger parties. As a single-issue party, the Prohibitionists likewise developed pretty much on their own.

The 1912 and 1924 Progressive parties were offshoots of the Republican party, while the Wallace party seceded from the Democrats. Between 1924 and 1948 no group took the Progressive party label. After the 1948 election, Democratic Senator Glen Taylor of Idaho, the vice presidential nominee, deserted the Progressives and returned to the Democrats. Former Vice President Henry Wallace broke with the party when it failed to support the United Nations' position on the Korean War. Even before this, extreme left-wingers and Communists gave the party support and took over its leadership after Wallace's departure. It condemned the Korean War in its 1952 campaign while being led by a wealthy San Francisco lawyer, Vincent Hallinan. It polled only 133,000 votes.

Unlike the Progressives, the Dixiecrats were a regional party which split with Truman and the Democratic National Convention over civil rights issues. Its presidential nominee, Governor J. Strom Thurmond of South Carolina, had his name entered in 16 states, including all in the South. He succeeded in carrying Alabama, Louisiana, Mississippi, and South Carolina, where he ran as the official "Democrat." The party fell apart and four years later Stevenson carried all four states. Ironically, several of the Southern states which failed to follow the Dixiecrats in 1948 voted for Eisenhower. The Dixiecrat group provides an illustration of a regional rather than national party and its position on civil rights and racial questions is unlikely to attract widespread following in other sections.

The Greenback and Populist parties of the last century were strongly sectional in character and arose out of agrarian discontent. They demanded a radical change in government policies in order to improve the lot of both the farmer and the worker and to curb the growing power of the industrial East. Strictly speaking, these parties were neither splinter nor Marxist but contained some elements of both. They survived longer than splinter groups but did not continue to live as did the Socialists and Prohibitionists.

A number of splinter parties organized on a state-wide basis have survived several elections. In most cases these parties represented the liberal-radical wing of the party and became somewhat more extreme in viewpoint if not doctrinaire and ideological and purported to some extent to have a class basis. The four best known of these are the Farmer-Labor party in Minnesota,[5] the Progressive party in Wisconsin, and the American Labor and Liberal parties in New York. The first two enjoyed great popularity during the 1930's, mainly because of agrarian discontent and the depression. Both elected governors and United States senators. Since 1940 they have declined in influence. The Farmer-Labor party was formed in 1918 and exerted considerable influence in surrounding states as well as in Minnesota as the so-called "core of revolution in the Middle West." The party later strongly supported the New Deal and for a time reduced the Democratic party to a relatively poor third in elections. Beginning in 1938 the Republican trend resulted in a defeat of its congressional candidates and many of the Farmer-Laborites deserted to the Republicans.[6] Disintegration continued to beset the party and in 1944 it voted itself out of existence to enable its remnants to merge with the Democrats for the purpose of reelecting President Roosevelt and electing New Dealers to Congress.

In 1934 Robert M. La Follette, Jr., and Philip La Follette, like their father a decade earlier, broke away from the Republican party and founded the Progressive party. The party was remarkably successful in its native Wisconsin and in 1938 Governor Philip La Follette, with much fanfare, announced the launching of a national progressive party. The movement collapsed when the independents and liberals to whom he appealed

---

[5] A brief history of the Farmer-Labor party and the Non-Partisan League of North Dakota is given in Chap. 6. See also J. R. Starr, "Labor and Farmer Groups and the Three-party System," *Southwestern Social Science Quarterly*, Vol. 17 (1936), pp. 7–19.

[6] At the height of its power the Farmer-Labor party was a well-oiled machine. The death of one of its leaders, Governor Floyd B. Olson, also was a considerable factor in its decline.

showed no enthusiasm and the party's congressional candidates, who were entered in five states, had no success. Wisconsin Progressives were sorely troubled over foreign policy, the La Follettes themselves being isolationist. This issue was undoubtedly one of the major reasons for the declining influence of the party in the state elections after 1941. With their forces at a low ebb, the Wisconsin Progressives met in 1946 and decided to dissolve, most of the members and Senator La Follette ostensibly returning to the Republican fold. This marked an end to the three-party system in Wisconsin. The Republicans, however, were in no mood to welcome them back, and Senator La Follette lost out in the Republican primary, bringing to an end a 21-year career in the Senate.

The American Labor party was created in New York in 1936 out of Labor's Nonpartisan League, a Democratic auxiliary.[7] Many supporters of President Roosevelt and Senator Robert Wagner were dissatisfied with the flavor of the New York City Democratic organization, Tammany Hall, and the party was used to attract voters who disliked to vote under the Democratic label. In 1944 a struggle ensued between the right and left wings and when the latter was victorious, the right seceded and formed the Liberal party. The program and activities of these two parties were reviewed in Chap. 5.[8] It should be noted, however, that the two parties are now so far apart ideologically that no *rapprochement* seems likely. Both have endorsed major-party candidates and the nominees have run on such tickets as Republican-Liberal, Democratic-American Labor. With the growing unpopularity of the extreme left wing among the electorate, the Liberal party, beginning in 1950, became the stronger of the two parties. In 1953 it ran its own candidate for mayor of New York and he polled 468,000 votes, while the ALP candidate polled only 54,000 votes.

Historically there have been numerous third parties in American municipal elections, especially when the major parties placed unsatisfactory candidates in the field. "Good Government," "Commonwealth," and "Fusion" are some of the labels under which independents have run. With few exceptions these parties and their successes have been short-lived, due to the inability to offer inducements to keep an army of precinct and other party workers intact.

CONTEMPORARY MINOR-PARTY GROUPINGS

Prohibitionists. Aside from the Marxist parties, only the Prohibitionists have remained as a permanently and nationally organized minor

---

[7] Chap. 5 gives an account of the labor parties in New York. For a history of the American Labor and Liberal parties see Hugh A. Bone, "Political Parties in New York City," *The American Political Science Review*, Vol. 40 (1946), pp. 272–282.

[8] See pp. 115–117.

party. The Prohibition party is also the oldest minor party, having first nominated a candidate for president in 1872. Its high point was reached in 1892, when it polled 271,000 votes. Early in this century many prohibitionists worked within the major parties to bring about national prohibition and this resulted in a decline in membership; since 1920, it has seldom polled over 100,000 votes. It suffered in 1952 along with all minor parties and polled only 73,000 votes in the 20 states where it was on the ballot. The group is moralist rather than class in character and its major strength comes from church groups and older persons. Until very recently it was a one-issue party but now its platform contains statements on political and economic problems.[9]

Socialist Parties. The Socialist Labor party was formed in 1877 as an outgrowth of the Social Democratic Workingmen's party. It was German in origin and clung to its German heritage. Originally its meetings were conducted in German and the party was reinforced by new waves of German immigrants exiled from their country after the enactment of anti-Socialist laws under the Bismarck regime. As a result, it never became a prominent part of the American labor movement, and its efforts to bore from within the Knights of Labor and the American Federation of Labor were unsuccessful.[10]

Under Daniel De Leon's leadership, the group embarked on a dual unionism venture by founding the Socialist Trade and Labor Alliance with a view to supplanting the AFL, which was unresponsive to the idea of politically supported socialism. De Leon envisaged unions as the framework for a socialist society and attacked what he called the "ridiculous geographic constituencies in Congress." He called for occupational representation by trades, which he felt would eliminate the conflicting interests in the capitalistic society. In 1896 the party entered national politics but captured only 39,000 votes. It has never polled 100,000 votes and does well to poll 50,000 in a national election. Many socialists would not accept De Leon's leadership and flocked to the banner of the Social Democrats and Eugene V. Debs in 1898. In 1901 the Socialist label was taken by the Debs group and has prevailed to the present.

The Socialist party has by far the most impressive record of all the Marxist parties. In 1912, with Debs's name entered in all states, it polled over 900,000 votes. Debs opposed the entry of the United States into World War I and conducted his 1920 campaign from a prison cell. At this time he polled the largest single vote ever cast for a Socialist presidential nominee—920,000 votes. Since 1920 the Socialist vote has declined

[9] See Roger Babson, *Our Campaign for the Presidency* (Chicago: National Prohibitionist, 1941).

[10] See O. M. Johnson and H. Kuhn, *Socialist Labor Party during Four Decades: 1890–1930* (New York: Labor News, 1931), pp. 11 ff.

and in 1952 Darlington Hoopes received only 18,300 votes and the party was on the ballot in only 14 states.

What are the differences between the Socialist and Socialist Labor parties which have influenced them to follow separate causes? The latter has been more theoretical, doctrinaire, and visionary. It has followed a long-run point of view of predicting the inevitable collapse of capitalism. The Socialist Labor party alone accepts De Leon and the theory that trade-unions must be the weapon to bring about socialism and serve as the pillar of a socialist system. It makes no compromise with capitalism, believing only in revolution and reform. In some states the party places its nominees under the label of "industrial government," symbolic of De Leon's emphasis on functional representation and unionism. The party asserts that it is "the only party with a truly Marxist program" and advocates the overthrow of the state, replacing it with a large industrial union. In 1952, it polled more votes (29,300) than the Socialists.

In contrast, the Socialists have been more opportunistic and have dealt with contemporary economic and social issues as they arose. The Socialist party has appealed to all labor groups and has been friendly to craft unions, while the Socialist Labor party has favored industrial unionism. The more specific program of the Socialists calls for the setting up, by parliamentary methods, of a cooperative commonwealth of socialism through social ownership of basic means of production, especially the heavy industries.[11] In this respect the American Socialists are in agreement with the British Labor party. For many years white-collar workers, professionals, and the intelligentsia were attracted to the party when it was led by Norman Thomas, who stepped out as leader before the 1952 campaign. More of these have supported the party in elections than the proletariat or the "great unwashed."

After the poor showing in 1952 the party decided to concentrate on education instead of diverting what little money and energy it had on campaigns. How long the party adheres to this policy remains in doubt, for leadership and general economic conditions could easily lead the Socialists to reverse this approach and again enter the electoral arena.

The Communists. Communist political groups aroused little interest in the United States until the successful revolution in Russia in 1919. In 1921 they united under the label of the Workers' party, which changed to Communist in 1929. From the beginning the Communists, like the Socialists, were beset with internal fights and in 1928 the Trotskyite wing was thrown out of the party and became the Socialist-Worker party;[12]

[11] Norman Thomas has written many books and articles on socialism. See especially *A Socialist's Faith* (New York: W. W. Norton & Company, Inc., 1951).

[12] See James Oneal and G. A. Werner, *American Communism* (New York: E. P. Dutton & Company, Inc., 1947). On Communist strategy to 1945, see Barrington Moore

it has run candidates for office under that label on occasions and polled 9,000 votes in 1952 for its teamster-presidential candidate, Farrell Dobbs. The Communists differed sharply from the Socialists, whom they bitterly fought, in the acceptance of physical force to overthrow the bourgeois state and establish a dictatorship of the proletariat. Socialists also never agreed with the opportunism of the Communists.

The history of the Communists is a fantastic story of intrigue, expediency, and sharp reversals of policy. The party has been alternately pacifistic and then pro-war. In 1938 the American Communist party officially severed its connections with the Communist International, disclaimed the use of force, and came out for majority rule and the Bill of Rights. It applauded the Russo-German nonaggression pact and opposed American rearmament, but later fervently demanded American rearmament and intervention when the Soviet Union and Germany went to war. It supported the war effort and became much less revolutionary in utterance and resolved itself from a party into an "educational" organization called the Communist Political Association.

At the end of World War II it threw out Earl Browder, elevated William Z. Foster to the leadership and changed to a new militant Marxist program.[13] A new constitution pledged itself to democracy and denounced the use of force, but the tone of its new supporters took on a revolutionary emphasis. It began again to run candidates for local office under the Communist label, though it voted to endorse Henry Wallace for President in 1948 rather than run its own candidate.

The turnabouts and opportunism are understandable only in terms of the consistent loyalty to the "party line," first of the Comintern, then the line of the official policies of the Soviet Union. Although not always fully apparent to many fellow travelers who worked in the party, the leadership invariably used the party as an instrument of Soviet foreign policy. This factor served as its undoing and led to its going underground. From 1946 on, there were wholesale desertions within the party membership and many deserters gave testimony to congressional committees and to the press on the membership and activities. The most serious blow came in 1950, when members of the national executive committee were convicted under the Smith Act of advocating and teaching the overthrow of the United States government by force and violence. Following this, numerous state and local party officials were indicted and convicted of conspiracy. When Congress passed the Communist Control Act of 1954,

Jr., "The Communist Party of the USA: An Analysis of a Social Movement," *The American Political Science Review*, Vol. 39 (1945), pp. 31–41. Communist membership in the United States has declined rapidly since World War II. It was estimated at 70,000 in 1947, 55,000 in 1951, and 22,000 in 1954.

[13] An account of this important transition is covered in *The New York Times*, July 26, 27, 28, 29, 1945.

Communists were no longer able to function through a party. The Act outlawed the Communist party on the ground that it was an illegal conspiracy to overthrow the government. Actually its members had largely gone underground before the passage of the law.

Following the party line of the Soviet Union was not the only distinguishing feature of the American Communist party. Its rigid internal discipline and tactics made its influence far out of proportion to its numbers. Hard work and zealousness enabled its members to permeate the leadership councils of some interest groups. Delinquent dues-paying members and dissenters were purged and ousted. The Communists attempted, with some success, to infiltrate transportation and communications unions, ostensibly in order to tie up the country in the event of a general strike. Many locals were expelled from national unions when this was detected. Spreading of dissension, confusion, and discontent also marked the tactics of the group. These techniques were far more important than electioneering.

The gradual exposure and final official recognition of the conspiratorial character of the Communist movement brought out the names of many fairly prominent Americans as onetime members or supporters who voted Communist as a protest (as did many who voted Socialist). Some were attracted during the depression by the Communists' vigorous championship of the "underdog" and during the war by the Soviet effort against Nazism and fascism. Many persons who have voted Communist or Socialist never fully accepted Marxism nor did they, like the party members, pay dues and take an oath to support the collectivist society.

The activities of the Communists hurt to an unknown extent all minor parties which were not splinters. They were called "subversive" by some and state legislatures made it increasingly difficult for minor parties to get their candidates on the ballot. With their advocacy of the use of force if necessary, Communists do not fit the requirement of constitutionalism or of the ideals of democracy and peaceful change. The Socialist party operated within the American constitutional framework but this distinction was not always recognized by all anti-Communists. The fight against Communists was used by some ultra-right-wing enthusiasts to attack all political liberalism, progressives, reformers, and Socialists. One rightist averred that a Communist is nothing more than an "excited Socialist." The attacks on liberals and radicals were denounced by many persons, including President Eisenhower. Nonetheless, many non-Communists found themselves put on the defensive by those who made undiscriminating attacks. Communism, as a result, has had profound effects on American political life beyond the activities of a comparatively small number of its leaders, most of whom are in jail, out on bail, or have gone underground.

BRITISH POLITICAL PARTIES

The point has been stressed that the American party system closely fits its own society. The same may be said for party arrangements in other lands, because democracy wears different faces in different countries. Differences in party systems are more than variations in party structure, organization, discipline, and leadership. Their wellsprings arise from sociological conditions, the governmental structure, and the disposition of power in the community. As members of the British Commonwealth of Nations, Australia and Canada might be expected to have essentially the same party system, but the variations between the Canadian two-party and the Australian three-party arrangements are marked. The latter, for example, has a "Country party," which was created out of agrarian discontent with the machinations of urban professionals and businessmen. Neither Canada nor Great Britain may be said to have a counterpart of the Country party. Australian Labor is less doctrinaire than British Labor and Canada has no Labor party. But Canada has a strong provincial party, the Cooperative Commonwealth Federation, which is based in cooperatives and socialism, interests which in England and Australia are absorbed by one of the major parties. Thus, the party systems are not easily exportable because they rest upon their own cultures. Some devices and techniques, however, may be transported and prove useful. At this point a brief examination will be made of certain characteristics of parties in Britain, Canada, and Europe.

Development and Cleavages. English parties antedated American parties by over a century and began as a contest between the Whigs and the Tories; gradually they gave way to the contemporary Liberals and Conservatives respectively. Until World War I each party was alternately in power for considerable periods of time. Each had quite clear-cut policies in contrast to the American Whigs and Democrats and later the Republicans and Democrats. For example, on home rule for Ireland the issue between Liberals and Conservatives was quite sharp, as it was over the question of reconstructing the House of Lords. In the present century, however, these two English parties have found themselves in general agreement over fundamentals.[14]

After 1918 the Liberals were torn with internal strife and the Labor party assumed the stature of a third major party. It acceded to power in 1924 but without a majority and was replaced by a Conservative gov-

[14] On interpretations of British parties see the symposium edited by S. D. Bailey, *The British Party System* (London: The Hansard Society, 1952); H. M. Stout, *British Government* (New York: Oxford University Press, 1953), Chaps. 10–12; D. E. Butler, *The British General Election of 1951* (New York: St. Martin's Press, Inc., 1952), and especially Ivor Bulmer-Thomas, *The Party System in Great Britain* (London: Phoenix House, 1953).

ernment after less than a year. Labor again came to office in 1929 but
without a majority. From 1931 to 1945 a Conservative coalition was in
control, due to the depression, the war, and the defection of the Laborites
from Ramsay MacDonald.

In one of the most stunning election surprises the Labor party was
swept into power in the general election of 1945, removing the popular
wartime Prime Minister, Winston Churchill. The Conservatives were
not returned to power until 1951, and even then they failed to poll a
majority of the popular vote (see Table 16).

Table 16. Major Party Strength in the British House of Commons

Party	Major party representation in Parliament				Popular vote, 1951
	1935	1945	1950	1951	
Conservative...	387	189	297	321	13,900,000
Labor.........	154	393	315	295	13,700,000
Liberal........	20	12	9	6	723,000

The Conservative and Liberal parties today bear considerable resemblance respectively to the Republicans and Democrats in the United
States. Both are heterogeneous in membership and regard themselves as
the bulwark against socialism and champions of private enterprise. Liberals are quicker to embrace state intervention and extension of social insurance as methods of heading off public ownership. For example, the
Liberals supported the Lloyd George-Keynesian program for national
development projects to conquer unemployment, believing they would
offer new opportunities for private enterprise. Liberals advocated the
Beveridge plan for social services, which they felt would preserve both
"freedom and welfare."

Sharp internal quarrels have weakened the Liberals since World War I.
But a more important reason for their decline is the rise of the Labor
party, resulting in the Liberals being ground between the other two
parties. The single-member district, as in the United States, favors two
parties. The Liberals, with a creditable popular vote of well over two
million in 1945, were able to elect only nine members to the House of
Commons. The cabinet system also contributes to a certain polarity with
the clear emergence of a "Government side" and an "Opposition side."

Labor differs from the other two parties both in composition and policy. While it makes appeals to all groups as do its rivals, the backbone of the party rests in the trade-unions, socialist and cooperative societies and constituent organizations. These groups nominate candidates who, upon endorsement by the National Executive Committee, run as official Labor candidates. Intellectuals and persons from diverse ranks have gravitated to the party but it remains essentially a working-class party committed to socialist principles. During its period in office following World War II, it nationalized the Bank of England, civil aviation, coal mining, tele-communications, inland transportation, electrical and gas utilities, health services, and the iron and steel industry. The party also succeeded in passing a law restricting the veto power of the House of Lords.

To some extent the Conservatives followed a "me too" program when they returned to power in 1951. They denationalized only trucking trans-port and the iron and steel industry and made comparatively minor modifications in the social-welfare program. Although they did not ex-tend the various social-welfare programs they made little effort to undo them.

In summary, there is a wider cleavage between Conservative and Labor-ites than between the former and the Liberals. In the popular mind the two major parties today stand for something rather definite in economic, political, and international policies. British parties have more cohesion on matters of broad policy than their American counterparts. The per-sonnel differences of the respective parties in Parliament are rather strik-ing.[15] Conservative members of Parliament are recruited from the upper middle to upper classes. Nearly a third are connected with families having a hereditary title and six out of seven attended a famous public school. Occupationally, they come from business and the professions. About a quarter of the Labor party members are teachers and miners and there are a liberal number of railwaymen and workers. Similar to the Conserva-tives, many Labor members are professionals and barristers. Although class lines are more pronounced than in the United States, there is a con-siderable degree of heterogeneity of party membership in the electorate and leadership ability is needed in order to unify the divergent ele-ments of each party both within and without Parliament.

Cabinet System. In England one commonly speaks of "the party in the country" and "the parliamentary party." The cardinal feature of the latter and of the British system is the importance of the cabinet. The cabinet is called "the keystone of the political arch, the pivot around which the whole political machinery revolves." In a general election for the House of Commons, the winning party takes control of the govern-ment and its leader becomes prime minister; the minority leader becomes

---

[15] Some interesting data will be found in J. F. S. Ross, "The Personnel of the Parties," in Bailey (ed.), *The British Party System,* pp. 168–176.

head of "His (or Her) Majesty's Opposition." A prime minister becomes leader of both the cabinet and the ministry; the cabinet is composed of inner circle ministers. The cabinet prepares legislation and becomes, with the ministers, responsible for carrying out national policy. If the cabinet loses the confidence of the House of Commons by being defeated on a major policy vote, the entire ministry resigns or appeals to the electorate. If the party is defeated in a general election, the new majority party forms a cabinet and takes control of the government.

The concept of an organized opposition in Parliament has no counterpart in the United States. Her Majesty's Opposition is a highly significant institution. The Opposition is wedded with the majority party in common allegiance to the Queen (or King) and to a general way of life. While the cabinet furnishes the actual advisers to the Queen the Opposition exists as potential advisers. At all times the Opposition is actual and visible, a group to whom the nation can turn at any time it feels the need for a change or an alternative government. The Opposition holds itself in readiness to take over the helm and to wage an immediate campaign. The leader of the Opposition sits in the House and helps to provide a cabinet opposition. By contrast, the defeated presidential candidate as "titular" leader resides away from Washington, and makes no effort to lead the opposition in Congress.

BRITISH AND AMERICAN PARTIES CONTRASTED

British and American parties present many contrasts other than the differences in cleavages and in the role of the opposition. The party leaders, the prime minister, and his cabinet exercise strong disciplinary control over party members in Parliament. Yet the party members remain a check on the prime minister and government and serve as a sounding board for the country. By contrast, an American President and his Cabinet are separated from the legislature. A majority of the President's own party can vote against him on a policy or override his veto, and both will still remain in power for a specified time. The President, therefore, has less actual control over his party in terms of formulating, defending, and executing broad national policies.

American and British parties offer their greatest contrast in terms of their control over the national legislature. Party organization in the House of Commons is more complete and discipline more strict in policy matters than in the House of Representatives. Whereas Americans choose their party leader (presidential nominee) in a national convention, in England the members of Parliament make the choice. Similar differences exist in making the party platforms. American national conventions take place quadrennially, whereas in England the national party conferences meet annually. The convention in England is for the purpose of formulating broad party policies and programs, making speeches, and fostering morale rather than for drafting the party's platform in the American sense of the word, because the party's group in Parliament formulates its own national program. Members of Parliament nevertheless look to the annual conference for support and defense of their activities in Commons. Simultaneously, the conference holds them accountable and is free with its criticism of the program formulated by its members in the House of Commons.

3. Functions in each party.

The British party conferences differ somewhat in detail, degree of influence, and function in each party.[16] In general, they are important in the transaction of party business, discussion of issues, criticism of the party's record in Parliament, and in the adoption of resolutions. Members of Parliament are not invariably bound by the resolutions but realize that they may be called upon to defend their positions at the conference. To some extent the conferences may be likened to a party legislature, dominated, however, by the executive committee. As a regular part of the party machinery, they are useful in formulating policy and in keeping the party's platform up to date. American writers have urged the use of annual meetings but Democratic and Republican leaders remain unenthusiastic because of the expense and because conferences may publicly air schisms within the ranks.

4. Organization

In organization, considerable difference exists between British and American parties.[17] The basic unit of the three major English parties is the local constituency organization composed of all party members. Local associations are run by a small executive committee and a paid party agent, whose job is to win the constituency in the election. Local associations are united in a national union, which maintains a central party office and runs the annual party conference.

5. election machinery in Britain is central.

The central office is the coordinating agency whose function is to plan, direct, and win elections. It works closely with the leaders in Parliament and has a hand in drafting the party's parliamentary program. The fact that Britain follows the "unitary" as opposed to the "federal" principle in the United States makes the number of local organizations fewer in number and somewhat less in importance. There is no local collection of funds in Britain, so all candidates depend for support on central headquarters, a practice widely at variance with American tradition. Unlike American practice, British parliamentary candidates must be approved by the national as well as local party organizations. Domination by the National Executive Office reflects itself also in the power to expel a party

unitary
federal in U.S.

[16] A useful discussion of the conferences is given by James K. Pollock, "The British Party Conferences," *The American Political Science Review*, Vol. 32 (1938), pp. 525–536.

[17] The following chapters are devoted to American party organization, hence only brief reference is made here.

member. There are cases on record where the national office has expelled Members of Parliament for opposition to the party's policies, an action which has no counterpart in American parties.

The party system took root in Parliament first and it took a long time developing into a regular party organization in the country. National party headquarters and representative constituency associations did not appear until after the middle of the nineteenth century. In local government the party system did not develop until much later. The system of democratic local government was not inaugurated until 1835 and there was a tendency for persons to run as "independents" during most of the rest of the century. Contests for local offices sometimes resulted in a Conservative-Liberal contest but the "nonpolitical" character was the rule. In the last 25 years, and especially since World War II, the party system has spread rapidly into local government. This was due to an extension of the franchise and the importance of social-welfare measures to the localities.[18] The local Labor party leaders turn to their national office for guidance and advice. Both major parties now publish elaborate campaign materials for local elections. These emphasize the parliamentary accomplishments of the party and the role of local councils in carrying out the national program. There is some criticism in Britain, as in the United States, that local elections can be won or lost over national instead of local issues and that the two should not be fused in local elections. In England the extensive social-welfare programs require some degree of party control if they are to be effective on the community level. In the absence of strong mayors or appointive managers, party control helps to provide a much-needed coordination. There is little sentiment in the United States for projecting national party authority into municipal elections.

As **Norton Long notes**,[19] what stands out in any comparison of the British and American party systems is the

real source of discipline and authority [in the former and] the voters' paramount interest in their member as a supporter of a cabinet and a program, and . . . the devotion of local party leadership to national policy and leaders.

This contrasts with the American tradition that a President should refrain from interfering in the primaries of his party, a tradition that justifies voting for a Roosevelt and a Byrd on the grounds that both are good men, a tradition that even goes so far in its ambivalence towards the logic of party government

18 See L. G. Harvey, "The Party in Local Affairs," *National Municipal Review*, Vol. 52 (1953), pp. 227–231.

19 "Party Government and the United States," *Journal of Politics*, Vol. 13 (1951), pp. 190–191; published by the Southern Political Science Association in cooperation with the University of Florida. This article is most relevant to many aspects considered in the preceding and succeeding chapters.

as to condemn Wilson's appeal for a Democratic Congress as narrowly partisan. . . . The interests of local party leaderships, when not hostile to Washington, frequently extend no farther than a shrewd appreciation of the value of keeping the voter regular.

In Britain the parties are highly nationalized, centralized, and disciplined and are able to take reasonably specific stands on public questions, whereas in this country the real seat of power is in the state or local organizations, which do not have to take orders or follow instructions from the national office. Each system has its merits and limitations. A British M.P. is not free to vote as he likes but is compelled to follow the decisions of the party council or else run the risk of being disciplined if he opposes the party decision too often. An American congressman is a much freer agent, responsible mainly to the voters and to his local party organization. Traditionally he resides in the district from which he is elected and he has a strong sense of loyalty to it. In England it is not axiomatic for the M.P. to live in his district and his sense of obligation to it is less; representatives are chosen more on class and party lines than as individuals. The American system of decentralization makes difficult party unity in Congress even on very vital issues which may appear in the party platform, and a congressman knows he will probably not be penalized by the national committee if he refuses to accept its program.

THE CANADIAN PARTY SYSTEM

America's sprawling northern neighbor has a most interesting political system, one using a combination of British parliamentary principles and American expedients. The Canadian party system, like that of the United States, must operate in a federal system requiring a local, provincial, and Dominion organization but within the framework of a cabinet government instead of presidential leadership. Canada is divided into great economic regions, each of which is capable of being diversely affected by a given national policy. To control the Dominion government, a party must carry at least two sections. In this respect, plus the factors incident to federalism, the parties in Canada resemble those in the United States in character, and sectionalism takes on a commanding importance. Geographical and sectional considerations have helped to fasten on Canada a two-party system in the national field. The national parties are, in effect, federations of provincial parties; the latter, unlike the British parties, collect the funds and essentially run the Dominion elections. Provincial associations usually meet annually to consider party policies and candidates are nominated by party conventions. In nominations, therefore, Canadian parties resemble their American counterparts much more than the British, where choice resides in the parliamentary group of the party and the central office.

An important characteristic of the Canadian system is the leadership of a particular man, a practice which has no parallel in England, where adherence to party principles competes with loyalty to a leader, or in the United States, where local leaders have no impelling obligation to follow the national leader. Professor Clokie says: [20]

In Canada more than anywhere else it is possible to define a party as being a body of supporters following a given leader. Parliamentary elections are primarily occasions on which the electors choose between party leaders as prospective prime ministers. Each voter knows that he is not so much voting for Candidate X as a Member of Parliament as expressing his desire that Candidate X's leader should form the Cabinet. Party leadership has thus become institutionalized.

An extreme example of the long leadership of one man was that of W. L. Mackenzie King, who led the Liberal party from 1917 to 1948, a tenure probably without parallel in any democratic nation in this century.

On the surface it would seem that the prime minister and parliamentary leaders might enforce the same discipline on members as is possible in England because of the threat of dissolution. Actually discipline is much less great and the leadership is not disposed to enforce the party line too strongly. For one thing, the cabinet must adjust itself to the demands of sectional interests and is forced to effect compromises in this respect. It cannot refuse nomination to an insurgent; it can only try to get the local constituency to deny him renomination. If the dissenter has strong backing in his province, this is an ineffective weapon.

The sectional and provincial politics of Canada have produced two important minor parties and other small groupings which bear but a vague resemblance to the Non-Partisan League, Progressives, and Populist groups in American history. These parties have been able to control a provincial government without at the same time securing a formidable amount of representation in the national government. Some of the radical elements among the western farmers combined with labor and socialist groups in that area to form the Cooperative Commonwealth Federation in 1932. By 1944 the CCF overwhelmingly controlled the government of Saskatchewan and constituted the official opposition party in British Columbia, Manitoba, and Ontario. Since 1949 the strength of the CCF has been ebbing in the provinces and in parliament. In the Pacific Coast province of British Columbia, the Progressives, Conservatives, and Liberals formed a coalition for the purpose of keeping the CCF from gaining control of the government. They decided to break up after passing a preferential-voting law by which they believed would be assured that one or the other would control the government. To the amazement of every-

20 H. M. Clokie, *Canadian Government and Politics* (1944), p. 91. By permission of Longmans, Green & Co., Inc.

one, the Social Credit party, irreverently called the "Socreds," was able under this system to win the British Columbia election in 1953. In 1944 this party captured the province of Alberta. The CCF and SCP exemplify how a group with a specific program may become strong locally without being able to rally enough country-wide strength to pose a serious national threat.[21] The Canadian Parliament elected in 1953, for example, was composed of 173 Liberals, 50 Progressive Conservatives, 25 from the CCF, 15 from the SCP, and 3 others. The huge electoral victory for the Liberals was their fifth in a row and started them on their nineteenth consecutive year in office.

EUROPEAN PARTIES AND POLITICS

It is almost impossible to generalize about political parties and politics on the Continent/except to say that they offer some very material differences from those of the United States, Britain, and Canada. European political programs and parties are difficult to classify because their strength is both changing and deceptive. The "People's Democracies" of Eastern Europe have been largely consolidated under Communist authority. Where parties once existed representing such important movements as liberalism, socialism, agrarianism, authoritarianism, and communism, all but the last-mentioned no longer have a chance to operate in the manner of political parties in Western Europe. The latter countries, with few exceptions, lived for a time under autocrats or a military dictatorship and occupation for at least some of the time since 1939 and their political institutions underwent some change. Postwar reconstruction made survival and rehabilitation the first order of business after 1945 but reformist social movements were struggling for the adoption of both reform and recovery.

The crosscurrents of politics in Europe are so complex that they are most difficult to understand, but political parties have become the implement through which most of these are struggling for power and accommodation. Religious schisms, clericalism, nationalism, neutralism, communism, ultraconservatism, pro- and anti-European alliance, revisionism, socialism, agrarianism, and monarchism are among the great forces contending for influence in numerous countries. These have not been integrated into two major parties and there seems little prospect that they will be. Hence, one of the most singular characteristics of European politics is its expression through multiple parties. This is by no means a postwar phenomenon but has been accelerated by the aftermath of

[21] On recent developments of these minor parties see article by H. L. Mathews, *The New York Times,* July 25, 1953 and D. E. McHenry, *The Third Force in Canada: The Cooperative Commonwealth Federation, 1932–42* (Berkeley, Calif.: University of California Press, 1950).

Expression through multiple parties .

World War II. Countries such as West Germany and Italy are shaking off both the prewar totalitarian state and the war itself and have broken out with a rash of parties. The new state of Israel, as reflective of its internal turmoil, has 17 distinct political parties, 15 of which elected members to parliament! With the exception of the Scandinavian countries, coalition government has been necessary because no one party has been able to muster a stable parliamentary majority.

PR and Italian Cleavages. In order to secure representative assemblies reflective of diverse interests, European nations commonly use some system of proportional representation (PR), which apportions membership in the legislature according to the voting strength polled by each party for its list of nominees. This has made it less easy for any party to win control. Recognizing this, the De Gasperi government (Christian Democratic party) [22] in Italy put through a revision in 1948 which would presumably permit it and its allies to secure a majority in the Chamber of Deputies. De Gasperi had a majority at the time the law was passed. The controversial revision in the PR system provided that the coalition of parties winning over 50 per cent of the popular vote would receive $64\frac{1}{2}$ per cent of the 590 seats in the chamber. All other parties would receive collectively only $35\frac{1}{2}$ per cent of the seats.

Prime Minister De Gasperi made this law a campaign issue in the 1953 elections and made a ministerial coalition with five other parties; the right and left opposition likewise formed their coalitions. [23] The results of the election (see Table 17) were disappointing as the ministerial group failed to get its majority.

A few items on Italian parties are illustrative of the social and political ferment and alliances in Italy and in some other nations. The Communists have been able to poll the second largest number of popular votes and the desire of most of Italy to avoid control by them is a prime issue. The Christian Democrats are aided by Catholic Action Committees and the bulk of the middle-class vote in the cities and the more prosperous peasants. They warn the middle class of the dangers of communism and of civil war which might result from the right versus the left. The left has been a combination of the Communists and the Socialists, which insists it should be invited into the ministerial coalition because it repre-

[22] Catholic parties are found in most European nations save in Scandinavia and have regarded themselves as the "center." The Catholic Church has stood as an important barrier to the triumph of communism in postwar Western Europe. In the new Federal Republic in Germany the Catholic party, called the Christian Democratic Union and led by Dr. Konrad Adenauer, became the major government party. A useful summary of German parties was published by the Office of the U.S. High Commissioner for Germany in 1952, under the title *Elections and Political Parties in Germany, 1945–1952.*

[23] See especially C. A. L. Rich, "Political Trends in Italy," *Western Political Quarterly,* Vol. 6 (1953), pp. 469–488.

Table 17. Parliamentary Strength in Italy, 1953

Party	Chamber of Deputies		Senate	
	Percentage	Seats	Percentage	Seats
Christian Democrats.....	40.08	262	40.7	116
Social Democrats.......	4.51	19	4.1	4
Liberals...............	3.11	14	3.0	3
Republicans...........	1.61	5	0.9	
South Tyrol Populists...	0.45	3		
Other.................	0.10		1.5	2
Ministerial Parties....	49.87	303	50.2	125
Communists...........	22.60	143	20.9	54
Socialists.............	12.70	75	12.1	28
Other.................	1.90		2.5	5
Left Opposition.......	36.70	218	35.5	87
Monarchists...........	6.85	40	7.1	16
Neo-Fascists...........	5.83	29	6.1	9
	12.68	69	13.2	25
Other	0.22		0.1	

sents the working classes. The left takes a "neutral" stand on the cold war and has objected to the Christian Democrats' insistence that Italy be integrated into the Atlantic Community. The Social Democrats have been impatient with the slowness of the Christian Democrats to undertake economic reforms and the former are plagued by internal quarrels which have hurt them during elections. Yet the Christian Democrats need the votes of this and the other small moderate parties or they will be forced into a new center-left coalition with the Socialists.

French Parties. Some reformers hoped that the postwar Fourth Republic of France might go over to a two-party system facilitated by an electoral law using a plurality to elect a general ticket in a fairly large district. General de Gaulle, however, chose to adopt a proportional representation plan which would encourage the growth of several large parties and discourage small splinter groups and independents. It is doubtful, however, if Frenchmen would have been satisfied with a two-party coalescence. The first National Assembly of the Fourth Republic (1946 to 1951) was governed largely by a left-of-center coalition, while the Second Assembly, elected in 1951, saw a shift to the right of center.

As in Italy, the desire to keep the Communists from control of the government and from becoming members of the ruling coalition has been at the base of much French politics. The Communists have been much stronger in France. In the first election in 1946 they polled more votes than any other party and elected 168 to the Assembly, with their nearest rivals, the Popular Republicans and Socialists, winning 162 and 108 seats respectively. The Communists not only have a vigorous tightly knit

Table 18. Party Distribution in the French National Assembly, 1954

Socialists..................	105
Communists...............	100
MRP (Popular Republicans).	88
RPF (Gaullists).............	84
Radical Socialists..........	75
Independent Republicans....	54
Peasants..................	46
Republican and Social Action (ex-Gaullists).............	32
UDSR....................	23
Overseas Independents.......	14
Other or vacant............	6
Total...................	627

organization but dominate the French Confederation of Labor, a leading labor union; they also have considerable support among the youth and intellectuals. An electoral law of 1951, designed to reduce Communist strength in the Assembly, did succeed in accomplishing that result in the subsequent election.[24] The election strengthened the center groups and reduced Communist representation to 100 seats (see Table 18). Nevertheless, they still polled 26 per cent of the popular vote. The large Communist vote distinguishes France, and also Italy, from all other countries in the non-Communist world.

The Socialists, though gaining a few additional seats in 1951, have declined in popular appeal and have been torn from within. In effect, they have lost ground because they sacrificed electoral advantage in an effort to block the far left or right. The Socialists still draw some proletarian support and have strength with the anticlerical bourgeois of small-town and rural France, the professionals, and civil servants.

The Catholic-inspired MRP (Popular Republicans), under the leader-

[24] This law provides that any coalition of parties which secures a majority of the total vote in any district is entitled to all of the representation. It helps to block the Communists because the other parties generally refuse to let them in the coalition.

ship of Georges Bidault, is inclined toward socialism also and toward "corporatism" and "pluralism." The party advocates "collectivities" such as the family, the profession, and local community which would be given special status distinct from other groups and perhaps eventual representation in the upper house of Parliament. On this program as well as MRP's efforts to obtain state aid for church schools, the Socialists are in disagreement. The two, however, have worked together to form a center coalition. Bidault once phrased his party's objective as an attempt to "govern in the center with right-wing methods to attain left-wing ends."

In the political spectrum the Radical Socialists, despite their name, occupy the center, with the Independent Republicans and Peasant party to their right. The Radicals are traditionally anticlerical but are essentially *laissez faire* in the economic sphere. Because they are in the central strategic position, they have often received the premiership and important cabinet posts. The wartime underground groups survived through the UDSR (the Democratic and Socialist Union of the Resistance), which has worked closely with the Radicals, whom it resembles in program.

The prewar rightist doctrines were resuscitated under various labels, the most successful of which were the Independent Republicans, the Peasants, and the Gaullists. The first two of these stand for the old libertarian ideal of *laissez faire* and reduction of taxes and public expenditures. The Peasant party has the support of the more prosperous farmers and represents an important growing political self-consciousness among farmers. Banking and industrial interests and the urban bourgeois give considerable support to the Independent Republicans. On the basis of the 1951 election these two groups acting together possess a potential veto over the formation of a center coalition cabinet.

The Rally of the French People (RPF) or the Gaullists has a contradictory if not vague program. Its supporters are accused of being pro-Fascist, pro-royal, and ultraconservative but its support suggests this is inaccurate. It wins votes among workers as well as capitalists and has some radical backers. De Gaulle seeks a strong, stable government and something of a corporative state. Several of his deputies have seceded from the party and the future of his group is in doubt. Fortunately for the Western democracies, the French coalitions have up to this writing not been of the extreme left or right. Yet the instability of "a new cabinet every Sunday" has delayed the welding of a solid Western European community.

Disraeli once said, "England is not governed by logic, she is governed by Parliament," and another distinguished Englishman, R. H. Tawney, commented, "It is a commonplace that the characteristic virtue of Englishmen is their power of sustained practical activity, and their characteristic vice a reluctance to test the quality of that activity by reference to principles." Looking at the party system on both the British Isles and the Continent, there is a certain logic to their systems in the sense that the political parties have grown out of tradition, heritage, and the psychology of the nation. Britain, the United States, and the Scandinavian nations have been spared a strong indigenous Communist movement capable of delivering a mass vote such as in France and Italy. On much of the Continent which has escaped totalitarian rule, the swirl and eddy of political currents has forced constant regrouping of coalitions, now to the left, now to the right, but, fortunately up to the present, avoiding the extreme pendulum in either direction. The inner contradictions of parties reflect the contradictions of society. If the parties reflect the popular will and if that will is contradictory, it should surprise no one that the parties appear contradictory. All democratic party systems appear to have their contradictions and their checks and balances; this has been the salvation and genius of government by parties as opposed to government by authoritarian fiat.

TWO PARTIES OR MULTIPLE PARTIES?

The contention that a democracy can operate efficiently only under a two-party system is widely held. The relative stability of the American, British, and Canadian governmental systems is cited in support of this view. That it is possible to provide a stable government and yet operate through a multiparty system is shown in Switzerland. The Swiss have four parties, each of considerable strength—the Radicals, Conservatives, Farmers, Social Democrats—and several smaller ones. Proportional representation has undoubtedly favored the growth of these parties as the single-member district and plurality principle have promoted the interests of the two-party system in the United States. One may also point out that in Finland, Norway, Sweden, and Denmark, with their three or four major parties, governmental crises similar to those of France have not resulted.

Both two-party and multiparty systems have advantages and disadvantages. The existence of several parties permits the organization and effective articulation of a variety of opinions in the legislature. Political groupings, therefore, are generally though not necessarily welded on the basis of principles. One has a greater opportunity of finding a group which better represents his interest when he has the choice of several parties. Under a multiple-party system, however, certain of the groups sometimes become too inflexible in attitude or uncooperative to the extent of consistently refusing to compromise on legislation. When this happens, instability results because the only way to control the legislature is through a coalition capable of producing a majority. This requires the obtaining of agreements of blocs to enter a coalition. It is not easy to locate responsibility for the failure to enact a policy in these instances. In France, a defect has resulted from locating power around individuals, such as a De Gaulle, a Bidault, or a Schuman rather than around principles and policies.

Admittedly, the individual frequently experiences political homelessness under a two-party presidential system, leading him to turn to political action through affinity with interest groups which more accurately reflect his basic needs. In the United States, many persons have remained skeptical of obtaining their ends in either of the two major parties and have resorted to third parties such as the Populists, Non-Partisan League, and the present-day Socialist and labor parties. In Canada the CCF and Social Credit parties have attracted many liberals who found no hope in the Liberal or Conservative parties. It is sometimes pointed out that the two-party system in the United States has resulted, locally and regionally, in a one-party or perhaps a "nonparty" system. To live up to the merits claimed for it a biparty system must grant truly what it implies, namely, that one can turn to an opposing party with some hope for its success. When an actual two-party system of real alternatives is offered to the voter in his state and local government, it appears to have merit over the multiple-party system because it can operate with an effective majority and it can at the same time provide large segments of the voting public with an adequate channel of political expression.

The one great virtue of the two-party system nationally cannot be overlooked—the provision of fairly consistent parliamentary majorities. With the great necessity for compromise between the large interests composing each party, permanent if imperfect unity has been given to the nation. Although the party is kept together by "organization" leaders in the United States, whose primary interest is in electoral success rather than policies, electoral success comes from votes. This has forced the parties to pass legislation favoring the group interests and to balance and harmonize these interests. Spoils alone cannot keep a party in control nationally forever; sooner or later it must push legislation demanded by the large constituency.

Representatives in the legislature under a multiparty system may reflect the varied currents of social thought and of classes. But this very representation may accentuate community splits while the two-party system tries to work out an over-all average of group interests by playing down the shades and nuances within its ranks. As Sir Ernest Barker has said, "The system of two parties leaves room for a margin of imprecision, or an area of incalculability, which is a safety-valve in the working of a democratic State."

It is sometimes argued by two-party adherents that their system is peculiar to English-speaking worlds and is a sign of political maturity and stability. This overlooks coalition regimes of anti-Labor parties in Australia and New Zealand and that England found coalition in wartime a successful arrangement. Multiparty systems have worked reasonably well and given stability to the Scandinavian countries and to Switzerland. The former have a tradition of efficiency and stability and have not run into the serious clerical and economic issues which have encouraged the formation of rival groups. Their economic system has accommodated both capitalist and socialist enterprises and led to a fair degree of prosperity. Their parties, moreover, fall somewhat naturally into two blocs rather than several. Swiss conservatives and progressives have been willing to make concessions and they know that the national referendum will be used to invalidate their proposals if they depart from the popular will. Every type of party system and each individual party is in need of constant improvement required by the demands of a rapidly changing political order. Political parties have a tendency to become a vested interest and their leaders may resist changes in organization and principles which might affect their own positions within the party. A party may continue to operate on a few basic principles but its program must undergo change. A dynamic democracy requires a dynamic party system capable of improving its efficiency and of enlisting, reflecting, and carrying out the wishes of its constituents.

SELECTED REFERENCES

On minor parties in the United States a brief recent general work is W. B. Hesseltine, *The Rise and Fall of Third Parties: From Anti-Masonry to Wallace* (1948). On the Socialist Labor party the New York Labor News Company has issued many works including Daniel De Leon, *As to Politics* (1941), *Reform or Revolution* (1940), and *Socialist Reconstruction of Society* (1940); O. M. Johnson and H. Kuhn, *Socialist Labor Party, 1890–1930* (1931); Arnold Peterson, *Daniel De Leon: Social Architect* (1941).

For the Socialist party see James H. Maurer, *It Can Be Done* (1938); Harry W. Laidler, *American Socialism: Its Aims and Practical Program*, 2d ed. (1937), and *History of Socialist Thought* (1927); Norman Thomas, *After the New Deal, What?* (1936), and *A Socialist's Faith* (1952).

On the Communist party *The Daily Worker* (New York) and party publications offer the best sources for contemporary data. See also the various reports by the House of Representatives Special Committee to Investigate Un-American Activities. Among the more pertinent books on the subject are Harold D. Lasswell and Dorothy Blumenstock, *World Revolutionary Propaganda: A Chicago Study* (1939); William Z. Foster et al., *Party Building and Political Leadership* (1946); Earl Browder, *The People's Front* (1938), and *The Communist Party of the U.S.A.* (1936); Benjamin Gitlow, *I Confess: The Truth about American Communism* (1940). Recent developments are reviewed by Benjamin Moore, Jr., "The Communist Party of the U.S.A.," *The American Political Science Review*, Vol. 39, pp. 31–41.

World War II uprooted many of the party systems on the continent of Europe, thereby dating many of the older works on European parties. Periodical articles are, however, providing an increasing body of information on current European politics.

The annual editions of the *Political Handbook* include election statistics and data on party strength in all nations.

For purposes of a general survey of the character of parties abroad the textbooks in comparative government are usually adequate. Among those published since 1951 are R. G. Neumann, *European and Comparative Government* (1951); Taylor Cole (ed.), *European Political Systems* (1953); G. L. Field, *Governments in Modern Society* (1951); J. T. Shotwell (ed.), *Governments of Continental Europe* (1952); H. Beukema et al., *Contemporary Foreign Governments* (1953); F. A. Ogg and H. Zink, *Modern Foreign Governments* (1953); F. Marx (ed.), *Foreign Governments* (1952).

Some useful comparisons and contrasts of various party systems are found in J. A. Corry, *Elements of Democratic Government* (1947), pp. 137–177. Works on specific parties not included in the footnotes are Louise Overacker, *The Australian Party System* (1952); D. E. McHenry, *The Third Force in Canada: The Cooperative Commonwealth Federation, 1932–42* (1950); S. M. Lipset, *Agrarian Socialism: The Cooperative Commonwealth Federation in Saskatchewan* (1950); *Christian Democracy in Italy and France* (1952); Ben Arneson, *The Democratic Monarchies of Scandinavia* (1949). For an excellent analysis of the organization, philosophy, and comparative aspects of political parties see Maurice Duverger, *Political Parties: Their Organization and Activity in the Modern State* (1954).

1. Types: Splinter & ideological
   1. Sectional 2. Single purpose

2. Contemporary minor parties. p. 306

3. British party system.
   1. Labor Party
   2. Conservative
   3. liberal

4. British and American Parties contrasted
   315

PART FOUR

Party Organization and Leadership

CHAPTER 14

The Party Hierarchy

The value of such a close-knit and far-reaching organization can be demonstrated. If the workers in the individual election districts succeed in getting ten voters, who otherwise might not have been interested, to the polls, the total would run close to 90,000 votes and many an election in New York State has been decided by a smaller margin. . . . A strong organization can do more than merely assist voters to the polls on election day. The members distribute propaganda, defend the party position, hold rallies, and carry on other very necessary activities.

—JAMES A. FARLEY

The functions of a political party are so many and varied that in the party, as in a pressure group, there is an imperative demand for a network of organizations or political committees. These committees are needed to manage the periodic national, state, and local conventions. In some states like New York they are charged with making nominations for state-wide offices. The management of a campaign requires a veritable army of workers, both staff and line. Money must be raised and publicity distributed. In some states political committees are charged by law to perform special duties. For example, the Maryland constitution requires that a vacancy in the General Assembly is to be filled by the governor with a person "whose name shall be submitted to him in writing by the State Central Committee of the political party with which the Delegate or Senator, so vacating, had been affiliated in the County or District from which he or she was elected." This is an exceptional constitutional provision, but the laws of numerous states impose equally important functions on the parties.

The need for organization goes even further. Some group of officials must determine policies between the meetings of party conventions. Charges against the party or its members can ill afford to go unanswered and the party and its leaders need to be kept before the public eye. The need for a permanent publicity staff, therefore, becomes obvious. Permanent headquarters must be kept open to provide continuity to the party and to keep it together between conventions and elections. Finally, the actual promotion of the internal party interests demands some form of organization. Patronage positions are to be filled, factional quarrels mediated, and prospective members recruited into the ranks. Building

331

the membership and promoting party harmony require the touch of the specialist—the professional politician.

Party organization has its formal, official, "paper" aspects with lines of authority neatly drawn. But there is an informal, "behind-the-scenes" direction which is usually more important than the regular committee structure. A gradual evolution took place from informal, amorphous, caucuslike organization to a more definite, regular framework which came to be recognized by statute and custom as the party committee system. But extralegal guidance did not disintegrate with the formalization of party structure.

The organizational patterns of the major parties are predicated on the assumption that a party committee is needed for each electoral area. These committees fall into the three broad categories of national, state, and local, with a multiplicity of committees and officers within each division. The regular committees are the national, state central, county central, ward or district in the cities, and precinct. In addition, there are an infinite number of other committees such as congressional and senatorial groups designed to help in the reelection of incumbents, and regional associations to discuss policy and area-wide organizational questions. Within the states and counties one sometimes finds congressional district, judicial, state senatorial and assembly district, probate, village, and township committees. These are semipermanent in character and often are brought into being for a specific function, usually to aid in the campaign of a judge, a state legislator, or some local official. There are also endless numbers of clubs, youth, men's, and women's auxiliaries.

The functions of the network of committees are often imprecisely defined; some are imposed by law and others appear in the bylaws of the party. The committees are frequently as little or as much as the imagination and ability of their leaders make them. Power centers within the local groups vary from state to state, but, more often than not, the county unit is the key to the strength or weakness of organization.

A hierarchy of conventions parallels the committee system. They perform certain nominating functions, adopt resolutions, ratify decisions of executive committees, and serve as a general forum for the party. They act as a safety valve in airing, testing, and settling factional disputes.

In the following pages and in the next chapter attention is focused on the committee system, organizational arrangements, and leadership. As these are read, two important facts should be kept in mind. First, the moving forces in the power of the organization are often the leaders, generous contributors, and persons who are able to raise money. They are often behind the scenes or in unofficial, supplementary organizations which are temporary in character. Regular official executives in these circumstances vary from mere figureheads without having any controlling force, to simply being one among several other equals of an unofficial group.

Second, a fairly general characteristic of party organization is its loose structure and low level of activity and organization in the precincts. Millions of Americans have never had their doorbells rung by a precinct captain and the chances are they do not even know if there is one in their district. A public-opinion poll in Washington state found only 13 per cent of the respondents who could recall ever having been approached by a worker from a political party for the purpose of discussing candidates or the party program. In one eastern county of that state, only one of 60 Democratic precinct committee positions was filled and anyone volunteering for such a job would probably be welcomed with open arms and no questions asked. Even in Seattle, with its comparatively highly developed organization, it is not unusual for one-fifth of the precincts to be without a committeeman and it is doubtful if more than half of the precinct leaders are at all active.

At the height of the presidential election in 1948 the executive director of the Republican National Committee reported that 357 counties in the nation had no Republican county chairman or executive. In Oregon that same year the Democrats had operating organizations in only 13 of 36 counties. In an interesting study of Minneapolis, R. L. Morlan found that there was not one ward in the city where the organization covered every precinct and that, "except in the weeks just preceding an important election, roughly 100 of the 634 possible precinct captaincies will be unfilled and not over half of the remainder are filled by actual party workers who can be depended upon all of the time." [1]

NATIONAL ORGANIZATION

National Committees. Until 1920, the national committees were composed of one man from each state, territory, and possession. With the ratification of the Nineteenth Amendment, one woman was added from each area. In 1952 the Republicans gave each state an opportunity to add a third national committeeman in the person of the state chairman of the states carried by the party in the previous presidential election. Electing a Republican governor or majority Republican delegation in Congress also entitles a state chairman to sit on the committee. Women in the party and Southerners sharply opposed the new rule for it diluted their strength on the committee.[2] The rule is designed to give impetus to the party organization to carry the state and to bring state chairmen into the national hierarchy. Also, the Northern and Eisenhower Repub-

[1] "City Politics: Free Style," *National Municipal Review*, Vol. 38 (1949), pp. 485–490.
[2] For debate on this Rule 22 see *Proceedings of the Twenty-fifth Republican National Convention*, pp. 278–289.

licans felt that the national committee would be more truly representative since Southern states rarely cast their electoral vote for the Republican candidate. While the anti-Taft forces captured a majority of the convention delegates, a clear majority of the national committee were pro-Taft and the former felt this showed the unrepresentative character of the committee.

Another rule permits the Republican National Chairman, on request from a majority of the national committee, to appoint an advisory committee consisting of all state chairmen, state vice chairmen, and other party officers as well as Republican officeholders. It seems doubtful if this group will be convened very often.

The national committee is chosen every four years by the national convention. In practice, this is only ratification, for each state chooses its own members by means of a party primary, a state convention, or selection may be made by the state's delegation to the national convention.

National committees set the time and place for the national convention and meet occasionally to discuss broad problems of strategy, policy, and finance. During campaigns the energies of the national committeeman and committeewoman are expended in promoting the party's ticket in his or her state. Seldom do the committee members participate in the work of the national headquarters.[3]

The size of the staff and budget of the national committees has grown tremendously since the 1930's. In the off year of 1953 the Republican National Committee expended $1,312,000 for staff, literature, radio, and television. A few 1952 campaign bills were included in this figure. The Democratic counterpart spent $815,000. In past years the staff of the national headquarters increased greatly during election years and was sharply reduced after each campaign. Both parties now keep a large permanent staff between elections. The number of paid employees in Republican headquarters remained at about 100 in 1953 and 1954 while the Democrats employed 50 and 60 respectively. In presidential campaign years, however, the staff is enlarged considerably. At the peak of the 1952 campaign the Republicans had 386 and the Democrats had 251 paid employees.

There are a number of divisions and departments in each national office operating under titles descriptive of public relations, nationalities, occupational, youth, research, and women's activities. Of greatest importance is the development in recent years of a women's division and a publicity division. The former was a natural outgrowth of the adoption

---

[3] The permanent headquarters of both major parties are in Washington. A campaign headquarters during presidential elections is usually set up separately, often in New York City.

of the Nineteenth Amendment and the consequent demand that women be given a formal place in the party councils. These auxiliaries devote special attention to helping the party's women nominees and to preparing materials designed to appeal to women voters.

In times past the national committee of the minority party virtually lapsed into "innocuous desuetude" in the wake of an election. After taking severe beatings in 1920, 1924, and 1928, the Democratic National Committee deemed it well to accept Alfred E. Smith's suggestion to set up a full-time publicity organization.[4] First a permanent executive committee was established by National Committee Chairman John J. Raskob, who in turn appointed Charles Michelson in the summer of 1929 as director of publicity. "Charley the Mike," as he was popularly called, soon turned out daily and weekly criticisms and statements on the Hoover Administration. His genius in building up publicity against the party in power paved the way for the Democratic comeback of 1932. The Republicans soon saw the virtue of a permanent publicity bureau and established a research and editorial division in 1936.[5] Michelson relied largely on former newspapermen to do the Democratic publicity job, while the Republicans used mostly advertising men.[6] Today both parties use many veteran newspapermen in their publicity divisions.

These agencies have rapidly grown in importance and influence. During campaigns they prepare and distribute literature, press releases, and pictures and send out "aids" to local committees. Former Democratic National Chairman James A. Farley once remarked, "The publicity department has a big role to fill in setting the tone of a campaign, and our side had an advantage in the presence of Charles Michelson, the wise old fox." Between elections the publicity divisions collect and prepare data for their party's legislators, often for insertion in the *Congressional Record,* release news stories, and in general act as a clearinghouse for materials of interest to the party. In campaigns they have gathered valuable data on opponents' voting records for use by individual congressmen and local organizations. The Democrats put out a popular monthly magazine called *The Democratic Digest.* From time to time the Republicans have published a monthly newspaper or journal. In a number of states

[4] For a description of the origin and early work of this body see Thomas S. Barclay, "The Publicity Division of the Democratic Party, 1929–30," *The American Political Science Review,* Vol. 25 (1931), pp. 68–71.

[5] After the overwhelming defeat in 1936, the Republican National Chairman John Hamilton went to England to study British party organization. Upon his return the permanent staff of the national committee was reorganized and expanded. American major party organization still does not operate so effectively as do the British parties.

[6] For a comprehensive survey of the Democratic publicity division in action see Theodore M. Black, *Democratic Party Publicity in the 1940 Campaign* (New York: Plymouth, 1941).

a semiofficial monthly paper is issued by interested partisans under such titles as *The Oregon Democrat, The Republican Call,* and *The Roosevelt American.* In the United States, however, the publication of a party newspaper has never reached the importance of the party press of many other nations.

The organization and operation of these high-powered publicity divisions is one of the most significant developments in party organization in the present century. A number of local organizations, taking a page from the national committees and political interest groups, are establishing publicity and research divisions designed to operate the year round. The national committees have come to realize that in order to perform their publicity functions effectively, a competent research staff is needed. The party in power has found that a permanent headquarters helps Presidents in terms of advice, information, and in the release of data provided by the Chief Executive. Although the party can command the research staffs of various executive agencies in preparing materials for their own use on public issues, it also needs a permanent party headquarters staff to carry on research and publicity. A well-staffed national office is even more essential to the party out of power to assist party leaders in Congress by providing them with ammunition for speeches and publicity, thus keeping the party in the public eye, and preparing attacks on the program of the incumbent party.

In summary, the two national party headquarters have become huge service agencies for the party's candidates and officeholders and for the state and local committees. They estimate financial needs, raise funds, and make allocations. The top officials determine campaign strategy and the staff carries on the activities necessary to implement the decisions. This is likely to involve speech writing, arranging for radio and television time, answering the opposition, sponsoring "workshops," preparing campaign "guides," issuing "fact sheets," and any number of other activities. Both parties have built up libraries in their headquarters and maintain files upon files of newspaper clippings and statistics. In addition to their campaign functions, the national committeemen and their staffs act as stimulators and cheerleaders for the state and local committees. National committees afford a channel of communication between the party leaders and their constituents in the states, independently of congressmen. The committee of the party in control of the administration looks after patronage matters. In the Eisenhower Administration this function was formalized considerably by directing the agencies to notify the Republican National Committee of all vacancies which could be filled without violation of Civil Service regulations. The Committee in turn asked Republican congressmen to recruit candidates for the positions.

Congressional and Senatorial Committees. Both parties in both houses of Congress have committees whose principal purpose is that of aiding the reelection of incumbents and the party's nominees. The House and Senate committees are anomalous in the party hierarchy, being neither superior nor subordinate to the national committees. The former have their own budgets and allocate money to candidates on the basis of presumed need. Like the national committees, the congressional groups now have permanent paid staffs and remain open year round. The National Republican Congressional Committee is the largest of the four committees and had 31 paid staff members in 1954. The committees have their offices on Capitol Hill, thus affording incumbents easy access to them. Between elections these committees compile legislative histories and voting records of opponents, write speeches and scripts, handle the public relations of the party's congressmen, arrange radio and television appearances, and act as a general service agency. Although these committees receive little public attention, they are far more important to the legislators elected from marginal districts than is generally realized.

Interestingly, the first congressional committee was formed out of protest against the national committee. In 1866 the latter committee was under the control of President Johnson, who took the issue of his reconstruction program into the congressional elections of that year. Fearful that they might lose control to pro-Johnson men, the Radical Republicans formed a Republican Congressional Committee to aid their own reelection. The outcome of the election from their point of view was so successful that the organization was continued. The Democrats soon established a similar group. In recent years these committees have received substantial aid from the national committees in the form of loans and subventions, which have led the congressional and senatorial committees to look more favorably on "cooperation." In mid-term elections they can expect less help from the national committees. At times the congressional committees have worked closely with state and local committees.

The present Republican Congressional Committee is composed of one Republican from each state having representatives of that party. The state delegation names its member subject to approval by the Republican caucus in the House. The Democrats follow the same practice, but in addition the chairman of the committee can appoint a committeeman from each state not having Democratic representation in the House and also a committeewoman from each state in the Union. The Democratic committee can become, potentially, more than twice as big as its Republican counterpart.

Before 1913 the state legislatures appointed the members of the United States Senate. With the ratification of the Seventeenth Amendment that

year, providing for popular election of senators, the need arose for some
campaign assistance for them. Accordingly, in 1916 the Republicans established a Senatorial Campaign Committee. Its size averages about
eight senators, appointed by the chairman of the Republican caucus for
a term of two years. In practice no senator who is a candidate for reelection is a member of the committee during a year when he is seeking his
own reelection. A Democratic Senatorial Committee was similarly formed
in 1918 and now consists of nine members, appointed by the Democratic
leader of the Senate after consulting the candidates for reelection.

THE NATIONAL CHAIRMAN

The real generalissimo of the party during a campaign is the national
chairman who, in practice, is chosen by the party's nominee for President
and ratified by the national committee. Vacancies in the office between
elections, of course, are filled by the national committee. With the party
in power the person is sure to be one who is *persona grata* to the President. Since the defeated candidate has much less control over his party
the same situation does not necessarily prevail in the minority party after
the election. The majority party chairman in practice is not the party
boss. In the final analysis if the President and national chairman disagree, the latter customarily resigns; the Roosevelt-Farley feud of 1940
offers a case in point.

Functions. No comprehensive study of the functions of national chairmen has yet appeared. Former National Chairman James A. Farley once
stated that the job of chairman was to "promote harmony, teamwork,
and united action in the interests of party success at the November balloting." This is a modest understatement of the role of many national
chairmen, including Mr. Farley. The first outstanding national chairman
was Mark Hanna who became a close adviser to McKinley and provided
an important link between the President and business. James Farley during his eight years as national chairman from 1932 to 1940 handled
patronage matters, perfected organization and vote-getting techniques
to a remarkable degree, and advised Mr. Roosevelt on political matters.[7]
In recent years the winning party has often given the chairman the Postmaster Generalship, since this office is in a strategic position with reference to patronage. One of the big tasks of the national chairman is to
take patronage requests to the President, a function especially difficult
and onerous in the first year of a new President. The chairman has become the final arbiter in patronage controversies, because he is the person

[7] Farley's book *Behind the Ballots* (New York: Harcourt, Brace and Company, Inc.,
1938) provides an interesting insight into the activities of one national chairman. Also
see Herbert Croly, *Marcus Alonza Hanna* (New York: The Macmillan Company, 1912)
for an intimate glimpse of one of the most powerful national chairmen of all time.

who places endorsements and recommendations on the President's desk.

Generally speaking, national chairmen are not regularly consulted on policies and many make a practice of studiously avoiding such matters in order that they may not become identified with a factional wing of the party. While Franklin Roosevelt seldom sought the advice of Farley, the national chairman nevertheless went to members of the House and Senate to request them to vote as the Administration wanted. Mr. Farley relates one instance where he spent an entire day phoning Democratic members of Congress to vote against bringing up a war referendum resolution. "This appeal by telephone," he wrote, "had an influence in blocking consideration of the resolution." [8] It may be noted, however, that this action was justified on the basis of his "right and duty" as a Cabinet officer rather than as national chairman. Other chairmen have met with little success and with much resentment when they tried to influence the votes of party members in Congress.

The national chairman is also called upon to be a trouble shooter. He travels about the country talking with state and local leaders, helping to mend political fences, and healing breaches within the party ranks which were caused by heated primaries, personal factionalism, and disputes over patronage. Chairmen try to keep their ears to the grass-roots ground on the reaction of public opinion and party leaders to the administration in power. The chairman of the party in power is required to be ambivalent and ambidextrous. He must be an agent of the President but give the impression that he is subordinate to the congressional leadership of his party. He must get money from the rich but keep up the appearance that his party is financially poor and operating on the basis of small contributions from large numbers of people. Deserving party workers expect him to obtain large numbers of fair-paying jobs without appearing to be sacking the merit system. He is expected to fire his listeners with oratory and state his party's policies in black-and-white terms but not become a prima donna taking the spotlight from the President or important party bigwigs in Congress.

Prototypes. What type of person is chosen as national chairman? There are many different prototypes, defying classification. With very few exceptions, however, they enjoy the reputation of "regularity" and have come up through the ranks of practical politics, having been outstanding local leaders. National Chairman Farley had a genius for organization and the national organization became a Farley organization filled with men personally selected by him and strongly devoted to "Big Jim." His remarkable memory for names and faces made him popular from one end of the nation to the other. Edward J. Flynn, who succeeded him, had long been the political boss of the Bronx and a practical politician

[8] *Op. cit.*, p. 362.

thoroughly schooled in the rough-and-tumble of urban politics. Flynn found himself caught between many Farley sympathizers who resented anyone taking the latter's place and the New Dealers who were often contemptuous of the "organization Democrats." [9] Farley and Flynn concentrated on organizational and patronage matters and rarely had anything to do with trying to influence the President on national policies.

To Robert E. Hannegan fell the job of Democratic National Chairman in January, 1944; [10] prior to that time he had been a successful ward leader. Many times he reiterated his credo as "I'm a practical politician, just a regular, 100 per cent organization, strictly partisan Democrat." Like his predecessors he went in strongly for patronage and was not averse to being called a "spoils politician." Unlike Farley and Flynn, however, Hannegan often took a hand in advising President Truman on policies, particularly as they affected Democratic fortunes. He was, of course, in a position to do this by reason of being in the Cabinet (Postmaster General). While most national chairmen are careful to avoid being identified with certain prospective nominees, Hannegan violated this precedent by aiding Truman's cause at the 1944 Democratic National Convention. Chairman Hannegan also alienated the Southern conservatives when he differed with them over legislation to control labor.

Though the chairman usually refrains from endorsing a candidate, he may be associated with a certain faction and his tenure will depend to some extent upon the dominant faction of the national committee. Governor Dewey's personal friend Herbert Brownell, Jr. retained the chairmanship only a short time after the 1944 election and was succeeded by Carroll Reece, who was friendly to the Taft wing. After his nomination for President in 1948, Dewey chose Hugh Scott of Pennsylvania as national chairman. This choice of a comparatively unknown figure was understood to have been made in return for the support of the Pennsylvania delegation led by Senator Edward Martin. Although Scott was selected as chairman, Governor Dewey appointed Brownell as his campaign manager—an unprecedented arrangement. Dewey's loss of the election caused much bitterness and Scott was ousted by the pro-Taft forces in favor of Guy Gabrielson, who avowed his role would be simply that of "an impartial presiding officer" to work for party unity.

Eisenhower's nomination, as expected, led to the replacement of Gabrielson by the pro-Eisenhower Arthur Summerfield of Michigan, who had been a leader for the General at the national convention. President Eisen-

---

[9] Flynn's own story on how he viewed his job as national chairman deserves reading; see his autobiography *You're the Boss* (New York: The Viking Press, Inc., 1947), Chap. 13.

[10] See Fred Rodell, "Robert E. Hannegan," *American Mercury*, Vol. 63 (1946), pp. 133–141.

hower appointed Summerfield as Postmaster General and the latter decided not to retain his chairmanship. Following this, Wesley Roberts,[11] who was shortly succeeded by Leonard Hall, was appointed chairman. Both were acceptable to major factions of the party. Hall brought to the office long experience as a congressman and onetime chairman of the Republican Congressional Committee.

The Democratic National Committee followed tradition in appointing Stephen Mitchell, a Catholic, as chairman in 1952. Mitchell was a personal friend of Adlai Stevenson. He lacked political experience, however, and many old-line Democrats were not fully satisfied with the choice. He remained in office, however, after Stevenson's defeat and did much to improve the party's financial status and to heal the breach between the Northern and Southern wings. He was succeeded in 1955 by Paul M. Butler of Indiana, also a Stevenson supporter. Mr. Butler was the first national committeeman in many years to be elevated to chairman.

The personalities and abilities of the national chairmen have determined the stature of the office. Those possessing energy and imagination have been able to improve the party's organization and activities. To be filled successfully, the office requires tact, extensive traveling, patience, endurance, and resourcefulness. The office of national chairman has increased in importance, as has the permanent staff of the national committees. Chairman Mitchell was voted an annual salary of $25,000, while Chairman Hall was unsalaried. Only a few of Hall's predecessors received salaries.

STATE CENTRAL COMMITTEES

At the apex of state and local organization is the state central committee. Unless it is fixed by law, the state central committee sets the date for the state primary and in several states it may decide whether a primary or convention may be used to nominate. It chooses the time and place for the state convention and occasionally for the county and city meetings. In Pennsylvania and Maryland the state committee is legally recognized as the governing body for the party in the state. Vacancies to state offices because of death, removal, or resignation are often filled by consultation with the state committees. The Arkansas Republican party rules, for example, require endorsement by the committee for Federal appointments.

The most important function of the state central committee, as of its national counterpart, is the management of the campaign, with all that it implies. This requires close cooperation with the national committee and the various local committees and the creation of a state executive com-

[11] Roberts was a publisher from Kansas. An investigating committee in Kansas found him guilty of certain improprieties in connection with public buildings in the state and he resigned the chairmanship.

mittee when the committee itself is unwieldy. With the important power of campaign management in the hands of the committee, it is small wonder that sharp fights occur within the party for control of the state executive committee. In recent years Southern Democratic conventions have seen many quarrels between pro- and anti-New Deal wings, each of which has at times set up a rival organization and sent two sets of delegates to the national convention.

State central committees derive their membership in a great variety of ways. The Indiana body is chosen in a straight line of authority pyramided from the bottom. Precinct committeemen elected in the primary collectively form the county committee; the various county chairmen form the congressional district committee, and the congressional district chairmen form the state committee. The Missouri committee is composed of four persons from each congressional district committee. In New Hampshire all county committeemen automatically comprise the state committee. In Michigan and Iowa the state convention chooses the committee members. In other states members are chosen by congressional district primaries, state senatorial or assembly primaries, county primaries, or conventions in the same subdivisions. In California, Minnesota, Wisconsin, and Vermont the party nominees for state offices form a council, which in turn chooses the state central committee. In spite of this diversity, the majority of states choose their central committeemen through the direct primary or state convention. This makes the personnel of the state body independent of the county or city committees. In a fashion similar to the "rotten borough" composition of state legislatures, the larger cities are underrepresented on the state committees. A committeeman usually serves for two or four years and may hold his position for several terms unless a different faction of his party gets into control.

With the larger committees, efficiency calls for direction by the state chairman as executive. His position resembles that of the national chairman in terms of promotion of the campaign and the fostering of party harmony. In the absence of a definitive study, it is hard to generalize on the stature of the chairman and the influence of the state central committee. Competent students of government seem to agree that the chairman is seldom the real boss in the state. Conspicuous exceptions to this were Rorabach of Connecticut and Poulson of Ohio, who as state chairmen were for a long time the bosses of their respective parties.

COUNTY COMMITTEES

The party committees in the 3,073 counties of the nation are a basic and usually vigorous part of the hierarchy. Their powers and functions resemble those of the national and state committees and include managing conventions, conducting campaigns, and supervising the operation of the organization throughout the county. County committees in general operate in an atmosphere of considerable independence from the state committee and at the same time are often without much influence over township or other local committees in the county. There are important exceptions to this. In New York, for example, the state election law places local control of the party in the county committee, and most of these committees wield a powerful influence over the village, assembly district, and diverse other committees located within the county.

County Organization. The composition and selection of county committeemen defy generalization. Michigan and Vermont permit the candidates for office to name their county committeemen. Many states authorize each precinct to choose a committeeman, who in turn serves as a member of the county organization. In some states the county convention names all the members of the county committee. Regardless of the unit used to designate a committeeman, there is an increasing tendency to permit the party voters to select the members of the county committee.

In addition to the county committee there is a wide assortment of other committees, some of which cross county lines, such as judicial and congressional district committees. Others, usually within the county boundaries, appear under diverse titles of ward, state senatorial and assembly districts, school and sanitary districts, and township and precinct committees and demonstrate that parties operate at and on all levels of local government. Most of these are used for campaign purposes and perform few functions between elections. A person seeking office in the legislature, for example, may become disgruntled at the assistance he is receiving from the county organization and, with a group of friends, create an assembly district committee to aid his candidacy. These become "candidates' committees" rather than party committees.

County Chairman. The key figure in the counties is the chairman of the committee and in many states he represents the county on the state central committee. He is important in the party's councils and often the director of the campaign in the county. The county chairmen are in a strategic position to distribute the patronage commonly associated with that level of government. In rural areas the county chairman is usually the actual as well as the titular leader of the county. In modern times, these chairmen are within an easy drive of all the villages and townships in the county. Many chairmen regularly visit the county's judicial officials, mayors, and local political leaders. The county leader can, therefore, personalize politics to a greater extent than his urban colleague; in this respect he resembles the city precinct captain. A rural county chairman spends much of his time talking with farmers and village merchants. A central Illinois chairman told the author he knew every farmer in the county by name and in many cases knew the members of his family. In urban areas there are many persons who do not know their county or municipal leader, but in rural areas it appears that the chairmen make themselves well known to the voters.

URBAN ORGANIZATION

In the larger municipalities, a more complex organization has developed. There is usually an over-all city committee or a county committee where a city and county are nearly coterminous. Below are the inferior committees variously designated as wards or districts, which in turn are composed of precincts. A brief description of the hierarchy in three different cities will illustrate the varying forms of organization.

Baltimore. Baltimore is not within a county and there is, therefore, no county party organization. Instead a city committee is used. The Democratic committee is composed of three persons from each of the six state legislative districts into which the city is divided. Baltimore's Republican counterpart is composed entirely differently, with two from each district, two from the city at large, and one from each of the city's 28 wards. The ward representatives serve as ward executives and are in command of the party's activities in their respective areas The Democrats have 28 ward executives but they are named by the city committee. Each ward leader appoints the precinct captain. There are about 700 precincts, so that the ward leader has many appointments to make. The variation between Republican and Democratic organization is fairly typical of many other cities, and this makes it necessary for an observer to study both parties in order to gain an accurate picture of party organization in the city.

Chicago. Party organization in Chicago centers about the ward.[12] A ward committeeman is elected by the voters in the party primary in each of the 50 wards for a term of four years. Collectively, these committeemen form the city committee. The ward leader, by virtue of his position, is automatically a member of the county central committee, which sends delegates to the state convention. The state convention in turn chooses the candidates for the Illinois Supreme Court, the trustees of the University of Illinois, and some of the delegates to the national conventions. Ward committeemen are also members of the judicial circuit convention, which nominates candidates for the Superior and Circuit courts.

As is customary in most other cities, each ward is divided into precincts. Illinois law requires a precinct to average about 400 and not more than 600 voters. These boundaries are altered after each election. Mobility of population, however, often increases the size of a given district well beyond 600 or decreases it below 400 before the next apportionment is

[12] For a description of the party organization and politics in Chicago see Harold F. Gosnell, *Machine Politics: Chicago Model* (Chicago: University of Chicago Press, 1937).

made. The ward committeeman appoints the precinct captains, who are on the spot in every election. Those who fail to deliver the votes or who prove to be inefficient are removed for more promising captains. While the turnover among ward leaders is slight it is rapid among precinct leaders.

New York City. No city-wide political committee or organization exists in the nation's largest city. The city is composed of five boroughs, each of which is a county and maintains its own complete organization, as it must do by state law. Consequently, there are five autonomous and unrelated centers of control within each municipal party. To complicate matters, the rules for county organization vary from borough to borough, and few in the party have any clear conception of their own committee's rules, let alone those of the other four counties in the city.[13] Each county is divided into state assembly districts. In most of the counties the enrolled voters choose the district leaders but in New York County these leaders are elected by the county committee members of their respective districts. In Brooklyn a majority of the district leaders may replace a county leader at any time.

In 1953 a law limited membership on county committees to a maximum of four committeemen from any election district. This resulted in reducing the New York County Democratic Committee from 11,762 to 3,471 members. Before the law went into effect, there were throughout all New York City 35,861 Democratic and 12,855 Republican committeemen! The absurdity is evident by the fact that, if well attended, city-wide committee meetings would have to be held in a ball park and would require hours to take the roll. The fantastic sizes, even under the new law, mean unwieldy committees which lend themselves in practice to control from the top through a leader and an executive council. The decentralized and large municipal organization results in interborough rivalry and the lack of an effective mechanism to act on city-wide problems.

Personal Organizations. The patterns used in these three cities are merely incomplete illustrations of the highly diversified form of municipal parties. In California cities and in Detroit, for example, the wide use of nonpartisan elections has resulted in less formal party structure and the machine itself is of less significance in municipal elections. In such cases, party organizations are strongly personal and cluster about mayoralty and city-wide candidates, with considerable shifting and fluidity of allegiances. This stands in contrast to the more or less permanent urban

---

[13] A description of the complicated Bronx County organization is given in Edward J. Flynn, *op. cit.*, pp. 9–10; see also Roy V. Peel, "The Political Machine of New York City," *The American Political Science Review,* Vol. 27 (1933), pp. 611–618. For a general work on the city and the state see Warren Moscow, *Politics in the Empire State* (New York: Alfred A. Knopf, Inc., 1948).

machines, which are kept together year in and year out regardless of the changes in the party fortunes of the nominees. In nearly all organizations and regardless of form, personal friendships constitute an important welding and binding influence.

LOCAL EXECUTIVES

Local Committeemen. Much of the success or failure of a political party rests in the "unit cell of the party structure," the precinct or voting district. Sometimes there is a precinct committee, but more often party affairs on this level are run by a captain or leader. Even if a committee exists, the captain is likely to be the dominant figure. These local committeemen work year round in the interest of the party. During primaries and elections they circulate petitions, get out the voters on registration and election day, distribute campaign literature, and in general work to promote the success of the organization's nominees. They are called upon to explain and to work for favorable votes on referendum propositions, especially those affecting the party. Problems and sentiments of the area are reported by precinct captains to the ward leader, a function highly useful during elections. It is not unusual for precinct committeemen to serve as election officers in their precincts.

Beyond the administration of election routine the job is likely to be what the captain can make it, subject of course to the character of the district. In many communities he functions as a broker between the citizen and his government. If the citizen has a complaint about his tax assessment, the precinct captain will help him to get an adjustment or advise him how to proceed. Voters in his district go to him about all sorts of services—street repairs, police protection, waste collections, water supply, recreational facilities, and so on—and the precinct captain takes up their problems with the proper authorities and is usually able to secure the desired action. Bail, counsel, or other assistance is given to those who run afoul of the law. All that the precinct captain asks for in return is that they turn out to vote—and vote right.

Diverse other activities have included securing physicians for those in need of medical care but who have little financial means, settling neighborhood quarrels, securing passports, furnishing travel information, and aiding aliens in the naturalization process. Service is rendered to rich and poor regardless of party affiliation. One enterprising worker took to the county chairman the problem of one of his constituent's sons, who had been denied admission to the state law school. The chairman exercised his "contacts" with the law-school authorities and the boy was admitted.

Of the People. The leaders springing from the well over 100,000 wards and precincts represent a cross section of their parties and constituencies.

It is not easy to "type" these leaders, and studies of local committeemen in such widely scattered areas as upstate New York cities, Philadelphia, Chicago, and Seattle reveal considerable variation in background.[14] For example, 42 per cent of Republican precinct leaders in Seattle were women, compared to only 5 per cent in Chicago. Government employees constituted about 20 per cent of the precinct committeemen in upstate New York and Seattle and over 50 per cent in Chicago and Philadelphia. Sharp contrasts were found in education. Those having a college education in the New York cities constituted but 12 per cent of the committeemen in 1932, 20 per cent in Chicago in 1936, and 53 per cent in Seattle in 1951. Marked increase in college attendance between the time the studies were made might account for some, but certainly not all, of the difference.

Long residence in the area is a general prerequisite for becoming a precinct captain. More than two-thirds of those in Chicago had lived in that city 30 or more years and 60 per cent had been 10 or more years in the district. Despite the great influx of newcomers to Seattle, over 50 per cent of the precinct leaders had lived there over 30 years. Gosnell concluded that in Chicago "a fairly long apprenticeship seems to be necessary for appointment as precinct captain. At least one-half of the 1936 committeemen had been engaged in political work for more than ten years. . . . It appears that one has to be well acclimated to Chicago politics before taking part in it." [15]

Local leaders generally represent the predominant nationalistic stock and prevailing religion of their locality. Philadelphia division leaders were found to [16]

. . . have the same race, and nationality origins in the given area which they represent. In a Negro division, one or both of the organization leaders are apt to be colored. The Italian, Irish, Jewish, and Slavic sections choose men of their own sort; so do the highly cultured, well-born communities, on the one hand, and the industrial and slum districts on the other.

Amateurs make up a large portion of the party workers in England, but in the United States a premium is put upon professionals. Mr. Dooley's

[14] Data here are from W. E. Mosher, "Party and Government Control at the Grass Roots," *National Municipal Review*, Vol. 24 (1935), pp. 15–18; D. H. Kurtzman, *Methods of Controlling Votes in Philadelphia* (Master's thesis, University of Pennsylvania, 1935); J. T. Salter, *Boss Rule: Portraits in City Politics* (New York: McGraw-Hill Book Company, Inc., 1935); Sonya Forthal, *Cogwheels of Democracy: A Study of the Precinct Captain* (New York: The Frederick-William Press, 1946); H. F. Gosnell, *Machine Politics: Chicago Model* (Chicago: University of Chicago Press, 1937); Hugh A. Bone, *Grass Roots Party Leadership: A Case Study of King County, Washington* (Seattle: Bureau of Governmental Research and Services, University of Washington, 1952).

[15] *Op. cit.*, p. 66.

[16] Salter, *op. cit.*, p. 41.

philosophy is not far wrong as applied to this group in the party—"Politics ain't bean-bag. 'Tis a man's game. . . . 'Tis a profissional spoort. like playin' baseball f'r a livin' or wheelin' a truck."

In the first instance, then, the local leader springs from the people around him. He reflects their weaknesses and aspirations. One whose education is inferior or whose background is at wide variance can succeed only by exercising extraordinary tact. The same applies to a leader of superior education and experience, lest he be considered "high-brow" or "high-hat." The precinct or ward executive has learned with Plunkitt of Tammany Hall: "There's only one way to hold a district; you must study human nature and act accordin'. . . . To learn real human nature you have to go among the people, see them and be seen. . . . I know what they like and what they don't like, what they are strong at and what they are weak in, and I reach them by approachin' at the right side." The successful local politician, or for that matter politicians from the top to the bottom rung, has a keen interest in people. If he does not have his own political club, he is a "joiner" of others. He goes to church and attends its various social activities and always has time to stop and visit with his constituents.

Many other attributes will aid the local leader, such as abounding energy, resourcefulness, persistency, and gregariousness. Unflagging loyalty to the party and its leaders is a common characteristic of the precinct executive. Those wishing to rise in the party soon learn the importance of loyalty. While the higher-ups supply the strategy and brainwork, the real success of the grass-roots politician is apt to be measured by the organization by the legwork.

Such in brief are some aspects of the formal structure of the major parties in the United States. This description by no means explains the operation of the system. Indeed, the real party forces are explained by an appreciation of the various extralegal mechanisms and the personalities operating them. The clubs, machines, bosses, and leaders become the driving forces behind the operation of the party. The machines and leadership will be considered in the following two chapters.

POLITICAL CLUBS

In many urban and in a few rural areas the political club, usually organized along ward or district lines, has become a most important extralegal unit of the party. These clubs received a high degree of development at the hands of Tammany Hall, which worked out an elaborate club system, with one or more clubs in each assembly district. These clubs are a central gathering place for citizens and aliens of all age groups. Social contacts provide the setting for making "business" deals and for getting votes. The people of the neighborhood go to the political club for service and information on many subjects. Some New York clubs give a dance once a year for their members; others provide an all-day picnic in Central Park. The club is what the district leader or captain makes it. Time permitting, a resourceful leader will weld the club into a powerful vote-getting and service institution. He may prescribe dues, bylaws, and organizational matters to facilitate this. He may attach a lawyer or judge to the clubhouse to render free legal advice or a doctor to give free service to constituents unable to pay a fee. Professor Peel has accurately referred to New York clubs as the "ganglia of politics." [17]

The clubs have been threatened by such other competing recreational facilities as the low-priced automobile, motion pictures, radio, and television. Old-timers deplore the disappearance of such colorful activities as political chowders, ox feasts, and the bonfires in front of clubhouses on election nights. However, the clubs are still a force in party organization, and new clubs appealing to the young people and to women are in ascendancy. From the famous Hendricks and Tammany clubs in Boston sprang the once powerful "Czar" Martin Lomasney and James M. Curley, and Martin Behrman got his start from the famous Choctaw Club in New Orleans.

Political clubs similar to those of New York City are rarely found elsewhere but in many cities there are clubs which operate out of the homes of various leaders and which rent halls a few times a year for dances and meetings. In the Los Angeles area there are about 25 Democratic clubs chartered by the county central committee. Unlike Eastern clubs, they seldom own property and clubhouses and virtually no patronage is given out through them. These clubs are often formed around a candidate or leader or specific ideology, such as the militant Fair Deal. Although club constitutions often prohibit preprimary endorsements, the club serves as a breeding ground for political candidates and a springboard of personal ambition. Many clubs attempt some educational programs and try to keep the party going between elections. Some regularly send resolutions to Congress and the state legislatures.

Recent years have seen the creation of clubs for youth, usually called the Young Democratic or Young Republican Club. They have little in common with the organization political clubs just noted and seldom have a clubhouse. Young people's clubs are nationally federated and are usually established on a city, county, or other governmental unit basis; several have been created on college campuses. The main function is apparently social and recreational and to promote interest and camaraderie within the party. Young men and women are recruited into the party ranks through these clubs. Unusual leadership in these clubs sometimes

[17] For the most comprehensive description of political clubs see Roy V. Peel, *The Political Clubs of New York City* (New York: G. P. Putnam's Sons, 1935).

helps a person to get on a political committee. Generally, these clubs are separate and distinct from the regular party committees and conventions, and they are given no recognition by being granted positions on a political committee or delegates to various conventions. Many ambitious members of these clubs are dissatisfied with their status and are seeking some form of recognition. Party regulars, however, are inclined to frown on giving the "youngsters" a voice in the party councils. This attitude is undergoing change, particularly on the national level. The chairman of the Young Republican National Federation has been made an ex-officio member of the Executive Committee of the Republican National Committee. Both the Democratic and Republican youth federations operate out of the respective national committee headquarters.

EVALUATION

A frequently heard criticism of party organization, especially from within the party, is that it fails to operate locally as a full-staffed, well-disciplined unit on a year-round basis. Part of this is due to one-party dominance. An overwhelmingly Republican precinct may not appear to need a captain and Democrats regard activity there as love's labor lost. Even where there is two-party competition, many persons doubt the influence of committeemen or that they are the "bone and sinew" of the party. Accordingly, they are unwilling to take over a precinct position.

Criticisms of the Committee System. In terms of the mission of coping with present-day problems, the party committee system is unrealistic if not outmoded. That the committees are unable to handle many if not most matters is evident from the very fact that the "paper" organization described here has given way to control by bosses and leaders, many of whom hold no position in the committees. The thousands of committees present a confusing picture both to committeemen and to the citizen. Very little is actually known of the functions party committees perform or are supposed to perform. The legal provisions or the party rules for party committees are often ambiguous and bewildering, and few committee members have seen or know the content of their organization's bylaws. Not much is known of the work of committees in the formulation of party policy, the building of party organization, or the administration of committees, and little thought appears to be given to the methods by which committees could be made responsible agents of party government. One is forced to look to the informal group behind the legal machinery to find the real seat of power in the party. The national committees, for example, exercise no control comparable to the annual party conferences or executive councils characteristic of many British and European parties.

The persistent proliferation of political committees outside the regular party organization carries an implicit criticism of the latter. If the statutory committees were satisfactorily performing the functions which the membership believe they should perform, there would not be much need for the multiplication of organizations. Many *ad hoc* clubs and auxiliaries arise out of dissatisfaction and frustration with the policies of the county committee and it is not unusual for them to oppose the latter on public policies. Young Republican and young Democratic organizations often show more concern with resolutions and policies than the regular organization.

One of the reasons for discontent is that party chairmen usually wear the hat of neutrality in the party primaries and very often on policy proposals. The California Republican Assembly rose from the feeling that the state organization was inept and lackadaisical in pushing party policies and, moreover, that it was indifferent to nominations.[18] This group forms candidates committees for purposes of making endorsements in the primary and seeking out promising persons in the party to support for public office. In addition, the assembly sponsors public forums, local projects, and research. So successful have been its activities that it is often referred to in the press as "the G.O.P. of California." Democrats in the state have recently formed a similar organization known as the Democratic Council.

A Republican women's group, Pro-America, was formed out of discontent with the regular organization's preoccupation with patronage, lack of militance in fighting the left, and its general neutrality in Republican primaries, nonpartisan municipal elections, and on initiative and referendum propositions. New groups nearly everywhere stem from a feeling that parties have functions to perform, which for one reason or another are being slighted by the official party organization. It bears repeating that the selection of candidates is the most essential function of party leadership and the inhibition on the leadership in exercising this role has led to the formation of unofficial organizations. Many believe this neutrality in nominations is of doubtful merit.

A serious weakness of the party structure, especially on the local levels, is the failure to work out profitable relationships between committees of different areas, owing to the excessive decentralization of parties. The rule here is to live and let live, and interference from another committee even with reference to a common problem is resented. The unsatisfactory character is perhaps best shown in the problems of metropolitan planning and the integration of services. Each party is organized on the basis of a geographical district, whereas such vital matters as transportation, parking, health, and recreational systems defy election district, municipal,

[18] For a discussion of several of these "volunteer" groups and the reasons for their creation see Hugh A. Bone, "New Party Associations in the West," *The American Political Science Review*, Vol. 45 (1951), pp. 1115–1125.

and county lines. Parties are interested only in their district, resulting in *ad hoc* attitudes toward problems common to the whole metropolitan area. No committee exists for developing policies associated with metropolitanism, and there is seldom extralegal, let alone formal, consultation on these matters.

While most party organizations suffer from myopia and provincialism in the problems of metropolitan areas, one example may be cited of the benefit of intercommittee cooperation. The Maryland National Capital Park and Planning Commission was created to have supervision over the Maryland-Washington metropolitan district. The Commission is empowered to work out a regional plan for the district, including zoning, recreational facilities, land use, and highways. Seeing the potentialities of this plan, the Montgomery County (Maryland) Democratic organization made regional planning an integral part of its program and threw its influence behind the Commission. It cooperated with party and civic groups in the District of Columbia to bring metropolitan planning to Montgomery County. This is a notable exception to what is generally a lack of concern about civic issues on the part of local party organizations.

Considerations in Improvement. The student of party organization cannot escape the fact that the organization of parties rests on a local basis but many of the real policy issues are national. The interests represented in the national party platforms have little relation to state and local units. This suggests that local committees should take more interest in the national party program and consider more seriously how they might relate themselves to it. Local party activity can be perhaps geared somewhat more to this fact than it has been in the past. Increased methods of democratic control, simplification of organizational structure, and the analysis of the party organization at all levels are a part of the process of improving party organization.

It should be remembered also that the criticisms of party organization are only one side of the coin. They assume (1) that everyone in the party is agreed on the mission and purpose of the county, state, and national hierarchy and (2) that the committees are the proper authorities to perform these functions and that, moreover, they possess the competence to do so. Many groups such as Pro-America, the California Republican Assembly, men's and women's auxiliaries perform valuable services in making preprimary endorsements, taking positions on referendum propositions, and on candidates for nonpartisan offices. There may be real wisdom in party chairmen and committees remaining neutral in these contests, for to take an official position on such matters is to run the risk of losing votes and fanning the fires of factionalism. For the Democratic State Central Committee to support a daylight-saving-time proposition is to alienate rural votes, but for the Young Men's Democratic Club of Indianapolis to do so may mobilize city voters without hurting the party in the country. The same applies to nominations. *Narrow interest*

Persons joining political parties have widely varying interests. They have anxieties, frustrations, and ambitions which can be partly met through such partisan political association. Some wish to further right-wing or leftish viewpoints. Others may be primarily interested in meeting people and in the social side of parties, and still others may desire the excitement of campaigning, attending rallies, conventions, and the like. The existence of many organizations both within and without the regular organization gives people a chance to fit themselves into party work in accordance with their interests and perhaps abilities. Often men's, women's and youth clubs are formed to promote ultraliberal or ultra-conservative policies and like-minded persons gravitate to the same niche in the party. Criticisms of the unwieldy size as well as the number of committees may overlook the virtues of giving hundreds of party workers a chance to attend conventions and meetings and acquire some feeling of participating in the decisions of the party.

Finally, the proliferation of organizations may reflect an alertness on the part of certain persons within the party to the need for party action in new fields. An example of this is the growing importance of regional associations such as the Western States Democratic Conference and the Republican Midwest Conference.[19] These groups meet periodically to discuss regional problems such as resources, water, and agriculture and attempt to focus the attention of the party's lawmakers on regional interests. The formal party hierarchy makes no provision for an intermediate group between the national and the state committees, yet there is a recognition that many problems such as river development cut across regional lines. The regional associations are composed of the national committeemen and committeewomen, state chairmen, and often other officials living in the region. At some of these meetings a "party platform" for the area has been adopted and campaign strategy discussed. All in all, the regional associations fill an important need and their potential has scarcely been more than tapped.

Modernization of party organization with a view to developing a dynamic party system consonant with the pace and requirements of contemporary life has become one of the great needs of our time. Before a realistic streamlining of the parties can take place, it is necessary to collect and analyze information on the party hierarchy. The student of parties and the party members themselves might begin by seeking the answers to these questions in his own locality:

[19] See *ibid.*, pp. 1121–1125.

1. How does one get elected to local party committees? Who are its members?
2. What are the functions of the local committee?
3. How are the officers of the state, county, ward, and district chosen and who appoints the standing committees? How responsive is the party organization to the will of the membership?
4. What party matters are regulated by law and which by the party's bylaws?
5. How does the pattern of party organization affect the attitude of parties toward state and metropolitan problems? Do the various committees cooperate on problems of the metropolitan area? How are jurisdictional problems settled?
6. Is a local party platform formulated?
7. Where is the locus of power in the party hierarchy?
8. Are there any functions now performed by party associations outside the regular organization which might better be performed by the latter?

SELECTED REFERENCES

There are relatively few works devoted to party organizational matters. One is forced to rely mainly on periodical and newspaper accounts and various manuals put out by the political parties. Some helpful general accounts include James A. Farley, *Behind the Ballots* (1938) and *Jim Farley's Story* (1948); Jesse Macy, *Party Organization and Machinery* (1904); Charles Michelson, *The Ghost Talks* (1944); H. F. Gosnell, *Machine Politics: Chicago Model* (1937); Sonya Forthal, *Cogwheels of Democracy: A Study of the Precinct Captain* (1946); V. O. Key, Jr., *Southern Politics* (1949); Ralph M. Goldman, *Party Chairmen and Party Faction, 1789–1900* (University of Chicago Ph.D. dissertation, 1951). Some useful articles will be found in *The Annals of the American Academy of Political and Social Science*, September, 1948, 1952.

A few of the especially pertinent periodical articles are W. E. Mosher, "Party Government and Control at the Grass Roots," *National Municipal Review*, Vol. 34 (1940), pp. 15–18. In *The American Political Science Review* see Marguerite J. Fisher and Betty Whitehead, "Women and National Party Organization," Vol. 38 (1944), pp. 895–903; Sonya Forthal, "The Small Fry and the Party Purse," Vol. 34 (1940), pp. 66–76, and in the same volume, Leon Weaver, "Some Soundings in the Party System: Rural Precinct Committeemen," pp. 76–84; J. T. Salter, "Party Organization in Philadelphia: The Ward Committeeman," Vol. 27 (1933), pp. 618–627; W. S. Sayre, "Personnel of Republican and Democratic Committees," Vol. 26 (1932), pp. 360–362; H. F. Gosnell, "The Political Party versus the Political Machine," *The Annals of the American Academy of Political and Social Science*, Vol. 169 (1933), pp. 21–28.

1. National committees
2. congressional and senatorial committees.

CHAPTER 15

Machine Politics

> The professional politicians operated, under the direction of the managers and the wire-pullers, with such uniformity and with such indifference or insensibility to right and wrong, that they evolved the idea of a piece of mechanism working automatically and blindly—a machine. The effect appeared so precisely identical that the term "machine" was bestowed on the organization as a nickname, which it bears down to the present day.
>
> —M. OSTROGORSKI

A theme running through the previous chapters is that "political party" is not expressed in any one group. There is a party-in-the-electorate, consisting of voters supporting its candidates. Although difficult to describe at times, there is a party in Congress and in the administration. To many people party signifies the officialdom of the organization from precinct executives to the national chairman. All these expressions of party have many interests in common, the major one being victory on election day. But each has certain functions to perform which are not the immediate concerns or responsibilities of the others.

Within local party organizations there are leaders and interests strongly guided by self-preservation, personal ambition, and perhaps aggrandizement, who would utilize the organization for personal as well as party ends. Whenever one succeeds to top power in this group he is often called the "boss," and the workers carrying out his orders constitute the "machine." Yet there is something to Edward J. Flynn's comment, "It is only the 'leader' you don't like who is a 'boss'; and the 'organization' you don't like that is a 'machine.'" In this chapter attention is given to certain aspects of party activity associated with political machines.

POLITICAL MACHINES

While "machine" and "organization" are often used as synonymous terms, it is sometimes desirable to use them to designate different bodies within the parties. In the broadest sense, the organization consists of the whole gamut of workers from the bottom to the top who are assisting the party as a whole. The committee system is thought of as the party organization. But a distinction can be made between machine and organization by connoting the former as the smaller group which is in actual control or striving for control and which becomes preoccupied with such

355

machine is an organization that is so formed to win elections matters as patronage and the perpetuation of its own power within the organization. Historically, the machine has often been willing to use unethical practices to maintain its power.

Stated another way, in almost every city, county, and even state, a group comes into control of the party by various paths. This may be a faction, a "wing," or a group which wishes to dominate the party for love of power, for personal or selfish motives, or for any number of other reasons. When this group gets strong enough to elect its own slate, dominate a nominating convention, control a lion's share of the patronage, it is called a "machine," a connotation which in the popular mind is bad. The machine is seldom synonymous with the city, town, county, or state central committee. As such, it has an extralegal basis. It may even be operating against the official party organization. Its leaders may hold no public office or even a prominent office in the party. The machine is interested in the welfare of its own members first and of the party secondarily. Often each wing or faction of a party has its own machine seeking to gain control of the party, such as the Byrd and anti-Byrd factions of the Democratic party in Virginia. A "machine" administration has also been distinguished from a "reform" administration by its greater emphasis upon patronage and its general lack of interest in over-all political issues of good government. It has scorn for "civic-minded idealists" and "reformers."

While the great depression of the 1930's brought political repercussions in the national government, forcing it, as was true in many other democratic countries, to move toward the left, American municipal machines made few changes or concessions in their political philosophies. The national government solved the major economic difficulties such as unemployment and helped to bail out some cities financially, but the people could give little thanks to the machine for this. However, such machines as Kelly-Nash in Chicago, Hague in Jersey City, and Pendergast in Kansas City were eager to identify themselves with the national administration and to capitalize on its popularity with the rank and file of voters. This, rather than their support of the New Deal program, explained their backing of the national ticket. Further, there is evidence that as the Federal government rendered more and more personal services to urban dwellers, the machine, especially in New York and Philadelphia, felt the ill effects in part. However, the collapse of Tammany Hall and the Vare machines with the arrival of the New Deal cannot be explained purely in terms of economic factors. Local factors, including the illness and death of Vare in Philadelphia and the expulsion of Curry by Tammany Hall, were of greatest importance. That most machines were able to survive the failure to solve acute local problems is testimony to the fact that their roots are deep enough to keep them from being blown over by economic crises. Moreover, the business of the machine is to elect candidates rather than to concern itself with policies.

The activities and support of the machine everywhere are rooted in the sociological and political complexion of the district as well as in the degree of political consciousness and public morality. Yet the common denominators of the successful personal or party machines have been based, in one degree or another, on patronage, financial support from diverse elements, an army of devoted followers, and usually a strong personal attachment to the leader, boss, or small clique. They are identified with the *status quo* and conservatism and their financial supporters and followers likewise are unenthusiastic about crusades or reforms. Party machines then become an interest group and fight all attempts to do away with their vested positions. For this reason reformers usually must look to unseating the machines before they can hope to achieve their ends. The machine out of power is likely to represent a conservative interest as well and frequently joins with the "in" machine against the insurgents and crusaders who would inaugurate a program damaging to their constituents.

MACHINE POLITICS: CONTROL

Ostrogorski saw the hierarchy of the machine as divided into the three categories of the "boys," the "henchmen," and the "boss." The first are the "chief performers in the primaries" who do the legwork and much of the dirty work of politics. They corral voters and carry out orders from higher-ups, orders which have at times called for fraud and strong-arm methods. Henchmen are of various ranks and social position, who manage the boys and subordinate politicians as a sort of vicar working for the boss. "Apart from political service the henchman owes the boss personal homage, just as his historical prototype, the vassal, owed it to the lord." [1] At the top, of course, is the boss or chief, who gives orders to the henchmen but who also must defend and protect them and try to forward their political ambitions.

This description by the French scholar does not fit all political machines today but the general outlines remain essentially the same. For the machine, the primaries most of the time are more important than the final election. The successful political leader is one who is able to construct a personal machine to support him. Personal machines become rivals for control of the party and are built up somewhat apart from the regular party machine or organization. After the primary, the party workers have the alternative of supporting the candidates of the successful machine and leader, deserting to the opposition party or sponsoring an

---

[1] M. Ostrogorski, *Democracy and the Party System in the United States*, p. 231. Copyright 1902 by The Macmillan Company. By permission of The Macmillan Company.

insurgent movement by running their own candidates as independents. The first course of action is the most common.

Once a machine is in power its major objective is to retain its position in the face of challenges from within its own party. This means victory in succeeding primaries. First, every effort is made to avoid a contest in the primaries in the interest of "harmony." This calls for painstaking work months in advance of the primary. Local leaders must be canvassed as well as those who contribute financial support to the machine. Deals may have to be made with certain factions threatening a revolt; this may call for minor concessions. Scattered individuals cannot successfully challenge the decisions of a machine and attempts will be made to cut off the support of those suspected of building up a rival organization. This requires talking with business, veterans', labor, racial, religious, and nationalistic groups in an effort to keep them in line and from going over to the "enemy."

In one of the most candid descriptions of how a boss and machine control, Edward J. Flynn, the undisputed Bronx leader for a quarter of a century, explained his success in terms similar to those above and told why victory is easier for the regulars: [2]

The organization at all times has its own personnel in each small unit. An insurgent who questions the decisions of the machine must first place a man or woman captain in every Election District. This is not an easy task. The organization is in existence and is active 365 days of the year. It is difficult to build up in two or three months what it has taken the organization years to achieve. . . . There have been primary fights. But in every instance the organization has won, because all its forces could be centered in the troublesome district. The result has been that the insurgent not only was defeated, but overwhelmingly so.

He proudly includes a verbatim transcript of an executive committee meeting of Bronx County in 1945, wherein all the candidates for the Democratic primary from municipal court justices to the mayor were nominated and unanimously ratified. From the opening gavel to the vote for adjournment took 10 minutes! He notes: [3]

There were no objections, for everything had been arranged in advance. The very smoothness of the proceedings exemplifies practical politics in action. For within the periphery of that meeting may be found, one by one, the axioms on which practical politics are based, beginning with the votes cast and extending to the highest office—the presidency of the United States.

Not all leaders are able to operate so successful a machine, but they find inspiration in this illustration.

[2] *You're the Boss* (New York: The Viking Press, Inc., 1947) , pp. 226–227.
[3] *Ibid.,* p. 220.

conclusion of machines

In conclusion, the party machine is an interest group. Its objectives may be at variance with the party as a whole. The public officials it helps elect must placate it. Among its major objectives are to control the distribution of favors and perquisites and to select as many public employees as possible. The distribution of patronage, management of perquisites, and domination of the primary are the machine's major methods of control.

Attention may now be turned to consider some of the elements which make party machine harmony possible.

PATRONAGE

Federal Patronage. Appointment to office of one's friends is not America's contribution to the art of politics nor an innovation of the nineteenth century. English kings made many appointments to colonial posts on the basis of personal favoritism or to pay obligations. Presidents Washington and Adams filled the new government's agencies with Federalists. Partial justification was made on the grounds that the Federalist Presidents naturally wished to launch the new government with men who believed in strong national authority.

While great progress is being made in extending the merit system in the national government, the fact remains that patronage on a substantial scale exists. The rapid increase in functions in recent years has increased Federal personnel to degrees unheard of 50 years ago. With the creation of many new agencies during the early days of the New Deal, Postmaster General Farley, dispenser of the patronage, found himself overwhelmed with job seekers. Taking a page from the book of that skillful party builder, Mark Hanna, Farley set about to systematize and record certain rules in black and white where all congressmen could see them (in the *Congressional Record*). The following statement sets forth his agreement with the Texas group: [4]

The two senators are to control the following patronage: District and appellate judges, district attorneys, United States marshals, internal revenue collectors, customs officers, postmasters in their respective home cities, all state-wide appointments requiring confirmation of Senate.

The congressman in each district is to control, subject to above, all postmasters in his district, all appointees in his district to be made by Mr. Morgenthau, the Reconstruction Finance Corporation, the Census Bureau, the Agricultural Department, the Treasury Department, and other appointments in his district not statewide.

[4] *Congressional Record,* 74th Cong., 1st Sess., p. 225. Farley's philosophy of patronage is considerably more ethical than that of municipal bosses because he emphasized the importance of ability and qualification. His viewpoint is worth reading; see *Behind the Ballots* (New York: Harcourt, Brace and Company, Inc., 1938), pp. 223–238.

The amount of Federal patronage available today is uncertain. When the Republicans returned to power in 1953, newspapers were full of statements of disappointment that so few Federal jobs were available. During President Eisenhower's first year, about 20,000 Republicans were appointed to jobs in the executive establishment.[5] During the Roosevelt-Truman Administrations a great many appointees were brought under civil service regulations. The Eisenhower Administration, moreover, was dedicated to retrenchment in Federal employment. It is much less easy for a President today to build up a "national machine" in the form of thousands of Federal jobholders who can be counted upon to work enthusiastically at party work the year round.

There appear to be about nine hundred patronage jobs in Congress such as doorkeepers, clerks, sergeants at arms, aides, and lesser jobs. The limited amount of jobs available to an individual congressman is hardly enough to build a successful machine but, nonetheless, provides some personnel to the legislator which will be helpful in campaigns.

There is a struggle in each state regarding control over the distribution of Federal positions. Often the jobs are funneled through the national committeeman and sometimes through the municipal boss or county chairmen. United States senators have sometimes been the major "clearinghouse" for distribution. Governor Thomas E. Dewey of New York worked out an arrangement whereby he controlled Federal patronage coming to the state under the Eisenhower Administration.[6] In New York, recommendations for the less important places originated with the county chairmen and were reviewed by the state chairman and the two members of the national committee before transmission to Washington. At this stage the governor could wield the veto power. Certain appointments within congressional districts were reviewed by the Republican representative or, if within a Democratic district, by Senator Irving Ives, a Republican. For the more important offices such as Federal judges and attorneys, Mr. Dewey's approval was required.[7] The major objective of this arrangement was to see that the governor's status would not be undermined by those within the party who were for Senator Taft for President or were opposed to the governor for other reasons.

Local Spoils. Political patronage is found in the largest degree in the counties, townships, and local districts. In 1953, county government employees, exclusive of teachers and school employees, numbered 473,000.

[5] See *The New York Times,* Jan. 17, 1954. At the end of that time there remained only about 200 reasonably good jobs for the 2,000 who were seeking them.

[6] For details see *The New York Times,* Jan. 6, 1953.

[7] This was in sharp contrast to former Governor Herbert H. Lehman, a Democrat. Postmaster General Farley, then also Democratic National Chairman, was the patronage arbiter in the state because he was more the Democratic boss of the state than Mr. Lehman.

The counties constitute a Garden of Eden for patronage since only a few of them have a central personnel system or civil service regulations. Probably no more than one-fifth of the jobs are covered by a merit system. More than half of the municipal employees are under civil service regulations but in 1953 the National Civil Service League reported that only 814 out of 1,347 cities over 10,000 operated under such regulations. In the same year only half of the states had a state-wide merit system.

In all these areas there is plenty of elbowroom to fill jobs with "one of the boys" and to give rewards for their political support. Wiser machines fill many prominent posts with men of good reputation who serve as "window dressers" by giving an air of respectability. White and Smith found that party committees often endorse and secure the appointment of able personnel who are genuinely interested in the public welfare.[8] Still other appointments are given on the basis of race, religion, language, class, or other distinctions; this is the essence of good politics. Beyond this, many jobs on the local levels are given as rewards, with no questions asked as to the person's education, qualification, or ability. Tradition sets the pattern for the filling of other positions. In one state legislature it is customary that the job of sergeant at arms be given to a certain county, and there ensues a struggle between the regulars and other factions of the county organization as to who shall name the man. Similarly, watchmen, doorkeepers, aides, and the like may be apportioned on a geographical basis. County patronage is controlled by the county officers as a rule. For offices in Chicago appointed by the governor only, ward committeemen submit the names to the county leaders, who in turn present them to the governor.

The more powerful municipal machines have entrenched themselves through a constantly expanding army of jobholders. McKean in his study of the Jersey City machine discovered a fantastic increase in employees and estimated in 1940 "the political army at 20,000, or about one adult in every twenty in Hudson County." [9] When the Tammany machine was replaced by the La Guardia administration in New York, an investigation showed [10]

. . . 834 exempt positions which are used for the most part for rewarding political henchmen. The city pays to this group of 834 exempt employees $2,300,000 a year. Since they are nearly all chosen by direct orders of county and district political leaders, the city is in effect sustaining the political machine by feeding its officers.

[8] See *Politics and the Public Service* (New York: Harper & Brothers, 1939).

[9] Dayton David McKean, *The Boss: The Hague Machine in Action* (Boston: Houghton Mifflin Company, 1940), p. 127.

[10] New York City Commissioner of Accounts, *Investigating City Government in the La Guardia Administration* (1937), p. 9.

The extension of the merit system offers one way of controlling machine patronage. But if the organization can get control over the civil service authorities, little is gained by the use of the merit system. Most of the employees both of Jersey City and of Hudson County, for example, are theoretically protected by civil service regulations but employees may be dismissed for reasons of economy or by the abolition of the positions they hold.

Some official patronage is available in the judiciary. Judges can appoint bailiffs, clerks, and several court positions, and machines are apt to refuse renomination to judges who do not award these jobs to the party faithful. But judges can be far more useful to the machine in the matter of financial perquisites. Refereeships, guardianships, and receiverships offer opportunities for obtaining profitable fees and bankruptcy cases are often lucrative. Fees of this kind can be given to members of the machine and help build up financial support for it. Due to the spread of nonpartisan election of judges and the exposure of judges using their prerogatives in a partisan way, judicial spoils are not so widespread as they once were but they are by no means nonexistent.

THE CASE FOR PATRONAGE

Over the years considerable rationalization has been made for patronage. It is argued that "patronage is the price of democracy" and that "charity begins on the public payroll." Patronage is presumed to have originated in antiquity and in human nature. In the field of business and the professions, favors and jobs are often the result of friendships and based upon a *quid pro quo;* therefore, it is natural to find similar practices in politics.

Party politicians generally argue that patronage is essential to the retention of the party system. Jobs provide the incentives for hard work in service to the party. There can be little doubt that patronage has been useful to party organizations and that it is the *sine qua non* of machines. Machine politics is usually strongly rooted in jobs. Hundreds of persons will work in a party organization without hope of direct benefits, but a basic cog of a personal machine is likely to rest on promises of diverse favors and spoils. "Spoils" may include not only jobs but various types of honors, favors, preferments, and preferences, some legitimate and some improper. Bosses and machines make promises to their loyal workers that they "will take care of them." This may include a job in a business concern which supports the machine and not necessarily a political appointment.

If one grants that political parties are essential to the operation of democratic government, patronage is viewed as helping the party system. In practice, it is a method of financing parties out of the public treasury and is a method of enforcing party discipline. Parties in turn help furnish the personnel of government by providing "qualified" men and women for government work. As previously noted, even supporters of the merit system admit that many political appointments do include capable persons.

President Jackson and others have supported patronage on the grounds of the desirability of frequent rotation in office. The public, it is held, needs to be protected from the evils of long tenure in office and frequent turnover encourages industry and efficiency. The giving of jobs, moreover, is a sign of responsiveness to the people and will help keep government close to them.

Finally, the giving of political appointments is condoned on the ground that the executive needs to have men around him who are personally loyal to him and to his principles. Giving him a large number of appointments will help to build up a popular following needed for putting over his program. Jobs are given out not only on the basis of party affiliation but with cognizance of race, religion, ethnic background, section, and faction. Patronage reflects these interests and represents them. The Democrats awarded many positions from doorkeepers to judgeships during the New Deal with these factors in mind. They built up much support among minorities not only because of an attractive legislative program but also because jobs given to the "underdogs" gave them status in the community.

THE CASE AGAINST PATRONAGE

Thanks to dramatization by reform and good-government leagues, the evils of patronage are now fairly generally recognized in terms of public administration. Political patronage interferes with the building of a career service and attracting competent people into administration. It is reasonably well established that patronage is costly, not necessarily because political appointees are incompetent or dishonest but because frequent rotation means training new employees. In Michigan the patronage system was found to result in an annual turnover of about 25 per cent with an estimated cost of a half million dollars in breaking in new employees.[11] While many instances may be cited where the parties appointed qualified people for office, the annals are full of cases where ill-prepared and dishonest persons were appointed.

Our primary concern here is the influence of patronage on party politics rather than on public administration. An indictment against the system is that it fosters the building of a machine whose major objective is not so much good government as self-perpetuation. Appointees are expected to do favors for the machine and the bidding of the boss. Such appoint-

[11] See J. K. Pollock, "The Cost of the Patronage System," *The Annals of the American Academy of Political and Social Science,* Vol. 189 (1937), pp. 29–34.

ments may freeze out competent, independent persons seeking positions but who are unwilling to serve the machine in all of its requests. An appointee serves the machine first and the party second, and sometimes the interest of the machine and the party are not the same.

In many cities patronage has corrupted rather than strengthened parties and its excesses have caused enough revulsion among the voters to cause defeat at the polls. Preoccupation with patronage, as seen in the previous chapter, has diverted attention from other party functions and built up unofficial party groups at the expense of the regular organization.

The contention that patronage is a requisite for operating a political party is open to debate. That party organizations can be built upon other than extensive job appointments has been demonstrated by British parties. One of the most competent party organizers in American history, James A. Farley, wrote: "I am convinced that with the help of a few simple ingredients like time, patience, and hard work, I could construct a major political party in the United States without the aid of a single job to hand out to deserving partisans." [12] On a Federal level, Eisenhower was elected without the benefit of a huge army of Republican officeholders. Any number of other candidates for President have duplicated the same feat. In numerous Western cities, where municipal elections are non-partisan and where a merit system exists, the parties have been forced and were able to build an organization without benefit of municipal jobs. Their organizations, moreover, are able to conduct effective campaigns in state and Federal elections.

There are many county chairmen and party officials who find the dispensing of patronage an onerous task and who would just as soon not be bothered with the job. Some complain that it causes more party rifts than it heals and takes time which might be better devoted to other party activities.

Few would disagree that mayors, governors, and Presidents should have freedom to choose their top policy makers, aides, and Cabinet officers on the basis of party and other considerations. But the application of party tests to certain technicians and jobs lower in the echelon is now widely challenged. The political neutralization brought about by the Hatch Acts, the unionization and professionalization of the career service, and the extension of the merit system into more and more divisions of government mean a decrease in the influence of patronage in political parties. The parties are having to learn how to live with less patronage and to develop new motivations for party activity.

[12] *Op. cit.,* pp. 232–233.

MONEY AND MACHINES

Money is oil to the machine in its drive for self-perpetuation. Some bosses give orders to their henchmen to purchase votes outright or make election bribes, but this practice is becoming much less common. Money is paid to cast fraudulent votes or to tamper with the registration and election machinery in order to get the "right" count. The machine of Thomas J. Pendergast in Kansas City and Jackson County, Mo., was one of the most powerful ever seen in the United States. Registration and voting figures reached fantastic proportions. At one time the United States Census listed the total adult population over twenty-one in Kansas City at 60 per cent but Pendergast had about 65 per cent of the total population registered. In one ward, 23,469 voters were registered though the census figures showed a total population, babies and all, of but 18,478! [13]

General Sources. Money is garnered from a host of sources. No two machines raise money in the same ways or in the same proportion. In times past "rake-offs" were made by getting the city council to deposit public moneys in banks willing to pay a large premium for the honor of acting as depository. A president testified under oath that his trust company paid a rate of 3 per cent or $2½ million over a period of years to the Quay machine in Philadelphia. Special interests sometimes pay the machine to block harmful legislation, but laws have helped to bring these sources of revenue under control. Machines past and present have thrived on assessment of public officeholders by means of threats or through "2 per cent" or "5 per cent" clubs whereby each employee was required to give a stipulated percentage of his salary to the cause. Various corrupt-practices acts likewise have reduced this source substantially, but ways are still found to evade these laws.

Some of the worst machines have been the result of an alliance between corrupt business and corrupt politicians. Machines antagonizing the business interests as a whole soon find themselves in a precarious position. It was once commonly believed that only big business kept the "ring" in control, the Tweed Ring in New York providing an illustration. In the present century the fabulous utility owner, Samuel Insull, worked with both Republican and Democratic machines in corrupting Chicago's government. It was reported that he threatened to purchase the Democratic organization for a half million dollars.[14] Big business has probably re-

[13] See Ralph Coghlan, "Boss Pendergast," *Forum*, Vol. 97 (1937), pp. 67–72.

[14] For an illuminating article on Insull's relations with machines see Donald Richberg, "Gold Plated Anarchy: An Interpretation of the Fall of the Giants," *Nation*, Vol. 136 (1933), pp. 368–369.

ceived more than its share of the blame. Mayor Hague of Jersey City alienated both the railroads and several large corporations and still remained in power.

During the period of rapid urbanization and business expansion it was common practice for machines literally to blackmail corporations desiring franchises and licenses to operate. For example, an electric company in Illinois might wish to serve Gary, Ind. A Gary councilman might introduce a bill, perhaps with no thought of pushing it, which would make impossible or difficult the operation of the utility in the Indiana city. The councilman would then approach the company to find out what it was willing to offer for withdrawal of the bill. Telephone, gas, water, and street-railway companies often found themselves victims of devices like this, even as late as 1900.

Medium-sized and small businesses have also had their alliances with the machines. Real-estate interests and those interested in tax fixing, tax adjusting, or tax lowering have had their share in "greasing the palm." Tax assessors often find themselves in a position to exercise wide "discretion" in valuing property. Assessors can either carefully probe or overlook tangible and personal property, and sizable contributions to party funds may lead assessors to be more lenient toward the owner. Reform in the administration of the tax machinery in recent years has reduced this form of bribery, but it has by no means disappeared. The O'Connell Ring, which ruled Albany, N.Y., for over a generation, made a huge success of the tax-assessment racket. Local Democratic leaders have notarized hundreds of appeals for reduction of assessments, and the larger property owners have found it to their advantage to employ O'Connell lawyers to handle their appeal cases. Van Devander [15] found that property owners were rewarded who "voted right."

Wise and frugal home owners in New York's capital city long ago learned not to enroll as Republicans. In 1938 only 6,930 out of the city's registrants admitted their Republicanism, as compared with 51,035 enrolled Democrats. Presumably, few of the 6,930 Republicans were property owners. It was too costly.

Another variation of this technique to extort money from legitimate businesses is found in the use of strict interpretations of city council ordinances which would force the enterpriser out of business. Honest builders are approached by an inspector, who points out an "interpretation" in the building code which will open them to prosecution unless the builders are willing to contribute. A Senate investigation found that Hoboken and Jersey City motion-picture operators paid large amounts for the nonenforcement of certain Sunday closing laws. Pressure is occa-

[15] *The Big Bosses*, p. 82. Copyright 1944, by Charles Van Devander, reprinted by permission of Crown Publishers.

sionally used to force those wishing to operate newsstands or other street-corner businesses to pay exorbitant license or other fees in order to avoid a narrow construction of a town ordinance which would put them out of business. In addition, illegal businesses such as gambling, numbers, prostitution, and underworld rackets have bought protection from the machine. These activities are carried on only with the blessing of the police, who are controlled by the machine.

"Honest Graft." Another source of revenue is what Tammany District Leader George Washington Plunkitt called "honest graft." A portion of his classic statement on the subject deserves repeating here.[16]

> Everybody is talkin' these days about Tammany men growin' rich on graft, but nobody thinks of drawin' the distinction between honest graft and dishonest graft. There's all the difference in the world between the two. Yes, many of our men have grown rich in politics. I have myself. I've made a big fortune out of the game, and I'm gettin' richer every day, but I've not gone in for dishonest graft—blackmailin' gamblers, saloonkeepers, disorderly people, etc.—and neither has any of the men who have made big fortunes in politics.
>
> There's an honest graft, and I'm an example of how it works. I might sum up the whole thing by sayin': I seen my opportunities and I took 'em.
>
> Just let me explain by examples. My party's in power in the city, and it's goin' to undertake a lot of public improvements. Well, I'm tipped off, say, that they're going to lay out a new park at a certain place.
>
> I see my opportunity and I take it. I go to that place and I buy up all the land I can in the neighborhood. Then the board of this or that makes its plan public, and there is a rush to get my land, which nobody cared particular for before.
>
> Ain't it perfectly honest to charge a good price and make a profit on my investment and foresight? Of course it is. Well, that's honest graft.
>
> Or, supposin' it's a new bridge they're goin' to build. I get tipped off and I buy as much property as I can that has to be taken for approaches. I sell at my own price later on and drop some more money in the bank.
>
> Wouldn't you? It's just like lookin' ahead in Wall Street or in the coffee or cotton market. It's honest graft, and I'm lookin' for it every day in the year. I will tell you frankly that I've got a good lot of it, too. . . .
>
> I've told you how I got rich by honest graft. Now, let me tell you that most politicians who are accused of robbin' the city get rich the same way.
>
> They didn't steal a dollar from the city treasury. They just seen their opportunities and took them. That is why, when a reform administration comes in and spends a half million dollars in tryin' to find the public robberies they talked about in the campaign, they don't find them.
>
> The books are always all right. The money in the city treasury is all right. Everything is all right. All they can show is that the Tammany heads of depart-

[16] Quoted in W. C. Riordan, *Plunkitt of Tammany Hall* (New York: McClure, Phillips, 1905), pp. 4–5. This extract is taken from a new edition of the book (with introduction by Roy V. Peel) published by Alfred A. Knopf, Inc., in 1948, pp. 3–4, 6–7.

ments looked after their friends, within the law, and gave them what opportunities they could to make honest graft.

Entrenchment with Private Groups. Machines also entrench themselves by breaking up organizations which in any way threaten their bailiwick. The Hague machine's success, to a considerable degree, rested in its abilities to keep labor unions, especially the CIO, taxpayers' associations, good-government leagues, and similar groups from getting a foothold. The "toleration," if not tacit approval, of this machine by businessmen, veterans, and the local hierarchy of the Catholic Church helped to explain its long tenure. As Frasier [17] points out, the Pew-Grundy machine in Philadelphia is geared in with industry, finance, and labor, and the longevity of the machine

. . . lies largely in the fact that it was organized by and for the "best people" as well as the politicians. Many of the best people are stockholders and directors in corporations which profit from a complacent Council and the influence which the Philadelphia Republican machine can exert upon a State Legislature.

Many American municipal machines have resorted to force when other methods fail. The Crump and Biggs organizations of Tennessee as well as the Pendergast and Hague machines have a sordid record of the use of strong-arm methods in assaulting watchers and voters at the polls and "restraining" irate citizens from making speeches or exposing damaging evidence to the powers that be.

THE POLITICAL BOSS

What Is a "Boss"? The party boss has most of the characteristics which make for a successful precinct or ward leadership but possesses much else. Most bosses spring from the ranks of lesser leadership. Bosses are of divergent types, and the term does not lend itself to easy definition. Most observers will agree that Tweed, Platt, Vare, and Penrose were political bosses in the old-fashioned sense of the word, with recent counterparts in Crump of Memphis and Hague of Jersey City. Many admired and continued to vote for Mayor Fiorello H. La Guardia of New York City but referred to him as a "boss." Yet in terms of what he did in the interests of good government for his city, La Guardia obviously cannot be classed with Tweed. President Franklin D. Roosevelt was affectionately called "the boss" by some of his own appointees in Washington. Simi-

[17] Alan Frasier "Philadelphia: City of Brotherly Loot," *American Mercury,* Vol. 57 (1939), pp. 279 ff. See also Robert Allen (ed.), *Our Fair City* (New York: Vanguard Press, Inc., 1947), for an account of the political machines of many of the larger American cities in which the close connections between machine politics and business are exposed.

larly, if Roosevelt was a national boss, it is certainly in a different sense than applied to Mark Hanna.

It is also an oversimplification to say that a man is a "boss" to his enemies and a "leader" to his friends. Some have argued that those who control the party without holding a public office, such as Pendergast and the many Tammany leaders, were bosses in the real and odious sense because the electorate never chose them to exercise responsible leadership.[18] This contention breaks down when one observes some of the office-holding bosses. Ed Crump moved to Memphis from Mississippi at seventeen, became active in ward politics, and within 10 years became the Democratic boss. He became mayor, county trustee, and congressman. Regardless of which position he held, he kept complete power over every Federal, state, county, and city employee in Shelby County. Edward J. Kelly became mayor of Chicago in 1933 and retained the joint position of mayor and boss for 14 years. However, during his first 10 years his control was shared with Pat Nash, who preferred to remain behind the scenes to exercise his control. Frank Hague became mayor of Jersey City in 1917, a position which he held for 30 years. Prof. Harold Zink in one of the best available studies of municipal bosses found a considerable number held positions at one time or another in the city council and state legislature and 4 of the 20 he studied served in Congress.[19] It is true, however, that at the height of their power many held no public office and only a minority ruled from any high titular positions in their organizations.

Prototypes. Cartoonists and popular opinion notwithstanding, bosses defy typing. Some are classified as "urban," "state," or "rural" bosses, but this gives little clue to their personality traits and techniques of behavior. A large number of Irish names appear among the ranks but some of the most successful bosses were non-Irish. A great many are without extensive formal education yet one of the greatest, Boies Penrose, was a college graduate who produced some reputable treatises on government. Gen-

[18] Theodore Roosevelt saw a boss as a "man who does not gain his power by open means, and usually by corrupt means," and who operates chiefly behind closed doors with the "use of that great greed which gives in order that it may get." On the other hand, Roosevelt regarded a leader as one of high motivation who "fights openly for principles and who keeps his position of leadership by stirring the consciences and convincing the intellects of his followers, so that they may have confidence in him and will follow him." *Autobiography of Theodore Roosevelt* (New York: Charles Scribner's Sons, 1920), pp. 148–149.

[19] *City Bosses in the United States* (Durham, N.C.: Duke University Press, 1930), pp. 48–51. Charles Van Devander, *The Big Bosses*, has given an incomplete but useful description of some of the bosses and machines in operation in New York, New Jersey, Massachusetts, Pennsylvania, Alabama, Tennessee, Missouri, Illinois, and California.

erally, however, the overlords have not been academic men and their approach to politics was strictly pragmatic and opportunistic.

In considering the traits of bosses past and present no common formula of psychological attributes is observed. Zink found many city bosses were generous to the poor, loyal to their henchmen, interested in religion, and reasonably moral personally. His conclusion that there is no "typical" urban boss and that there is no "distinct species" is borne out by substantial evidence of bosses.   *Conclusion.*

It is of some value to observe two general prototypes in terms of the behavior and operation of bosses. One is the blustery, vociferous, loud-spoken type which relies heavily on showmanship and rabble rousing. Perhaps the greatest municipal boss of the nineteenth century, the swaggering, jovial Boss Tweed, offers an example of this type. Another illustration is William Hale ("Big Bill") Thompson, mayor of Chicago from 1915 to 1923 and 1927 to 1931. "Big Bill," with his cowboy hat, halter, burro, and parades with elephants along Michigan Boulevard, made an international reputation as a clown and buffoon of the first order. His bizarre campaign methods included bringing onto the stage a cage containing two rats, which he called by the names of his two opponents. He let the rats out of the cage while women shrieked and men looked on with excitement. Then "Hizzoner" would say, "You can see what will happen if you let a couple of rats loose in this city." As a rabid Anglophobe he adopted the slogan "Kick the snoot of King George out of Chicago" and proceeded to have American history textbooks which he suspected of pro-British leanings taken out of the public schools. There were thousands of Irish and Germans to whom "Big Bill's" words against the British were applaudable. He thrived on publicity, whether good or bad. When one of his opponents called him a hoodlum, he told his audiences, "Come on out, hoodlums, and bring another hoodlum with you to the polls!" While Thompson diverted the people's attention with these antics his political associates were busily engaged with spoils politics, gangster alliances, and scandals in public contracts and on the school board.

Huey Long, the "Kingfish" from Louisiana and one of the most ruthless and dangerous state bosses in the nation's history, followed much of the same blustery showmanship. However, Huey's greater cunning, thirst for power, and aspirations to become President made him a more serious threat to democracy.[20] Long's assassination was viewed with relief in both high and low places, for he was an example of *l'état, c'est moi.* One of his former henchmen, Gerald L. K. Smith, continued to use Huey's demagogic tricks to rally support for isolationist and nationalist causes.

---

[20] See Harnett T. Kane, *Louisiana Hayride* (New York: William Morrow & Company, Inc., 1941).

Sheriff Birch Biggs, the Democratic boss of a portion of eastern Tennessee, offers a striking example of a hearty, noisy, rough-and-tumble ruler. For a score of years he and his son Broughton had alternately been sheriff of Polk County. His ten-gallon hat and free-swinging revolver were not of the drugstore variety. Opponents have likened him to European dictators because of his terroristic methods. His influence was projected far beyond his county and he was an influence in the election of state-wide officers. Crump saw fit to make alliances with Biggs.[21] The sheriff-boss also gave lie to the statement that political bosses exist only in big cities; Biggs's bailiwick was overwhelmingly rural. Related to this type of boss, at least by temperament, were tough, boastful, pugilistic Richard T. Croker of Tammany Hall, from 1886 to 1902, and, to a lesser extent, Frank Hague.

Croker was succeeded by a person of an entirely different personality, Charles F. Murphy, who was boss from 1902 to 1924. Cold, silent, shrewd, he was content to remain behind the scenes and out of the public eye. The former boss of Kansas City and one of the greatest American city bosses, Tom Pendergast, offers one of the best recent illustrations of a highly successful boss who kept out of the limelight and did much of his business from a Democratic club retreat known for its secret doors. Few people ever saw the boss. He inherited and built up the political machine started by his saloonkeeper brother Jim and remained in control until 1939. "Big Tom" had an unusual knack of dealing with "enemy" Republicans.[22] In quiet and devious ways many of the smaller fry of the Grand Old Party were led around to giving covert support to the boss and his machine. Daniel P. O'Connell of Albany resembles Pendergast in many respects. The four O'Connell brothers captured control of Albany in 1922. One of them dropped out and the other two died. Dan then took over the machine. His practice is to avoid crowds and he is almost shy in meeting people. Pat Nash of Chicago also operated unobtrusively behind the lines. The business interests who constitute the real bosses of the Philadelphia machine offer other examples of leaders who avoid parades, dramatic escapades, and demagogic oratory.

However different in temperament bosses may be, they possess a flair for the game of politics and a love for it. Most of them enter politics at an early age and work up through the ranks. They must possess the ability to make decisions rapidly and with a sense of what course of action

[21] For a description of this little-known boss see Charles Van Devander, "Mailed Fist in Tennessee," *American Mercury,* Vol. 58 (1944), pp. 539–546, and Chap. 7 in the same author's *The Big Bosses.* Ed Crump, often called the last of the old-style bosses, and Biggs both died in 1954.

[22] On Pendergast and his environment see William Reddig, *Tom's Town* (Philadelphia: J. B. Lippincott Company, 1947).

will help to aid themselves and their machine. No boss who aspires to remain in his post can afford to go back on his word. He makes promises to his friends and keeps those promises. Bosses are usually motivated in part by financial gain and most of them have done well in this respect. Yet pure acquisition of wealth does not alone explain their occupation. Many are sustained by the power and prestige of their position. Bosses show remarkable ability to withstand the onslaughts of reformers and the resiliency to make a comeback if defeated.

LIFE AND DEATH OF BOSSES AND MACHINES

Sources of Strength. As we have seen, bosses and machines thrive on patronage, increased public payrolls, "honest graft," and money obtained both from the upper and the underworld. Gambling, slot and pinball machines, burlesque, and racing and betting interests of various kinds are often found ready to aid a boss who will give them protection.[23] The Kefauver Crime Investigation Committee turned up evidences in city after city of alliances between corrupt business and corrupt politics.

Legitimate business interests are frequently found supporting a boss or keeping silent. This may be due to the fact that the machine is in a position to control assessments. In the early days of the Hague regime, one newspaper sharply criticized the boss. Soon it found its property assessments drastically increased and all but one of the local theaters withdrew their advertising. After some time the criticism stopped and some of the paper's employees were put on the city payroll. The triple device of assessments, advertising boycotts, and patronage tempered much criticism of Hague. Many municipal ordinances, if enforced, would be annoying to businessmen, and some of them have been willing to tolerate boss rule if the boss will not enforce Sunday closings, building regulations, and so on. The alternative to boss rule is often presented as a "reform" regime which would be a greater anathema to business.

Control over the police force through the power to appoint and remove policemen at will was a real source of strength to many of the old-style bosses. As an elected city commissioner, Hague became director of public safety and cracked down on both policemen's and firemen's unions in the interests of cleaning up the city. After filling the police force with men loyal to himself, he proclaimed over the radio that Jersey City was the "most moralist city in America." Cars were stopped and searched, vagrants arrested, and "radicals" deported. When Hague was in a police station once, two boys were brought in for truancy. The youths told the mayor that they would prefer jail to school, and he suggested to the assistant superintendent of schools that they be given jobs. When told that

[23] On boss rule and alliances with the underworld in Chicago see Virgil W. Peterson, *Barbarians in Our Midst* (Boston: Little, Brown & Company, 1952).

this was not possible under the law, Hague replied, "Listen, here is the law; I am the law. These boys go to work." The phrase "I am the law" gave him a national reputation as the "City Führer."

Bosses gain power and remain in power by affecting alliances with various groups. Abe Ruef of San Francisco was closely allied with organized labor.[24] Hague for many years made his city an "open-shop" one and received backing of many businesses. His crusade against Norman Thomas and radicals brought support of some veterans and right-wing groups. Some, but not all, of the Catholic clergy supported certain of his causes. Almost invariably, underprivileged ethnic groups have been befriended by the boss and machine and have been willing to support its slate in primaries and elections. Many persons inveighing against boss rule overlook the fact that bosses remain in power because they have the backing of important voting and financial elements. In the final analysis, a political boss is about as strong as his machine and the machine must be able to control the primary and to deliver in the general election.

Factors Weakening Boss Rule. Many observers profess to see a replacement of the boss and the machine by the leader and the organization. City machines, it is asserted, can no longer elect whom they please, when they please, and how they please. The retirement of Kelly in Chicago, Hague in Jersey City, Jim Pendergast in Kansas City, the ejection of the McFeely brothers in Hoboken, and the serious electoral setbacks for the Pew machine in Philadelphia are but a few of the more spectacular illustrations of the wane of the old-style boss. Tammany Hall has undergone much reorganization and is trying to go "respectable."

City-manager governments and effective political action by good-government groups have resulted in a decline of the system of overlord and fiefdom. Among the other factors weakening the old-time machine are the use of voting machines, extension of the merit system and the growing literacy, prosperity and independence of the first generation of immigrants. Federal and state assumption of welfare services, the growing political consciousness of the electorate, and political activity of organized labor are having their influence. Ed Crump once said, "Most people don't know anything at all about how to vote. . . . If you put Judas Iscariot on the ballot, he'd get 1,000 votes in Shelby County." [25] This "Crumpism" is becoming less true as the voter is becoming increasingly interested in policies and concerned over the local tax base.

Many of the old-line machines and bosses are feeling the sting of law

[24] Ruef was an honor man in philosophy and ethics at the University of California. On his political career see Walton Bean, *Boss Ruef's San Francisco* (Berkeley, Calif.: University of California Press, 1952).

[25] H. B. Hinton, "Crump of Tennessee: Portrait of a Boss," *The New York Times Magazine*, Sept. 29, 1946.

enforcement and Federal indictments. Tom Pendergast was convicted of evading the Federal income tax. Enoch L. ("Nocky") Johnson, who had been boss of Atlantic City for 30 years, was sent to the Federal penitentiary in 1941 for similar reasons. About the same time, the former blacksmith James J. ("Jimmy") Hines, boss of Harlem and adjacent districts, was sent to Sing Sing through the action of young District Attorney Thomas E. Dewey, who proved that Hines was the political protector and financial beneficiary of a ring of gamblers engaged in the New York numbers racket. Where it can be used, this method is effective. Probation was granted to all three only with the understanding that they never again engage in politics. Arthur Samish, powerful liquor lobbyist, was sometimes called the "secret boss of California" because of his influence over many state legislators and with government agencies. His career was also terminated by running afoul of income-tax laws. Mayor James Curley of Boston was sent to the Federal penitentiary in 1947 for mail fraud. Upon his release, "Uncle Jim" returned to the mayoralty and his friends, meanwhile, had kept his machine intact but Curley was later defeated at the polls.

Future of Machine Politics. Textbooks today give less attention to bosses and machines and the pathology of municipal politics than they did a generation ago. Yet investigating committees continue to show unholy alliances between politics and certain interests. It appears unwise to write off the influence of bosses and machines. The number of old-type bosses is still considerable regardless of semantics. Party organizations still require leadership, as do all political associations, and the line between machine and organization is perilously thin at times. Leadership and organization are here to stay and a future is assured to both.

The future leader and his organization, however, will employ somewhat different practices and methods. Indeed, perhaps the greatest difference between the older and newer type of organization rests in methods. The organization in many cities from now on must rely upon influencing the vote. Instead of dispensing favors to religious and nationalistic minorities in return for votes, it places a member of the bloc on the ticket for a high state or local office. The Curley machine in Boston gave important positions during the campaign to representatives of all racial groups.[26] The organization of today makes promises to Negroes, labor, and other blocs which it must live up to if it gains control of the government. Legislation is being substituted for the free beer party. Rulers are taking a greater interest in policies.

[26] This had the added value of tempering racial appeals. See J. S. Bruner and S. J. Korchin, "The Boss and the Vote: Case Study in City Politics," *Public Opinion Quarterly,* Vol. 10 (1946), pp. 1–23.

Party organizations are more and more identifying themselves with respectable as contrasted with underworld elements. Prominent persons are given a place in the organization, and in some instances persons with specialized education are brought into the ranks either as advisers, research men, or regular party workers. Mayor Martin Kennelly of Chicago, who took over the reins from Kelly, was a prominent businessman who brought the backing of the better elements in the city to his office.

Some of the smoothest operating state organizations today are controlled by top officeholders who operate in the open and assume responsibility for decisions and patronage. Examples are afforded by Governor Dewey of New York and Senator Byrd of Virginia. Their influence extends even down into urban machines, which were formerly impervious to the state organization. The contrast in method of operation between these leaders and Platt and Penrose is considerable.

Whether contemporary organization leaders are more scrupulous may be debated, but they are certainly more cautious and careful. The use of alliances with the entrenched respectability, interest in public policy and legislation, publicity, and utilization of representatives from voting blocs in the organization are not new but rather are receiving increased emphasis. The use of publicity and mass communication by political leaders is also bringing about changes in the older form of operation.

Hope for the abolition of corrupt leadership rests in the simplification of governmental machinery, the extension of jobs according to merit principles, and widespread civic consciousness. In the final analysis much rests with honest, dynamic leaders who make of public office a public trust. Van Devander has pointed out that in California, for example, advertising and propaganda have supplemented bribery as a means of political control, and vote stealing and fraudulent counting are extremely rare.[27]

SELECTED REFERENCES

The general works cited at the conclusion of the preceding chapter devote considerable space to political bosses and machines. James Bryce, *American Commonwealth* (1922–1923), and Ostrogorski, *Democracy and the Party System in the United States* (1910), provide a valuable insight into these matters, as does Chap. IX in Robert C. Brooks, *Political Parties and Electoral Problems* (1933). See also the extensive bibliography in Brooks, pp. 248–251. Various works of Lincoln Steffens relate the abuses of machine rule in many cities and states; see particularly his *Autobiography* (1931) and *The Shame of the Cities* (1904).

Literature on political bosses and machines may be found in profusion. Among the better general works are Harold Zink, *City Bosses in the United States* (1930); Charles Van Devander, *The Big Bosses* (1944); H. F. Gosnell, *Machine Politics: Chicago Model* (1937); G. M. Reynolds, *Machine Politics in New Orleans, 1897–1926* (1936);

[27] *Op. cit.*, Chap. 12.

D. H. Kurtzman, *Controlling Votes in Philadelphia* (1935); Frank R. Kent, *The Great Game of Politics* (1923); M. R. Werner, *Tammany Hall* (1928); Lloyd Wandt and Herman Kogan, *Lords of the Levee* (1943); J. T. Salter, *Boss Rule* (1935); Charles E. Merriam, *Chicago: A More Intimate View of Urban Politics* (1929); Allen A. Michie and Frank Rhylick, *Dixie Demagogues* (1939); S. P. Orth, *The Boss and the Machine* (1919).

Lengthier accounts of particular bosses include W. L. Riordan, *Plunkitt of Tammany Hall* (1905); H. F. Gosnell, *Boss Platt and His New York Machine* (1924); Webster Smith (pseud.), *The Kingfish: Huey P. Long* (1938), and on the same subject, H. T. Kane, *Louisiana Hayride* (1941); on Frank Hague, Dayton D. McKean, *The Boss* (1940); S. S. McKay, *W. Lee O'Daniel and Texas Politics* (1944); Denis Tilden Lynch, *Boss Tweed* (1927); Alfred Henry Lewis, *Richard Croker* (1901); Robert Douglas Bowden, *Boies Penrose: Symbol of an Era* (1937); Robert Vale and Walter Davenport, *Power and Glory: The Life of Boies Penrose* (1931); M. M. Milligan, *Missouri Waltz: The Inside Story of the Pendergast Machine by the Man Who Smashed It* (1948).

Bosses seldom write autobiographies but Thomas C. Platt and Edward J. Flynn have obliged in *Autobiography of Thomas Collier Platt* (1910) and *You're the Boss* (1947). The latter merits reading by every student of machine politics as one of the most candid accounts of urban organization.

Pol. is anyone who runs for or who holds elected public office or pol. party office or who is actively associated with candidates, elected public officials pol. parties or independent orgn. in an effort to influence the outcome of elections

CHAPTER 16

Political Leadership

Political science without biography is a form of taxidermy.
—HAROLD LASSWELL

Government, political parties, and machines are operated by men of varying abilities, standards, and ethics. They have ample opportunities to operate these institutions for good or for evil. Popular assumption has it that those who conduct the government to serve their own ends are "politicians"; those who selflessly promote the common good are regarded as "statesmen." Dictionaries customarily give two definitions to the word "politician" as: (1) "one who seeks to subserve the interests of a political party merely; especially one who uses politics for private advantage, a political schemer," (2) "one skilled in political science or administration, a statesman." Pragmatists sometimes define a statesman as a "dead politician." No useful purpose is served here in attempting to argue the meaning of the term. The student of political science is better served if he considers a politician as a technician in the art of governing and politics as a respectable calling. Accordingly, there are honest and dishonest politicians, able and incompetent politicians, much as there are both highly skilled and honest doctors and those who are quacks.

Governmental functions are roughly divided into "politics" and "administration." The former is concerned with the determination of public policies, the management of public opinion, and the whole process incident to this. Administration is the execution of policy and theoretically does not begin until after a policy has been defined. Both require technicians and specialists. The border line between politics and administration is constantly shifting. Some speak of the person engaged in the former as a "politician" and the latter as an "administrator." Yet certainly the most successful governors and Presidents are both. To the campaign chairman, the management of an election is more of an administrative than a policy task. All of this merely underlines the difficulty of securing common agreement on the concept of a politician. Our use of the term implies no opprobrium. We are concerned with the broader question of leadership in the field both of policy and of administration, keeping in mind, however, that the successful bureaucrat or administrator is generally required to possess certain qualifications, expert knowledge, and abilities quite different from those who excel in the art of vote getting and in the leadership of public opinion. Both functions must be performed well; many public men have shown competence both on the floor of·Congress and also as directors of administrative agencies. Others have best advanced their careers by remaining either in the field of administration or in legislative positions.

American literature is rich in political biography. Extensive reading of the lives of great political leaders will repay those who desire an intimate view of the great game of politics. To understand better the government and politics, which supply him with services from the cradle to the grave, the citizen needs to study as well the leaders of his own county, district, and section. Would-be political leaders have much to learn from observing the success or failure of politicians in their own precinct, on their campus, or in their lodge. What constitutes effective leadership in Seattle does not invariably apply in New Orleans or in Denver. What works on the east side may not work on the west side. The techniques of control must and do vary. This is not to conclude, however, that there is a complete absence of pattern or formula for political behavior. J. T. Salter in his portraits of the character of Philadelphia ward politicians found common denominators which have wide applicability in other municipalities.[1] Prof. W. B. Munro in a study of political leaders found some similarity of personality traits but, unlike Salter, found no great correlation between local bosses and the dominant nationality groups.[2] A reading of Zink's and Van Devander's studies of urban political bosses, as noted in the preceding chapter, shows certain common traits among powerful leaders.[3] To understand a political situation the personality and methods of the leader must also be understood and a study made of the environment and its influence on the leader.

Can the traits for successful leadership in politics be set down as a formula or an irreducible minimum? Would the qualifications which made an individual a great leader in business, science, or medicine guarantee a successful career in politics? Should the recognized absence of some of these qualities discourage an individual from pursuing a political career? Studies in the psychology of leadership have, as yet, failed to give categorical answers to these questions. Lincoln, Cleveland, and the two Roosevelts came from diverse backgrounds and represented some sharp contrasts in temperament, yet all achieved success in state and national politics. Some outstanding generals failed to become great

[1] See *Boss Rule* (New York: McGraw-Hill Book Company, Inc., 1935).

[2] See *Personality in Politics* (New York: The Macmillan Company, 1924).

[3] Harold Zink, *City Bosses in the United States* (Durham, N.C.: Duke University Press, 1930); Charles Van Devander, *The Big Bosses* (New York: Howell, Soskin, Publishers, Inc., 1944).

presidents. Many business leaders have had an unsatisfactory political career. Herbert Hoover had a distinguished record as Secretary of Commerce and as a businessman but failed to become a popular party leader.

PRESIDENTIAL LEADERS

The presidency of the United States demands the highest type of leadership in the nation, if not in the world. The stature of the office requires almost a superman to carry out effectively its functions. Over a period of years the President has assumed many extralegal duties and has seen his constitutional and legal obligations expanded. The President is leader of his party, with all that this connotes. At the same time he is the chief administrator and the chief legislator. As party leader he must spend some time in patronage matters, and patronage may embarrass him when, as an administrator, he wishes to extend the merit system and reorganize and consolidate the myriad of bureaus and boards. As the chief legislator, both the nation and Congress look to the President for proposals to promote the public welfare. His reelection usually depends on his record of handling public issues. As a representative of the nation, he is called upon to meet with the heads of foreign governments, formulate foreign policy, and act as Commander in Chief of the Armed Forces.

Presidential Types. Some efforts have been made to type our Presidents. Jackson, Wilson, and the two Roosevelts were vigorous and dynamic leaders who mastered the techniques of mobilizing public opinion and their party for the purpose of crusading for causes and fighting special privilege. They thought in terms of the "Square Deal," the "New Deal," and the "New Freedom" for the masses of the people.[4] Opposite in temperament and action were Buchanan, Taft, and Coolidge, who made no great effort to give strong and determined popular leadership. Lincoln is placed between these two groups. Though not outstanding as an aggressive leader before he was inaugurated, Lincoln rose to the crisis confronting him and became a statesman of distinction. Many others, once in the White House, have risen to unexpected heights because the office required them to use latent powers of leadership.

A number of our Presidents were known as a "politician's politician," including Van Buren, Garfield (and his successor, Arthur), Harding, and Truman. What is actually required to be a politician's politician is not too clear. Generally this has meant wide experience in organization politics and perhaps an overdeveloped sense of party regularity and loyalty. Surely the term implies close proximity to the organization leaders

[4] For a brief but useful summary of the "great" presidential leaders see Henry Steele Commager, "What Makes for Presidential Greatness?" *The New York Times Magazine,* July 22, 1945.

and often easy social relationships with them. Many of these Presidents lacked the ability to lead public opinion. As applied to the five Presidents mentioned it does not imply personal dishonesty but respect for observance of the rules of the game.

Regardless of temperament, successful Presidents do not deviate too far from the mood and temper of the country. Theodore Roosevelt at the end of his second term said that the country was tired of crusading and needed a quiet and staid person who would consolidate the gains of his administration and give the country a "rest." Harding and Coolidge fairly typified the urge for normalcy, whereas Hoover, as the "engineer," personified at the time of his election the emphasis on prosperity, science, and technical management. In 1952 the nation felt the need for order, stability, and the bringing to an end of the Korean War. It turned to a popular military figure and overlooked his lack of experience in elective public office. At the end of his first year in office, Eisenhower retained a high popularity primarily because he accomplished these things.

Political experience is considered a prerequisite to nomination for the presidency, Willkie and Eisenhower being conspicuous exceptions. The office of governor offers one of the best steppingstones to the White House. Of the last 12 Presidents, half of them came from this office (Cleveland, McKinley, the two Roosevelts, Wilson, and Coolidge), while several defeated presidential nominees (Hughes, Cox, La Follette, Smith, Landon, Dewey, and Stevenson) were also governors. Of the remaining Presidents, Harrison, Harding, and Truman were senators; Taft and Hoover Cabinet officers, and Eisenhower a professional military man. Most Presidents are in their fifties at the time of their inauguration and over half were lawyers.

Attributes and Methods. Our more successful Presidents have possessed political skill, tact, and sagacity. Lincoln as the first person elected by a new party was beset with a torn nation. An important element in his success was his use of patronage and the selection of his Cabinet. In a careful study of Lincoln's astuteness in filling positions, H. J. Carman and R. H. Luthin conclude: [5]

His wise use of patronage in holding the party together was a necessary antecedent to the formulation of any statesmanlike policy concerning the nation; . . . as a politician, he utilized the patronage in holding together diverse conflicting factions in common purposes—the preservation of the Union, the success of his administration, and the rewarding of the faithful—is only to enhance the greatness of Lincoln . . . Had he not wielded the patronage so skillfully— something that his predecessor James Buchanan and his successor Andrew Johnson did not do—probably his administration would not have been as successful.

[5] *Lincoln and the Patronage* (New York: Columbia University Press, 1943), p. 336.

Oratorical ability, if not showmanship, is an important trait. Lincoln, the two Roosevelts, and Wilson were masters of phraseology. Franklin Roosevelt had the use of the radio and made the most of it. Gifted with a remarkable voice and simplicity of expression, he used the microphone for "fireside chats" to "let the citizen in on his government" and to explain the great crises facing the nation. Lincoln by some standards was not a great orator. Yet he possessed an extraordinary fund of anecdotes and the ability to mix wisdom, humor, and nonsense in his speeches. His anecdotes usually illustrated an important point and his logic and phrases during the Lincoln-Douglas debates made him into a national figure. Wilson prior to his political career was one of the most popular after-dinner speakers in the East.

Theodore Roosevelt was a dramatist who portrayed the strenuous life. He invited boxers and wrestlers to the White House, rode horses, climbed mountains, and hunted lions in Africa. His statement "Damn the law, I want the canal built!" endeared him to millions who were sensing the growing emergence of the United States as a world power. He, like many other Presidents, possessed a personal magnetism and had the faculty of giving the impression that he liked the person to whom he was talking.

Successful Presidents have possessed an instinct for what the people were thinking, and a consciousness of social direction. "T.R.'s" statement of his leadership has become a classic: "I really did not 'divine' how the people were going to think; I simply made up my mind what they ought to think, and then did my best to get them to think it." Andrew Jackson typified the hatred of the masses for "the money monopolists of the East" in his assault on the Bank of the United States. Lincoln's phrases on the need for national unity, Wilson's "New Freedom," Roosevelt's "New Deal" and his statement "The only thing we have to fear is fear itself" reflected answers to anxieties and desires. With social insight, these men became interpreters of social movements and had a perception of possible courses of action. Franklin Roosevelt had an unusually keen sense of timing and some facility for forecasting the actions and impulses of the people.

Wilson and Theodore Roosevelt were adept at balancing interests and clinging to the middle of the road while at the same time pushing through progressive legislation. The stronger Presidents have shown a similar adroitness in holding together the dissident elements of their party. Great resourcefulness and adaptability to the times and environment are important attributes. Political leadership requires diplomacy in handling men and ideas. One of the great tasks of democracy is the accommodation of conflicting social classes and of sectionalism. Compromise is the essence of democratic leadership.

Our statesmen-presidents have compromised over methods but, when the occasion called for it, they displayed a rare courage. Though not a great party leader, Cleveland enjoyed vast prestige because of his indomitable courage to do what he believed right. He dared the wrath of many special interests when as mayor of Buffalo, governor of New York, and President he wielded the veto power to protect the treasury and to further his concept that a "public office is a public trust." Harry Truman had many detractors and had less success in keeping his party together than his predecessor but his courage was widely applauded.

Harold Gosnell [6] has summarized the qualities which enabled Franklin Roosevelt to get ahead in politics:

He had charm, optimism, confidence, generosity, faith, a vibrant voice, a handsome physique, a good memory, courage, a fine sense of humor, an excellent digestion, freedom from worry, a great gift for words, calmness, poise, and patience. He liked to use his talents to win the attention and affection of others. If one does not enjoy speaking, late and irregular hours, long trips, meeting strangers, riding on trains, planes, and ships, holding innumerable conferences, making difficult decisions, answering mountains of letters, writing speeches and public papers, losing one's privacy, then one should keep away from politics.

Not all successful Presidents possessed the same qualities to the same degree, but they possessed most of them.

STATE AND CONGRESSIONAL LEADERS

Congressmen, governors, mayors, and state and local executives, like Presidents, are of innumerable prototypes. No sure-fire formula exists for guaranteeing nomination, election, and success in a public elective office any more than there is a comparable key to success in business or the professions. Some prerequisites and attributes, however, are found helpful if not indispensable to a career in American politics.

Native Sons. The "native son" factor in local politics is strong. In his study of American governors from 1930 to 1940, Professor Perkins found that out of the 178 who held office, 116 were born in the state that they governed.[7] As might be expected, governors are a product of their environments and conform reasonably well to the customs and social complexion of their states. The West and South have seen many governors who have risen to office by means of breezy, colorful campaign techniques such as "Ma" Ferguson and Lee ("Pappy") O'Daniel of Texas and "Alfalfa Bill" Murray of Oklahoma. A Scandinavian name has long

[6] *Champion Campaigner: Franklin D. Roosevelt* (New York: The Macmillan Company, 1952), p. 220.

[7] John A. Perkins, "American Governors, 1930 to 1940," *National Municipal Review*, Vol. 29 (1940), pp. 178–184.

been considered an asset, if not a necessity, for those seeking the governorship in Minnesota. The melting-pot character of New York made it possible for three men of widely differing backgrounds and religions to become the state executive. Alfred E. Smith, an Irish Catholic, literally rose from the "sidewalks of New York." Franklin D. Roosevelt was of wealthy Dutch and Protestant parentage, while Herbert H. Lehman, the son of a German Jew, was a businessman (textiles and banking) before entering the public service. Governor Wilbur L. Cross, who called himself a "Connecticut Yankee," campaigned in the best personal-contact and town-meeting tradition. The overwhelming majority of governors in New England have been native-born.

Experience and Occupational Status. Few can hope to become governors without having held one or more public offices first. Of the governors in the decade studied, 95 per cent had held two and three offices before becoming state executives.[8] Many served as mayors, legislators, or judges, thereby gaining valuable administrative as well as policy-determining experience. At the same time, they were party regulars or had rendered yeomen's service to the party. Wilbur Cross of Connecticut and Woodrow Wilson of New Jersey offer exceptions to the rule of becoming successful governors without previous political experience.

The position of governor calls for high qualities of leadership. As the leader of his party, he must keep dissident elements together. Since many state offices are elective, he is not in a position to appoint his "cabinet." The rural-urban conflict, as in Pennsylvania, Ohio, Michigan, and Illinois, requires careful balancing. Local interests, headed by county and city party leaders, must be placated, especially in matters of patronage. Still other governors have had to deal with a powerful city boss, either because of an election debt to the boss, or because the latter controlled the state legislature or various state administrative agencies. In such cases, the boss, not the governor, is the real leader of the party. Gubernatorial aspirants also recognize the value of civic and party support. In keeping with general political tradition, governors and lesser officeholders are usually "joiners," members of a church, and attend countless dinners, conventions, and social affairs. No opportunities to maintain personal contact with the people are overlooked.

Governors and national legislators generally come from the more privileged classes and many are successful business executives, although law represents the most popular occupation.[9] In the state legislatures, lawyers and farmers predominate. However, a proportionately larger number

---

[8] *Ibid.*, pp. 182–183.

[9] On the background of national lawmakers see Madge M. McKinney, "The Personnel of the Seventy-seventh Congress," *The American Political Science Review*, Vol. 26 (1942), pp. 74–75.

of farmers are found in the state bodies than in Congress. Many one-time teachers are in Congress, whereas they are few in number in state assemblies. Senator Josh Lee of Oklahoma asserted that his former students were responsible for his election. Very few of the nation's lawmakers are affiliated with trade-unions. This is surprising in terms of the strength of organized labor. However, most congressmen are professed friends of labor, and the record of labor legislation and of farm measures in recent years shows that influence in Congress cannot be measured in terms of the number of one's own group elected to that body.

Service to Constituents. An examination of the activities of congressmen shows that, except during campaigns, few have developed systematic programs either for their district or the nation. Representative Sol Bloom of New York City, who held office for a quarter of a century and who was chairman of the House Foreign Affairs Committee during the crucial years from 1939 to 1947, was typical of many solons.[10] In spite of his position he made little effort to discuss public issues with the voters of his district. His continued reelection was due in a large measure to personal services for constituents. He maintained an office just off Times Square to handle requests for those who were unable to come to Washington. To 1942, his office had handled 300,000 cases, including the securing of jobs, expediting the issuance of passports and visas, immigration service, and information about customs and laws. The politics of those who sought help was not asked, and he had the reputation of serving all who applied.

Policies Also Important. Undoubtedly many legislators believe that the key to leadership—and reelection—lies in performing well the various "errand-boy" functions and that securing a new post office for one's district is regarded as more important than a vote on a tax bill or other measures. However true this may be, a legislator's voting record is becoming more and more important. Labor unions, the League of Women Voters, and various other organizations now print and distribute copies of the voting records of representatives and senators for public scrutiny. Roll-call records, committee work, and other functions are becoming known, making it less easy for legislators to remain in office purely on a record of servicing constituents. At the same time, for example, that Mr. Bloom was rendering service to his district, he was making an impressive record in voting for far-reaching social legislation and in working with his committee to bring American foreign policy in line with the nation's commitments.

While a great many, if not a majority, of national and local executives

[10] Two volumes containing sketches of some 45 governors and other state and national politicians are those edited by J. T. Salter and published by The University of North Carolina Press, *The American Politician* (1936) and *Public Men* (1946).

owe their reelection to services to constituents, there are many whose identification with causes pleasing to their voters played a prominent part in their tenure in office. Senator Joseph O'Mahoney with his attack on corporate monopoly, Hamilton Fish, the crusading isolationist, and the battlers for liberalism exemplified in Maury Maverick, Claude Pepper, Jerry Voorhis,[11] and Robert Wagner are a few of those drawing great voting strength from their advocacy of policies. Senators Paul Douglas, Robert A. Taft, and Arthur Vandenberg, to mention but a few, championed such widely varying causes as ethics in government, labor union regulation, and bipartisan foreign policy respectively. Each made many enemies and many friends but all achieved national reputations because of the tenacity with which they pursued their interest. Governor Earl Warren made a huge success of the politics of nonpartisanship while Governor Thomas E. Dewey made a name for himself as an administrator and vigorous party leader.

Political leaders generally find they cannot go too far beyond the ideas and opinions of their constituents and they accordingly dramatize the issues of the moment. But the politicians to whom posterity has given recognition were not content with mirroring opinion. Rather they proceeded on the assumption that political leadership is an educational job as well. As Lincoln once remarked of Douglas' followers, "It's my business to make some of the blind followers see." One prominent state legislator publishes a pamphlet at the end of each session telling of the major legislation enacted and the reasons for his vote. This analysis, sent to thousands in his district, also points out what the legislature failed to accomplish and what is unfinished. The same document solicits voters' opinions on the record. Though highly exceptional, the practice has resulted in enhancing his position in the community, not to mention his repeated reelection.

INDEPENDENTS IN POLITICS

Compromise in Politics. The great majority of political leaders know when and how to compromise. Indeed, the art of compromise and the science of alternatives are regarded as the essence of politics. In his speech on conciliation, Edmund Burke said, "All government, indeed every human benefit and enjoyment, every virtue, and every prudent act is founded on compromise and barter." Prof. T. V. Smith, once a United States representative, said of the politician that "the zigzag path of his compromises in the past we call civilization." Representative Donald O'Toole, on the other hand, has remarked, "Avoid compromise because compromise in politics is death." Norman Thomas and other minority-

[11] See Voorhis, *Confessions of a Congressman* (New York: Doubleday & Company, Inc., 1947).

party leaders have usually taken the position that they would rather be right than be President. Mr. Thomas could undoubtedly have had a successful political career if he had compromised and accepted a major-party label, but he refused to resort to such expediency and the Socialist party itself refuses to join with a majority party, even in municipal elections, to support good-government candidates.

Many reformers and others who say "I don't want my boy to be a politician" proceed on the assumption that opportunism and expediency are *ipso facto* bad and hypocritical. Reformers, moreover, often have unhappy experiences and commit political suicide through an unwillingness to compromise. One Texas lawmaker after his retirement from Congress remarked, "When I stopped running for office I quit a'lying to the people." Thus it is presumed that prevarication, acceptance of machine dictation, and the compromise of convictions and principles are essential for political achievement. These assumptions are based partly upon misunderstanding and partly upon lack of knowledge of when and over what to compromise. No hard and fast rules exist but honesty and the general welfare have not been compromised by those who were later to be called statesmen. As T. V. Smith phrased it: "A man is not a good man who will compromise the core of himself—that is, the final principles by which he lives. But a man is not a good citizen who does not meet other citizens halfway." [12]

The degree to which one must acquiesce in the interests and dictates of the party organization will remain a problem for years to come. When should one abandon the practice of "boring from within" his party and attempt independent political action? Generally the greatest chance of election and reelection resides in having the support of a major party organization. When the organization imposes its will to the extent of dictating how one should vote and the methods to be used, a problem of integrity arises if the organization views are out of harmony with one's better judgment. After much soul searching a number of persons have resorted to independent political action. The pages of history are full of failures of those who have attempted this path. Martin Van Buren, Millard Fillmore, Theodore Roosevelt, Robert La Follette, Sr., and Henry Wallace went down to defeat for the presidency when they bolted a major party and headed a third-party ticket.

Successful Independents. A glance at congressional membership over the years reveals that few independents get into Congress. Representative Vito Marcantonio for many years forged a powerful personal machine capable of drawing a sizable bloc of Republican and Democratic votes. On occasions he captured simultaneously Republican, Democratic, and American Labor party primaries. His strength rested in entrenching him-

[12] *The Legislative Way of Life* (Chicago: University of Chicago Press, 1940), pp. 77–78.

self with racial, religious, and nationalistic minorities in his New York City constituency.

The careers of Senators Robert La Follette, Jr. of Wisconsin, George Norris of Nebraska, and Wayne Morse of Oregon have served as an inspiration to independents. La Follette and Norris were able to beat both parties in attempts for reelection. Morse's test will not be made until 1956. Although all these men achieved national reputations as independents, it is significant that none of them were first elected under that label. All began their career as Republicans but became associated with the politics of insurgency and later left the party. All became champions of a militant liberalism and social legislation. Prof. Claudius Johnson summarized the Norris riddle in three words, "honesty, courage, and independence." [13] Norris' name is closely associated with the unicameral legislature of Nebraska, the abolition of the Lame Duck Session in Congress, and the resolution in the House of Representatives which resulted in shearing the Speaker of the House of important powers. La Follette was coauthor of the Congressional Reorganization Act and won acclaim for his investigating activities. His devotion to putting through the former kept him from keeping his political fences mended in 1946 and his attempt to get nominated as a Republican failed, thus terminating a distinguished career.

Several persons have been successful in being reelected as mayors on independent or third-party tickets. Fiorello La Guardia was notably successful in this respect. He served in Congress, then as mayor of New York City for 12 years. During his political life, which consisted of running for office 14 times, the mayor ran under nine different party labels and under as many as four in a single election. He was correctly referred to as a "man without a party" and a "one-man party."

Several elements contributed to his comparatively long tenure as a municipal executive. For one thing, he made good government good politics. After suffering years of corrupt rule, the voters found in La Guardia a person of unimpeachable honesty who rehabilitated the municipal departments. He crusaded against gamblers and racketeers, crying out, "Tinhorns, thieves, dirty chiselers, I'll run 'em outa town"— and he did! Though much of a boss himself, the mayor denounced over the radio, by name, local political bosses and machines. While he beat Tammany at the polls, he never succeeded in destroying it.

La Guardia had no organization support, but the trade-unions, underprivileged, civic associations, and the huge Italian and Jewish populations rallied behind him on election day. While political bosses use machines

---

[13] See J. T. Salter, *The American Politician* (Chapel Hill, N.C.: The University of North Carolina Press, 1936), p. 77. This volume and its companion *Public Men* (1946) provide some excellent sketches of American political leaders.

to provide "bread and circuses," the mayor had the city dispense the "bread" through the orderly channels of municipal departments, while he himself provided the "circuses." The "Little Flower" was one of the most colorful politicians and showmen of the twentieth century. He was always in the thick of battle and ready to speak at any time and in any place on almost any subject. In a fireman's hat he chased fires all over the city, barking orders to the firemen. He led bands (his father was a bandmaster) in Central Park, had a fist fight on the steps of the City Hall, and "socked" a heckler in Detroit. Equally illustrative of his showmanship, the impeccable "Little Flower" pulled lamb chops from his pocket to show how little food value one could get for 30 cents.

Of La Guardia it may be said that he brought reform leadership to his city but that he did not always resort to reform methods to do so. He fought hard and ruthlessly for good causes. Where many reformers would refuse to use these methods even if they lost the cause, La Guardia used them and saved the cause.

It may be repeated again that those who have made a political career as independents nonetheless almost invariably started with the help of a political party. Reelection came as a result of association with good government or popular policies and help from nonparty groups. The road of an independent is a long and hard one. Party label is an almost indispensable need for a governor, congressman, or other elective official where the partisan ballot is used.

NONPARTISAN LEADERS

There are many opportunities for political leadership outside the pale of party politics. In earlier chapters mention was made of persons who have made a career in leading political interest groups. Writers often overlook the fact that thousands of persons today run for and are elected to public nonpartisan offices and many have made a career in such offices. Minnesota and Nebraska select their state legislators on a ballot without party designations. Nearly all the municipalities in the Far West and a great many elsewhere elect their city councils on a nonpartisan ballot. A great many mayors, boards of education, judicial, county, and other local offices are similarly elected. In fact, nearly one-half of the nation's voters are called upon to make some of their electoral choices from a nonpartisan ballot.[14]

Nonpartisan elections and politicians have not received the study they

---

[14] R. S. Childs says that nonpartisan elections are "in use in 61 per cent of American cities and, in Southern one-party states, the Democratic primaries provide a similar condition in many more." See "500 Non-political Elections," *National Municipal Review*, Vol. 38 (1949), pp. 278–282. Political parties are fighting, with some success, a rearguard battle to preserve partisanship in the counties.

merit. Does a successful career in nonpartisan politics require different attributes than for a partisan office? Are campaign techniques different? What is the relationship between the party organization and so-called "nonpartisan candidates"? These and many other questions are matters of importance for continued study.

Upon the basis of observations of the Minnesota and Nebraska legislatures and of the city councils of Minneapolis and Detroit, Charles Adrian advanced several interesting hypotheses about nonpartisan elections and officeholders.[15] It was found, for example, that incumbents have a real advantage in reelection, with the result that the council or legislature is composed of a relatively higher percentage of experienced members and making for conservatism. The voter becomes familiar with the names of incumbents and, in the absence of party labels and overriding campaign issues, casts his ballot for the incumbent. Newspapers are conservative and the publicity given to conservative candidates is helpful to them. A study of Seattle's city councilmen bears out the same conclusion.[16] In that city many persons have served for years and years on the council and have made a career of it. The average served by 1953 council members was 13 years. Councilmen have not particularly aspired to elective partisan offices.

This gives additional evidence for Adrian's finding that most successful nonpartisan politicians do not move up into higher partisan ranks. Segregation of political leaders according to either partisan or nonpartisan is fairly customary. Nonpartisan elections, moreover, have restricted the channels of recruitment for both partisan and nonpartisan, that is, candidates for offices are recruited from the respective party or nonparty ranks. On the other hand, there is considerable evidence that nonpartisan offices have attracted persons into public life "who would never become candidates under the traditional method since they would be unwilling to become entangled in the ordinary processes of party politics." Partisan considerations have entered into Seattle mayoralty races much more than in councilmanic contests.

Nonpartisan candidates do not have the support of party organization and finances, except covertly. They are in competition with party candidates for funds and many find it difficult to secure money. The reverse may also be true that there are people who are willing to donate to a nonpartisan candidate but would refuse to support a partisan campaign. It is most important for a nonpartisan leader to build a name for himself

[15] "Some General Characteristics of Nonpartisan Elections," *The American Political Science Review*, Vol. 46 (1952), pp. 766–776; and "The Origin of Minnesota's Nonpartisan Legislature," *Minnesota History*, Vol. 33 (1952), pp. 155–163.

[16] Gordon McKibben, *Nonpartisan Politics: A Case Study of Seattle* (M.A. thesis, University of Washington, 1954).

in community groups and with municipal and good-government leagues. These groups usually render public endorsements and may provide a platform and audience for the candidate. In many cities such leaders have the active support of a group which plays about the same role as a party organization, though usually without a definite label. The parties themselves occasionally make public endorsements, but generally their support is not so direct or apparent. The candidate must build up his own name and organization and bring himself to the attention of the voters; newspaper support is often crucial.

Because voting "for the man" is basic in a nonpartisan election, Adrian believes there is a tendency for candidates to avoid issues and to rely on name and personality. In Seattle's experience it would be hard to prove this one way or another. In partisan campaigns for state legislative and local offices there is also a notorious avoidance of taking a firm stand on issues. It may be noted again that there are many exceptions to these contentions about the nature of nonpartisan leaders. As such, nonpartisan elections afford a challenging area of research and a challenge to those seeking a political career. The opportunities for leadership in towns, villages, and the smaller cities are improving. As a general practice, experience in lesser political offices is a practical prerequisite to being elevated to municipal executive. There are increasing opportunities through the channel of nonpartisanship for local political leadership.[17]

THE POLITICIAN

Motivations. Psychology is useful to the student of government in helping to explain how leaders are able to obtain favorable reactions from their constituents. It is also helpful in explaining leadership itself in terms of the motivation of the leader. The seeking of political positions is explained in general terms of compensations and satisfactions. It is much less easy to reduce this to specifics. Several studies have been made on the relationship between bodily structure and personality, motivations, and frustrations, and so on. By use of psychological methods and personal interviews and observations, Harold Lasswell has rendered a useful, though provocative, contribution to the analysis of political leadership.[18] He advanced the general theory of the political man in terms of private motives, their displacement onto public objects, and their rationalization in terms of public interests. He found that political agitators as a class

[17] For those interested in "nonpolitical" elections and politics an inspiring account has been prepared by Richard S. Childs, *Civic Victories: The Story of an Unfinished Revolution* (New York: Harper & Brothers, 1952). The *National Municipal Review* is a storehouse of articles on these subjects.

[18] *Psychopathology and Politics* (Chicago: University of Chicago Press, 1930); and *Power and Personality* (New York: W. W. Norton & Company, Inc., 1948).

are strongly narcissistic, that is, given to fixation to oneself or self-adoration. Administrators differ from agitators "by the displacement of their effects upon less remote and abstract objects." Their lack of interest in abstractions is due mainly to the lack of need for using abstractions as a diversion for their own emotional problems. The agitator and orator, often without intimate friendship, satisfy this need by receiving approbation and applause from crowds. Lasswell later developed a typology based upon three rage types—uninhibited, partially inhibited, and inhibited.

The inducements and motivations for precinct, ward, and other leadership posts in a political party have received considerable attention. Gosnell and Forthal in their studies of precinct captains in Chicago [19] found hope of obtaining concrete economic reward the most common motive for entering politics. The economic reasons included keeping their own and their friends' tax assessments down, enhancing business contacts, selling goods or services to government agencies, securing immunity from punishment for violations of the law, and obtaining patronage. In many other areas economic rewards appear much less important. Persons seek party positions because they like the prestige and social contacts which go with the job. There is a sense of pride which the politician may feel in being important in people's lives. The motivations and drives which lead persons to seek party or public offices are highly varied and not easily identifiable but they remain a fascinating problem for analysis and speculation.

Functions. From this survey of party organization and leadership, the role of public men should become fairly obvious. The politicians keep the government running. As Alan Valentine has phrased it, "Politicians are the domestic servants who do the nation's political housekeeping. They perform the daily chores which the average citizen ignores and does not even understand." [20] Through influencing nominations and elections they influence and furnish the personnel of government.

In one degree or another public men dramatize, formulate, and give expression to public aspirations and policies. The job is not only one of bringing forth policies, it is also a matter of interpretation of policies and programs to constituents. Educators and former legislators T. V. Smith, Jerry Voorhis, George Outland, Howard McMurray, and many others have noted the educational aspects of political leadership as one of the most important. McMurray once commented, "I operate politically on the basic assumption that political leadership is essentially an educa-

[19] See H. F. Gosnell, *Machine Politics: Chicago Model* (Chicago: University of Chicago Press, 1937); Sonya Forthal, *Cogwheels of Democracy: A Study of the Precinct Captain* (New York: William-Frederick Press, 1946).

[20] "The Politician as Housekeeper for the Nation," *Saturday Review of Literature,* Apr. 12, 1947, p. 21.

tional job and that people are educable." Reformers probably emphasize policies and education more than their less crusading colleagues but all elective officeholders try to make their constituents "see."

The championship of policies has not obscured, for the public man, his prime obligation as a conciliator, mediator, and compromiser of group conflicts and interests. This is the aspect which makes politics for him "the art of the possible," the building of solutions through compromise and barter. This requires not only imagination, patience, and understanding but the ability to work with fellow politicians. Floyd M. Riddick,[21] for example, has noted that the successful qualities of a floor leader in Congress

. . . are not necessarily great powers of intellect, but bargaining power, cool-headedness, good temper, firm will, and the ability to appreciate services rendered by another man. A leader must soon learn that Representatives enjoy recognition. . . . He must be a good organizer of men, and above all, know how to work with them. These qualities may make a very successful leader even though the person lacks the attributes of a forceful and persuasive public speaker.

Finally, the American politician, probably more than his foreign brother, is expected to render personal services to his people. Most of a legislator's correspondence and even callers are concerned with personal problems and local benefits rather than with legislative questions. Veterans seek to press claims through their congressmen, businessmen want government contracts, many others seek jobs or free legal advice or a host of other services. Congressmen are now being given assistants who can run errands for constituents but most city councilmen and state legislators do not receive such help. They are aided in many cases by the party official who performs these services as a broker between the government and the citizen. Politicians are often damned for spending time on so many nonlegislative matters but many constituents consider this a part of their function. "Politician" is sometimes an opprobrious term, but how many of his detractors could perform any better his role of compromiser, interpreter, advocate, educator, and errand boy? His is one of the least dispensable positions in modern society.

SELECTED REFERENCES

There are hundreds of political biographies of public men. There are biographies of all the Presidents, many congressmen, governors, and local leaders. Some of these appear in the footnotes of the chapter. A few of the general works on political leaders include C. E. Merriam, *Four American Party Leaders* (1926); J. T. Salter (ed.), *The American Politician* (1936) and *Public Men* (1946); Graham Wallas, *Human Nature in Politics* (1921); W. B. Munro, *Personality in Politics* (1924); Ordway Tead, *The Art of Leadership* (1935); A. W. Gouldner, *Studies in Leadership* (1950); H. H. Jennings, *Leadership and Isolation* (1943); W. F. Whyte, *Street Corner Society* (1937).

[21] *Congressional Procedure* (Boston: Chapman & Grimes, Inc., 1941), p. 70.

PART FIVE

Nominations and Elections

Weak pres:

1. Lack of ability
2. Had a narrow view of the pres. functions.
3. Unable or unwilling to muster needed pol. ~~support~~.
4. Had a limited party appeal.
5. Were dominated by or unable to lead congres

CHAPTER 17

The Selection of Candidates

The right of popular government is incomplete, unless it includes the right of the voters not merely to choose between candidates when they have been nominated but also the right to determine who these candidates shall be.

—THEODORE ROOSEVELT

In the United States, legislative positions, the higher executive positions, and many judicial offices are filled by popular election. Totalitarian nations likewise fill many of their positions by this method. A basic difference exists, however, in the choice of candidates to stand for election. In the totalitarian countries the ruling party draws up a list of its nominees with little or no help from outside sources. The voter then is allowed to subscribe to or disapprove of the list. If he disapproves of the nominees, he has no alternative nominees to support but must be content with merely voting no. Frequently he is not even permitted to write in an opposing name. Since all parties are outlawed save the one in power, the result of this system is essentially the same as appointment of the palace guard by an absolute monarch.

Universal suffrage can have a real meaning only if the process of the selection of one group of persons to run against another group for election is a vital and lively process, followed by the presentation of rival slates to the electorate. A democratic society profits little if in the general election the voters' choice is limited to mediocre, ill-qualified, or boss-controlled candidates. The League of Women Voters and other supporters of good government are trying, with varying success, to focus attention on the fundamental importance of the nominating process. In spite of these efforts, nominations are not yet receiving sufficient interest, and popular participation in selection has failed to keep pace with interest in election. The subject is often regarded as dull and confusing by the citizen and he has failed to realize his obligation or his part in this aspect of the political process.

Nominating machinery in the United States has progressed from the relatively simple to the complex, from mere self-announcement to a system of conventions and primaries. In early America, where persons in an area generally knew each other, candidates for a local office presented themselves to the electorate on their own announcements. Some feeling existed that the office should seek the man; where this occurred town meetings met and offered the nomination to a certain person. He accepted and agreed to run as an obligation to the community. The more common practice, however, has been and still is for the man to seek the office.

Even in early America, self-announcement was not completely satisfactory, especially in areas more thickly populated and of wider expanse. Here prominent individuals gathered to name individuals for office; in time these became informal caucuses. With the growth of political parties, party leaders and officeholders assumed the function of designation; the making of nominations became a most if not the most important activity of political parties. People whom the party refused to nominate (especially in the West and South) continued recourse to self-announcement. As the parties assumed the nominating function, a long struggle began as to the extent of participation by the party members in the choosing of candidates. This struggle to control party nominations forms the basis for the development of nominating machinery in the United States. Three major methods have been used by the parties to name candidates—the caucus, the convention, and the direct primary. There are many variations of each of these methods and a review of their uses and development requires separate treatment of each.

THE CAUCUS

Operation and Use. The nominating caucus as popularly understood today is a preliminary and private meeting of certain self-appointed members of a political party for the purpose of selecting candidates.[1] The caucus was used even before the establishment of parties in colonial Boston and became a widely used method for choosing candidates in small areas.[2] The Committees of Correspondence and patriotic clubs offered

---

[1] The term "caucus" is used in a number of different senses today. The nominating caucus is to be distinguished from the meetings or conferences of party members in a legislature for the purpose of deciding committee assignments and the party's position on public issues; the party caucuses are often referred to as the Senate Republican caucus, the House Democratic caucus, etc. Before 1830, there were at least three types of nominating caucuses—the informal type held by local party leaders, the legislative caucuses composed of party members of the legislature, and mongrel or mixed caucuses in which legislators and outside representatives united to select party candidates. In some New England states today the caucus is a precinct meeting of all enrolled party members called for the purpose of nominating candidates; more properly, this resembles a primary, for it is an open rather than a secret meeting and includes all party members instead of a few. The term itself may have originated with the Algonquin Indians in the word Kaw-Kaw, meaning "the talk," or been derived from a word meaning secret meetings of shipyard mechanics, known as "caulkers" meetings.

[2] On the evolution of the caucus see F. V. Dallinger, *Nomination for Elective Office in the United States* (New York: Longmans, Green & Co., Inc., 1897); M. Ostrogorski, "The Rise and Fall of the Nominating Caucus, Legislative and Congressional," *Ameri-*

a basis for experience with informal, private conferences. The description of the early caucus appearing in Samuel Adams' diary in 1763 has become immortal, and these few lines indicate that it was little different in form from many caucuses of the present.[3]

> This day learned that the Caucus Club meets at certain times in the garret of Tom Dawes, the Adjutant of the Boston Regulars. He has a large house . . . and the whole club meets in one room. There they smoke tobacco till you cannot see from one end of the garret to the other. There they drink flip I suppose and they choose a moderator who puts questions to the vote regularly; and selectmen, assessors, collectors, firewards, and representatives are regularly chosen before they are chosen in town.

It might be added that Adams himself later received the nomination for representative from Boston through this system.

After the Revolution, the choice of state-wide candidates posed a problem because of the difficulties of transportation and communication. Caucus members at one end of the state could not easily confer with those at the other. Soon, therefore, a convenient device developed known as the "legislative caucus," where the respective party members of the state legislature met while in the capital, decided upon, and publicly announced the ticket for state-wide offices.

Since George Washington had no opposition, the problem of nominating presidential and vice presidential candidates did not arise until 1796. By this time the legislative caucus principle was so well established that convenience pointed to the formation of a congressional caucus to handle the problem. In order, Adams, Jefferson, Madison, and Monroe received their nominations from the respective Federalist and Republican caucuses. The lack of effective opposition to three Republican Presidents led the device to go virtually without challenge until 1824. The Federalists, however, replaced the congressional caucus with meetings of party leaders from various states.

Meantime, in the states there was discontent with state legislative caucuses on the part of the counties and districts which were not represented in the state legislature. In effect, the absence of party membership in the legislature from a certain county deprived the county from a voice in state-wide nominations. As a remedy, mixed caucuses were evolved to permit delegates from nonrepresented districts to sit with legislators for the purpose of making nominations. Actually, this was a hybrid caucus-convention institution and demonstrated a recognition that all electoral

---

can Historical Review, Vol. 5 (1900), pp. 255 ff., and *Democracy and the Organization of Political Parties* (New York: The Macmillan Company, 1922), Vol. II, pp. 3–280.

[3] *Life and Works of John Adams* (Boston: Little, Brown & Company, 1856), Vol. II, p. 144.

districts deserved to participate in selecting party designees for governor and other state offices.

Evaluation. In the early days of its operation the legislative caucus had much to recommend it. It was simple and inexpensive. It overcame the geographical barriers standing in the way of canvassing party leaders in the communities. The caucus also placed nominations in the hands of the party's representatives and provided the voters with some guidance in the selection of candidates. Nominations were made by men who were in government and who had some knowledge of the talents and abilities required for public office. More than this, the caucus members were widely acquainted with men who possessed the requisites for public office.

In spite of its merits, the caucus was short-lived and was criticized on many grounds. First, it gave the legislature undue influence over the executive. The executive, it was argued, felt responsible to the legislators who nominated him instead of to the party or its rank-and-file membership. Potentially the caucus might lead to cooperation and harmony between the two branches, but it could also result in legislative dominance and executive dependence. The popularity of the legislative branch also began to decline, and it was natural for the public to express less confidence in the legislators' choices.

Foremost among the objections to the caucus was its undemocratic character. The few, it was held, dictated the choice of personnel to the many. It lent itself to "bargains" and "deals" as well. The onslaught against the caucus came from the growing equalitarianism of the West, dramatized in the person of Andrew Jackson. Jackson, who had been nominated in 1824 by the Blount County, Tenn., convention, climaxed the battle against the caucus. Jackson and his supporters made an issue of "King Caucus," knowing that the congressional caucus would not nominate the general. He would not permit his friends to attend the congressional caucus and made his battle against the institution the people's battle as well. That the whole system of nomination was under attack was shown by the fact that William H. Crawford alone was selected by a poorly attended Republican caucus and the method of choice was made an issue against him. Adams and Clay were nominated by various state legislatures and Jackson by a county convention. John C. Calhoun became the candidate of all anticaucus factions for the vice presidency. The death knell was rung on the congressional caucus in 1828, when no nominees were placed in the field by it. With the congressional caucus discredited, the device could not hope to survive in the states.

RISE OF THE CONVENTION

The unpopular character of the caucus provoked a steadily increasing volume of dissatisfaction. A body of younger men within the parties began to protest the arrogance of those who controlled the caucus and, with an enlargement of the suffrage, counseled the people to demand a voice in the selection of the candidates. Even while the caucus was in wide use, the Middle Atlantic states were employing, for purposes of county nominations, the delegate convention. The county was the electoral unit in these states, and in New Jersey and Delaware the state legislative caucus was not used. About 1804 Republicans in these two states decided the delegate convention would be a useful device for welding opposition to the Federalists and the idea was put into effect. Capitalizing on the democratic impulses which condemned the caucus as aristocratic, politicians in nearby states also began to champion the idea of a state nominating convention. In 1824 a call for a state nominating convention at Utica, N.Y., was issued for the purpose of choosing candidates for governor and lieutenant governor. The convention consisted of as many delegates as there were representatives in the state legislature. By the end of the decade the state convention became widely used throughout the Northeast.

The convention method for choosing presidential candidates was first used in 1831 by the Anti-Masonic party. A few months later the Maryland legislative caucus issued a call to National Republicans to meet in Baltimore for a similar purpose. Various committees and permanent officers of the convention were chosen to perfect the organization. An address to the people was drafted by a group of persons meeting in Washington a short time later; this corresponded roughly to a party platform. President Jackson saw the virtue of this device and, working through the New Hampshire Democratic caucus, he had the Democrats called together with the object of selecting Martin Van Buren as his running mate. Jackson let it be known that the delegates were to favor Van Buren for Vice President "unless they wished to quarrel with the general." He was also responsible for pushing the convention to adopt the rule of requiring nominees to obtain a two-thirds majority vote of the convention, a rule which was retained in Democratic National Conventions until 1936.

The displacing of the county, state legislative, and congressional caucuses by the convention was an important victory for more democratic control of the nominating process. In theory at least, the convention possessed outstanding merit. The hierarchy of conventions from local areas to state-wide and eventually to national meetings provided a progressive hierarchy of deliberative bodies which could consider both candidates and issues. Here divisive interests within the counties and states could be compromised and ironed out. Nationally, the evils of sectionalism could be mitigated. In matters of policy and party platform the convention offered a vehicle for reducing extreme factionalism and diverse viewpoints. Compromise nominations would result in balanced tickets from all parts of the state or county. Nominations would more likely include able but not widely known men who, under the caucus system, remained in political oblivion. The delegate convention appeared to offer an excellent example of representative democracy. Supposedly, the people would choose the best and most outstanding men to represent them in the convention. The Constitution itself could be pointed to as the product of a convention of wise men. The men chosen to participate in the conventions, moreover, would have to answer to the voters of their party for the nominations made and policies drafted.

NOMINATING CONVENTIONS IN PRACTICE

Experience with the convention on state and local levels failed to bear out these merits. Most of the weaknesses of the convention system in the nineteenth century were due to their unrepresentative composition and undemocratic organization and procedure. A basic part of any convention system is the choice of delegates to the convention. If the convention is to be subject to popular control, the basis of representation in that body is a matter of real importance. The unit of representation and apportionment of delegates is left to the party committees so that when delegate districts are drawn up by the party there is a tendency to resort to gerrymandering in favor of the faction in power. Many "packed" and unrepresentative conventions resulted from party gerrymandering.

Character of Delegates. In practice, delegates were chosen to various town, district, or county conventions by a town meeting or caucus of party voters; the county and district conventions in turn selected delegates to the state, and later national, conventions. The delegates chosen to attend conventions were seldom the wisest or the most public-spirited members of the party. As always, the independent voters were not well organized and were often ineffective in the meetings called to select delegates. On the other hand, the factional and machine leaders were well organized and successfully chose either themselves or their own men as delegates to attend the convention. All too frequently the "best" persons failed to participate in the selection of delegates.

The breakdown of the process of choosing delegates was shown in the low estate of the composition of the Cook County, Ill., convention in 1896. Of its unwieldy body of 723 delegates, over 150 either had criminal records or had been tried for crimes, 148 were political employees, and over one-third were saloonkeepers.[4] Conventions of this quality were easily dominated by corrupt bosses and the many delegates owing their jobs to the machine were expected to "take orders." Underworld elements

[4] See *Review of Reviews,* Vol. 16 (1897), p. 322; and R. M. Easley, "The Sine-qua-non of Caucus Reform," *The American Political Science Review,* Vol. 16 (1922), pp. 322–324.

were in a position, through their men in the convention, to influence the choice of nominees. The buying and selling of places in the convention also was not unknown.

Manipulation. Not only was the composition of the conventions a mark against the device, but the procedures and behavior of those bodies themselves were even worse. Careful deliberation frequently gave way to indecorum, commotion, and emotion. The hidden managers prepared in advance both the organization and the agenda of the convention. Robert M. La Follette [5] described one convention in these words:

> Away in some retired room behind locked doors the masters of the machine sit in quiet conference. They have issued their orders to those in nominal control. The program of the convention is all prepared. The temporary and permanent chairmen have been "elected" in advance. . . . These men have been selected by masters of the machine with considerate judgment. There will be no mistakes made. Men designated in advance will be recognized by the chairman for all important motions at the "right time." All troublesome points of order will be decided in the "right way."

In spite of this care, machines were not always certain that things would be so "uneventful" or that their nominees would be chosen without a floor fight. Ingenuity in this case sometimes dictated the calling of a "snap" assembly which met a few hours before the scheduled convention and made the designations before the arrival of all the delegates. Those notified of the "changed hour" of the convention were, of course, the machine delegates, and when the noncontrolled members appeared for the meeting, they were met with a *fait accompli.* Another technique was the scheduling of the meeting in a small hall incapable of seating all the delegates. The machine delegates filed into the hall early and transacted the business while the insurgents and others were scrambling to find seats in the convention room. Violent methods of keeping certain delegates from attending the convention also came in for their share of use. If all else failed, the presiding officer might resort to parliamentary tricks to steam-roller candidates and policies even against the will of the majority. Since the whole convention procedure was without governmental regulation and in control of the party managers, fraudulent nominations could not be contested. The realization that conventions needed some public regulation came about at the time of the Civil War and in 1866 California passed such a law. However, by the time regulatory action was taken on anything like a general scale, the convention system was well on the road to decline.

Appraisal. Though the convention offered a chance to democratize nominations, it failed to elicit widespread popular enthusiasm. Voters

[5] Chester L. Jones, *Readings on Parties and Elections* (New York: The Macmillan Company, 1912), pp. 60–61.

did not go to the polls in large numbers to choose delegates to the convention, and many considered it an uninteresting burden. Public-spirited members of the party too often shunned the opportunity of seeking a place in the convention. If they were not "too busy," they regarded the job with cynicism, since the convention, they believed, would put over machine nominations by hook or crook. Others who were delegates often found themselves hopelessly outnumbered and ineffective in the face of such professional perversion of the convention. Out of the dissatisfaction with the convention method grew a demand to place nominations on a more democratic basis; the device developed for this was the direct primary.

In appraising the convention several points are to be considered. Not all conventions, of course, were controlled and many were wholesome expressions of representative government; far too many, however, were operated in the interest of the few. Not all the evils noted appeared in one place at one time but many took place whenever there was ardent factional rivalry. As the doctrine of spoils was extended it was inevitable that its advocates would use the nominating system, in this case the convention, to further the job interests of the party leaders. The increase in the number of elective offices and the rotation-of-office principle helped also to make a mockery of any lengthy deliberation in the convention and the tendency for factional slates was natural when nominations had to be made for a number of offices. In rural areas where individuals were well known to each other the delegates could be called upon to answer for their acts. The growth of cities with their shifting populations led to greater anonymity of the delegates with greater opportunities for abuses where there was no public regulation of the convention. With the development of the industrial revolution came the scramble for utility franchises and special privileges for the private interests, who in turn sought the control of the conventions. These factors, leading to an ever-widening gap between voters and delegates, made it extremely difficult for the convention system to fulfill the expectations of honest popular control of nominations.

Uses Today. In spite of appalling abuses characterizing the state and local nominating conventions from time to time, the institution has been retained in some states. Connecticut [6] uses the convention method for making nominations for all state offices. Indiana and New York nominate their state-wide elective officers by means of a state convention. In Connecticut, the convention method of nomination is used for virtually all local offices as well as for state-wide offices. In only a few towns are local officials designated in the primary. All enrolled members of the party

[6] Rhode Island used the convention until 1948; at that time it began to use direct primary, which was provided for in 1947.

may attend the town or city convention, which makes the nominations for the myriad elective town officials. The city conventions and the town conventions in turn choose delegates to senatorial, congressional, probate, and state conventions, which make the respective nominations for state senators, United States representatives, probate judges, and state officers. The state convention, in addition to making the six state-wide congressional nominations, designates the candidates for United States senator and congressman-at-large. Names are placed before the convention and roll calls are taken much in the fashion of the national nominating conventions. The delegations of most of the larger towns and cities operate under the unit rule, which binds the entire delegation to vote for the candidate who receives a majority in a caucus held by the delegation. In practice, the town conventions and ward caucuses in the cities of Connecticut are not well attended and it becomes easy for an organized group to obtain a voting majority.[7] At times, however, the state and lesser conventions are just as spirited and deliberative as national conventions. New York uses a hybrid system, with the direct primary for nominating candidates for local offices and the state convention for designating the state offices and certain judgeships. Unlike Connecticut, however, New York provides for the voters to choose the members of the state and judicial conventions by means of the direct primary.

The caliber of men nominated for governor and United States senator by delegate conventions compares favorably with states choosing gubernatorial candidates by means of the primary. In recent decades the few convention states have selected candidates for governor as distinguished, and in many cases more so, as those in the states using the primary. At the moment there seems to be little likelihood that the convention system in Connecticut, Indiana, and New York will give way to the direct primary. Similarly, in those states where the primary is used there seems to be no disposition to return to the convention system. The convention is retained in many direct-primary states today for purposes of governing the party and for framing the party's policies and resolutions.

THE DIRECT PRIMARY

Importance. In contrast to the oligarchy of the caucus and the indirect choice of nominees through the convention system, the primary is an election closely resembling the final or general elections. Aspirants seeking nomination customarily campaign, distribute literature, and seek to impress the party members with the "strength" which they can add to the ticket. Primary contests are often as heated as general elections

---

[7] In Connecticut the larger cities are divided into wards; the meeting of registered voters in the ward to make nominations for delegates to the city convention is known as a "caucus."

and deep-seated party cleavages are brought to the fore. Contests are frequent between the machine and nonmachine factions of the party. They may constitute a fight between the factions of the machine, illustrated by pro- and anti-Byrd in Virginia, and the defeat of the Pew-Grundy-Owlett slate by Senator James H. Duff in Pennsylvania in 1950. Primary contests may also center around policies such as conservatism and progressivism. In the South there have been sharp races between pro- and anti-Fair Deal Democrats, as exemplified in the bitter campaign between Willis Smith and Frank Graham in 1950 in North Carolina. Racial questions were brought into this campaign and resulted in the defeat of the incumbent Graham, an administration supporter. Floridians will not soon forget the heated Smathers-Pepper primary the same year. Since 1940 numerous Republican primaries have reflected the pro- and anti-internationalist schism in the party and were often tied to the support or opposition to Governor Dewey or Senator Taft.

It was observed earlier that a large number of states and local districts are, practically speaking, one-party areas. It is hard to overemphasize the importance of the primary in these areas because it is, in effect, the general election. In *U.S. v. Classic* the Supreme Court recognized that the primary in some states effectively controlled the choice of the person elected and that the primary was an integral part of election. Several studies of the South show that this is fully recognized by Southern electors where contested Democratic primaries will bring a turnout of votes which favorably compares with a general election in two-party areas. The data on elections to the House of Representatives collected by Cortez Ewing suggest that at least half of the representatives elected had only to overcome the hurdle of primary nomination to be reasonably sure of election.[8] This places an enormous power and responsibility in the hands of the major-party voters. The fact that labor unions, business groups, and other associations spend large sums of money to secure nominations is a further recognition of the crucial nature of the primary.

Another factor lending importance to the primary is that, with the exception of the South, there is usually much less turnout of voters in the primaries. This means that where there is a race in the primary, the organization, party, or private association which can mobilize its supporters behind its slate will have the best chance of winning. Furthermore, the less conspicuous the office, the greater is the chance of the individual with organization backing to win designation. This is because of the lack of interest displayed by many voters in these contests.

Origin and Development. The origin of the direct primary is somewhat obscure but is generally considered as having been adopted by the

[8] "Primaries as Elections," *Southwestern Social Science Quarterly*, Vol. 29 (1948–49), pp. 293–298.

Democratic party in Crawford County, Pa., in 1842. The Republicans abandoned their delegate convention in this county in 1868 and adopted rules to provide for nominations at the primary,[9] which became known as the "Crawford County System." Several other counties went over to the primary system soon after. At this time the primary system was optional and voluntarily instituted by the local party organizations. It soon was characterized by many of the same abuses as the convention, with manipulation and fraudulent counting of ballots. Men of different or no political faith invaded party primaries and often succeeded in controlling them. Some parties attempted to regulate their primaries by the adoption of rules, which of course had no legal sanction. The ineffectiveness of these regulations led to indignant demands for public control.

California and New York enacted the first statutes to protect "the elections of voluntary associations" and to "protect primary meetings, caucuses, and conventions of political parties."[10] The law of the former state was an optional statute adopted voluntarily by any political associations or parties which wished to invoke its protection. A few other states also adopted optional laws. Development in Idaho followed a somewhat different pattern. In 1903 the state began to regulate party nominating machinery by requiring a primary election to select delegates to the nominating conventions.[11] Gradually allegiance tests, the date of primaries, and public payment of primary expenses were added to the laws of several states. By 1900 most of the present features of primaries had appeared, but as yet no state had enacted a mandatory law placing the primary on the same footing as the election. Until this was done the growing demand for greater popular participation in the nominating process was bound to be frustrated by interested politicians and economic group pressures.

From the appearance of the primary in 1842 until the first mandatory state-wide adoption in 1903, a real battle was fought between the stalwarts and machine on the one hand and reformists and progressives on the other. The Old Guard fought hard to save the convention system, but the gradual pressure of the Populists, Progressives, and others who were incensed at its abuses was too much to defeat.

[9] On the origin of the primary see James H. Booser, "Origin of the Direct Primary," *National Municipal Review*, Vol. 24 (1935), pp. 222–223, and E. C. Meyer, *Nominating Systems* (1902), p. 146.

[10] On the history of primary legislation see C. E. Merriam and L. Overacker, *Primary Elections* (Chicago: University of Chicago Press, 1928), Chaps. 1–5.

[11] The study of the primary in Idaho is especially interesting because the state went from this primary election for delegates to conventions to a direct primary. After ten years the primary was repealed and the convention restored by law. In 1931 the primary was reenacted. See Boyd Martin, *The Direct Primary in Idaho* (Stanford, Calif.: Stanford University Press, 1947).

The development of the primary was not limited to any one section of the country, but proceeded more rapidly in those areas where social and economic discontent was greater. The dominance of the Democratic party in the South led to an early use of the primary so that a real election might be held prior to the perfunctory final elections. In state after state, the Democratic party in the South before 1890 adopted the primary idea, and some legislative regulation was instituted in South Carolina as early as 1888. Strong democratic inclinations led Western counties to substitute the primary for the convention. In 1902 Mississippi passed a state-wide mandatory primary law but left the conduct of the primary to the party committees.

When Robert M. La Follette became governor of Wisconsin, he succeeded in pushing through a mandatory state-wide primary system in 1904. For nominating purposes the convention was completely abolished and its functions assumed by the primary. The Wisconsin law set the pattern for other states, though the latter have ended up with a great number of variations in application and detail.[12] The progressive movement aided adoptions and by the end of Wilson's administration all but four states had primary laws and during the New Deal era three of these, Utah, New Mexico, and Rhode Island, adopted the primary. Connecticut alone retains the convention system. In some Southern states the primary is optional at the discretion of party committees. Primaries of all parties are held simultaneously in a state and for the most part at public expense.

PARTY CONTROL AND NOMINATIONS

Unofficial Designation. The control over nominations by party organizations and leaders failed to disappear with the spread of primaries. Many county chairmen remain officially "neutral" in primaries but many do not. The control and influence of the organization in the primary is sometimes official, but probably more often unofficial. But in the latter instance party voters become well aware of the organization in the absence of any public announcement as word is passed around among precinct leaders and newspaper columnists give the tip-off. Often selections are decided upon in a preprimary "parlor" caucus. Following this, efforts are made, in the interest of "team play" and "harmony," to dissuade factions from running these candidates. Professor Porter has shown that this and other methods in the primaries for county offices in Iowa resulted

[12] On the variations see Arthur Harris and Carl Uhr, *Direct Primary Elections* (Berkeley, Calif.: Bureau of Public Administration, University of California, 1941). A comprehensive bibliography dealing with the primaries in specific states will be found at the end of the following chapter.

in the absence of contests in over half the counties.[13] Senator Albert W. Hawkes of New Jersey, in seeking renomination in 1948, found that a group of county leaders "agreed" on R. C. Hendrickson as his successor. Hawkes first decided to challenge the organization and run against Hendrickson but later withdrew with a blast against "machine rule." Hendrickson was nominated and elected.

In New York City, county chairmen get together and try to draw up a slate for city-wide offices in order to avoid primary fights. In 1953 a poll of Democratic party leaders showed opposition to renomination of Mayor Vincent Impellitteri, and he failed to get endorsement. The mayor ran in the party primary and was defeated by Robert Wagner. After due consideration, Impellitteri decided not to run in the general election as an independent and Wagner won the election. Political machines in New York City regularly prepare a slate to be "ratified" by the county committees. Aspirants for municipal offices there, and elsewhere where such practices prevail, know that the organization's active and strong endorsement carries fair promise of success; they cannot take lightly, therefore, the prospects of running without organizational support. At the same time, the party organization in a great many if not most places is unable to dominate the primary as successfully as it did the convention. The primary has given the voters of the party a means of disapproving the choices of the organization, which at times the voters have used, thus weakening the grip of the party organization over nominations.

Preprimary Conventions. In Colorado, Utah, Rhode Island, and New Mexico the role of party organization in slatemaking is formalized by law.[14] This is accomplished by means of a preprimary convention whereby the organization may endorse or present a set of candidates. In Colorado there are a series of preprimary party assemblies from the local to state levels. One ballot only is cast for each office and any candidate receiving 20 per cent of the vote is endorsed by the assembly. New Mexico's arrangements resemble those in Colorado. Nebraska likewise followed the Colorado pattern but dropped the plan in 1954 after having used it for

[13] "The Deserted Primary in Iowa," *The American Political Science Review,* Vol. 39 (1945), pp. 732–740.

[14] Dates of adoption: Colorado 1912, Utah 1948, Rhode Island 1948, New Mexico 1952. For accounts of these preprimary convention systems see the report prepared by the National Municipal League's committee on direct primary, of which J. P. Harris was chairman, *A Model Direct Primary Election System* (1951). See also C. B. Judah and O. E. Payne, *New Mexico's Proposed Pre-primary Designating Convention* (Albuquerque, N.M.: The University of New Mexico Press, 1950); R. S. Childs, "Rhode Island Tries Primary," *National Municipal Review,* Vol. 38 (1949), pp. 126–129; R. N. Ballard, *The Primary Convention System in Utah* (Salt Lake City, Utah: University of Utah Press, 1947).

10 years.[15] The Republican assemblies in California likewise make endorsements but the California groups are unofficial volunteer associations not under party rules.[16] In 1954, the Democrats formed an analogous group known as the Democratic council and made preprimary endorsements. Utah's plan requires the selection of two candidates, a provision which may actually assure rather than reduce primary contests. In Rhode Island the regular party committees instead of a special convention select the nominees. Candidates who receive the party endorsement have an asterisk by their names and are given first place on the ballot or first column on the voting machine.

It is not easy to generalize on the basis of experience the merits, criticisms, and results of these official methods of party participation in the primary. There appears to be some evidence the parties endorse suitable candidates, especially in terms of voter appeal, and discourage entry by persons having little support. It has helped insurgent movements in Colorado. Although it is argued that the preprimary convention aids incumbents and organization men, candidates receiving endorsements have not invariably won. Convention preferences in Nebraska usually won, but not always the first preference. A reason for dropping the system in Nebraska was the feeling that it contributed to party disunity.

Open versus Closed Primaries. Many party leaders oppose direct primaries on the ground that they diminish party responsibility for nominations, a function which is probably the most important one performed by parties. But party officials have recognized that primaries are here to stay and have centered their fire on trying to obtain primary systems which will give them the greatest amount of control. Direct primaries vary considerably in detail but are often broadly designated as "open" and "closed," with party leaders generally favoring the latter.

In the closed primary only those persons willing to submit to a test of party membership may cast their votes, thus making it difficult to shift from one party to another. There are two methods by which tests are imposed, enrollment and challenge. The enrollment is more widely used and requires the voter to state his party affiliation at the time of registration or when he appears to vote in the primary. Persons giving no party membership may not vote in the primary. Persons can change parties at the next opportunity for registration or file a declaration with a clerk a certain period of time prior to the primary. It is easy to shift party allegiance.

Under the challenge system the voter declares his party affiliation when

15 See A. C. Breckenridge, "Pre-primary Trial Dropped," *National Municipal Review*, Vol. 43 (1954), pp. 186–191.

16 On the California assemblies see Hugh A. Bone, "New Party Associations in the West," *The American Political Science Review*, Vol. 45 (1951), pp. 1115–1125.

he applies to vote in the primary. If he is challenged, the presiding officer asks him to assert that he belongs to the party, supported its candidates at the last election, or that he intends to vote for them at the coming general election.

Party organizations believe the closed primary helps to promote party responsibility because it limits the decisions on the party's candidates to persons who are willing either by oath or enrollment to be publicly known as party members. It closes the "party" election to independents and to adherents of the opposition party who might come over and "raid" the primary by voting for weak candidates. There also appears to be some psychological value and moral obligation when one declares a party faith and tests of party faith may help to fix alignments and encourage party responsibility.

Eleven states operate under an "open" system. With some deviations, two main practices are used. In Wisconsin, the party voter receives the ballots of all parties, which are identical in size and shape. He marks the ballot of the party of his choice and deposits the ballots of other parties in a blank ballot box. The blank ballots are later destroyed by officials. The voter, therefore, may keep his party identity secret in each primary election. Michigan, Montana, and Utah follow essentially the same plan. In another type of open ballot, used in Minnesota, Idaho, and North Dakota, there is a single or blanket ballot with a separate column for each party. The voter checks the party column in which he wishes to vote and marks the various nominees of his choice. Should he cross and vote in another party column for some candidate, his ballot is rejected. The Washington ballot is the most lenient of the open primaries and permits the voter at his discretion to cross back and forth, voting, for example, in Republican primaries for governor, then crossing over and voting for one of the Democratic contestants for some other office. This is facilitated by giving the voter a single ballot, as in Minnesota, but instead of grouping candidates by parties, the contestants are grouped by office. This permits those who have no strong party affiliation to vote for the person whom they think best qualified in any party, for any office.

The open primary has its share of critics. It is pointed out that a primary should be a method of settling intraparty quarrels over personalities without interference of outsiders. Furthermore, it is argued that party responsibility and self-control are broken down. The primary is open to "raiding," that is, the machine of one party will vote in the other party's primary to try to defeat its greatest vote getter. By beating the opposition's best candidate in the primary, the chances for defeating that party's nominee in the final election are improved. Although it is theoretically possible for Republican voters to raid Democratic primaries for the purpose of nominating weak candidates, or vice versa, such practices are infrequent. It is more common for private interests to enter open primaries to try to defeat contenders unfriendly to their interests. Some labor unions, for example, urge their members to cross party lines for this

---

SAMPLE PRIMARY ELECTION BALLOT

Thurston County

TUESDAY, JULY 11, 1944

To Vote for a Person Mark a CROSS in the Square at the Right of the Name of the Person for Whom You Desire to Vote

UNITED STATES SENATOR — Vote for One
- HERB SIELER................Republican ☐
- HOWARD E. FOSTER.............Republican ☐
- CLEMENT L. NISWONGER........Republican ☐
- JOHN A. HOGG.................Democrat ☐
- JOSEPH A. MALLERY...........Republican ☐
- EDWIN L. RICE...............Republican ☐
- WARREN G. MAGNUSON..........Democrat ☐
- MARTIN F. SMITH.............Democrat ☐
- HARRY P. CAIN...............Republican ☐
- STELLA ALENE BLANCHARD......Republican ☐
- CAMERON SHERWOOD............Republican ☐
- GORDON B. DODD..............Republican ☐
- J. PARKHURST DOUGLASS.......Republican ☐
- CHARLES ARLIN NAVE..........Republican ☐
- ....☐

REPRESENTATIVE IN CONGRESS
Third Congressional District — Vote for One
- CHARLES SAVAGE..............Democrat ☐
- FRED NORMAN.................Republican ☐
- MARION SEXTON...............Democrat ☐
- ....☐

JUDGE OF THE SUPREME COURT
Position No. 1 — Vote for One
- WILLIAM J STEINERT..........☐
- ....☐

Position No. 2 — Vote for One
- GEORGE B. SIMPSON...........☐
- ....☐

Position No. 3 — Vote for One
- CLYDE G. JEFFERS............☐

JUDGE OF THE SUPERIOR COURT
Position No. 1 — Vote for One
- JOHN M. WILSON..............☐
- ....☐

Position No. 2 — Vote for One
- D. F. WRIGHT................☐
- ....☐

GOVERNOR — Vote for One
- MARIUS RASMUSSEN............Republican ☐
- ARTHUR B LANGLIE............Republican ☐
- LOUIS A. WASMER.............Republican ☐
- MON C. WALLGREN.............Democrat ☐
- CHAS. A. DEBOLT.............Republican ☐
- ....☐

LIEUTENANT GOVERNOR — Vote for One
- VICTOR ZEDNICK..............Republican ☐
- CHARLES R. MAYBURY.........Republican ☐
- CHARLES J. McDONALD.........Republican ☐
- B J. DAHL...................Republican ☐
- GEORGE F. COTTERILL.........Democrat ☐
- JOHN T. McCUTCHEON..........Republican ☐
- LOREN E. VINSON.............Democrat ☐
- VICTOR A. MEYERS............Democrat ☐
- ERLE C. BEST................Republican ☐
- OSCAR F. PETERSON...........Republican ☐
- ....☐

SECRETARY OF STATE — Vote for One
- BELLE REEVES................Democrat ☐
- AGNES M. GEHRMAN............Republican ☐
- W. P. MURPHY................Republican ☐
- M. J. SCHMITT...............Republican ☐

STATE TREASURER — Vote for One
- W. S. LINCOLN...............Democrat ☐
- HOMER R. JONES..............Republican ☐
- CARL HUGO CARLSON...........Republican ☐
- RUSSELL H. FLUENT...........Democrat ☐
- ....☐

STATE AUDITOR — Vote for One
- CLIFF YELLE.................Democrat ☐
- HAROLD QUICK................Republican ☐
- MARK BARTLETT...............Democrat ☐
- EMMETT H. SHAW..............Republican ☐
- PETER K. REILLY.............Republican ☐
- MERRITT DUSTIN..............Republican ☐
- ....☐

ATTORNEY GENERAL — Vote for One
- SMITH TROY..................Democrat ☐
- NEWTON C. McCOY.............Republican ☐
- WALTER C. HINMAN............Republican ☐
- CORNELIUS C. CHAVELLE.......Republican ☐
- GEO. E. CANFIELD............Republican ☐
- ....☐

SUPERINTENDENT OF PUBLIC INSTRUCTION
Non-Partisan Ballot — Vote for One
- PEARL A. WANAMAKER..........☐
- DONALD B. BAKER............☐
- ....☐

COMMISSIONER OF PUBLIC LANDS — Vote for One
- PROGRESSIVE JACK TAYLOR.....Democrat ☐
- SAM J. CLARKE...............Republican ☐
- ALDRICH W FENTON............Republican ☐
- ART RITCHIE.................Republican ☐
- J. W. BOWERMAN..............Republican ☐
- ARCHIE McLEAN...............Republican ☐
- OTTO A. CASE................Democrat ☐
- ....☐

STATE INSURANCE COMMISSIONER — Vote for One
- WILLIAM A. SULLIVAN.........Democrat ☐
- COLONEL GEO. B. LAMPING.....Republican ☐
- WM. G. (BILL) BROOKS........Republican ☐
- ....☐

STATE SENATOR
22nd District — Vote for One
- GERALD SOPHY................Republican ☐
- MERT FRANCIS................Democrat ☐
- CARL MOHLER.................Democrat ☐
- ....☐

STATE REPRESENTATIVE
22nd District — Vote for Two
- CHESTER E. (CHET) BAKER.....Republican ☐
- JOHN A. STEEN...............Republican ☐
- THOS. P. ALLEN..............Republican ☐
- L. A. "ANDY" LAMERE.........Republican ☐
- GEORGE F YANTIS.............Democrat ☐
- LEVY JOHNSON................Democrat ☐
- E. K. FRISTOE...............Republican ☐
- ....☐

COUNTY COMMISSIONER
District No. 1 — Vote for One
- D E. (DON) COURSER..........Republican ☐
- BOYD G. ANDREUS.............Republican ☐
- H. W. (HANK) BOLENDER.......Republican ☐
- JOHN F HAMILTON.............Republican ☐
- CHESTER F NYE...............Democrat ☐
- ....☐

COUNTY COMMISSIONER
District No. 3 — Vote for One
- JOE C. PETERS...............Republican ☐
- EMIL J. LEWIS...............Republican ☐
- HAROLD ROBBINS..............Democrat ☐
- ALBERT RUTLEDGE.............Democrat ☐
- ....☐

The "wide-open" primary ballot used in the state of Washington. On the closed-primary ballot, candidates are grouped by office, and only candidates from one party are included.

purpose; for that matter, the CIO Political Action Committee has been able to do this to some extent even within the prescribed limits of the closed primary.

The open primary can save the independent voter embarrassment in a community where it is socially respectable to belong to a given party.

In this instance he need not declare his party affiliation and is free from the stigma of voting "Republican" or "Democratic." The open-primary ballot allows free movement from one party to another and guarantees secrecy similar to that in a general election. If the system can provide an opportunity to select men who seem more likely to promote the general as contrasted with only the party welfare, it may claim an additional virtue. Unfortunately, definitive studies of either the virtues or the defects of the open-primary ballot are wanting and many of the contentions on both sides are based more on conjecture or on special cases than on over-all operation.[17]

NONPARTISAN PRIMARIES

In the "nonpartisan" primary the candidates run irrespective of party affiliation and the ballots carry no party labels. The persons receiving the first and second highest number of votes for the office become the candidates at the election, though frequently it is provided that any candidate who receives a majority of the votes in the primary is declared elected. In many cities only a single election is held; the candidate who receives the highest vote for each office is elected. The nonpartisan primary is predicated on the assumption that freedom from partisanship is desirable in the nominations for certain offices, mainly local and judicial public offices. Because these positions are essentially administrative, it is thought desirable to eliminate the influence of national and state party labels and to free the officials from the pressures which might be exerted by party heads.[18]

In theory, if not always in practice, the nonpartisan primary possesses considerable merit for local offices. The troublesome problem of party tests is avoided, and national party issues will not be infused into local elections. Municipal partisan primaries and elections are replete with illustrations of the interjection of the extraneous issues of national and state politics. In the choice of judges and school officials particularly, nonpartisanship is to be encouraged. Proponents believe more efficient management of these offices may be obtained through the elimination of party politics. On the whole, advocates of the nonpartisan primary be-

---

[17] Daniel M. Ogden, Jr. in his studies of the Washington blanket primary finds little evidence of "raiding" and believes it a highly advantageous type of primary; see "The Blanket Primary and Party Responsibility in Washington," *Pacific Northwest Quarterly,* Vol. 39 (1948), pp. 33–38; and "Washington's Popular Primary," *Research Studies of Washington State College,* Vol. 19 (1951), pp. 139–161; see also C. O. Johnson, "The Washington Blanket Primary," *Pacific Northwest Quarterly,* Vol. 33 (1942), pp. 27–39.

[18] As noted in the preceding chapter, a great many cities use nonpartisan primaries for the selection of councilmen. Nonpartisan nomination of state and local judges, school officials, and for various township and local offices is also fairly widespread. For a chart showing the use of nonpartisan primaries see Harris and Uhr, *op. cit.,* p. 25.

lieve the system encourages independent candidates and independent voting. In some jurisdictions final elections are eliminated for these offices in which candidates in the primaries obtain a majority vote. If this primary fails to obviate the need for a final election, it at least reduces the number of names on the ballot in the general election. However, all types of primaries are a sifting and eliminating process and result in a reduction of the number of candidates in a final election.

Many party politicians oppose nonpartisan primaries because it takes away some control over patronage and nominations. In many cities the nonpartisan primary has not seriously handicapped the party machines and they have learned to live with it. Not infrequently the parties actually enter nominees in the primary without benefit of label. Word is passed "down the line" that certain candidates are "ours." Open, official party endorsements, however, are usually avoided. As noted in the preceding chapter, there are still many independents in nonpartisan primaries and elections who run and win without any party's tacit endorsement and who remain truly nonpartisan. It is naïve, however, to assume that in the larger cities nomination and election can be won without an organization. Political interest groups, good-government leagues, and personal organizations give help of one kind or another.

A higher degree of political literacy is required of voters in nonpartisan primaries. Some effort must be expended to learn which interests are behind a candidate. As it stands today, the nonpartisan primary's usefulness is limited essentially to local positions. It has not been seriously advocated for selecting governors or congressmen, and is used only in Minnesota and Nebraska for selecting state legislators.

Preference for the closed, open, or nonpartisan primary is not simply a matter of weighing the assets and liabilities of each type. In the final analysis the choice rests in a large measure on one's general outlook on the role of the party in state, county, and local elections. Those who dislike party allegiance for nominations on the local level and who place a premium on voting for candidates on the basis of personal merit, principle, or independence incline toward the open and nonpartisan primary. As a result many reformers and independents in politics (especially during progressive times) champion these two forms of primaries. They believe that the closed primary has a tendency to put party discipline above personal integrity. For those who have a strong sense of party allegiance and affiliation, the closed primary seems a better method of preserving party politics and discipline. Though some profess to see a decline of partisanship in recent years, the open and nonpartisan primaries have made little headway since World War I.

SOME PROBLEMS OF THE PRIMARY

In addition to the difficulties incident to particular types of primaries, such as raiding and the enforcement of party tests, there are several problems, in part technical, which confront the direct-primary system. These include getting names on the ballot, the position of the names, multiple filing, the drafting of a platform, and plurality elections. The first two of these are problems of general elections as well.

Entry Requirements and Long Ballot. In the largest cities the primary ballot often becomes unbelievably long, carrying a hundred or more names. It is not surprising, therefore, that attention is given from time to time to reducing the number of names. The problem becomes one of permitting every serious candidate who has obtained a reasonable following to obtain a position on the ballot, without at the same time having the ballot cluttered with the names of irresponsible persons who stand no chance of nomination and who may have been placed on the ballot to detract votes from the more deserving.

Two general methods are used to secure a position on the ballot. One of these is through presenting a petition signed by a required number of voters. The number may be reckoned on a percentage basis or may be a flat figure. In Maine, for example, 1 per cent of the party vote for the office in the last election is necessary, while in Colorado there must be 300 signatures for a state office and 100 for a county or local office. A second method is that of announcement of candidacy and the payment of a filing fee. This is a practice borrowed from the British parliamentary elections, which require a deposit of £150. This system is widely used in the South and in numerous other areas. Filing fees for members of Congress seldom exceed $250. Often failure to poll a certain percentage of the votes results in forfeiting the fee. Neither petition requirements nor filing fees have resulted in consistently short primary ballots. Larger filing fees might reduce the number of applicants but they would result in charges that the provisions were undemocratic and weighted in favor of the wealthier.

There is some evidence that when the voter is unfamiliar with the names of would-be nominees for a given office, he tends to check a name on or near the top. The person at the top of the list, therefore, possesses some advantage. To get around this, nearly half of the states require that the ballots be printed so as to rotate the names. In this case an equal number of ballots would be printed with each aspirant's name first. Some states merely print the ballots with the names in alphabetical order and in a few states position on the ballot is determined by lot. It is a travesty both on the electoral procedure and on political intelligence that the order of the names on a ballot should be of any importance.

"Cross-filing." About 40 states require an aspirant to be a member of the party whose nomination he seeks but several other states have no such requirement and generously permit a person to seek the nomination of as many parties as he chooses.[19] These "double filing" or "multiple nominations" provisions lend encouragement to independents and bolters but highly confuse the political picture and obscure whatever political issues may exist between the parties. To a considerable degree they accomplish the same result as an open primary by allowing voters of one party to support a candidate who is nominally of another party.

In California it is common practice for a person to seek the nomination of more than one party and to run for office under as many party designations as he is able to capture. Governor Earl Warren and Senator William Knowland of California were successful in winning both Republican and Democratic nominations. In fact, a large number of nominees for the more important offices have been able to win both primaries. A good many party leaders have opposed the system but office seekers in both parties have endorsed the provision and Mr. Warren declared himself strongly in favor of cross-filing. An initiative to abolish the practice was narrowly defeated in the 1952 election.

In New York also there is double filing, though less than in California. In 1944 Representatives Vito Marcantonio and Adam C. Powell were successful in obtaining triple designations—Republican, Democratic, and American Labor. In the same election, nominees with two-party labels were found in 41 out of 45 congressional districts. Major-party aspirants often find it advantageous to enter the Liberal or ALP primaries and run with the support of a minor party. In 1947 a law was passed requiring that candidates for nomination be enrolled members of a party unless the appropriate party committee grants permission for a person to enter its primary. This has resulted in less double filing and it contributed to the defeat of Marcantonio but James Donovan secured permission to enter and was able to win the primaries of the Republican, Democratic, and Liberal parties.[20]

Plurality Nominations. As long as only two candidates present themselves for nomination, one is certain to obtain a majority and presumably enter the general election with the backing of a majority of his party. It often happens that the race has three or more candidates. If no one obtains an absolute majority under a plurality system, the nomination

---

[19] On filing provisions of direct primary election laws see Harris and Uhr, *op. cit.*, pp. 14–17; and R. W. Binkley, Jr., *Double Filing in Primary Elections* (Berkeley, Calif.: Bureau of Public Administration, University of California, 1945).

[20] In Texas the law allows a candidate to be listed on the general election ballot as the nominee of more than one party. In 1952 the Republican party put 15 Democratic candidates on its ballot, including Governor Allan Shivers.

goes to the one who obtains the highest vote. On the surface this seems fair, but the minority nomination may lead to dissension within the party and a weakening of it in the final election.

Ten Southern states have a runoff primary in the event that no one obtains a majority. This contest is limited to the two highest competitors. The runoff has served the peculiar purpose of the Democratic primary, the winning of which is tantamount to election. Iowa and South Dakota provide for a postprimary nominating convention whenever none of the candidates is able to poll 35 per cent of the vote.

Proposed Revisions. Primary laws are being constantly revised, looking toward their improvement. The National Municipal League has drafted a model law which contains some fundamental revisions of the system.[21] The major features of the plan are (1) adoption of the short ballot by removing all except major policy officials, (2) authorization for endorsements by political party organizations or conferences with appropriate designation of endorsed candidates on the ballot, (3) adequate provisions for individual filing, (4) placing the primary in the autumn within one or two months of the final election, and (5) mandatory use of the primary for all political parties polling 10 per cent or more vote at the preceding general election. The model suggests that the choice of a closed, open, or blanket type of primary should depend upon the "party traditions and history within the state." These proposals merit consideration.

MINOR-PARTY NOMINATIONS

For the smaller parties the primary is both unnecessary and unsuitable, for there are rarely any contests. Direct primaries are regulated by state laws and all legal political parties are subject to statutory provisions. If minor parties are recognized as legal parties, they would become subject to state laws, in many instances running counter to their principles. The Socialist party, for example, has elaborate party laws and tests of membership which are more strict than those of the major parties; therefore the Socialists are not satisfied with the relatively simple tests of party membership employed by the Republican and Democratic parties. In most states the Socialists hold no primary and rely on the regular independent petition process to get their nominees' names on the ballot for the general election. Nomination is made by mailing ballots to dues-paying members, who mark their choices and return the ballots to the state committee or central authority, which counts the votes and announces the nominations. Norman Thomas and others have criticized numerous state legislatures for making minor-party and independent nominations difficult through advancing filing dates and imposing al-

---

[21] *A Model Direct Primary System,* prepared by Joseph P. Harris (1951); see also Harris, "A New Primary System," *State Government,* Vol. 21 (1948), pp. 140–144.

legedly unreasonable financial and petition requirements but the legislatures are not inclined to ease the requirements.[22]

CONCLUSION

Americans as well as European observers are bewildered at the complexity of nominating processes in the United States. In Europe, comparatively greater cohesion in matters both of personnel and policy has
made for more or less easy agreement on candidates. Practically speaking,
the selection function is performed by party executive committees. Disagreement within the parties, boss rule, and political independence led
to the demand for the democratization of the nominating process from
caucus to convention to primary or a mixture of the last two. None of
these three methods is without faults, and all have recognizable virtues.
The primary has increased the voter's burden and the long ballot often
becomes the tool of the political machine which has prepared the slate
and mobilized its army to elect its candidates.

Many proponents of the primary failed to realize that the same groups
which had sometimes dominated the caucus and convention could dominate the primary. They overlooked the important fact that leadership
is quite as necessary in the nominating process as in elections. Leadership
is of necessity a matter of numerical minority. When the leadership is
out of harmony with the membership, it becomes the latter's function
to replace it. For this reason it is the duty of all to participate in the
primary election, a duty often shirked. The primary is a shotgun behind
the door to hold at bay inferior candidates or those proposed by unscrupulous bosses. The gun has not been used often enough!

SELECTED REFERENCES

See the end of the following chapter.

[22] For an account of the difficulty of minor parties in securing a place on the ballot
see Hugh A. Bone, "Small Political Parties Casualties of the War?" *National Municipal
Review,* Vol. 42 (1943), pp. 524–528.

CHAPTER 18

National Conventions

At last after a session of several days, the end is reached; the convention adjourns *sine die*. All is over. As you step out of the building you inhale with relief the gentle breeze which tempers the scorching heat of July; you come to yourself; you recover your sensibility, which has been blunted by the incessant uproar, and your faculty of judgment, which has been held in abeyance amid the pandemonium in which day after day has passed. You collect your impressions, and you realize what a colossal travesty of popular institutions you have just been witnessing. A greedy crowd of officeholders, or of office seekers, disguised as delegates of the people, on pretense of holding the grand council of the party, indulged in, or were victims of, intrigues and maneuvers, the object of which was the chief magistracy of the greatest republic of the two hemispheres—the succession to the Washingtons and Jeffersons. . . . Yet, when you carry your thoughts back from the scene which you have just witnessed and review the line of Presidents, you find that if they have not all been great men—far from it—they were all honorable men, and you cannot help repeating the American saying: "God takes care of drunkards, of little children, and of the United States."

—M. OSTROGORSKI

The Constitution made no provision for the nomination of the Chief Executive but provided that he be chosen by electors. Following President Washington, the Federalists and their opponents contested for the presidency and some method was needed for uniting various groups and factions around a candidate, and a caucus of members of Congress was used for the purpose.[1] The congressional caucus never became thoroughly institutionalized and was used primarily by the Jeffersonian Republicans. A group of party leaders in New York designated Pinckney in 1808 and Clinton was nominated in 1812 by friends in the state legislature and ratified by a state convention. Crawford, the last congressional caucus candidate, was nominated by only 66 of the party's 264 legislators. The Anti-Masonic party held a national nominating convention in 1831 and it was soon taken up by the major parties. The national convention has developed into one of the most remarkable institutions in the world and is properly regarded as one of the greatest political shows on earth. In no other nation is the selection of the national candidates and the

---

[1] See W. G. Carleton, "The Collapse of the Caucus," *Current History*, Vol. 25 (1953), pp. 144–150; S. E. Morison, "The First National Nominating Convention, 1808," *American Historical Review*, Vol. 17 (1912), pp. 744–763.

formulation of ostensibly serious policies placed in the hands of a convention of about 3,000 howling delegates and alternates.

THE CALL TO CONVENTION

Choice of Site. The national committees set the time and place of the
conventions and allot the delegates to each state. In recent years both
major parties have tended to meet in the same city and auditorium two
weeks apart. The Republicans traditionally convene first, in late June
or early July. An important consideration in the choice of a city is the
willingness of local groups to put up a minimum of $200,000 and to
provide huge hotel and meeting place facilities. Chicago and Philadelphia
have become the favored cities with occasional choices elsewhere.

Political considerations sometimes dictate the location. In 1928, with
Alfred E. Smith's nomination apparently assured, the Democrats went
to Houston in an effort to placate the South. The Republicans, fearing
defection of the Middle Western farm belt, held their convention the
same year in Kansas City.

Following the choice of a location, the national committees communi-
cate the decision to the state and territorial committees in what is known
as the "call to convention." Included in the call are specifications on the
general methods of choosing the delegates, together with the number of
delegates to which each state is entitled, according to the rules adopted
by the preceding convention.

Apportionment Problems. The Democrats have had relatively few serious quarrels over the allotment of delegates or votes to the states. At
first they gave each state as many votes (often several delegates were sent
with a single vote between them) as it had members in both houses of
Congress, irrespective of political affiliation. This representation was
doubled in 1852, and, as territories were created, it became common
practice to give them from two to six delegates each, as well as six to
the District of Columbia. As a bonus to states going Democratic, two
additional votes were added in 1944, and the number was raised to four
in the following convention. This results in giving slightly more voting
power to the South, which generally remains loyal. The South is still
agitating for additional representation in Democratic National Conventions and the problem of apportionment is not necessarily settled for all
time.

The South caused the Republicans many problems and in 1916 they
abandoned the formula which they had borrowed from the Democrats.
In 1912, for example, four Southern states with about 50,000 Republican
voters had as many votes in the convention as Pennsylvania with 750,000
loyal partisans. Delegates from the South were more or less of the local
"paper" organization and recipients of Federal patronage. This gave an

incumbent Republican President a sizable block of delegates subject to his control. In 1912, the control of Southern delegations by President Taft assured his renomination in the bitter contest with Theodore Roosevelt. The upshot was to modify the rules so as to give each congressional district but one delegate and it could earn an additional delegate by polling 7,500 votes for any Republican elector in the preceding presidential election.

Subsequent changes were adopted which gave a bonus of three delegates to each state if it went Republican in the preceding presidential election, and raised from 7,500 to 10,000 the number of Republican votes necessary for a congressional district to be entitled to two delegates. In 1940, the rules were changed again to permit a state to earn its bonus by electing a Republican senator and provided that unless a district cast 1,000 votes for a Republican President or congressional nominee, it would lose its delegate. Later bonuses were raised to six per state and the congressional district requirement was lifted from 1,000 to 2,000 votes. The present allotment is shown in Table 19. To these are added about 25 delegates from the various territories and the District of Columbia.

Table 19. State Representation in Republican National Convention, 1956

Delegates-at-large *	*District delegates*
Four for each state	One for each congressional district which
Two for each representative-at-large	cast 2,000 Republican votes at the last
Six additional if the state went Republican or elected a Republican governor or United States Senator at the last election	election One additional delegate for each congressional district which cast 10,000 Republican votes at the last election

* Republican national rules recommend election of district delegates, while delegates-at-large are selected in a state convention. State laws take precedence over these rulings.

Selection of Delegates. Methods of choosing the delegates are by the party committees, conventions, and presidential primaries, with the overwhelming majority designated by the last two. In 1952, 17 states held presidential primaries in one or both parties. Arkansas and Georgia, whose laws are optional, held no primaries.[2] In the Republican convention 590 votes out of 1,206 were cast by delegates from states using primary elections, with a somewhat similar number in the Democratic

[2] For summary and commentary on state laws see *Preference Primaries for Nomination of Candidates for President and Vice President,* Hearing before the Senate Subcommittee on Rules on S. 2570, 82d Cong., 2d Sess., Mar. 28, 1952. Louise Overacker, *The Presidential Primary* (New York: The Macmillan Company, 1926), is the major work in the field; she notes that primary laws are as different from each other as fingerprints.

convention.[3] However, in some of these states some delegates were named in state conventions and probably no more than one-third of the delegates were actually selected in a public primary.[4]

Most of the state conventions and primaries are held between early March and June. During this period, and even before, presidential aspirants and their supporters are traveling and speaking, trying to get delegates selected favorable to their cause. In the convention states efforts are made to line up support in local caucuses, county and state conventions. Parliamentary maneuvering, imposing of unit rules, and the like characterize the battles in state and district conventions where the national convention delegates are chosen.[5] These conventions are usually predominantly composed of party officials and are likely to choose delegates who favor a candidate known for his "regularity." Senator Taft, for example, received more support from convention than from presidential primary states. The primary permits the rank-and-file members to vote and provides an opportunity for some candidates who have little popularity with party leaders to demonstrate if they have strength with the party's voters.

PRESIDENTIAL PRIMARIES

Forms. Presidential primaries were designed to give the people a more effective control over the presidential nominating process and came in with the direct primary law in 1905 in Wisconsin; at one time primaries were in use by over half the states. The laws differ so much in detail and application that it is not easy to classify them. Of the 19 states using the presidential primary, 16 have the closed primary; Minnesota, North Dakota, and Wisconsin have open primaries. Many states permit write-ins and the tremendous write-in vote for Eisenhower in Minnesota (1952) and for Stassen in Pennsylvania (1948) did much to aid their causes. Most states permit aspirants to have their names on the ballot only with their consent but in two or three states consent is not required.

[3] States where one or both parties selected some or all of their delegates at a primary in 1952 were Alabama, California, Florida, Illinois, Maryland, Massachusetts, Minnesota, Nebraska, New Hampshire, New Jersey, New York, Ohio, Oregon, Pennsylvania, South Dakota, West Virginia, Wisconsin, and the District of Columbia. Montana will begin using the primary in 1956.

[4] Maryland held a presidential primary that resulted in instructing the Democratic delegation but actual selection of the delegates occurred in the state convention.

[5] The story of the selection of delegates to the 1952 conventions of both parties from each of the states was prepared by a cooperative project of the American Political Science Association and makes available a rich source of data and analysis on the selection of delegates. This has been published in five volumes under the title *Presidential Nominating Politics in 1952* (Baltimore: Johns Hopkins Press, 1954). For an interesting case study of the selecting of delegates by state conventions see O. Douglas Weeks, *Texas Presidential Politics in 1952* (Austin, Tex.: Institute of Public Affairs, University of Texas, 1953).

From the voter's standpoint, there are three major varieties. One type allows him to vote directly for delegates to the national convention; a second permits him to express a preference for one of the candidates for the presidential nomination. Nine states permit some combination of the two, that is, voting both for delegates and expressing a preference. Of these states, only Nebraska and Oregon bind the elected delegates to the support of the winner of the preference ballot. In practice, only Arkansas and Maryland hold preference tests without at the same time electing delegates.

Primary Strength and Nomination. A close scrutiny of the campaign, as conducted in the primaries, raises a question as to how important demonstrated success in them is in terms of getting the party's nomination. Warren G. Harding ran fourth in the 1920 primaries but received the Republican nomination. In 1940 Wendell Willkie eschewed the Republican primaries, while Dewey, Taft, and Vandenberg conducted rather vigorous campaigns, only to see Mr. Willkie nominated. Ironically, Mr. Willkie entered the 1944 primaries, while Governor Dewey stood extremely aloof of the primary contests, only to receive the nomination. Governor Bricker of Ohio also actively sought the nomination in 1944 without success. However, Bricker's popularity among the delegates, partly due to his extensive preconvention campaign, led to his designation as Vice President. On the other hand, the presidential primaries have often greatly influenced the outcome, as in Oregon in 1948, when Stassen's defeat by Dewey caused his boom to burst while Dewey went on to victory. Eisenhower's very strong showing in the New Hampshire and many other primaries in 1952 did much to weaken the Taft boom and aided immeasurably in the General's nomination. His supporters pointed to the primaries and said, "Taft can't win but Ike can." Senator Kefauver beat President Truman in New Hampshire's "popularity contest" and went on to pile up enormous votes in Democratic primaries. Governor Stevenson refused to let his name be entered in any primary yet won the Democratic nomination.

Notwithstanding the incongruity which often appears between performance in the primary and capturing the nomination, the primaries do serve many useful purposes. They place potential nominees before the party voters and provide something of a testing ground by revealing sources of strength and weakness in the candidate's appeal and may result in eliminating certain prospective nominees. On occasions they bring out issues such as the nationalist-internationalist debate in the Republican party and in general heighten interest in the national conventions.

One of the reasons why the potentially democratic device has failed to give enrolled party members an effective method for controlling decisions in the national conventions is that voters seldom have a chance to express a preference on all or even a majority of the leading contenders. Aspirants generally do not enter their names in states where they believe they cannot make a good showing. Taft and Eisenhower faced each other in only about two states where the outcome could be considered significant. Party leaders backing a local favorite son resent "outside interference" and bring pressure on party workers to defeat a prominent outsider in the primary. Only in Maryland, Montana, Nebraska, and Oregon are the delegates elected placed under obligation to support the preference of the voters, and in the former actual instruction is given by the state convention after surveying the results of the preference. Finally, while the voters can vote for delegates who may (or may not) pledge themselves, there are many states where no preference vote is available and delegates are left to make their own interpretations of their election.

Future of Presidential Primaries. An honest difference of opinion exists on the wisdom of placing strong compulsion on the delegates. The long insistence of a state delegation for its favorite son leads to unnecessary and absurd delay in the national convention. The candidate finally nominated must be one on whom the major-party elements have compromised and secured a minimum of agreement. Delegates must have some freedom of action to accomplish this consensus on presidential and vice presidential nominees. After delegates arrive at the convention, their views, after talking with other politicians, often undergo changes and many feel they must vote differently in the interest of choosing a candidate who can win. Many Taft and Kefauver supporters underwent this conversion in 1952. Yet voters in the presidential primaries feel that unless they can bind the delegates to some extent, the primary system has failed to fulfill its potential as an expression of party opinion. They point out that numerous state conventions "instruct" their delegates to the national conventions and that primaries should be accorded the same privilege.

The use of a direct primary to select delegates to the national convention has made little headway since 1920. Senator Paul Douglas and Representative Charles Bennett took the lead in 1952 in advocating a nationwide primary and have received some support for it in and out of Congress. The Gallup poll reported that 83 per cent favored a nationwide primary election that would choose presidential candidates in place of the present national convention.[6] Those advocating primaries are con-

---

[6] The Douglas-Bennett bill provides for Federal aid to the states for each vote cast in a presidential preference primary and the delegates elected from each state would be pledged to vote for the national candidate who had achieved a plurality of votes in the primary. The pledge would be binding on the first ballot and thereafter until released by his candidate or when the candidate's vote fell below 10 per cent of the votes cast in the convention.

cerned with decisions being made in "smoke-filled" rooms. In many Republican state conventions in 1952 there were bitter charges of "fraud," "strong-arm methods," infiltration, and parliamentary dishonesty in the choice of delegates; several of these issues had to be settled by the national convention itself. It is only natural that this caused some persons to look with favor on the extension of primaries.

If the primary is to have a more demonstrable influence on nominations for the presidency, it must be adopted by a good many more states, overcome the great dissimilarity of laws in the states now using the system, and impose stronger compulsion of the delegates chosen in the primaries. There must be some way of getting the principal presidential aspirants to contend with each other in the primaries. Nebraska experimented with this in 1948 with a "people's primary," which enabled enrolled party members to vote their preference for the seven leading Republican contenders. The voters responded to the opportunity with an increase of 300 per cent in turnout over the previous all-time record.[7] Party leaders, however, did not like this "popularity contest" and repealed the law before it could be used again in 1952.

THE OPENING OF THE CONVENTION

The opening day sees the convention city covered with a mantle of decorations. Hotels are teeming with delegates, news reporters, and party leaders. Many aspirants have a suite of rooms, and sometimes an entire floor of a leading hotel, which takes on the character of a campaign headquarters. The convention hall itself is bedecked with flags, banners, and batteries of lights, microphones, and amplifiers. Inside and outside the hall literature and buttons are being passed out urging support for favorite sons, and bands whip up lively tunes to stir the spirits of the delegates as they gather to "pick a winner." Frequently parades for certain nominees are formed and not infrequently clowns, animals, and circus performers are brought to nearby streets to entertain bystanders and to kindle enthusiasm for the prospective nominees.

Keynote Addresses. The first session is called to order by the national chairman and welcoming speeches by the mayor of the city and governor of the state generally follow. After the national chairman has delivered his address the gavel is turned over to the temporary chairman, who usually delivers the "keynote" address. This speech supposedly outlines the job for the convention. In terms of flamboyant oratory, extravagant phraseology, and castigation of the opposition, it has few equals. With an ever-increasing crescendo the minority party keynoter calls upon his party to "save the nation" from the party in power. The eloquence of Democratic keynoter Claude Bowers in 1928 concluded with: [8]

---

[7] For an extensive account of this primary see *The New York Times,* Apr. 15, 1948.
[8] *The New York Times,* June 27, 1928.

We shall win because our cause is just. The predatory forces before us seek a triumph for the sake of sacking. Their shock troops are the Black Horse Cavalry whose hoof beats have made hideous music on Pennsylvania Avenue during the last eight years. They are led by the money-mad cynics and scoffers and we go forth to battle for the cause of man. In the presence of such a foe "he who dallies is a dastard and he who doubts is damned." In this convention we close debate and grasp the sword. The time has come. The battle hour has struck. Then to your tents, O Israel.

The keynote address of the party in power conversely asserts that the nation dare not be returned to the hands of the opposition and that a strong America can be maintained only if the party is retained in power. Governor Robert S. Kerr of Oklahoma, Democratic keynoter in 1944, warned against a return to the "poverty" of the Republicans and roused the delegates with these concluding words:

We have stormed the beaches of poverty and discouragement and fear, and seen the hearts of the people filled with new life, lifted with new hope and buoyant with superb confidence. We have overrun the ramparts of special privilege and reaction and planted the banner of Democratic liberalism high on the hill of human progress. Let our opponents, who have grown fat in a prosperity they could not build for themselves, do their worst. Under our great Commander in Chief we will not retreat! We will not falter in mid-passage! We will win!

Senator Alben Barkley's ringing keynote address in 1948 resulted in a thunderous ovation and demonstration and won for him the vice presidential nomination, even though up to that time President Truman had not placed his stamp of approval on the Kentucky senator. By contrast, the keynote speeches in 1952 by General MacArthur and Governor Dever were ponderous and failed to "electrify" the conventions.

The Standing Committees. Before the delegates can begin the exciting and dramatic business of nominating speeches, certain routine affairs receive attention. These are handled by four committees on permanent organization, credentials, rules and order of business, and platform and resolutions. At the first or second session the state and territorial delegations are instructed to send to the platform the names selected by the delegations to serve on the four committees. The credentials, rules, and permanent organization committees usually consist of one person from each state and territory.

It falls to the committee on permanent organization to present the permanent officers of the convention. This is a routine matter, since the permanent chairman has been agreed upon far in advance of the convention and the lesser temporary officers such as the secretary are usually named as permanent officers. After the permanent chairman has been named, a committee is appointed to escort him, amid the plaudits of the membership, to the rostrum.

The permanent chairman's first job is to make a speech in his own right. Many of these addresses differ little in tone from the keynote speeches. The opposition is berated, the virtues of his own party are extolled, and with rhetorical eloquence the chairman points out the serious job facing the convention and the party. Because of the difficulty of maintaining order and the need at times for quick decisions, the permanent chairmanship goes to a seasoned person with some knowledge of parliamentary procedure. The last few Republican conventions chose Joseph W. Martin, Jr. of Massachusetts, former minority floor leader and later Speaker of the House of Representatives, as their chairman; the Democrats selected respectively Senator Alben Barkley of Kentucky and majority floor leader of the United States Senate, Senator Samuel D. Jackson of Indiana, and Speaker Sam Rayburn.

The convention is called upon to see that only bona fide delegates are seated and to decide contests where there are disputes over membership in a state delegation; this is performed by the credentials committee. The party rules require each delegate and each alternate to file his credentials with the national committee a few weeks prior to the convention and delegates are seated temporarily on the basis of this list. The committee on credentials must review and certify this list before the delegates can be seated. Its report is, therefore, presented before either the adoption of a platform or the nomination of presidential and vice presidential candidates.

At most conventions this is a routine matter, but exceptions, when they occur, are apt to be important, for the convention can be disrupted unless an amicable settlement is worked out by the committee reasonably early in the convention. For example, in the Republican convention of 1912 there were many contested seats between the Roosevelt and Taft forces; the credentials committee ruled all contested seats in favor of the President. Incensed at what they considered the "steam-roller" tactics of the Taft machine, the disqualified as well as accepted Roosevelt delegates bolted and formed a third party. The Republican credentials committee was called upon to decide between rival Georgia delegations in 1948 and voted by the close margin of 26 to 24 to seat the pro-Dewey delegation. Georgia delegates in 1952 again provided the convention with real fireworks by sending delegates representing two factions of the party. The credentials committee first held hearings on the matter, with the nation following the proceedings over television. A majority of the committee were Taft supporters and decided on seating the Georgia faction favoring the senator. Eisenhower strategy decided the issue should be taken to the floor of the convention and a minority report was presented. This proved to be the high point of excitement for the convention because it represented a test of strength.[9] The convention voted 607 to 531 to adopt the minority report, a favorable omen for Eisenhower. Following this, a similar problem over rival slates of delegates sent from Texas was settled the same way.

As the name implies, the committee on rules and order of business prepares the agenda for the convention and recommends rules of voting procedure. For example, it fixes the length of nominating and seconding speeches and demonstrations and recommends rules for the party and the succeeding convention. This committee is in a position to assume some leadership in bringing about reform in the choice and allotment of state delegations and in the operation of the national convention itself.

Credentials and rules problems come during the "temporary organization" stage and are often accompanied by parliamentary tilting by supporters of the contenders for nomination. The permanent chairman Joseph Martin was not able to take over until well into the third day of the 1952 Republican convention.

Another example of the important quarrels which take place during the temporary organization stage was provided by the 1952 Democratic convention, which was delayed in getting down to its business of adopting a platform and nominating candidates by a bitter wrangle over the "loyalty oath." Northern Democrats recalled that in 1948, President Truman was kept off the ballot in Alabama, and in several other states, J. Strom Thurmond was placed on the ticket as the Democratic candidate for President. In an effort to see that this would not happen to the 1952 nominee, Senator Moody of Michigan introduced near the close of the first day his modified "loyalty resolution." It provided that: [10]

No delegate shall be seated unless he shall give assurance to the Credentials Committee that he will exert every honorable means available to him, in any official capacity he may have, to provide that the nominees of the convention for President and Vice President, through their names or the names of electors pledged to them, appear on the election ballot under the heading, name or designation of the Democratic party.

The resolution was passed by a voice vote and Stevenson was able to run under the Democratic banner in all states. At the Democratic state convention in Texas in September, it was agreed that the Stevenson-Sparkman ticket would appear in the Democratic column but a resolution was adopted urging every Democrat in Texas to vote for Eisenhower.[11]

[9] For debate on the Georgia case see *Proceedings of the Twenty-fifth Republican National Convention, 1952,* pp. 164–196.

[10] *The New York Times,* July 23, 1952.

[11] See Weeks, *op. cit.,* pp. 86–88.

In 1954, the Democratic National Committee in a "harmony" meeting agreed to try to prevent a renewal of the loyalty oath in the 1956 convention.

THE PLATFORM

The first document to be considered as a party platform was, oddly enough, drafted by a group of self-styled "young men" in the National Republican party after the party's convention in 1831. This declaration of principles consisted of planks almost exclusively "anti" or negative in character. The practice was omitted in 1836 but revived by the Democrats in their national convention in 1840. Since then party platforms have become an integral part of the convention and party system. It is not always easy to define what a platform is since there have often been long preambles and appended resolutions which are apparently not intended as a part of the platform.[12] Today platforms profess to be a guide to the principles and policies which the party will carry out if elected to office.

Preparation. The platform is prepared and presented by the committee on resolutions to the delegates for debate and amendment. Resolutions committees are generally composed of one man from each state and one woman from each state having women in its delegation. Appropriately, many outstanding persons have been appointed to these committees. For example, on the 1944 Democratic body were 11 United States senators, including Senator Harry S. Truman of Missouri, as well as two governors, and several former governors, senators, and representatives. Representative John W. McCormack, House majority floor leader, served as chairman and read the document to the convention. The Republican committee, headed by Senator Robert A. Taft, likewise was composed of numerous Federal and state officeholders and Alfred M. Landon, the party's 1936 presidential nominee.

Because of the alleged importance of the platform, lengthy committee deliberations are needed and these are begun in advance of the opening day of the convention by a subcommittee of the resolutions group. The resolutions committee is not only a forum before which factions in the party argue; it is also besieged with pleas of the various interest groups. In this respect it resembles a legislative committee. Spokesmen for the Farm Bureau and other agricultural associations appear before it to obtain a plank favoring specific farm programs. Representatives of the CIO and AFL present their ideas on what should be the party's attitude toward labor, and leaders of business seek assurance from the committee that the party will record its approval of the private enterprise system and

[12] The 1952 platforms are in the appendix. Kirk Porter, *National Party Platforms* (New York: The Macmillan Company, 1924), contains all party platforms from 1840 to 1924.

a minimum of governmental controls. Women's organizations, especially the Woman's Rights party, are perennially seeking an "equal rights for women" or similar plank. Veterans and temperance groups, to mention only two others, can be depended upon to seek inclusion of their interests in the platform. The resolutions committee tries to iron out differences on controversial issues raised by party and private groups in order to avoid a floor fight. The platform is finished in time to be presented to the delegates before the nominating speeches and the balloting.[13]

Senator Taft took 45 minutes to read the 4,500-word platform in 1944, only to have it adopted within 20 seconds after the reading with fewer than one-fourth of the delegates on the floor and only about 500 spectators in a gallery capable of seating thousands. In view of the hours of labor in its preparation, the small attendance was a gloomy anticlimax to its makers. However, the fact that the platform contained enough compromises to avoid much of a floor fight was considerable compensation to its drafters.

Floor Debates. The acceptance by the conventions with little or no debate is by no means the rule. In almost every convention there is at least one large issue over which the platform committee has a battle, and on many occasions the controversy has to be settled on the floor of the convention. In the 1924 Democratic convention a strong minority called for a bold declaration in favor of the League of Nations and for religious freedom. The last-mentioned largely concerned the quarrel over the supporters and enemies of the Ku Klux Klan. After a bitter and acrimonious debate the minority planks were defeated, in the case of the Klan by only one vote.[14]

Great excitement occurred in the 1948 Democratic convention when neither the Northern nor the Southern extremists were willing to accept the compromise statement of the resolutions committee on civil rights. After an hour of debate on the floor, the delegates turned down a states' rights plank submitted by Southern delegations on a roll call of 925 to 309. When the Southern delegation insisted on submitting the states' rights plank, which would have largely nullified the general plank proposed on civil rights by the resolutions committee, a minority group of members of the resolutions committee submitted a plank praising President Truman for his "courageous stand" on civil rights and pledging the party to the specific measures contained in it. This plank was anathema to the Southern delegations, which already were threatening to bolt the party. Although a majority of the delegates in the interest of party har-

[13] An exception to this occurred in 1944, when the Democrats literally "sandwiched in" the presentation of the platform between the nominating speeches and the roll call.

[14] An interesting account of this battle is found in William Allen White, *Politics: The Citizen's Business* (New York: The Macmillan Company, 1924), pp. 71–84.

mony would have preferred the general plank submitted by the resolutions committee, which might have avoided the split and the formation of the Dixiecrat ticket, nevertheless, when forced to vote on the measure, the large industrial states of the North voted for the amendment and it carried 651½ to 582½. Without waiting for the presidential nominations, half of the Alabama and all of the Mississippi delegations walked out of the convention.

Character of the Platform. If the voter expects to find specific issues and clearly defined party policies in the platform, he will be sorely disappointed. As a guide to the program to be carried out by the victorious party, the platform is also of little value. Rather the resolutions are largely composed of vague and general propositions. They run in a large part to the "we point with pride, we view with alarm" theme rather than to definite promises. As Lord Bryce once observed, their purpose appears to be "neither to define nor to convince, but rather to attract and confuse." Platforms also are strongly negative in character, revealing the widely held view of many politicians that people prefer to vote *against* rather than *for* something. In the resolutions, as in campaigns, the voters are encouraged to vote their fears. The party in power warns against returning the nation to the "outs," and the opposition's document warns against continuing the present regime in power.

The reasons why the platform is an unsatisfactory guide to the party's contemplated program are many. In general, they result from the nature of the parties themselves, i.e., a heterogeneous composition representing progressive and conservative wings and a widely diversified social and economic complexion. The platform, like the party organization, attempts to weld together discordant elements and to mean all things to all men. Unlike the Marxist, agrarian, labor, or other minor parties, the major parties are concerned about offending large financial contributors or a sizable voting segment. With dexterity, the resolutions seek to avoid alienating any group, except possibly the Communists, and at the same time to put something in the platform to please the large minorities.

The Democrats in recent elections, with little hope of corralling isolationist-nationalist votes, were more forthright on foreign policy. Both platforms are always committed in a general way to "farm prosperity," "free enterprise," aid to preserving small business, and to reduce taxes (often couched in careful terms). The party out of power inveighs against bureaucracy while the "in" party remains silent on bureaucrats. As always, generous promises are made to veterans. Since 1840, it has become axiomatic for the major parties to demand "rigid economy in government."

Although platforms tend toward sameness, there have been important exceptions. Planks over prohibition, foreign policy, and social security have shown marked differences. The 1952 Republican platform upheld the Taft-Hartley Act but urged the adoption of such amendments "as time and experience show to be desirable, and which further protect the rights of labor, management, and the public." The Democratic platform called for categorical repeal of the Taft-Hartley law. The Democrats declared in favor of Federal aid to education; the Republican platform was silent.

While there is an essential similarity in the two major-party platforms, the Democrat documents have been somewhat more specific. One reason for this is the fact that, with the exception of 1888, the Republican convention has always met first. This provides the Democratic platform with a knowledge of what and whom it has to fight and to capitalize on weaknesses appearing in the Republican statement. More than this, a minority party can always be more specific in its platform, both in criticizing and in making promises which are definite. From the Civil War to 1932 the Democratic party was the minority party most of the time, and under the leadership of Franklin Roosevelt it stood for rather specific policies in the fields of labor, business, agriculture, and foreign affairs.

Nominees Influence Platform. Resolutions are often left purposely vague in order to permit the presidential nominee to add his own interpretation and to develop certain planks into full-blown campaign issues. If a policy were too specific, the candidate might be restricted or limited and, if he departed from the plank, the object of embarrassment. The Democratic convention in 1928, for example, pledged its nominees to "an honest effort to enforce the Eighteenth Amendment." Yet its candidate Alfred E. Smith notified the convention of his opposition to prohibition and used it as an issue in the campaign. In "dry areas" strong disapproval was expressed of Mr. Smith's departure from the party's platform.

The Republican platform in 1952 was silent on mandatory price supports for agricultural products, while the Democratic resolutions pledged support "at not less than 90 per cent parity." In a major campaign speech on farm policy, however, Eisenhower said he favored 100 per cent parity. On the controversial provision to give title to the submerged coastal lands to the states neither platform took a specific stand. Yet Eisenhower, campaigning in the South, pledged a Federal quitclaim law and "a return of tidelands to the states." Governor Stevenson, when pressed for his position on the matter, met personally with Governor Shivers of Texas and announced that he would abide by the United States Supreme Court decision upholding Federal ownership. The Texas governor immediately came out for Eisenhower and kept the tidelands issue in the forefront of the campaign. Thus the amplification of their position on the question by the two candidates served to overcome the silence of the platforms and undoubtedly contributed to the Eisenhower victory because the General took the politically popular position. Governor Dewey both in 1944 and 1948 elaborated considerably on his party's foreign policy planks and committed himself to much more of an internationalist viewpoint than was apparent in the platforms. Wendell Willkie did likewise in 1940.

Significance of the Platform. Platforms are not always rigidly followed by the winning party and are sometimes viewed, therefore, as meaningless. When a party embarks upon a policy not stated in its resolutions, political opponents decry the action as a violation of party principles. Involvement in war in 1917 and 1941 and the Democratic promise in 1932 to reduce Federal expenditures 25 per cent are cited by partisans as violations of party promises. President Roosevelt's so-called Supreme Court "packing" plan and the lend-lease proposal, neither of which appeared in the Democratic platform, provoked further criticisms of "betrayal of the platform." It seems doubtful, however, if the nation would have tolerated a drastic reduction of expenditures in 1933 for it would have meant no relief programs. Public-opinion polls showed majority support of lend-lease in 1941, and the course of international events in the two world wars led the minority members of Congress to vote almost unanimously with the Democrats for a declaration of war. Over a half year elapses between adoption of the platform and inauguration, and, in a world of rapidly changing events, slavish adherence for four years to a platform, subject at best to wide interpretation, seems an unreasonable expectation from any point of view.

The very nature of the platform keeps it from being an ironclad party program and it should not be regarded as such. The President and congressional leaders in effect make their own platform and, in the absence of periodic party conferences as is found in England, the practice seems most efficient and desirable. As the responsible agents of the party in power, the President and his congressional supporters must formulate policies. To follow a platform drafted in a convention by men in many cases having no public responsibility would invite confusion and division of power, not to say absurdity.

What then are the significance and utility of a platform? If perfectionism can be discarded as a standard, the platform may be regarded as a useful device for rallying divergent interests to a general credo of faith and principles. In some respects it may be compared with similar statements issued by private-interest organizations. The fact that not all businessmen fully subscribe to the bylaws or declarations of the Congress of American Industry does not necessarily mean that no such resolutions should be formulated. So it may be argued by party adherents. Regarded in this light, party declarations help to unify the conglomerate groups and attempt to establish a few common goals and principles. Party resolutions also help to awaken the electorate on contemporary problems and the weaknesses of the opposition; as such they constitute a focus and a base for debate and discussion during the campaign. During the last century the platforms assumed more significance than in this one because the nominees were not expected to depart too far from the precepts adopted at the convention. The greater latitude which is taken by the candidates today, however, has led to campaign debate on a larger number of subjects and has resulted, in effect, in broadening the platform.

The fact that the opposition in succeeding years points out the discrepancy between promise and performance indicates some usefulness of the platform as a yardstick. Often the resolutions are a measuring stick for the party in power as well. It is erroneous to fall into the cynical habit of believing that the resolutions are honored more in the breach than in the observance. If one will measure the remarkably specific and progressive Democratic platform of 1932 with legislation passed during the succeeding four years, he will find an impressive record of promises and fulfillments.

THE PRESIDENTIAL NOMINATION

Nominating Addresses. With resolutions and routine matters out of the way, the delegates enthusiastically file into the convention hall for the big show, the great drama for which they have been waiting—the nomination of a presidential candidate. The chairman asks the secretary to call the roll. In alphabetical order from Alabama to Wyoming each state's name is called and each is entitled to put forth a name. States often have agreements to yield to another for purpose of placing names in nomination. In the 1944 Republican convention, for example, Alabama yielded to Nebraska, thus permitting the chairman to give the floor to the representative of the Nebraska delegation, Governor Dwight Griswold. After long and boisterous applause the governor began,

We are here to restore the Presidency of the United States to the American people. (Applause.) We are here to bring Washington, D.C. back into the United States. (Applause.) We are here to make the American people masters in their own household. (Applause.) For that job we have the means and we have the man. (Applause.)

In hard-hitting terms Mr. Griswold berated the opposition and extolled the record of the "governor of New York," who had broken rackets, fought political corruption, and revitalized his state. Withholding the person's name, as is customary until the end of the nominating address, the speaker concluded, "I give to you the nominee of the Republican party, the spokesman of the future, Thomas E. Dewey!" History repeated itself when Alabama yielded to Pennsylvania in 1948 to permit Senator

Edward Martin to place before the convention the man "who for years has belonged to all America, tried, tested, and true, America's next President—Thomas E. Dewey!"

On both occasions, as with all nominating addresses, the announcement of the name was a signal for the demonstration. As if an electric button had been pushed, Dewey banners appeared throughout the sections reserved for the delegates and supporters marched through the aisles holding aloft pictures of Dewey and bearing such inscriptions as "Dewey will win!" "America wants Dewey," "Dewey, the people's choice." Music blared from the band in the balcony. In the galleries, visitors waved flags and hats in rhythm with the music. After the demonstration and parade had proceeded for about 30 minutes, the chairman vigorously pounded the gavel and ordered the sergeant at arms to clear the aisles of the paraders and demonstrators.[15] A few minutes later order was restored, the "fake," as the trade calls the demonstrations, was over and the convention proceeded with its business. This consisted in numerous seconding addresses for Governor Dewey, followed in turn by nominating speeches for other hopefuls, demonstrations, and seconding addresses. In 1948 the Taft and Stassen supporters tried to outdo the Dewey demonstration with novelties, balloons, and cheering squads and songs. Radio commentators reported that they were successful in this endeavor. The 1952 Republican nominating addresses and demonstrations lasted over six hours, with adjournment at three o'clock in the morning. On occasions when many names were placed before the convention, it has taken from 10 to 20 hours to complete the roll call for placing nominations.

Balloting. Following the completion of the nominating and seconding addresses, a roll call of the states for voting on the nominees is taken. By reason of the "unit rule," a number of states in the Democratic convention cast their votes in a bloc. Concisely, the rule allows a state convention to instruct its delegation to cast the entire vote of a state in accordance with the desires of a majority of its delegation. In this case the national convention enforces the instruction given to the state delegation. The Republican convention does not recognize state instructions to abide by the unit rule.

In both major-party conventions a simple majority is now needed for nomination. Prior to 1936, the Democrats always operated under a rule requiring a two-thirds majority to nominate. This rule coupled with the unit rule often resulted in longer and more vociferous conventions than those of the Grand Old Party. The two-thirds rule was originally spon-

---

[15] In the past demonstrations commonly lasted an hour for leading candidates, with cheerleaders and stunts to keep the "show" going. Recently demonstrations by agreement have been limited to 20 to 30 minutes and seconding addresses have been limited to four in number per candidate.

sored by a Southern Democrat ostensibly to create a "more imposing effect." From its inception it received continued stanch support from the South, and efforts by Democrats from the North and West to modify it were defeated on numerous occasions. In effect the rule operated to enable a section to force a compromise on nominees if necessary. The Solid South, supplying as it did the most consistently reliable Democratic strength, regarded the two-thirds majority as a safeguard against the choice of a nominee considered unfavorable to its interests.

Roosevelt supporters in 1932 felt certain of a majority for their nominee but were less sure of a two-thirds majority and they were successful in getting the rules committee to recommend a change that, after failing to nominate on the sixth ballot, the convention would abide by a simple majority rule. When it became apparent that this proposal would provoke a floor fight with possible harm to the Roosevelt candidacy, his managers got the rules committee to agree to shelve the matter and to recommend that the 1936 convention consider the abolition of the two-thirds rule. With the aid of National Chairman James A. Farley, the 1936 convention abolished the two-thirds rule. This was possible largely because Roosevelt was renominated by acclamation and this issue was, therefore, not concerned with any personality at the moment. The possible loss of strength to the South was somewhat compensated by a change of rules in subsequent conventions rewarding bonuses of delegates to each state going Democratic in the preceding presidential election.

In 1924, with the Democratic convention operating under the two-thirds rule, the battle between Smith and McAdoo continued unabated until a compromise choice was agreed upon. The convention took two weeks to nominate. Since that time both parties have been able to arrive at a nomination after six or less ballots. Even so, the calling for a poll of individual delegates by states and recesses between ballots have caused long delays. Stevenson was nominated on the third ballot, which took virtually all day and into the early morning hours. By the time he appeared for his acceptance address, the bulk of the radio and television audience, at least in the East, had been lost.

The delays between balloting, the polling of individual state delegations, and so on are exasperating and make no sense to the listening and viewing audience. Under the surface, however, the delays are largely for the purpose of working for consensus, for consummating deals and bargains, and to give floor leaders an opportunity to make phone calls to aspirants and trying to get delegations to switch their votes from favorite sons. Managers for the leading contenders are looking for "breaks" which will stampede other delegations to switch their votes. Harding and Willkie did not start out with many votes but picked up strength on each ballot to emerge with the nomination. When the Minnesota delegation broke from Stassen to Eisenhower, there was a race to the Eisenhower bandwagon. One never knows when the "regulars" may emerge with a Harding or when a popular leader like Bryan may throw his strength to a Wilson.

Vice Presidential Nomination. After the presidential nomination is agreed upon, the convention proceeds to name a candidate for "second place" on the ticket. Names are placed in nomination and a ballot taken in the same manner as for the President. This is usually an anticlimax, for the delegates are emotionally spent and colorful demonstrations are missing. An effort is made to get the matter over quickly so delegates can hear the acceptance addresses and start home. Most of the time the vice presidential nomination has been "negotiated" and the delegates are "told" who is to be the nominee. Nixon was literally selected in a "smoke-filled room" where Republican governors and other officeholders representing both Taft and Eisenhower factions arrived at agreement. Feelings were high between Northern and Southern Democrats and it seemed to dictate the choice of Senator Sparkman of Alabama, whose voting record was reasonably acceptable to the Northern wing. Since Senators Russell and Kefauver were presidential contenders, discretion dictated that neither of them be given the place.

The nomination may often be a consolation prize to a section or faction; Garner of Texas, Bricker of Ohio, and McNary of Oregon provide conspicuous examples. The presidential nominee is always consulted and may actually make the decision himself. Roosevelt indicated his preference for Wallace in 1940 and for Truman in 1944, while Dewey selected Bricker in 1944 after Warren declined. Many delegates were unhappy with Roosevelt's choice of Wallace and about 500 of them voted for other candidates.

It would be hard to support the view that consistently good vice presidential selections have been made. This is because the choices are so strongly motivated by factional and sectional appeasement. Indeed, many persons have been selected who possessed few qualifications for a potential President. This suggests that more sober consideration should be given to vice presidential nominations.

EVALUATION

Many American writers have agreed with Ostrogorski that national conventions are "a colossal travesty of popular institutions." Sheer size of the conventions and the methods of selecting delegates make for control by means of backstairs deals and hotel room compromises of professional party leaders rather than a grass-roots expression of the party members. Former Democratic National Chairman Edward J. Flynn once wrote that every national convention is controlled by less than 100 persons and that "the average delegate takes practically no part in the work of the convention other than voting when he is required to do so." [16] Most of the real work of the convention goes on behind the scenes, and the floor activities are merely the results of agreements reached outside the convention itself. This, it should be noted, is true of almost all large conventions, and necessarily so. Delegates themselves often owe their position to the organization and are far from free agents. Although much of the work is done in secret, it does not follow that the unseen activities are invariably sheer connivance to frustrate the popular will.

Critics also point to weak selections by the convention. They note that important qualities of availability may run to the candidate's family life, his place of residence, or his religion, thus debarring competent persons on these grounds. Vote-getting ability, party loyalty, a capacity to work with machine politicians, though legitimate considerations, are likewise felt by many to be given undue consideration. It cannot be denied that since 1832 some mediocrities have been nominated and some elected and that highly competent men have been passed over for the less competent and well qualified.

Some scholars profess preference for the British parliamentary system which results in bringing to the prime ministry what Lord Bryce called a "natural selection" of "highest gifts to the highest place." In effect, this is to prefer the cabinet system to the presidential system and is not particularly a question of method of nomination. There seems little prospect of public acceptance of a cabinet system or a return of the nominating function to the congressional caucus.

Notwithstanding valid criticisms of convention organization and procedures, a strong case exists for the preservation of the institution. Negatively, the device is convenient and there are serious problems in finding an acceptable alternative. As noted a moment ago, few critics would favor revival of the congressional caucus and few would be prepared to leave nominations to the national committees or other small body of the top organization in the party. National committeemen as spokesmen for the state party organizations would tend to follow the pattern of orthodox politics and considerations.

For years the proposal to nominate by a national party primary system has had some distinguished proponents. Senator George Smathers sponsored a Constitutional amendment to enable Congress to enact a national primary law.[17] The extension of state presidential primary laws

[16] *You're the Boss* (New York: The Viking Press, Inc., 1947), p. 97.

[17] Space prohibits an analysis and evaluation of this proposal and various other issues of national nominating procedure. There is a comprehensive discussion by Paul T. David, Malcolm Moos, and Ralph Goldman in *The National Story*, which appears as Vol. 1 of *Presidential Nominating Politics in 1952*, Chaps. 5–6.

as proposed by Senator Paul Douglas would not do away with nomination by the national convention, while the Smathers proposal would permit Congress to abolish the convention in favor of a nationwide vote. A primary system faces formidable practical problems such as the need for acceptance of a plurality vote, a runoff primary, a preferential vote, or entrusting the national committee or other body to designate if no candidate received a majority vote. Would the second highest person receive the vice presidential nomination or would some other system be used to designate him? Potentially, the national primary might result in disregarding the sectional and factional considerations and leave the party without unity and cohesion in the general election. From the point of view of candidates, a national primary might well be more expensive and exhausting than the present system. Proponents of the primary, of course, can offer rebuttals for all these points but the arguments nonetheless remain impressive.

One of the most serious shortcomings of the proposed primary system is also the strength of the national convention—the lack of the advantages of deliberation and compromise which now characterize the convention. The convention works to assure the nomination of a candidate approaching the mean. It passes over extremists in favor of persons who, though maybe not first choice, are acceptable. It is here that a case can be made for the smoke-filled room where party managers appraise the vote-getting potential of contenders in terms of the temper of the times.[18] To select a person out of tune with the times and who is an anathema to certain groups and wings of the party is to invite disaster at the polls. The 1952 conventions provided good illustrations of the tendencies of such meetings. Senator Taft appeared the logical, most deserving candidate and was in the popular mind "Mr. Republican." Governor Warren and former Governor Stassen were associated with the liberal wing of the party but were not popular with conservatives. MacArthur appealed to some of the most vociferous of the right wing. Eisenhower occupied the middle ground, much as Dewey had done in 1944 and 1948. The General was not a New Dealer but neither did his name appear on a labor law unpopular with union leaders nor was it associated with isolationism. Moreover, public-opinion polls seemed to indicate he could win—something that the other aspirants were unable to show. Democrats passed up Averell Harriman, who was associated as a pro-Fair Deal, Americans for Democratic Action, labor candidate, and Senator Russell, whose support was sectional and factional. Senator Kefauver had alienated many Truman and Southern Democrats and was referred to as a man who was neither able to run with the hares nor hunt with the hounds. He did show up

[18] On this point see the comments of James M. Burns, "The Case for the Smoke-filled Room," *The New York Times Magazine,* June 15, 1952.

well in the Democratic primaries but, to the delegates, Governor Stevenson was a better approximation of the mean. Eisenhower and Stevenson appeared to be capable of uniting the diverse factions in their parties better than anyone else. The enormous popular vote of both candidates and the absence of any serious third-party threat suggest the nominations in 1952 achieved their potential. Not every convention, of course, has been able to do this.

The role of the convention is more than simply nominations. It is a colorful conclave and deeply imbedded in the American tradition. Delegates return home with news, gossip, and a feeling that they have experienced a great act in party life. They bring enthusiasm and leadership to the ensuing campaign. Many help to assuage the disappointed back home by explaining why a certain man was nominated and another was not. The delegate relates his visits to hotel rooms where he met the party's factotums and candidates. His faith has been affirmed and his spirits reinforced. If he did not get his man nominated for President, he may very well have seen his favorite receive second place and he probably got something in the platform which was pleasing to him. Not every delegate comes home "pepped up" but it is fair to say the great majority do and they are willing to close ranks and take on the "enemy." These are psychological values which are not to be overlooked. Rightly or wrongly, the delegate believes he comes home a better Republican or Democrat much as the Legionnaire, Shriner, or Rotarian comes home from his convention with a greater feeling of loyalty.

Perhaps the greatest virtue of the convention is that it works. From the voter's standpoint, the convention process is reasonably simple, understandable, and an illustration of democracy at work. To the practical-minded loyal partisan it is reasonably satisfactory. The conventions of the present century appear, on the whole, to have placed before the voters better choices than the last. Friends of the convention process, however, are by no means satisfied and recognize the need for improvement. Among the oft repeated suggestions are the following.

First, an effort might be made to reduce the size of the convention and to make it more representative. This inevitably brings up the questions on apportionment and on the selection of delegates. Delegates traveling a long distance to the conventions sometimes have their way paid by a presidential hopeful and are not therefore free agents. Many excellent representatives of the party do not become delegates because they cannot afford it. Conventions are likewise often overcrowded with party officialdom and officeholders. The use of preference primaries and merits of selection by state convention need reappraisal both as to implications and to the perfection of their mechanics and operation. Many voters remain perplexed by the primary ballots.

Television and radio have happily brought a reduction of the length of speeches and demonstrations. Both parties are considering ways of overcoming the tedious delays of the individual polling of delegations. Balloting in the 1952 Democratic convention took all day and evening and proceeded with agonizing slowness, largely because many delegations were polled man by man. The Kefauver forces used it to stall for time, others wanted to put their fellows' votes on record, and still others apparently wanted a few seconds in front of television cameras. Whatever the reason, it made tedious viewing and listening and the individual polling might have been done in a speedier fashion. One may also hope for a reduction in the number of favorite sons nominated, but hope and realization are likely to be hard to reconcile. Convention rules and mechanics have undergone improvement and there is room for further changes. Perhaps a careful study of the finding of the Cooperative Research Project of the American Political Science Association will open up new insights into the improvement of national conventions.

SELECTED REFERENCES

The basic works on nominating systems, practices, and procedures include Charles E. Merriam and Louise Overacker, *Primary Elections* (1928); Arthur Harris and Carl Uhr, *Direct Primary Elections* (1941); Illinois Legislative Council, *The Direct Primary Ballot* (1940); S. D. Albright, *Ballot Analysis and Ballot Changes since 1930* (1940) and *The American Ballot* (1942); Joseph P. Harris, *Election Administration in the United States* (1934) and *Registration of Voters in the United States* (1929); Louise Overacker, *The Presidential Primary* (1926). Two old but useful works on the caucus, conventions, and primary are E. C. Meyer, *Nominating Systems: Direct Primaries versus Conventions* (1902); and F. W. Dallinger, *Nominations for Elective Office in the United States* (1903). See also Benjamin Glassman, *A. B. C. of the Direct Primary Law*, 3d ed. (1938); and C. H. Woody, *The Direct Primary in Chicago* (1926). Louise Overacker's articles on "Direct Primary Legislation" in *The American Political Science Review*, Vol. 24 (May, 1930), pp. 370–380; Vol. 26 (April, 1932), pp. 284–300; Vol. 28 (April, 1934), pp. 265–270; Vol. 30 (April, 1936), pp. 279–285; Vol. 34 (June, 1940), pp. 499–506, give a comprehensive review of changes in primary laws during that decade.

The student is urged to study the laws governing nominations in his own state. Articles or books are available on the direct primaries in most of the states. Clarence Berdahl has a wealth of material on party primary tests in "Party Membership in the United States," *The American Political Science Review*, Vol. 36 (1942), pp. 16–50; 241–262. Volumes on certain states include Boyd A. Martin, *The Direct Primary in Idaho* (1947); A. F. Lovejoy, *La Follette and the Establishment of the Direct Primary in Wisconsin, 1890–1904* (1941); L. M. Holland, *The Direct Primary in Georgia* (1945); R. D. Boots, *The Direct Primary in New Jersey* (1917); P. Beckett and Walter L. McNutt, *The Direct Primary in New Mexico* (1947); and James K. Pollock, *The Direct Primary in Michigan, 1909–1935* (1943).

Of value to the student of national conventions are the *Proceedings of the National Convention* published quadrennially by the political parties. A few of the more useful general works include J. B. Bishop, *Presidential Nominations and Elections* (1916); T. H. McKee (ed.), *The National Conventions and Platforms of All Political Parties, 1789–1905* (1906); W. J. Bryan, *A Tale of Two Conventions* (1912); K. H. Porter (ed.)

National Party Platforms, 1840–1924 (1924); W. A. White, *Politics: The Citizen's Business* (1924); H. L. Mencken, *Making a President* (1932); Harold Laski, "The Conventions and the Presidency," *Harper's Magazine,* July, 1940, pp. 166–171; T. M. Plaisted, "Origins of National Nominating Committees and Platforms," *Social Studies,* Vol. 30 (1939), pp. 199–206; J. S. Murdock, "The First National Nominating Convention," *American Historical Review,* Vol. 1 (1896), pp. 680–683; and James Reston, "The Convention System: A 5-Count Indictment," *The New York Times Magazine,* July 11, 1948. The comprehensive five-volume work, *Presidential Nominating Politics in 1952* (1954), is indispensable to the student of national conventions.

The discerning appraisal of two eminent foreign scholars of our nominating system is always worth reading and rereading; James Bryce, *The American Commonwealth,* Vol. II, and M. Ostrogorski, *Democracy and the Party System,* especially Chaps. VI–VII. E. Stanwood, *A History of the Presidency,* Vols. I–II (1912; 1916), gives an intimate glimpse into a number of national conventions.

CHAPTER 19

Political Campaigns

"The time has come," the Walrus said,
"To talk of many things:
Of shoes—and ships—and sealing wax—
Of cabbages—and kings—
And why the sea is boiling hot—
And whether pigs have wings."
—*Through the Looking-Glass*

"Nobody has ever been able to formulate a code of political ethics," said Charles Michelson, onetime Democratic publicity director. "Despite the fine altruistic language of party platforms, the habit has always been to smite the opposition, regardless of Marquis of Queensberry rules, whenever and however the opportunity offers." The political campaign offers no better example of this statement. Americans place a high premium upon entertainment as evidenced by the popular esteem enjoyed by motion-picture performers and radio stars, especially comedians and singers. The Barnum and Bailey road shows, boxing matches, and professional sports draw millions of spectators every year. High on the list of American drama is the political campaign. Its directors know the value of "good show" and they know how to stage one which will appeal to the voter's love for drama. Millions of dollars are spent to present nominees to the public. Behind every speech, rally, or piece of literature go careful thought and planning. The planning and execution of a political campaign can be divided into the following: (1) the preparation of the over-all grand strategy; (2) the selection of issues and the working out of detailed strategy; (3) the development of the organization and use of subsidiary organizations; (4) the counteroffensive; (5) campaign techniques; (6) the issuance of paid advertising and campaign literature; (7) finance. The first five of these are considered in this chapter; the last two in successive chapters.

THE GRAND STRATEGY

The over-all strategy of a presidential campaign is decided as soon as possible after the national conventions. It may even be done before the conventions when a President's renomination is assured or when it seems reasonably certain that a particular favorite son will receive the party designation. No generalization can be made as to the persons who decide this strategy. These matters are confidential and full details are seldom known until biographies are available, and even then biographers are often unable to obtain the complete story. In the case of the two Roosevelts and Willkie, the men themselves had much to do with deciding the strategy. The McKinley and Harding campaigns were largely in the hands of seasoned party leaders and bosses, who dictated the general nature of the campaign. The national chairmen and high-ranking party leaders invariably have a part in deciding the type of battle to be waged.

Stay Home or Stump? The first decision to be reached is whether to use a front-porch or a barnstorming campaign. Several factors are to be considered here. First, the assets and liabilities of the party candidate as well as the opposition's candidate must be carefully appraised. If the candidate has a magnetic personality, excellent platform appearance and oratorical ability, is possessed of great stamina, and is not too well known, an intensive stumping campaign is generally employed. Here the candidate will be seen and heard with "every handshake a vote" and "every speech thousands of votes." William Jennings Bryan typified this method. He traveled 18,000 miles and visited 29 states in 1896, generally speaking several times a day. Wendell Willkie broke this record in 1940. Many Republicans were of the opinion that Willkie made too many speeches and that his almost daily appearance on the radio hit the point of diminishing returns with the voters. In 1944 Thomas E. Dewey attempted to avoid this error and made only a comparatively few speeches. Most of these were several days apart and delivered in widely varying localities from San Francisco to Boston.

The stay-at-home, front-porch method resulted in a huge success for Lincoln, McKinley, and Harding. In these instances, effective press relations and publicity, excellent speeches by others for the nominees, and a hard-working organization resulted in their election. Lincoln's first campaign was skillfully managed. Strategy dictated that this little-known rail splitter stick resolutely to his home town and avoid making speeches that would too clearly expose his views. The Lincoln cause was aided by a four-cornered fight for the presidency and a party platform which was a masterpiece of political craftsmanship. In 1932 President Hoover remained in the White House, saying that he was too busy grappling with problems of the depression to campaign. At the eleventh hour he made a cross-country tour, but in the judgment of several of his managers the trip was too late. Rightly or wrongly, many Republicans believed his refusal to get out and publicly answer charges made by Governor Roosevelt was responsible in a large part for his defeat.

Both in 1940 and in 1944 President Roosevelt was forced partially to abandon the position of being too busy to campaign. One cannot know the full reasons for this change of tactic. Certainly it was due in part to the fear of his managers that the vigorous speeches and the appearances of his opponents were making serious inroads on the Democratic cause. A rumor persisted in 1944 that Mr. Roosevelt was ill. To offset this the President made a tour of several large cities in an open car to enable the voters to see for themselves that he was fit to carry the enormous burdens of office. In New York City he went through with a parade in the face of a driving storm—a convincing demonstration of his ability to take it. This is illustrative of how the grand strategy of staying at home had to be revised in light of conditions and changes in the political picture.

President Truman chose to follow a different strategy than his predecessor and conducted an extensive cross-continental tour with hundreds of brief rear-platform addresses. This strategy was dictated in part by the belief that Truman was highly effective in informal, "off-the-cuff" speeches, but was unimpressive in formal platform addresses and over the radio.[1] In part it was also due to the fact that Truman began the campaign as the underdog, according to the public-opinion polls, and it was believed that he could hardly hope to win by merely remaining in the White House. Governor Dewey also conducted a barnstorming campaign in 1948 even though his managers felt his election was certain without it. Failure to make the traditional campaign swing would, they feared, be regarded as a sign of snobbery or arrogance and the 10,000-mile trip was in the nature of a holding operation.

President Truman's "whistle-stop" campaign in 1948 was called a "miracle of electioneering." During the campaign many Republicans criticized his technique as both undignified and futile. Nevertheless, his victory led the Republican high command to urge Eisenhower to conduct a nationwide tour in 1952. For one thing, the General was well out in front in all public-opinion polls, and dozens of informal chats and platform appearances seemed advantageous for purposes of keeping up enthusiasm for him. For another, the whistle stops permitted the Republican nominee to meet local party leaders and to help heal the rift caused by the bitter fight over the nomination. Finally, extensive appearances would give an added boost to Republican state and congressional candidates. Eisenhower visited every state except Maine, Vermont, Mississippi, and Nevada and he invaded many large pivotal states twice. There is no accurate estimate of the millions who saw him during the 11,000 miles which he traveled by train and while he delivered 40 major and about 230 whistle-stop speeches. An additional 22,000 miles were traveled by

[1] The Truman technique in "riding the circuit" very much resembled the style of a state or local candidate, with hundreds of appearances from the rear platform of his special train.

plane, which probably set an all-time record for total miles traveled during a single campaign.

Barnstorming became the dictated strategy for the Stevenson cause but for different reasons. The Illinois governor was not well known and it was necessary for him to be seen and to meet party workers and candidates. His eloquence led hundreds of local communities to pressure his managers for a personal appearance by the governor. It was even more imperative for Stevenson to reach national audiences and he could not hope therefore to devote as much time and energy to local stops as Eisenhower. Nevertheless, Stevenson traveled 32,500 miles, 27,140 by air. He gave 21 nationally televised speeches, about 210 others, and went into 32 states.

One of the most remarkable characteristics of the 1952 campaign was that, notwithstanding the availability of radio and television, stumping the country became the order of the day. President Truman repeated his 1948 tactics by traveling from coast to coast and making some 211 speeches in 27 states. Republicans, remembering his success in 1948, sent several senators right behind him as a self-styled "truth squad" to answer the President. Senator Taft also campaigned intensively for the Republican ticket, appearing in about half the states. When the extensive itinerary of Senators Nixon and Sparkman is added to those above, it seems clear that 1952 broke all barnstorming records.

Sometimes the failure to "ride the circuit" and to make widespread public appearances is due to a manager's fear that the candidate will be unable to handle hecklers and himself well. Harding's strategists were unsure of his ability to answer questions and were concerned that he might make blunders and unpolitic errors if he made numerous appearances and submitted himself to questioning. The front-porch technique is quite frequently employed in state and local campaigns. This strategy may be used when a candidate appears far ahead, or when he seems assured of a large "coattail" vote, or is too low on funds to afford much travel expense. Popular incumbents often successfully employ the method of "staying on the job" and refraining from delivering widespread campaign speeches.

Attack or Defend? Another factor entering into over-all strategy is the balance between offense and defense. When an incumbent is running for reelection against an opponent who has little in his record to attack, the incumbent may be easily forced into a defensive position. His main attack is most likely to be limited to the opposition's lack of experience; beyond this he will have to defend his own record. If his policies have been popular, this tactic may be successful; illustrative instances were the last three Roosevelt campaigns. In each case the President enjoyed a superior position. He largely ignored his opponents and did not mention them by name. By contrast, Herbert Hoover in 1932 was forced to defend an administration which was caught in the throes of a depression.

Party managers are pragmatists but they often are slow to change methods. Many proceed on the assumption that the voter would rather vote against a candidate or a policy than for someone or a program. As a result, the nominee is always advised to concentrate his guns on his opponents, "go easy" on presenting a positive, or at least a dangerously concrete, program, and avoid being placed on the defensive. A high-ranking party manager, in delivering an off-the-record speech (1939) before a group of political scientists, phrased it in these terms: "In politics a man's liabilities are much more important that his assets. People vote against things, not for them. In considering nominees of our own party, we first see if they have any serious liabilities. If they have, we think it best to reject them even though they may have many excellent qualities and abilities. When the opposition has a candidate, we comb everything in his past, from his boyhood to the present, to see what we can get our hooks into, and then we go to town on those things." Many, even within this man's party, would debate this proposition and point to several national elections where such tactics failed. Yet one sees evidences, especially in state and local elections, where mudslinging, vitriolic attacks, and purely negative speeches form the basis of the campaign.

THE SELECTION OF ISSUES

Personalities are customarily regarded as more important than policies in a campaign. Regardless of this axiom, some issues have to be discussed by those seeking office. How are these issues selected? Broadly speaking, campaign arguments grow out of the (1) political and economic environment of the moment and (2) the nature and imagination of the nominee and his managers.

Conditions Govern Choice. Many issues are cut out for the parties even before the national or state conventions or before the primaries. In 1944, it was axiomatic that the Republicans would seize as issues the building of a large wartime bureaucracy, the internal quarrels between rival agencies, and conflicting orders and policies. These would bulwark the attack against the Roosevelt Administration regardless of whether Dewey, Willkie, Taft, or any other Republican were nominated. At the same time the Democrats were in a position of warning the nation against changing the Commander in Chief and the "team" in the midst of successfully prosecuting the war. President Truman chose to make the record of the Eightieth Congress the central issue of the campaign, selecting such questions as housing, price control, social security, and the Taft-Hartley Act. This was largely due to the fact that, as governor of New York, Dewey had been able to remain aloof from these issues and had an administrative record which was essentially good, and Democratic strategists regarded the weakest part of the Republican armor and its greatest liability to be the behavior of Congress. These issues, then, were essentially determined by the situation of the moment, and each party found itself circumscribed accordingly, being handed a certain line of attack by virtue of the nature of things.

For the party out of power, the strategists have usually decreed that the "theme and variation" should center around the mistakes and shortcomings of the party in power without too much emphasis on a positive program. The 1946 congressional elections offer a case in point. From the Republican national chairman down to the lowest precinct captain and in the speeches of nominees, the major theme was the "bungling," "bureaucracy," and "confusion" at Washington. The meat and other shortages were seized upon as general evidence of incompetency in Washington and, by implication, of all Democrats running for office. The politics of protest likewise sets the stage in state and local contests.

Another set of issues is built around the concept of guilt by association. For decades the Democrats have charged the Republicans with being dominated by moneyed interests, "Wall Street" and "reactionary big business," and "private-interest moneyed lobbies." Republican orators have countered with allegations of a communistic and socialistic interest behind the Democrats and that the party is dominated by "pinks" and left-wing labor leaders. In local elections, the "outs" commonly charge the party in power with machine politics, boss rule, and alliances with undesirable elements or the underworld.

The Politics of Evasion. Campaigners are frequently as concerned with what to avoid as with what to include in the way of issues. Both candidates desire to avoid controversial issues which may cost themselves votes. "Gentlemen's agreements" not to bring up certain issues are sometimes made by the respective campaign managers in local races. Incumbents may side-step debate on embarrassing questions by saying, "My record speaks for itself," even though the record scarcely indicates the officeholder's position. Thomas E. Dewey skillfully avoided discussion of several serious state issues and promises of things to be done in his next term as governor. His policy of "no comment," silence, and failure to take a forthright position in gubernatorial campaigns did not hurt him, but many believed it cost him heavily in votes in his 1948 bid for the presidency. Leaders in the Byrd Democratic organization in Virginia often avoid speechmaking on the theory that their faithful following need no oratorical arousing to bring them to the polls and that speeches would merely stir up opposition and aid opponents.

Governor Dewey's "unity and teamwork" which he urged in 1948 was the prototype of Wilson's "New Freedom" generalizations in 1912. Both

Wilson and Dewey seemed assured of victory if they were able to avoid taking a stand on controversial issues. Calvin Coolidge in 1924 and Franklin Roosevelt in 1932 avoided being specific on a great many matters. Dwight Eisenhower received the nomination for President without campaigning in the primaries and without making his views known on most public questions. To a considerable extent his successful campaign for the presidency was conducted on generalities.

The politics of evasion seems predicated in part on the assumption that people hear what they want to hear and see what they want to see. Among partisans, from lukewarm to zealous, there is a tendency to be influenced by preconceptions that a candidate agrees with them or that they somehow do not know where he stands on an issue when they stand on the other side. Four weeks before election day in 1948, Elmo Roper noted that his polling studies showed that most Dewey voters were unfamiliar with how the governor stood but thought he agreed with them. Roper remarked that Dewey appeared "to be all things to all men." "On the civil rights issue, Mr. Dewey draws the support of voters favoring exactly opposite things, and more than that, each side thinks Dewey agrees with them." [2]

The Eisenhower-Stevenson Campaign: A Contrast. Several additional axioms, strategies, and problems of selecting issues in American campaigns may be illustrated by reference to the 1952 election. In most respects the Eisenhower campaign was essentially traditional and conventional. The General, even before the national conventions, was shown in public-opinion polls as likely to be the victor over any Democrat nominated. His wartime record was successful and well known and he had no public elective office record which could be attacked. Given the general public displeasure with the course of the Korean operation and the existence of dishonesty and Communist infiltration in some Federal agencies, Eisenhower found himself the beneficiary of mounting protest against the party in power. Similar to Wendell Willkie, the General likened his campaign to a "crusade" and attached to it a strong moral appeal. In Buffalo, for example, he told his listeners: [3]

You and I and millions of Americans are now engaged in a great crusade—a fighting crusade for Americans who want again to hold their heads high, for Americans who want again to be proud of the men and women in their government. . . .

As a nation we are what we are because of what we believe. We believe in God and in the supremacy of moral law. We believe that man is more than a machine; we believe that he is made in the image of God. We believe that

2 *New York Herald Tribune,* Oct. 7, 1948.
3 *The New York Times,* Oct. 24, 1952.

governments are not instituted to be the masters of man's destiny. We believe they should defend, encourage and release man's God-given ability to be the master of his own destiny. . . . This miracle of America has been proof of the power of moral and spiritual forces to bind us together. Faced with a moral and spiritual challenge the people of America have never failed.

Eisenhower repeatedly talked of the "mess" in Washington and the "scandal-a-day administration." He made numerous direct appeals to women to sweep the grafters out of Washington. "I know what can be done," he said, "with a good broom in the hands of a morally indignant woman. For the women of America in a special sense are the keepers, the defenders of our moral values." Without calling Stevenson by name or accusing him of corruption, Eisenhower, nonetheless, insisted that "the candidate of the Administration party has been taken over body, boots, and breeches by the Administration."

In a bid to those who felt insecure in terms of peace but who desired tax reductions and a balanced budget, Eisenhower used the slogan "security and solvency." For the states' righters he condemned "the idea of whole-hog Federal government" and spoke of the people getting "their region out of hock to the Federal government." On foreign policy the Republicans stressed the "stumble-fumble-bumble" of the Truman Administration, blaming it directly or indirectly for the loss of China to the Communists and for following policies which encouraged the aggression into South Korea.[4] In seeking the vote of independents, Eisenhower stressed that he was "not a politician," that he would bring an administration of *expertise,* and would keep the social gains of the preceding administration.

Governor Adlai Stevenson conducted what *The Christian Science Monitor* called one of the most "unorthodox" campaigns in American history. He recognized the handicaps under which he began the campaign by telling party workers that he was up against a candidate who had been a hero and household word for 10 years and that the only way he could win would be by reaching and "talking sense to the American people on all issues." [5] In doing this, Stevenson relied heavily on national television and radio networks to reach his audience and some of those speeches were reminiscent of the "fireside" appearances of Franklin Roosevelt. Eisenhower relied much less on formal speeches delivered over a nationwide hookup.

[4] Timing is an important factor in campaigning and Eisenhower's promise, late in the campaign, to go to Korea if elected, caught the Democratic high command off base and it was unable successfully to combat this appealing promise.

[5] It was a tribute to the quality of the Governor's speeches that an edition of his campaign addresses appeared while the campaign was still in progress—*Stevenson Speeches* (New York: Random House, Inc., 1952).

The unorthodox character of the Democratic strategy was shown in several ways. The Governor made Springfield, Ill., his headquarters instead of New York and Washington, and his campaign managers were, for the most part, amateurs. By contrast, the Eisenhower campaign was skillfully managed by professionals and showed a professional touch. Stevenson drew around him some excellent writers, interspersed his speeches with wit, anecdotes, and wisecracks far beyond the usual amount found in campaigns. He referred to the Republican party as having "a hopeless case of political schizophrenia" and constantly tried to portray the party as completely split between the followers of Taft and Eisenhower.

In his speeches the Governor often told the people what he thought they ought to hear rather than what they wanted to hear. He selected the South to take the unpopular stand on the highly controversial position against state ownership of the submerged coastal lands containing rich oil deposits, and on civil rights legislation. By contrast, Eisenhower soft-pedaled civil rights in his Southern speeches and came out for the popular position on the so-called "tidelands oil" question. Stevenson told the American Legion at its convention, "I should tell you now, as I tell all other organized groups, that I stand to resist pressures from veterans, too, if I think their demands are excessive or in conflict with the public interest, which must always be the paramount interest." In the same speech he criticized the excesses with which some self-styled patriots had trampled on civil liberties—a point which newspaper reporters felt applied to the activities of some local Legion posts. On several occasions he took a sharply critical view of the remarks of Senator Joseph McCarthy of Wisconsin, who had made serious charges of disloyalty against numerous Federal employees, General George Marshall, and certain other prominent Americans. It was Republican strategy to shy away from alienating the Wisconsin senator's supporters.

The Governor also tried to present the realities of the Korean situation and made no promises of an early termination of it. In Portland, Ore., he selected an editors and publishers convention to talk on "the one-party press" and said some things that were not well received, including, "it's not honest convictions honestly stated that concern me. Rather it is the tendency of many papers, and I include columnists, commentators, analysts, feature writers and so on, to argue editorially from the personal objective, rather than from the whole truth, . . . and I am, frankly, considerably concerned when I see the extent to which we are developing a one-party press in a two-party country." [6] On the issue of corruption, Stevenson argued that he was not "pro-corruption" and that there was no one running on a pro-corruption ticket and that corruption was not

[6] *Ibid.,* p. 103.

stamped out by simply damning politicians. He said, "You are not going to clean up crime and corruption until you clean up civil life. Who is going to do that? You are going to do it or it isn't going to be done."

Stevenson also differed from Eisenhower in refusing to give blanket endorsement to all Democratic candidates running for Congress. He incurred the ire of several senior Democratic senators because of this and because of his outspoken position on certain legislation.

Eisenhower drew enormous crowds wherever he went. James Reston of *The New York Times* traveled extensively with both the Eisenhower and Stevenson trains and expressed the views of most firsthand observers when he wrote: [7]

> . . . the size and manner of the crowds is striking. In a way, it is the difference between a crowd at a concert and a crowd at a football rally. General Eisenhower's crowds are larger and more enthusiastic. Governor Stevenson's are quieter and more attentive . . . when you pass along behind Governor Stevenson's car in a city street, the people look interested but slightly puzzled, but the people in the General's crowds are invariably smiling.
>
> In a hall, the reaction usually is the opposite. Mr. Stevenson's aim is so unerring, and his weapons so sharp that when he lets fly, his audiences are moved to laughter by the strike. General Eisenhower, on the other hand, is almost fiercely serious and his audience is correspondingly solemn. . . .
>
> The people out back of the train, who still have votes, respond to the General with enthusiasm. They like the little moral lectures that evoke groans from the press car. They like his looks and his expressive gestures. They like his angry little outbursts against corruption, and his essays on America. And what may sound like dynamic platitudes to some ears on the train . . . nevertheless usually win the loudest applause out on the station platform.

There is no way of knowing whether the Stevenson speeches and specific discussion of many issues resulted in a net gain or loss of votes. Undoubtedly many voters did not like his blunt talk and his humor and comments were too sophisticated for some. At the same time, the Governor won many votes by his candor. Surveys of reporters covering both the Eisenhower and Stevenson itinerary showed the big majority favoring the Governor because of his frankness and fresh approach. Intellectuals, writers, and college professors gravitated in large numbers to the Democratic candidate and thousands of people who were never before active in politics joined the ranks of the "Volunteers for Stevenson." But, as one reporter phrased it, "Do you win elections with brilliant speeches or with moral appeals and all-out attacks on crime, corruption, and Communism?"

[7] *The New York Times*, Sept. 17, 1952.

CAMPAIGN ORGANIZATION

Regardless of the general strategy and the issues or lack of them, the job of campaign organizations, in the first place, is to build up the candidate through publicity, stereotypes, and appeals. In the second place, the nominee and his supporters constantly emphasize that they will be successful and that all should jump on the band wagon. This is commonly known as "creating the illusion of victory." For the most part these objectives are carried forward by thousands of party and nonparty political committees. In California, the rather extraordinary practice prevails of candidates hiring a firm which specializes in managing campaigns of all kinds to conduct the campaign for them. Under a contract, these agencies take over the publicizing of a candidate just as they would advertise soap or a movie star.

National Organization. After the primaries and conventions, the organizational machinery is perfected. This consists in the opening of thousands of headquarters throughout the nation, which become the scene of bustle and feverish activity as the campaign gains in intensity. First, there are the national headquarters, which generally operate out of the permanent national offices of the national committees in Washington and from a temporary headquarters located in recent years in New York. Paralleling the geographical organization of the parties, a hierarchy of state, county, and local headquarters is established. A large number of divisions are created in the national offices for the purpose of preparing appeals for specific groups and evolving strategy for soliciting their votes. Among the sections usually found are those for Negroes, veterans, women, and farmers. Radio and television, newspaper, graphic, and finance are among the other divisions created to perform specialized functions.

In the larger states, the state organizations rent a suite of rooms in a large hotel for the G.H.Q., marking each room for a designated function. As local leaders come in for materials and advice they are referred to the appropriate section by a receptionist. The visitor is greeted with a "glad hand," and flattering pictures of the party's nominees adorn the walls; photographs with personal signatures of nominees are on the desks. On the first visit, at least, one is treated to optimism, enthusiasm, and the illusion of victory.

In presidential campaigns, the director and manager is usually the national chairman, who, with his staff, prepares and executes the policies for the presidential nominees. The chairman's job is an enormous one, requiring much traveling in order to help the state leaders guide the local organizations according to the national plan. It becomes his task to promote harmony and to reconcile differences between the local and national interests which appear to endanger the ticket. He assists state leaders in locating funds when needed and in supplying them with lists of speakers.

Campaign organization and activity in a national election do not, of course, show the same intensity in every county and state. Practically speaking, presidential campaigns are regional in character, with the most effort expended in the large doubtful states. Managers in each party draw up a list of states considered as crucial and requiring maximum effort. Presidential nominees, for example, seldom appear north of Boston or in the deep South,[8] since it is assumed the electoral results there are a foregone conclusion. Vermont and New Hampshire, moreover, have few electoral votes. Many other small-vote states, such as Wyoming, Delaware, and Nevada, are not always favored by visits from the top aspirants unless there is an important senatorial contest. Of the remaining states, there are upward of a dozen usually regarded as politically doubtful. In these, organization is made more complete and campaigning is intensified. Presidential and vice presidential nominees make widespread appearances there, and the national committees expend much money for publicity in them. In recent years California, Illinois, Indiana, Massachusetts, Michigan, New Jersey, New York, Ohio, and Pennsylvania have been highly crucial. Collectively they have 226 electoral votes; any nominee carrying all or most of them is almost certain to win. (A majority vote in the electoral college is 266.) Certain other states are at times regarded as exceptionally vital, especially if the opposition seems assured of several of the above states. These include the farm-belt states and border ones such as Oklahoma, Kentucky, and Maryland.

Local Activities. The decentralized character of the party system results in much of the burden in both national and state elections being carried by the local organizations in rural and urban areas, through the channels of the county, municipal, ward, and election-district organizations. One of the first jobs of local leaders is to build up a large staff of volunteer workers who will personally solicit votes, do odd jobs around headquarters, address envelopes from registered voters' lists, pass out literature, and talk persuasively to visitors. Some enterprising urban leaders prepare lists of persons capable of performing certain jobs on short notice. Files will show that Jones and Smith can effectively operate a sound truck, Brown, a union man, can reach the boys at the factory at closing time. Mrs. Powell is a persuasive speaker before women's clubs, Gerry makes a particularly good chairman for rallies in the Negro or Italian district, etc. Journalists, script-writers, and radio entertainers are brought in for purposes of ghostwriting, digging out materials on the opposition, and management of rallies. In order to make certain the women will vote,

[8] In this respect the 1952 election was atypic, with Eisenhower and Stevenson both invading the South.

many organizations now supply competent baby sitters to take care of children while the mother goes to the polls to register, vote, or to serve a few hours at campaign headquarters as a secretary. Even the assistance of agricultural college professors is sought for materials on speeches dealing with farm matters in some states! In addition to volunteers, paid secretarial help and workers to function on registration and election days must be recruited.

Nominees for Congress and for the state senate and assembly frequently open offices in their own district and bring together a staff over and above that of the regular party organization. Almost every candidate for a state-wide and often local office has his own campaign manager. This enables the nominee to concentrate on local issues and to make exclusive use of his employees or of personal friends who may not be too enthusiastic over the rest of the party's ticket. In spite of the efforts of state chairmen to promote solidarity, the creation and operation of scores of local campaign headquarters results in decentralization, duplication, and occasional inconsistencies in the campaign, but their existence promises emphasis upon local issues which otherwise are lost in the larger campaign. When the presidential nominee is in the state, however, every effort is made to present the ticket as a team. All candidates sit on the platform together while party loyalty and straight-ticket voting is stressed. "Coattail" riding is one of the oldest practices of party politics.

A key figure in every election is the county chairman, who works out ways to help nominees for county and state legislative positions and plans the itinerary for the state motor "caravans" which come through. County chairmen usually preside at rallies, submit substance for brief speeches on local problems by gubernatorial or other nominees who do not live in the district and who have little or no knowledge of local sentiment. The chairman, of course, is the mobilizer of district and precinct leaders and his office or home is often the campaign headquarters.

In recent years, the various auxiliary party committees and clubs have taken over an increasing burden of the campaign both in activity and in fund-raising. The various Young Democratic clubs in many states actually did more on behalf of Stevenson than the regular organization. In many communities there is a tacit understanding that certain party auxiliaries will assume primary responsibility for the campaign of certain of the party's candidates in the areas.

Independent Campaign Committees. To an increasing degree, independent political action committees are taking over a vital part of campaign organization. At times these groups occupy a room in the state or party headquarters but more often they operate their own office. Where the latter is the practice, a system of liaison has to be worked out between the regular and nonparty organizations in order to avoid working at cross-purposes. The independent campaign organizations of lawyers, doctors, farmers, laborers, and a host of racial and nationalistic committees probably rival the regular committees in importance.[9]

In 1952 hundreds of Citizens for Eisenhower clubs had much to do with electing delegates to the national convention, thereby assuring the general's nomination. After the convention these organizations took over the burden of creating thousands of additional local clubs to make special appeals to independent voters. The national office, operating out of New York, acted as a clearinghouse for volunteers and took special pains to provide a great many things for women to do, such as giving parties, operating a "coffee hour for Eisenhower," and telephone canvassing. It financed the very expensive election eve television and radio show which cost $285,000, and spent two or three times as much on spot announcements over these media during the campaign. A Gargantuan quantity of work was also done in turning out publicity and in mobilizing speakers. A major job was to handle the advance publicity on Eisenhower's appearances. In carrying out this function, men were sent two days ahead of Eisenhower with balloons, signs, "band wagons," and other paraphernalia. Strategy, speeches, and local rallies for Eisenhower, however, remained essentially in the hands of the Republican national chairman. The organization had one mailing of 1,690,000 in Illinois, reaching virtually every family. By the end of the campaign, the national office had a record of some 15,000 local clubs having more than 2 million active workers.

Democratic presidential nominees have also had the assistance of many independent political committees. As previously noted, labor's political action committees were especially active for Roosevelt, Truman, and Stevenson. In 1952, the Volunteers for Stevenson operating out of Chicago carried both a large financial and organizational burden for the Illinois Governor. Unlike the Eisenhower counterpart, it sponsored many broadcasts and influenced strategy and was not formed until after the conventions. In many parts of the nation the Democratic party was so demoralized that little campaigning would have been done were it not for the Volunteers for Stevenson.

There are some recognizable merits in the activities of the independent

[9] These groups draw up an imposing roster of names and throw themselves into the drive for votes. Their activities often parallel those of the party, such as ringing doorbells, operating sound trucks, mailing literature, and sponsoring radio and television shows. Illustrative of titles of these committees: Farmers for Roosevelt Committee, Servicemen's Wives to Reelect Roosevelt, Mission Volunteers for Willkie, Minute Women for Dewey and Bricker, Thomas E. Dewey Italian-American Committee, Allied Democrats, Inc., Veterans for Truman and Barkley, Independent Physicians for Eisenhower and Nixon, and Youth Committee for Stevenson. Many other groups appear under patriotic, ethnic, and class labels.

campaign groups. They help with finances and bring into the activities persons who ordinarily would refuse to serve under a Republican or Democratic label. An advertisement sponsored and paid for by a party organization may be heavily discounted while the same advertisement sponsored by local attorneys, businessmen, and teachers may carry more weight. The Volunteers for Stevenson relied on advertisements bearing the signature of well-known writers, scientists, college professors, and other professionals. Some citizens' committees can make special appeals to classes and to nominal followers of the opposition party which are not susceptible to the lures of the regular party organization. A number of the independent committees are essentially fictitious or "paper" organizations, for they never meet and are simply devices of the candidate, and often paid by him, to use the names of prominent citizens as a basis of indicating broad support.

Party leaders are not invariably enthusiastic about nonparty committees which they have neither formed nor are able to control. These organizations usually lack a professional touch and may demand a voice in the determination of campaign policy. More than this, leaders of the independents sometimes ask for patronage after the elections. Some precinct leaders resent what they consider interference with their prerogatives and feel that independents are operating at cross-purposes with the over-all strategy. As a general rule, the parties and candidates welcome the support of independent committees—a case of not looking a gift horse in the mouth.

To summarize, American campaign organization, like the party system itself, is highly decentralized, resilient, and often based on expediency. Where in Europe the campaign is usually run from a constituency or a national headquarters of the party, it may be run from one or more of the following in the United States: (1) the regular party headquarters and high command, (2) auxiliaries of the party, (3) the candidate's own headquarters staffed by both party friends and independents, and (4) independent nonparty committees such as labor and medical political leagues, the Citizens for Eisenhower or the Volunteers for Stevenson.

SOUND AND FURY

A century ago everyone turned out to the political rally, if for no other reason than to witness one of the few good shows of a lifetime and to share in the excitement. As newspaper circulation developed and as the farmer could be reached by postal delivery and then by the radio and television, it was widely predicted that the old-fashioned log cabin, hard-cider rallies, and torchlight parades would be outmoded. Mass communication brought some changes in campaign methods and techniques but the rally and parade are still among the great traditions.

Prior to the appearance of the candidate at a rally, bands, songs, speeches, and entertainment are used both for purposes of amusement and to make the crowd receptive to the appearance of the candidate. In one of Eisenhower's Eastern appearances, the audience was treated to an accordion player, a hook-shot basketball artist, and a Broadway show troupe, while in Seattle a big ice follies show preceded his arrival. In both cases the crowd was instructed in how to chant "We like Ike" just before the General stepped on the platform to face the audience and the television cameras. The build-up for the appearance of presidential nominees is designed to result in a rafter-shattering hullabaloo when the head of "the next President of the United States" first appears.

Those witnessing the massive rallies in New York's Madison Square Garden or the monster outdoor shows in Chicago's Soldier Field and the Los Angeles coliseum do not soon forget the "big show." At the last-mentioned there are often a troupe of wild West cowboys led by a Hollywood actor and a group of cowgirls in a riding exhibition around the billiard-cloth grass of the coliseum infield. Movie heroes by the dozens attend the rally and entertain the crowd until the appearance of the nominee, who rides into view with the giant spotlights playing upon him.

What may have been lost in color by the absence of torches is now compensated for by noise of motor caravans and screeching motorcycle escorts. Wendell Willkie rode hundreds of miles in cities standing up in an open automobile, waving at crowds and pushing from his eyes the showering confetti. Dwight Eisenhower similarly toured hundreds of miles in the open streets with arms stretched high in a characteristic gesture.

The ingenuity of the campaign technicians is shown in the "staged" act which provides the nominee with a chance to drive home, in unorthodox fashion, one of his issues. Frank R. Kent's story about Congressman Hill of Maryland deserves repetition here: [10]

Stalking into a crowded hall, Mr. Hill would walk to the table on the stage where, under his instructions, a pitcher of water and glass had been placed. Picking up the pitcher he would start to pour himself a drink. Suddenly and dramatically he would throw the water out of the window or dash the glass to the floor. "What is this," he would shout, "water? We don't want water in this district. We want beer; and boys if you send John Phillip Hill to Congress he'll get it for you." Then he would grab an American flag (also planted), the band would strike up, and the crowd would go crazy.

Huey Long was a past master at capitalizing on "unexpected events," both staged and spontaneous. When campaigning in the Louisiana heat, some crying infant usually interrupted his speech. On hearing the wailing,

[10] *Political Behavior* (New York: William Morrow & Company, Inc. 1928), p. 99.

the "Kingfish" would stop his speech and wave to one of his henchmen in the audience, who in turn would go to the mother and deftly pick the child from her arms. After giving the baby a drink of cold water and patting it lightly once or twice, it would stop the whimpering. Thereupon, "Papa" Long would launch into a discussion of the virtues of motherhood and proceed to give advice on how to raise children. If a dog voiced its grief during one of Huey's harangues, the speech was interrupted while a helper took the dog and played with it, again providing Long with the opportunity for extemporizing on pets. Such tricks were assidu- ously cultivated to show that the "hero" was a home lover just like the humble folk who gathered to hear him.

Governor "Big Jim" Folsom of Alabama actually appeared barefooted during some of his campaign appearances in 1946. Eugene Talmadge considered his red suspenders an indispensable adjunct during his cam- paigns. Whenever weather permitted, the champion of white supremacy in Georgia shed his coat, proudly revealing his shining galluses.

Unorthodox campaign showmanship is not a sectional characteristic. One candidate for a state-wide office conducted a diaper-pinning contest on the streets of Seattle. Congressman and thrice mayor of New York, Fiorello La Guardia was not above seizing a cabbage from a vegetable wagon and holding it aloft shouting, "My opponent's head." Other campaign tricks in the "Little Flower's" repertoire consisted of making beer on the streets of New York to dramatize the evil of prohibition and challenging his opponent to debate with him in Yiddish. Governor Harry Nice of Maryland put on hip boots and waded out into Chesapeake Bay to shake the hands of oyster fishermen saying, "If you reelect me there will be so many oysters in Chesapeake Bay that you won't be able to even get a rowboat in it!" Among other things, he was pictured shaking hands with a bewhiskered mountain hermit, barging into barbershops to solicit votes from those stretched out for shaves, and delivering a ser- mon before a Negro congregation in Baltimore.

Invective continues to be a part of campaigns in a number of com- munities. Indeed one wonders if any progress has been made in elevating the level of the campaign oratory used by local party spokesmen. In 1840, one Democratic orator called General Harrison a "clodpoll, a dun- derpate, a ninnyhammer" too ignorant to know "a bee from a bull's foot." Jackson was seen as an "adulterer, a gambler, and a murderer," Pierce as a "coward" and "drunkard," Lincoln a "vulgar village politician and fourth-rate lawyer," Bryan a "lunatic," and Henry Clay was de- nounced for running the campaign of John Quincy Adams "like a shy- ster, pettifogging in a bastard suit before a country squire." In our own century one of Mayor Thompson's opponents remarked in a campaign address, "The people have grown tired of this blubbering, jungle hippopotamus defending his gangsters and crooked contractors by slobbering insults. . . . He calls me loony. Did you ever see a lurching, shambling imbecile with the flabby jowls of a barnyard hog, whose diseased brain didn't defend its own lunacy by snarling at others?" [11]

Harold L. Ickes, "the old curmudgeon," added spice and invective to the Roosevelt and Truman campaigns. In 1948 Democrats used his "Thomas *E*lusive Dewey, the candidate in sneakers" to a great degree and appreciated his remark about Truman that "at least he is earthy and without cant." In 1952 Senator Nixon charged that "Stevenson holds a Ph.D. degree from Acheson's college of cowardly communist containment—the State Department."

Whispering campaigns are never officially countenanced but nevertheless commonly appear. It was rumored that "Al" Smith was a "boozer" and had arranged to have the Vatican moved to Washington, and in the South the rumor was spread that Herbert Hoover had a Negro concubine. Franklin Roosevelt's health and mental soundness were the subject of whispers in all his presidential campaigns. Mrs. Roosevelt meanwhile was the subject of fabulous tales, comparable to some of those told of Mrs. Andrew Jackson. In 1932, with thousands of unemployed, it was rumored that Hoover employed twoscore Chinese coolies on his "estate" in California, thus depriving deserving American laborers of those positions. In local elections, private appeals to prejudice, the conjuring of hate and fear, and the pitting of religious and racial minorities against each other excel those used in presidential campaigns. Although the fair-minded citizen denounces this practice and no votes are won by it among thinking people, the device persists, causing hatred, division, and rancor within the body politic.

MUSIC AND VERSE

Music was the "language of the soul"—and of the campaign to the Whigs as they paraded through the streets in 1840 drinking hard cider, displaying banners emblazoned with a log cabin, and singing:

> Let Van from his coolers of silver drink wine,
> And lounge on his cushioned settee,
> Our man on his buckeye bench can recline,
> Content with hard cider is he,
> The iron-armed soldier, the truehearted soldier,
> The gallant old soldier of Tippecanoe

Music is an indispensable item in the campaign pantry. Bands, phonograph records, soloists, and orchestras are a part of the programs of rallies

[11] Fletcher Dobyns, *The Underworld of American Politics* (New York: The Author, 1928), p. 34.

and parades. Some candidates entertain the crowd by playing instruments and reciting made-up parodies. The Democrats used a specially written song and hand clapping piece in 1952 called "Don't Let Them Take It Away." Martial music and patriotic songs are employed to attract attention, stir the emotions, and soften up bystanders and audiences for the orators to follow.

Nicknames of nominees, provided they have a common, folksy appeal, are regarded as an asset by managers and find their way into campaigns. From history come the well-known Presidents such as "Old Hickory," "Old Rough-and-Ready," "Honest Abe," "Unconditional Surrender," and "Silent Cal." Stephen A. Douglas was the "Little Giant," Blaine the "Plumed Knight," Bryan the "Great Commoner," Smith the "Happy Warrior," Hoover the "Great Engineer," and Landon a "Kansas Lochinvar." Familiar titles of senators and governors in the last generation include "Honest John" Bricker, Huey Long, the "Kingfish," "The Man" Bilbo, "Ma" Ferguson, "Long Tom" Connally, "Puddler Jim" Davis, "Happy" Chandler, "Cotton Ed" Smith, and "Alfalfa Bill" Murray.

As a brand of American humor, a premium is placed on campaign slogans which will capture the popular imagination. First use was made of this device in 1840, when a Whig huckster came through with "Tippecanoe and Tyler too," and swept the incumbent Van Buren out of office with "Van, Van is a used up man." In 1946, the Republicans coined "A porterhouse on every platter" and "Had enough? Vote Republican!" The latter will go down in history with "Free soil, free speech, free labor, and free men," Lincoln's "Vote yourself a farm," Harding's "Back to normalcy," Hoover's "A chicken in every pot, two cars in every garage," "McKinley and the full dinner pail," and Bryan's "Sixteen to one" and "Let the people rule." Alliterative slogans which say nothing and mean nothing, but which have the political virtue of sounding as though they do, are also favorites, for example: "Keep cool with Coolidge," "Land Landon with a landslide," or "Win with Willkie." On a few occasions the opposition has pinned a damaging and costly phrase on its rivals. Scott's soldiers coined "Old Fuss-and-Feathers" for him and the campaigners put it to good use; Blaine was associated with the remark "Rum, Romanism, and Rebellion," and Hoover with the "Hoover depression," and to the pounding of drums it was asked, "Polk, Polk, who is Polk?" Not even puns or rhymes escape use. In the last generation voters have been told, "McAdoo'll do," "Dewey will do it," "Vote for Landon and land a job." Partisans of Senator Vandenberg urged people to "Get on the Van wagon" and asserted, "One good term deserves another"; Senator Ives's supporters chorused, "All in favor say Ives!" The Republicans in 1944 misconstrued a story with reference to President Roosevelt and his relationship with Sidney Hillman, leader of the CIO Political Action

Committee. From Governor Dewey on down, the slogan was "Clear it with Sidney" and served as a formidable campaign issue.

In the great game of politics sloganeers come and go but shibboleths enjoy a hardy immortality. It seems doubtful that campaign slogans win or lose elections and there is no way of learning how many votes are gathered or lost by them. Like a catch phrase in advertising, if the slogan is repeated often enough, it may come to stand for something in the public mind. Lincoln's "A house divided against itself cannot stand," and the use of "He kept us out of war" by Wilson's spokesmen, formulated in each case a simple campaign appeal which undoubtedly dramatized an issue. Though not particularly meaningful at first, the "Full dinner pail" of McKinley, the "New Freedom" of Wilson, and the "Square Deal" and "New Deal" of the Roosevelts symbolized in one way or another a program and a personality to millions of Americans.

Verse of the crudest sort has found its way into some campaigns. One entitled "Traitors Three," consisting of 12 stanzas, was circulated clandestinely in 1940. It related the story of "Brutus, Arnold, and Franklin D.," who were comparing exploits, and concluded with President Roosevelt's boast:

> They believed in me both husbands and wives,
> But the little pigs ran for their lives,
> They alone knew they were no longer free,
> As I killed them off with the greatest of glee.
>
> I fooled these yokels, both old and young;
> I was the greatest scoundrel to remain unhung.
> I've ruined their country, My Friends, and then,
> I placed the blame on Nine Old Men.
>
> Brutus stood there filled with awe.
> Arnold sat with fallen jaw.
> Then Brutus said, "We've had our fling,
> Get up now, Arnold, and salute your King!"

In the same campaign Democratic journalists ribbed the Republicans with lengthy verses, a portion of which read:

> For seven long years they've played for votes
> But never mentioned six-cent oats.
> They say this New Deal stuff is rotten
> But never spoke of five-cent cotton.
>
> For seven long years they've wept aloud,
> And cussed "this money-spending crowd,"
> They say of liberty they've been shorn
> But not a breath of eight-cent corn.

RADIO AND TELEVISION IN ELECTIONS

Radio was first used extensively in the campaign of 1928, and its use has increased with subsequent elections. Originally only the voices of nominees were carried as they addressed rallies. On several occasions "Al" Smith's speeches were extemporaneous and therefore were not particularly well prepared for the radio audiences. Managers came to realize that the immediate political audience was different from the listener miles away and thereafter each speech was written with the "microphone approach." Today each nominee's speech is carefully drafted with the radio listener in view. A number of campaign addresses are specifically prepared for the radio and delivered without benefit of the ballyhoo of a visible audience. This technique is gaining increased use in state and local elections where candidates are not able to afford numerous rallies or to purchase radio time in the late evening when rallies are normally held. The fact that the cost of radio time is the largest single item in many campaign budgets in itself demonstrates the high value which the parties place on this form of reaching the voters.

Before the advent of radio, presidential candidates were less restrained in expressing their position on sectional problems. The radio, however, can prove embarrassing, for what is said in one section of the country is heard elsewhere and may be damaging to the nominees' causes. One of Governor Dewey's California speeches, strongly New Deal in tone and calling for liberalized credit, brought heated reaction from some of the conservative Eastern interests.[12] Radio has, indeed, helped to "nationalize" the character of national campaign addresses and in general has caused the candidates to speak with greater temperance lest they offend the literary sensitivities of independents and nonpartisans. In "the good old days" the rabid partisans came to rallies to hear a knockdown namecalling feast and appeals to local prejudices, but, thanks to radio in a great degree, addresses of this character are disappearing.

Radio has brought American entertainers into political campaigns on a big scale. The Hollywood for Roosevelt Committee put on a large-scale two-hour network show in 1940 and 1944, composed exclusively of big names from screen and radio; the Dewey-Warren Hollywood group put on a similar show on election eve. The "all-star cast" put on skits, read famous patriotic addresses, and gave eloquent testimonials. Serious messages were interspersed with appropriate gags from comedians and songs from favorite crooners and singers. Throughout the campaigns both Republicans and Democrats sponsored five-minute speeches by actors and actresses, carried over large networks. Reports on these programs reveal that volumes of fan mail and large listening audiences resulted. The suc-

[12] See editorial, *The New York Times,* Sept. 22, 1944.

cess of this campaign technique offers additional evidence that campaigning is a drama and that the professional actor's services add an appealing touch to the proceedings.

In the same vein the radio offers an excellent vehicle to exploit the value of testimonials. Each party is on the alert to bring to the microphone prominent lawyers, journalists, writers, educators, political bolters, and outstanding past and present local or state officeholders. Time is rented on the radio for them to appeal to their admirers to support a certain candidate. Another radio device, gaining in popularity, is the spot announcement given at the juncture providing for a station identification. A 15-to-60-second recording is played, repeating the campaign slogan or giving a terse admonition in support of a candidate.

Much of what has been said about radio in campaigns applies equally to television. Both have opened new vistas for the campaigner while not displacing the older methods of campaigning. These mass communications media have added to, rather than restricted or revolutionized, the old campaign techniques. They have brought the proceedings of the political rally into the home and many managers complain that the rallies are less well attended as a result.

It is frequently asked if television is an effective vote-getter and what kind of a campaign TV show will gain the largest audience. The impact of television on campaigns remains a moot point because of lack of evidence and careful study. The medium first saw wide use in 1950, even though there were only about eight million television receivers in the country. Governor Thomas E. Dewey made spectacular use of the medium in this campaign by staging, shortly before the election, a marathon when he remained before the television cameras the better part of 18 hours. During this time he answered questions phoned in or telegraphed to the studio. By 1952 the number of sets had tripled but there were still many states and areas unreached by television. Beginning in 1956 television will pretty well blanket the country and a better opportunity will be afforded to study the influence of television.

A few possibilities and potentialities of campaigning by television are already apparent. It gives the unknown candidate a chance to become a familiar personality almost overnight. Senator Estes Kefauver became known through the televising of the Senate Crime Investigation hearings and was catapulted into being a serious contender for the Democratic nomination. Television greatly helped the comparatively unknown Adlai Stevenson to reach millions of voters in record time. It also probably helped to swell the number voting in the election.

The showmanship as well as expense of campaigns is accentuated by television. On election eve the Eisenhower forces put on a two-hour combined radio-television show which blanketed the nation. Pickups of voters in various parts of the country, high-powered entertainment, and the appearance of the Eisenhower and Nixon families featured the show. Senator Nixon put on two highly dramatic telecasts, one on his work with the House Committee on Un-American Activities, the other explaining his personal finances. In the latter his wife sat beside him and the cameras played on her from time to time. Several newspaper reporters were of the impression that those viewing this show on television were far more moved emotionally than those hearing it on the radio. It was almost universally conceded that Nixon's amazing performance netted him votes.

After 1928 several opponents of Franklin Roosevelt were no match for his unusual radio personality. It may well be that being photogenic on television will become a "quality of availability" in the future. In Los Angeles a television training school was used to coach Republican speakers who planned to appear on television.[13]

Radio and television would provide an excellent chance for face-to-face debate between the principals of the campaign and to open themselves to questions from the audience. George V. Denny, who has put radio to such worthwhile use in his "Town Meeting of the Air," perennially invites the presidential nominees to appear on his program at the same time but has always been met with polite refusals. The League of Women Voters has had only limited success in sponsoring public forums (sometimes broadcast), where nominees speak from the same platform. Governors Dewey and Stassen engaged in a national radio debate in 1948 prior to the Republican National Convention. Gubernatorial candidates in the South Carolina Democratic primary likewise often speak from the same platform, though seldom for radio broadcast.

Perhaps a major contribution which television and radio could make to American political life is to substantially shorten the length of the campaign. In every election, radio station managers report that listeners are drastically reduced in number by the long weeks of wearisome radio speeches of the candidates. One television critic said the American people were suffering from "drooping eyelid" long before the end of the campaign. One Columbia Broadcasting Company official has recommended that national nominating conventions be held September 1, with a shortening of the campaign to a seven-week period.[14] This could be facilitated by combined use of radio and television with fewer appearances over these media. It would result, he believes, in less wearied listeners and viewers, less cost to the parties, and much greater conservation of

[13] See Frank Washburn, "The Television Panel as a Vehicle of Political Persuasion," *Western Speech,* Vol. 16 (1952), pp. 250–251.

[14] William S. Paley, *Television and the Presidential Campaign* (New York: Columbia Broadcasting System, 1953).

the energies of the candidates. Notwithstanding the merit of proposals to shorten presidential campaigns, little progress has been made because party leaders feel they need all the time they can get to campaign for votes.

THE PSYCHOLOGY OF CAMPAIGNING

"There's only one way to hold a district," said Plunkitt of Tammany Hall, "you must study human nature and act accordin'. You can't study human nature in books. . . . To learn real human nature you have to go among the people, see them and be seen. . . . I know what they like and what they don't like, what they are strong at and what they are weak in, and I reach them by approachin' at the right side." [15] A onetime league organizer gave the following instructions for seeking money or possibly votes: "Find out the damn fool's hobby and talk it. If he likes religion talk Jesus Christ, if he is against government damn the Democrats, if he is afraid of whiskey preach prohibition, if he wants to talk hogs, talk hogs—talk anything he'll listen to, but talk, talk until you get his Goddamn John Hancock to a check for six dollars." [16]

Although the best interests of a healthy political society are not promoted by pampering prejudice, a careful analysis of the political composition of the electorate of one's own district is useful to the campaigner, the lawmaker, and the public official. Techniques which succeed in Augusta do not necessarily bring about the same response in Dallas, Iowa City, or Walla Walla. Political and social environments vary from place to place and even from time to time. More and more research into voting behavior and related areas is being carried on by the parties and candidates in order to understand the characteristics of one's district.

In planning campaign strategy it is not only desirable to know the demography (income, occupation, age, sex, ethnic background, religion, etc.) of the voting population but it is also helpful to recognize that at election time the electorate broadly falls into four groups. First are the hard-core following of the party and the candidate. Second are the loyal partisans who seldom aid the party but who can usually be depended upon to vote a straight ticket. A third group may be thought of as party sympathizers, or persons who have a nominal party attachment, but who can be enticed from their party from time to time. Perhaps these voters may be spoken of as "latent" Republicans and "latent" Democrats. Finally, there are the complete independents who have little or no feeling of party affinity and who gravitate from one party to another to vote for "the best man."

15 W. L. Riordan, *Plunkitt of Tammany Hall* (New York: Alfred A. Knopf, Inc., 1948), pp. 33–34.

16 Quoted in Samuel Lubell, *The Future of American Politics* (New York: Harper & Brothers, 1951), p. 138.

There is no way of knowing how many millions of voters fall into each of these categories and the lines of the divisions are not necessarily distinct. In their study of the 1948 election, Angus Campbell and R. L. Kahn estimated there were many more latent Democrats than latent Republicans, especially among nonvoters.[17] In 1952, the Gallup poll estimated that there were 21,500,000 Democratic voters, 18,500,000 Republicans, and 15,000,000 independents. Since over 61 million persons voted and the Gallup estimate accounted for the political leanings of only 55 million, it leaves a considerable number unlabeled. Careful research precinct by precinct of the electorate in a given legislative district might, however, give a reasonably accurate estimate of the party attachments of the voters which would be of real value to campaign managers.

It should also be recognized that a campaign will or may produce one of three effects—activation, reinforcement, and conversion.[18] Some persons will not vote or get excited enough about elections unless their latent predispositions are aroused. Campaigners try to activate this group, many of whom stay home. Other voters need to be told they are right; they like additional evidence for and rationalizations of their views. Finally there are those who may actually be converted by the campaign and who do not make up their minds until near election day. This group appears to be comparatively small, but its votes may prove to be crucial in a close election.

In recognition of these groups and factors, common sense dictates that most of the energy be directed toward winning the votes of the party sympathizers and independents. The nominal sympathizers of one's own party need to have their loyalties renewed to keep them from straying from the party or from not voting. At the same time one is trying to activate and hold these adherents, an attempt must be made to drive a wedge between the nominees and lukewarm adherents of the opposition party. For the independents, the symbols of party loyalty are not very effective and other appeals will have to be used to convert them. While demogogic appeals to "Americanism" and "bureaucracy" may help to reinforce the loyal partisans and hard-core groups to bolster their courage and spur them on to greater campaign activity, they do not necessarily convert the independents. A "pocketbook" appeal to the latter, who are property owners and taxpayers, a school appeal for parents, a recreation

[17] *The People Elect a President* (1952), Chap. 3.

[18] For a fuller discussion see the study of Erie County, Ohio, by Paul Lazarsfeld, Bernard Berelson, and Hazel Gaudet, *The People's Choice: How the Voter Makes Up His Mind in a Presidential Campaign* (New York: Columbia University Press, 1948). For an interesting study of variables influencing the voter, such as party identification, candidate and issue orientation, see Angus Campbell, Gerald Gurin, and Warren Miller, *The Voter Decides* (Evanston, Ill.: Row, Peterson & Company, 1954).

program for the sportsman, and so on may win more votes in local elections than emotional appeals based on generalities.

Part of the psychology of campaign appeals is based upon the desire of a listener to have a frame of reference and standard of judgment for judging issues and men. If the candidate can contribute to this desire, he has made some progress toward gaining a chance for a friendly hearing with the voter. A listener is more susceptible to suggestion when he has no adequate mental context upon which he may base an interpretation of an event. In the many areas of foreign affairs, the hearer often has no knowledge and may therefore accept "snap" and "superficial" suggestions and remedies. A man with a rigidly structured mental context may be completely unsusceptible to ideas coming from an out-group, while uncritically accepting those from his own group. Thus, the rabid partisan is generally quick to believe his own candidates and equally quick to accuse the opposition of barefaced prevarication. For this reason astute campaigners try to "know their audiences" and adapt their speeches accordingly.

Campaigns provide an especially good opportunity to make use of "myths." The definition of this term varies but the concise description of Robert MacIver is useful in this connection. MacIver sees a social myth as "a value-impregnated belief" which is "alogical" and not amenable to proof.[19] In a campaign, the candidate uses the myth to knit his followers, to explain and to rationalize the world for his listeners, and to voice their aspirations for the good life. The myth often is strongly based in emotion and people become emotionally involved with it. The myth can be used to analyze what is happening and to predict what will happen to the listener and the myth if the opposition wins. Words such as Americanism, bureaucracy, corruption, justice, freedom, equality, and individualism are related to the myth if, indeed, they do not become the myth itself.

Campaigns give the observer of political life an unusual opportunity to study the use of myths because most of the myths we live by are brought out and pointed up during a campaign. Campaigners try to relate their programs to the myths of the moment in a way to resolve doubts and to give assurances to the worried voter. The myth, symbols, and propaganda devices are found in every society and are a part of the technique in the struggle for power and influence. Some attention will now be given to these, especially as they appear in American elections.

SELECTED REFERENCES

See the end of the following chapter.

[19] *The Web of Government* (New York: The Macmillan Company, 1947), pp. 4 ff.

CHAPTER 20

Propaganda and Campaign Literature

Always the storm of propaganda blows. Buy a paper. Read a book. Start the radio. Listen in the railroad car, in the bus. Go to church, to a movie, to a saloon. And always the breezes of personal opinion are blowing mixed with the doctrines of propaganda or the chatter of spelling spiels.

—CARL SANDBURG

For all of its hyperbole and absurdities, the mere existence of a political campaign represents real progress in the march of civilization. Where men used to seize power by force or a *coup d'état* they are now forced in many countries to use persuasion to engineer consent. To gain consent, systematic methods are employed which have come to be known as "propaganda." At this point in our study of parties, pressures, and public opinion, we may stop to consider the uses of propaganda and force as political techniques. Most but not all of our illustrations relate to the great mobilization of propaganda during elections because these occasions afford one of the best opportunities for examining propaganda.

WHAT IS PROPAGANDA?

Propaganda is to be distinguished from education by its methods and techniques rather than, as is often thought, by its objectives. There can be propaganda for virtue as well as for sin, for good causes or for bad ones. One may educate for democracy as well as propagandize for it. A basic difference between education and propaganda is that the former encourages suspended judgment until all possible evidence can be accumulated by scientific analysis. Education emphasizes objectivity and uses reason and knowledge for the purpose of arriving at conclusions. Propaganda tries to do the job by a short cut, to gain acceptance or rejection of an idea, cause, or a candidate without a full examination of the evidence. Where the true educator will not use deceit or falsehood, the propagandist is not always above employing both, and appeals to emotions are part of his techniques. The propagandist may not be in possession of full evidence or may be too impatient to use the involved process of education for his cause; very often he is fearful that a careful analysis of some aspects of the evidence will weaken his case. Propaganda is sometimes used because of a lack of respect or faith in the intelligence of the reader. In the call for action, it is believed that responses will be

467

more vigorous if based upon emotional reactions. For this reason, propaganda is apt to be more barefaced and crude in time of war than during peace.

It is relatively easy to distinguish between extreme propaganda at one end and pure education at another. In between are thousands of shades of education and propaganda, and as one moves toward the center from the extremes it is much less easy to define where education ends and propaganda begins. A detailed consideration of the various definitions of propaganda is fruitless here but a brief reference to a few commonly cited statements about propaganda will indicate the attributes associated with the term.

Prof. L. W. Doob speaks of propaganda as "the attempt to affect the personalities and to control the behavior of individuals towards ends considered unscientific or of doubtful value in a society at a particular time." [1] In contrast, education is defined as the "imparting of knowledge or skill considered to be scientific or to have survival value in a society at a particular time." [2] Prof. H. D. Lasswell sees propaganda as "a technique of social control, or as a species of social movement. As a technique, it is the manipulation of collective attitudes by the use of significant symbols (words, pictures, and tunes) rather than violence, bribery, or boycott." [3] Viewed in this light propaganda becomes concerned with language aimed to influence mass attitudes on controversial issues. It bombards the reader and listener through symbols and words and, unlike education, is not concerned primarily with transmitting skills, insights, or noncontroversial attitudes. Some educators, incidentally, are not content to regard this as the function of education, but, on the contrary regard education as also a process of indoctrination of both controversial and noncontroversial attitudes. Closer to Lasswell than to Doob is Prof. H. L. Childs, who refers to propaganda as "the conscious attempt to manage the minds of other and more numerous publics." [4] N. J. Powell takes an even broader view in seeing propaganda as "the spreading of ideas or attitudes that influence opinions or behavior or both." [5]

---

[1] *Public Opinion and Propaganda* (New York: Henry Holt and Company, Inc., 1948), p. 240. In an earlier work, *Propaganda* (New York: Henry Holt and Company, Inc., 1935), p. 89, Doob gave a broader definition of "intentional" propaganda, speaking of it as "a systematic attempt by an interested individual (or individuals) to control the attitudes of groups of individuals through the use of suggestion and consequently, to control their action."

[2] *Public Opinion and Propaganda,* p. 237.

[3] *Propaganda and Promotional Activities: An Annotated Bibliography* (Minneapolis: University of Minnesota Press, 1935), p. 3.

[4] "Pressure Groups and Propaganda," in E. B. Logan (ed.), *The American Political Scene* (New York: Harper & Brothers, 1936), p. 226.

[5] *The Anatomy of Public Opinion* (New York: Prentice-Hall, Inc., 1951), p. 7.

The term "propaganda," like "lobbying," is often used to fit the exigencies of the user. Many students of parties and interest groups regard propaganda as the use of suggestions and symbols directed, usually, by an organized group toward preconceived ends. For the most part, the literature on propaganda is devoted to strategy and tactics rather than to ethics, definitions, and theories. As Powell has said, "We may take propaganda and public opinion as two interrelated points in the process of communicating ideas, attitudes and beliefs. Public opinion is what takes place before or after, despite or because of propaganda's effects." [6]

The evil connotation of the term can be traced in part to the disillusionment following World War I. All intelligent citizens, however, recognize that propaganda is an ill-defined term but that, correctly understood, it has legitimate uses. What is needed is a full understanding of propaganda techniques and the ability to recognize these devices whenever they are employed by an advertiser, interest group, political party, public official, or campaign orator.

PILLARS OF PROPAGANDA

Believing that the confusion of conflicting propaganda and the babel of voices assailing the public emphasized the need for analyzing propaganda, a group of educators formed the Institute for Propaganda Analysis in 1937. Until it went out of existence with the advent of World War II, it produced numerous studies analyzing the methods of the propagandist. Perhaps its greatest contribution was the attempt to formulate, in simple terms, seven widely used techniques used by special pleaders, viz., name calling, the glittering generality, transfer, testimonial, card stacking, band wagon, and plain folks.[7] Concisely, the Institute attempted to give the public a measuring stick for the detection of propaganda. These techniques may be included in our somewhat broader analysis of propaganda devices.

Defamation and Guilt by Association. Defamation is one of the oldest techniques in politics, yet surprisingly, no comprehensive work has ever been published on its use in the United States. There are times when individuals and organizations deserve to be defamed and the names applied to them are altogether descriptive. More often than not, the terms are incorrect and highly exaggerated. Many leftist groups follow the propaganda line of condemning conservatives as "reactionaries" and "fascists," while the right has referred to those championing reforms in the *status quo* as "Communists," "socialists," and "pinks." Some members of the medical hierarchy have labeled even the mildest proposals for sickness compensation and preventive medicine as "socialized" medicine, a

[6] *Ibid.,* p. 5.
[7] See Institute for Propaganda Analysis, *Propaganda Analysis,* Vol. 1 (1937), pp. 1–4.

term designed to frighten people from a careful study of the plans. Labor leaders have long dubbed even mild bills to regulate labor as "totalitarian," "fascist," "un-American," and "slavery." President Roosevelt was called, in campaign leaflets, a "Communist," a "Communist sympathizer," a "warmonger," a "tool of the fifth column" with an insatiable "lust to become a dictator." Willkie was identified by some of his unscrupulous opponents as a "Nazi sympathizer," a "tool of Wall Street," and "pro-German." Dewey was sneered at by some opponents as being the "darling of Wall Street," the "Pawling dictator," and the "boy wonder." During the 1940 campaign, a leaflet appeared over the signature of the Loyal American League of Rhode Island, with the caption, "The Nazis Endorse Willkie." These extracts show how Willkie's German background was exploited:

The people of America were shocked last week when the Republican candidate for President, Wendell L. Willkie, born of German parents, was endorsed in a full front-page editorial in the official newspaper, the *Free American Deutscher Weckruf and Beobachter*.

Is Wendell Willkie an American or a German Nazi? Surely if he had American blood and spirit in him he would repudiate Hitler's indirect endorsement and would condemn the American German Nazis as Arch Enemies of America. Fellow Americans of Rhode Island, follow this German-Willkie situation carefully.

Some of those working for direct aid for England and France before Pearl Harbor attempted to strengthen their cause by pointing out that many antiwar committees contained anti-Semites, pro-Communists (before the Russo-German war), pro-Germans, and other undesirables. Numerous sincere opponents of these measures, therefore, were pilloried for their views and charged as guilty of being anti-Semitic or pro-Nazi because of association. Interventionists likewise were accused of being pro-British and later pro-Communist.

The composite photograph is a technique sometimes used as a guilt-by-association device. In 1950, Senator Millard Tydings of Maryland was shown, by means of fake photography, as though he were talking with Earl Browder, onetime Communist candidate for President. The picture stirred such controversy that it was investigated by a congressional committee. Republican opponents of General Eisenhower in the New Hampshire primaries in March, 1952, attempted to represent him as friendly to Communists by means of a photograph purporting to show him drinking with Russian Marshal Zhukov. The caption ran: "Zhukov, Communist General, Decorates Drinking Partner Eisenhower at Frankfort, Germany." Many photographs appear during the campaign which do not directly attack the candidate but which stir anxiety about his associations or advisers.

"Color" Words and Oversimplifications. A common form of name call-ing is the "color word," which editorializes the point while seeming to present a statement of fact. This has, unfortunately, crept into many newspaper dispatches. The *Chicago Tribune* in a front-page news story referred to the Agricultural Adjustment Act as the "farm dictator bill." In the same paper prohibitionist and price-control enforcement officers were frequently called "snoopers," "do-gooders," and "busybodies." Other color words found in the current propagandist's vocabulary of name call-ing include "sovietize," "Tory," "alien," "outside influences," "trouble-maker," "utopian dreamer," "yes man," "left-winger," "bureaucrat," "fel-low traveler," "planner," "subversive," and "welfare stater."

An opposite technique from name calling is the use of virtue words to gain support for one's cause. In a burst of virtue, one campaign leaflet called a nominee for Congress a "courageous, passionate fighter for social justice, a progressive, loyal American" who would give his constituents "clean, humane, and efficient government." It is an axiom of politics that one must always favor the "public interest," "social justice," more "democracy," "constitutional government," "freedom," "liberty," "unity," "the people," "peace," "private enterprise," "progress," "civilization," "Christianity," "loyalty," "the American way," "honor," and "truth." No one can quarrel with these, but the terms are often so ill-defined and their employment so glib in campaign propaganda as to render them poor guides for judging a candidate's qualifications or ability.

To make his point, the propagandist commonly resorts to a black-and-white presentation which makes the person completely accept or com-pletely reject a proposition. Business groups have said, "You must be for either democracy or socialism; there is no middle way." The listener, if he accepts democracy, must apparently be for capitalism, the implica-tion being that a socialist cannot be a democrat. The fact that democratic socialism does exist and is possible is completely overlooked by the propa-gandist who wishes to sell a special brand of capitalism. James A. Roe, a conservative former congressman, admonished his listeners that they must be "either-or": "There is only one type of Americanism and that is true 100 per cent Americanism. This so-called talk of liberalism is a misnomer. It is the wolf of communism in sheep's clothing and the people of Amer-ica must not fall for it. Now is the time for all good citizens to stand up and be counted. We are either for our Government or we are against it, for there is no middle road." [8] These words were spoken at a time of tension with the Soviet government and when Congress was considering the outlawing of the Communist party in the United States and other strong measures against its party members. By implication, those who

[8] *Long Island Star-Journal,* Apr. 26, 1947.

believed in preserving civil liberties for liberals as well as for Communists were against the government and for communism.

Card Stacking. Special pleaders and propagandists invariably rely upon the use of "evidence" in the form of statistics, quotations, and "circumstance." This can be, and often is, one of the most pernicious of propaganda techniques because it may lead the conscientious citizen to feel that he is making a decision on the basis of fact and reason. It is as Antonio remarked to Bassanio in "The Merchant of Venice," "The devil can cite scripture for his purpose." During World War II all governments were apparently guilty of misusing figures about their own and the enemies' losses and about the damage done to the enemies' resources, proving Lord Ponsonby's observation, "When war is declared, truth is the first casualty."

In the great battle over postwar price control, both sides resorted to card stacking in the citation of figures to defend their position. The public was flooded with statistics and counterstatistics. Reputable agencies such as the Bureau of Labor Statistics and Dun and Bradstreet had their figures presented by both sides. The discrepancy lay in the failure to give full citations or to explain exactly what the figures meant.

The citation of a phrase or sentence, taken out of its context, from the speech of an opponent is an old campaign device. In one Republican campaign newspaper appeared the inflammatory headline, "Wallace Praises Dictators, Slams Priests in Book Ms.," beneath which the article opened as follows: "Many people will be surprised to learn that Henry A. Wallace, Roosevelt candidate for the vice-presidency, once praised Dictators Lenin, Stalin, and Mussolini and repeated religious criticisms which are certain to horrify many good Christian Americans." [9] The remainder of the story was utterly devoid of substance which could justify the headline. Actually, the article took a few passages from a study made by Wallace of sixteenth-century religious leaders and from these attempted to show that Wallace was in favor of contemporary totalitarianism and anticlericalism.

Innuendo is one of the cleverest tricks of the propagandist trade. This often consists of imparting information in such a way as to leave the impression that results of a course of action or the election of a candidate will be a near calamity. If, at a later date, the originator is shown to be incorrect, he can defend himself by insisting that he was misunderstood or wrongly interpreted.

The use of innuendo and insinuation and the playing upon fears and anxieties to gain support for a cause are shown in a printed sheet distrib-

[9] *The Inside Story,* Vol. I, No. 2. Published in 1940 by the Missouri State Republican Committee.

uted in front of a Minneapolis high school in 1940, with the suggestion that the message be taken home to parents:

Do *you know* that the next move will be a law like this one [Selective Service] drafting women and young girls?

Do *you know* that under this law women and girls are to be used to make the most dangerous munitions? That some of them will be "on duty with the armed forces"?

Do *you think* that the morals of your daughters can be safeguarded under such conditions?

You have only this one election to save the lives of your sons and daughters.

OTHER PILLARS

Transfers. Issues and causes are also often beclouded by the employment of transfers and testimonials and by exhorting the reader or listener to join causes supported by the "people," the "plain folks." This consists of taking some institution or symbol which is revered and transferring its prestige to gain acceptance for its own cause. Among the more widely used are the Constitution, the Bill of Rights, the Declaration of Independence, the church, the Bible, the Cross, and Uncle Sam. These stir the emotions and help to create a favorable mind-set or place the listener or reader in a friendly, receptive mood. As has been pointed out, campaigners frequently allude to historic documents and quote from them at strategic times to "prove their point."

The testimonial attempts to transfer the prestige of some prominent person, who enjoys a large following, to further the objectives of the group. Interest and citizens' groups frequently have an imposing list of "knowns" as "honorary members" on their letterhead. In political campaigns the parties constantly play up the names of journalists, clergymen, popular entertainers, civic leaders, and others who have endorsed their nominees and, wherever possible, solicit a sentence or two from the personages to be used in the campaign. More often than not, the names are drawn from the past. Presidents Washington, Jefferson, Jackson, and Lincoln are certain to be brought into every campaign to indicate that these men are on "our side." Testimonials are a mainstay in advertising anything from cereals to tooth paste and come from popular baseball heroes, radio artists, and Hollywood stars.

One of the most widely distributed handbills issued over the signature of the Republican National Committee in 1940 used both transfer and card stacking in an attempt to stop Mr. Roosevelt's reelection. In parallel columns were listed sketches of six persons supporting and opposing the third term, with a sentence purporting to show their position. The three in opposition were Washington, Jefferson, and Jackson, and the reader was left to accept the views of these "loyal" Americans or those of a Communist leader, a political boss, and a Secretary of the Interior who had made many enemies. Much of the anti-third-term literature misconstrued the position of the founding fathers.

On the Band Wagon. In every election all parties exhort the readers to get on the band wagon and follow the crowd by voting for the "winners," who, of course, will be their own nominees. Every effort is made to create an illusion of victory and the voter is exhorted not to throw away his vote by casting it for the opposition or for a minor-party candidate. The "we" feeling is employed to get a solid vote from the various minorities. Campaign leaflets tell why all Catholics, or Irish, or Jews, or Negroes, or farmers, and so on are mobilizing behind a particular cause or candidate. All independents and others are asked to vote for the good-government nominee who will win a brilliant victory over the political machine. President David Dubinsky of the International Ladies' Garment Workers' Union pointed out that "all" workers must find themselves on the side of the New Deal since "every labor-baiter, every reactionary, every pleader for special interests hates the New Deal and is rooting for Dewey. In behalf of the leadership of our union, I make this final appeal to you to come out in full strength and vote for President Roosevelt for a greater, expanded New Deal." [10] The parade with its marchers and martial music, the packed political rally, the huge and boisterous demonstration are all a part of the campaign to show that "everyone is doing it." Perhaps the greatest master of band-wagon showmanship in this century was the Nazi leader who staged public emotional orgies practically without parallel.

The "Common Man." Reference may be made to one other technique, often associated with band-wagon appeals, and which the Institute for Propaganda Analysis has called "plain folks." This is the effort to win confidence and support for one's candidate or leader by picturing him as just a plain person like his neighbors and the masses. In American political campaigns this manifests itself through the wide dissemination of photographs depicting the nominee as a real man of the people. The Republican National Committee in "humanizing" their candidate published a 15- by 24-inch mat for newspapers and posters carrying six striking poses of Governor Dewey as a plain citizen. Under one of them, which showed Mr. Dewey stroking a cow, was the caption: "Down on the farm Dewey inspects one of his cows at his Pawling, New York, home. Although he does not claim to be a farmer, Governor Dewey understands farm problems and speaks the farmer's language." Another showed him sitting on a desk, informally talking with labor leaders about their problems, and still another being sworn in as a prosecutor and gang buster.

[10] *Justice*, Vol. 26 (Nov. 1, 1944), p. 2.

In a flattering portrait with Mrs. Dewey, he was called a "family man" with "two husky sons." "Mrs. Dewey," it was asserted, "leaves politics to her husband, centers attention on her home and family." Pictured shaking hands with his minister, the reader was told that this was "Church Worker Thomas Dewey, a vestryman of St. Peter's Protestant Episcopal Church in Albany, N.Y. The Deweys attend church regularly, give Sunday-school picnics at their farm at Pawling, say grace at meals. Mrs. Dewey sometimes plays the organ in the little church near their farm."

Republican literature featured "Ike and Dick" as "a couple of regular guys" who are "God-fearing men," "family men," and "scrappers." Adlai Stevenson was photographed in an Indian blanket in Pendleton, Ore., Robert Taft wearing a sombrero in Texas, Franklin Roosevelt fishing, and sharing sandwiches at a factory. The coonskin cap of Senator Estes Kefauver was used to lend color to his campaigns. Wendell Willkie was portrayed with rolled-up sleeves, hair falling over his brow, engaged in husking corn. "Alf" Landon and Frank Knox were photographed as two-fisted horseback riders, a folksy appeal reminiscent of Theodore Roosevelt.

Humble origins and birthplaces are always depicted as essential qualifications and have been used, whenever possible, from Jackson to the present. Few presidential nominees today can claim having been born in a log cabin, but campaign managers see a value in dramatizing their candidate as springing from modest little Independence, Mo., or Abilene, Kan. In Texas an effort was made to play down Eisenhower's Republican label by concentrating on the appeal "Vote for Texas-born Ike."

LITERATURE AND PUBLICITY

One hundred million pieces of campaign literature were shipped from the Chicago headquarters of the Republican party in 1896 and the same party spent about a half million dollars on posters and Harding lithographs in 1920. Charles Michelson, onetime Democratic publicity chief, said that at least one hundred million pieces of literature were distributed by his party in 1936, and R. D. Casey estimates that 361,000 press releases were issued by the Republicans in the same year.[11]

Advertising columns of newspapers are usually open to all candidates. Many campaign managers remain skeptical of this form of political advertising and less space appears to be bought for this purpose by the national committees than in former years. For local elections, advertising in newspapers is still one of the most frequently used methods of getting

11 For two highly informative articles on campaign literature see Casey, "Republican Propaganda in the 1936 Campaign," *Public Opinion Quarterly,* Vol. 1 (1937), p. 43; and "Party Campaign Propaganda," *The Annals of the American Academy of Political and Social Science,* Vol. 179 (1935), pp. 96–105.

the voters' attention. The support of newspaper columnists and also editorial endorsement are sought. When obtained, the candidates often have thousands of reprints distributed. The Volunteers for Stevenson did a great deal of advertising by means of reprints.

American ingenuity in finding methods of disseminating campaign appeals appears unlimited. Nearly everyone has seen messages carried through franked mail, handbills, leaflets, dodgers, broadsides, calling cards, "open" and personal letters, windshield and envelope stickers, and automobile bumper signs. A candidate by the name of Hamburger distributed a luscious-looking printed hamburger, the exact size and shape of the famous sandwich, and a person named Egg put out an eggcup inscribed "Vote for a Good Egg." Brewers in Washington state used beer bottle caps to promote their cause in an impending initiative proposition. Some nominees have publicized their wares on free kites and free soldier hats for the kiddies. Billboard advertisements first came into effective use in 1916, and have remained ever since. Candidates' pictures have adorned telephone poles about as long as anyone can remember and it is quite certain that great-grandfather saw the faces of candidates on wooden fences.

Perhaps the newest type of conveyance is the colored picture book fashioned after the Walt Disney publications and portraying à la "Dick Tracy" and "Superman" the life history and exploits of the candidate. Millions of copies of a 14-page colored magazine on Harry S. Truman were sent out by the Democratic National Committee in 1948, and a similarly flattering colored book appeared on behalf of Stevenson in 1952. In the latter year the Republicans put out two bitter and highly emotional colored sequences entitled "Yalta to Korea" and "Crime, Corruption, and Communism." Labor opponents of Senator Taft in Ohio issued a caustic colored book portraying the senator as a "tool of the exploiters" and a foe of the consumers and underprivileged. Several objective observers felt the material was so overdone, if not libelous, that it boomeranged against its sponsors.

The method of dispersion is conditioned in part by the geographical situation, financial resources, and the nature of the constituency. Rural voters can often be reached best through mailing pieces, urban voters through the dissemination of handbills at bus and subway terminals. Billboard and newspaper advertising along "institutional" lines may be a good investment for state and city-wide committees. Political parties in Seattle use a unique "traveling-billboard" idea by placing large signs on the city transit buses. An advertiser who uses 100 signs has his message carried 90,000 miles in the course of a week, with a million stops. Political advertising is also sometimes used on the inside of the buses. After the initial shock, the public, the parties, and the city government accepted the idea and it has proved popular. The city, moreover, found the income highly useful in balancing the books and the transit system showed no partiality because it accepted business on a first-come, first-served basis.

A more conventional practice in many cities is the use of banners extending across the street, above the traffic, presenting candidates and slogans to motorists and pedestrians. Pamphlets probably hold greater appeal for the independent voter, while those who have little interest may find their attention caught by sensational circulars, cartoons, or a post card received the day before election.

The national committees generally print and distribute to local committees tons of literature setting forth the general appeals and issues, leaving the choice of method of dissemination to the local organizations. Most of the local committees also print their own supplementary materials, emphasizing the virtues of local nominees and issues incident to the constituency. Appeals have to be general and national in scope and devoid of matters which might receive an unfavorable reception in some localities.

Literature over the signature of the Republican National Committee in 1952 bore down heavily on universal appeals of condemning the Democratic Administration for "appeasing the Chinese Communists," corruption, and the "mess in Washington," and gave these among many reasons to show it was "time for a change." One widely distributed leaflet said that "a vote for Ike and Dick is a vote against communism" and "a vote for Ike and Dick is a vote for morality" and "a vote for Ike and Dick is a vote for prosperity without war." Democratic institutional literature dwelt upon "the prosperity team—Stevenson and Sparkman" and the social gains for labor, farmers, electricity users, the aged and others under the program of the Administration. It warned of a recurrence of depression if the Republicans were to gain power with the appeal "don't let them do it again."

Campaign publicity issued by the national committees, though clearly propaganda, is usually proper and legitimate, being marked by restraint when compared to that issued by private groups and individuals. For obvious reasons, excessively emotional and irrational appeals to race, religion, class, or family affairs involve much less responsibility if left in the hands of private, temporary, and amorphous groups. In spite of this, some objectionable and inflammatory publications have come from the party committees, especially the state and local ones. For example, much offensive matter appeared in a six-page pamphlet issued by the St. Louis Democratic Campaign Headquarters, Negro Voters Division. Each page contained grotesque and uncomplimentary cartoons of Mr. Willkie, showing him as an octopus with arms reaching out to take slush money from the utilities' consumers, squeezing telephone subscribers, charging high electric rates, and so on. Another cartoon showed a sheriff, blackjack in hand, standing in the door of the railroad station at Elwood, Ind. (Willkie's boyhood town). On the station a sign read "No Negroes Allowed"; beneath the picture, the Republican nominee was quoted as saying, "I learned my liberalism right here at home."

NONPARTY CAMPAIGN LITERATURE

The volume of campaign literature issued by nonparty organizations is unbelievably large. It is generally specific in appeal, hard-hitting, and often libelous and scurrilous. Leaflets over the names of the "Irish-Americans of Middletown," "Italian-Americans of Homewood," "Mothers of America," "Glenwood Friends of Freedom," "War Veterans' Mission League," "Christian Factfinders" tell why the Irish, Italians, mothers, freedom lovers, veterans, Christians, and whatnots should vote against the opposition and for their candidate. Two general types of nonparty groups publish campaign materials. First of these are especially formed political committees whose *raison d'être* is the election, and which, after the campaign, go out of existence. It is not unusual for such organizations to be fictitious, existing only in the mind of the copy writer of the advertisements or the pamphlet bearing the author's name. The second is composed of permanently organized interest groups to whom the campaign is merely incidental to the larger cause. In the case of the latter, the literature attempts to relate the campaign issues to the general objectives of the group and the election is also used to increase the membership and mailing list of the association. In terms of financial accountability, the reporting of expenses under the corrupt-practices laws, and character of appeal, the distinction between these two types of political organization is important.

Temporary Political Committee Publicity. The strictly nonparty political committees make great use of testimonials and appeals to a class or fraternal interest. They often work closely with the party organizations and receive assistance from the party organizations in preparing materials and in campaigning. As noted previously, they carry much of the financial burden of an election and relieve the parties of certain responsibilities and duties. The voter can usually identify these groups and their literature is easily recognized for what it purports to be—election propaganda. Most of these groups address their message in the form of paid newspaper advertisements and leaflets to a special audience.

A group calling itself the Rhode Island Democrats for Willkie showed ingenuity in issuing a leaflet under the title, "Where Do I Come In?" purporting to tell how each of 20 occupational, ethnic, and other groups should vote. Only four groups were voting for Roosevelt—the fifth columnists, Fascists, Communists, and New Deal politicians. The following appeals, chosen at random, are illustrative of the type commonly issued by the auxiliary political committees.

Catholic. I would vote for Willkie because the Catholic Church teaches self-denial, discipline, love, and courage. The New Deal preaches spending, something-for-nothing, class hatred, and fear. Its government Reorganization Plan tried to put Catholic schools under state control. Willkie promises "toil and sweat" but he "hates no man, fears no enemy."

Doctor. I would vote for Willkie because the New Deal has threatened to put doctors under political control. Under its scheme for socialized medicine, the sick man can no longer choose his doctor. Willkie believes in individual liberty. "May the best man get the patients."

Negro. I would vote for Willkie because Roosevelt put an ex-Ku Klux Klan member on the Supreme Court and failed to support the antilynching bill. He talked a lot about equal wage scales in the South, where most of our people live, but did he establish them? The New Deal has wrecked the cotton-growing industry in the South and transferred it to Brazil. I believe Willkie is like Abraham Lincoln and really fair-minded.

The Citizens for Eisenhower and Volunteers for Stevenson put out very large quantities of specific interest appeals. One of the latter groups distributed an appeal to veterans, which carried cartoons by Bill Mauldin and said in part, "Right now we're looking for a President who can help to prevent the next war. Adlai Stevenson can and will do that. Dwight Eisenhower can no longer be considered an independent; . . . he is now a private in the ranks of the McCarthys, the Jenners, the Tafts. The general, who speaks so harshly of regimentation, represents the most regimented way of all—the military"; and "Stevenson is the choice of the pfc's." Citizens for Eisenhower issued a frontal attack on "Stevenson's mess in Illinois" and accused the governor of failing to cope with crime and corruption in Illinois and with failure to bring honest and competent men into his administration. Both of these independent groups sought to corral the support of labor, farm, business, youth, women's, and many other groups.

Interest-group Publicity. Pressure groups commonly engage in political activity during elections. Labor unions have long exerted efforts on behalf of certain candidates and the good-government leagues become additionally active during campaigns, not only for nominees but on referendums and constitutional amendments. The journals of labor, farm, business, medical, educational, and other groups often bring especially prepared messages of the aspirants, roll-call votes, or other aspects of a nominee's public record, and sometimes make endorsements. Some of these magazines have a circulation running into seven figures and serve the purpose of affirming rather than converting. Where the outcome of an election directly affects the objectives of the group or the welfare of its membership, it seems altogether fitting for an association to enter the political arena. The voter must be on guard, however, when independent groups seize the opportunity, under the *laissez faire* of a political campaign, to circulate inflammatory doctrines and to interject ideas which have little or no relevance to the election but which promote their own struggle for power.

Examples of these include politico-religious appeals and racial biases. Several of the former have used campaigns as a vehicle for preaching anti-Catholic doctrines. The *Herald of the Epiphany* issued a special edition on July 15, 1940, offering evidence of a "quasi-alliance between the Roosevelt Administration and the Catholic Church." Another publication, *The Monitor,* mailed a "startling disclosure" all over the nation asserting:

> According to a recent news story, Henry A. Wallace, Candidate for Vice-President, has left the United Presbyterian Church and joined the High Episcopal or Anglo-Catholic Church. Inform all your friends of this startling piece of news. Do your American duty. Support the Republican ticket in the coming election. It's the Protestant Party! The Backbone of our Democracy.

A billboard in Philadelphia in 1940 bore this sign:

SAVE YOUR CHURCH
DICTATORS HATE RELIGION
VOTE STRAIGHT REPUBLICAN

The Church League of America published a leaflet which it claimed was being mailed to 100,000 ministers warning them that a third term meant "less support for churches." After citing the Declaration of Independence and Constitution the document said in part:

> The Wagner Act is an outstanding example of recent cyclonic reform, upheaval, and world-wide trend to substitute the rule of men for the rule of laws. The Wagner Labor Act, under the guise of protecting collective bargaining, more than offset its good with its evils. First it tied the hands of every employer (large and small) so that any criminal—any Communist—or any racketeer could go into any plant and start organizing the employees into a dues-paying corral regardless of the merits of the case. Second—even more destructive to our American System—was the scheme by which a three-man Labor Board was created to act as prosecutor, judge, and jury in thousands of cases where professional labor organizers clashed with employers.
>
> As private enterprise is being taxed more and more by the executive, ever-growing demands for big government arise—and as the growth of bureaucratic obstructions and red tape tends to strangle human initiative and stifle opportunity for more employment—it is inevitable that there will be less and less from the profits of business to go for the upkeep of educational institutions, churches, and the wide network of human agencies they maintain.

There are those who probably never fully realized that the only alternative to the support that comes to free institutions from private enterprise must necessarily be some form of government subsidy.

For a number of years anti-Semitic groups capitalized on alleged "communistic" New Deal policies to spread their doctrines during election years; their propaganda thus differed from other campaign materials in that the primary aim was to foster anti-Jewish sentiment and only secondarily to defeat President Roosevelt.[12] Gerald Winrod's *The Revealer,* of Oct. 15, 1936, purported to chart President Roosevelt's Jewish ancestry back to 1862, asserting, "It shows why he has given hundreds of liberals, socialists, and Communists powerful positions in the national government. It reveals the origin of the sinister spirit which today animates the White House." In a similar vein the Edmondson Vigilante bulletins advised, "Vote Republican . . . and save the U.S. from absorption into the Jewish Empire." An airplane dropped vicious anti-Semitic literature over New York City during one campaign.[13] Similar crude appeals have been made in Italian, Polish, German, and other communities. One of the worst of these was the following message, printed on small cards, by a housing association in Philadelphia and distributed to white tenants in a neighborhood near a Negro section and a Jewish school building:

"To the White People of North Philadelphia: You have got to help protect our homes. The Niggers and Jews are taking all our houses. Now the Republicans have put the Niggers and Jews on the ticket. Don't vote for them. Vote the straight Democratic ticket. Keep the Jews and Niggers out."

Further exhibits of scurrilous and defamatory literature would only emphasize the point that elections are often used by undemocratic groups to disseminate pernicious propaganda. Reputable party and civic leaders have denounced these materials and have deplored their entry into campaigns. It is clear that these appeals have no place in an election or, for that matter, in American life.

ANONYMOUS LITERATURE

Unidentified campaign literature raises some problems separate and distinct from those issued by bona fide political organizations. The content of anonymous publications has been, by far, more vicious and inflammatory than the foregoing exhibits of party and nonparty groups. Those charged with enforcing corrupt-practices laws obviously meet with

---

[12] On the background of anti-Semitic groups using the election to further their program see Donald S. Strong, *Organized Anti-Semitism in America* (Washington, D.C.: Public Affairs Press, 1941).

[13] A full reproduction of these leaflets may be found in Hugh A. Bone, *Smear Politics* (Washington, D.C.: Public Affairs Press, 1941), pp. 28 ff.

special difficulties in the case of literature bearing insufficient identification. Such material constitutes a threat to open and aboveboard party activity and is a menace to the public, for it seems probable that its influence is relatively unaffected by the lack of careful identification. An important trick of many propagandists is to veil the sources of fact and information. To evaluate the political propaganda, the voter must know its source, and the absence of this information imposes at the outset a serious handicap as to the validity of the contentions.

Anonymous political advertising divides itself into two categories: (1) the complete absence of either a sponsor or an address, (2) insufficient or fictitious identification. A Senate Campaign Expenditures Committee made a comprehensive study of campaign literature and reported that "two-thirds of the 1940 campaign material, exclusive of that officially issued by the regular party organizations, was placed in circulation by unidentified individuals and groups. These sponsors were further concealed behind a shield of total or partial anonymity." [14] In this campaign, anonymous literature was especially pernicious and abundant, indicating great expense but with no record or report of its sponsors. Literature completely devoid of identification grossly misrepresented the conscription program and made the crudest appeals to racial and religious prejudice. Though anonymous, many of these pieces were found in as many as 30 different states, indicating that some central sponsoring group, rather than local cranks, masterminded their publication and distribution.

In attacking the selective service bills, one message printed on attractive green paper said the bills would "empower the President to determine the amount of government bonds you must buy . . . another New Dealer has introduced a bill to *conscript all children* in Elementary and High Schools into compulsory physical training from 4 to 8 hours per day under *Government Control*. Vote for Willkie." Other warnings were sent out over the open-letter caption "To Mothers of America" carrying similar warnings. A 12- by 18-inch broadside in black and red type flooded several Middle Western cities predicting:

WAR BY JANUARY
IF YOU VOTE DEMOCRATIC ON NOVEMBER 5TH.
THE DEMOCRATS LIED TO YOU IN 1916 AS THEY ARE
LYING TO YOU TODAY—THEY ARE MAKING PROMISES
OF OLD.
THEIR EVERY ACT IS A STEP CLOSER TO WAR!
A VOTE FOR ROOSEVELT IS A VOTE FOR WAR.
A VOTE FOR WILLKIE IS A VOTE FOR PEACE.

[14] Report of Senate Campaign Expenditures Committee, 77th Cong., 1st Sess., p. 15.

Pictures of Mrs. Roosevelt visiting a Negro educational institution were captioned, "This is Mrs. Roosevelt a goin' to a nigger meetin' " and distributed in the South. The pictures were completely unidentified but someone went to great expense to prepare them.

Because most persons are sophisticated enough to discount obviously anonymous literature, publications often bear the name of an apocryphal organization to make it appear bona fide. Titles such as the "Rank and File Research Committee," "Loyal American League of Rhode Island," "Mothers of the United States," and so on have published materials without benefit of a street address and were found after an election to be nonexistent, though some readers may have been duped into believing the organizations to be responsible ones.

A post-office box or mailing permit is a popular device to cover up sponsorship; thousands of copies of a 61-page booklet went out over an Oklahoma City permit in 1940 saying that the cost of printing and mailing was met through "popular subscription by the fellows—the plain people, liberty loving and democratic." The content was pseudointellectual and strongly anti-Roosevelt without a single reference to Mr. Willkie.

In addition to the issuance of publicity by amorphous, ephemeral organizations which disappear on election day, many personal advertisements are fictitious. Newspaper advertisements and leaflets have appeared over these signatures and without an address: An Eisenhower Booster, A Patriot, A Worker, A Farmer, An American, A Voter, A Democrat for Dewey, and A Disabled Veteran for Truman.

CONTROL OF POLITICAL ADVERTISING

When cognizance was taken of the large volume of anonymous campaign literature and of its character—a character which was harmful to national unity and to the body politic—demands arose that Congress take steps to eradicate the menace during campaigns. Public acknowledgment of the responsibility for the publication of political advertising came in the form of an amendment to the Federal election laws in December, 1944.[15] The law provides that no person shall publish or distribute any political statement relating to a candidate for a Federal office which does not contain the name of the person responsible for its publication or distribution. If a corporation or association is responsible for the material, the names of the officers must be attached.

Campaign literature issued during the presidential elections since the law took effect has been studied by the respective congressional committees. There are still cries of "scurrilous literature" but there seems to have been a considerable reduction in racial and religious bigotry themes

[15] Public Law 544, Chap. 706, 78th Cong., 2d Sess.

and more particularly of anonymous publications in general. The law does seem to have put an end to the large number of unsigned full-page and half-page newspaper advertisements. If the legislative approach is to be effective, state laws requiring identification of the sponsors of campaign materials must supplement the Federal act. Today only about half of the states have laws requiring paid political advertisements to be so identified and many of these states do not require the name and address of the sponsor to accompany the statement.

Laws requiring the disclosure of the identity of the sponsor seem both desirable and wholly within the framework of a free press. The prevention of abuses of the franking privilege during political campaigns also appears a proper sphere for legislative action. It seems doubtful that legal restrictions should go beyond this point, even if they could surmount constitutional hurdles against placing limitations on freedom of expression. It appears inadvisable to prohibit the printing and circulating of scurrilous literature because of the difficulty of defining what is "scurrilous." The zealous partisan considers most of the attacks against his candidate as defamatory, and no one could hope to obtain agreement on what constitutes "smear" literature.

Several other remedies are available for mitigating some of the problems raised here and for affording more sufficient protection for the reader. There is need for better enforcement of existing laws, notably corrupt-practices legislation, and the calling to account of those organizations failing to report expenditures for campaign propaganda. One or two properly publicized libel and slander suits against malicious personal attacks might have a salutary effect on the quality of printed materials. Action of this type, however, must be carefully planned else the suit might boomerang.

In the final analysis, the cure for smear politics will come from public opinion. Aroused electorates are in a position to exact a higher standard than the law demands, as may be witnessed by outcries and action against those expending excessive money on elections. A few—but not enough—civic leaders, radio commentators, and newspapers have conducted campaigns against reprehensible political methods. Organizations such as the Minnesota Antidefamation Council are rendering a valuable service in collecting data on "hate" groups and deserve greater popular support. Of assistance to the individual is education in propaganda analysis. The citizen who can recognize propaganda is in a position to expose those groups who seek to make a "sucker" of their fellow man. Mass propaganda is here to stay; a universal recognition of the symbols and tactics used by the propagandist will equip the citizenry to assay the pleas of those who would sell ideas and men.

THE USES OF CAMPAIGNING

Little Discussion of Specific Policies. Political campaigns in this country are rarely marked by a clear-cut contest on principles, policies, or programs. Candidates avoid taking sides on controversial issues, particularly if they have a good chance of winning, for to do so might alienate large blocs of voters. They follow instead the practice of voicing general appeals and broad objectives, about which there can be little disagreement. Usually only candidates whose chance of winning is slight dare to take definite stands on issues. It is for this reason that third parties are always specific and definite in their promises. They are not afraid of losing votes and may win them by taking definite positions.

Our political campaigns are often criticized because of the lack of definite issues. Many issues are touched on during the campaign, but when the votes are counted, there is seldom a definite mandate from the voters on any single issue. As has been recently pointed out, a national election is not a true referendum or mandate on issues of foreign affairs because foreign policy is secondary to domestic questions.[16] The decision is essentially between the "ins" and the "outs." Because of our governmental system, with its checks and balances, separation of powers, division of powers between the executive and the legislative and judicial branches, as well as between the Federal government and the states, it is rarely possible for either party to be able to formulate and carry through a consistent governmental policy for which it may be held responsible. Added to these considerations is the patent fact that both the major national parties are largely decentralized, and the candidate for neither party is able to speak with assurance for his party.

While the absence of campaigns on definite issues and programs is often voiced as a major criticism of our party system, something can be said in its defense. Political campaigns do not provide a suitable occasion for decision, as a rule, on specific issues and programs. They are so charged with extravagant statements, with praise and abuse, with prejudice and lack of calm deliberation, that it is perhaps fortunate that few issues are decided directly as a result of a campaign. Specific promises made in the heat of a campaign with the hope of winning votes often later embarrass the candidate when he is elected to office and public interest requires a different decision. Also, while the platforms and statements of the parties and their candidates are usually vague and consist largely of glittering generalities, the record of each party, its leader-

---

16 On this point the student should consult Thomas A. Bailey, *The Man in the Street: The Impact of American Public Opinion on Foreign Policy* (New York: The Macmillan Company, 1948). A feeling, however, that Eisenhower might bring an early end to the Korean War probably won many votes for him in 1952.

ship, and where its support comes from are known and well understood by the voting public, and the performance of the party, when it comes into power, rarely differs greatly from the expectations of its followers. The record of the party rather than its campaign promises constitutes at least some guide to its future performance.

Do Campaigns Win Votes? Are votes actually won or lost as a result of the enormous amount of time, energy, and money expended during a campaign? [17] Party workers believe so. James A. Farley attributed Mr. Truman's 1948 success to a last-minute switch in votes brought about by the President's campaign. Defeated party members commonly express the view that victory was lost because of campaign mistakes. In their election post mortem, victorious campaign managers and their cohorts receive congratulations for a "brilliant performance" and strategy.

Notwithstanding the nearness of the 1948 electioneering feat of President Truman, objective students of politics are less inclined than party enthusiasts to believe that electoral outcome is due to campaign techniques. It seems doubtful, for example, whether any type of campaign would have brought a Landon victory in 1936, and it is open to question whether different strategy would have resulted in success for Willkie in 1940, for Dewey in 1944, or for Stevenson in 1952. The respective personal strength of the nominees themselves, the course of events, as well as the temper of the voting public at the time, are likely to have more effect than the propaganda battle. Polls show that millions of voters make up their minds soon after the primaries and conventions, and many even earlier, and that electioneering brings no appreciable change in voter sentiment. Moreover, the loyal and ardent partisan will vote in every election regardless of the campaign, and he is unlikely to be changed by any argument of the opposition. He accounts for the bulk of the crowd at political rallies and is the most avid reader of the publicity of his own party; campaign activities merely strengthen rather than change his conviction. For this reason, election activities, if they are to have any value, must be directed to other than the party "regular."

Reliable data on the influence of campaigning are limited and the information possessed relates largely to presidential elections. For the fraction of voters who are not partisans, campaigns appear to reinforce views and stimulate registration and voting. In very few cases is there evidence that voters are actually converted by campaign publicity and speeches. The stunning victory of Truman in 1948 provoked and will

[17] Few careful studies have been made of the influence of political campaigns. The best analysis of how the voter makes decisions is a study of Erie County, Ohio, by Paul F. Lazarsfeld, Bernard Berelson, and Hazel Gaudet, *The People's Choice: How the Voter Makes Up His Mind in a Presidential Campaign* (New York: Columbia University Press, 1948).

continue to provoke debate on whether his campaign determined the outcome, thus affording the exception to what had long been regarded as the rule. It will be some time, if ever, before a definite answer can be made. This election, if it did nothing else, showed that the illusion of victory can be a great delusion and that the influence of campaigns offers a challenging field of study.

On the state and local level, where voting strength is close or nearly even between rival parties, a vigorous campaign plus get-out-the-vote efforts have turned the tide. The strategic use of evidence of political corruption accompanied by doorbell ringing has, at times, resulted in a victory for fusionist and good-government parties in municipalities. On initiative and referendum propositions, city-manager plans, and constitutional amendments, appeals frequently decide the outcome. Success in these cases is due primarily to mobilizing the sporadic and apathetic voters by dramatizing the evils of continued rule by unscrupulous political machines and bosses. Perhaps the greatest single use of American political campaigns lies in stirring up the independent and occasional voter to a point where he believes his vote will count for something.

Beyond getting out the vote and arousing civic interest, the campaign does bring the personalities before the public and it focuses attention, however imperfectly, on some problems and issues, thereby providing some clue to differences between candidates and parties. Those actively engaged in electioneering undoubtedly enjoy the thrill of taking part in a great democratic process. As a result of the oratory and ritual directed to him, the voter feels that there has been a healthy debate resulting in a wholesome collective judgment. These less tangible and psychological aspects seem real and few Americans would advocate an abandonment of campaigns. Most sincere observers of American elections believe, however, that our campaigns would be vastly improved by a reduction in their length, fewer speeches, and less high-pressure, emotional oratory.

SELECTED REFERENCES

Although there is no definitive work on campaign organization and techniques, the political parties themselves issue many pamphlets and materials on the subject. The larger newspapers, particularly *The New York Times,* present day-to-day descriptions of specific campaigns and constitute important sources on the matter.

Interesting insights may be obtained from James A. Farley, *Behind the Ballots* (1938) and *Jim Farley's Story* (1948); Charles Michelson, *The Ghost Talks* (1944); E. J. Flynn, *You're the Boss* (1947); R. V. Peel and T. C. Donnelly, *The 1932 Campaign* (1935); H. A. Bone, *Smear Politics* (1941); T. M. Black, *Democratic Party Publicity in the 1940 Campaign* (1941); A. Campbell, G. Gurin, and W. E. Miller, *The Voter Decides* (1954); O. Carlson and A. Blake, *How to Get into Politics: The Art of Winning Elections* (1946); A. Campbell and R. L. Kahn, *The People Elect a President* (1952); and P. F. Lazarsfeld, B. Berelson, and H. Gaudet, *The People's Choice: How the Voter Makes Up His Mind in a Presidential Campaign* (1948).

For a guide to the extensive literature on propaganda see B. L. Smith, H. D. Lasswell, and R. D. Casey, *Propaganda, Communication, and Public Opinion: A Comprehensive Reference Guide* (1946). The various textbooks in public opinion and propaganda are useful for presenting background for the study of campaigns; see especially Albig, *Public Opinion* (1939); Smith, *Public Opinion in a Democracy* (1939); Childs, *Introduction to Public Opinion* (1940); Doob, *Public Opinion and Propaganda* (1948) ; Irion, *Public Opinion and Propaganda* (1950); Powell, *Anatomy of Public Opinion* (1951); Ogle, *Public Opinion and Political Dynamics* (1950); MacDougall, *Understanding Public Opinion* (1952), and the book of readings by Katz, Cartwright, Eldersveld, and Lee, *Public Opinion and Propaganda* (1954).

CHAPTER 21

Party Finance

The mazuma, the jack, the shekels, the kale,
The velvet, the you-know-what,
The what-it-takes, a roll, a wad,
Bring it home, boy,
Bring home the bacon.
Start on a shoestring if you have to.
Then get your first million.
—CARL SANDBURG

Political parties operate elaborate machinery to perform their functions. To oil the machinery money is needed. Money has always been a
factor in American elections, but large-scale finance is a development of
the last 75 years. It is estimated that $25,000 was spent by the Democratic
National Committee to elect Buchanan, while the newly formed Republican National Committee disbursed $100,000 on Lincoln's behalf. This
may be compared with reported expenditures in 1944 by the same committees of $2,056,000 for Roosevelt and $2,830,000 for Dewey. Party
expenditures rose and fell on many occasions between these dates but
exhibited a general upward trend.[1] For years, expenditures and financial
practices of political committees and individuals have been of public
concern. State and Federal legislatures perennially investigate the sources
and expenditures of party funds, but outcries against the excessive
amounts involved continue. Much of the criticism is warranted; but
some of it results from a lack of knowledge of party financial needs and
from a failure to understand the difficulties of control.

THE HIGH COST OF CAMPAIGNS

It is impossible to ascertain the cost of a presidential election or even
of a state election. One could scarcely estimate the cost of a national
campaign within five million. Because of the requirement for filing expenditures, however, one can discover the sums spent by the major politi-

[1] Much interesting, valuable, and historical information on the growth of party
finance will be found in James K. Pollock, *Party Campaign Funds* (New York: Alfred A.
Knopf, Inc., 1926); Louise Overacker, *Money in Elections* (New York: The Macmillan
Company, 1932); and in Earl R. Sikes, *State and Federal Corrupt Practices Legislation*
(Durham, N.C.: Duke University Press, 1928).

489

cal committees such as the national committees. Table 20 shows the reported expenditures by these committees since 1900. Actually, reported figures are not very meaningful except to suggest that they are very large. A great many political committees appear not to have reported their expenditures. A House committee in 1946 looked for organizations which were presumably engaged in activities calling for reportable expenditures and announced that only 47 out of 117 political committees had re-

Table 20. National Committee Expenditures

Year	Republican	Democratic
1900	$3,000,000	$ 425,000
1908	1,900,000	700,000
1912	1,076,000	1,135,000
1920	4,022,000	1,318,000
1928	4,065,000	3,157,000
1932	2,041,000	1,993,000
1936	6,892,000	4,531,000
1940	2,242,000	2,197,000
1944	2,829,000	2,056,000
1948	2,736,000	2,127,000
1952	2,937,000	2,602,000

Source: Figures given for direct expenditures in certain elections are chosen with a view to illustrating variations in expenditures. Figures for 1900 and 1908 are unofficial; 1912 and 1920 figures are taken from Pollock's *Party Campaign Funds* and subsequent figures from official congressional committee reports.

ported.[2] Over $23 million were actually reported for the 1952 general election,[3] but a survey by *The New York Times'* correspondents estimated $32,150,000 as the "rock bottom figure" and several congressmen and newspapers estimated that $85 million would be nearer correct. The lowest estimates indicate a national average campaign expenditure of 54 cents per voter, varying from 43 cents in Wyoming to $1.19 in Connecticut. In expenditures reported, 12 states spent from one to four million dollars each on the presidential campaign.

[2] See summary in *Congressional Record,* Mar. 20, 1952 (daily edition), p. A1840.

[3] The student of government owes a debt of gratitude to the *Congressional Quarterly* for its excellent periodic compilations of reported campaign expenditures. On the 1952 election see especially its *Weekly Report* for July 17 and Oct. 2, 1953, and Dec. 1, 1952. Some of the figures for 1952 appearing in the next few paragraphs are taken from these compilations. Louise Overacker has provided articles on the financing of several presidential elections in the issues of *The American Political Science Review* (1933, 1937, 1941, 1945).

Reported expenses, moreover, do not include money spent by the thousands of county, city, district, and nonpartisan miscellaneous other committees. Money expended to elect a Democratic sheriff or county judge, for example, usually helps the state or national nominees, since party workers encourage straight-ticket voting. No figures have been compiled on the sums used by county committees during presidential election years but it is known to be large. The county committees in Pennsylvania did report their expenses in 1944 to the Senate Campaign Expenditures Committee—a figure of $1,265,000.[4] One may assume figures approximating a million dollars from county committees in many other states.

Turning to the mid-term congressional elections one finds millions of dollars spent on behalf of nominees for the national legislature. In the 1946 general election, political organizations filed accounts totaling $12,-205,000 [5] with the Clerk of the House of Representatives. Nearly half of this amount was expended by the Republican and Democratic state central committees. When opponents charged Senator Taft of Ohio with spending over $5,000,000 on his reelection campaign, the senator testified that the cost was but $612,000.[6] In the 1952 senatorial race the reported accounts show the Jackson-Cain race in Washington costing $137,000; Smith-Alexander in New Jersey, $63,000; and Mansfield-Ecton in Montana running to $59,000. House contests between Small and Lankford in Maryland were reported as $33,000. The fact that many candidates get free endorsements or sharp criticisms of their opponents by newspaper and radio columnists may be highly advantageous and worth money but is not reflected in expenditures.

These figures on national elections, moreover, do not reflect primary or nominating expenses. Sums expended in the senatorial primaries of 1944 were: Arkansas, $317,000; Louisiana, $48,000; Missouri, $86,000; Oregon, $93,000; and Washington, $38,000.[7] In the South the cost of the Democratic primaries greatly exceeds that of the general election. In 1944 in the Democratic senatorial primary in Alabama, $12,000 was expended while only $100 was spent on the general election. Respective figures in Florida were $39,000 and $8,000; in North Carolina $22,000 and $1,250; and in South Carolina $11,000 and $2,000. In Georgia and Louisiana no expenses were reported for the general election. In several Northern states over $20,000 was spent in the 1946 senatorial primaries.

Large amounts of anonymous campaign literature suggest expenditures

[4] *Report of Senate Campaign Expenditures Committee, 1944,* 79th Cong., 1st Sess., Rept. 101, 1945, pp. 241–242.

[5] *Report of House Campaign Expenditures Committee, 1946,* 79th Cong., 2d Sess., Rept. 2739, 1947, p. 53.

[6] *The New York Times,* Nov. 28, 1951.

[7] *Report of Senate Campaign Expenditures Committee, 1944,* pp. 122–132.

of money not accounted for in the reported expenses. Similarly, other expenses, often of questionable sort, are not reflected in the official records of campaign receipts and expenditures.

The high cost of campaigns is also reflected on state and local levels. One candidate for governor in Pennsylvania was reliably reported as having spent $134,000 out of his own pocket for campaign purposes. The fantastic sum of $1,000,000 was allegedly spent by a gubernatorial nominee in Vermont. A glance through reports filed by senatorial aspirants in 1946 shows that "personal" expenditures varying from $5,000 to $12,000 were fairly common; the highest reported figure for an individual primary expenditure was $18,000.[8] In the 1945 mayoralty race in New York approximately $2 million was spent on behalf of the candidates.

The high cost of campaigning does not end with merely campaigning for public office. Large amounts are often poured into an election to carry or to defeat a referendum proposition or a constitutional amendment. The California Retail Chain Stores Association and its leaders reported an expenditure of $1,142,033 to defeat a referendum on a chain-store tax.[9] Although this is an exceptional figure, large amounts are frequently spent on legislative propositions.

Campaign expenditures are subject to much fluctuation. Hotly contested races require more money than hopelessly one-sided races. One-party areas generally see large primary-campaign costs with small outlays for the general election. At all times, however, the parties must be prepared to raise money both during and between elections. There is a growing tendency to maintain local party headquarters and clubs on a year-round basis, with the result that party expenditures not directly related to campaigns are increasing.

WHY CAMPAIGNS ARE COSTLY

A major reason for the great financial outlays for presidential campaigns is that a potential electorate of 90 million must be reached. In other large nations, the chief executive is not popularly elected and the number in the electorate is smaller. Party managers believe their nominees must be seen either in person or in complimentary portraits, and this requires thousands of miles of travel and the wide distribution of pictures. One is reminded of the remark attributed to Governor "Al" Smith when he first viewed the magnificent spaces of Wyoming: "My, I'd hate to run for Congress out here—I'd have to run so far." National

---

[8] *Report of Senate Campaign Expenditures Committee, 1946,* 80th Cong., 1st Sess., Rept. 1, Part 2, 1947, pp. 53–61.

[9] Other figures on referendum expenditures are found in V. O. Key, Jr., and W. W. Crouch, *The Initiative and Referendum in California* (Berkeley, Calif.: University of California Press, 1939), Chap. 5.

and local candidates are expected to reach all the inner and outer recesses of their constituency by automobile, train, and plane, and these cost money. In comparing expenditures today with those of yesteryear, it must be remembered that inflation has hit the campaign pocketbook hard, with every item from travel to rentals rising sharply.

Today radio and television usually constitute the largest single item in the campaign budget. These costs alone ran to $2,083,000 for the Republicans and $1,428,000 for Democrats in the 1952 presidential election. A 30-minute coast-to-coast television network broadcast costs about $75,000.

Other publicity items come high. The Republican National Committee spent $48,000 for Willkie buttons and both parties find it costs them $2,000 to $3,000 for a single page in a metropolitan newspaper and as much in many magazines. Billboards, posters, and campaign literature are expensive and vary considerably in price from state to state. Space on 25 billboards in Seattle for one month costs over $1,000. When State Senator Richard L. Neuberger of Oregon was considering running for the United States Senate, an advertising firm prepared a campaign budget for him. To give an idea of what might face him, he was told a state-wide radio network would run about $3,000 for a half hour. "To herald my excellence with lapel buttons, match book covers and nail files alone," he writes, "would cost $5,000. A photographer's bill in one campaign in the nearby state of Washington came to more than $2,000. The candidate had to be snapped doing dishes, gaffing a salmon, pitching hay, picking apples. It mattered not that ordinarily he did none of these things. It was a way to sell him to the voters in a handsomely illustrated brochure." [10]

"Overhead expenses," including rent, postage, telephones, and the like, cost the Democratic National Committee a quarter of a million dollars in 1944. A candidate for the legislature nowadays is reminded that the cost of post cards alone to 50,000 voters would be $1,000. In the larger cities a suite of rooms in a hotel or other building is rented for campaign headquarters and in most smaller cities some rooms are rented. In addition, enormous sums are expended for travel and hiring of halls for political rallies and speeches.

Another item, if computed on a national basis, which would run into a large figure is the payment of party workers and watchers, particularly on election day. It is common for many to receive from $10 up to drive people to and from the polls and to do other odd jobs. One candidate paid persons a dollar an hour to telephone potential voters. Public-relations firms are now paid a good fee to manage the campaigns of those

[10] "It Costs Too Much to Run for Office," *The New York Times Magazine*, Apr. 11, 1948, p. 59.

who can afford it. In times past, the payment of party workers was one of the largest items in the budget. This often resulted in corruption in the form of "kickbacks" to political leaders, bribes to voters, purchase of liquor for purposes of intoxicating voters and in paying election board members to spoil the ballots of the opposition party. There is much less of this today and the great proportion of the money is spent on legitimate items connected with publicity and organizational work.

The allocation of the national Republican campaign dollar in the 1954 election is shown in Table 21. It will be noted that about one-fifth

Table 21. Allocation of Combined Campaign Dollar of the Republican National, Senatorial, and Congressional Committees in 1954

Item	Amount
Radio and television	$0.20
Aid to candidates	0.19
Publicity	0.13
Contingent	0.09
Administration	0.06
Executive	0.06
Special groups	0.06
Field forces	0.05
Patronage	0.03
Centennial	0.03
Women's activities	0.03
Young Republicans	0.02
Research	0.02
Finance	0.02
Speaker's bureau	0.01
	$1.00

of the money went in the form of direct aid to candidates through the senatorial and congressional committees.

SOURCES OF INCOME

Importance of Nonparty Committees. The student of party finance is often baffled by the proliferation of fund-raising political committees. With 8,000 elective offices in the United States, it is difficult to estimate the amount of money spent on nominations and elections, and there is bound to be vigorous competition for the campaign dollar. Formerly the national committees made subventions to the state and auxiliary committees and state committees gave subventions to the county committees. The passage of the Hatch Act in 1939 brought about a decentralization of campaign finance and there is much less tendency for the national committee to channel its funds to local committees. In fact, the national committees carefully husband expenditures for they are allowed to spend only $3 million a year.

The tendency is to create "independent," "nonpartisan" committees to take over the major burden of collecting and distributing the campaign money. Committees are organized under such titles as the Hollywood Democratic Committee, Republican Citizens Finance Committee of Illinois, Democrats for Dewey, and so on. In Table 22 the sums spent by

Table 22. Reported Campaign Spending of Select Groups, 1952

Republican

Republican National Committee	$2,937,168.10
Citizens for Eisenhower-Nixon	1,551,168.86
Republican Finance Committee of Pennsylvania	1,505,945.10
United Finance Committee of New York	1,401,447.76
United San Francisco Republican Finance Committee	256,019.19
Republican State Finance Committee of Delaware	203,653.08
National Professional Committee for Eisenhower and Nixon	121,489.79

Democratic

Democratic National Committee	2,602,651.23
Stevenson-Sparkman Forum Committee	800,780.03
Democratic Campaign Committee of Philadelphia	306,581.32
Illinois Volunteers for Stevenson	108,545.14
CIO Political Action Committee	505,721.70
International Ladies' Garment Workers' Union	265,345.10
Labor's League for Political Education	249,257.92

Other

Christian Nationalist Crusade	210,482.37
Progressive Party	113,662.85
Americans for America	73,365.65
Socialist Labor Party	55,728.33
Prohibition National Committee	47,114.92
Policyholders Protective Association	27,149.81

SOURCE: Compiled from *Congressional Digest Weekly Report*, July 17 and Oct. 2, 1953.

the respective national committees and those of six independent committees illustrate the fund raising and spending of independent groups. The six groups supporting Republican candidates spent over $5 million and the six pro-Democratic committees spent well over $2 million. The table, moreover, does not reflect expenditures by scores of other committees.

Republican and Democratic state committees spend a great deal to aid the cause. The Senate Campaign Expenditures Committee reported that Republican and Democratic state committees in 1944 spent $9,261,000 and $2,033,000 respectively.

Individual and Family Contributions. Individual contributions constitute a major source of revenue for the major parties. Thousands of
persons from all walks of life contribute from a few cents to many dollars
to the party. The Democrats and labor unions used the slogan "a buck
for Roosevelt" to raise quite a bit of money and a great effort was expended to obtain large numbers of $5 contributions for the Stevenson
campaign. As the financial basis is broadened, a larger number can be
expected to take an interest in the party; the party, moreover, feels less
obligated to a few "wealthy angels." Each party keeps a "list" of potential
donors who are phoned or written to at the beginning of each campaign.

In spite of the growing trend to increase the number of donors, large
contributions by a comparatively small number of individuals still account for a major share of party revenues. During 1952, the six top Republican and Democratic political committees received 55 per cent of
their total receipts in 2,407 contributions of $1,000 or more.[11] Many con-
tributions are family affairs. In 1944, eight families contributed almost
a half million dollars to the Republican cause. The Du Pont and Pew
families each gave about $100,000 and the Mellons contributed $60,000.
The Democrats did less well, but received $20,000 each from the Field,
Higgins, and Warner families.[12] Even in mid-term elections family contributions are high. In 1950, 34 members of the Du Pont family, together
with seven executives in one of its companies, contributed a combined
total of $98,000 to Republican candidates.

Other Sources. Legislative investigations continue to show that gambling, slot- and pinball machine, book-making, race track and similar
interests are usually willing to make contributions to persons running
for public office who will be friendly to them. An effort is made to keep
these contributions from becoming public knowledge because it is likely
to be harmful to the recipient even where the businesses are legitimate.
In state and local races many businesses are "tapped" and often feel
obligated to contribute. Federal laws prohibit business corporations and
labor unions from making direct contributions to general election campaigns although they are presumably free to help out in primaries. There
are usually fewer restrictions in the state laws and organized interests
frequently contribute to campaigns. But there is a great tendency to
cover up exact sources through the creation of "independent" political
committees.

Persons running for public office generally contribute to their own
campaign. No generalization can be made as to the amount given by

[11] See *Congressional Quarterly Report,* July 17 and Oct. 2, 1953.
[12] Compiled from the *Report of Senate Campaign Expenditures Committee, 1944,*
pp. 140–151.

nominees, since personal wealth, the nature of the campaign, and political expediency are factors which must be taken into consideration. A few political machines have formulated a specific figure to present to a candidate who wishes to run for office. He is simply told that in order to get the backing of the organization and some contributions from the party's treasury, he is expected to put up a certain amount from his own pocket. There are cases on record where wealthy would-be candidates for a governorship have given $100,000 in an effort to secure the nomination, but these are rare. By and large, expenditures by the candidates themselves represent a very small portion of the total figure expended in the election. This may be contrasted with the practice of the Conservative party in England. Parliamentary candidates there usually give up to £100 to their local constituency associations. In addition, the party, as in the United States, relies heavily on voluntary contributions. The Conservative party's expenditures run large because it employs full-time professional electioneers, drawing from £500 to £800 a year in pay. In 1939 there were about 400 of these electioneers.

The Socialist and Communist parties have relied heavily on regular dues to raise funds. Members are expected, in order to remain in good standing, to pay a certain percentage of their salaries into the party coffers. Another practice is to charge a small fee for admission to a political rally or meeting. In addition, funds are solicited at the meeting by "passing the hat" after an appeal by the speakers for funds.

The British Labor party's main income is from an annual affiliation fee of sixpence (7 cents) per member. Generally speaking, parliamentary candidates do not contribute large sums to local organizations. Unlike the Conservative party, the Labor party places great reliance on unpaid local election agents during campaigns. The Labor party found in 1945, however, that affiliation dues and voluntary workers could not meet the expenses of the campaign and the party turned to raising large sums from voluntary contributions.

Regular dues and assessments are very infrequently used by the major parties in the United States, and, with few exceptions, no charge is made for attendance at political rallies. In some areas, usually in cities, money is raised by means of membership "contributions" to political clubs and organizations. These are usually not specifically earmarked for a campaign but rather for the general upkeep of the party and the club. Seldom are the contributions of a specified amount but are left to the discretion of the donor. At one time assessments were made on officeholders during campaign years. Under this plan "2 per cent" or even "5 per cent" clubs were organized, whereby the incumbent was expected to pay that fraction of his salary to the party organization. Such plans have now been pretty generally outlawed by corrupt-practices legislation among Federal employees but are by no means extinct on the local level.[13] The techniqu_ which, practically speaking, accomplishes the same purpose, is now to call them "voluntary contributions." Political employees are more or less expected to contribute and when they ask what amounts are "right," are supplied with a "reasonable figure."

The widely employed Jackson, Jefferson, and Lincoln Day dinners operate as a form of special assessment. Persons holding jobs receive invitations to attend a dinner for a price ranging from $5 to $100 per plate. Some party bigwig is usually present to deliver a fighting political speech and entertainment is provided. Sometimes it is hinted that if one cannot attend, a check would nonetheless "be appreciated." It is not unusual for a dinner to raise $200,000, and the 1940 Jackson Day dinner yielded $400,000. Despite some cries of unethical, there seems little inclination to abandon this money-raising bonanza. State and local dinners were the major method by which the Democrats reduced their 1952 deficit.

Party members are ever alert to find new sources. The Democrats sold the 1936 *Book of the Convention,* personally autographed by President Roosevelt, for $100 each and raised nearly a million dollars. Heated charges that this was "racketeering" led to its early abandonment. Efforts are sometimes made to sell literature, speeches, and newspapers; minor parties have employed this with some success.

Motivations for Contributions. In the literature on democracy and politics there are three policy values which continue to appear. First, money alone should not be the deciding factor in who shall hold public office. That only the well to do should be able to run for office is a denial of the Jeffersonian-Jacksonian tradition. A second value, closely following the first, is that qualified, competent persons, irrespective of status, should be able to seek, with same chances of success, a public office regardless of their finances. Third, persons elected to public office should be free agents in the sense that they are not indebted to a special group which will make demands on them to "pay off" in the form of pressing for a public policy not in the general interest.

Speeches on money in elections and laws regulating campaign finance emphasize these policies but inner contradictions are ever present. Undoubtedly vast numbers of people become campaign donors for idealistic reasons often stated in the virtuous phrase "good government." Others give out of personal friendship or admiration for the candidate. Apparently college professors in unprecedented numbers dug down in their

[13] Municipal employees paid the Hague machine in Jersey City 3 per cent of their salaries to "collectors" in their departments as "campaign contributions." In the last two years of the administration (1948–1949) $341,000 was collected; see report of the city commission summarized in *The New York Times,* June 23, 1950.

pockets and contributed small sums on behalf of Adlai Stevenson. This was not done because the Illinois governor promised Federal aid to higher education and better salaries for professors. Labor union leaders likewise contributed to the Stevenson cause but he had come out for the repeal of the Taft-Hartley law. Were the motives of the professors purer than those of union leaders? Many citizens gave money to the Eisenhower campaign because they "liked Ike" and felt he would "clean up the mess in Washington." Oil interests were likewise heavy contributors and liked the Eisenhower-Nixon pronouncements on tidelands oil. Are the motives of the "citizens" to be applauded and those of the petroleum industry criticized?

Campaigns are the arenas for contenders of power. It is only natural that economic interests hoping to preserve or to change the *status quo* in public policy will be mightily interested in the outcome of an election. And it follows that they will contribute to campaigns. The economic interests of large contributors to the 1944 presidential campaign are shown in the chart on page 500. Although both parties obtained large sums from all types of business interests, Republicans received more help from bankers, manufacturers, and utilities, while the Democrats enjoyed an advantage with brewers, union and professional people, amusement industries, and officeholders. With the change of the party in power in 1953, a similar chart in 1956 will undoubtedly show substantial shifts in financial support. After Mr. Truman's unexpected victory in 1948, checks from many businessmen poured in from all over to help erase the "deficit" in campaign coffers. Almost every interest desires to curry some favor with the party in power. Even if it opposed the party, it will try to make its peace with it. In local elections, proprietors quite often give to rival candidates so as to be on the winning side no matter who is the victor.

The important thing is not that private economic interests donate to campaign funds; it is rather the degree to which the recipient feels obligated to promote their interests as well as the type of demands which donors make upon those elected to office. There is also the question as to whether this places at a disadvantage large segments of the population who do not or cannot afford to contribute. There are many candidates who refuse contributions from certain people and interests for these as well as many other reasons. The candidate and political committee are often placed in the position of having to judge and evaluate the economic motivation of those who are willing to give. The recipient is faced with the question of whether generous donors want a *quid pro quo* for their contributions, such as tariff favors, antitrust exemptions, government contracts, oil leases, licenses, loans, protection from legal prosecutions, key appointments, or special legislation.

The motivation for campaign gifts by officeholders appears reasonably clear. They have a stake in the jobs they hold and the programs they espouse. The veiled threat of withheld endorsement or removal from office may be present as an "incentive" for donations. Some persons have

ECONOMIC INTERESTS OF CONTRIBUTORS TO CAMPAIGN FUNDS*
(In amounts contributed to National Committees, One Thousand Club, and United Republican Finance Committee of Metropolitan New York, 1944)

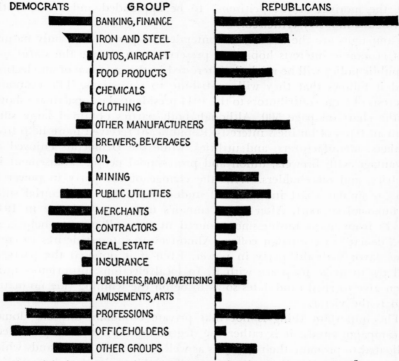

DEMOCRATS	GROUP	REPUBLICANS
	BANKING, FINANCE	
	IRON AND STEEL	
	AUTOS, AIRCRAFT	
	FOOD PRODUCTS	
	CHEMICALS	
	CLOTHING	
	OTHER MANUFACTURERS	
	BREWERS, BEVERAGES	
	OIL	
	MINING	
	PUBLIC UTILITIES	
	MERCHANTS	
	CONTRACTORS	
	REAL ESTATE	
	INSURANCE	
	PUBLISHERS, RADIO ADVERTISING	
	AMUSEMENTS, ARTS	
	PROFESSIONS	
	OFFICEHOLDERS	
	OTHER GROUPS	

* These data drawn from Louise Overacker, "Presidential Campaign Funds, 1944," *American Political Science Review*, vol. 39, (October 1945), pp. 916

given because they wanted nomination or appointments. Among officeholders, a large number of "fat cat" contributions come from those occupying diplomatic posts in American embassies and legations abroad. The appointment of wealthy party members to diplomatic positions is an old custom.

To summarize, persons contribute to political parties for a wide variety of reasons. Idealism, political ideology, economic interest, the seeking of favors both legal and illegal from government, and the retention or acquisition of a public job are among the major motivations. Criticism of the sources of campaign income of one's opponent may be the result of a rationalization of one's own motivations. A highly successful political manager told the author that over the years he had learned that the best way to maintain the independence and integrity of his party's officeholders was to secure funds from among the party's own job holders and officialdom. "I found the gambling interests and many legitimate business interests ready to give money, but they always wanted something in return and the price was often too high," he said. "The same was true of the labor boys and I did not want to be obligated to them either. I found that if we raised our own money from among ourselves, then we could run our own show and run the government for all the people instead of for a special interest." This rationalization is intriguing, but disregards the degrading effects of forced campaign contributions on the public service. For most campaigns today, not enough money can be raised from officeholders to fill the requirements. Moreover, this does not solve the financial problem for the party out of power. Over the years the public became concerned with the income and outgo of campaign moneys and by statute set up certain values and restrictions. In effect, the laws told what sources of income and expenditure were to be considered a violation of the rules of the game. We may now look at these public policies in the field of party finance.

CORRUPT-PRACTICES LEGISLATION

The regulation of party finance, especially as to campaigns, has aimed at four major objectives: (1) publicity of sources of income and expenditures, (2) limitation on sources of income, (3) limitation on expenditures, (4) prevention of bribery and pernicious political activity. The regulation of the use of money in elections is in the first instance a state function. The thousands of elective state and local offices, as well as primaries, are under exclusive control of the states. Concurrently, the states and the national government legislate for congressional elections.

State Laws. An oft-repeated theme of this volume has been that of the extreme variation between the states, and the so-called corrupt-practices legislation is no exception. One may obtain a full picture of the allowable financial practices of a given state only by a careful study of the election laws of that state because the state laws follow no single pattern.[14] In 1890 the first law was passed in New York and applied only to the expenditures of the candidates. Within 10 years, 17 other states

[14] On state laws see Sikes, *op. cit.*, and the tabulation found in S. S. Minault, *Corrupt Practices Legislation in the 48 States* (Chicago: Council of State Governments, 1942, mimeographed).

had passed laws. Today all states have some law, though in many cases it is very rudimentary and does little more than outlaw bare-faced corruption and purchase of votes.

Wisconsin has one of the most comprehensive laws and requires every candidate and secretary to file a sworn and itemized statement of receipts and disbursements, including details of every sum of more than $5. Disbursements are made only through the candidate or a party or personal campaign committee. Limitations are placed on the amount spent both for nomination and election and numerous legitimate expenditures such as rental of halls, postage and literature, travel and expenses of speakers. Campaign advertisements must bear the name and address of the author. Corporations doing business in the state may not make direct or indirect contributions. One especially interesting proviso is that payment may not be made for services to be performed on the day of either election or the primary. Newspapers and periodicals are not permitted to solicit or receive compensation in return for political influence.[15]

A few generalizations on state laws can be made. Three-fourths of the states prohibit contributions from corporations and about 40 states limit the amount as well as the nature of campaign expenditures; of these, almost half apply the limitations to the candidates alone. Some two-thirds of the states require the filing of accounts after the primary and general elections. Most states apply their laws to both primaries and general elections but a few states impose limitations only in the primaries.

Three general methods are employed to restrict the amounts expended. One method is simply to name a flat sum, as in New Jersey where a nominee may not spend more than $50,000 in the primary and the same amount in the general election. A second practice holds the candidate's expenditures to a certain percentage of the salary connected with the office. For local offices in Wisconsin only one-third and in Iowa one-half of the annual salary of the office sought may be spent. A third plan is illustrated by Virginia, where nominees (in the primaries) are permitted to spend 15 cents for each vote cast for the candidate receiving the largest number of votes in the preceding gubernatorial election.

Federal Legislation. Federal laws, like those of the states, have been experimental, with Congress having the advantage of observing state legislation. Charles Evans Hughes, William Jennings Bryan, and Theodore Roosevelt took the lead in advocating the passage of legislation requiring publicity. The first law in 1907, however, forbade corporate contributions and it was not until 1910 that the publicity feature was added. Congressional investigations played a prominent part in adding amendments, all of which were incorporated in the Federal Corrupt Practices

[15] See Election Laws, Chap. 12, Secs. 1–29, as amended in 1951.

Act of 1925.[16] Two important additions were made during the New Deal —the Hatch Acts of 1939 and 1940 and the War Labor Disputes Act of 1943. The latter prohibited union contributions to political campaigns, a restriction also placed in the Taft-Hartley law.

The publicity feature of the law is based upon the assumption that the public is entitled to know who is making a contribution, the amount donated, and the amount expended. Each treasurer of a political committee must file statements with the Clerk of the House in March, June, and September of each year. On the first day of January, a statement covering the whole preceding year must also be filed. The name and address of any person contributing as much as $100 within the calendar year are to be included. The statement must also show (1) the total of the smaller contributions; (2) the total of all contributions; (3) the name and address of any person to whom an expenditure of at least $10 was made during the year, together with the amount, date, and purpose of the expenditure; and (4) the total of all the expenditures. The same practice must be followed by any person who spends $50 or more for the purpose of influencing an election in two or more states. Finally, candidates for election to the House and Senate are required to file statements before and after the election.

Maximum expenditures of candidates for the House and Senate are limited to $2,500 and $10,000 respectively. As an alternative the nominee is permitted to spend 3 cents per vote for the total number of votes cast for all the candidates for the office which the candidate seeks, provided such amount does not exceed $25,000 for the Senate or $5,000 for the House. Actually these allowances are easily exceeded, since the office seekers may spend an unlimited amount for subsidiary expenses such as traveling, postage, and telephone service. The 1940 amendments to the Hatch Act sought to place a limitation on the size of contributions by providing that no political committee shall receive contributions amounting in total to more than $3 million in any calendar year.[17] No individual may give to a committee an aggregate sum of more than $5,000.

One of the oldest forms of regulating the direct or indirect misuse of money is the prohibition of bribery, fraud, and intimidation. To protect the Negro in his right to vote, Congress in 1870 and in 1871 penalized bribery, impersonation, and other corrupt practices. These acts were repealed in 1894, but in 1918 the antibribery law was reenacted. This law makes indirect or direct bribery of voters in congressional elections an offense against the national government.

Abuses of the spoils system, especially the levying of political assess-

[16] See U.S. Code of 1925, Title II, Secs. 241–246; and Title XVIII, Secs. 208–213; *Statutes at Large,* Vol. 48, p. 1070.

[17] Revised by Public Law 772, 80th Cong. 2d Sess.; Title 18, U.S.C., Secs. 608, 609.

ments on officeholders, led to another form of congressional regulation of money in elections. In 1867 an act was passed to protect navy-yard employees from such assessments. The Civil Service Reform Act of 1883 (Pendleton Act) prohibited any employee of the United States from soliciting or receiving any "assessment, subscription, or contribution for any political purpose whatever." No classified officer or employee may be solicited anywhere for political funds by a congressman, senator, or Federal officeholder or by any person whatever in a building used by the Federal government. Nonofficeholders, under this act, may solicit so long as they do not enter a government building. Employees are also protected against demotion or discharge for refusing to make a political contribution. These sweeping provisions received court approval and have gone a long way toward reducing the evils of political assessments.

Though not directly related to money, the provisions of the 1939 Hatch Act designed to prevent "pernicious political activities" may also be mentioned here. Under this law all Federal employees except those occupying policy-determining positions are not permitted to take an active part in the political management of a campaign or to use their authority to bring about "the election or nomination of any candidate" for a national office. The following year the Act was extended to state and local employees who engaged in full-time activities financed, in whole or in part, by the national government or whose main employment is in a federally aided activity.[18] The general interpretation and enforcement of the Hatch Act is made by the U.S. Civil Service Commission.

THE RESULTS OF LEGISLATION

Federal corrupt-practices legislation has resulted in a marked reduction in the "shakedown" practices employed on Federal employees. Statements of contributions and expenditures and the requirement of statements between as well as during campaigns have provided some record on party finances. Inquiring reporters now have the opportunity to get facts and figures and the public is given a great deal more information on income and expenditures of party committees and candidates than it was a half century ago.

The select committees of Congress charged with investigating campaign finance have, through hearings and reports, made available much valuable data. Much illuminating data, however, remain buried in committee files and are not carried in the press. Congress commends the committees for their work but has acted on only a few of the legislative remedies which they have proposed. The least that may be claimed for these in-

18 See *Statutes at Large,* Vol. 55, p. 1197; Vol. 54, p. 767. For a useful article on the subject see L. V. Howard, "Federal Restrictions upon the Political Activity of Government Employees," *The American Political Science Review,* Vol. 35 (1941), pp. 470–489.

vestigations and laws on finance is a keener appreciation of party financial problems and practices.

The effects of state legislation are disappointing in almost every respect. American genius for finding loopholes in and getting around the law is nowhere better illustrated than in both the Federal and state corrupt-practices legislation. The laws have not appreciably diminished the use of money in elections, if indeed that was their purpose. Campaigns continue to be accompanied by cries of "slush fund," charges of excessive expenditure, and "hush money," as well as "coercion," if not outright bribery.

An enumeration of the shortcomings of Federal legislation should begin with their limitation to final elections and the exclusion of primaries and conventions. This enables candidates to spend large sums of money in obtaining a nomination. In this process, trips, campaign literature, and advertising help the nominee to get his name before the public and to campaign on a grandiose scale. This is especially important in states, as in the South, where a primary nomination is tantamount to election. Illustrative of this was one individual in Maryand who spent $88,000 to obtain the Democratic senatorial nomination, but spent only $2,000 between the primary and the general election to defeat his Republican opponent.

The provision prohibiting life insurance companies, business corporations, and labor unions from making contributions to political committees has been circumvented by individual contributions. There is nothing to prohibit persons from donating to a party out of their earnings and later being recipients of bonuses from the corporation. In 1940 and 1944 the People's Committee to Defend Life Insurance and Savings received large sums of money ($70,000 in 1944) from insurance salesmen and other persons to propagandize the allegation that the Roosevelt Administration jeopardized life insurance and investments. One insurance company sponsored a radio-network news commentator who, throughout the campaign of 1944, spent much of broadcast time in bitterly attacking the "fourth term" and the New Deal in general. Congressional investigating committees concluded that these practices were all within the letter of the law. However, in operation they came close to violating the spirit of the law and demonstrate the difficulty of regulation.

Organized labor likewise found a way to participate financially in the 1944 campaign. Before the Democratic National Convention, the CIO Political Action Committee collected $647,000 from trade-unions. Two-thirds of this fund was used prior to the national convention to influence primary contests and for "educational purposes." After the convention the remainder of the fund was frozen. Officers of the PAC pointed out that this was within the definition of corrupt-practices legislation, since the union funds were used before nominations were made. Several union officials argued that funds could also have been raised and expended during the campaign, since the PAC was not a "labor organization" within the meaning of the law and since financial separation between the CIO and the PAC was complete. In spite of this assertion, criticism continued because of the close relationship in personnel between the CIO as a union and the PAC as its political arm. It was argued that the law in effect was being violated because the union men were actually giving time to the campaign.

The use of private personnel in campaigns is by no means new. For years numerous legislative investigating committees, both national and local, have given what amounts to leaves of absence to the staff during elections so that they may work in respective campaign headquarters. The government continues to pay the salary of staff members, but their time is devoted to helping the party rather than furthering the committees' activities. There are evidences of some businesses also allowing their employees to promote party candidacies on the companies' time.

When the Hatch Act was passed, it was generally believed that the $3 million and $5,000 limitations for committees and individuals meant the over-all expenditures. The parties and contributors placed no such interpretation on the law. Rather they operated under the assumption that no one committee might spend more than $3 million. Thus, the national committee might raise and expend this sum while each state or even local committee might likewise do so. The same liberal construction was placed on the $5,000 maximum individual contribution. For example, two members of the Pew family of Pennsylvania each contributed a total of $22,750 to 14 different political committees. One of the most important ways by which the law is circumvented is through the development of independent political committees potentially capable of expending $3 million each. As earlier noted, the total sums expended in presidential elections many times exceeded the $3-million limitation because of the decentralization and splintering of party finance. The Hatch Act limitations have tended to make the parties depend upon organizations other than the official party committees as agencies for raising money and conducting campaigns. This dispersing of fund-raising and expending has undermined the publicity features of the law by making it difficult to locate all those responsible for financing.

A loophole in regulating funds is the lack of a clear-cut definition and interpretation of a "political committee." Many organizations which attempt to influence an election refuse to report their expenses, claiming they are an "educational organization." For example, the National Committee to Uphold Constitutional Government offered in 1940 to send generous quantities of literature and "No Third Term" buttons free to any persons or groups. When confronted with a demand that it file a statement, this group did so under protest, offering the argument that it was not seeking the election of any candidate. Incidentally, the Committee reported a sum of $377,000 expended during the campaign! In the same election, pieces of campaign literature were distributed over the signatures of 133 organizations and individuals; of these only 6 filed statements with the House of Representatives. A special House investigating committee found one organization had "an annual budget for 'educational' work approximating $1½ million, and among other things regularly supplied 500 radio stations with 'briefs for broadcasters.'" The same committee discovered many educational, patriotic, and other organizations disseminating literature and propaganda which was often designed to "inculcate broad sociopolitical attitudes" which were easily definable as favorable to one set of candidates in any given campaign. The printing and distributing of campaign literature is certainly an activity designed to influence the outcome of an election; to the extent that any group engages in this practice, it is assuming a function commonly associated with a political committee. Yet most of these "educational" associations profess to be "nonpartisan" and "nonpolitical."

In spite of the progress made in the prevention of pernicious political activity, many methods of subtle persuasion, intimidation, and coercion continue to be used. Public employees still find themselves accosted by party agents outside of government property. Pressure, not always too gentle, is oftentimes exerted on employees to attend Jackson Day and other "dinners." Local officials do not always feel obligated to abide by the orders of the U.S. Civil Service Commission. A case in point was an investigation by the Commission of the Pennsylvania State Department of Health, which is financed partly by Federal funds. The Secretary of Health, according to the Commission, called a number of his staff to a meeting at the Republican State Headquarters and told them the party needed money and that the Hatch Act did not forbid "voluntary contributions." [19] A bureau chief told his subordinates that contributions might be made to him in his office. One other employee was charged with taking an active part in the campaign by serving as vice-chairman of a county committee. After hearings on the case the Civil Service Commission ordered the dismissal of all from their positions. [20] At once the state administration replied that it would either ignore or contest any such

[19] *The New York Times,* Feb. 16, 1945.

[20] See "Report and Order of U.S. Civil Service Commission in the matter of Alexander H. Stewart and the Commonwealth of Pennsylvania," No. 124 (1945). The Supreme Court upheld a removal of an Oklahoma official by the U.S. Civil Service Commission in a somewhat similar case; see *Oklahoma v. U.S. Civil Service Commission,* 330 U.S. 127 (1947).

order from the Civil Service Commission. Pennsylvania refused to remove the officials and the Federal government withheld funds accordingly. In effect the taxpayers of Pennsylvania suffered because the state administration refused to discipline employees who were found to have violated the law. Unfortunately there are other illustrations of the same attitude on the part of state and local officials toward the Civil Service Commission.

Many other ways are found to evade the spirit of the law, such as contributing or receiving free newspaper space and radio facilities. It may be fairly said that many weaknesses of corrupt-practices laws are the result of the basic failure to fix responsibility for spending. Until it is clearly determined who can spend, diffusion of responsibility results in abuse and ineffectiveness of laws. British laws have helped this situation by providing that no person except the candidate or the agent designated by him may spend to further his campaign.

AVENUES OF IMPROVEMENT

Revision of the Law. The Hatch Act has imposed limitations that do not limit and prohibitions that do not prohibit. The congressional committees investigating campaigns regularly recommend amendments in the law but Congress seems unwilling to follow the suggestions.[21] The $3-million limitation on committee expenditures and the $2,500 and $10,000 restrictions for House and Senate candidates, or the alternative of three cents per vote, have long proved to be unrealistic in view of inflation and the use of radio and television in campaigns. What the figure might be raised to, of course, is a moot question.[22] It is possible that increasing the sum which can be expended might curb somewhat the great decentralization of finance in presidential campaigns and make the national committees more of the responsible fiscal agent.

A redefinition of the term "political committee" is in order so as to cover so-called "educational" and propaganda organizations whose activities seek to influence the vote cast for Federal officers during and between campaigns. Several congressional committees have suggested the creation of an agency of Congress empowered to require disclosure of opinion-molding, civic, patriotic, educational, and other organizations so that they might no longer masquerade under a nonpolitical label while engaging in political activity.

---

[21] For a detailed account of proposed reforms see *Proposed Amendments to Federal Corrupt Practices Act*, Report of the Senate Subcommittee on Privileges and Elections, 83d Cong., 1st Sess., 1953.

[22] Several Senate investigators have suggested a $10 million figure for political expenditures, $10,000 for House and $25,000 for Senate candidates.

It would be better to make a single person from each party committee exclusively responsible for receiving, disbursing, and reporting all finances connected with a campaign. The same requirement should be imposed on independent and nonpolitical committees and apply with equal force to primaries, conventions, and general elections. State laws are particularly deficient in some of these matters which fix financial responsibility.

British experience has shown the wisdom of the unions using separate levies and funds for political purposes. The minority is protected while at the same time the majority of the union is enabled to engage in political activity deemed desirable to the union's interests. This principle might well be extended to all multiple-purpose organizations which at times engage in campaign activity.

The publicity feature is basic in most corrupt-practices laws in the United States and seems altogether worthy. Many states, however, require no publicity during a campaign but merely the filing of reports a month after the election. This obviously does not give the voter a chance to see, before election, who is paying the political bills of the campaign.

This points up the fact that a major weakness of controlling money in elections is due to lack of enforcement. Clerks of the legislature and secretaries of state are little more than repositories for the records filed. Occasionally legislative investigating committees turn up evasions of the law—but not until well after the fact and rarely unseat a legislator for failure to file. In some communities there are unwritten gentlemen's agreements that only a certain percentage of the campaign accounts are to be filed. A vigilant enforcing body could track down and expose these and other evasions of the law. Many careful observers of corrupt-practices laws believe they are purposely kept vague, full of loopholes, and unenforceable so as not to handicap persons who can secure ample funds. Whether this is true or not, substantive changes in the laws will not be very effective without stringent enforcement.

Regulation of Nominations. Political scientists, journalists, and numerous congressional committees have long recommended that reform of the corrupt-practices laws should begin with their extension to primary campaigns and nominating conventions. By every logic nomination and election are but facets of the same process—the selection of public officeholders. It is hard to argue that money spent for seeking the nomination should go unregulated, while money spent in the general election should be subject to restrictions. There is no doubt of the power of the states to regulate the primaries and conventions, and the state legislatures which have failed to enact laws on this subject should proceed to do so.

Prior to 1941 the decision in the Newberry case seemed to preclude congressional regulation of the primaries. The decision rendered by the

Supreme Court in the *United States v. Classic*,[23] however, opens the door for Congress to regulate the congressional primaries. In this case, Classic, a New Orleans politician, was found guilty of election frauds in conducting a primary election to nominate a candidate for Congress. In finding that a primary election is an election within the meaning of the Constitution and Statutes the Court said, in part:

. . . We think that the authority of Congress given by Section 4 (Art. I of Constitution) includes the authority to regulate primary elections when, as in this case, they are a step in the exercise by the people of their choice of Representatives in Congress. . . .

The right to participate in the choice of representatives for Congress includes . . . the right to cast a ballot and to have it counted at the general election whether for the successful candidate or not. Where a state law has made the primary or where in fact the primary effectively controls the choice, an integral part of the procedure or choice, the right of the elector to have his ballot counted at the primary, is likewise included in the right protected by Article I, Section 2.

By the same token the national conventions and the state and local conventions which designate nominees for Federal office would seem to come under the purview of Congress. Hence preconvention expenses and presidential primaries can and should be subject to regulation by Congress. Until the law is extended to include the nomination process, the purpose of Congress to publicize and restrict campaign contributions and expenditures cannot be effectuated.

Government Subsidization. It is customary for political parties to raise their funds by means of dues and from voluntary contributions of individuals and groups. We have seen the problems and abuses of this system as applied to American parties. For the individual candidate, collecting money for his campaign raises serious practical and ethical problems. If the nominee is known to be hostile to the banking, manufacturing, liquor, or real-estate interests, he runs little chance of securing aid from persons who have made their money from such enterprises. To accept money from them may be to invite a "little friendly advice" and pressure where legislation is concerned.[24] To accept money from labor organizations likewise has its liabilities. Many unions are not so wealthy as is popularly believed and the law may be easily violated unless care is taken not to use union funds directly for a campaign. Gifts from slot-

---

23 313 U.S. 299 (1941).

24 On the moral and practical aspects of individual campaign finance see Neuberger, *op. cit.* A Senate committee stated that "there are some men grown poorer in Congress who find it impossible to make ends meet and therefore, unconsciously or otherwise, hesitate to alienate groups whose support financial or ballot-wise, they may need at the next election." *Ethical Standards in Government,* Report of the Senate Subcommittee of the Committee on Labor and Public Welfare, 82d Cong., 1st Sess., 1951, p. 3.

machine interests and the underworld or near-underworld constitute a potential liability as well as a moral question. It is all very well to say, "Let the politicians pay their own way," but in many cases qualified, able, and honest men of moderate means are discouraged from running for office for financial reasons alone. The democratization of party finance is not only a question of increasing the number of contributors; it is also a matter of trying to equalize campaign resources.

One proposal is for government subsidization of the cost of elections. Some would pay the nominees' expenses out of the public treasury; others would give each political party a specified sum of money. President Theodore Roosevelt, in his annual message to Congress in 1907, recommended that Congress provide an appropriation "for the proper and legitimate expenses of each of the great national parties, an appropriation ample enough to meet the necessity for thorough organization and machinery." In addition, a party would be allowed to receive only a fixed amount beyond this from individual donors. Another plan would permit no individual contribution but only government subsidies. One legislator favoring this system said, "If, as a Senator, I had received campaign donations from cattle ranchers and then voted away part of the upland meadows of the public domain to be overgrazed and eroded, the American people would be nicked for more financially than if I got a $50,000 campaign fund directly from the United States Treasury." [25]

Objections to public aid come from taxpayers. Minor parties feel that they should receive a contribution and major parties object to subsidizing the smaller parties. The problems of arriving at the amount and of deciding how to prorate subsidies among the various parties are difficult but not insurmountable ones. By and large, however, there seems to be no great enthusiasm for outright subsidization of political committees or candidates.

There is, nevertheless, a considerable amount of indirect public financial aid to parties. Direct primaries in most cases are paid for out of the public instead of the party treasury. Several states and many municipalities have experimented with the use of candidates' pamphlets. These are prepared and distributed to each registered voter by the election authorities. Each candidate is given a certain amount of space which permits him to put his case before the voters at a nominal cost. Oregon has used the voters' pamphlet with considerable success since 1908.

The publicity pamphlet has real potentialities as an instrument for political education and for raising the quality of campaign literature. As a means of defraying party expenditures, it is of little importance, since in many cases the cost of printing is borne, in whole or in part,

[25] *Ibid.,* p. 61.

by the parties. Even so, the main reason for discontinuing these pamphlets in several states has been the expense involved. Several states and cities aid nominees and parties through the provision of free radio time over publicly owned stations. Where time is granted to the minor- as well as major-party candidates, it has helped considerably to equalize the use of radio facilities. There is much to be said for this type of assistance. Proposals have been made from time to time that the national government purchase several hours of radio network time for each party. In view of the fact that the proceedings of the national conventions are carried gratis by the networks, together with various preconvention speeches of would-be nominees, the suggestion has never received serious consideration in Congress.

DO CAMPAIGNS COST TOO MUCH?

Implicit in much of the discussion of money in elections and of corrupt-practices laws is the assumption that campaigns cost "too much." But do they? And how much is too much? Will money buy an election? Some years ago George Lundberg, after studying 156 elections, found that in 14 out of 15 cases, reported campaign expenditures constituted a reliable index of the outcome of the election.[26] These elections were prior to the widespread use of radio and television in campaigns. Professor Lundberg's study, of course, limited itself to reported expenditures and there is no way of telling of the influence of unreported sums. Franklin D. Roosevelt was elected four times and Harry Truman once with sums reportedly considerably less than their Republican opponents. This suggests that the personal appeal of the candidates and their programs had more influence on the voters than expensive publicity.

On the local level one might find some persuasive illustrations of the influence of money. Money can buy name familiarity on billboards and posters and it can purchase other methods of bringing the nominees' names before the electorate. It is here that the candidates with meager financial resources may suffer and where it may result in their losing elections. Nominees who have made a name for themselves by being prominent in civic affairs may be able to win municipal or state legislative races without spending much money. Persons well known for their activities in veterans', union, and philanthropic activities can often obtain a group vote without heavy spending. Endorsements of municipal leagues and citizens' associations and word-of-mouth support may be worth more than hundreds or even thousands of dollars of contributions and expensive publicity. This is not to argue that the citizen should be unconcerned about money—or the lack of it—in elections. But it is to say that money

[26] See "Campaign Expenditures and Election Results," *Social Forces,* Vol. 6 (1928), pp. 452–457.

is not the only factor or alternative available to candidates and that the inarticulate (and sometimes articulate) premise of many that money and victory at the polls go together needs objective appraisal.

In asserting that campaigns cost too much, one overlooks that in modern America huge sums are spent on public relations and publicity. Tobacco and soap companies spend millions and millions of dollars to push their wares and if one regards selling a presidential candidate as an advertising job, campaign expenses may not be compared unfavorably with commercial advertising. In a publicity-conscious nation, political managers believe they must follow some of the techniques of the business world. If campaigning is regarded as an advertising job, then advertising rates will have to be paid and campaigning will be done within the framework of the familiar highly competitive advertising setting of the nation.

There is no easy way to curb the use of money in elections given the publicity atmosphere within which campaigns are conducted, the unrealistic character of some of the provisions of corrupt-practices laws and the highly decentralized character of raising and expending funds. The legislature itself can help by refusing to seat persons who appear to have stepped beyond the bounds of propriety. The Senate refused to seat Frank L. Smith of Illinois and William S. Vare of Pennsylvania largely because of the sources and size of their campaign incomes for nomination. Congressional committees continue to ferret out information on campaign finance which deserves more attention in the press than it has received and all too often the data are made public too late.

If voters can become fully armed with the facts before election day on who is paying the bills, they might find themselves in a better position to judge whether a candidate, party, or independent committee spent "too much." Expenses incurred in the primaries should be made available long before the general election. An original objective of laws regulating the use of money during campaigns was that of publicity. This is still sound policy provided there is full publicity. Concentration of responsibility and the publicity of moneys received and spent, of "loans" which in the final analysis are "gifts," offer greater promise than detailed provisions. *Sub rosa* financial practices and anonymous receipts and expenditures are harmful to an enlightened electorate. If something could be done to overcome the confusion resulting from the multiplication of fund-raising groups and the long ballot which leads to competition for funds and for further muddying of the financial waters, the public would be better able to reappraise the whole question of money in elections.

In conclusion, it should be emphasized again that money in elections today is one of the great unsolved problems. A university president was approached to run for the United States Senate and was candidly told that his campaign would cost a half million dollars. Experienced political observers in California point out that it may easily cost nearly a million dollars to run for governor and $50,000 to $100,000 for Congress in those districts where there is a contest. For lesser offices such as the state legislature and city council in many areas, candidates unable to spend from $5,000 to $10,000 have found themselves considerably handicapped. Indeed, the influence of money is likely to be of greater importance in these local races than in gubernatorial or presidential contests. Any number of persons who would make good public servants have failed to file when confronted with these financial realities. It is not simply a question of the inability of persons to raise money. The money can very often be raised for the candidate, but it may come from sources to which he does not wish to be in debt. Although direct promises are not necessarily exacted by the donors, many potential candidates decline to run because they believe that eventually they may be placed under obligation.

SELECTED REFERENCES

A useful compilation of periodical literature on 1952 campaign finance has been made by Isabella M. Hayes, *Financing Presidential Campaigns* (University of Maryland Library, 1953, mimeographed). The hearings and reports of the House and Senate Elections and Campaign Committees offer some of the best available data on campaign finance and provide indispensable sources of information on Federal elections. Many of these are cited in this chapter. Basic questions and considerations involved in remedial legislation are well covered in the *Report of the Special House Committee to Investigate Campaign Expenditures,* 82d Cong., 2d Sess., 1953, H. Rept. 2517.

The story of money in elections and party financial practices is told in a number of volumes. Works giving valuable historical data include Earl R. Sikes, *State and Federal Corrupt Practices Legislation* (1928); James K. Pollock, *Party Campaign Funds* (1926) and *Money and Politics Abroad* (1932); R. C. Brooks, *Corruption in American Politics and Life* (1910); Louise Overacker, *Money in Elections* (1932); and Frank R. Kent, *The Great Game of Politics* (1926), Chaps. 19–22. Louise Overacker, *Presidential Campaign Funds* (1946) and S. S. Minault, *Corrupt Practices Legislation in the 48 States* (1942), bring the several older references up to date. For a number of years *The American Political Science Review* (1933, 1937, 1941, 1945) has carried Dr. Overacker's articles on the financing of presidential campaigns. Two works on cases involving excessive expenditures for senatorial nominees are Spencer Ervin, *Henry Ford v. Truman H. Newberry* (1935); and C. H. Wooddy, *The Case of Frank L. Smith* (1931).

CHAPTER 22

Registration and Election Administration

Yed'd wonder what's wrong wid the nation
  The way the elections was done.
'Twas proportional riprisintation
  An' in consequince iveryman won!
                —*Punch* (on the Irish elections)

The molding of public opinion, the use of campaign propaganda, and various other efforts of political education have been of major concern to this point. All these, however, are likely to be frustrated unless the people's will is honestly and fairly recorded at the polls. It is of little profit for one to be prepared to cast an intelligent ballot if that ballot is marked by someone else who has impersonated him. Nor is there any profit in casting a vote if the vote is falsely counted. In order to facilitate the recording of opinion at an election, machinery is necessary. As in the case of nominations, the administration of elections has proceeded from the simple to the complex. The checking of those who have fulfilled the voting qualifications and the balloting in the United States have developed into two essentially different operations—registration of voters and the election administration. Both, however, are primarily interested in the prevention of fraud.

THE FUNCTIONS OF REGISTRATION

In early rural America the recognition of each individual claiming the right to vote was relatively easy for he was usually personally known to the election officers or could be identified by a fellow citizen.[1] All that was needed was appearance on election day. If identification became necessary, an affidavit was easily obtained from neighbors. It soon became apparent that this simple system was inadequate. Even in rural areas, strangers appeared on horseback demanding the right to vote and officials were loath to challenge them. As urbanization and social mobility increased, immigrants and newcomers swarmed into the community. Unscrupulous persons began to perpetrate fraud and hire "repeaters"

---

[1] The major work on the history and operation of registration is Joseph P. Harris, *Registration of Voters in the United States* (Washington, D.C.: Brookings Institution, 1929).

to go from one station to another to vote, usually under assumed names. Investigation of many persons became imperative in order to combat these practices. The purpose of registration became one of preparing a list of electors prior to the day of election in order to make possible an investigation of their qualifications.

Massachusetts took the first step toward excluding those who did not fulfill the necessary qualifications when it established a registration system about 1800. Other New England states followed soon after, but the majority of the states did not create registration machinery until after the Civil War. Registration laws frequently followed an exposé of election frauds. At the outset, registration was limited to the cities and in many states it is still found only in predominantly urban areas. Today all states except Arkansas and Texas have registration laws. In these two states the voter must present his poll-tax receipt, which, for all practical purposes, is a form of registration.

Generally speaking, in European countries the government assumes the duty of preparing a complete registration of voters in contrast to the United States, where the voter himself assumes the responsibility for his registration. On the Continent, the frequent censuses of the population are used to add and to strike out names. Great Britain sends out canvassers to check the election lists against persons actually living in the area and to add new names.[2] As a result, the records are kept reasonably up to date without placing the burden of a personal appearance on the voter. Systems of this type, a few of which are found in the United States, are commonly designated as "nonpersonal." In the urban and suburban areas, and in many rural areas of the United States, the elector must assume the responsibility of presenting himself before the registration officials. This is known as "personal" registration.

Following the registration, lists of voters are compiled in alphabetical order in each election district. On election day the voter, through his signature or other identification, claims the right to a ballot. Unless he has previously registered, he is not entitled to vote. Registration procedure, therefore, arose out of the need for eliminating the grosser abuses of repeating and impersonation, and the machinery has undergone much change since its appearance in Massachusetts a century and a half ago. An evaluation of registration in terms of the fulfillment of its objectives may be made after an examination of the major developments in procedure.

ESSENTIAL FEATURES OF A SOUND SYSTEM

Criteria. The major issue in registration in the United States has centered around the question of a permanent or periodic system. In the

---

[2] Milwaukee and Boston use the police to check up periodically on registered voters.

latter, the voter is required to register before each election or at regular intervals. Under permanent registration, only initial registration is required and the registrant's name remains on the list as long as he continues to live at the same address and remains qualified as a voter.[3] About one-fourth of the states still use the periodic type. Each system needs to be judged in terms of its effectiveness.

Among the more important criteria of an effective system are: (1) Does it prevent fraud? (2) Are the lists kept up to date and accurate? (3) Is each voter properly identified before he is allowed to vote? (4) Is the system convenient for the voter so that it will result in registering a high percentage of qualified electors? (5) Is the administrative setup in accordance with sound public administration such as a competent staff and location of responsibility? (6) Is it economical?

Periodic or Permanent Registration? Proponents of the periodic method claim as a leading virtue that it keeps the voting lists up to date by canceling them and making it necessary for all voters to register again.[4] This not only helps to eliminate fraud, it also removes the names of deceased persons, former residents, and the uninterested who might be bribed to turn out at a last-minute election-day get-out-the-vote campaign. Those favoring periodic registration contend that the permanent system encourages attempts to vote deceased registrants.

Where periodic registration is accompanied by genuine personal investigation, there is something to be said for it. Experience has shown, however, that annual and biennial registration is not a guarantee against fraud. Corrupt machines have used repeaters on registration day, sending them from poll to poll to register. In "flophouse" districts precinct captains have rounded up transients on registration day with the knowledge that they will be absent on election day and with the plan to use repeaters to vote these names. Vacant lots and buildings may be used for fake addresses. Under any system there should be some house-to-house canvass in districts with a highly mobile population and there should always be provision for positive identification of the voter at the polls through his signature.

A serious shortcoming of periodic registration is the inconvenience to the voter. Usually only a very few days are set aside for registration. Persons who are ill or out of town during this period find it difficult to register. In New York City, where one must register annually, the inconvenience often becomes intolerable. In presidential elections, queues

---

[3] For a digest of registration provisions see J. P. Johnson and J. J. Lewis, *Registration for Voting in the United States* (Chicago: Council of State Governments, 1946).

[4] For a useful evaluation of registration systems and essentials of sound procedure see the National Municipal League's mimeographed report, *A Model Registration System* (1954).

over a block long and lengthy waiting periods are fairly frequent. Some persons become discouraged and drop out of line.

Permanent registration is much more convenient for the voter since it avoids frequent reregistration. Persons changing residence in the city can often have their registration transferred by simply notifying the

Table 23. Percentage of Eligible Voters Registered in Selected Cities, 1948, 1950

City	% eligible citizens registered, 1948	% eligible citizens registered, 1950
Cities with Permanent Registration		
Boston.............	78.5	78
Chicago............	88.5	84.5
Denver............	78.5	77
Kansas City........	64	60
Los Angeles........	75.5	78.5
Philadelphia.........	78	73.5
San Francisco.......	84.5	79
Cities with Periodic Registration		
Buffalo, N.Y........	68	57.5
New York City......	65	55
Rochester, N.Y.......	70	60
Schenectady, N.Y....	71	60
Syracuse, N.Y........	72.5	60.5

SOURCE: *A Model Registration System* (mimeographed, prepared by the National Municipal League, 1954).

authorities and giving their new address. Because of its convenience, a higher percentage of eligible voters at a given moment are generally registered (see Table 23).

No registration system is completely fraudproof but careful checkups and canvasses keep the voter lists reasonably accurate under the permanent system. The experience in a great many large American cities with permanent registration, such as Chicago and Detroit, shows that fraud can be controlled as effectively as under a periodic system. The use of the signature identification of the voter under either form of registration affords considerable protection against illegal registration.

Permanent registration appears to be cheaper in the long run, although comparisons of registration costs are difficult because it is not always possible to allocate the overhead and clerical costs involved in elections and registration since the two operations are performed by the same officials. In six cities with annual registration, the average cost over a period of years was 72.2 cents per registered voter compared to 29.8 cents in six cities with permanent registration during the 1920's.[5] Registration costs have gone up materially since then but in few large cities today does it exceed 55 cents (see Table 24). In 1951 in New York City the

Table 24. Costs per Registrant of Permanent Registration, 1951, 1952

Boston	$0.54	Milwaukee	$0.15
Chicago	0.41	Philadelphia	0.55
Detroit	0.10	San Francisco	0.22
Los Angeles County	0.22	Seattle	0.12

SOURCE: *A Model Registration System* (mimeographed, prepared by the National Municipal League, 1954).

comparatively light registration cost 40 cents per registrant and 21 cents in 1952. It must be remembered, however, that everyone must be re-registered annually, which runs into an enormous cost. New registrations under permanent systems seldom exceed one-tenth of the total registration. In a few cities having permanent registration a house-to-house canvass is made or a spot mail-check, these adding to the costs.

Other Considerations. Certain other procedures and practices are important to an effective system of registration, whether periodic or permanent. One of these has already been mentioned—signature identification at the time of registration and again at the polls. Another is the conduct of registration by a competent staff selected on a merit rather than on a patronage basis. This should provide better trained personnel and assure freedom from political considerations. During rush periods before the election, and especially under the periodic system, field deputies may be appointed, a practice used in several Western States. Temporary transfers from other departments may also be used. To concentrate responsibility, there should be centralization of administration in a single office and preferably headed by a single commissioner appointed by the state or municipal executive.

Under permanent registration, precinct officers as a general thing should not be used. There are not enough new voters to be registered each year to justify their use. Registration should normally be done by the prospective voter appearing in person at the central office. Where outside registration is needed, special deputies can be sent from the office

[5] See Harris, *op. cit.*, pp. 104–108.

to do the job. The permanent staff can also conduct canvasses where needed. Precinct officials of party machines have been known to conduct fraudulent canvasses. Registration should be conducted throughout the year except for the last few weeks preceding the election. This enables the authorities to check and to prepare the precinct lists.

Although rarely needed, provision should be made for persons denied registration to appeal the decision to the top registration officer and to the courts. Numerous states have an arrangement which permits absentee registration where electors are serving in the Armed Forces or are temporarily away from their residence when they become qualified to vote.

Several procedures are in use to keep the records up to date. These are basic if permanent registration is to be successful. Persons transferring their residence within the jurisdiction of the registration office should be permitted to transfer their registration either by applying in person or submitting a written request to the office. All states having a permanent system provide for this except California and Pennsylvania. Health officers should be required to report to the registration office the names of persons over twenty-one who have died in order that their registration may be canceled. Sporadic mail and police checkups are used to detect fraud and to correct the records. Detroit has successfully used the mail checkup. The registration office submits lists of registered voters to the post office, and for a small fee secures the standard address. Letter carriers indicate whether persons reside at their registered addresses, or if they have moved, their new addresses.

In the permanent system it is important to cancel the names of non-voters from the list so as to eliminate deadwood. In many places this is done after the person has failed to vote in two succeeding elections. To extend a longer period of grace is to fail to eliminate names of persons who have very likely moved.

The clerical, record-keeping, legal, and other details of registration need not concern us here, but it may be pointed out that both the theory and the procedure of registering voters are real challenges in public administration. A good permanent-registration law should be uniform throughout the state so that citizens are not confused or discouraged by a complicated system. Within a state, procedures must be flexible in order to take cognizance of the problems raised in big cities as compared with suburban and rural communities. To a certain extent, then, procedures must be flexible and tailor-made while at the same time operating within the framework of common essentials. The student of government should look upon registration as well as many other administrative processes as capable of further simplification. Permanent registration, which has the essential features just noted, meets the criteria of a sound system reasonably well. Unless there is an equally good system of election administration, a sound registration procedure will bear little fruit in terms of curbing fraud.

ELECTION ADMINISTRATION

Election Officials. Election administration is now almost completely a governmental function calling for: (1) the identification of registered voters and the distribution of a ballot to each recognized voter; (2) the operation of polling booths and voting machines; (3) the counting of the ballots.[6] These functions are commonly placed in the hands of a bi-partisan precinct election board which is very frequently the same board conducting the registration and the primary election. Members of the board, who number three or four, are usually designated as inspectors or judges and are assisted by clerks. The local boards are appointed in various ways, including nomination by a city or county board of elections, the city or county council, popular election, or, as in Oregon, the county court judge. With a few exceptions, notably California, appointments are made on a patronage basis, i.e., by and with the advice and consent of party chairman or district captain. Where there are three on the precinct board, not more than two may belong to the same party, and the clerkships likewise are distributed on a party basis. The reason for bipartisan appointments is that theoretically security is provided, with each party watching the other. In many areas this has resulted in jobs being handed out as patronage to incompetents and perhaps to persons selected with a view to defrauding the ballot.

Election judges must obviously be of intelligence and high character if corruption of the ballot is to be avoided. Yet the only legal requirement is likely to be literacy. New York requires the inspectors to have some knowledge of their duties and in the cities a written examination is required. For a long time this procedure was ridiculously perfunctory since the "right" people, in terms of politics, always managed to pass the tests. Some improvement has taken place but the examination still only tests one's ability to copy accurately. Once having passed the test, one remains eligible for reappointment without examination, although every year the inspectors must take instruction in the operation of voting machines. Although there is no dearth of persons for the position of election judges, the problem of securing enough really competent inspectors such as bank or other clerks is widely existent.

[6] Professor Joseph P. Harris has published a definitive companion volume to his *Registration of Voters in the United States.* See *Election Administration in the United States* (Washington, D.C.: Brookings Institution, 1934).

Procedure. On election day the board opens the polls [7] between 6:00 and 8:00 A.M., and sits for some 12 continuous hours. When the voter appears to vote, the registration books are checked to see if he is duly registered. He is usually required to sign a pollbook, and his name is entered by the official in another pollbook. If he is found to be qualified and identified, he is given a ballot initialed by the election board.[8] From here he goes into a booth closed off by a curtain and proceeds to mark the ballot. After he has completed this marking, the voter folds the ballot and gives it to one of the judges, who deposits it in the ballot box. In some cases, the law requires the voter to place his own ballot in the box.

Where voting machines are used, the person steps inside the booth and pulls a hand lever, which draws a curtain, completely shutting him from view and simultaneously preparing the machine for recording his vote. When he has pressed down all the levers of his choice, on the face of the machine, he pulls the lever opening the curtain and simultaneously recording the vote and preparing the machine for the next voter. To assist the voter, sample ballots and instruction cards or replicas of the face of a voting machine are made available at the polls. The elector may request assistance in marking his ballot or in operating the voting machine.

Because election boards are composed of partisans who are personally interested in the outcome of the election, some protection is needed for the major and minor parties as well as for the independent candidates. Most election laws permit each party to have "watchers" at or near the guard rail in each precinct, with the authority to challenge any voter and to inspect the records. The watchers are also allowed to be present to examine the ballot boxes or machines before the polls open and during the count, until the returns are available. Watchers have to be extraordinarily adept at detecting impostors and fraud and possess, in addition, a thorough knowledge of the election law. Unfortunately, conscientious watchers may not be effective in the controlling of chicanery because of intimidation, violence, and shanghaiing; others have been bribed. Professor Salter quotes a Philadelphia ward leader's technique of "persuading" two Roosevelt watchers to change sides: "I gave them both the price of a breakfast and made them dissatisfied with the $2 they were getting from the Roosevelt group. I hinted that the leader was holding

---

[7] Elections are now generally held in public buildings such as schoolhouses, police stations, or other suitable establishments. This is a vast improvement over the first century of American politics, when polling stations were commonly located in saloons and barbershops, with the municipality often paying extortionate fees for rentals.

[8] In some states the candidates and referendums are on separate ballots and this requires the use of two or more ballots.

out on them. Next I paid them each $10—and promised them a job I didn't have; this got them outside for the rest of the day." [9]

Counting. The generally arduous job of counting begins as soon as the polls are closed; in some places the count may be started before this time. Depending upon the length of the ballot, from two to ten hours are required to complete this task. Election laws usually prescribe in detail how the votes shall be tallied, such as recording in duplicate by two separate clerks, with cross checking on the final results. Recounts often show the existence of errors even in the hands of honest clerks and judges. The reason for this is fairly obvious. Most counters, having been in the polling station all day, are extremely weary and many are far from competent to perform the tedious task of counting a short ballot, let alone the widely prevalent long ballot.

In order to overcome errors resulting from fatigue and to speed up the count, upward of a dozen states have placed the counting in the hands of a separate board. Members of the board arrive at the polling place a few hours before the closing and, where permitted by law, take the ballots to a special room and begin to tabulate. Despite the advantages of having a fresh group of counters, the plan involves certain practical difficulties, the most important of which is the securing of personnel and the limitations of space. Experts in public administration believe a sounder practice to be a central count such as is used in Great Britain. Under this procedure the ballot boxes are taken to a central station, where, under the supervision of experienced clerks, the ballots are counted. Indiana requires this procedure in populous counties and a central count where election is by proportional representation. Precinct jealousies and alleged public impatience to hear immediate returns are obstacles to widespread adoption in the United States.

When the precinct count is finished, the tally sheets are certified and sent to the central election authority, which "canvasses" or adds the totals of all precincts and announces the results. For state offices, the results are sent to the secretary of state, who makes the official tabulation. It may be several days or even weeks before the final official results are announced. To satisfy an anxious electorate and the press, the unofficial procedure in municipalities is to phone precinct results to police headquarters. Quick tabulations are made, figures in strategic precincts are analyzed, and within a few hours unofficial results are made public with obviously defeated nominees conceding the election to their opponents.

An opportunity is usually afforded as a matter of right, and certainly when there is evidence of fraud, for the results to be contested by the losers. When such is demanded, a recount is made and sometimes results

[9] *Boss Rule: Portraits in City Politics* (New York: McGraw-Hill Book Company, Inc., 1935), p. 46.

in a reversal of the results. Some states require the petitioner to finance the recount. Recounts can be conducted inexpensively and it is sound policy to have the public bear the cost as a protection of the sanctity of elections. The validity of returns is usually left to the courts or to the central canvassing board. Contests over legislative positions are settled by Congress or by the state legislative assemblies respectively. Professor Barnett finds that this procedure has not been too partisan in Congress, but in state legislatures the majority party tends to favor its own party's candidates.[10] There is much to be said for turning over contested elections for the legislature to the courts.

Expense. Election administration is expensive. In his survey of election costs, Professor Harris found that in many cities the combined registration and election costs exceeded $1.00 for each vote cast. Among the higher figures were: Kansas City, Mo., $1.54; Columbus, $2.13; Dayton, Ohio, $1.76; and Cleveland, $1.45.[11] In the 1945 mayoralty and councilmanic (PR) vote the cost to New York City was $1.40 per vote. Among the lowest costs, according to Harris, were 37 cents in Minneapolis and Salt Lake City, 67 cents in Denver, and 56 cents in Milwaukee.[12] Major items of expenditure include the rental of buildings where public ones are unavailable, excess of workers in many precincts, and high printing costs for paper ballots.

Most students of elections believe these expenditures capable of reduction. A number are of the opinion that the voting machines will reduce the cost of election administration. This is debatable not only because the initial outlay for the machines is great, but also because of the upkeep on the machines and the larger cost for the instruction of the election board. Once the initial cost of installation is completed, however, subsequent elections should be cheaper because paper ballots will be unnecessary, precincts may be combined for voting purposes, and fewer persons will be needed to administer the election. Voting machines which will record PR are not yet practical, so where that system is used the utility of voting machines is limited.

Despite their cost, voting machines are vastly superior to paper ballots in the more populous counties. Indeed, it is hard to justify the use of the paper ballot in these jurisdictions. The assurance of honesty and accuracy, not to mention speed, far outweighs other considerations. At least half the states now authorize the use of voting machines and their use is mandatory in many cities. Objections that the machines are too complicated to operate or confusing to the voter are little more than rationaliza-

10 See V. M. Barnett, Jr., "Contested Congressional Elections in Recent Years," *The Political Science Quarterly*, Vol. 54 (1939), pp. 167–215.

11 *Election Administration in the United States*, pp. 386–387.

12 *Ibid.*

tions of political partisans who long for the "good old days," when too often elections were conducted in the spirit of contentedness and corruptness.

BALLOT FORMS

In early America both viva voce and paper ballots were used. With the rise of parties a ballot was printed at party expense for the convenience of the voters. Party-printed ballots were colored and included only the names of the candidates of the party, with the X already printed on them. All the voter needed to do was to walk to the ballot box and hand the ballot to the officials. Unofficial ballots led to bribery and made it difficult to vote other than a straight-party ticket. These abuses led to the eventual adoption of a new form of secret ballot, which had been introduced in Australia as early as 1856. It was not until 1888, however, before the first two states, Kentucky and Massachusetts, applied it. Today this ballot is used in some form in all states except South Carolina, where the ballots are still prepared in various ways.

In its true form, the Australian ballot was (1) provided by the government, (2) distributed only at the polls, (3) marked in a private booth, (4) without party designations, and (5) with the names of all candidates arranged by offices.[13] Substantial modifications of this ballot were made in the United States. The main forms today are designated as the Massachusetts office-block and Indiana party-column types. Massachusetts followed the Australian system of grouping names on the ballot according to the office sought. As used today, the party designation accompanies each name (see sample ballot of California). The arranging of names by offices encourages discriminating voting instead of an indiscriminate voting according to party label; it does not, of course, eliminate incompetent nominees.

Party leaders were stunned at this Massachusetts form because it seriously interfered with straight-party voting. Within a year they devised, first in the state of Indiana, a way to overcome the obstacle through a party-column ballot. Today, some 28 states use this form. A list of all party candidates is placed in a single column with a circle at the top opposite the party name (see Louisiana ballot). By marking the circle at the top the voter can, in a second, cast a ballot for every party candidate for every office. A few states put the names in a party column but omit the circle, requiring the voter to go down the column checking each candidate. Persons desiring to split their votes between various parties leave the party circle blank and check each choice individually, or mark the party circle and put a cross in squares of candidates' opposing parties where they wish to depart from the general party line. Party emblems

[13] The "nonpartisan" ballot used in numerous municipal elections today bears the closest resemblance to the original Australian form.

Office-block ballot form as used in California. As a general rule (Pennsylvania excepted) there is no provision in this type for straight party voting.

SAMPLE BALLOT

MARK CROSSES (X) ON BALLOT ONLY WITH RUBBER STAMP; NEVER WITH PEN OR PENCIL

(Fold Ballot to this Perforated Line, leaving Top Margin exposed)

GENERAL TICKET—17th Congressional, 38th Senatorial, 68th Assembly District

INSTRUCTIONS TO VOTERS: To vote for a candidate of your selection, stamp a cross (X) in the voting square next to the right of the name of such candidate. Where two or more candidates for the same office are to be elected, stamp a cross (X), after the names of all the candidates for that office for whom you desire to vote, up to, but not to exceed, however, the number of candidates who are to be elected. To vote for a person not on the ballot, write the name of such person under the title of the office in the blank space left for that purpose. To vote on any question, proposition or constitutional amendment, stamp a cross (X) in the voting square after the word "Yes" or after the word "No," as you desire. All marks, except the cross (X), are forbidden. All distinguishing marks or erasures are forbidden and make the ballot void. If you wrongly stamp, tear or deface this ballot, return it to the Inspector of Election and obtain another.

STATE

Governor — Vote for One

FRANK F. MERRIAM, Republican
Incumbent

ROBERT NOBLE, Commonwealth

CULBERT L. OLSON, Democrat
State Senator

RAYMOND HAIGHT, Progressive
Counsellor at Law

Lieutenant Governor — Vote for One

ELLIS E. PATTERSON, Progressive
Assemblyman

GENEVE L. A. SHAFFER, Townsend

WALTER SCOTT FRANKLIN, Republican
Doctor and Rancher

Secretary of State — Vote for One

FRANK C. JORDAN, Republican, Democrat
Secretary of State

NELLIE S. HARRISS, Prohibition

LEO GALLAGHER, Communist
Lawyer

Controller — Vote for One

HARRY B. RILEY, Republican, Democrat, Progressive, Townsend
State Controller

ANITA WHITNEY, Communist

ELLEN G. PRITCHARD, Prohibition

Treasurer — Vote for One

CHARLES G. JOHNSON, Republican, Democrat
Incumbent

LEGISLATIVE

State Senator Thirty-Eighth District — Vote for One

HARRY W. FRANCIS, Progressive

ROBERT W. KENNY, Democrat, Republican
Judge of the Superior Court

Member of the Assembly Sixty-Eighth District — Vote for One

FRED REAVES, Democrat
Assemblyman

CHARLES M. SMITH, Republican

JUDICIAL

For Chief Justice of the Supreme Court

Shall WILLIAM H. WASTE be elected to the office for the term expiring January 1, 1951?

	YES
	NO

For Associate Justice of the Supreme Court

Shall WILLIAM H. LANGDON be elected to the office for the term expiring January 1, 1951?

	YES
	NO

For Associate Justice of the Supreme Court

Shall JESSE W. CURTIS be elected to the office for the term expiring January 1, 1951?

	YES
	NO

For Associate Justice of the Supreme Court

Shall FREDERICK W. HOUSER be elected to the office for the term expiring January 1, 1951?

	YES
	NO

For Presiding Justice, District Court of Appeal, Second Appellate District, Division One — Vote for One

---

QUESTIONS AND PROPOSITIONS SUBMITTED TO VOTE OF ELECTORS

1 — LABOR. Initiative. Defines what constitutes lawful and unlawful picketing, boycotting and display of banners. Prohibits unlawful picketing and boycotting, and mass picketing, obstruction or interference with use of public highways, stores, storerooms or places of business; etc. | YES / NO

2 — REGULATION OF POISONS. Initiative Measure. Defines "poison" and regulates conduct thereof; prescribes duties of pharmacists, etc. | YES / NO

3 — MOTOR VEHICLE TAXATION AND REVENUE. Senate Constitutional Amendment 30. | YES / NO

4 — HIGHWAY AND TRAFFIC SAFETY COMMISSION. Initiative Constitutional Amendment. Creates Highway and Traffic Safety Commission. | YES / NO

5 — FISHING CONTROL. Initiative measure presented by, and not acted on by, Legislature. | YES / NO

6 — TAXATION OF INSURANCE COMPANIES. Senate Constitutional Amendment 33. | YES / NO

13 — REVENUE BOND ACT OF 1937. Referendum of act of Legislature (Chapter 31, Statutes 1937). | YES / NO

14 — REMOVAL OF JUDGES UPON CONVICTION OF CRIME. | YES / NO

15 — JUDICIAL COUNCIL. Assembly Constitutional Amendment 36. | YES / NO

16 — RETIREMENT OF JUDGES. Assembly Constitutional Amendment 1. Adds section 27 to Article VI of Constitution. | YES / NO

17 — INITIATIVE. Senate Constitutional Amendment 26. | YES / NO

18 — STATE MONEY. Senate Constitutional Amendment 31. | YES / NO

19 — LENDING OR GIFT OF PUBLIC MONEY. Senate Constitutional Amendment 32. Amends section 31 of Article XIII of Constitution. | YES / NO

COUNTY QUESTIONS

PROPOSED COUNTY CHARTER AMENDMENT NO. 1. Shall the Charter of the County of Los Angeles be amended by amending Section 4 (g fixing the salary of members of the Board of Supervisors of $5,000 per year, to become effective with respect to the term of the supervisors of the second, fourth, and fifth supervisorial districts beginning in 1940 and with respect to the terms of supervisors of the first and third districts beginning in 1942? | YES / NO

PROPOSED COUNTY CHARTER AMENDMENT NO. 2. Shall the salaries of the Sheriff, District Attorney and Assessor be fixed in the charter at $10,000 per year? | YES / NO

PROPOSED COUNTY CHARTER AMENDMENT NO. 3. Shall the Charter of the County of Los Angeles be amended by amending Section 34 to provide that the County Forester and Fire Warden to detect a flood control employment as to officers and to exclude jurisdiction over parks, playgrounds, beaches and other recreational areas? | YES / NO

PROPOSED COUNTY CHARTER AMENDMENT NO. 4. Shall the Charter of the County of Los Angeles be amended by amending Section 33, relating to Civil Service, to place the Chief Deputy County Assessor in the classified service, to require and provide for the placing of certain members of the Commission and Committees in the unclassified service? | YES / NO

PROPOSED COUNTY CHARTER AMENDMENT NO. 5. Shall Section 34 relating to the Civil Service Commission, be amended by providing that after the permanent separation of an officer or employee in the classified service, who has been absent without pay for such period to provide that such service shall be effective, if such service is repeatable? | YES / NO

PERFORATED LINE

1268

53

were originally used to aid illiterate voters. Republican workers told the illiterates or near-illiterates to mark the circle beside the eagle or the "bird with pants on." Several ballots still contain the Republican eagle and Democratic crowing rooster or star.

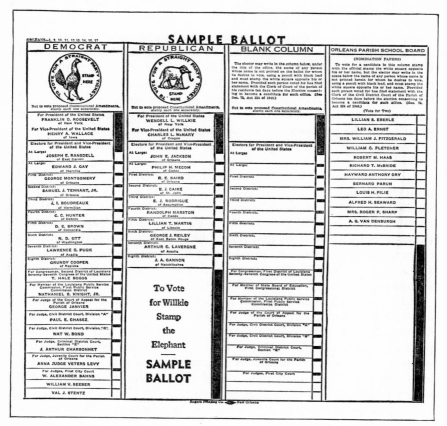

Party-column ballot with party emblems as used in Louisiana. Third column may be used for "write-in" candidates. A majority of the states use party column forms.

Most party regulars prefer the party emblem as an inducement to voting a straight ticket. They argue that this simplifies the voter's task, "voter" in this case meaning the loyal partisan. The office-block ballot has greater appeal for the independent voter, as it requires him to look over the candidates for each office and mark them (or refrain from marking them) accordingly.

Absentee Voting. In all but about six states, some provision is made for civilian absentee voting; this poses special problems in election administration. Laws on this subject defy classification or uniformity. About one-half of the states make a special provision for those who are too ill or physically disabled to go to the polls to vote.[14] Nearly all the states require that the absentee be within the territorial limits of the United States to qualify. Although New Hampshire extends its provisions only to presidential elections, the common practice is to apply it to all elections.

The details in administration likewise show variation. Minimum provisions, however, include application to the appropriate election officials and full identification of the voter. In order for the ballot to be valid, it must be attested by a notary public or other officer that the person entitled to vote actually marked the ballot. In most cases, the ballot must be in the hands of one's election board by or on election day. From this stage on, the election officials are charged with checking the voter's identity on the pollbooks and counting the ballots.

More recently, a greater problem has concerned the servicemen's vote. Indeed, the original impetus for absent voting came during the Civil War and each subsequent war has brought new questions. The size of the military personnel in World War II made the soldier vote of crucial significance and resulted in bitter controversy. Congress was so slow in enacting a law in 1942 that scarcely 100,000 soldier ballots were cast in the congressional elections that year. The 1942 law provided that in time of war, notwithstanding any provision of state law relating to registration and elections, those in the Armed Forces who were otherwise qualified should be entitled to vote for all elective officials.

It became evident in 1944 that the service personnel and their friends and relatives back home would demand something better for the presidential election. The Administration and the War and Navy officials prepared a measure (Green-Lucas bill) which would permit distribution of ballots through a War Ballot Commission directly to those in the service.[15] This simplified ballot was to be available to members of the merchant marine and to civilian employees of the United States overseas. Federal participation was to be limited to general elections at which Federal officers were chosen.

A seething controversy arose in Congress. Republicans generally denounced it, fearing the sizable vote among soldiers for the Commander in Chief; for similar reasons Northern Democrats were enthusiastic about it. This placed the balance of power for enactment in the hands of

14 For a useful summary of variations of absentee voting laws see Paul S. Steinbicker, "Absentee Voting in the United States," *The American Political Science Review*, Vol. 32 (1938), pp. 898–907; see also James K. Pollock, *Absentee Voting and Registration* (Washington, D.C.: Public Affairs Press, 1940); and G. F. Miller, *Absentee Voters and Suffrage Laws* (Washington, D.C.: Daylion Co., 1949).

15 A useful survey of the bill and the controversy over it is given by Boyd A. Martin, "The Service Vote in the Elections of 1944," *The American Political Science Review*, Vol. 39 (1945), pp. 720–732.

Southern Democrats, and they soon made their position clear. Publicly, the Southern congressmen vigorously opposed the proposal on constitutional grounds—that it violated states' rights by granting Congress the authority to determine suffrage qualifications. Practically speaking, the opposition was principally aroused because the bill would enfranchise thousands of persons, especially Negroes. The battle was won by the states' rightists and the bill was enacted without benefit of the President's signature.[16] The bill limited the use of the Federal ballot (which included the names only of Federal officers) to those states which failed to set up adequate machinery. Where the state ballot was used, the Federal government facilitated the transmission and return of marked ballots. The military personnel in effect was governed by the voting laws of the respective states.

Only 20 states made any use of the Federal form and only 84,000 ballots were cast under this alternative. The controversy was not without beneficial results because it led to improvement in state soldier-voting laws. The number of service votes was higher than anticipated, with approximately 2,700,000 ballots or 5.6 per cent of the total popular vote. Congress repealed the Federal short-ballot form in 1946, leaving the question of soldier votes entirely in the hands of the states. The Selective Service Act of 1948 banned the poll tax as a requirement for voting for Federal officers by inductees but not by volunteers. A committee of the American Political Science Association in 1952 recommended that absent servicemen should have the right to vote both in time of war and peace without the poll-tax ban and that the states liberalize and standardize service voting procedures.[17] Congress has shown little interest in acting on the recommendations.

ELECTION FRAUDS

The history of election days in the United States is filled with pathology. Corrupt seekers of power have left no stone unturned in working out ways and means of defrauding the ballot box.[18] Before the adoption of the Australian ballot about a half century ago, corruption was of unbelievable extent. Colored ballots were printed and passed out by party leaders and, in the absence of privacy for marking the ballot, watchers could easily make certain that floaters and bribed voters would vote

---

[16] 56 STAT. 753.

[17] *Voting in the Armed Services: Message from the President Transmitting the Report of the Special Committee on Service Voting, American Political Science Association,* 82d Cong., 2d Sess., H. Doc. 407, 1952.

[18] Fraudulent elections are not limited to any one nation. Many elections in Eastern Europe since World War II have been characterized by colossal fraud. No election may be considered as a mandate or a reflection of public opinion in any nation unless the honesty of it is first assured.

"right." Names were purposely put in peculiar combinations on the ballot to confuse even the more intelligent voters. When some states required all names to be placed on white paper, different grades of paper were used to achieve something of the same result. These abuses, as noted earlier, led to the adoption of an official ballot. It was not long, however, before techniques, administrative and otherwise, were developed to overcome the setbacks the corrupt interests had suffered from the introduction of the secret ballot. Some of the more common methods may be mentioned.

One practice is to take advantage of so-called "illiterates." Here an election judge spies a first or supposedly "sucker" voter and marches into the polling booth with him to demonstrate how to vote this "complicated" long ballot. Once inside, the judge deftly wields the pencil, marking an X in the party column, before certain names, and on referendum propositions. The uninitiated often does not wish to engage in an argument and acquiesces. If a protest is made, the judge may innocently proclaim "misunderstanding" of the voter's instructions.[19] This "assistance" dodge is also used in some foreign sections, where intimidation may easily take place. It was used in former days to make certain that bribed voters marked their ballots the "right" way.

Another technique, much less extensively used today than formerly, is for the machine to line up its voters and repeaters early in the day, so that the long line causes the honest voter to turn away rather than to wait. Upon returning later, the latter learns that someone has already voted under his name. If he protests, he may receive a threat of indictment for attempting to vote twice, and the obliging policeman backs up the precinct boss.

Stuffing the ballot box with checked-off votes and "weighing" it in advance (i.e., deciding who gets what and by what margin without opening the box) can be successfully accomplished only through collusion of the opposing election judges. This may be done in order to work out a bargain or deal and to steal the votes cast for a minor-party, independent, or reform candidate. When votes are found, during the count, for independents or "do-gooders," the ballots are destroyed and marked ballots, evenly distributed or prorated by agreement for machine candidates, are substituted. Unquestionably, third parties are robbed of many votes because of insufficient watchers or cheating in the count.

Election laws generally provide that ballots which are torn or marred by pencils are invalid. This makes possible further cheating on the count

[19] Two of the author's students received this treatment in the 1936 election in a Chicago South Side district and reported that several other voters were literally muscled out after their ballots were marked by tough-looking inspectors.

by spoiling the ballots cast for the opposition. One device is "short penciling," which consists of concealing and waxing a piece of lead in the palm of the hand or under a fingernail. As the ballots are spread in front of the tabulator, he may make an X in the party-column box at the top of a ballot and simply count the X, thereby voting for all members of his party. Or he may mark one or two vacant squares or run pencil marks over part of the ballot, thus spoiling the entire ballot. Effecting erasures or tearing the ballot are two of the additional methods of causing spoliation.

Even after the count, the sudden failure of the lighting system or a sleight of hand results in the substitution of a new tally sheet. There are also cases on record where the ballot box used during the day at the polls is destroyed and replaced by an entirely new ballot box prepared by the political boss.

At one time, bribing, together with a faulty registration and identification system, accounted for a large share of fraud. The organization secured a list of all previously registered dead persons and voters who moved away and registered as well a number of persons under false names. Floaters were then hired on election day to go from precinct to precinct and vote under these names. Where a party worker did not trust his floaters he employed the "Tasmanian dodge." This necessitated stealing an official ballot early on election day, filling it out for the organization, and handing it to the "stinger," as the floater was called. The stinger appeared at the polls, received a blank official ballot, went into the booth and exchanged ballots. The organization-marked ballot is then handed to the election judge and the blank ballot is returned to the briber. The blank is then marked and given to another floater and the process is repeated ad infinitum. A small army of floater-repeaters can cast several hundred fraudulent votes in this manner.

Falsifying the people's will by stuffing the ballot box and manipulating the tally sheets is often supplemented by intimidation, coercion, and violence. These range from mere "suggestion" of the "healthy" way to vote to strong-arm work, such as kidnaping and waylaying watchers or arresting political workers of the opposition party on trumped-up charges of breaking the election laws. Fist fighting, election-day massacres, and activities by hoodlums are by no means uncommon in many of the nation's cities. In some instances, the police force is bribed or compelled to overlook election-day irregularities. Though much less common than in former years, violence, unfortunately, is still a part of the election-day procedure in some areas. In the 1946 election, a Republican worker was waylaid on the way to the polls in Manhattan's Eighteenth Congressional District and received a beating resulting in his death.

Complete figures on the extent of fraud, of course, can never be known. In 1926, Professor Harris found that from 42 to 47 per cent of the votes cast in 23 Chicago precincts were fraudulent.[20] Moreover, a recount on several referendum propositions in a number of precincts in the same city divulged errors up to 9 per cent in the count.[21] Even in the face of these figures, there is no reason for complete disillusionment because the amount of corruption varies from place to place and in thousands of precincts an honest and an accurate vote is recorded. Moreover, fraud is much less prevalent than even a generation ago; this is due to the innovation of practices, procedures, and devices coming as the result of outcries from honest citizens.

REMEDIES

The elimination of fraudulent election practices is possible if the recording of the people's will should come to be viewed as basically a problem in public administration and not as a party function. As noted in the case of registration, placing election administration in the hands of nonpartisan personnel instead of bipartisan boards is one of the first steps toward sound administration. The great majority of election frauds today are perpetrated by the election officers, hence some method of selection which will take their selection away from corrupt party machines is essential to honest elections. Local boards, whether used in precincts or in larger areas, should be appointed by and responsible to an election commissioner or central authority. Services of the Civil Service Commission might be used in recruiting clerks, recorders, counters, and those operating various election paraphernalia. Much fraud is possible because of the collusion of the local election boards or because of an incompetent staff—nonpartisanship and a "professional" attitude in administering elections would result in a more honest vote.

The preceding pages have demonstrated that, in the next place, honest balloting and counting are impossible unless based upon a sound registration system. The Tasmanian dodge and repeating voters take place when voting lists contain deadwood or where identification of voters does not include the signature or other methods of detecting impersonation.[22] For this reason reform of registration procedures and election administration must proceed simultaneously. Good laws governing these do not in and of themselves guarantee honest elections, but they will go far to

20 *Registration of Voters in the United States,* p. 356. Harris, *Election Administration in the United States,* Chap. 9, presents a comprehensive account of election frauds.

21 D. M. Maynard, "Fraud and Error in Chicago Referendum Returns," *National Municipal Review,* Vol. 19 (1930), pp. 164–167.

22 Chain voting may also be broken up by using detachable serially numbered stubs on the ballot. If the election judge carefully observes and compares the numbers on the stubs and ballots, the dodge technique is easily detectable.

preserve the sanctity of the ballot and to establish public confidence in the election results.

Another opportunity for substantial improvement deserves mention— the use of voting machines. Voting machines, as earlier noted, are superior to paper ballots not only in terms of speed and efficiency but also in faithfully totaling the vote. Spoiled ballots, cheating by addition (or subtraction), and such devices as the Tasmanian dodge are eliminated. Machines are not susceptible to rigging and "doctoring up." Complete secrecy is assured because a ballot cannot be marked for identification and the machine prevents one from casting a defective or spoiled ballot. Should the voter pull up the levers before his vote is recorded, i.e., before the curtain is pulled back, he will fail to cast a vote. Simple instruction in the operation of the machine, however, will reduce this to a minimum. When a recount is necessary, only the inspection of the counters and tabulation is required, and this spares both time and expense. A recount should be permitted as a matter of right within a specified time after the election. Most states have such laws. Irrespective of the expense, impartial experts are generally agreed on the superiority of voting machines over paper ballots. Probably no more than a third of the ballots cast in a presidential election are recorded on voting machines. Voting machines are impractical in mountainous areas and where population is sparse. Absentee ballots, of course, are on paper. Obviously, paper ballots will continue to be widely used and methods of preventing the fraudulent use or counting of them remain an important problem.

An item too often overlooked in administration is that of the police force. If the public is to have confidence in election administration, the polling stations must have effective policing both inside and outside. Election laws forbidding loitering require the strictest enforcement. Party workers and campaigners, except for watchers, should be forbidden proximity to the polls. And the watchers themselves require watching to see that they keep within the letter and spirit of the law.

PROPORTIONAL REPRESENTATION SYSTEMS

An extended discussion of systems of representation is beyond the scope of this book. We have had occasion, nonetheless, to mention functional and PR and their influence on the party system in Europe. Likewise, gerrymandering and some of the results of the single-member district operating under the plurality principle were observed. It is convenient at this point to note briefly American experience with certain alternative vote forms. These raise special problems in election administration, especially in the marking and counting of ballots, but involve for the parties much more than simply these technical problems. At one time preferential voting systems were used in several American cities but they have been

Full view (above) and the face (see opposite page) of a voting machine are illustrated.
the extreme left. (*Automatic Voting Machine*

largely abandoned.[23] Two forms which are in use in the United States today for the purpose of assuring some minority representation are the cumulative vote for the Illinois House of Representatives and the Hare system of proportional representation.

Cumulative Voting. Illinois adopted its system in 1870 for the purpose of remedying faulty sectional representation while retaining the principle of majority rule. Three persons are elected from each district and the voter is given three votes. If an X is placed for one candidate, he receives three votes, if two persons are marked, each receives one and one-half votes, and if three are checked, each person receives one vote. This plan helps to assure the election of one person from the minority party in each district because the party voters are urged to "plump" or concentrate all three votes on the party's candidate. To work satisfactorily, each party must carefully assess its strength in each district and limit the number of nominees. Illinois laws permit a quota to be placed upon the number of entrants in the respective party primaries, a task entrusted to the state senatorial district committees. This is an important function for the committees and they are often criticized for "manipulation" or for

Where the law permits, a straight ticket may be voted by pulling the party lever at *Corporation, Jamestown, New York.)*

[23] For a discussion of systems of preferential voting see G. H. Hallett, Jr., *Proportional Representation—The Key to Democracy* (New York: The Macmillan Company, 1940).

over- or underestimating the party's strength with the voters. A so-called "setup" may be arranged by the two committees agreeing which shall put up one, and which two, in the general election. Naturally, factions will denounce the setups but these "arrangements" generally reflect political reality.

Blair believes the long experience in Illinois has demonstrated beneficial results.[24] It has resulted in less turnover in legislative personnel in the lower house than has been true in neighboring states and has helped to reelect experienced lawmakers. The system has avoided alternate huge Republican and Democratic majorities because a party seldom makes a sweep of all seats. It has approximated in representation the voting strength of the parties. Finally, the system has resulted in electing a working majority but with an effective minority. Cumulative voting, however, has not commended itself to adoption by any other states.

Proportional Representation. Cumulative voting is minority rather than proportional representation. Under the latter, third parties have a much better opportunity to elect their nominees, although third parties have elected their candidates at times in the Illinois system.

The Hare system attempts to give each element in the voting population representation closely corresponding to its numerical strength through the use of the single transferable vote.[25] Nominations are made by petition and placed on a simple ballot. The ballot is marked with numerals 1, 2, 3, 4, 5, and so on, in order of the voter's preference. He may rate only one candidate, thereby losing a chance to have his vote transferred if his first and only choice is eliminated after the first count, or express preferences for several or all of the remaining nominees. At the conclusion of the voting, the ballot boxes are locked and transported to a central place for counting.

The process of counting is complicated, difficult, and not easily understood by the average voter. First, an election quota must be obtained, i.e., the smallest number of ballots needed by a candidate to win. Mathematically, the formula may be expressed as follows:

$$\frac{\text{Total number of valid votes}}{\text{Number of seats to be filled} + 1} + 1 = \text{the electoral quota}$$

If 100,000 votes were cast in a PR election to select nine persons, a quota of 10,001 would be reached as follows:

$$9 + 1 = 10 \div \frac{10,000 + 1}{100,000} = 10,001 \text{ quota}$$

---

[24] George S. Blair, *Cumulative Voting in Illinois* (doctoral dissertation, Northwestern University, 1951); see also his article of the same title, *National Municipal Review*, Vol. 42 (1953), pp. 410–414.

[25] For a description of the operation and merits of PR consult Hallett, *op. cit.*

After the quota is established, ballots are sorted according to first choices. Following our figure above, anyone receiving 10,001 first choices is declared elected. If the candidate received 11,000 first choices, he received 999 more votes than he needed and they are distributed according to second choices. These 999 ballots may be taken from the top or bottom of the pile, selected at random, or from a proportionate share of second preferences. After the transfer, first and second choices are added together, and those obtaining the quota are elected. Several counts or transfers may be necessary in order to elect the required number of persons.

Table 25. Majority Party Representation in New York City Council under Proportional Representation

Year	% of final vote		% of council	
	Democrats	All others	Democrats	All others
1939	60	40	67	33
1941	61	39	65	35
1943	57	43	59	41
1945	59	41	61	39

Proponents of PR claim several theoretical and practical advantages over the single-member-plurality system. Under PR, comparatively few votes fail to help elect someone.[26] Besides avoiding wastage of ballots, PR assures the minority party and the larger other minorities some representation and reduces overrepresentation of the majority party. A striking case of the need for a more equitable system was shown in the 1943 councilmanic election in Baltimore. The Democrats polled 67,370 votes to 50,452 for the Republicans. Yet the 43 per cent Republican vote did not elect a single candidate, and the 57 per cent Democratic majority elected the entire council. By contrast, the results of four PR elections (Table 25) in New York City showed the majority party receiving representation far more in accordance with voting strength. PR also gave minorities like the Labor, Liberal, and Communist parties seats on the council.

PR was repealed in New York City in 1947, after having been used in four elections. The election results immediately reverted to the old

[26] See George H. McCaffrey, "Proportional Representation in New York City," *The American Political Science Review,* Vol. 33 (1939), pp. 841–852, and in the same journal, Belle Zeller and Hugh A. Bone, "The Repeal of P.R. in New York City—Ten Years in Retrospect," Vol. 42 (1948), pp. 1127–1148.

pattern with the election of 24 Democrats, one Republican, and no minor-party members on the council. While PR was in effect, the Democrats always had the majority to which they were entitled but a more effective minority opposition was elected to the council.

Among the claims for PR are that it curbs gerrymandering, provides for automatic reapportionment, eliminates primary elections, and gives insurgents and newcomers some opportunity to win over the candidates of the political machine. Since nominees are chosen from a larger constituency than is the case with a single-member district, PR may help to minimize purely local considerations in the choice of a nominee. Ballots are tabulated at a central counting place by competent persons under honest supervision and with less opportunity for the chicanery sometimes employed in precinct counting under the conventional system.

The use of PR for the election of members of Congress and the state legislatures has not been seriously considered, although the National Municipal League has recommended it for the latter. A considerable number of cities have experimented with PR, often coupled with the city-manager plan. Cleveland and New York City abandoned PR but Cincinnati and several other cities still use it.

In practically every city where it is used, PR has been under attack and citizens' movements favoring it have had to fight a constant battle against repeal referendums. The spearhead of the opposition usually comes from the two major parties and more likely from the party commonly in the majority. The latter likes the "99 per cent majority" which it may be able to elect under the plurality system and opposes PR for the very reason that it does give representation in accordance with voting strength. Organization politicians dislike the loss of control over nominations and the potential loss of some power to independents, insurgents, and minority candidates who commonly fare better under PR. The argument that PR results in voting along racial and religious lines is not impressive because appeals to religion and nationality and the use of the "balanced ticket" of minorities were well established in many American cities long before the use of PR. For many citizens, the fact that the system is complicated and that they do not understand it has led them to be wary of it as "alien." Opponents point to the unstable governments of Europe as evidence that the system is divisive and likely to prevent a majority of any one party.

In the United States, PR will continue to be an issue only for the election of city councils and for the governing bodies of private organizations. Those who believe that governing bodies should represent social, economic, and political interests according to fairly exact mathematical quotas find much merit in the Hare system. For those believing in strong partisan government in the city councils, PR does take away some control over nominations and may make uncertain an effective majority. In view of the successful experience of many nonpartisan city councils chosen on at-large basis, there is some doubt if a strong partisan majority is a necessary adjunct of good city government. If the Hare system is to succeed in cities, the council should be kept small and constituencies city-wide or at least small enough to keep the ballot from being so long as to confuse the voter with a lengthy list of unfamiliar names.

SELECTED REFERENCES

The two most comprehensive works on election administration are Joseph P. Harris, *Registration in the United States* (1929) and *Election Administration in the United States* (1934). Prevailing registration systems will be found in the *Book of the States,* and the digest prepared by J. B. Johnson and J. J. Lewis, *Registration for Voting in the United States* (1946); see also A. L. Powell, *Registration of Voters in Louisiana* (1940); J. K. Pollock, *Absentee Voting and Registration* (1940); Office of War Information, *State Absentee Voting and Registration Laws;* G. F. Miller, *Absentee Voters and Suffrage Laws* (1949); National Municipal League, *A Model Registration System* (1954). Several states have issued manuals on their registration and election procedure.

Facsimiles of ballots used by various local, state, and national governments will be found in Carl O. Smith, *A Book of Ballots* (1938). See also S. D. Albright, *The American Ballot* (1942). *The American Political Science Review* and *National Municipal Review* carry numerous articles on registration and election administration. On PR the two major works for and against are respectively G. H. Hallett, Jr., *Proportional Representation—The Key to Democracy* (1940), and F. A. Hermens, *Democracy or Anarchy? A Study of Proportional Representation* (1943). The student would profit by an intense study of the election laws and their administration in his own locality.

PART SIX

Popular Participation and Opinion Measurement

CHAPTER 23

Suffrage

It is a personal injustice to withhold from any one, unless for the prevention of greater evils, the ordinary privilege of having his voice reckoned in the disposal of affairs in which he has the same interest.

—JOHN STUART MILL

Every society and community is faced with the question of who shall participate in the control of government and upon what basis. Monarchies, aristocracies, and dictatorships have allowed only a minimum or no control by the people. Democracies and republics are known for permitting a larger number to have a share in determining the policies and personnel of government. It is often remarked that "in a democracy everyone can vote." Such is not the case. In the United States at a given time scarcely more than 50 per cent of the total population is eligible to vote. The other half has failed to meet the qualifications set forth by the various state laws in order to be entitled to cast a ballot. Throughout history, from the Greek democracies to the present, suffrage has been denied, or permitted, on the basis of age, citizenship, religion, race, ownership of property, criminal record, residence, payment of taxes, group affiliation, intelligence or literacy, or for many other reasons.

If a vote is to be meaningful, it must be accompanied by some opportunity to express a choice or to choose between alternates. The constitution of the Soviet Union provides for broad suffrage and is highly democratic in tone. But the voter has only one person for whom to vote and the process of placing that candidate in nomination is carefully controlled. Persons are permitted to scratch out the name of the nominee but this must be done without secrecy. This suggests a second element, namely, that a ballot be cast in secret and without fear of personal recrimination or violence. Unless public law or the political system provides for these two conditions, the elective franchise is not an effective method of popular control.

The privilege of suffrage has been a demand of those seeking political emancipation and a voice in the management of government. Historically, voting was associated with ownership of property, the holding of titles, or some special status in society. Revolutionary theorists have usually exalted the "people" and demanded suffrage for at least some classes

543

formerly without it. In the first half of United States history, the great battles over suffrage centered around property requirements because the equalitarian doctrines of the Declaration of Independence brought about little liberalization of the suffrage in the new state constitutions. There was a dire need for a strong, stable government and it was believed that property owners had a deeper concern in the conduct of government than the propertyless. Even Jefferson was not enthusiastic about what the hordes in the cities might do to his dream of an agrarian America. He championed freedom of the press and public education but not the abolition of freeholding requirements; his native Virginia, incidentally, did not abolish this restriction until 1850.

The impetus for abolition of property qualifications came from Western frontiersmen who accepted the doctrine of equalitarianism. If one man was as good as another, then denial of the ballot was without justification. Jacksonian democracy struck down taxpaying and property-owning requirements for suffrage but many such qualifications remained in one form or another through the rest of the century. Following the attack on this limitation, the great battles over enfranchising Negroes and women took place. Like the propertyless (which many of them were) the struggle for the ballot became a struggle for political and also social and economic emancipation. It became a badge and symbol of freedom.

Although the pages of history are filled with the claim that voting is a natural right, in practice it has been a right conferred by the state. In full-fledged autocracies, the ruler and his guard for all practical purposes decide who shall vote and the terms of the suffrage. In a unitary state such as England, the Parliament makes the suffrage laws which are in effect throughout all counties and boroughs. Federalist governments, with their division of power between the central and provincial authorities, pose a problem less simple of solution. The Swiss constitution resolved the question by fixing the requirements for Federal elections and letting the cantonal constitutions state the qualifications for the voting in local elections.

There was some sentiment for nationalizing the suffrage laws in the Constitutional Convention of 1787 in the United States but suffrage matters were left to the states for several reasons. The framers of the Constitution were not interested in broad, universal suffrage. The wide diversity of voting qualifications in the 13 states and the probable impossibility of achieving consensus among the drafters themselves were important barriers. Furthermore, suffrage matters would probably add fuel to the anticipated conflict over ratification. After the Civil War, the Supreme Court formally stated the obvious in holding that the Constitution "does not confer the right of suffrage upon anyone, and . . . the United States have no voters of their own creation." Although the states possess the reserved right to decide eligibility for voting in all elections, there have been and will continue to be efforts to amend the Constitution on some suffrage matters. After historic debate, the Constitution was amended to take away from the states the power to deny the ballot to a person because of sex or race. Several attempts have been made by Congress to nationalize the election laws in such matters as the soldiers' vote and the poll tax. Although the casual observer may believe that suffrage issues are now pretty well settled in the states, there are still certain issues and proposals which are being debated. The more important of these are reviewed here.

SUFFRAGE QUALIFICATIONS

Age. In his annual message on the State of the Union in 1954, President Eisenhower recommended that suffrage be conferred at the age of eighteen. Immediately a constitutional amendment was submitted and reported favorably by the Senate Judiciary Committee. Prospects of it receiving a two-thirds majority vote in both houses were never bright. But this revived a question which was widely debated in the state legislatures during World War II. Impetus was given to the proposal by reason of the Federal law which inducted men into the armed services at eighteen, an argument summarized in the slogan "Old enough to fight, old enough to vote." Under the leadership of Governor Ellis Arnall of Georgia, an amendment to confer voting on the eighteen-year-olds was adopted in 1943. No other state followed the lead although South Carolina extended the eighteen-year rule to the Democratic primaries in 1946, only to repeal it shortly thereafter. The extent to which the prestige of Eisenhower will be used to revive the issue in the states remains to be seen. It may be noted that several other nations have lowered the age requirement below that of twenty-one.

Proponents point to the extension of school attendance and the increased college enrollments to support the view that young people can be depended upon to use the franchise fairly wisely. It is argued that it will increase political interest among them and aid the political parties in the recruitment of youth. Opposition expresses itself in terms of the "immaturity" or "emotional instability" of the "youngsters" and tradition for age twenty-one remains strong. Notwithstanding some compelling arguments for lowering the voting age, the burden of proof will rest upon those advocating the change. To date, the eighteen-year-old voter proposal has no support from powerfully organized groups such as the veterans and farmers.

Residence. Since colonial days every state has made voting contingent upon a period of residence in the state, and usually in the county and precinct. About two-thirds of the states require a year's domicile in the state, from 60 to 90 days in the county and 30 days in the precinct. Maine requires only three months' residence in the state, while Michigan and several other states require six months. At the other extreme are a few states which require two years' residence. One of these, Mississippi, reduces the period to six months for clergymen.[1]

Residence qualifications can be justified on the basis of combating fraudulent voting by nonresidents and on the grounds that the prospective voter needs some opportunity to appraise the local situation before casting a ballot. On the other hand, they result in disfranchising temporarily large numbers of voters who change their residence. There appears little justification for lengthy state residence requirements, particularly with respect to national elections.

Granted the essential justice of a domicile requirement, the question arises as to what is the most reasonable length of time. Often the requirement is used to encourage or discourage new residents and workers. The two-year "waiting period" in some states is undoubtedly motivated by a desire to preserve the *status quo* and to keep political control from falling into the hands of migratory workers or away from a sudden influx of laborers due to the opening of a new industry. This requirement is often coupled with a poll tax and literacy test designed to discourage newcomers from exercising the franchise. Under modern conditions, the prolonging of residence beyond one year seems to have no justification.

Foreign observers and many Americans are amazed that residents of the District of Columbia cannot vote unless they are citizens and hold legal residence in a state which permits them to vote by absentee ballot. Taxes paid by residents of the capital are greater in amount than those paid by the citizens in numerous states. Residents of the district have many organizations demanding suffrage and inveighing against "taxation without representation." The political parties perennially promise the franchise to the area but do not act.

The obstacles to enfranchisement are both legal and practical. Legally, the area is not a state and cannot vote in Federal elections and Congress has failed to grant municipal home rule. The latter could be done by a simple act of Congress but Congress appears loath to give up its control over the District of Columbia. Some opposition to local home rule comes from business interests which fear that it might result in higher taxes. As long as the Federal government denies the suffrage to residents of the district, it is under obligation to assume a part of the cost of local government. Questions of fair sums of appropriation out of the national treasury in lieu of taxes would be bound to raise some questions. Southern members of Congress have opposed home rule for the district because of its large Negro population, and have feared that their enfranchisement

[1] A table showing residence requirements will be found in W. B. Graves, *American State Government* (Boston: D. C. Heath and Company, 1941), p. 115.

might in some way lead to an increased demand that the Negro be permitted to vote in Southern states. Obviously, this opposition cannot be defended under democratic principles, but the demands of the League of Women Voters and other civic groups in the district have so far been unavailing.

Poll Taxes. The imposition of poll taxes took place around the turn of this century and was instituted as only one of a number of disfranchising devices aimed mainly at the Negro. Some historians believe the poll tax was designed to stem the rising tide of Populism. Conclusive evidence on this point is difficult to find, but it seems highly probable that in some areas ruling groups regarded the poll tax as a means of minimizing Populist influence. The Populist party, for example, was a "poor farmer" party and was making inroads in the legislatures and in Congress. Many poor whites objected to the poll tax because of the burden which would fall on them. Proponents replied that the poll tax was necessary to preserve "white supremacy" and that the Negroes would be less likely to pay the tax since they were more neglectful and would lose the receipts anyway. At the same time it was alleged that the money would be used for public education. The slogan "Disfranchise the darkies and educate the white children" provided the propaganda in concise terms.

Over half the Southern states have now abolished the poll tax but it remains as a qualification in Alabama, Arkansas, Mississippi, Texas, and Virginia.[2] Opponents of the practice have long tried, without success, to get Congress to outlaw the poll tax by statute for Federal elections or to propose a constitutional amendment to abolish it for all elections. The statutes require a payment of from $1 to $2 usually several months before the Democratic primaries.

The case against the poll tax rests on many grounds. It has served to deter the financially poorer elements from voting. Poll-tax repeal in Florida and Louisiana was followed by increases in Democratic primary participation ranging from one-quarter to two-thirds.[3] In 1948 in South Carolina about 141,000 people voted in the presidential election. The poll tax was abandoned in 1950, and in 1952 there were 341,000 votes cast for President. While lifting the tax was not exclusively responsible for more than doubling the vote, it was a material factor. Local personal machines have used the device to entrench themselves by block buying

[2] Literature on the poll tax is abundant. See especially F. D. Ogden, *The Poll Tax* (doctoral dissertation, Johns Hopkins University, 1951); F. P. Graham et al., *The Poll Tax* (Washington, D.C.; Public Affairs Press, 1940); Hearings before a Subcommittee of the Senate Committee on the Judiciary, 77th Cong., 2d Sess.; and Donald Strong, "The Poll Tax: The Case of Texas," *The American Political Science Review*, Vol. 38 (1944), pp. 695–696.

[3] See Strong, *op. cit.*, pp. 702–703.

of the poll-tax receipts and distributing them to "friends" of the organization. The argument that the poll tax keeps the illiterate from voting is not impressive, for literacy tests can accomplish the same purpose. The threat of Federal action is leading many in the South to recommend state action. The Southern Conference for Human Welfare, the Southern Women's Committee to Abolish the Poll Tax, the Southern Electoral Reform League, various good-government leagues, and other liberal groups are marshaling facts and attacking the law. They argue on a point precious to the Southerner, states' rights. In order to head off Federal action and preserve states' rights, they contend, the states must change the provision themselves. With the poll tax under strong attack from both the outside and the inside of these states, it would seem only a matter of time before its abolition.

Literacy Tests. Each state originally had the sensible requirement that in order to receive the franchise, one must be of sound mind. Beyond this, the states, until about a century ago, required no test of literacy or intelligence for voting. However, with the elimination of property and taxpaying tests, proponents of a narrow suffrage were compelled to look elsewhere for restrictions. One of the devices found was that of literacy. Today some 18 states employ restrictions of this character and a few other legislatures are empowered to create such provisions. A geographical basis is noted in this connection. Eight of the states with this limitation are found in the South. Nearly all of the Atlantic states from Maine to Florida, the three Pacific Coast states, Arizona, and Wyoming require evidence of literacy. This requisite is curiously absent from all the Middle Western states, suggesting that reasons other than pure logic or faith in education were paramount. Broadly, immigration and the resulting desire to control the influence of foreign-born citizens were important in New England and in the Far West, while the literacy tests in the South were used against the Negroes and the whites in the lower strata. Native American and Know-Nothing societies brought about a literacy test in Connecticut in 1855 and in Massachusetts in 1857. In the latter states these groups, together with the Whigs, hoped to weaken the Irish-Democratic alignment.

The character of these laws shows great variation, from the mere requirement of a signature in California to a full-fledged comprehension test in New York. Most accept simple evidence of the ability to read and write English. Several Southern states require a prospective voter, at the time of registration, to read a paragraph in the Constitution. Since these tests are administered by the regular election board, they can be strictly or leniently administered to enfranchise or disqualify. Property owning or other alternatives may exempt one from the test. With immigration now restricted to a quota, there seems little justification (if any originally existed) for literacy tests to keep the ballot from the foreign-born.

It is one thing to require evidence of the ability to read and write one's name or simple English. It is quite another to pass an examination showing the ability to comprehend. In 1923 New York passed a law which is the most far-reaching type of literacy test in the nation. The examination is prepared and administered by the state educational authority, the State Board of Regents. Actually this is an intelligence test aimed to limit suffrage to those with at least the intelligence of a ten-year-old. If one can furnish evidence of having graduated from eighth grade, the test is waived. From the standpoint of administration the New York system is far superior to the plan of leaving it in the hands of partisan election officials. A surprising number of persons fail the examination. In 1944, 9.3 per cent or 18,695 out of 199,586 persons were unable to pass the examinations. The majority of those failing the test are foreign-born who have not satisfactorily mastered the English language.

The law has received wide approval from many educators and political scientists as a successful method for weeding out those who are lacking the necessary equipment for comprehending political issues and policies. At the same time, many party leaders have opposed it as "undemocratic." Some educators approve the principle but object to the type of test on the ground that it fails to measure intelligence or the ability of a person to understand a newspaper or printed matter. The argument over the value and nature of intelligence tests from our point of view can be left to educational psychologists.

NEGRO SUFFRAGE

The struggle of Negroes for suffrage and for political power is still going on. It was infused with reconstruction politics in order to keep Northern control over the South. It is now bound up with customs in the South and the struggle for power among the white population. Earlier we saw that Negroes are gaining additional strength through labor unions and various other organizations.[4] Out of this complex picture, a few aspects may be singled out for consideration.[5]

[4] See pp. 104, 187–188.

[5] For other short accounts see S. B. Weeks, "The History of Negro Suffrage in the South," *Political Science Quarterly*, Vol. 9 (1894), pp. 671–703; W. A. Mabry, "Disfranchisement of the Negro in Mississippi," *Journal of Southern History*, Vol. 4 (1938), pp. 318–333, and various publications of the National Association for the Advancement of Colored People. For longer accounts see Paul Lewinson, *Race, Class and Party: A History of Negro Suffrage and White Politics in the South* (New York: Oxford University Press, 1932); Charles S. Mangum, Jr., *Legal Status of the Negro* (Chapel Hill, N.C.: University of North Carolina Press, 1940); Gunnar Myrdal, *An American Dilemma*, Vol. I (New York: Harper & Brothers, 1944), especially Part I; and Henry L.

Early History. Slaves had no legal status and hence no claim to vote. In colonial America free Negroes who were able to meet the regular requirements could vote. After the Revolution in both the North and South racial discrimination was common. Indeed, at the outbreak of the Civil War, Maine, Massachusetts, New Hampshire, Rhode Island, and Vermont were the only states where the "color line" was not drawn, and in these states the number of Negroes was very small. Even the democratic West gave the vote only to white males. The problem of Negro suffrage became acute after the Civil War. The reconstruction program added three amendments to the Federal Constitution destined to bring about great changes in the Negro's social and political status. The Thirteenth Amendment (1865) emancipated him, the Fourteenth conferred citizenship (1869), and the Fifteenth (1870) forbade the denial of suffrage "on account of race, color, or previous condition of servitude."

Prior to the ratification of the Fifteenth Amendment, Congress had imposed Negro suffrage on the ten Southern states as part of the policy of reconstruction. This was done through the Reconstruction Act of Mar. 2, 1867. This aspect of the program was without the approval of Presidents Lincoln and Johnson. The new state constitutions also were required to permit Negro suffrage. The reconstructionists, however, were realists enough to know that these provisions could be circumvented. Hence the Fifteenth Amendment was added to give permanency and Federal sanction to the newly awarded right to vote. Only a few supported the Fifteenth Amendment on the basis of natural rights and democracy. Congress pushed Negro suffrage because it best served the radical Republican program of reconstruction. The withdrawal of the military governors and Federal troops in 1877 paved the way for exclusion of the Negro from political life and the reestablishment of white control.

The use of the gerrymander for a time bottled up the Negroes in a few districts. Poll taxes and literacy tests came into use. When many whites found themselves disfranchised by the literacy test, the alternative was sometimes added of exemption from the test if one owned a certain amount of property. An ingenious alternative was provided in the "grandfather clause." This law provided that anyone who was the descendant of a person who was qualified to vote before the Reconstruction could vote even though he failed to fulfill certain other qualifications. By this law illiterate whites could qualify by claiming that they were descendants of persons who voted prior to 1867, while Negroes could claim no such exemption from the test. In 1915 the United States Supreme Court invalidated the grandfather clause as a violation of the Fifteenth Amend-

Moon, *Balance of Power: The Negro Vote* (New York: Doubleday & Company, Inc., 1948).

ment.[6] This decision did not, however, bring about the enfranchisement of Negroes in the Southern states, which have utilized a number of legal devices to keep the Negro from voting.

Current Restrictions. Earlier we saw that the poll tax and literacy tests keep the ballot from many Negroes. To these may be added a long list of administrative techniques. As a matter of fact, it is not so much the provisions of the law as the discriminatory administration of the law by white election boards that results in keeping the Negro from voting. In some communities the "problem" is solved for white election authorities by merely failing to provide any polls in which the Negroes may vote. If the Negroes go into areas where there are polls, they are told that they are "out of their own election district." Others are simply told that they "do not have enough education" or they "fail to fulfill other requirements for voting." Literacy tests when administered by election boards are especially susceptible to administrative manipulation. Negroes are often asked to define such complicated terms as "mandamus," "civil code," and "due process of law." A Negro law professor in Mississippi, for example, was asked to explain "due process" but, after giving the board a learned answer, was told that his answer was not "reasonable," and under the law of that state he was rejected. Several states require applicants to be able to read the Constitution "and give a reasonable interpretation thereof," which permits the white election officials to reject Negro applicants by ruling that their explanation is not "reasonable."

In Alabama persons specifically disqualified from registering and voting include those convicted of robbery, burglary, assault and battery on the wife, bigamy, living in adultery, or vagrancy.[7] It has been somehow found easier to enforce these provisions against a prospective Negro than a white voter. Testimony has been presented to investigating committees that Negroes attempting to vote were arrested on trumped-up charges of drunkenness and disorderly conduct. "Character tests" are still found in Georgia and Louisiana. These require Negroes to be vouched for by whites or to be known to the election registrars. Such tests are obviously subject to abuse.

A Senate Campaign Investigating Committee amassed much evidence in 1946 that registration officials made every effort to keep Negroes from registering in Mississippi. Officials were candid in admitting that they counseled Negroes in advance not to try to register and if they did appear, they were asked "more difficult questions on governmental organization than the whites." [8] Registration procedure is a powerful weapon to keep

[6] *Guinn v. United States*, 238 U.S. 347.

[7] Noted by Prof. Charles W. Smith, Jr., "The Negro in Alabama Politics," in a paper presented to the American Political Science Association, Dec. 27, 1940.

[8] A fairly comprehensive account of this hearing is given in *The New York Times*, Dec. 3 and 4, 1946.

Negroes, newcomer whites, and "troublemakers" from voting. Lowell Mellett,[9] newspaper columnist and former Federal official, reports the "economical" operation of the Byrd machine in Virginia in this connection:

You're a newcomer, so you ask your nearest neighbor where one goes to register. He doesn't know, nor does your next nearest neighbor. So you go over to the county seat. If you're persistent, you will find someone who can and will tell you. You go to the place indicated, and, if there's anybody at home, you are told that isn't the place any more. Yep, it used to be, but it's been changed. Guess the feller over to the courthouse didn't know. The place to get registered now is at Old Man Smith's over on the other side of Blossom Corners. You take the little dirt road that runs off to the left catty-cornered across from the grocery store at Blossom and foller it 4 mile, mebbe 5 mile. . . . No he ain't got any phone; you'll have to drive over and see if he's home.

Old Man Smith isn't at home the first time. The second time Mrs. Old Man Smith is a little doubtful about calling him in out of the garden but she is persuaded . . . and he is called in. But he hunts for his spectacles. They are hard to find. Then he hunts for the book. It is even harder to find although he is sure he left it right there on top of that other book when that lady came over to register just before Easter. Then there isn't any ink in the bottle, and he doesn't suppose you've got a fountain pen. Fortunately, you have.

The brown crackling pages of the books are turned to one bearing your initial and there you inscribe your name, the first fresh name to decorate that page in a long time, judging by the appearances.

So you are registered, you hope, and it may turn out that you really are; it doesn't always, as some would-be voters discover when they show up at the polls.

When other methods fail, intimidation, threat, or actual use of force is sometimes resorted to. The Ku Klux Klan has threatened the Negro with physical punishment. An investigation was made of the election activities of the late Senator Theodore W. Bilbo as they related to keeping Negroes from the polls. A number of Negro war veterans told a Senate committee that they were beaten up when they tried to vote.[10]

[9] *Washington Evening Star*, Feb. 20, 1945. A CIO director in Virginia reports, "It is plain to see that a Negro would have had very great difficulty in getting his name on the [registration] books. Here are the circumstances: the place of registration was a home in a small white workingmen's neighborhood. It would be an odd and unusual sight for a Negro to be coming down that street. Secondly, the registrar was a lady. Thirdly, the place of registration was her front parlor. Fourth, she kept a very large dog. Fifth, her husband sat attentively by while the registration was going on."—From Committee of Editors and Writers of the South, *Voting Restrictions in the 13 Southern States*, a pamphlet published by the authors, Atlanta, Ga., 1945, pp. 20–21. In the same work Hartnett T. Kane says of registration of Negroes in Louisiana, "He is told to come back tomorrow, we are fresh out of application blanks, we will send you a notice when we are ready for you. He is kept away by all sorts of tricks." The keeping of registration books in the home, however, is seldom practiced in other states.

[10] *The New York Times*, Dec. 3, 1948.

This fact was not denied by any of the white registrars called to testify. Senator Bilbo in his campaign speeches was quoted as saying that "red-blooded Anglo-Saxon men must use any means to keep Negroes from voting. If you can't do it otherwise, visit their home the night before election. If you're arrested you'll be tried before a white judge." [11] When asked by a reporter, "Wasn't that in effect to intimidate any Negroes who might have differed with your interpretations of the law and to keep them from voting?" the senator replied, "Well, call it what you may. It's good diplomacy and good strategy to keep them from voting." [12] On another occasion, however, Senator Bilbo said that the preelection-night visit was meant to be only that of "peaceful persuasion."

White Primaries. A most important issue in the current suffrage picture as it applies to Negroes is the white primary. This is fundamental not only because of Negro suffrage and the overwhelming importance of Southern primaries but also because it involves the nature of a political party. It raises again the question of what is a political party. Is a party a public or a private matter? Even before the adoption of the direct primary for nominations, Negroes had been excluded from participation in the affairs of the Democratic party in the South. As primaries came into use many specific party rules limiting participation to whites in the primaries were adopted in many states. In some instances, however, white factions continued to accept some Negro votes. Texas took the lead in sanctioning this exclusion by legislation.[13] A long series of legal niceties has resulted and, if space permitted, would be worth a chapter.

Dr. L. A. Nixon, a Negro physician, challenged the Texas white primary law (enacted in 1923) as a violation of the Fifteenth Amendment and the law was declared void by the United States Supreme Court.[14] The state then enacted a law authorizing the state executive committee "to prescribe the qualifications of its own members." As expected, the state executive committee proceeded to adopt a resolution permitting only qualified white Democrats to vote in the party's primary. Dr. Nixon was again denied the ballot and fought the case to the Supreme Court. The Court invalidated the ruling on the grounds that the legislature had no authority to vest such power in an executive committee independent of the party.[15] To do so was to make the committee an organ of the state and the exclusion of Negroes by a committee so authorized was a denial

[11] *New York Post,* Dec. 3, 1948.

[12] From a transcript of this program, "Senator Bilbo Meets the Press," *American Mercury,* Vol. 63 (1946), pp. 525–534.

[13] See O. D. Weeks, "The White Primary," *Mississippi Law Journal,* Vol. 13 (1935), pp. 133–153, and "The Texas White Primary System," *Southwestern Social Science Quarterly,* Vol. 13 (1932), pp. 1–26.

[14] *Nixon v. Herndon,* 273 U.S. 536 (1927).

[15] *Nixon v. Condon,* 286 U.S. 73 (1932).

by the state of equal protection of the laws. Texas Democrats were not long in overcoming this ruling by calling a party convention which adopted a white rule for the primary.

This action now presented the Court with a new question, the legal nature of parties. In a unanimous opinion the Court upheld the white primary which had been adopted at the party convention.[16] Parties were viewed as being voluntary associations and "not creatures of the state." The cost of conducting the primary, it was noted, was not borne by the state but entirely by the party. As a private association, then, the Democrats were within their rights and the state was depriving no one of equal protection. This appeared to settle the issue in Texas once and for all. But in other states, where government financed the Democratic primary, white primaries were on less secure ground.

The question was not long settled. In 1941, the decision handed down in *United States v. Classic* ruled that the primaries were an integral part of elections and, therefore, within the scope of Federal action [17] and said that interference with the right to vote in a Louisiana Democratic congressional primary was in effect "an interference with the effective choice of the voters at the only stage of the election procedure when their choice is of significance." In relying on the "unitary character of the electoral process" as set forth in the Classic case, the Court in the *Smith v. Allwright* [18] case reversed the *Grovey v. Townsend* ruling. Concisely, the Court viewed the Texas primary as an integral part of election. It noted that the state regulated many aspects of the primary and that it was therefore discriminating when it permitted the white primary. Such action, the Court held, violated the Fifteenth Amendment.

The Allwright decision was widely denounced by Southern Democrats as "a political decision of a political court," but condemnation of the Court did not solve their problems. South Carolina returned to the good old days by repealing, in 1944, every law governing the primary. This left nominations uncontrolled by law and placed their management entirely in party hands. The following year, the Georgia and Florida supreme courts upheld the right of Negroes to vote as Democrats in primary elections in these states. Arkansas set up two primaries, one for Federal, the other for state and local nominations. Negroes, in compliance with the Allwright decision, were allowed to participate in the primaries for Federal nominations, but not for state and local affairs. This system

[16] *Grovey v. Townsend*, 295 U.S. 45 (1935). At the time the decision was rendered, the Newberry decision was still the ruling law. In effect, the Newberry ruling said that the Federal government had no jurisdiction over the conduct of primaries.

[17] 313 U.S. 299. See Chap. 23 above. This ruling reopened the way for a testing of the legality of state primary laws applicable to the election of Federal officers which discriminated against Negroes.

[18] 321 U.S. 649 (1944).

was later repealed and an increasing number of Negroes are voting in the primaries. In several other states numerous politicians had advocated the South Carolina plan but waited for a test of its legality.

In 1947 Judge J. W. Waring, a Southerner, declared the nomination procedure invalid and asserted it was "pure sophistry" to find "any natural difference" in the governance of the South Carolina primary before and after the private-club plan was adopted.[19] The Circuit Court quickly upheld the decision, emphasizing that no election machinery could be countenanced whose purpose was to deny the Negro "an effective voice in the government of his country or the state or the community in which he lives." The Supreme Court declined to review the lower court decision. Another suit in 1948 compelled admission of Negroes to membership in the party. Several states then repealed their limitations.

Political Participation. The legal barrier to Negro participation in Democratic primaries is thus conclusively removed. The extent to which new subterfuges can be found is yet to be demonstrated. There is a tightening up of registration machinery and the use of literacy tests may become more important. In Alabama, for example, an amendment adopted in 1951 empowered county registrars to determine the fitness of those seeking to register, such as being of "good character" and "embracing the duties and obligations of citizenship." In 1950 South Carolina adopted a law designed to reduce Negro participation in Democratic primaries. It requires that voters must be able to "both read and write" a section of the state constitution. The requirement is waived if the person owns $300 in property and has paid all taxes on it.

The "custom" of Negroes to refrain from voting is still present and the removal of the obstacle to active citizenship through the ballot will not result in a mass Negro vote in the South. Enfranchisement of the Negro will continue to be modified by the pattern of racial relationships in the local community.

Although fragmentary data of Negro registration and voting in certain cities and counties are available as a result of special studies, it is impossible to obtain reliable figures on the number of Negro voters in the country at large. Negro leaders have estimated that about 1,180,000 Negroes were registered in 1952 in the 12 Southern states.[20] This included about 175,000 in Texas, out of a Negro population of 886,000, and 120,913 in Florida, in a total registration of 1,213,000. These figures showing the fractional character of registered Negroes are fairly typical of the other

[19] For the decision and its appeal see *Elmore v. Rice*, 72 F. Supp. 516 (1947), 165 F. 2d 887 (1947), and 68 Sup. Ct. 905 (1948). See also O. Douglas Weeks, "The White Primary: 1944–1948," *The American Political Science Review*, Vol. 42 (1948), pp. 500–570.

[20] For a state-by-state summary see *The New York Times*, Aug. 11, 1952.

states. Very few reliable estimates are available on the number of Negroes actually voting. Governor James Byrnes of South Carolina said that 60,-000 Negroes voted in the general election of 1952 in his state. Increases in the Negro vote have been largely in the urban areas, and in states which have a proportionately smaller Negro population. Negroes are participating in increased numbers in nonpartisan municipal elections.

Evidence indicates that Southern Negroes are largely Democratic in sympathy and recognize that the party is a more effective channel to work through than the Republican. The Republicans as a rule have been as "Lily-white" as the Democrats, so Negroes have found no special advantage in becoming Republican. A few Negroes have been elected to party offices.

As may be expected, Negroes in the South as yet have few opportunities for nomination and election to public office. There are some isolated instances, however, where they have been elected to municipal offices. A Negro was elected to the city council of Richmond, Va., and the president of Atlanta University was elected to the city board of education in 1953. The Supreme Court's ruling outlawing segregation in the public schools in 1954 will mean that Negroes will give increased attention to voting in school elections and probably will encourage a larger number of Negroes to seek positions on the school boards.

In summary, the Negro in the South is participating in elections to a greater extent than formerly and is finding fewer obstacles in the cities to voting than in rural areas. Numerous white groups are aiding him in seeking the franchise and the courts have struck down many legal obstacles. Social custom which discourages Negroes from voting is a powerful factor. It is no longer so much a threat of violence as it is the fact that in many communities if a Negro attempts to vote he will incur the hostility of influential white citizens of the community. The failure to vote is commonly attributed to "apathy," but it would be more accurate to credit it to social pressure combined with the discriminatory administration of the election laws.

Although the Negro's struggle for franchise is concluded in the North, the sizable amount of nonvoting among Negroes has caused concern and embarrassment to their leaders. Both major parties seek his vote and when the balance between the Republicans and Democrats is close in the Northern cities, the Negro vote can, potentially, swing an election. This has led both parties to court the Negroes through promises of distribution of patronage, fair-employment practices and public-housing laws and other favors. In predominantly Negro neighborhoods, precinct and district leadership positions are given to him. It appears that Negroes no longer cast their votes in blocs for Republican candidates, and there is a developing tendency for them to cast their votes on other lines than the racial issue. When this is fully accomplished, opposition to Negro voting may decline in areas outside the North. Fear of a "Negro voting bloc" has been a deterrent to the granting of franchise.

As for elective positions, the Northern Negro has not fared as well as many of their leaders hoped.[21] Only a few Negroes have been elected to Congress or to important positions in the Northern states. Many, however, are elected to city councils and the state legislatures. A number have received reasonably important administrative positions, though not those of higher rank. For legislation benefiting their welfare Negroes must still look to the white legislator, but the lawmaker in turn cannot ignore the fact that his tenure in a considerable measure may rest upon justifiable services to and understanding of the group he so long held in bondage.

WOMAN SUFFRAGE

Developments. The dramatic movement toward woman suffrage, covering over a century and a half, is replete with amusing incidents and with heartaches, with female persistency and with male arrogance. Franchisement is only a part of woman's long struggle, still in progress, for social, economic, and political emancipation both here and throughout the world. Women had only limited success in acquiring the right to vote in national elections before the present century. Woman suffrage was established in New Zealand in 1893, but not in France until 1944. It is still absent in many nations of the world.

To modern Americans many of the arguments used against franchisement for women seem ridiculous, but at the time of their utterance they were far from amusing to either side. Most of them stemmed from the fundamental proposition that women were inferior to and subordinate to men. Accordingly, woman suffrage, which was identified with equality, was condemned by many religionists as a violation of God's law and natural law. Man's world under common law regarded them as minors. Obviously, then, the ballot could not and should not be trusted to minors. In this respect the status of woman and the Negro slave was remarkably similar.

Many men recognized that political equality would eventually result in economic equality, with consequent female competition in the vocations. This fear of upsetting the *status quo* in the social system, though usually cloaked by one of the other objections, became a very real one to many men in the later stages of the movement.

The movement for elective franchise for women in America is a long and involved story. Here we can only sketch the major developments.

[21] For an excellent analysis and presentation of data on the Negro in politics see J. E. Miller, "The Negro in Present-day Politics with Special Reference to Philadelphia," *The Journal of Negro History*, Vol. 33 (1948), pp. 303–343.

In the United States the struggle was connected with several other movements, including (1) the general effort to secure political and economic rights, (2) the contest over emancipation and the eventual enfranchisement of the Negro, (3) the Populist movement and liberalization of suffrage in the West, and (4) the Progressive era. The feminists first strove to secure equality before the law. In 1776 a few women protested taxation of their sex without representation. Attention was then turned to securing property rights for married women. By the 1840's a definite movement for reform was under way. At a historic local convention at Seneca Falls, N.Y., a "Declaration of Sentiments," modeled after the Declaration of Independence, was drafted. It drew up a list of grievances against man and pointed out how he subjugated woman legally, religiously, educationally, economically, and morally. The Declaration concluded with a demand for full rights and privileges of citizenship, which included the right to vote. Although this failed to bring enfranchisement, it soon resulted in reform legislation granting important property rights to married women.

In the meantime, many women were learning the techniques of agitation by joining abolitionist societies. They found striking similarities between the theories advanced for emancipation of the Negroes and their own cause. But the male abolitionists on the whole were unenthusiastic about tying their cause to that of the "hyenas in petticoats" and the "unsexed women in bloomers." These statements referred to some of the extremists, who wore long-legged boots and short petticoats or bloomers. Momentarily the slavery issue and the Civil War overshadowed the cause.

The final decade before the adoption of the Nineteenth Amendment in August, 1920, was full of excitement and successes in the states. The various suffrage associations were combined into a unified National American Woman Suffrage Association, with headquarters in the nation's capital. Alice Paul, who had worked with the English suffragettes, brought new life and militancy to the organization. The Progressive movement was flowering and women secured a voice in the Bull Moose national convention. By the use of parades, speeches, bands, street dances, and all the arts of propaganda the suffragists pressed their cause. By 1916 women had acquired the right to vote for presidential electors in 11 states, and both major-party platforms that year gave approval to "state action" in granting suffrage. By the close of World War I in 1918 some 29 states permitted women to vote in some form.

While this battle was being waged in the states, Miss Paul was busy organizing spectacular appeals for a Federal amendment and lobbyists were busy working on members of Congress. During the war the White House was picketed and many who resisted arrest for this and other demonstrations were put in jail. While in jail, they resorted to a hunger strike, which further dramatized and publicized the cause. Other developments help to bring about the final drive for a constitutional amendment. Women were in the factories and participating in all aspects of the war effort, a fact which placed them on strong ground for demanding political equality. Women had also contributed much to the cause of temperance and prohibition and in turn were helped by these groups. The organized liquor interests were portrayed as the real foes of woman suffrage. In the idealism of the war the suffragettes proclaimed that if women were given the ballot, they would "purify" politics and help to break up corrupt machines. President Wilson finally championed Federal action and early in 1918 urged Congress to act. The House gave immediate approval, and the necessary two-thirds was mustered in the Senate a year later and ratified by the necessary 36 states in time to become effective in the 1920 election.

Results. Woman suffrage has resulted in fulfilling neither the dire forebodings of its opponents nor the rosy predictions of its proponents. Woman suffrage did not bring an end to political bosses or corruption. The female vote has been similar to the male and women appear to vote fairly generally as their husbands do.[22] Women were rather slow to take advantage of their victory until 1928. Thereafter they came to the polls in increasing numbers and in 1942, due to the wartime reduction of the male vote, more votes were cast by women than men. In several American communities since then there appear to be more women registered to vote than men.

The extension of suffrage carries with it the opportunity for women to run for public office. Figures are unavailable on the number of women serving in city councils and school boards but it is not at all unusual for them to get elected to these bodies; a proportionately small number of women are found in state legislative assemblies, less than 300 out of 5,000 legislative seats. It is unusual for more than 10 of the 531 members of Congress to be women and comparatively few have been elected to important state offices. Several women, however, have received appointment to important Federal and state administrative positions in recent years. The Republican National Committee reported that in 1953, 1,200 women occupied "positions of high policy and administrative authority" in the Federal government.[23]

Probably the most important result of woman suffrage is the increasing number of women who have become interested in public affairs since 1920. This is shown by growing memberships in women's clubs devoted

[22] On this point see W. A. Lydgate, *What America Thinks* (New York: Thomas Y. Crowell Company, 1944), pp. 118 ff.

[23] See *Women in the Public Service*. This is a useful digest of positions held by women in the national, state, and local governments.

to the study of government and politics. Campaign organizations rely heavily on women for the many office duties in headquarters and for various types of campaign activity.

Women received equal representation on the national committees in 1924 and often on the state and county committees of the parties. Women's auxiliaries are taking over an increased share of the work of the parties at all levels. In the national conventions they serve in equal numbers on the resolutions committees but in much fewer numbers on the three other committees. Women have had less success in being selected as delegates to the national conventions. A record high of 129 women delegates and 260 alternates were elected to the 1952 Republican National Convention, while the Democrats have often elected more than 200 women delegates.

NONVOTING

Extent and Variations. It has long been popular to view with alarm the low vote cast in the United States both in national and municipal elections in comparison with European democracies. Participation, moreover, shows sharp fluctuations in both presidential and local elections. In 1948, for example, only 49 million voted in the presidential election, while 61.5 million cast ballots in 1952; the eligible voters who balloted were estimated at 48 and 61 per cent. It is estimated that 79 per cent of the eligible voters turned out in the 1896 contest between Bryan and McKinley, the highest percentage voting in any national election in this country.

Apathy is far more prevalent in municipal elections than in state and national ones. A study of 45 cities in Los Angeles County over a 17-year period showed the turnout for voters in national elections was from 68.4 to 80.6 per cent of those eligible.[24] During the same period, the vote in city elections ranged from 10.3 to 60.9 per cent, with an average turnout of 41.1 per cent. It is not unusual to see bond and school issues defeated in American cities because 10 per cent of the registered electorate failed to vote. Within a given state there is often wide variation in the percentage of eligible voters who cast their ballots. In one Maryland gubernatorial vote there was a 22.8 per cent vote cast in Worcester as compared with 56.5 per cent in Calvert County, and the vote in the Democratic primaries in 1942 ranged from 10 to 80 per cent.

Millions of persons for one reason or another fail to register. Quite a number of these are not able to register because they do not fulfill the suffrage requirements. There is no way of knowing how many are involved but it is probably considerable. They may be soldiers away

[24] L. W. O'Rourke, *Voting Behavior in the Forty-five Cities of Los Angeles County* (Berkeley, Calif.: University of California, Bureau of Governmental Research, 1953).

from home, persons who have recently moved, those who did not pay their poll taxes, and so on. In statistical counts everyone over twenty-one years of age is often classed as a potential voter irrespective of his ability to qualify as a voter. When this kind of count is used, of course, the percentage of nonvoters looks large.[25] The number of persons who are registered but fail to vote is much smaller. In a narrow sense these are the true nonvoters. During the 1940's the polling agencies estimated that about one in six persons who were registered failed to vote in presidential elections or somewhere under 20 per cent. However, as the term nonvoter is loosely used to embrace all persons over twenty-one years of age who fail to vote, most studies of the "slacker" vote use this as a base.

Group Interest and Electoral Participation. Electoral inaction follows a strongly but by no means completely sectional pattern as shown in Table 26. In 1952, about 24 per cent voted in Mississippi at one extreme to about 80 per cent in Utah at the other. Maine ranked fairly low while its neighbor, New Hampshire, ranked fourth highest. Low Negro participation lowers the Southern voting record. The lack of vigorous party competition also appears to cut down the vote, and turnout between the states shows some variations from election to election.

Public-opinion polls, with allowances made for some error, have revealed some interesting data on who are the nonvoters. Again nonvoting varies from election to election. The Survey Research Center of the University of Michigan found that about 60 per cent of the farmers failed to vote in 1948 and the figure was reduced to 34 per cent in 1952; figures for college graduates in the same elections were 28 and 11 per cent respectively.[26] At the same time, the number of Negro nonvoters remained almost constant in the two elections, 70 and 68 per cent respectively. It is possible, however, to make a few generalizations. Men vote in larger numbers than women, though this margin is narrowing; white voters greatly exceed those of other races; the prosperous and those living in better quarters exercise suffrage in larger numbers than poorer people; persons over fifty years of age turn out considerably better than those under fifty, and the more highly educated voters exceed those of less formal education.

The National Opinion Research Center found some interesting vari-

[25] The United States Senate compiled a state-by-state, county-by-county list of this type. It listed all persons twenty-one years of age and then the number who voted in the 1948 presidential and 1950 gubernatorial elections. See *Comparison of Potential Voters and Actual Votes Cast by Counties in Each State in 1948–1950*, 82d Cong., 2d Sess., S. Doc. 150 (1952).

[26] See "Political Issues and the Vote: November, 1952," *The American Political Science Review*, Vol. 47 (1953), pp. 359–385. Nonvoting figures for several other groups will be found in Table 11, p. 268.

Table 26. Electoral Participation by States in 1952

(Ranked by states from lowest to highest)

0–45%	46–69%	70% and over
1. Mississippi........ 24.3	10. Florida......... 50.0	25. California........ 70.0
2. Alabama.......... 24.9	11. North Carolina.. 52.1	26. Kansas.......... 70.2
3. South Carolina.... 30.7	12. Arizona......... 52.6	27. Missouri......... 71.2
4. Georgia........... 30.8	13. Maryland....... 57.5	28. Wisconsin....... 71.4
5. Virginia.......... 31.3	14. Kentucky....... 60.0	29. Nevada.......... 71.5
6. Arkansas......... 37.8	15. Oregon......... 62.7	29. Washington...... 71.5
7. Louisiana......... 40.4	16. New Mexico..... 63.5	30. Colorado........ 71.6
8. Tennessee......... 42.6	17. Maine.......... 64.5	31. Wyoming........ 71.8
9. Texas............ 42.8	18. Pennsylvania.... 65.0	32. Minnesota....... 72.6
	19. Michigan........ 65.6	33. Montana......... 73.2
	20. Vermont........ 66.5	34. South Dakota.... 74.0
	21. New York....... 68.0	34. Massachusetts.... 74.0
	22. Nebraska........ 69.1	35. Indiana.......... 74.5
	23. Ohio............ 69.2	36. Illinois........... 75.0
	23. Oklahoma....... 69.2	37. Iowa............ 75.2
	24. New Jersey...... 69.6	38. Connecticut...... 75.9
		39. North Dakota.... 77.2
		40. West Virginia.... 77.4
		41. New Hampshire.. 77.8
		41. Rhode Island..... 77.8
		42. Idaho........... 78.5
		43. Delaware........ 79.1
		44. Utah............ 79.6

SOURCE: Adapted from *AFL News-Reporter,* Jan. 23, 1953, and *Congressional Record,* Jan. 29, 1953, p. A349. Note ties for 23d, 29th, 34th, and 41st places.

ables in the nonvoters in the 1940 election.[27] Economic status outweighed education. For example, those with only a grade-school education but who were in the upper fourth economically outvoted those who had attended college but were in the lower fourth in income. A larger percentage of managerial, white-collar workers, and those in the professions are voters, followed in order by farmers and manual workers. Service workers, which include domestics, barbers, policemen, and the like, voted in fewer numbers than any other occupational group. Among religious groups, Jews voted in the largest numbers, 84 per cent; followed by 72 per cent of the Catholics and 66 per cent of the Protestants. This pattern of voting by religious groups is generally characteristic. The Protestant percentage is lowered by the many nonvoters in the South

[27] See G. M. Connelly and H. H. Field, "The Non-voter—Who He Is, What He Thinks," *Public Opinion Quarterly,* Vol. 8 (1944), pp. 175 ff.

and by the fact that rural areas, which are predominantly of that faith, vote in far fewer numbers. The Survey Research Center in 1948 found that 60 per cent of rural dwellers failed to vote, while the corresponding figure in the towns and cities was 39 per cent, and in the metropolitan areas, 17 per cent.

Political Activity and Involvement. Democracy implies the participation of all in the control of government. Popular control in the first instance is a matter of voting for candidates and casting a negative or affirmative answer on proposed constitutional amendments, initiatives and referendums, and recall of public officers. Only about a dozen states have provisions for recall, and these are for the most part west of the Mississippi River. There are 20 states which have provisions for initiative and referendum on state statutes. Nearly every voter at some time or another is called upon to vote on local bond issues and amendments to the state constitution. As a general rule, the vote cast on measures is considerably less than for candidates. When interest groups are directly involved, they mobilize their voters. Farmers turn out to vote on daylight-saving time and margarine, the school forces on educational propositions, the veterans on bonuses, the recreationists on parks and fishing matters, and property owners on increased millage on real estate. Where there is not direct involvement there is a tendency to pay less attention to these propositions, notwithstanding appeals to "good citizenship" to vote. Indeed, referendums and initiatives are generally sponsored by organized interests who pay the cost of collecting signatures and running the campaign. Victory at the polls is more likely a victory for good advertising than the result of a great popular uprising.

People often fail to vote on measures because they do not understand or feel the importance of the issue. Their failure to vote on candidates is due partly to the same reason, but the motivations are probably a little more complex. Professors Merriam and Gosnell found indifference the most important single cause of nonvoting in Chicago.[28] Yet, one may ask, why the indifference? Illness, disgust with politics, ignorance of the candidates, bad weather, oversight of registration, and so on were given as other reasons for failure to vote.

The fact that the better-educated and more prosperous vote in larger numbers may indicate an appreciation of their stake in society and a concern for the preservation of the *status quo*. This is at least a hypothesis worthy of examination. The Survey Research Center's sample of 1948 voters indicates that voting participation increases with the level of information on public affairs. If it is assumed that the better-educated are better informed on public questions, then the reason for their larger

[28] *Non-voting* (Chicago: University of Chicago Press, 1927).

voting turnout is understandable. The fact that the younger and the foreign born usually vote in fewer numbers than the older and native Americans illustrates further that assimilation in the community and a sense of involvement in its life and affairs seem to increase voting participation. Negroes offer an exception to this, but the Negro vote is gradually increasing.

These factors have led to the advancement of the thesis that "a large vote favors the Democrats, a small vote, the Republicans." Generally the more prosperous, older, and better-educated voters in the New Deal years appeared to favor Republican presidential candidates. Nonvoting among them was less. Presumably, if the younger and lower income groups could be brought to the polls in larger numbers, the Democrats, particularly those running for Congress, would be helped. This view may have general merit but it has probably been exaggerated. The large vote for Eisenhower in 1952 suggests the need for some revaluation of this proposition, particularly when it is noted that he received (according to the Survey Research sample) a majority of the votes of those placed in the category of young people, of grade-school education, and low income. However, Eisenhower was regarded not as a Republican but rather as an "independent" or "nonpartisan," and the Democratic candidates for Congress did very well considering the size of the Eisenhower vote.

The relationship between voter participation and partisan advantage in municipal elections is not easily established or demonstrated. The percentage of persons casting their ballots in city elections is sometimes in inverse proportion to the excellence of city government. A small vote may indicate satisfaction with the incumbents or with a good slate of candidates put up by the citizens' committees. Connelly and Field found that nonvoters are more inclined to be satisfied with the conduct of their politicians and stay home on election day.[29] In a sense this is a manifestation of the politics of protest. If citizens are satisfied with an incumbent and feel his election is assured, many do not take the trouble to vote. If they are disgusted, they go to the polls to throw the rascals out. Viewed in this light, voting and nonvoting constitutes a fever chart.[30] Except for an issue involving a violent constitutional upheaval, it should not be concluded, however, that a small vote is invariably desirable in terms

[29] *Op. cit.*, pp. 175–176.

[30] For a development of this thesis see Francis G. Wilson, "The Inactive Electorate and the Social Revolution," *Southwestern Social Science Quarterly*, Vol. 16 (1936), pp. 73–84. He writes: "In a society in which only fifty per cent of the electorate participates it is clear that politics does satisfy in a way the desires of the mass of individuals in the state. As the percentage of participation rises above, let us say, ninety per cent it is apparent that the tensions of political struggle are stretching to the breaking point the will of the constitutional."

of stability and order. A large protest vote can often force the party in power to make needed concessions in the direction of social amelioration.

Popular control and political involvement are by no means matters of suffrage. They include activity in a political party, a political interest group, citizens' associations, letter writing to public officials, and related efforts. Data here are less complete than that for voting. Woodward and Roper made a study of political participation and set up an index of four categories—very active, fairly active, fairly inactive, and very inactive.[31] They found a pattern somewhat similar to that of voting, namely, activity increases as one mounts the economic and educational scale. At the same time, many upper groups were not active and plenty of persons in the lower economic level were politically active.

POPULAR CONTROL AND VOTING

Compulsory Voting. "Get-out-the-vote" campaigns are usually commended, yet there is no inherent virtue in a large vote unless those who vote are informed and vote intelligently. A large vote could be obtained by a system of compulsory voting, with fines for failure to register or vote; a few nations use this method.[32] Military dictatorships in Latin America have sometimes found it convenient to use forced voting. In the 1948 election in Paraguay, only one name appeared for presidential candidate, the government's nominee. Write-ins were not allowed. Nonvoters were fined and voters were given a government-attested stamp to place on their registration cards. The card had to be shown whenever the owner wished to secure any form of government service. Those who failed to vote incurred the risk of being unable to obtain a marriage license, a passport, or other essential documents. Although a few American state constitutions permit compulsory voting, no such legislation has been enacted. Our national character and psychology do not provide fertile soil for forced voting to take root. Compulsory voting laws are not promising as a method of encouraging the use of the franchise in the United States.

Voting numbers could be increased considerably by the removal of obstacles to registration. Stringent residence requirements, poll taxes, discriminatory administration of literacy tests, periodic registration, and the like undoubtedly discourage millions of persons from either trying to register or being able to fulfill the qualifications for registration. There are certain suffrage requirements which are based upon expediency rather than on sound democratic philosophy. It behooves each generation to

[31] "Political Activity of American Citizens," *The American Political Science Review,* Vol. 44 (1950), pp. 872–885.

[32] See Herbert Tingsten, *Political Behavior* (London: P. S. King & Staples, Ltd., 1937), Chap. 4.

reexamine the voting requirements in its own state in the light of an enlightened and broadened popular control.

A Shorter Ballot. In the quest for more meaningful popular government, Jacksonian tradition saw the answer as voting and more voting. As the state and local governments added more administrative services, it was assumed that people must choose the officials charged with performing such functions. Succeeding generations placed on the ballot such positions as animal and hide inspectors, sanitary commissioners, school superintendents, state university trustees, and dog wardens, to mention only a few. Not only legislative and executive, but judicial officials as well were added. Initiative, referendum, recall, and direct primaries lengthened the ballot and increased the voters' burden. These developments led to such a fantastic absurdity in one case as a ballot 12 feet long and consisting of almost 500 names. No person can hope to vote intelligently for all the officers or propositions on a long ballot.

Democracy does not require popular election of all officers. The long ballot results in boss rule, which is a negation of democracy. What is important is to control the government and this can be done more effectively by the election of a few conspicuous, responsible officers than by the election of many minor officials. Political scientists are unanimous in believing that the short ballot is one of the first requisites for a more satisfactory popular control.

Briefly, the short ballot principle would restrict the officers popularly elected to those concerned with policy determination. Elections at a given time would be limited to one level of government, namely, (1) presidential and congressional, (2) congressional mid-term, (3) gubernatorial and state legislative, (4) mayor and city council, and (5) county. The separation of Federal, state, and local elections, while desirable, is no remedy for the long ballot; thus the basic concern of the short ballot is simply the drastic reduction of the number of elective offices. Under the short ballot judges and administrative officials would be appointed. The names of presidential electors should be eliminated from the ballot, replacing them with only the names of the presidential and vice presidential candidates. This presidential short ballot is used in many states today.

The principle of the short ballot is sometimes shocking to Americans because of the overemphasis placed upon control of government by voting. In Canada, England, and elsewhere very few public officers are selected at the polls. Through separate elections, the Englishman is called upon to vote only for a member of Commons, a county or borough councilor, borough auditors, and perhaps a parish councilor. At the typical British election the voter casts his ballot for only one person. Among the notable advantages of this plan are the centralization of responsibility for both policy determination and administration, the increased possibility for greater efficiency in administration, and the simplification of the voter's task. Sometimes in the American states the governor is of a different political faith from his fiscal officers, school superintendent, and other administrative officials. The governor's subordinates in these instances owe their appointment to constituents instead of to their chief and this results in confused and decentralized administration. Dispersion of responsibility for administration is likely to be even greater on the municipal and county levels. A short ballot would spare administrators and judges the often onerous and energy-wasting job of campaigning and leave them free to concentrate upon performing their duties efficiently.

Since the drive for a shorter ballot began a half century ago, mountains of evidence and argument have been presented to show the undesirable results and blind voting which accompany the "tablecloth" ballot. Progress has not been so rapid as hoped for. A few states have amended their constitutions, abolishing some elective offices. Yet it is still common to find six or more administrative offices on the ballot. Very little headway has been made against the great offender—the county government. County-manager adoptions proceed at a snail's pace and county reorganization has not often resulted in any substantial reduction in the number of popularly chosen officers.

The story as applied to cities is a happier one. Nearly every city has a shorter ballot than it had in 1910. The transformation from weak to strong mayor-council systems has given the mayor the power to appoint his department heads, and under the commission form the commissioners themselves become department heads. City-manager plans in over 1,200 municipalities now place the selection of personnel largely in the hands of the manager.

The voter's burden would also be decreased through the adoption of a four-year term for members of the state legislature and the United States House of Representatives. These changes have highly respected proponents and may in time be adopted. Longer tenure for legislators, however, is not purely a question of eliminating a mid-term election for the voter, it must also be reviewed in terms of its effect on party responsibility, responsiveness of the legislature to changes in public opinion, and the effect of a four-year as opposed to a two-year term on the individual legislator.

Voter Education. Education is the panacea offered for curing most of our ills, and perhaps education as such is often overrated. The teacher and student of government are, nevertheless, correct in their belief that a promising method of increasing popular control of government is the long road of political education. This does not consist of compulsory citizenship courses in the schools, but the schools can play a part. Civic or adult education must become a greater channel for enlightenment than ever before. The press, radio, motion pictures, and political parties must strengthen their part. The programs of the League of Women Voters, labor unions, business and professional men's clubs, citizens' associations, ethnic groups, and even churches are devoting more and more attention to political education. Political activities of these organizations, moreover, provide a means of exerting influence in the government.

Political education propagated by organized groups is often unrealistic, inaccurate, or prejudiced. One reason for the shortcoming is the failure to perceive objectives beyond what appears to be the interest of the group's clientele or to relate the organization's goals to the broader ones of genuine reform and responsible government. Labor unions have been known to side with party organizations to oppose enabling acts for city-manager systems. Farm organizations have likewise sometimes joined with an entrenched political bureaucracy to resist county reorganization. A meritorious plan for consolidation of counties in a certain state a few years ago was defeated when patriotic organizations denounced the whole idea as "un-American." Other well-meaning groups have joined with dubious groups to defeat ratification of a new state constitution or proposals for calling a constitutional convention. Party organizations too often regard the beginning and the end of their work as getting out the vote. Reformist citizens' and women's groups are quite generally clear on worthy goals but weak on an understanding of the realities of practical politics and political action. It is, unfortunately, not enough to have one's heart in the right place.

Education in popular control of government might begin with an analysis of the functions and limitations of voting. It would show that the ballot is at best a very imperfect test for registering public opinion or even exercising democratic control of government. In the nature of things, the voters usually do little more than express approval or disapproval of the administration. The ballot is the ultimate sanction whereby public opinion controls government, but more refined tools of democratic control are necessary on the multitude of popular issues. An understanding of voting within the framework of the theory and practice of representative government and the meaning of majority rule is a prerequisite to intelligent voting and other forms of civic participation.

The realistic and useful citizen is one who knows that voting for candidates is an important but nonetheless small part of political participation. He is concerned with reformation of governmental organization and procedure in the interests of greater responsibility and effective control. On the local level this requires a knowledge of how his city and county are really governed and the accessibility of information which will bring him into contact with proposals such as the city- and county-manager plans, metropolitan government, and reorganization, which promise to bring more efficient and centralized management. When this is done, John Q. Citizen will be able to act with sincere groups in bringing changes before the voters and in voting on the proposals submitted to the electorate to achieve them. He is now in a position to assume some leadership in his citizens' association, nonpartisan committee, and political party in gaining acceptance for charter or constitutional amendments which make popular government more meaningful.

SELECTED REFERENCES

Two excellent historical works on suffrage are Kirk H. Porter, *A History of Suffrage in the United States* (1918); and A. E. McKinley, *The Suffrage Franchise in the Thirteen Colonies* (1905). See also D. O. McGovney, *The American Suffrage Medley* (1949). The various qualifications for voting in all the states may be found in the *Book of the States, 1945–46,* p. 88. Among the many discussions of the poll tax, the following are the most helpful: F. P. Graham et al., *The Poll Tax* (1940); L. B. Boudin, "State Poll Taxes and the Federal Constitution," *Virginia Law Review,* Vol. 28 (1941), pp. 1–25; Jennings Perry, *Democracy Begins at Home* (1944); and *The Poll Tax,* published by the American Association of University Women (1942).

On Negro suffrage see Paul Lewinson, *Race, Class, and Party* (1930); C. S. Mangum, Jr., *The Legal Status of the Negro* (1940); Gunnar Myrdal, *An American Dilemma* (1944), especially Vol. I; Ralph Bunche, *The Political Status of the Negro,* a research memorandum (unpublished, Harlem Library, New York, 1940); Kelly Miller, *The American Negro as a Political Factor* (1910); Henry L. Moon, *Balance of Power: The Negro Vote* (1948).

A monumental four-volume work on woman suffrage was edited by Elizabeth Cady Stanton et al., *History of Woman Suffrage* (1881–1902). See also Ida H. Harper, *The History of Woman Suffrage* (1922); C. C. Catt and N. R. Shuler, *Woman Suffrage and Politics* (1923); Doris Stevens, *Jailed for Freedom* (1920); Emmeline Pankhurst, *The Suffragette Movement* (1931); National American Woman Suffrage Association, *Victory: How Woman Won It. A Centennial Symposium, 1840–1940* (1940); and Annabel Paxton, *Women in Congress* (1945). The most up-to-date materials on women in politics are provided by the regular publications of the National League of Women Voters, Washington, D.C.

Some of the better works on voting and nonvoting problems and on electoral behavior are Louis H. Bean, *Ballot Behavior* (1940); Charles H. Titus, *Voting Behavior in the United States: A Statistical Study* (1935); Harold F. Gosnell, *Getting Out the Vote* (1927) and *Why Europe Votes* (1930); James K. Pollock, *Voting Behavior: A Case Study* (1939); Herbert Tingsten, *Political Behavior* (1937); Charles E. Merriam and Harold F. Gosnell, *Non-voting* (1924).

CHAPTER 24

Opinion Measurement

What I want is to get done what the people desire to have done, and the question for me is to find that out exactly.

—ABRAHAM LINCOLN

One of the recurring problems of this volume has been that of popular control of government. In a government based upon the popular will, the press, radio, television, the political interest group, and the political party seek to influence public opinion and bring it to bear on the government. Much of our discussion to this point has dealt with these matters. The public official wants to know both preponderant opinion and minority opinion and, moreover, which is which. With James Bryce he often says to himself, "Such is the din of voices that it is hard to say which cry prevails, which is swelled by the many, which only by a few throats." The quest of the conscientious public servant is one of ascertaining opinion and evaluating it.

Many congressmen assiduously study their mail and communications from back home in the form of telegrams, newspaper editorials, and talks with constituents. These often highlight complaints and requests for action but provide an imperfect measurement of the general status of opinion. By reading his mail with discretion and making proper discounts for certain deluges of messages on certain matters, he is able to form some estimate of needs, moods, and attitudes.

The ballot box is the oldest and simplest form of recording public opinion. It records the choice between candidates and the "yes" and "no" on propositions. The election shows that voters prefer A to B, but beyond this point what is revealed? Was A's victory a mandate to lower taxes, reduce foreign aid, repeal the Taft-Hartley law, and for rigid price supports for farm products? Seasoned political observers are cautious in attributing defeat or victory to any simple factor and in attaching too much significance to the so-called "electoral mandate." Personal popularity, machine support, or other factors may result in returning a congressman with a poor voting record. The ballot box does not tell *why* people voted as they did nor can it measure the *intensity* of an individual or collective opinion. To answer these questions, follow-up studies which attempt to isolate qualitative factors and weigh them are necessary.

570

Election outcomes, however, may reveal discontent or confidence with incumbents and, though vague, are an important way of recording opinion.

Many newspapers conduct straw votes on certain public issues and on elections. Some of these simply ask readers to cut out coupons and mail them in, others have reporters stop persons on the street or go from door to door on a sampling basis. These polls are apt to get responses from the most interested and their samples are more or less random rather than based upon a scientific formula. In 1936 the *Literary Digest,* using mail ballots, predicted a Landon landslide over Roosevelt, with the latter obtaining only 41 per cent of the popular vote. Roosevelt received 60.7 per cent of the vote and the magazine was liquidated. Since that time newspaper and magazine polls have enjoyed less prestige, but predictions of electoral outcome are still a favorite pastime.

Social scientists have not contented themselves merely with studies of the manifestations of public opinion nor with analysis of opinion-forming agencies. Quantitative scientific description of attitudes and interests has become one of the many new fields of social science. Commercial agencies make great use of market-analyst authorities to determine public attitudes toward products. Radio and television advertisers hire analysts to discover the popularity of their programs and have been known to drop singers, commentators, and entertainers who fail to "rate" on the Hooper poll. The techniques used in commercial polling have been carried over into the field of elections and attitudes toward public issues. Many organizations do both types of polling. Among the better-known polls which also do pre-election polling and often conduct surveys on public issues are the American Institute of Public Opinion (AIPO), popularly called the Gallup poll because of its director Dr. George Gallup; the Roper polls, some of which are carried in *Fortune* magazine; the Crossley poll, which specializes in radio-listener opinions, and the Princeton poll, conducted by specialists in various fields. These are often called "scientific" polls because of the greater care with which the groups select the sample, prepare the questions, and evaluate the results. The student of politics is particularly interested in their pre-election surveys on candidates and various polls taken between elections on public issues.

PRE-ELECTION SURVEYS

Table 27 presents the results of the leading polls in recent presidential elections. Figures for the 1952 polls are not included because they were circumscribed with qualifications not present in the previous elections and an erroneous impression might be gained by simply putting the figures in the table. The poll directors were extraordinarily careful and overly cautious in 1952 because of the results of their 1948 forecasts.

Table 27. Polling Results in Presidential Elections

Election year	Actual Democratic vote	*Literary Digest*	Gallup poll	Roper poll	Crossley poll	Princeton OPOR	Denver NORC
1936	60.7	40.9	53.8	61.7	53.8	....	....
1940	55.0	....	52.0	55.2	....	....	....
1944	53.8	....	53.3	53.6	52.2	53.3	51.7
1948	49.9	....	44.5	37.2	44.9	....	....

SOURCE: All figures are in percentage. The Denver and Gallup poll figures in 1944 apply only to civilian vote. For an analysis of the polling results in each of these elections see Jerome H. Spingorn, "These Public Opinion Polls," *Harper's Magazine*, Vol. 178 (1938), pp. 97–104; Daniel Katz, "The Public Opinion Polls and the 1940 Election," *Public Opinion Quarterly*, Vol. 5 (1941), pp. 52–78, and "The Pol's and the 1944 Election" by the same author in *Public Opinion Quarterly*, Vol. 8 (Winter, 1944–1945), pp. 468–482.

Nationally, Eisenhower received 55.1 per cent of the votes for all candidates. The Crossley poll gave him 47.4 per cent, Stevenson 42.3, and the remaining per cent reported as undecided. Gallup gave 47 per cent to Eisenhower, 40 per cent to Stevenson, and 13 per cent recorded as undecided. He then equated the undecided, first on a 2 to 1 Democratic basis, which came to 51 per cent for Eisenhower, 49 per cent for Stevenson. With a 3 to 1 Democratic allocation, the race ended 50-50. Gallup foresaw in any event a "tight race for the popular-vote majority." The Princeton Research Service saw Eisenhower with a 50.2 per cent lead. Roper found 10 per cent undecided but gave a small edge to Eisenhower.

Considering the magnitude of the task, the Gallup and Roper polls forecast the electoral victories of Mr. Roosevelt in 1936, 1940, and 1944 with a fair degree of accuracy. From the beginning, all the polls showed Mr. Dewey well ahead in 1948. In September Mr. Roper announced that President Truman had only 37.2 per cent of the popular vote. He regarded the race as over and said there would be no further reports unless a change were indicated. Shortly before election day Roper reiterated his earlier forecast and Crossley and Gallup gave the President less than 45 per cent of the popular vote in their final statement. President Truman repeatedly criticized the results and called them "sleeping polls."

The stunning error of the polls was the object of widespread discussion and resulted in soul searching by the pollsters themselves. Most of them agreed the major error rested in their allocation of the silent or undecided vote. Dr. Gallup estimated that 75 per cent of this vote went at the last moment to Truman and that there was a large eleventh-hour switch from Wallace to Truman which the polls failed to detect.[1] There were, moreover, an unusually large number of "don't know" and "late deciders," probably enough to make for considerable error when not properly weighed or evaluated. Two other factors may have been important. Organized labor quietly mobilized its forces prior to and on election day and the polls completed their surveys several days in advance of election day. Many respondents concealed their intention to vote for Truman by "don't know" answers, for Truman was on the side of less prestige. This included both labor and farm voters.

With public confidence in the polls badly shaken as a result of the 1948 pre-election forecasts, the pollsters approached the 1952 elections with the caution of once bitten, twice shy. As noted earlier, they were careful to hedge, particularly in estimating where the undecided vote would go. In his final poll Roper said, "There are enough people still undecided to throw this election either way." An Associated Press dispatch the day before the election reported that the four major polls "inclined to think Eisenhower is ahead" but "none of them flatly predicted he would win." In some ways the 1952 result should have been easier to forecast because it was a clear contest between Eisenhower and Stevenson with no formidable third parties to complicate the picture. Yet the polls greatly underestimated the strength of Eisenhower. Because of the care they took in presenting variations on the basis of equating the undecided vote, the margin of error cannot be determined. In ten key pivotal states, all of which went for Eisenhower by comparable margins, Gallup found two going to Stevenson, one tied, with Eisenhower just barely ahead in a few others. One week before the election the Princeton Research poll found Stevenson leading in 25 states and Eisenhower in 23 states, with the latter, however, ahead in popular and electoral votes. Even if Eisenhower had been given all of the undecided vote, his popular strength would have been 52.7 per cent, a figure quite a bit short of his demonstrated strength. From any point of view, there was a considerable margin of error in 1952, but the fact that Eisenhower did win saved the polls from the sharp popular criticism which they received in 1948.

A few generalizations may be made about the pre-election forecasts of the reputable polls during the five presidential elections from 1936

[1] See statements by Crossley, Gallup, and Roper in *The New York Times*, Nov. 4, 1948. For fuller analyses of the errors see F. Mosteller et al., *The Pre-election Polls of 1948* (New York: Social Science Research Council, 1949); Daniel Katz, "An Analysis of the 1948 Polling Predictions," *Journal of Applied Psychology*, Vol. 33 (1949), pp. 15–28; and the symposium in *International Journal of Opinion and Attitude Research*, Vol. 3 (1949).

to 1952. During the first four, the Gallup poll consistently underestimated Democratic strength while the Roper poll in the first two overestimated it. Improved techniques cut down the Gallup margin of average state error from 6.0 per cent in 1936 to 3.6 per cent in 1940 and 2.4 per cent in 1944. The poll allows itself a margin of error of 4 per cent. In every election this maximum deviation was exceeded in eight or more states. Taking the 188 state forecasts of the Democratic vote in the elections from 1936 to 1948 as presented by Gallup, about 45 per cent of the cases came within 4 per cent of the Democratic vote.[2] Over half the forecasts ranged from −4 to +4 per cent, or a spread of 8 per cent, of actual Democratic percentage. Each reader will determine for himself the degree to which this is a reasonably precise measurement. With the exception of 1948, the pollsters have had the luck to be on the winning side and certain margins of error have been overlooked. The rather substantial underestimation of Eisenhower strength in 1952 also indicates the need for continued improvement in polling techniques before their estimates can be considered reliable in future elections.

Perhaps the most important conclusion to draw is that every election is different, with a different set of imponderables and variables. Voters behaved rather similarly during the polling on Mr. Roosevelt's three reelections. But in 1948 it was Truman, not Roosevelt, who was running and voters were slow to make up their minds, or at least to express them, a factor less present than formerly. In 1952, the pollsters had a tendency to give more of the undecided vote to Stevenson because of the 1948 experience. But the voters did not behave that way. The silent vote had either made up its mind for Eisenhower and was not telling or else gravitated at the last moment in wholesale numbers to him. In view of the great popularity which Eisenhower showed in polls prior to his nomination, the former is probably more likely the case.

Pre-election polls will be of increased use and interest as they are able to supply additional information other than answers as to who is going to carry what states in an election. The Survey Research Center's pre-election and postelection study [3] and some others have attempted to ascertain how, why, and when the voter makes up his mind in addition to the general demography of the voters. Persons were interviewed not only to ascertain for whom they intended to vote, but also on their perception of the candidates and attitudes toward campaign issues. The latter questions were asked immediately after the election. Dewey, for

---

[2] See Mosteller, *op. cit.*, p. 64.

[3] Angus Campbell and R. P. Kahn, *The People Elect a President* (Ann Arbor, Mich.: Ann Arbor Institute for Social Research, University of Michigan, 1952); see also P. F. Lazarsfeld, B. Berelson, and H. Gaudet, *The People's Choice* (New York: Columbia University Press, 1948).

example, was found to be identified with the business interests and somewhat "smug" and "patronizing," while Truman was for "the common man" but "incompetent" and "inefficient." Foreign policy presumably played no great part in the voter's thinking about the election, while rent control and the Taft-Hartley law did. As questions of depth of feeling, perception of issues and candidates, and the relationship of issues to party identification can be worked into pre-election polls so as to yield reliable data, their value to candidates, party managers, and the general public will be increased. These are virgin areas for research and exploration.

POLLING ON ISSUES

Counting the ballots for candidates and on propositions is a simple and decisive method of determining public opinion on candidates and on a few issues. Pre-election polls are interesting but not particularly helpful after election day. If democracy is to rest on public opinion, it is of great importance to ascertain public thinking on national and local issues. Many polling agencies today purport to do this and their findings are widely reported in the press and made available to government authorities. In fact, pre-election polling on candidates is only a side light for a polling agency such as the Gallup organization. It spends most of its efforts polling the public on issues. Many of the techniques for polling on candidates and on issues involve essentially the same problems, but the latter raise some problems not found in an election poll. From the standpoint of administration, a poll involves the following steps: (1) designing the plan, (2) constructing the questionnaire, (3) preparing the sample, (4) interviewing, (5) tabulating and editing the schedules, (6) reporting, with evaluation preceding the report, (7) public relations.[4]

Sampling and Timing. Prior to 1936 the *Literary Digest* had been able to forecast accurately by conducting a mail poll of several million voters. But its debacle in 1936 showed that a large poll in itself would not assure accuracy of results. The Gallup poll seldom samples more than 60,000 and usually polls less than a tenth of that number, with a high level of stability reached in any subsection with only 400 interviews. To illustrate this point, the poll notes that in a question on the NRA in 1936, the addition of 29,500 cases to the first 500 resulted in a difference

[4] A definitive work on polling is Mildred Parten, *Surveys, Polls, and Samples* (New York: Harper & Brothers, 1950). Her work also includes a bibliography of 1,145 titles. Two highly useful shorter works are S. C. Dodd, "Dimensions of a Poll," *International Journal of Opinion and Attitude Research,* Vol. 3 (Fall, 1949); and the pamphlet *The New Science of Public Opinion Measurement,* published by the American Institute of Public Opinion Measurement. George Gallup, *A Guide to Public Opinion Polls,* and Hadley Cantril, *Gauging Public Opinion,* both published in 1944 in Princeton, N.J., are likewise useful.

of 0.6 per cent in the national findings. The first 500 cases reported 54.9 per cent against reviving the NRA and the entire 30,000 resulted in a figure of 55.5 per cent.

The important thing is an adequate cross section, with a proper distribution according to age, sex, education, occupation, income status, party affiliation, religious and ethnic background, and residence. Census figures are consulted in the preparation of the sample. Not all elements such as religion and race are necessarily included in every sample but are taken into consideration if the question is apt to be biased by omitting a representative sample of them. The types of samples are quota, probability, and pinpoint; the first-mentioned being more widely used.

The quota sample applies the same percentage of the sample as appears in the general population. If 20 per cent are under age thirty and live in rural areas, then 20 per cent of the sample will be the same, and so on. Sufficient data on the population are not always available and this may bias the sample. Figures are not always obtainable, for example, on income distribution. Each interviewer is given a quota of, say, men, workers, or others and he is free to select the specific persons he will interview provided he meets his quota.

Probability sampling is generally used with area sampling and concentrates on opinion in strategic sections such as a state, a county, or pinpointed within a few blocks. A random sample of individuals is then selected within the area and a list of individuals to be interviewed is prepared. This method does not rely on the chance selection of persons to be interviewed, as is the case in the quota method, and it eliminates interviewer discretion in the choice of respondents. This sample is more expensive to prepare than the quota and will not be successful unless the character of the population to be polled is reasonably well known.

The Gallup organization is trying to make greater use of a variation of probability sampling, which Dr. Gallup calls "pinpoint" or "precinct" sampling. This was experimented with extensively in the 1950 congressional and 1952 presidential elections and, he notes, "proved superior to any other method we have tried." [5] The sampling units are representative election districts, with the interviewers calling at every nth dwelling unit, and interviewing one person in each. The number of adults in the family is recorded in order to correct any size of family bias. In 1952, the sample consisted of 119 precincts and its results approximated almost precisely the actual voting strength of Eisenhower and Stevenson. In the 1954 election for the House of Representatives the Gallup poll selected 105 precincts for a pre-election survey. In these areas Republican strength

[5] See Gallup, "The Future Direction of Election Polling," *Public Opinion Quarterly*, Vol. 17 (1953), pp. 202–207. This type of sampling was used on a more limited basis prior to 1950.

was overestimated by only 0.06 per cent, which Dr. Gallup claims as his best record. As the polling agencies use area sampling more and quota sampling less, their forecasts are likely to be more nearly correct. One serious problem still confronting the poll taker is the sorting out of persons who will vote from those who will stay at home. In polls on public questions, of course, it matters little whether the person votes or not.

The rapidity with which conditions change points to the need for checking dates of the poll and also for repeated polling in order to keep the polls up to date. Attitudes toward foreign aid, tax reduction, armaments, and so on undergo fairly rapid shifts. Events change many people from having no opinions to adopting opinions. President Truman's popularity took very sharp rises and falls. Although Senator Joseph McCarthy was much in the headlines prior to the Eisenhower election, it took only one year of the new administration for most people to make up their minds about him. The Gallup poll showed the following changes in public views on him.

	Per cent favorable	Per cent unfavorable	Per cent no opinion
August, 1951........	15	22	63
April, 1953.........	19	22	59
June, 1953..........	35	30	35
January, 1954.......	50	29	21
March, 1954........	46	36	18
May, 1954..........	35	49	16

A most remarkable change may be observed in the two-month period between April and June, 1953.

Wording the Question. Polling experts are aware of the great difficulty of wording questions which will elicit precise answers and which will not be obscure or have an implicit overtone resulting in inaccurate or worthless answers. Color words and adjectives can easily throw off the count. Several surveys show that a question such as "Are you in favor of a state-administered prepayment health plan to help budget medical expense?" will often result in over 50 per cent of affirmative answers. But when asked, "Are you in favor of socialized medicine?" an overwhelming majority reply in the negative. A great many union men replied negatively to questions on whether they favored the Taft-Hartley law, but when queried on several individual provisions of it, answered affirmatively. In an experimental poll with university students, 89 per cent answered "no" to the question "Should every worker be forced to join a union?" When the question was worded "Is it proper to require wage earners in an industry to join the union when the union controls a majority of the employees?" the response was 37.6 per cent favorable.[6]

A great many issues cannot be settled by a mere "yes" or "no" answer and a series of alternative answers may provide a more accurate reflection of opinion. For example, a simple affirmative or negative answer on whether one feels the United Nations is effective would not yield a too meaningful picture of public opinion. A poll of 4,585 male college students attending eleven universities, however, gave a somewhat clearer picture of opinion. This poll gave the student several alternatives in answering the question "How effective do you think the UN has been?"[7]

Extremely effective	1%
Fairly effective	46
Fairly ineffective	36
Extremely ineffective	12
No opinion	3
No answer	2

Care must be taken as to the order in which alternatives are presented on some issues because there is a tendency to choose a middle way when the first and last answers represent the extremes.

Learning the intensity or depth of an opinion becomes important for considering the permanence and degree of crystallization of public opinion and may be helpful to molders of opinion who may wish to modify prejudice. There are some attempts to measure intensity of feeling by providing the respondent with an opportunity to reply in such terms as "strongly approve," "mildly approve," "makes little difference," "mildly disapprove," "strongly disapprove," or similar phrases. This is an important area which has not yet been thoroughly developed.

Interviewing. The reputable polling agencies have learned that much of the success and reliability of their efforts rests upon the interviewer and they have eliminated the obviously biased poll takers. Some interviewer bias is almost certain to exist and this is sometimes overcome by selecting an equal number of interviewers who reflect the major biases an issue may arouse. An unintentional bias can result when the interviewer fails to establish rapport with the respondent. Training in interviewing overcomes a good deal of this. Experience shows also that no matter how well trained the poll taker may be, he may fail to get complete or correct answers from certain types of persons or in certain

---

[6] See Paul Studenski, "How Polls Can Mislead," *Harper's Magazine,* December, 1939.
[7] See E. A. Suchman, R. K. Goldsen, and A. M. Williams, Jr., "Attitudes toward the Korean War," *Public Opinion Quarterly,* Vol. 17 (1953), pp. 171–184.

neighborhoods. For example, in some areas there may be a suspicion that the poll taker is a "stooge" for the boss, a "city slicker," and Negroes may be inhibited in the presence of white interviewers. Personality traits and language difficulties may accentuate barriers and interfere with successful rapport. Care is needed in developing a neutral vocabulary in interviewing quite as much as in the specific questions asked.

POLLING BY SPECIAL INTERESTS

A growing number of candidates for public office are hiring polling organizations to discover moods, reactions, and attitudes which will help them with their campaigns. Nominees try to discover what public questions are of greatest concern to their constituents and their views on certain alternatives, with the view of gearing campaign speeches in these directions. Some congressmen have polls conducted on questions particularly important to them. Polling, however, is expensive and this technique favors candidates and incumbents who have the wherewithal to hire interviewers.

Special-interest groups are making increased use of polls to test sentiment among members on policies specifically concerning the organization. Leaders consider their position strengthened if they can point to the results of a poll. On rare occasions the organization will hire a reputable polling agency to do the job. Most of the time the poll is conducted by the staff of the organization itself, with the result that the poll is operated in a much less scientific manner than, for example, the *Fortune* surveys. Mail ballots, telephone calls to leaders, and various other methods are usually employed with a view to eliciting as near unanimous response as possible on a particular issue. Polls operated by medical associations among physicians, trade associations among businessmen, and union votes on strikes are conducted with much less reverence for objectivity. An "educational" program frequently precedes the vote and "90 per cent" majorities are by no means unknown. One of the best-known polls is the referendum system of the United States Chamber of Commerce and was described and evaluated in Chap. 4.[8] Even this poll, which is better operated than many private group surveys, appears weighted on the side of the views of the national leadership.

Obviously, an interest group is a group with an interest to protect and enhance, and it is, perhaps, expecting too much of any private organization to conduct an unbiased vote on an issue directly connected with its own livelihood. However, the group and public interest would be well served by the introduction, development, and extension of impartial institutional polls.

[8] See pp. 79–80. Also consult the Chamber's pamphlet *The Referendum System and Methods of Voting* (undated), obtainable from the national office in Washington, D.C.

THE GOVERNMENT AND POLLS

Government Surveys. Public officials make use of polls conducted by private associations and operate several on their own. Results of polls are often cited in the *Congressional Record* by congressmen in support of their own position. Administrators observe results as applied to the programs under their jurisdiction. The State Department, for example, has great interest in polls on foreign policy and the Agricultural Department on farm questions. No systematic study, however, has ever been made of the influence that polls have on legislation and administration; many congressmen have stated publicly that they pay little attention to the polls and are uninfluenced by them.[9] Kriegsberg found that a group of congressmen rated mail, talking to people, and newspapers as more useful than polls in discovering public opinion.[10] It should be noted, however, that some congressmen have had polls taken in their constituency both during and between campaigns.

The government itself has conducted a considerable number of surveys on such diverse subjects as labor force and employment, consumer finances and purchases, housing, health, real property, and youth needs and problems. One of the first government agencies to enter the sample social-survey field was the U.S. Department of Agriculture. Answers in many cases were admittedly to serve as guides for administrative decisions.

One of the best known agricultural surveys is the referendum, which is an election rather than a poll. Referendums are held on a variety of subjects and often are required by law before a Federal program can go into effect. Agricultural referendums were used 695 times up to 1941 in 40 states.[11] A provision was included in the 1938 farm legislation whereby the farmer is asked whether he wishes marketing quotas to be established for corn, cotton, peanuts, rice, tobacco, or wheat for any marketing year. The Secretary of Agriculture is authorized to call for a vote on a commodity whenever he finds that in a given year the normal supply will exceed the demand. The poll is conducted by the Department and a two-thirds majority is required before the orders or program go into effect.

[9] See G. F. Lewis, Jr., "The Congressmen Look at Polls," *Public Opinion Quarterly*, Vol. 4 (1940), pp. 229–231. In the survey of 117 congressmen, only 9 per cent indicated polls were useful to them in ascertaining the desires of their constituents and 30 per cent said they are useful "in part."

[10] "What Congressmen and Administrators Think of the Polls," *Public Opinion Quarterly*, Vol. 9 (1945), pp. 333–337. Of a congressional group, 33 per cent regarded polls as helpful and 24 per cent considered them as injurious to the working of democratic government.

[11] See L. V. Howard, "The Agricultural Referendum," *Public Administration Review*, Vol. 2 (1942), pp. 9–26.

On the surface, the agricultural referendum is a democratic device by which the opinion of farmers may be measured and made effectual. It promotes self-government and gives constituents a chance to help in determining public policies which affect them. Professor Howard notes that farmers have responded well and that in the South more farmers cast ballots on the referendums than all the voters cast in presidential elections.[12] However, the farmer votes "yes" or "no" on a specific program submitted to him by the government and not particularly on the desirability of one marketing program over another. Agricultural authorities usually conduct an "educational" program in advance of the voting and the interesting question is raised as to whether neutrality on the part of the government is or can be possible.

The agricultural referendum is an interesting experiment in popular control of government and represents a novel attempt on the part of government to become a poll taker of one of the largest occupation groups. The government is further projecting itself into its role of molding public opinion in favor of its policies; while the method is different, the role is the same. Partisan use makes the referendum a potential instrument for coercing a group into acceptance of a program which the members neither understand nor approve. However, a vote on a proposal without a statement from the agency explaining it would be unrealistic. If an agency proposes a program, it presumably believes in it. The important question when the government uses this electoral device is whether the statements are factually correct.

The National Labor Relations Board sets up machinery for conducting an election on representation for purposes of collective bargaining. These issues are simpler and the Board is not in the position of selling a program to the unions but merely acts as an umpire.

Public Regulation. Numerous bills have appeared in Congress calling for the denial of the use of the mails for poll taking, for investigation and audit, and for various other forms of regulation. Some individual lawmakers have expressed the view that election polls should be eliminated altogether. Regulation is urged mainly on the theory of the potential band-wagon effect and on the theory that an erroneous result could be obtained through the use of money and dishonesty to produce a distorted picture of opinion. The alleged band-wagon effect, as noted before, possesses little validity. The matter of money and honesty, especially on questions of issues, is, however, a valid point. Public officials who may be guided by these opinions are entitled to know the nature of the sponsorship of the polls, methods of procedure, and financial backing of the organization. Managers of the established polls have indicated the desirability of a public audit and have welcomed a thorough public

[12] *Ibid.*, pp. 2–3.

investigation. This is in addition to the self-policing of public-opinion research by the interested organizations and universities. It is to the credit of the Gallup poll that it has voluntarily submitted information of this nature. More than that, it has published materials on the details of procedure and its margins of error together with explanations of inaccuracies.

Elmo Roper goes even further to recommend the use by government, in competition with private agencies, of public-opinion polls. He believes that a governmental polling agency could be developed with a tradition and an objective staff such as characterizes the judiciary or the census agencies. His suggestion has not received the debate it merits. Perhaps the greatest stumbling block is Congress itself, which most certainly would be apprehensive that such a plan would usurp some of the representative functions of a lawmaker and might be turned into a weapon to favor the program of the party in power. In comparison with business, government makes relatively little use of polls. A great deal may be said for their use in order to provide more precise and accurate information on public opinion concerning governmental programs.

EVALUATION

Some have regarded the development of public-opinion polls as the greatest social invention of the era and believe their use provides governmental policy determiners with an opportunity to discover the will of the majority at all times on nearly all questions. The quickening pace of the modern age means rapid changes in opinion and the pollsters can, in a matter of days, report "the pulse of democracy." There is little doubt that the polls can be used to deflate extravagant claims of pressure groups seeking special privilege and reveal the views or lack of them among the generally inarticulate and unorganized minority. Polls may help to refute the deluge of synthetic letters to congressmen on a specific issue. There is some value in the ability of polls to reveal areas of ignorance and the extent of "don't know" or "never heard of" on certain policies. Polls were helpful to the government during World War II on the popularity of some types of war bond issues, morale among certain minorities, and attitudes on price controls.

The polls have their critics. Lindsay Rogers concludes his criticisms in in his book *The Pollsters* by saying: "So far as the pollers of public opinion are concerned, the light they have been following is a will-o'-the-wisp. They have been taking in each other's washing, and have been using statistics in terms of the Frenchman's definition: a means of being precise about matters of which you will remain ignorant." [13] Colonel McGuire

13 New York: Alfred A. Knopf, Inc., 1949, p. 239.

declares the polls "harmful to the continuation of our present system of government" and that they "undercut and discourage the influence of able and conscientious public men and tend to elevate demagogues to power." [14] Others see the polls as too mechanical and leading policy determiners around by the nose and discouraging leaders from independent investigation and thought. There are bound to be charges of bias, and criticisms of the sample, interviewer bias, and the administration of the poll. The reputable agencies, to their credit, have been self-critical in this respect and have constantly worked to reduce biases and factors causing errors.

Some other questions have been raised, such as the possibility of polling persons to excess, directing too many questions at them, and intentionally forcing an opinion. A basic concern is the accuracy on issues. Election predictions can be verified and the margin of error detected but results of polling on labor, foreign policy, the H-bomb, and so on cannot be verified. Despite the contrary evidence of the 1948 presidential predictions, some persons still believe that polls create a band-wagon effect.

Public-opinion polls will be useful if kept in the perspective that they are not an end in themselves. They should not be regarded as a mandate or gospel, and in times past, at least, some pollsters claimed too much for their results. Poll statistics do not impart much depth or meaning, these are dimensions that will have to be added by the interpreter and perhaps more by instinct than by science. Polls do not measure emotions (though intensity of belief is sometimes measured) or intangible factors important in public opinion. Great skill is needed in interpreting and evaluating the results of a poll if the data are to be useful as a guide to public opinion. Polls are but one of many means, all of them imperfect, of determining the popular will.

Polls can tell us what opinions are but still leave the problem of translating the opinions into instruments of policy. They may lead to the superficial belief that it is enough to measure opinions and to identify them. The student of democracy must regard polls as a beginning and not an end; the broader problem is to make both polls and opinions, if possible, effective instruments of democratic policy. As Lasswell [15] points out:

. . . no friend of democracy will believe that democratic processes have necessarily been strengthened by improving the mechanical proficiency with which we count heads. It is not only important that heads shall be counted but that heads shall be used. We need a public opinion realistically directed toward the

[14] "The U.S. Constitution and Ten Shekels of Silver," *Public Opinion Quarterly*, Vol. 4 (1940), pp. 232–235.

[15] In Douglas Waples (ed.), *Print, Radio, and Film in a Democracy* (Chicago: University of Chicago Press, 1942), p. 114.

support of policies conducive to the survival of a democratic society. This is what is meant by the reality value of public opinion.

The results of over a decade of private polling are refreshing in terms of faith in the common sense of the people. Elmo Roper [16] remarks that his experiences give him a

. . . profound respect for the wisdom of the American people as a whole and with it the firm conviction that if we can keep the power in the hands of the people and further develop techniques for making them vocal, we need never have fear that this country will ever face the situations now being faced in certain countries of Europe.

Lydgate, Gallup, and others have expressed similar pride in the opinions of the public and find the people frequently in advance of their lawmakers.

SELECTED REFERENCES

Mildred B. Parten, *Surveys, Polls, and Samples: Practical Procedures* (1950), presents the most complete analysis of the technical aspects of opinion survey and includes an indispensable bibliography. Other valuable works include Hadley Cantril, *Gauging Public Opinion* (1944); Louis Bean, *Ballot Behavior: A Study of Presidential Elections* (1940) and *How to Predict Elections* (1948); George Gallup and S. F. Rae, *The Pulse of Democracy* (1940); and George Gallup, *A Guide to Public Opinion Polls* (1944), a useful volume written for the lay reader; W. A. Lydgate, *What America Thinks* (1944); Claude Robinson, *Straw Votes: A Study in Political Prediction* (1932); National Opinion Research Center, *Interviewing for NORC* (1946); and Jerome Bruner, *Mandate from the People* (1944).

Periodical articles are extremely abundant, especially in the *Public Opinion Quarterly,* the *Journal of Applied Psychology,* and the *Journal of Social Psychology.* For purposes of this chapter, the following articles in the *Public Opinion Quarterly* are valuable: F. H. Allport, "Polls and the Science of Public Opinion," Vol. 4 (1940), pp. 249–258; H. Cantril, "Experiments in the Wording of Questions," Vol. 4 (1940), pp. 330–332; A. M. Crossley, "Experiments in Polling Technique," Vol. 5 (1941), pp. 83–86; H. F. Gosnell, "How Accurate Were the Polls?" Vol. 1 (1937), pp. 97–104; D. Katz, "Do Interviewers Bias Poll Results?" Vol. 6 (1942), pp. 248–268; Elmo Roper, "Classifying Respondents by Economic Status," Vol. 4 (1940), pp. 270–273; L. Warner, "The Reliability of Public Opinion Surveys," Vol. 3 (1939), pp. 376–390; S. L. Payne, "Some Opinion Research Principles Developed through Studies of Social Medicine," Vol. 10 (1946), pp. 93–98; G. M. Connelly, "Now Let's Look at the Real Problem: Validity," Vol. 9 (1945), pp. 51–60; E. Benson, C. Young, and C. Syze, "Polling Lessons from the 1944 Election," Vol. 9 (1945), pp. 467–493, and George Gallup, "The Future Direction of Election Polling," Vol. 17 (1953), pp. 202–207. Norbert Muhlen's three articles in *The New Leader* (Dec. 22 and 29, 1945, and Jan. 5, 1946) present some provocative ideas on the place of polls in a democracy.

[16] "Sampling Public Opinion," *Journal of the American Statistical Association,* Vol. 35 (1940), pp. 325–334.

PART SEVEN

The Party in the Government

CHAPTER 25

The Party in the Government

It is a rule of our politics that no vexed question is settled except by executive policy. Whatever may be the feeling of Congress toward the President, it cannot avoid an issue which he insists upon making. And this holds good of Presidents who lose their party leadership as with those who retain it. Tyler, Johnson, and Cleveland, although repudiated by the parties which elected them, furnished the issues upon which party action has turned.

—H. J. FORD

Mankind has certain desires, values, and aspirations which it wishes to realize. Some are fulfilled by the family, the church, the class, and interest groups. A large number of them require the institution of government for fulfillment. Government itself must be staffed by and controlled by human beings. Political parties have arisen out of a need for individuals and groups to pool their strength for an effort to win control of the government. The degree of responsibility of the party once in power varies considerably from nation to nation but in every democracy the party tries to provide the human element of government and to bring unity to it. A party's duration in power will be dependent in a large degree upon its ability to control the processes of government in a way to shape public policies which have the support of a very sizable group of the electorate.

So far as political parties are concerned, our major attention to this point has been focused upon the nature of parties in the electorate, their functions in nominating candidates, conducting campaigns, and the organizational arrangements in performing these functions. We have noted that the official party organizations have had to share these responsibilities with interest groups and specially created political committees. The major purpose of the nomination-campaign activities of a major political party in the United States is to win control over the executive and legislative establishments. From the public's point of view, the heart of the party system is its functioning in government. In this final section of the book, it is appropriate to give attention to party leadership and influences in the government.

THE PARTY IN CONGRESS

The basic merit of the two-party system, at least theoretically, is that it establishes majority rule. The party which captures a majority of the votes ordinarily controls the legislature and the executive branch, and can be held accountable by the public for the policies it puts into effect, while under multiparty systems, responsibility is diffused among the several parties which make up the coalition. The majority party in this country does act in concert in organizing the legislative body in electing the party leadership of each house, but on controversial public policies the parties have often been hopelessly divided. As the American society became more complex and urbanized and the problems of government more difficult, the major parties have often been unable to compromise their internal differences and to agree on a unified program.

Literature on parties stresses the need for "more responsible parties," "party discipline," "stronger parties," and so on. Writers are not fully agreed on questions of to whom the parties are to be responsible and for what, nor on the methods of discipline or how to make the parties stronger. Within Congress itself there has continued to be a recognition that some degree of party unity is needed on matters which transcend speakerships and committee assignments. Congress has experimented with a great many devices and methods for securing greater cohesion among party members on legislation. None of these has resulted in consistently developing an official "Democratic" or "Republican" policy which would satisfy the proponents of more responsible parties. Insurgency, threatened or actual, has led to a toning down of proposals to punish recalcitrants and deviationists.

Election Regularity. In a comprehensive research into party discipline during the last century, Clarence A. Berdahl found that while legislative voting record appeared to have little relevance in determining party membership on committees, it did have relevance in some but not all cases in terms of the failure to support the party's candidates for President.[1] Party members in Congress will forgive their fellows for refusing to support the party program in Congress but not necessarily for bolting the party's ticket on election day. Berdahl found, however, that there was no consistent criterion for exclusion from caucus or demotion in committee assignments; rather, the circumstances of the moment determined the action. Those senators who bolted to support Theodore Roosevelt in 1912 did not suffer loss of assignments, probably because the party was in the minority and several senators would have been involved. But some mem-

---

[1] See "Some Notes on Party Membership in Congress," *The American Political Science Review,* Vol. 43 (1949), pp. 309–321, 492–508, 721–734; also *Our Two-party System* (University, Miss.: Bureau of Public Administration, University of Mississippi, 1951).

bers of Congress from Wisconsin were ousted from places on key committees when they bolted Coolidge to support La Follette for the presidency in 1924. Republican William Lemke ran for President on the Union party ticket and was demoted to the lowest place on minor committees.

Senator Wayne Morse of Oregon consistently voted in opposition to the policies of his party but always supported the ticket in elections and by 1952 had built up seniority on two important committees. However, when he supported Governor Stevenson for President and after the election styled himself as an "independent," the Senate leadership moved him to the "foot of the class" of two minor committees. The significant point of this incident is that Morse took the unusual step of resigning from the Republican party instead of simply taking a "walk" from its presidential nominee. He asked to retain his membership on the powerful Armed Services Committee not as a Republican but as an independent and argued that he was still entitled to the "Senate seniority" which he possessed. But neither party would give him a place or would vote for extra seats so that he could retain his place.[2] Several of Morse's colleagues insisted that in effect one obtained seniority as party member, not simply as a member of the Senate.

The Democrats have been less troubled with bolters and more tolerant. However much Southern Democrats in Congress opposed their Northern colleagues on legislation, very few of them actually campaigned for Hoover in 1928, or for the Dixiecrats in 1948, or for Eisenhower in 1952. The few that did desert in the election were criticized but not disciplined and several lost their own reelection shortly afterward. The Democrats did impose severe punishment for Democratic Senator Rush Holt of West Virginia, in part because he was personally annoying and brash in ignoring Senate traditions. He deserted his party in 1936 to aid Republican candidates for President and United States senator. Shortly after the election, the patronage chairman of the Senate sent him a letter telling him that he could expect to lose some of his patronage positions because "there are newly elected Senators who wholeheartedly supported the Democratic party at the last election and who therefore have a sound claim to patronage positions among the attaches of the Senate." Rarely, however, is the punishment so harsh, yet examples like this are well known and incumbents who value their political life are careful about bolting the decisions of their party's primaries and conventions. Election regularity, it may be concluded, is a part of the rules of the game for party members in Congress. To deviate is to run some risk of losing perquisites and prerogatives in Congress.

[2] Debate on the subject is found in the *Congressional Record*, Jan. 13, 1953 (daily edition), pp. 334–347.

PARTY LEADERSHIP IN CONGRESS

House Caucuses and Conferences. Prior to 1917, what the Democrats called a "caucus" and the Republicans a "conference," generally formulated the party's position on leadership and organization and enforced the party will on these matters. The caucus was and still is composed of all members of the party. The extent to which the institution was utilized in drafting party position on legislation is in doubt. For at least a score of years prior to his being shorn of certain powers in 1910, the Speaker, working with the caucus, enforced party discipline and undoubtedly controlled the votes of most party members where a party position on policy was laid down. During President Wilson's first term, the Democratic caucus was a powerful instrument in pushing through the party's legislative program.

The House Democratic caucus rules were adopted early in the present century and provided that there was to be unity in "Democratic principles and doctrine" but in nonessentials "entire individual independence." [3] Wherever a matter is declared to be a party one, two-thirds of the caucus can bind the individual member to vote. On party measures, however, members had an "out" when they could show that the bills involved a "construction of the Constitution," or that to vote for the measures would be "contrary to pledges to their constituents."

As an instrument for binding members on party policies, the caucuses have been of little importance during the past generation. In 1949, the House Democratic caucus met only four times and reached a binding decision in only one matter—limiting the powers of the Rules Committee. House Republicans held eight conferences, several of which were devoted to bills such as rent control and housing, none of which sought to bind the party membership. But caucuses and conferences remain important for determining party positions on leadership, organizational, and personnel matters.

In 1910 the Republicans created a steering committee and the Democrats created a similar body in 1933. The steering committees grew out of a need for a policy-forming and executive committee within the caucuses. The Democratic Steering Committee in the House is composed of the speaker (when in control of Congress), the floor leader, whip, caucus chairman, several committee chairmen, and one representative from each of 15 geographical districts. The Republicans converted their steering committee into a "House Republican Policy Committee" in 1949.

---

[3] Texts of the rules of this caucus and of the Senate Republican caucus are found in George Galloway, *The Legislative Process in Congress* (New York: Thomas Y. Crowell Company, 1953), pp. 328–334.

It consists of 22 members, including the major party officers in the House and representatives from regional districts. The delegations from the various areas designate their own members on the policy group. According to the resolution creating the committee, its function is to serve as "an advisory committee to the leadership" and "no Republican member of Congress shall be bound by the decisions of this Policy Committee, but its suggestions should guide the minority to a firmer national policy."

House Rules Committee. The Rules Committee has become one of the most powerful committees, whose approval is necessary before bills may come before the House. Through its power to report special orders of business and on matters not hitherto introduced, it is the governing body in procedure and is most influential in the realm of policy, for it can accelerate, hinder, or bury legislation and decide what controversial measures shall be brought before the House. The Rules Committee fixes the timetable of the House and determines when bills shall come up, the duration of debate, and the time and manner of voting on them. It can bring in rules to limit amendments, give priority to those bills and amendments it favors, or obstruct those it opposes.

The Rules Committee can be circumvented by such devices as Calendar Wednesday, a motion to suspend the rules (which requires a two-thirds majority for passage), and favorable action on a discharge petition. All these devices are seldom used and are difficult to employ. A member of the House can refuse consent to having a bill placed on the unanimous consent calendar. Appropriations bills in the House, however, are privileged business and this committee is most powerful in its own area.

The concentration of power in the Rules Committee makes it potentially a useful agent of party control for smothering bills and resolutions for investigations sponsored by the minority. In theory at least, the Rules Committee is the agent of the majority and through its control over legislative procedure may vastly aid in furthering the President's program. In practice, this is often not the case because a majority of members of the committee may be in disagreement with the President and even other members of the House. The Democratic chairman of the Rules Committee bottled up the wages-hours bill for a long time and President Roosevelt found it necessary to oppose the chairman's reelection to Congress in 1938.

For a number of years under Roosevelt and Truman the Rules Committee was controlled by a coalition of Southern Democrats and Republicans who opposed many New Deal-Fair Deal bills and who interpreted their function to be much more than simply "a traffic director on a legislative highway." Instead of advancing the President's program, they made it more difficult to get it through the House. As a coalition, it was not an agent of party control but of coalition control. Like all other committees, this one is constituted on a seniority basis, with chairmen and ranking minority members likely to come from reasonably safe and conservative districts. Of the 12 members in the Eighty-third Congress, one-fourth were Southern Democrats, and the two ranking and therefore potential chairmen were from the South. Only one of the four Democrats on the committee was from the North. Of the Republican members, Leo Allen of Illinois was chairman and Clarence Brown of Ohio ranked next to him; both of them were supporters of Senator Taft before the 1952 convention.

There have been numerous rebellions against the Rules Committee. In 1949, after Mr. Truman was elected, Democratic leaders took steps to overcome the frustration they had felt at coalition domination and added several members to the committee from the majority party. They appointed Democrats from the North to these posts and adopted the "21-day rule" to take away the committee's absolute veto. To prevent a permanent blockade of legislation, the rule permitted a standing committee chairman to call up a bill for House action if the Rules Committee refused to do so after 21 days or if the Rules Committee had reported the bill adversely. The rule was effective in bringing up several measures such as Hawaii statehood, minimum-wages and anti-poll-tax legislation. These matters alienated the conservative coalition and they were successful in repealing the rule in 1951.

The Rules Committee soon showed itself intent on restoring its former prerogative by delaying for weeks a bill to authorize a much-needed wheat shipment to India until the bill was amended to meet a majority of the committee's wishes. Representative Chet Holifield commented before a Senate committee: "Until the 21-day rule is restored we can expect further situations in which a few men, strategically situated in the Rules Committee, can impose their will on Congress and prevent the enactment of legislation deemed by the House majority to be essential to the security and welfare of the nation." [4]

An unsuccessful effort was made to restore the 21-day rule when the Republican-controlled Congress took office in January, 1953. During the Eighty-third Congress, however, the Rules Committee was not the major stumbling block to President Eisenhower's legislative program. In fact, the committee helped to force out the Eisenhower proposal to extend the excess-profits tax when it appeared to be bottled up by Chairman Reed of the House Ways and Means Committee.

---

[4] See Hearings before the Senate Committee on Expenditures in the Executive Department on the Organization and Operation of Congress, 82d Cong., 1st Sess., June 1951, p. 52.

The Senate Rules Committee, in contrast, has no such control over legislation and performs only such housekeeping functions as assigning office space. It is the majority floor leader, rather than the Rules Committee, who exercises leadership over the agenda of the Senate but he has only limited powers and must have the support of his party. In the several state legislatures, similar rules committees often are real instruments of party control, and are used to push the governor's programs and to sidetrack bills opposed by the majority party. Rules committee chairmen in the states are not always constituted on a seniority basis and the governor's wing of the party can often obtain control of the rules committee. But the vagueness of party differences in the states and frequent unipartyism often means that dominance of the legislature is not necessarily party control or governor's control but coalition or factional control.

Senate Policy Committees. The Senate has party caucuses similar to the House. The rules of the Republican Senate Conference, as its caucus is called, specifically provide that its action shall not "be binding in any way on members in casting their votes," and the Senate Democratic caucus follows the same rule. Because Senate procedure is more informal, there is less need for the Rules Committee to perform the same functions of its House counterpart. There has been, however, a growing awareness of the need for greater party policy leadership in both houses. The Joint Committee on the Organization of Congress recommended in its report of 1946 that each party should establish party policy committees in the House and the Senate. This recommendation was adopted by the Senate, which now has Democratic and Republican Policy Committees, each with salaried staffs. Senator Robert A. Taft, first chairman of the Republican group, gave a considerable impetus to his committee.

The Democratic Policy Committee consists of nine members appointed by the party leader, while the Republicans have 23 members who are elected by the conference for a two-year term. Each committee receives around $65,000 a year for research and other staff members. As noted before, the House does not have such formally recognized policy bodies with a staff paid out of policy funds.

The policy committees meet frequently and help schedule bills for floor consideration, coordinate committee work, and advise on committee investigations and parliamentary procedures. They serve as a forum for presentation of individual views of party members on public policy and have sometimes issued statements on policy. One firsthand observer of the policy committees, however, concludes that [5]

[5] Galloway, *op. cit.*, p. 336.

as devices for coordinating legislative policy making and strengthening party leadership [they] have thus far failed to achieve their full potential. As instruments for promoting more effective liaison and cooperation with the President they have also been a disappointment, partly because of the lack of similar policy committees in the House of Representatives. Their limited achievements to date can be attributed to their composition, to the fragmentation of power in Congress, and to deep internal divisions within both of our major political parties.

The Republican Policy Committee in the Eighty-third Congress provided an illustration of both weakness and strength. On such highly controversial matters as the Bricker Amendment and the censure of Senator McCarthy, the committee did not even meet. Republican senators were badly divided on these issues. Some critics felt that the failure to reach a policy compromise on these and other issues indicated a general lack of usefulness of the committee.

On the other hand, the Eisenhower Administration hammered out its legislative program in a three-day session with Senate and House leaders early in 1953. The Republican Policy Committee took over the residuum of these meetings, made them the party's program, and a very large percentage of the policies adopted by the committee passed the Senate. Many Cabinet secretaries and Senate committee chairmen were brought before the committee to discuss details and to decide when certain bills should reach the Senate floor. At the end of each meeting the chairman, Homer Ferguson, met with members of the press to inform them of what had taken place in the session. Senator Ferguson sat in on most of the legislative meetings with President Eisenhower and was able to speak with a knowledge of the President's views. Minutes of each meeting were circulated to all Republican senators. Although no senator was bound to support the decisions of the committee, its views appear to have had some influence. It should be noted that the committee's staff did some effective work in preparing summaries of bills and policies.

Floor Leadership. Institutional leadership expressed through the standing committees, caucuses, and policy groups is buttressed by the personal leadership of the Speaker, and from time to time the Vice President, the floor leaders, and whips. These leaders devote their efforts to trying to tie together the loose, incongruous alliances which make up each political party. They try, with all their resources, to marshal majorities large enough to pass or to defeat bills.

The Speaker of the House, unlike his English counterpart, is a partisan officer. He keeps party interests in mind in making decisions on the floor of the House, in the appointment of select committees, and through his power of recognition and of addressing the House. Although he has the services of a parliamentarian, the Speaker is usually well versed in parliamentary procedure. Parliamentary law is highly important in getting legislation through or defeated and is oftentimes an important technique of party control. Speakers exercise considerable influence through personal negotiation with the Rules Committee chairman, the floor leaders, committee heads, and factional leaders. Sam Rayburn, who served longer than any other Speaker, was often instrumental in welding a majority by leaving the rostrum and going to the floor to debate and negotiate.

The floor leader in the House fills a position second only in importance to that of the Speaker. The public hears of him less but the work which he performs for his party is as vital as that of the Speaker, if not more so. His function is to integrate the forces of the party to work as a unit. Committee chairmen regularly consult with the majority floor leader in regard to special rules or the calling up of legislation for consideration. If the President and majority floor leader are of the same party, the latter is usually regarded as the leading spokesman for the administration. The views expressed by floor leaders Alben Barkley and John McCormack generally were accepted as representing those of Presidents Roosevelt and Truman, as Senators Robert A. Taft and William Knowland presumably spoke for Eisenhower.

Each party also has a whip, appointed by respective floor leaders. The whips in turn appoint several assistants, who are chosen on a sectional basis and thus facilitate contact with the entire party within a few minutes to an hour. These assistants quickly poll the various state delegations on certain matters and report to the whip. Information such as the party's stand on an issue can be sent quickly through the whips; they are also important in rounding up absent members and in trying to keep party members in line.

Mr. Barkley,[6] long-time Democratic floor leader, says of the office:

The majority leader of the Senate is expected to be the legislative spokesman of the administration. . . . It is his duty to confer with the President about the wisdom and propriety of recommendations that he makes to Congress, the chances of their enactment, sometimes even to suggest to the President that he call members of the Senate down to the White House and explain to them so that they may understand his measures, especially if they are inclined to be on the other side, so that he may give them his reasons for advocating the legislation, and so that there will be less controversy about it within his own party when it reaches the floor of the Senate. He must be the majority spokesman. . . .

[6] "The Majority Leader in the Legislative Process," in Amry Vandenbosch (ed.), *The Process of Government* (Lexington, Ky.: Bureau of Government Research, University of Kentucky, 1949), pp. 36 ff.

The man who is chosen by the members of his own party as majority leader in the Senate or the House has a great opportunity, a great duty, and a great responsibility.

Although the minority floor leader functions as the spokesman for the minority party in Congress, he does not customarily consult the party's titular leader, the defeated presidential nominee. Democratic Senator Lyndon Johnson of Texas was chosen minority floor leader in 1953 in an attempt to heal the North-South division within the party following the 1952 election.

In some respects the position of majority floor leader in the Senate is more important than in the House because the Vice President or president pro tem exercises less authority than the Speaker. The House floor leader, however, usually carries no standing committee assignments and devotes full time to floor leadership. The Senate leader usually retains some committee assignments. The Senate Democratic floor leader is chairman of the Democratic caucus, but this is not true of the Republican party. During the first session of the Eighty-third Congress, Minority Floor Leader Lyndon Johnson brought the Democratic Policy Committee together each Tuesday for lunch. This practice helped to overcome the disunity among Senate Democrats which had developed during the Eighty-second Congress when they were in the majority.

Evaluation. The party leadership devices in Congress work reasonably well in taking care of personnel questions, selecting leaders, and in deciding upon committee assignments. Members very seldom bolt the caucus decisions on the speakership, committee chairmanships, patronage, and related matters. Presidential nominations are often reviewed in the Senate conferences and decisions are reached on support or opposition. There are certain psychological values in meeting as a party group and talking over problems of personnel, election regularity, the President's program, and party faith in general. Party machinery is influential in determining priority of legislative consideration, rules and floor strategy, and in setting up congressional investigations. The House Rules Committee allocates equal time to each major party.

Although the party is influential in the choice of the Speaker and floor leaders and in the allocation of the number of seats on committees to be given to the Democrats and Republicans, its control is far short of dominant. Committee chairmen are chosen not by the party but by seniority and some highly anomalous situations arise from it. The parties are unable to control committee chairmen for they do not select them. Virtually every President has found certain congressional committee chairmanships in the hands of representatives of the opposite faction of his party. President Eisenhower was sharply opposed on several tax measures by Dan Reed, chairman of the House Ways and Means Committee, and by John Taber, chairman of the House Appropriations Committee.

Party machinery in Congress has no consistently great influence in policy directing or in establishing party accountability for legislative program. This is due to the great decentralization and fragmentation of political power in Congress into over a score of committees, groups, and leaders. The committee on political parties of the American Political Science Association suggests that "the proliferation of leadership committees means that in neither house of Congress is there a body of party leaders who have the power of managing party affairs in Congress and who therefore can be held accountable for it." [7] Further, as Victor Jones points out, "The principal difficulty with developing party policy committees into an effective group of legislative leaders is that there is no congressional party to be led. The task is to develop parties to govern and to oppose the government. This cannot be done by designating a group of men, some of whom are not leaders in fact, as a party policy committee while Congress sub-contracts its work to bipartisan committees and subcommittees." [8]

It is popular on Capitol Hill to say that the House Democratic Steering Committee "seldom meets and never steers." Smith and Field present some convincing evidence that it is a myth to assume that the party agencies such as the floor leaders, caucuses, and policy committees "are powerful authorities controlling procedures, committee structure, and legislative schedules and that they frequently dictate to members how they shall vote." [9] As they point out, the floor leaders, whips, policy and standing committee chairmen are often in disagreement with each other, with little possibility for or evidence of an official party position. The comparatively few policy committee statements appear more as propaganda for voters than as controls of the voting behavior of the party's congressmen. Few congressmen today claim these party institutions to be effective policy determiners. One veteran member could recall "only three or four caucuses called with the idea of binding members in the last two decades. Another congressman regarded as authoritative in procedural

[7] See the committee's report, *Toward a More Responsible Two-party System,* published as a supplement to *The American Political Science Review,* Vol. 44 (1950), p. 59.

[8] "The Political Framework of Stabilization Policy," in Max F. Millikan (ed.), *Income Stabilization for a Developing Democracy* (New Haven, Conn.: Yale University Press, 1953), p. 605.

[9] "The Responsibility of Parties in Congress: Myth and Reality," *Southwestern Social Science Quarterly,* Vol. 34 (1953), p. 25.

matters speaks of the caucus as 'completely abandoned' except for the organization of Congress." [10]

It is obvious that party machinery in the House can be most effective only when all the legal and extralegal officials work in concert, including the Speaker, floor leader, Rules Committee chairman, and the more important legislative committee chairmen. Policy committees and party steering groups in both houses must contend with the power that is often built up by committee chairmen. Representatives Dan Reed and John Taber and Senators Pat McCarran, Harry Byrd, Joseph McCarthy, to mention only a very few, have been able to challenge the national and congressional party leadership. Powerful legislative committee chairmen have been able to resist the demands of pressure groups which they do not like and at the same time promote the narrow interests of some groups which they like. Through the power to investigate the executive agencies, they are able to embarrass the executives in programs which the latter hope to get through Congress. The protection of seniority and the personal resourcefulness of chairmen make them potentially formidable opponents of a general party legislative program.

The effectiveness of party control and discipline is a variable thing because party arrangements are so casual. Quite often the minority party will have greater cohesion on roll calls when it is in the minority than when it was in the majority. The Democratic caucus was very influential in Wilson's first term and floor management was instrumental in getting through many measures during the first term of Franklin Roosevelt. At other times none of the groups appear to have any influence in obtaining a party vote. At all times, however, personality is important. The personal intervention of the Speaker or floor leaders, their prestige, and competence have had marked effects. Careful preparation by them has led measures to be accepted by the caucus or on the floor without much difficulty. Factional leaders are less likely to be successful in welding party unity than those who can stand between the factions and by forceful personal persuasion bring about some party cohesion.

Party discipline varies in the House and Senate, in state assemblies, and in city councils. An individual United States senator exercises considerable independence and may resort to filibustering to delay action on measures of his own party. Bicameralism in the American legislatures is a formidable obstacle to party unity and time and time again a party majority will be mustered in one house but fail to materialize in the other. This suggests that some measure of party discipline and harmony must come from outside the halls of the legislature, an influence capable of bringing together the party's representatives and senators on a program. The Chief Executive has provided the most important single force

10 *Ibid.,* p. 31.

to provide legislative and policy leadership. Before probing further into the problem of party discipline, it is well to look briefly at the leadership provided by the President and his advisers.

THE PARTY IN ADMINISTRATION

Executive Leadership. Grover Cleveland, who became accustomed to quarrels with Congress, once said that "the President and the President alone represents all of the people." When he became President, Dwight Eisenhower, like most of his predecessors, avowed he would be the non-partisan or bipartisan leader of all of the people. He saw his position not as a central point in the struggle of party politics but as an institution above the battle of partisanship. He first announced in the elections of 1953 that he would make no endorsements and stay out of politics. Party managers brought pressure on him and, as in 1952, caused him to reverse his position and state that he supported the candidacy of all Republicans. These two instances illustrate some profound truths, the implications of which are not always fully appreciated.

As Cleveland noted, the President is selected from a national constituency and is the object of pressures from every direction. He is expected to take a national point of view and to consider the welfare of the entire country. Legislators are selected from state and local constituencies and their immediate concern is the effect of proposals on their districts—and their reelections. The congressman may come from a one-party, an agrarian, a metropolitan or other district and be concerned primarily with certain parochial pressures and problems. It is inevitable in the very scheme of electoral areas that on certain policies there will be tugs of war between the President and Congress, and between the governor and the state legislature.

The duality of role and interest which has bothered Eisenhower and other Presidents grows out of the recognition that the President must be a national and world leader and that in the performance of these duties powerful interests may have to be offended. No person can be elected President without votes from independents and some disgruntled members of the opposition party. In Congress a President must have support from members of the opposition,[11] a case of building up a "concurrent majority" or at times a coalition of "concurrent minorities." If he becomes too strong a partisan, he stirs up a partisanship in members of the opposing party without necessarily carrying all the members of his own party and he may thereby lose his voting majority. On the other

[11] The 1953 session of Congress provided an illuminating illustration of this. In 43 important victories for the Eisenhower program in the Senate, the Democrats made up the difference between victory and defeat in 37, and 20 of the 31 House victories were accomplished only with Democratic help. See *The New York Times*, Oct. 29, 1953.

hand, if a President refuses to back his own party candidates vigorously at election time, he may lose some votes within his own party. Of President Eisenhower's blanket assertion that he would support every Republican for every office national or local, Arthur Krock commented in *The New York Times* that "if this is to be settled policy it is a peril-laden notice to all Republicans that they will not forfeit his partisan endorsement by opposing his programs. He didn't want to go that far, but neither did some of his predecessors who had the same experience." [12]

During the first century of the American Republic, Presidents tended to operate in practice, if not in theory, in one of three ways. Washington, the two Adamses, and Monroe saw the President as leader of the entire country and not especially as a party leader or leader of a particular faction. Jackson and Van Buren put themselves at the head of their parties and relied upon strong party leadership to put over their legislative programs. Another group of Presidents governed under what is sometimes spoken of as the "Whig concept." They were content to remain as nominal leaders and Chief Executives and leave major initiative for formulating policies and putting over a legislative program to powerful congressional leaders. To some extent each of these approaches worked reasonably well in their particular times. That they were able to do so illustrates the flexibility of the American system. [13]

Presidents in the present century more and more have come to be expected to provide leadership in legislation in party matters and to bring what order and cohesion to the party that they could. Wilson, the two Roosevelts, and Truman (in the latter part of his term) typified efforts at strong party leadership. The strengthening of the presidency and the President's emergence as a leader of his party and of public opinion have been aided partially by nationalization and Federal regulation of a large part of the economy. The rise of great nationally organized groups has permitted him to deal in person with the spokesmen for interest groups.

Eisenhower operated during his first year under something of the Whig idea. He ran the Cabinet and the Administration and let Senate Majority Floor Leader Taft assume much legislative initiative. However, the death of Taft left a serious gap in this leadership and Congress did not have a very impressive record of legislative achievement. The Senate became embroiled over the Bricker Amendment, which the President regarded as invading his prerogative. While the Amendment was defeated, the contest between the two branches of government continued during the

[12] See his column and also that of W. H. Lawrence on the same problem, Oct. 30, 1953.

[13] For a discussion of this point see A. N. Holcombe, "Presidential Leadership and the Party System," *The Yale Review*, Vol. 43 (1954), pp. 321–335.

Army-McCarthy hearings. Senator McCarthy maintained during this investigation that all Federal employees should turn over information on communism, corruption, and subversion, even if the information had been labeled secret by the executive. Many newspapers termed this a "constitutional crisis" and called upon the President to resist legislative encroachment. The President publicly opposed the McCarthy contention and received much Democratic support for his position. Congressional Republicans were divided on the matter. The result of his experiences with Congress led the President to attempt more vigorous legislative leadership.[14]

"Strong" governors tend to formulate the party's legislative program and through the speaker and presiding officers and floor managers exert pressure to put through the program. Governor Dewey's lieutenants have "lectured" party recalcitrants in the caucus, emphasizing that certain of his bills *must* pass. This system has resulted in numerous controversial bills passing the New York legislature by a 100 per cent party vote. This is by no means typical or even the rule in American states, but it does show that executives sometimes do bring a high degree of party responsibility to the state's government. In New York there were those within the party who privately resented the "executive dictation" and felt the legislature did not play a large enough role in the formulation of policy.

The President's direction of the party program in the legislature is not without limitation. He can and is expected to propose important legislative measures but it is Congress alone which can raise and appropriate public money for them. Congress has the function of sifting the President's proposals, amending them, and establishing priorities for them. Congressmen are quick to resent "presidential dictation" and to voice it vigorously. Pressure groups not liking the President's proposals side with congressmen in denouncing executive "interference" and demand a "restoration of constitutional government" and of the legislative prerogatives presumably "usurped" by the President. Senatorial courtesy and congressional investigations are sometimes used to embarrass the President and exercise some control over the administration. If the President is unpopular, his championship of certain measures may actually be a liability to passage in Congress. Near the end of President Truman's term, one member of Congress said on the floor of the House, "All I want to know is whether Truman is for a bill; if he is, I am automatically against it!"

The position of the Vice President is somewhat anomalous. Many holding the office were former congressmen and appeared to do little more than preside over the Senate. At the same time, the Vice President is a

[14] The Gallup poll at the end of Eisenhower's first year showed that 65 per cent of the respondents wanted the President to exert stronger leadership.

part of the administration's party and a representative of the President. Vice Presidents Garner, Wallace, and Barkley worked for enactment of the President's program. Nixon, more than any recent Vice President, conceived his role as one of the leaders of the party in the Administration and he particularly spoke for Eisenhower on many occasions. He assumed the role of peacemaker between the President and certain Republicans in Congress. When Adlai Stevenson accused the Republicans of being "half Eisenhower and half McCarthy," Mr. Nixon was selected by the Republican National Committee to give the official answer to Mr. Stevenson. At this time, Nixon said that President Eisenhower, and Eisenhower alone, was the leader of the Republican party.

Techniques and Methods. The constitutional functions given to the President in the legislative process are limited to the veto, the delivering of messages, and the calling of special sessions. The first of these is a negative instrument and not a trading device particularly useful in obtaining a legislative program. The annual and other messages delivered before Congress provide the opportunity for the Chief Executive to put the full force of his office and leadership behind specific legislative proposals. Recent Presidents have delivered some of their messages to Congress in person and their words have been carried to the nation by radio and television. The calling of a special session to act upon emergency matters presented by the executive has sometimes been very important in the states; it is used but rarely by Presidents. In 1948, President Truman called the Republican Congress into special session to enact price control and other legislation which the Republican National Convention had endorsed. As was foreseen, the special session did not enact the program, thus putting the Republicans on the spot.

The formulation and presentation of a party program are accomplished through numerous extraconstitutional and informal means. More or less regular meetings are held with the "Big Four," consisting of the two majority floor leaders and presiding officers. Chairmen of the important committees often join the entourage.

On rare occasions the President has taken a hand in party organizational matters in Congress. In 1937, Franklin Roosevelt intervened to obtain the election of Senator Barkley as majority leader. Vice President Garner received widespread approbation among Democrats, however, when he called it "an encroachment of the legislative branch no President of the United States ought to engage in." [15] President Truman saw the opposing wing of his party select as floor leader Senator McFarland of Arizona instead of Fair Dealer O'Mahoney of Wyoming in 1951, and other Presidents have seen their choices turned down. Nevertheless, Presi-

15 See B. N. Timmons, "John N. Garner's Story," *Collier's*, Feb. 28, 1948.

dents usually cultivate floor leaders to the hilt, once they have been chosen.

After his reelection in 1936, President Roosevelt saw several Democrats in Congress, many of them committee chairmen, oppose important parts of his legislative program while claiming to support him. He spoke out against several of these in the Democratic primaries, hoping the voters would nominate persons more in harmony with his views. Despite his great popularity, Roosevelt was unable to bring about defeat of these insurgents, with one or two exceptions. His opposition apparently helped rather than hurt their reelection. This illustrates to some extent the weak position of the President as leader of his party. He does not possess effective disciplinary powers such as the leader of a British party.

There is some merit in having the executive participate in his party's primaries for the purpose of obtaining a greater degree of party accountability. On the other hand, most Americans seemed to object to this practice and felt it involved a potential, practical danger. President Roosevelt did not use it in any subsequent elections, although in 1942 he suggested that those who favored a strong foreign policy before Pearl Harbor should be returned to Congress irrespective of party labels.

The most successful Presidents in terms of legislative leadership have been those who demonstrated real ability as party leaders and who were able to work with and secure the support of leaders of their party in Congress. This is accomplished in part by the building up of strength back in the constituencies, which in turn have influence on the representatives. Party leadership requires leadership of public opinion and informing the public of policy goals. President Roosevelt used the "fireside chat" on the radio to mobilize public support for his programs. President Eisenhower used a round-table television appearance with several of his Cabinet secretaries to dramatize the Administration's program. All Presidents make trips and deliver speeches in various parts of the United States; many of these touch upon policy matters. These trips give the President an opportunity to meet with local party officials.

Presidential Press Conference. The press conference in the United States is a unique political institution. Foreign leaders and correspondents express amazement at the give-and-take in these conferences between American newspapermen and their President and the various department heads. Presidents Cleveland and McKinley on infrequent occasions met a few carefully chosen correspondents at the door of the White House and gave out some news. To Theodore Roosevelt goes the credit for the inauguration of the press conference. With a flair for the unconventional, he invited friendly journalists to the barbershop and, while being shaved, and to the fascination of the reporters, expounded his views with gestures. President Taft varied this practice through what he called the "town hall meeting." In these cases, which were infrequent, he sat down with a group of newspaper-bureau heads in the Cabinet room and discussed matters of public policy. President Wilson was the first to make the conference a regular weekly affair by receiving correspondents in his private office. Presidents Harding, Coolidge, and Hoover continued the Wilsonian conferences, but with less success, largely because each of them required the journalists to submit written questions in advance.

Because of his easy camaraderie with newspapermen, President Franklin Roosevelt made the press conferences exciting and usually informative.[16] He abolished the rule that questions be submitted in advance in writing and added a high degree of informality to the meetings. President Truman called a press conference within five days after his inauguration and made considerable use of them throughout his tenure.

The press conference exists more or less by sufferance of the President, yet it has become a permanent institution. Great variation exists in the use made of the device. In his last year in office, President Hoover held but 12 meetings, while Roosevelt held 998 during his term in office, an average of 80 a year; Truman held 324, an average of 40 a year. President Eisenhower was slow to call his first conference and met with the press less frequently during his first year but experimented with having part of the conference broadcast and televised. Roosevelt and Truman utilized the conference to make some very important party as well as general announcements of policy.

It is a rule of press conferences that the President may not be quoted without his permission. Correspondents at times complain that this places a serious limitation on the value of the interviews, but the restriction permits the President to develop his points at random and to impart his thoughts to the press. Unlike a straight government press release, the conference helps the reporter to size up the man and to ask leading questions, which bring out information on subjects the reporters feel have wide reader interest. Some of the most sensational news since 1932 has been brought to the people by the presidential press conference. Governors, Cabinet heads, and other public officials also use the press conference with varying results. The success rests in the main with the executive and his personality and his willingness to give out information in this more or less informal manner.

The executive press conferences are sometimes compared with the "question period" in the British Parliament. Except for having the

---

[16] Walter Davenport gives an intimate account of Roosevelt's press conferences in his series "The President and the Press," *Collier's,* Jan. 27 and Feb. 3, 1945. For extensive accounts of the press conference see Merriam Smith, *Thank You, Mr. President* (New York: Harper & Brothers, 1946); and James E. Pollard, *The Presidents and the Press* (New York: The Macmillan Company, 1947).

common objective of obtaining information, the analogy is not correct. In England the administrative heads sit in Parliament, where the members may question them regarding the affairs of their departments.[17] Every member is entitled to put three oral and an unlimited number of written questions to the administrator. An important effect of this procedure is to alert the department heads and to exercise legislative and party control over the administration. The question procedure in England is more formal as compared with the informality of the American press conference and subject to certain guiding rules. Senators Fulbright and Kefauver have proposed an amendment to the Senate and House rules to permit heads of executive departments and independent agencies to appear and answer questions, but this proposal has received little support.

Other Aspects. The party in the administration reflects itself in numerous other ways. Party officials often influence administration and the latter must be sensitive to party pressures; conversely administrators, other than the President, are in a position to influence the party's programs. Illustrative of influence of parties on administration is the item of patronage. Those departments composed of a sizable number of employees whose positions are outside civil service regulations are besieged with requests to give jobs to the party faithful. Where jobs are filled under the civil service, employees may be ousted by the expedient of abolishing jobs. Chief Executives and heads of agencies may run into trouble if they do not reward "regulars" with appointments. Former Democratic National Chairman Edward J. Flynn [18] asserts that Mr. Roosevelt's failure to honor this rule caused much dissatisfaction. Many of the appointments, he notes,

went to men who were supporters of the President and believed in what he was trying to do, but who were not Democrats in many instances, and in all instances were not organization Democrats. This caused a feeling of resentment between the regular organization Democrats and the New Dealers. It did much to bring about the bad feeling so strikingly revealed in the convention in 1940. . . . If the President had continued to appoint Democrats and, in many instances, organization Democrats there would have been no serious opposition in the party to a third term in 1940.

Early in President Eisenhower's Administration similar complaints were voiced by organization Republicans that their patronage demands were

[17] On the question period see R. W. McCulloch, "Question Time in the British House of Commons," *The American Political Science Review*, Vol. 27 (1933), pp. 971–977, and the more recent account by Herman Finer, Report of the Joint Committee on the Organization of Congress, *Suggestions for Strengthening of Congress*, June, 1946, pp. 49–58.

[18] *You're the Boss* (New York: The Viking Press, Inc., 1947), p. 153.

not being recognized. In 1954, the Administration promised to consider these demands and to find jobs for deserving Republicans.

Patronage is at times instrumental in securing support for a presidential program, but in the long run it probably weakens as much as strengthens the Chief Executive's position. Because of "senatorial courtesy," the senators of the same party insist on the right to name all presidential appointees within their own state, except the postmasterships, which traditionally have been accorded to the representatives. Patronage disputes have incurred enmity in the Senate for many Presidents. After initial appointments, the President's influence gained through patronage declines. It is usually on lesser appointments that the patronage can strengthen the President's legislative hand. State and local executives also use patronage to secure support for their policies, but the large number of elective offices weakens, to a considerable degree, the use of patronage, since each elected official has patronage of his own over which the governor or mayor has no control. The padding of the payroll, the appointment of incompetents and political hangers-on, and the use of patronage to build an unscrupulous machine are detrimental to the public welfare and have little defense on the grounds of party cleavage or responsibility.

Party patronage practices in the filling of public offices often horrify independents and purists, who feel that this is "politics" of the lowest sort. Actually, these practices are not so bad as they appear. Any executive must have support if he is to be a responsible party leader and agent of the electorate. It is not unreasonable that he should appoint personal acquaintances and men who share his views. In most instances these men are of the same party affiliations. In launching the new Federal government, President Washington appreciated the need for men who would favor strengthening the national government and chose them instead of states' rightists. The loose character and composition of American major parties needs some cohesive force, however imperfect. Party loyalty in the case of patronage, congressional organization, and elections may help to obtain at least some unity in matters of policy.

It is not unusual for the Postmaster General to hold the position of national chairman in the party. Jackson and Lincoln Day dinners offer the occasion for virtually all Cabinet secretaries to appear before the various party conclaves and to deliver strongly partisan addresses. The secretaries have informal meetings with party leaders from time to time and hear about party matters and become aware of party interests. Rarely does a year go by but what some congressman or local party official calls upon his own President to fire a Cabinet or other officer "for the good of the party."

Administrators are in a position to encourage or discourage legislation in the attitude which they take toward proposed bills introduced by a congressman. Committee chairmen commonly call on administrators to prepare reports on bills before their committees. Unfavorable reports or unfavorable testimony may lead to having the bill sidetracked while a favorable report may advance the measure. The fact that numerous major bills are prepared in the executive branch has already been noted.[19] When these are strongly endorsed by the executive, they are likely to be regarded as party measures, particularly if the executive reminds his party followers that the bills are intended to fulfill campaign and party platform promises.

The independent regulatory commissions such as the Federal Communications Commission, the Federal Trade Commission, and the Interstate Commerce Commission raise special problems for the President and Congress. These groups have quasi-legislative functions which may have considerable influence on the administration's program. The Eisenhower Administration's power program showed considerable variation, at least in degree, from its predecessors. It emphasized "partnership" between the Federal government, the states, and private power companies in developing electric power. The Federal Power Commission is given authority to survey the water resources of the nation and pass on applications to establish hydroelectric projects along navigable waters and public lands. Naturally the Eisenhower program would depend to considerable extent upon the willingness of the FPC to grant permits to private companies and to the states. The FTC has the problem of enforcing prohibition of "unfair methods of competition," a function obviously involving policies toward business. Likewise, the other commissions have jurisdiction over policies which have a bearing on an administration program.

Commissioners are given tenure which often overlaps changes in party control of the executive. In filling vacancies on these commissions, Presidents are careful to inquire into the views of prospective appointees in such areas as the tariff, power, trade practices, and transportation. Several Presidents have had their troubles with the commissions or individual commissioners held over from the previous regime. Franklin Roosevelt found the FTC of different view on several matters and requested the resignation of one of the commissioners. He wrote to Commissioner Humphrey, "I do not feel that your mind and my mind go along together on either the policies or the administering of the Federal Trade Commission, and, frankly, I think it best for the people of this country that I should have a full confidence." The Supreme Court upheld Humphrey's resistance to removal, saying that Congress had limited the President's power to remove members of commissions on these grounds. Because of such limitations, Presidents may find it difficult to bring commission and

[19] See Chap. 7.

party policies into a successful working arrangement. Democrats criticized some of Eisenhower's appointments to the independent commissions. Yet, unless the President can integrate the policies of the independent commissions with those of himself and his Cabinet secretaries, parts of his program are bound to be frustrated. This is one of the important unsolved problems in American government.

In summary, the party in the administration includes the President and his immediate associates in the White House establishment, his Cabinet advisers, and heads of the more important agencies directly under the President. They develop, to a considerable extent, an official party program. Members of independent regulatory commissions are not regarded as a part of the President's political team. The thousands of civil servants are not directly a part of this group because their political neutralization has been established by law. While the opposition party often charges that public employees constitute an "army of voters" who support the incumbent President, there is little evidence to support this assertion. Party policy in the administration is often an *ad hoc* matter. Cabinet secretaries frequently make contradictory statements and presidential secretaries quickly issue "clarifications" on "misunderstandings." These illustrations show that the policies of the party in the administration, like the party in Congress, are evolved in a fragmentary way and that administrators make important party declarations often without clearance from their colleagues or even the President. Statements on foreign and defense policies have especially shown incongruities. Notwithstanding the integration which the President can give to a party program, Congress remains a power center. Unless it agrees to the self-denials and discipline implicit in the President's program, it will be difficult to put over the program of the party as formulated by the President.

PARTY POLITICS AND THE JUDICIARY

Theoretically, the administration of justice should be above partisanship. It is said that there is not a Republican or Democratic method of administering it and that partisan politics should not enter into judicial appointments because it might interfere with the high order of ability, independence, and integrity which is demanded of a judge. The British have never considered it wise to permit their judges to be subjected to the temptation incident to election and have made the judiciary entirely appointive. In some European nations, judges are appointed from among persons specifically trained for the bench. In the United States and England, however, judges come largely from the ranks of practicing lawyers. At this point, the similarity in the choice of judges in England and the United States ends.

Popular Election. In the American states, counties, and municipalities, not only the judges but many other court officers, sheriffs, and clerks are chosen by the voters. Candidates run for office as Republicans or Democrats in a great many cities and counties. In early America, justices were selected by the royal governor; following the American Revolution, appointment came from the state legislatures. With the spread of Jacksonian democracy and the rise of party organization, judges were nominated by the parties and elected by the voters. The parties have maintained the popular election system for judges because of the patronage at the disposal of the bench, such as auctioneers, clerks, guardians, receivers, referees, and trustees. These positions are distributed among political leaders and offer a source of revenue in the form of campaign contributions. Probate and surrogate jobs in most counties are lucrative to the party. Judges, therefore, are nominated not only on the basis of ability, but on vote-getting powers, possible strength to the ticket, and a willingness to turn over the patronage to the party. In municipal elections, the parties hail victories in judgeships as evidence of a trend, "a vote of confidence in the Eisenhower Administration," a "repudiation" of a state administration, and so on. Local party leaders appear to have made a reality, at least in their own minds, of the "party in the judiciary."

In many counties and cities today, few young lawyers can hope to become judges unless they align themselves with a political party and perform several years of yeoman's service. The party leaders say in effect, "You stay with us and someday you'll get to be a magistrate or judge." The young lawyer then becomes attached to a political club and perhaps serves as a counsel for a legislative committee. If he "works out all right," he may be elevated to a clerkship in the judge's office or become a referee, and so on, until a vacancy occurs in one of the smaller judgeships. By this time he has full understanding and appreciation of politics and patronage, an education not forgotten when occupying the bench. This is not to cast aspersions on the integrity of the decisions of judges or to accuse them of rank partisanship and favoritism in questions of law. In fact, many states have an excellent judiciary even though the judges are popularly elected. But it is clear that in matters of personnel the judge is loyal to his party and that the potential judge who possesses vote-getting ability stands a greater chance of elevation to the bench than one who does not have these qualities of "availability."

Federal Appointments. Justices to the Federal courts are appointed by the President with confirmation by the Senate. This has not kept political considerations from entering into judicial appointments, inasmuch as the Federal bench offers some patronage opportunities and also a chance to reward loyal party men who can qualify for the office. That party labels enter into the choice was shown by the demand of Republican Senator Wiley that more of his party be placed on the Federal bench. He noted that only 17 Republicans were among the 231 persons named to the Federal courts from 1932 to 1946.[20] As chairman of the new Senate Judiciary Committee, he called this "an indefensible overrepresentation of the present minority party" and added, "a fair representation of Republicans must be achieved." He stated, "I will do everything I can to reject any more New Deal appointments to the Federal judiciary." In this instance he drew a distinction between conservative Democrats, whom he might approve, and New Dealers, whom he would oppose to the last man so as to put an end to the "grossly lopsided Democratic leftist" character of the bench.

A number of Federal justices have come from the ranks of elected public officials, which again shows that political experience and partisanship are not discounted as qualities of availability. Chief Justice Hughes was a Republican governor from New York and his party's nominee for the presidency in 1916.

Chief Justice Fred Vinson (1946 to 1953) was a Democratic member of Congress and later served in President Truman's Cabinet before his appointment to the bench, and his successor, Earl Warren, was serving his third term as governor of California at the time of his appointment by President Eisenhower. In 1954 seven of the eight justices reflected a political background. Three of them were former United States senators, two were attorneys general, two others held executive positions in the Roosevelt Administration at the time of their appointment.[21]

More important than party politics are the social, economic, and political views of justices. These come into play for the reason that in spite of the so-called separation of powers with an independent judiciary, the courts have been given a share in the lawmaking process, the power of disallowance. Through judicial interpretation of statutes, the courts are in a position to expand or contract the powers of Congress and the executive orders of the administrative branch. Such historical decisions as *Dred Scott v. Sanford, McCullough v. Maryland, Gibbons v. Ogden, Rathbun v. United States, National Labor Relations Board v. Jones and Laughlin Steel Corporation, Schechter v. United States,* and *Yakers v. United States*

[20] *The New York Times,* Jan. 6 and 10, 1947.

[21] A journalistic but informative account of the Court members appointed by Presidents Roosevelt and Truman is that of Wesley McCune, *The Nine Young Men* (New York: Harper & Brothers, 1947). For a scholarly account of Court alignments from 1937 to 1947 see C. Herman Pritchett, "The Roosevelt Court: Votes and Values," *The American Political Science Review,* Vol. 42 (1948), pp. 53–67, and *The Roosevelt Court* (New York: The Macmillan Company, 1948). On the Court under Truman see Arthur Schlesinger, Jr., "The Supreme Court," *Fortune,* January, 1947.

indicate the large role assumed by the courts in the operation of our constitutional system and on the powers of Congress.

It is not surprising, therefore, that many Presidents have had battles with the Supreme Court and that the viewpoints of a prospective appointee are carefully analyzed by both the President and Senate.[22]

SELECTED REFERENCES

There are numerous textbooks and treatises on the organization and operation of Congress which treat in part with parties in Congress. Those especially useful are Floyd Riddick, *Congressional Procedure* (1941), Chaps. 2–5; P. D. Hasbrouck, *Party Government in the House of Representatives* (1927); George B. Galloway, *The Legislative Process in Congress* (1953), Chaps. 11–14, 18; Bertram M. Gross, *The Legislative Struggle: A Study in Social Combat* (1953), Chaps. 4–5, 7; Harvey Walker, *The Legislative Process* (1948), Chaps. 6, 9; Ernest Griffith, *Congress: Its Contemporary Role* (1951); James M. Burns, *Congress on Trial* (1949); Roland Young, *This Is Congress* (1945).

Other pertinent works include E. E. Schattschneider, *Party Government* (1942) and *The Struggle for Party Government* (1948); E. P. Herring, *Presidential Leadership* (1940); W. E. Binkley, *President and Congress* (1947); L. H. Chamberlain, *The President, Congress, and Legislation* (1946); *Toward a More Responsible Two-party System,* published as a supplement to *The American Political Science Review,* Vol. 44 (1950).

There is an abundance of periodical literature on the subject; many of the titles are cited in the chapter. *The New York Times Magazine* frequently carries articles on party leadership questions and the pages of the *Congressional Record* illuminate many battles within Congress on party leadership and policy questions.

[22] See C. G. Haines, *The Doctrine of Judicial Supremacy* (Berkeley, Calif.: University of California Press, 1932), and E. S. Corwin, *The Twilight of the Supreme Court* (1934).

CHAPTER 26

Toward Stronger Party Government?

The accomplishment of party government lies in its demonstrated ability for reducing warring interests and conflicting classes to cooperative terms.

—E. P. HERRING

Party government is the democratic and liberal solution of the problem of reconciling authority and liberty; they can manage interests without becoming oppressive.

—E. E. SCHATTSCHNEIDER

In the majority of legislative struggles in Congress, the parties are little more than observers. A great many bills are noncontroversial and pass without opposition and others provoke only a few dissenting votes based upon local considerations. On some very important measures, however, there are sharp cleavages, many of which cut deeply across party lines (see Tables 13 and 14 in Chapter 12). One observer of the operation of parties on the floor of Congress notes that they appear to desire the role of "neutrality" in legislative battles. The major parties, he says,[1]

if drawn in momentarily, the next moment may be back on the side lines. When they really get into a legislative struggle, it is usually at an advanced stage in combat, rarely before battle positions of conflicting contestants have been crystallized. Sometimes a tacit bipartisan understanding yields a party battle staged like a professional wrestling match. Spokesmen for opposing parties will grunt and groan through a series of phony routines, applying holds that are dramatic to the spectators in the gallery but harmful to nobody and ending up with a preordained finale.

Students of American government have long debated the question of party unity, cohesion, and discipline in matters of public policy in Congress and to some extent in the state legislatures. The party system is criticized by some as resulting in utter chaos and irresponsibility, and, on the other hand, is defended by those who feel it works as well as can be expected. Recent evaluations and discussions of the policy role of parties were stimulated by the report of the committee on political parties of the American Political Science Association. Under the title *Toward*

[1] Bertram M. Gross, *The Legislative Struggle* (New York: McGraw-Hill Book Company, Inc., 1953), p. 67; Chaps. 4–5 are particularly relevant to the problems considered in this section.

a More Responsible Two-party System,[2] the committee made recommendations for the weaknesses it saw.

The provocative Report produced numerous critiques which were in themselves revealing in that they differed with each other over the nature and effectiveness of the American party system.[3] One of them argued that recent party platforms were substantially similar, while another saw sharp differences between major-party platforms. Several interpreted the Report differently from others and some misconceived certain aspects and attributed more extreme viewpoints to the Report than was intended by its writers. The student of political parties will be rewarded by studying these and older writings on the subject of party responsibility. Only the aspects of the controversy which are related to the party in government are summarized at this point.

THE CASE FOR STRONGER PARTIES

Criticisms of the Existing System. In arguing for a greater degree of party discipline, most proponents begin by pointing to the alleged weakness and ineffectiveness of the existing system such as the absence of party votes on legislation, the independence of members of Congress, and the departure from articles of present party dogma. The familiar failure of successful candidates to deliver on platform and campaign pledges is cited as disturbing evidence of a lack of a sense of responsibility. Former Vice President Henry A. Wallace called on the party in Congress in 1946 to discipline those members who continued to desert the President by refusing committee appointments to "a member who turns his back upon the party." Mr. Wallace said: [4]

I say it is a fraud upon the voters when a candidate says, "I stand in full agreement with President Truman" if he then votes in Congress against the forward-looking program enunciated by Harry S. Truman. Unless a member of the majority party in Congress votes in favor of major issues upon which he and his party were elected the legislative branch of our government ceases to function.

[2] Published as a supplement to *The American Political Science Review*, Vol. 44, September, 1950 (hereafter cited as the Report).

[3] The rejoinders were not limited to political scientists but the most careful analysis of the Report appears to be made by them. Perhaps the four most frequently cited are Julius Turner, "Responsible Parties: A Dissent from the Floor," *The American Political Science Review*, Vol. 45 (1951), pp. 143–152; Austin Ranney, "Toward a More Responsible Two-party System: A Commentary," *ibid.*, pp. 488–499; M. S. Stedman, Jr. and Herbert Sonthoff, "Party Responsibility—A Critical Inquiry," *Western Political Quarterly*, Vol. 4 (1951), pp. 454–468; T. W. Goodman, "How Much Political Party Centralization Do We Want?" *Journal of Politics*, Vol. 13 (1951), pp. 536–561.

[4] *The New York Times*, Apr. 23, 1946.

Many other persons in and out of government have voiced similar sentiments.

In its case against what is called the "inadequacies of the present system," the committee on political parties held the view that unless there were better integrated parties in Congress, there would be a drift and dangerous inaction resulting in compensation by "overextending the presidency." [5] Fear was expressed also that there would be a disintegration of the two major parties leading to a splintering effect and a system of several smaller parties. "If the two parties do not develop alternative programs that can be executed," the Report held, "the voter's frustration and the mounting ambiguities of national policy might also set in motion more extreme tendencies to the political left and the political right." [6]

Senator Taft noted in 1941 that there would be no national convention to make declarations in policy before the 1942 elections and that the Republican National Committee had no authority to declare the party's views on foreign policy. In view of this he said, "I see no reason why each congressman and each senator should not run on his own foreign policy." [7] Many critics argue that the crucial role of the United States in the world is jeopardized by such a loose party system, which may be incapable of decision, and that the nation can no longer afford the luxury of extreme independence on the part of members of Congress. Walter Lippmann, a strong advocate of a bipartisan foreign policy, states that it "takes two organized parties, each with its recognized leaders in the field of foreign affairs. Today neither party is organized. Neither party has leaders in the field of foreign policy. In this chaos no Secretary of State can function successfully." [8]

Along somewhat similar lines is the expressed anxiety that the razor-thin margins which recent Presidents have obtained on some foreign policy matters and the failure to deliver a party vote on great national issues may lead to instability of government and the weakening of United States' world leadership. Other commonly voiced opinions are that prospective party members will become so cynical of party promises that they will be reluctant to join parties and that pressure politics will replace party politics.

Those who want to bring about stronger parties do not look upon their objective as an end in itself but have certain purposes in view, purposes which have not always been clearly stated. First they want

[5] On the committee's criticisms of the existing system see the Report, Chaps. 3, 12.
[6] *Ibid.*, p. 95.
[7] The fact that Mr. Taft strongly supported policy committees several years later may indicate he retreated somewhat from this view. However, many congressmen undoubtedly subscribe in principle to the views cited in this quotation.
[8] *New York Herald Tribune,* Mar. 27, 1950.

stronger government, and recognize the party as an instrument for enabling the government to cope with the problems of society in a more definite and positive manner. The strong government of Presidents Wilson and Franklin Roosevelt in their periods of strength was grounded to a considerable degree on their leadership of the party rather than simply an exercise of the constitutional powers assigned to them. The role of the United States in foreign affairs calls for it to be able to take leadership, which, it is feared, cannot be done under a weak party system.

A second objective of party reformers is a system which will bring a more meaningful and purposeful range of choice between alternatives of action. They want to see parties take definite stands and develop broad programs in order to afford the voter more clear-cut choices, largely as a means of achieving greater democracy, but partly also to enable government to carry on more effectively. Proponents of stronger national parties argue there is more need for emphasis on programs than ever before and that the formulation of policy alternatives should be a primary function of parties with the result that party labels will be comprehensible and meaningful to voters and constituent party members. Parties must be able to "bring forth programs to which they commit themselves and . . . possess sufficient internal cohesion to carry out these programs." [9]

Proposals. Recommendations for overhauling the present party system vary from those requiring constitutional amendments to those requiring only changes in party bylaws, congressional machinery, and public attitudes. In the former category is the suggestion of a modified form of cabinet responsibility. Proposals for a cabinet system would be difficult to operate under the present bicameral Congress and Americans are unlikely to take kindly to unicameralism or to weakening the Senate. Former Representative Christian Herter suggested that in the field of foreign policy the President make his proposals a matter of confidence with the sanction of resignation. Professor Elliott proposed that the President be given the power of dissolution of the House of Representatives once a term, thus compelling a House reelection.[10] Thomas K. Finletter likewise would give the President the power of dissolution, but would extend it to both houses and to both branches of the government.[11] He suggests placing the President, the House, and the Senate on a common six-year term with a joint executive-legislative cabinet responsible for preparing a legislative program. The Elliott, Herter, and Finletter proposals stop considerably short of the British system and would retain the President

[9] See Report, p. 18.

[10] W. Y. Elliott, *The Need for Constitutional Reform* (New York: McGraw-Hill Book Company, Inc., 1935).

[11] See *Can Representative Government Do the Job?* (New York: Harcourt, Brace and Company, Inc., 1945).

as a nationally elected independent official rather than simply as the majority leader in Congress.

Less revolutionary in character and perhaps easier to achieve is the plan for a legislative cabinet, which has found numerous converts both within and without Congress, among them a sizable number of political scientists. Under this plan the controlling party in Congress would appoint a group of its leaders in both houses, including the presiding officers, floor leaders, and chairmen of major committees, to formulate the party's legislative program and seek its adoption; the President would also be consulted on policies. If the two houses were controlled by opposing parties, the legislative cabinet would be bipartisan. The cabinet would be collectively responsible for legislation and when defeated in either house on a major party measure would resign. In this event the party caucus would choose a new floor leader and select new committee chairmen. Under this arrangement, writes Professor Chamberlain: [12]

> Our political system will not have been changed . . . individual congressmen will still vote their convictions or record the wishes of those who dominate their constituency. But it will be easier to judge the party in power by its works, as distinguished from its promises, and, perhaps, even its promises will be more significant than formerly.

"Party government" as a proposed system would also make some use of a legislative-executive cabinet. The term itself is not always clearly defined but implies concentration of power in the political party, as James N. Burns says, "in contradistinction to presidential government, congressional government, and cabinet government, not one of which . . . can safely and effectively master the problems arising in an era of chronic crisis." [13] Presumably there would be a single party-in-government capable of formulating the larger national policies, followed by the capacity for disciplining party members and using the machinery of government in a way that would realize the policies. Perhaps the leading proponent of party government is E. E. Schattschneider, who sees it as the most practicable and feasible solution of the problem of organizing American democracy.[14] Party government would carry over the cohesion and victory of election day to cohesion and victory in carrying out public policy. He sees party government as the only force capable of being above, if not

---

[12] L. H. Chamberlain, "Congress—Diagnosis and Prescription," *Political Science Quarterly*, Vol. 60 (1945), p. 445. Professor C. Perry Patterson, *Presidential Government in the United States: The Unwritten Constitution* (Chapel Hill, N.C.: The University of North Carolina Press, 1947), advocates a cabinet composed of members of the party majority in Congress, which would be responsible to such majority.

[13] *Congress on Trial* (New York: Harper & Brothers, 1949), pp. 193–194.

[14] See *Party Government* (New York: Rinehart & Company, Inc., 1942) and *The Struggle for Party Government* (College Park, Md.: University of Maryland, 1948).

controlling, the local political bosses, pressure groups, and the legislator-president, a power capable of harmonizing, synthesizing, and integrating these centers of power in the national interest. The essence of party government is that a party's members in Congress can be bound to vote on articles of party faith and program. In practice, this means the use of the caucus or conference to decide which matters are party matters upon which a line can be laid down. Enforcement of the party will against repeatedly recalcitrant members would be in the form of withdrawing patronage or removal from coveted committee assignments. If this fails, efforts would be made to get the party's voters to purge the member in the primaries. There are numerous cases where a drive has been made to defeat persons for renomination because they have so frequently voted in opposition to the majority of their party.

The Report steered away from both the cabinet system and party government but endorsed the principle that parties could and should be more "responsible." It emphasized a gradual change-over with a bit-by-bit change, starting by developing a strong national organization capable of providing leadership between national conventions, and strengthening party leadership in Congress.[15] On the latter point, it proposed consolidation of the various leadership committees into one for each party in each house, with frequent meetings between the respective committees of the two houses. The leadership group would be responsible for submitting policy proposals to the party membership, managing the legislative schedule, and overseeing committee assignments and structure. These committees would call frequent party conferences and work for a binding decision on legislative policy designed to carry out the party's program. Without calling for abandonment of the seniority principle for committee chairmanships, the Report nonetheless argued that party loyalty and personal competence should have priority over seniority on the major committees of Congress. The recommendation for a four-year term for members of the House of Representatives, with election in presidential years, is one which has widespread acceptance among political scientists irrespective of their views on the rest of the Report.

The committee revived the proposal suggested many years ago by Charles E. Merriam for a party council to serve as a major organ of leadership between national conventions. It recommended biennial national conventions reduced in size from the present nominating conventions. The party council would be composed of about 50 members, including representatives from (1) the national committee; (2) the congressional party organizations; (3) the state committees; (4) the party's governors; and (5) other groups such as the Young Democrats and Young Republicans and some to be designated by the national convention. The

15 See Report, Chaps. 6–10.

President and some Cabinet officers would serve as ex-officio members of the administration party while the defeated presidential nominee would serve on the opposition party council.

Among the duties of the council, which would meet at least four times a year, would be (1) to propose a preliminary draft of the party platform to the national convention; (2) to interpret the platform currently; (3) to consider and make recommendations to appropriate party organs in respect to congressional candidates; and (4) to make recommendations with respect to "conspicuous departures from general party decisions by state or local party organizations." Candidates as well as policies would be discussed in a preliminary way, all with a view to bringing together "the threads of party control and party leadership."

The committee believed that the party council would also be useful in helping to coordinate the numerous state and local organizations. It would try to get these local groups to think in terms of the entire party, imbue them with a stronger sense of party loyalty and overcome some of the diffusing, splintering tendencies caused by local autonomy and federalism. The council, moreover, would receive and discuss policies and views emanating from regional, state, and local party associations.

THE CASE AGAINST STRONGER NATIONAL PARTIES

Criticisms of the Report. The Report was criticized by those who felt it did not go far enough and by others who approved its goals and principles but regarded the proposals as unrealistic. Turner argued that several of the reforms would accentuate the present defects of the party system and would increase the tendency toward one-party districts. If local candidates were kept from insurgency, they might not be able to champion the views of their constituencies and it would be difficult for them to win elections. Insistence upon dogma, regardless of the popularity of the dogmas, would cause a decline of the opposition party's popularity (at that time the Republicans) and lead to a suicide of the minority party.[16]

Several critics accused the Report of underestimating present party responsibility and misconceiving the nature of parties. Turner, for example, insists that the parties do present clear alternatives to the voters and show distinct differences in voting behavior in Congress. He cites a large number of roll calls where the parties differed significantly. However, there is again the matter of interpreting roll-call votes, the standard of a party vote, and so on. The point was made earlier that differences may be greater on votes to recommit and on amendments than on final roll calls when the opposition recognizes that it is an "either-or" proposition. Debate on the degree of difference between the parties becomes

16 *Op. cit.,* pp. 151–152.

something of a standoff because each side can muster data which presumably will prove that there is or is not a substantial degree of party cohesion.

Another point offered in opposition to the Report is that its authors conceive responsibility as simply a matter of organization and that they have, as a result, resorted to suggesting "gadgetry." This, it is argued, is perceiving the problem in much too narrow a context and premise.[17] Parties arise from and reflect the cultural, social, and legal context of the society in which they operate. The present loose party system is the natural consequence of the nation's political system. It follows, therefore, that political behavior is not going to change simply by reorganizing parties.

An objection to stronger, well-disciplined national parties emanates from those who fear that centralization would quench the individualism of state and local organizations and that they would have to accept the dictates of a "central office." Griffith [18] feels it would hurt what he considers a virtuous system of independence in Congress.

The independent on a given issue is in a position to criticize and vote against a special interest; the disciplined man cannot do this if the desires or special interests have been incorporated into his party's program. The opportunity to urge his views in the councils of the party is a poor substitute for the sacrifice of his freedom at the time of the final, responsible decision; . . . the values associated with the localism of Congress would seemingly be eroded in the face of binding national-party programs.

Virtues of Tweedledum and Tweedledee. A number of scholars and observers of the American party system are reasonably content with its operation and feel that it is accomplishing all that can be expected of it. They are sometimes called the "tweedledum-and-tweedledee" school of thought, for they express satisfaction with the lack of clear-cut demarcation between the major parties. Arthur N. Holcombe suggests the best party system as "one in which each of the major parties was as nearly as possible a fair sample of all important factional interests in the country. Under such a party system the voters would possess the greatest freedom of choice between the candidates for important offices on grounds of merit and fitness." [19] Pendleton Herring is fearful of the potentialities of a highly disciplined party system in the hands of those wanting change, noting that if they "were able to gang up and force through a sweeping party program, while all those of the party against change were expected

[17] See especially Stedman and Sonthoff, *op. cit.;* Ranney, *op. cit.;* and E. S. Griffith, *Congress: Its Contemporary Role* (New York: New York University Press, 1951).

[18] *Op. cit.,* p. 167.

[19] *Political Parties of Today* (New York: Harper & Brothers, 1924), p. 145; see also his *Our More Perfect Union* (Cambridge, Mass.: Harvard University Press, 1950).

to stand by until an election occurred two or three years hence, the pent-up feeling and the resulting clash would probably blow the dome off the Capitol." [20]

Those defending the present party system make considerable point of the virtue of "consensus" rule as contrasted with "party" rule, or consensus rule as opposed to majority party rule. Consensus means the building up of a majority by the combining of major groups within the parties. No one group is able to have its own way or to muster a majority unless it can carry substantial fractions of other important groups. Sectional, local, party, and other interests would be protected and to some extent coalesced in the building of a consensus. Some have expressed the fear that majority rule of a single party would work harm to a section and would encourage government by class. If the Democrats were captured by labor interests and could deliver almost a 100 per cent vote, they might put over legislation detrimental to farmers, businessmen, and professionals. Republican rule conceivably could put over measures harmful to the South. Advocates of party responsibility argue that these "ifs" are unlikely to happen and that even if such majorities were obtained, the filibuster in the Senate, presidential veto, and perhaps the courts could be used to check such excesses. Consensus as a procedure has, however, long been a part of the American political system and the majority of American public policies have been enacted this way. Majority party leaders and the President have sought the votes of the minority party whenever they could get them and have attempted to conciliate all classes or most of them in order to work out compromises with minorities.

In summary, the case for the party system as it is rests to a considerable degree on the thesis advanced by A. Lawrence Lowell over a half century ago.[21] The parties are as they are because they are appropriate to the kind of government the people want. The people do not want full-blown majority rule but want it in sharply modified form so as to guarantee that minority rights will be protected. Contemporary defenders of the undisciplined parties support it because it means government by consensus or the "concurrent majority" and seems designed to avoid sharp swings to either the political left or right. The present decentralized arrangements give strength to the parties locally, foster localism in the representative system, and permit the lawmaker a high degree of independence. It is admitted that there are periods of drift in Congress and of voter frustration but that these are part of the process of building up consensus, or as Herbert Agar has suggested, "the price of union." [22] The

[20] *The Politics of Democracy* (New York: Rinehart & Company, Inc., 1940), p. 114.

[21] *Essays on Government* (1897).

[22] *The Price of Union* (Boston: Houghton Mifflin Company, 1950). Arthur W. Macmahon in his presidential address to the American Political Science Association

intraparty strife and conflicts, the friction between the President and Congress, bipartisan coalitions, the lack of programmatic unity, bargaining between interest groups and sections are all a part of the process of building consensus. Viewed in this light, these things, which are so often deplored by people both within and without the parties, are unavoidable and certainly understandable if not desirable. Parties have met the pragmatic test, they have blundered but they have muddled through, they built up consensus during wars and emergencies and have adjusted to as well as modified the Federal, separation-of-powers, presidential system. Given the cultural, legal pattern of American life, they have done as well as can be expected. In general, they have found the middle ground in American politics and have advanced this position in their own peculiar fashion.

THE PEOPLE'S CHOICE

There is a high amount of agreement among critics, and critics of the critics, that the American party system is remarkably flexible and loose-jointed. Within different congressional districts in the United States one can find what amounts to a no-party or one-party system, two-party systems, and even multiple-party systems. American parties are notoriously adaptable and, locally, have learned how to live in their environment.

The two major issues which stand out over the debate on the party system are (1) should the parties stand more definitely for principles and program, and (2) should there be more effective leadership, unity, and discipline within the parties? Even if an affirmative answer is given to both questions, there is disagreement over means and over degree. It is not our purpose to arbitrate the case for or against national parties, especially in Congress. The reader, moreover, has probably already made up his own mind on the subject. It is to state reality, however, that in the twentieth-century world we require a government which can cope with the problems, domestic and foreign, of society. Because a weak party system suited the needs of earlier eras does not mean it is necessarily suitable today. Each generation must reappraise its political institutions in the light of contemporary needs and realities. Both Congress and the Federal executive branch have recently undergone changes in structure and to some extent procedure. A persuasive case can likewise be made for reappraisal of and changes in party structure and outlook. The direct primary was one factor which helped to break down the former party structure of the old boss and machine dominance over nomination. Most persons believe this was good riddance. In some states, notably California, unofficial party organizations have taken over control of the primaries

has brilliantly stated the role of consensus and conflict; see "Conflict, Consensus, Confirmed Trends, and Open Choices," *The American Political Science Review,* Vol. 42 (1948), pp. 1–15.

and the party because the regular party organizations were incompetent. Whether this is a welcome development remains to be seen. In some local areas the weakness of the party organization has led to its being taken over, at least in fact, by pressure groups. This is a development fraught with serious implications and hardly to be welcomed.

Both those for and against the general recommendations in the Report are in rather general agreement that there should be close cooperation between the President and his party leaders in Congress and that the President should exercise effective legislative leadership. One of the ways of working out cooperative relationships between the legislature and the executive is a more effective party structure. The policy and leadership committees are potential instruments for fostering greater discussion of the important national and international issues and for focusing attention on parties as instruments for carrying out the will of the people. There is also general agreement on the need for constant surveillance of the power exercised by sectional and special-interest groups; the parties can be used as instruments for this function.

On at least one other count there should be general agreement and this is the development of a party which enables men and women to participate in an active and satisfying way. Increased political participation is fostered in part by democratizing party organization and enhancing the prestige of politics and parties. Many Americans, however, are likely to be attracted to parties only if they stand for broad principles and support definite programs. To these persons, parties which fail to do so become little more than a sham and a struggle for power and spoils. But opponents of parties based on specific principles and cleavages become concerned about this, especially if disciplinary action is taken against party officeholders who fail to support the party program. This is at the crux of the debate over so-called stronger party government.

To a great extent the kind of party alignments and system will be determined in the constituencies at the local level. If voters are convinced of the value of strongly disciplined parties, they can have this system. Party members can use the primaries and write to their congressmen to enforce loyalty to a national program if they wish, or they can support a man because he is a maverick or an independent. They can aid in the building of a second party where only one now exists and indicate their interest in a politics of policies to a greater extent than in a politics of personalities. Party government in Congress cannot be fully effective without making nominations in the constituencies binding. Thus the party in the country will determine in a large measure the character of the party in the government. All schools of thought can hardly fail to agree that the American two-party system will face increasingly difficult problems of domestic and international policies. Its capacity to cope with these problems will determine what changes in emphases and in organizational arrangements, if any, will be made in the system.

ETHICS IN GOVERNMENT

Although students of government are not agreed on the desirability of a stronger party system in the sense of party discipline, a moral strengthening of American politics can be generally welcomed. As more competent and honest men and women take positions in the party hierarchy and seek public office, the parties will be strengthened and the profession of politics elevated in popular esteem. In recent years there has been a growing interest in the question of morality in government, as evidenced by a considerable body of writing on the subject, congressional studies of ethics in government, and investigations conducted by the Kefauver committee into organized crime. In the 1952 campaign the issues of corruption and morality were injected into the speeches to a much larger degree than in many preceding campaigns.

Areas in Question. During the course of this volume we have noted many practices which appear to raise questions of public morality. As for party activity, there is first of all the question of campaign ethics. "The low plane of campaign ethics," writes George Graham, "is in part responsible for the low prestige of politics as a profession. It is thus a deterrent to entering politics, and in turn feeds back to lower political ethics still farther. Campaign mendacity, if unchecked, sets in motion a downward spiral." [23] Although considerable latitude and tolerance is allowed to campaigners, it is undoubtedly true that concern over excessive mudslinging, charges of disloyalty, personal and family smears, and the like deter some persons from entering public life.

As pointed out earlier, the financial obligations arising from seeking nomination and election may raise grave questions for office seekers and incumbents who do not possess their own funds for financing increasingly expensive campaigns. In 1952, it was dramatically brought out that some congressmen were not only beneficiaries of campaign funds coming in from outside their states from interests seeking special legislation, but that they received private funds for noncampaign expenses. These practices leave the public official open to the obvious question of whether he is or may become indebted to those interests helping him out financially in his legislative work.

Where the political party helps its candidates financially during campaigns and where the party does not become heavily obligated to a few interests, the nominees are freed to some extent from seeking help from

[23] *Morality in American Politics* (New York: Random House, Inc., 1952), p. 281. This book presents a broad discussion of ethics in various segments of American government and politics.

interests who may require special favors. If a party, however, is subservient to a few particular interests, its officeholders may not enjoy freedom in promoting the broad public interest or even the official program of the party itself. Since successful parties are those drawing voting support on a broad basis and stand for reelection on their program, the ethical questions involved in financing are of major importance to the parties.

There is also the question of ethics within government itself. H. H. Wilson has pointed out that individual congressmen often operate on a live-and-let-live basis and spring to the defense of colleagues under indictment or charged with unethical behavior.[24] Questions of propriety may be raised where legislators receive retainers from those who are interested in securing government contracts and favors. There are times when the investigating power has been misused, perhaps unethically, both to "get" an administrative agency or a person not liked by a committee chairman. Numerous congressmen have been convicted of taking salary "kickbacks" from their employees, padding the payroll, and other violations of Federal laws. Considering that there are only 531 members of Congress, these breaches of public faith are more numerous than they should be. "There is," says Graham, "no positive evidence in recent years that the House considers conviction of a crime a disqualification for the high office of serving in Congress." [25]

A duality of interest of both administrators and legislators is likely to occur when they maintain private practices and businesses while working for the public good. Many officials hold active membership in certain organizations. Others hold no membership but nonetheless are products of the business or professional groups to which they belonged prior to entering the public service. Consistent friendliness to certain causes and interests is obvious in the voting and other record of numerous officials. For administrators there are laws prohibiting the holding of financial interest in companies with which one might deal in an official capacity. Legislators are usually less inhibited in this respect. George Galloway notes: [26]

There's a law on the statute books (Title 18, Section 281, USCC) that makes it a felony for a member of Congress to represent a client for a fee before an agency of the Government or in court-martial proceedings. Conviction carries a penalty of a $10,000 fine or two years' imprisonment. Yet members of Congress are often found in the role of advocates before Government agencies, . . . and

---

24 *Congress: Corruption and Compromise* (New York: Rinehart & Company, Inc., 1951).

25 *Op. cit.*, p. 89.

26 *The Legislative Process in Congress* (New York: Thomas Y. Crowell Company, 1953), p. 389; see also pp. 380–391 for a useful summary of the problem of ethics and corruption in government.

whether a fee is involved is known only to the member and his client. Congress never asks.

One Congressman, accused of accepting a fee for private practice, did not even deign to acknowledge the charge. Another, who was paid for helping out in the negotiation of a Government loan for a factory, still enjoys all the privileges of his office.

Concern over public ethics and the questionable status which many accord to politicians is traceable to several causes. The Brandeisian view that bigness is inherently bad is still held in one degree or another by many people. Because government is big, so the story goes, there are many more opportunities for corruption. It is less easy to see government's operations and to supervise them. Without accepting this doctrine, it is nonetheless true that the size and impersonality of the government complicate the question of morality and perhaps raise suspicions.

Of much greater significance is the fact that persons are recruited from private life for public positions and often carry over the practices from private to public business. Yet government operates under a different standard, and practices such as gratuities, which are countenanced in private business dealings, are usually regarded as improper when applied to public business. Many government employees have been pilloried for yielding to pressures of "influence" and for accepting favors from private interests. But unless it is regarded as just as culpable to offer a favor as it is to accept one, private interests are not likely to see the fine distinction between government and private business.

Government reflects the values and standards of the society it serves and if the morals of society are low, it is difficult for government to rise far above them. The fact that public servants are criticized for their improprieties suggests that the public expects a higher standard of them than it does of those outside the government. In effect, a different standard of propriety is applied to government and to business. Politics is probably equally as honest as business and the professions when these different standards are equated.

Confusion over ethical standards also arises from the foremost principle of the public interest. A public action is presumably to be judged not in the individual interest but in the general public interest. But it is difficult to erect criteria to judge the public interest. Legislation defended by some senators is regarded as improper by others. For example, one senator criticized certain tax provisions in these words: "We have the law of depletion and allowance. I think that is improper. . . . I think it is improper that the insurance companies did not pay any Federal income taxes for two years. That amounted to $147,000,000, and here is a $9,000 mink coat that gets the headlines." [27]

[27] Hearings of the Senate Subcommittee on Labor and Public Welfare, Special Committee on Ethics in Government, 82d Cong., 1st Sess., June 20, 1951, p. 87.

It is not so much the absence of codes of public conduct which causes complications but the fact that there are double standards of morality. Legislators exact a higher standard of administrators than they do of themselves, and it was just noted that private and public affairs are operated under different rules and customs. Campaigners may reflect on the personal integrity of their opponents but on the floor of Congress they are expected to refrain from doing so. Of necessity, public servants enjoy certain immunities in pursuit of the public business which they would not enjoy as private citizens, and lawmakers are not held legally accountable for their utterances on the floor of Congress. Some congressional committees operate under a code of fair procedure and others do not. Committee members sometimes violate the code during the hearings and do so with impunity and without fear of being disciplined by the legislature or their parties.

There are still many instances where public actions cannot be easily judged. This is because the line between what is improper, possibly improper, and even possibly illegal is not always easily distinguished. In recent years the questions of "loyalty," "security risk," and "possible security risk" have confused the public and have often been associated in one way or another with morality.

Proposals for Improvement. There are many proposals and methods for improving the ethical standards of politics and politicians. Exposure through the channel of congressional investigations and the press remain important ways of calling attention to wrongdoing. Congressional committees have already drafted codes of legislative conduct and it has become a question of extending these codes and using them as the basis for disciplinary action—something that Congress has been loath to do. The New York legislature in 1954 adopted a code of fair procedure. In signing this bill, Governor Dewey expressed the hope that it might blaze a trail both for Congress and other states.

Among the other proposals advanced are amendments to the corrupt-practices laws which would set up a single responsible fiscal agent for the candidate and a more realistic statutory limitation on expenditures.

The decentralization of party finance has decentralized responsibility and often obscured contributions by interest groups. It may well be that some form of indirect government subsidization as well as stricter enforcement of existing corrupt-practices legislation is needed.

There are several other suggestions which, though they have not been adopted, still merit discussion. One of these is the increase in the salary of legislators and larger expense accounts. This would help to relieve the pressure of "implementing income." Another proposes that congressmen make public their income-tax returns or sources of income. Eisenhower and Stevenson, incidentally, did this during the 1952 campaign.

Several governors have called for legislation to do away with the "legis-lator-lobbyists" who represent clients before state agencies and are in a position to vote appropriations for agencies before which they are special pleaders. The United States, moreover, has still to devise a lobbying law capable of curbing improper pressure. "Improper" tactics, except for bribery, are not well defined and are left to the conscience of the lobbyist.

Such in brief are the problems of some aspects of reform in American politics. These are not matters exclusively for the individual, the bureaucrat, or the legislator. They should be concerns of the political parties and the parties will gain respect as they take more seriously questions of public morality and the behavior of their own officeholders.

There have been cases recently where the party's official or unofficial organization denied endorsement in the primary to those persons whose record raised questions of propriety and integrity. And it is a tribute to the party's voters that they too have at times defeated incumbents in the primaries whose conduct in office appeared unethical. In the final analysis, government operates in the context of society and the morality of the former is conditioned by the morality and standards of society. Ethical conduct in public office is partly a problem for the constituency level and for the local party organization itself. Honest politics can be good politics!

Conclusion. The fact that large segments of the population and the government itself are concerned about corruption and morality in government and politics is an encouraging sign. In many parts of the world graft is accepted as commonplace and some degree of it is more or less expected. By contrast, Great Britain has been able to maintain a strict and high standard of morality and most public servants in the United States exemplify a dedication to high ideals in the public service.

While corruption in public life has not been brought to an end, and given human nature as it is, will never disappear, this country has made great strides toward higher morality in the public service. A century ago some United States senators made no secret of taking money from an interest group as a fee for delivering a speech on their behalf on the floor of the Senate. It is less than a century since the debauchery of the reconstruction state governments ran rampant. Although the huge expenditures of governments today offer many more opportunities for graft than ever before, there is little evidence that corruption has increased at the same rate. What is more, the day of the old corrupt boss and machine, the venal legislature, the bribed voter, the stolen election, and the fixed judge is pretty largely past. But this does not mean that the nation has obtained the standards of ethics in the public service to which it should aspire.

We need to develop a political tradition and standard which will attract able, leading, patriotic citizens to public life. The extent to which they will do so, not for pecuniary gain, but for the recognition, prestige, and sense of service, offers the test of whether our political life is serving the nation. The need for the moral man applies to all levels of government and to persons of all ages. But the public life would be especially enriched by the entry of young persons of ability who will bring to it a high sense of devotion to public service. This applies to elective public office, administrative positions, advisory and consultant capacities, political parties, and political interest groups. The highest type of citizenship involves active participation in public affairs, intelligence, objectivity, leadership, and a high personal standard of public morality.

SELECTED REFERENCES

There is an abundance of periodical literature, both past and present, proposing and opposing stronger national parties; some of these articles are cited in the footnotes of this chapter. Major pertinent works are E. E. Schattschneider, *Party Government* (1942) and *The Struggle for Party Government* (1948); C. H. Berdahl, *Our Two-party System* (1951); J. M. Burns, *Congress on Trial* (1949); Julius Turner, *Party and Constituency: Pressures on Congress* (1951); E. P. Herring, *The Politics of Democracy* (1940); A. N. Holcombe, *Political Parties of Today* (1924); T. K. Finletter, *Can Representative Government Do the Job?* (1945) and *Toward a More Responsible Two-party System,* supplement to *The American Political Science Review,* Vol. 44 (1950).

Some of the volumes on ethical considerations in government include: George Graham, *Morality in American Politics* (1952); H. H. Wilson, *Congress: Corruption and Compromise* (1951); P. H. Appleby, *Morality and Administration in Democratic Government* (1952); P. H. Douglas, *Ethics in Government* (1952); C. W. Callender and J. C. Charlesworth, *Ethical Standards in American Public Life* (1952) and *Ethical Standards in Government,* a committee print of the Senate Subcommittee on Labor and Public Welfare, 82d Cong., 1st Sess. (1951).

The 1952 Platform of the Democratic Party

Adopted by the Democratic National Convention
at Chicago, Illinois, July 24, 1952

PREAMBLE

Our nation has entered into an age in which Divine Providence has permitted the genius of man to unlock the secret of the atom.

No system of government can survive the challenge of an atomic era unless its administration is committed to the stewardship of a trustee imbued with a democratic faith, a buoyant hope for the future, the charity of brotherhood, and the vision to translate these ideals into the realities of human government. The Government of the United States, administered by the Democratic Party, is today so entrusted.

The free choice of the Democratic Party by the people of America as the instrument to achieve that purpose will mean world peace with honor, national security based on collective pacts with other free nations, and a high level of human dignity. National survival demands that these goals be attained, and the endowments of the Democratic Party alone can assure their attainment.

For twenty years, under the dedicated guidance of Franklin Delano Roosevelt and Harry S. Truman, our country has moved steadily along the road which has led the United States of America to world leadership in the cause of freedom.

We will not retreat one inch along that road. Rather, it is our prayerful hope that the people, whom we have so faithfully served, will renew the mandate to continue our service and that Almighty God may grant us the wisdom to succeed.

TWENTY YEARS OF PROGRESS

Achieving Prosperity. An objective appraisal of the past record clearly demonstrates that the Democratic Party has been the chosen American instrument to achieve prosperity, build a stronger democracy, erect the structure of world peace, and continue on the path of progress.

Democratic Party policies and programs rescued American business from total collapse—from the fatal economic consequences of watered stock, unsound banks, useless and greedy holding companies, high tariff barriers, and predatory business practices, all of which prevailed under the last Republican administrations. Democratic policies have enabled the Federal government to help all business, small and large, to achieve the highest rate of productivity, the widest domestic and world markets, and the largest profits in the history of the nation.

The simple fact is that today there are more than four million operating business enterprises in this country, over one million more than existed in 1932. Corporate losses in that fateful year were over $3 billion; in 1951, corporate profits, after taxes, reached the staggering total of $18 billion.

Democratic policies and programs rescued American agriculture from the economic consequences of blight, drought, flood and storm, from oppressive and indiscriminate foreclosures, and from the ruinous conditions brought about by the bungling incompetence and neglect of the preceding twelve years of Republican mal-administration.

Economic stability, soil conservation, rural electrification, farm dwelling improvement, increased production and efficiency and more than seven-fold increase in cash income have been the return to farmers for their faith in the Democratic Party.

Democratic labor policies have rescued the wage earners in this country from mass unemployment and from sweat shop slavery at starvation wages. Under our Democratic administrations, decent hours, decent wages, and decent working conditions have become the rule rather than the exception.

Self-organization of labor unions and collective bargaining, both of which are the keystone to labor-management peace and prosperity, must be encouraged, for the good of all.

Unemployment is now less than 3 per cent of the labor force, compared with almost 25 per cent in 1932. Trade union membership has reached a total of 16 million, which is more than five times the total of 1932.

The welfare of all economic and social groups in our society has been promoted by the sound, progressive and humane policies of the Democratic Party.

Strengthening Democracy. We are convinced that lasting prosperity must be founded upon a healthy democratic society respectful of the rights of all people.

Under Democratic Party leadership more has been done in the past twenty years to enhance the sanctity of individual rights than ever before in our history. Racial and religious minorities have progressed further toward real equality than during the preceding 150 years.

Governmental services, democratically administered, have been improved and extended. The efficiency, economy, and integration of federal operations have been advocated and effectuated through sound programs and policies. Through cooperative programs of federal aid, state and local governments have been encouraged and enabled to provide many more services.

The Democratic Party has been alert to the corroding and demoralizing effects of dishonesty and disloyalty in the public service. It has exposed and punished those who would corrupt the integrity of the public service, and it has always championed honesty and morality in government. The Loyalty Program of President Truman has served effectively to prevent infiltration by subversive elements and to protect honest and loyal public servants against unfounded and malicious attacks.

We commend the relentless and fearless actions of Congressional committees which, under vigorous Democratic leadership, have exposed dereliction in public service, and we pledge our support to a continuance of such actions as conditions require them.

The administration of our government by the Democratic Party has been based upon principles of justice and equity, and upon the American tradition of fair play. Men who are elected to high political office are entrusted with high responsibilities. Slander, defamation of character, deception and dishonesty are as truly transgressions of God's commandments when resorted to by men in public life as they are for all other men.

Building Peace with Honor. The Democratic Party has worked constantly for peace—lasting peace, peace with honor, freedom, justice, and security for all nations.

The return of the Democratic Party to power in 1933 marked the end of a tragic era of isolationism fostered by Republican administrations which had deliberately and callously rejected the golden opportunity created by Woodrow Wilson for collective action to secure the peace.

This folly contributed to the second World War. Victory in that war has presented the nations of the world a new opportunity which the Democratic Party is determined shall not be lost.

We have helped establish the instrumentalities through which the hope of mankind for universal world peace can be realized. Under Democratic leadership, our nation has moved promptly and effectively to meet and repel the menace to world peace by Soviet imperialism.

Progress in the New Era. The Democratic Party believes that past progress is but a prelude to the human aspirations which may be realized in the future.

Under Democratic Party leadership, America has accepted each new challenge of history and has found practical solutions to meet and overcome them. This we have done without departing from the principles of our basic philosophy that it is the destiny of man to achieve his earthly ends in the spirit of brotherhood.

A great Democrat—Franklin Delano Roosevelt—devised the programs of the New Deal to meet the pressing problems of the 1930's. Another great Democrat—Harry S. Truman—devised the programs of the Fair Deal to meet the complex problems of America in the 1940's. The Democratic Party is ready to face and solve the challenging problems of the 1950's. We dedicate ourselves to the magnificent work of these great Presidents and to mould and adapt their Democratic principles to the new problems of the years ahead.

In this spirit we adopt and pledge ourselves to this, the Democratic platform for 1952.

OUR GOAL IS PEACE WITH HONOR

Peace with honor is the greatest of all our goals.

We pledge our unremitting efforts to avert another world war. We are determined that the people shall be spared that frightful agony.

We are convinced that peace and security can be safeguarded if America does not deviate from the practical and successful policies developed under Democratic leadership since the close of World War II. We will resolutely move ahead with the constructive task of promoting peace.

THE DEMOCRATIC PROGRAM FOR PEACE AND NATIONAL SECURITY

Supporting the United Nations. Under Democratic leadership, this country sponsored and helped create the United Nations and became a charter member and staunchly supports its aims.

We will continue our efforts to strengthen the United Nations, improve its institutions as experience requires, and foster its growth and development.

The communist aggressor has been hurled back from South Korea. Thus, Korea has proved, once and for all, that the United Nations will resist aggression. We urge continued effort, by every honorable means, to bring about a fair and effective peace settlement in Korea in accordance with the principles of the United Nations' charter.

Strong National Defense. Our Nation has strengthened its national defenses against the menace of Soviet aggression.

The Democratic Party will continue to stand unequivocally for strong, balanced defense forces for this country—land, sea and air. We will continue to support the expansion and maintenance of the military and civil defense forces required for our national security. We reject the defeatist view of those who say we cannot afford the expense and effort necessary to defend ourselves. We express our full confidence in the Joint Chiefs of Staff. We voice complete faith in the ability and valor of our armed forces, and pride in their accomplishments.

COLLECTIVE STRENGTH FOR THE FREE WORLD

We reject the ridiculous notions of those who would have the United States face the aggressors alone. That would be the most expensive—and the most dangerous—method of seeking security. This Nation needs strong allies, around the world, making their maximum contribution to the common defense. They add their strength to ours in the defense of freedom.

The Truman Doctrine in 1947, the organization of hemisphere defense at Rio de Janeiro that same year, the Marshall Plan in 1948, the North Atlantic Treaty in 1949, the Point IV program, the resistance to communist aggression in Korea, the Pacific Security Pacts in 1951, and the Mutual Security Programs now under way— all stand as landmarks of America's progress in mobilizing the strength of the free world to keep the peace.

Encouraging European Unity. We encourage the economic and political unity of free Europe and the increasing solidarity of the nations of the North Atlantic Community.

We hail the Schuman Plan to pool the basic resources of industrial western Europe, and the European Defense Community. We are proud of America's part in carrying these great projects forward and we pledge our continuing support until they are established.

Support for Free Germany. We welcome the German Federal Republic into the company of free nations. We are determined that Germany shall remain free and continue as a good neighbor in the European community. We sympathize with the German people's wish for unity and will continue to do everything we can by peaceful means to overcome the Kremlin's obstruction of that rightful aim.

Support for the Victims of Soviet Imperialism. We will not abandon the once-free peoples of Central and Eastern Europe who suffer now under the Kremlin's tyranny in violation of the Soviet Union's most solemn pledges at Teheran, Yalta, and Potsdam. The United States should join other nations in formally declaring genocide to be an international crime in time of peace as well as war. This crime was exposed once more by the shocking revelations of Soviet guilt as disclosed in the report filed in Congress by the special committee investigating the Katyn Forest massacre. We look forward to the day when the liberties of Poland and the other oppressed Soviet satellites, including Czechoslovakia, Hungary, Rumania, Bulgaria, Albania, Lithuania, Estonia and Latvia and other nations in Asia under Soviet domination, will be restored to them and they can again take their rightful place in the community of free nations. We will carry forward and expand the vital and effective program of the "Voice of America" for penetration of the "Iron Curtain," bringing truth and hope to all the people subjugated by the Soviet Empire.

Support for the Nations of the Middle East. We seek to enlist the people of the Middle East to work with us and with each other in the development of the region, the lifting of health and living standards, and the attainment of peace. We favor the development of integrated security arrangements for the Middle East and other assistance to help safeguard the independence of the countries in the area.

We pledge continued assistance to Israel so that she may fulfill her humanitarian mission of providing shelter and sanctuary for her homeless Jewish refugees while strengthening her economic development.

We will continue to support the tripartite declaration of May 1950, to encourage Israel and the Arab States to settle their differences by direct negotiation, to maintain and protect the sanctity of the Holy Places and to permit free access to them.

We pledge aid to the Arab States to enable them to develop their economic resources and raise the living standards of their people. We support measures for the relief and reintegration of the Palestine refugees, and we pledge continued assistance to the reintegration program voted by the General Assembly of the United Nations in January 1952.

South Asia: A Testing Ground for Democracy. In the subcontinent of South Asia, we pledge continuing support for the great new countries of India and Pakistan in their efforts to create a better life for their people and build strong democratic governments to stand as bastions of liberty in Asia, secure against the threat of communist subversion.

Collective Security in the Pacific. We welcome free Japan as a friendly neighbor and an ally in seeking security and progress for the whole Pacific area. America's security pacts with Japan and with the Philippines, Australia, and New Zealand are indispensable steps toward comprehensive mutual security arrangements in that area. Our military and economic assistance to the Nationalist Government of China on Formosa has strengthened that vital outpost of the free world, and will be continued.

Strengthening the Americas. In the Western Hemisphere, we pledge ourselves to continue the policy of the good neighbor. We will strive constantly to strengthen the bonds of friendship and cooperation with our Latin American allies who are joined with us in the defense of the Americas.

Disarmament Remains the Goal. The free world is rearming to secure the peace. Under Democratic leadership, America always stands prepared to join in a workable system for foolproof inspection and limitation of all armaments, including atomic weapons. This nation has taken the leadership in proposing concrete, practical plans for such a system. We are determined to carry on the effort for a real, effective disarmament.

We look forward to the days when a great share of the resources now devoted to the armaments program can be diverted into the channels of peaceful production to speed the progress of America and of the underdeveloped regions of the world.

Helping Other People to Help Themselves. Even though we cannot now disarm, we will go forward as rapidly as possible in developing the imaginative and far-sighted concept of President Truman embodied in the Point IV program.

We will continue to encourage use of American skills and capital in helping the people of underdeveloped lands to combat disease, raise living standards, improve land tenure and develop industry and trade. The continuance of ever stronger and more vigorous Point IV programs—sponsored both by this country and by the United Nations—is an indispensable element in creating a peaceful world.

Upholding the Principle of Self-Determination. In an era when the "Satellite State" symbolizes both the tyranny of the aggressor nations and the extinction of liberty in small nations, the Democratic Party reasserts and reaffirms the Wilsonian principle of the right of national self-determination. It is part of the policy of the Democratic Party, therefore, to encourage and assist small nations and all peoples in the peaceful and orderly achievement of their legitimate aspirations toward political, geographical and ethnic integrity so that they may dwell in the family of sovereign nations with freedom and dignity.

Expanding World Trade. The Democratic Party has always stood for expanding trade among free nations. We reassert that stand today. We vigorously oppose any restrictive policies which would weaken the highly successful reciprocal trade program fathered by Cordell Hull.

Since 1934 the United States has taken the lead in fostering the expansion and liberalization of world trade.

Our own economy requires expanded export markets for our manufactured and agricultural products and a greater supply of essential imported raw materials. At the same time, our friends throughout the world will have opportunity to earn their own way to higher living standards with lessened dependence on our aid.

Progressive Immigration Policies. Solution of the problem of refugees from Communism and over-population has become a permanent part of the foreign policy program of the Democratic Party. We pledge continued co-operation with other free nations to solve it.

We pledge continued aid to refugees from Communism and the enactment of President Truman's proposals for legislation in this field. In this way we can give hope and courage to the victims of Soviet brutality and can carry on the humanitarian tradition of the Displaced Persons Act.

Subversive elements must be screened out and prevented from entering our land, but the gates must be left open for practical numbers of desirable persons from abroad whose immigration to this country provides an invigorating infusion into the stream of American life, as well as a significant contribution to the solution of the world refugee and over-population problems.

We pledge continuing revision of our immigration and naturalization laws to do away with any unjust and unfair practices against national groups which have contributed some of our best citizens. We will eliminate distinctions between native born and naturalized citizens. We want no "second-class" citizens in free America.

OUR DOMESTIC POLICY

Economic Opportunity and Growth. The United States is today a land of boundless opportunity. Never before has it offered such a large measure of prosperity, security and hope for all its people.

Horizons of even greater abundance and opportunity lie before us under a Democratic Administration responsive to the will of the people.

The Democratic Administration has had a guiding principle since taking office 20 years ago: that the prosperity and growth of this nation are indivisible. Every step we have taken to help the farmers has also helped the workers and business. Every improvement in the status of the worker has helped both farmers and business. Every expansion of business has provided more jobs for workers and greater demand for farm products.

A STABILIZED ECONOMY

Combatting Inflation. The Democratic Administration early recognized that defense production would limit the amount of goods in civilian markets and subject our economy to heavy inflationary pressure. To prevent this from resulting in ruinous inflation, the Administration proposed pay-as-we-go taxation to keep the national debt as low as possible and to prevent excess money pressure on scarce goods and services.

Direct controls were also proposed to channel scarce materials into highly essential defense production and to keep prices down.

In 1951 and 1952 Republican Congressmen demonstrated their attitude toward these necessary measures when they sponsored amendments which would have destroyed all controls.

Prices. We shall strive to redress the injury done to the American people—especially to white-collar workers and fixed-income families—by the weakening amendments which the Republicans in Congress have forced into our anti-inflation laws.

We pledge continuance of workable controls so long as the emergency requires them. We pledge fair and impartial enforcement of controls and their removal as quickly as economic conditions allow.

Rents. We strongly urge continued Federal rent control in critical defense areas and in the many other localities still suffering from a substantial shortage of adequate housing at reasonable prices.

Full Employment. The Democratic Administration prudently passed the Employment Act of 1946, declaring it to be national policy never again to permit large-scale unemployment to stalk the land. We will assure the transition from defense production to peace-time production without the ravages of unemployment. We pledge ourselves at all times to the maintenance of maximum employment, production and purchasing power in the American economy.

Integrity in Government Finances. We solemnly pledge the preservation of the financial strength of the Government. We have demonstrated our ability to maintain and enhance the Nation's financial strength. In the six full fiscal years since V-J Day, our fiscal policy has produced a $4 billion budget surplus. We have reduced the public debt $17 billion from the post-war peak.

We have demonstrated our ability to make fiscal policy contribute in a positive way to economic growth and the maintenance of high-level employment. The policies which have been followed have given us the greatest prosperity in our history. Sustained economic expansion has provided the funds necessary to finance our defense and has still left our people with record high consumer incomes and business with a record volume of investment. Employment and personal incomes are at record levels. Never have Americans enjoyed a higher standard of living and saved more for contingencies and old age!

Federal Taxes. We believe in fair and equitable taxation. We oppose a Federal general sales tax. We adhere to the principle of ability to pay. We have enacted an emergency excess profits tax to prevent profiteering from the defense program and have vigorously attacked special tax privileges.

Tax Reductions. In the future, as in the past, we will hold firm to policies consistent with sound financing and continuing economic progress. As rapidly as defense requirements permit, we favor reducing taxes, especially for people with lower incomes. But we will not imperil our Nation's security by making reckless promises to reduce taxes. We deplore irresponsible assertions that national security can be achieved without paying for it.

Closing Tax Loopholes. Justice requires the elimination of tax loopholes which favor special groups. We pledge continued efforts to the elimination of remaining loopholes.

Government Expenditure. We believe in keeping Government expenditures to the lowest practicable level. The great bulk of our national budget consists of obligations incurred for defense purposes. We pledge ourselves to a vigilant review of our expenditures in order to reduce them as much as possible.

THE AMERICAN FARMER AND AGRICULTURE

We know that national prosperity depends upon a vigorous, productive and expanding agriculture.

We take great pride in our Party's record of performance and in the impressive gains made by American agriculture in the last two decades. Under programs of Democratic Administrations the net agricultural income has increased from less than two billion dollars to almost fifteen billion dollars. These programs must be continued and improved.

Resource Conservation. The soil resources of our country have been conserved and strengthened through the Soil Conservation Service, the Agricultural Conservation Program, the Forestry and the Research programs, with their incentives to increased production through sound conservation farming. These programs have revolutionized American agriculture and must be continued and expanded. We will accelerate programs of upstream flood prevention, watershed protection, and soil, forest and water conservation in all parts of the country. These conservation measures are a national necessity; they are invaluable to our farmers, and add greatly to the welfare of all Americans and of generations yet unborn.

Grass Roots Administration. We will continue the widest possible farmer participation through referenda, farmer-elected committees, local soil conservation districts, and self-governing agencies in the conduct and administration of these truly democratic programs, initiated and developed under Democratic administrations.

Price Supports. Under the present farm program, our farmers have performed magnificently and have achieved unprecedented production. We applaud the recent Congressional action in setting aside the "sliding scale" for price support through 1954, and we will continue to protect the producers of basic agricultural commodities under the terms of a mandatory price support program at not less than ninety percent of parity. We continue to advocate practical methods for extending price supports to other storables and to the producers of perishable commodities, which account for three-fourths of all farm income.

Abundant Production. We will continue to assist farmers in providing abundant and stable supplies of agricultural commodities for the consumers at reasonable prices, and in assuring the farmer the opportunity to earn a fair return commensurate with that enjoyed by other segments of the American economy.

The agricultural adjustment programs encourage the production of abundant supplies while enabling producers to keep supply in line with consumer demand, preventing wide fluctuations and bringing stability to the agricultural income of the nation. We pledge retention of such programs.

We pledge continued efforts to provide adequate storage facilities for grain and other farm products, with sufficient capacity for needed reserves for defense, and other emergency requirements, in order to protect the integrity of the farm price support programs.

Research. We are justly proud of the outstanding achievements of our agricultural research. We favor a greatly expanded research and education program for American agriculture in order that both production and distribution may more effectively serve consumers and producers alike, and thus meet the needs of the modern world. We favor especial emphasis on the development of new crops and varieties, on crop and livestock disease and pest control, and on agricultural statistics and marketing services.

Marketing. We must find profitable markets for the products of our farms, and we should produce all that these markets will absorb. To this end we will continue our efforts to reduce trade barriers, both at home and abroad, to provide better marketing and inspection facilities, and to find new uses and outlets for our foods and fibers both in domestic and foreign markets.

Farm Credit. We have provided credit facilities for all agriculture, including means by which young men, veterans of military service, and farm tenants have been encouraged to become farmers and farm home-owners, and through which low-income farmers have been assisted in establishing self-sustaining and fully productive farm units. We will not waver in our efforts to provide such incentives.

Crop Insurance. Crop insurance to protect farmers against loss from destruction of their crops by natural causes has been created and developed under Democratic Administrations into a sound business operation. This program should be expanded as rapidly as experience justifies, in order that its benefits may be made available to every farmer.

Rural Electrification. Democratic Administrations have established the great Rural Electrification Program, which has brought light and power to the rural homes of our Nation. In 1935, only 10% of the farm homes in America had the benefits of electricity. Today, 85% of our rural homes enjoy the benefits of electric light and power. We will continue to fight to make electricity available to all rural homes, with adequate facilities for the generation and transmission of power. Through the Rural Telephone Program, inaugurated by the **Democratic 81st Congress,** we will provide the opportunity for every farm home to have this modern essential service. We pledge support of these self-liquidating farm programs.

Cooperatives. We will continue to support the sound development and growth of bonafide farm cooperatives and to protect them from punitive taxation.

Defense Needs. We will continue to recognize agriculture as an essential defense industry, and to assist in providing all the necessary tools, machinery, fertilizer, and manpower needed by farmers in meeting production goals.

Family Farming. The family farm is the keystone of American agriculture. We will strive unceasingly to make the farm homes of our country healthier and happier places in which to live. We must see that our youth continues to find attractive opportunity in the field of agriculture.

The Republican Party Platform is loud in its criticism of our great farm programs. We challenge Republicans and other enemies of farm progress to justify their opposition to the program now in operation, to oppose the improvements here proposed, or to advocate repeal of a single vital part of our program.

A FAIR DEAL FOR WORKERS

Good Incomes. There can be no national prosperity unless our working men and women continue to prosper and enjoy rising living standards. The rising productivity of American workers is a key to our unparalleled industrial progress. Good incomes for our workers are the secret of our great and growing consumer markets.

Labor-Management Relations. Good labor-management relations are essential to good incomes for wage earners and rising output from our factories. We believe that to the widest possible extent consistent with the public interest, management and labor should determine wage rates and conditions of employment through free collective bargaining.

Taft-Hartley Act. We strongly advocate the repeal of the Taft-Hartley Act.

The Taft-Hartley Act has been proved to be inadequate, unworkable, and unfair. It interferes in an arbitrary manner with collective bargaining, tipping the scales in favor of management against labor.

The Taft-Hartley Act has revived the injunction as a weapon against labor in industrial relations. The Act has arbitrarily forbidden traditional hiring practices which are desired by both management and labor in many industries. The Act has forced workers to act as strikebreakers against their fellow unionists. The Act has served to interfere with one of the most fundamental rights of American workers— the right to organize in unions of their own choosing.

We deplore the fact that the Taft-Hartley Act provides an inadequate and unfair means of meeting with national emergency situations. We advocate legislation that will enable the President to deal fairly and effectively with cases where a breakdown in collective bargaining seriously threatens the national safety or welfare.

In keeping with the progress of the times, and based on past experience, a new legislative approach toward the entire labor-management problem should be explored.

Fair Labor Standards. We pledge to continue our efforts so that government programs designed to establish improved fair labor standards shall prove a means of assuring minimum wages, hours, and protection to workers consistent with present-day progress.

Equal Pay for Equal Work. We believe in equal pay for equal work, regardless of sex, and we urge legislation to make that principle effective.

The Physically Handicapped. We promise to further the program to afford employment opportunities both in government and in private industry for physically handicapped persons.

Migratory Workers. We advocate prompt improvement of employment conditions of migratory workers and increased protection of their safety and health.

STRENGTHENING FREE ENTERPRISE

The free enterprise system has flourished and prospered in America during these last twenty years as never before. This has been made possible by the purchasing power of all our people, and we are determined that the broad base of our prosperity shall be maintained.

Small and Independent Business. Small and independent business is the backbone of American free enterprise. Upon its health depends the growth of the economic system whose competitive spirit has built this nation's industrial strength and provided its workers and consumers with an incomparably high standard of living.

Independent business is the best offset to monopoly practices. The Government's role is to insure that independent business receives equally fair treatment with its competitors.

Congress has established the permanent Small Business Committee of the Senate and the Special Small Business Committee of the House, which have continued to render great service to this important segment of our economy. We favor continuance of both these committees, with all the powers to investigate and report conditions, correct discriminations, and propose needed legislation.

We pledge ourselves to increased efforts to assure that small business be given equal opportunity to participate in government contracts, and that a suitable proportion of the dollar volume of defense contracts be channeled into independent small business. The Small Defense Plants Administration, which our Party caused to be established, should retain its independent status and be made a continuing agency, equipped with sufficient lending powers to assist qualified small business in securing defense contracts.

We urge the enactment of such laws as will provide favorable incentives to the establishment and survival of independent businesses, especially in the provision of tax incentives and access to equity or risk capital.

Enforcement of Anti-Trust Laws. Free competitive enterprise must remain free and competitive if the productive forces of this nation are to remain strong. We are alarmed over the increasing concentration of economic power in the hands of a few.

We reaffirm our belief in the necessity of vigorous enforcement of the laws against trusts, combinations, and restraints of trade, which laws are vital to the safeguarding of the public interest and of small competitive business men against predatory monopolies. We will seek adequate appropriations for the Department of Justice and the Federal Trade Commission for vigorous investigation and for enforcement of the anti-trust laws. We support the right of all persons to work together in cooperatives and other democratic associations for the purpose of carrying out any proper business operations free from any arbitrary and discriminatory restrictions.

Protection of Investors and Consumers. We must avoid unnecessary business controls. But we cannot close our eyes to the special problems which require Government surveillance. The Government must continue its efforts to stop unfair selling practices which deceive investors, and unfair trade practices which deceive consumers.

Transportation. In the furtherance of national defense and commerce, we pledge continued Government support, on a sound financial basis, for further development of the Nation's transportation system—land, sea and air. We endorse a policy of fostering the safest and most reliable air transportation system of the world. We favor fair, non-discriminatory freight rates to encourage economic growth in all parts of the country.

Highways. In cooperation with State and local governmental units, we will continue to plan, coordinate, finance, and encourage the expansion of our road and highway

network, including access roads, for the dual purposes of national defense and efficient motor transportation. We support expansion of farm-to-market roads.

Rivers and Harbors. We pledge continued development of our harbors and waterways.

Merchant Marine. We will continue to encourage and support an adequate Merchant Marine.

OUR NATURAL RESOURCES

The United States has been blessed with the richest natural resources of any nation on earth.

Yet, unless we redouble our conservation efforts we will become a "have-not" nation in some of the most important raw materials upon which depend our industries, agriculture, employment and high standard of living. This can be prevented by a well-rounded and nation-wide conservation effort.

Land and Water Resources. We favor sound, progressive development of the nation's land and water resources for flood control, navigation, irrigation, power, drainage, soil conservation and creation of new, small family-sized farms, with immediate action in critical areas.

We favor the acceleration of all such projects, including construction of transmission facilities to load centers for wider and more equitable distribution of electric energy at the lowest cost to the consumer with continuing preference to public agencies and REA Cooperatives.

The Democratic Party denounces all obstructionist devices designed to prevent or retard utilization of the nation's power and water resources for the benefit of the people, their enterprises and interests.

The wise policy of the Democratic Party in encouraging multi-purpose projects throughout the country is responsible for America's productive superiority over any nation in the world and is one of the greatest single factors leading toward the accomplishment of world peace. Without these projects our atomic weapons program could never have been achieved, and without additional such projects it cannot be expanded.

The Democratic Party is dedicated to a continuation of the natural resources development policy inaugurated and carried out under the administrations of Presidents Roosevelt and Truman, and to the extension of that policy to all parts of the nation, North, South, East, Mid-West, West and the territories to the end that the nation and its people receive maximum benefits from these resources to which they have an inherent right.

The Democratic Party further pledges itself to protect these resources from destructive monopoly and exploitation.

River Basin Development. We pledge the continued full and unified regional development of the water, mineral, and other natural resources of the Nation, recognizing that the progress already achieved under the initiative of the Democratic Party in the arid and semi-arid States of the West, as well as in the Tennessee Valley, is only an indication of still greater results which can be accomplished.

Fertilizer Development. Great farming areas, particularly of the Mid-West and West, are in acute need of low-cost commercial fertilizers. To meet this demand, we favor the opening of the nation's phosphate rock deposits in the West, through prompt provision of sufficient low-cost hydro-electric power to develop this great resource.

Forests and Public Lands. We seek to establish and demonstrate such successful policies of forest and land management on Federal property as will materially assist state and private owners in their conservation efforts. Conservation of forest and range lands is vital to the strength and welfare of the Nation. Our forest and range lands must be protected and used wisely in order to produce a continuing supply of basic raw materials for industry; to reduce damaging floods; and to preserve the sources of priceless water. With adequate appropriations to carry out feasible projects, we pledge a program of forest protection, reforestation projects and sound practices of production and harvesting which will promote sustained yields of forest crops.

We propose to increase forest access roads in order to improve cutting practices on both public and private lands.

On the public land ranges we pledge continuance of effective conservation and use programs, including the extension of water pond construction and restoration of forage cover.

Arid Areas. In many areas of the Nation assistance is needed to provide water for irrigation, domestic and industrial purposes. We pledge that in working out programs for rational distribution of water from Federal sources we will aid in delivering this essential of life cheaply and abundantly.

Minerals and Fuels. The Nation's minerals and fuels are essential to the national defense and development of our country. We pledge the adoption of policies which will further encourage the exploration and development of additional reserves of our Mineral Resources. We subscribe to the principles of the Stockpiling Act and will lend our efforts to strengthening and expanding its provisions and those of the Defense Production Act to meet our military and civilian needs. Additional access roads should be constructed with Government aid. Our synthetic fuels, including monetary metals, research program should go forward. Laws to aid and assist these objectives will be advocated.

Domestic Fisheries. We favor increased research and exploration for conserving and better utilizing fishery resources; expanded research and education to promote new fishery products and uses and new markets; promotion of world trade in fish products; a public works and water policy providing adequate protection for domestic fishery resources; and treaties with other nations for conservation and better utilization of international fisheries.

Wildlife, Recreation. In our highly complex civilization, outdoor recreation has become essential to the health and happiness of our people.

The Democratic Party has devoted its efforts to the preservation, restoration and increase of the bird, animal and fish life which abound in this Nation. State, local and private agencies have cooperated in this worthy endeavor. We have extended and vastly improved the parks, forests, beaches, streams, preserves and wilderness areas across the land.

To the 28,000,000 of our citizens who annually purchase fishing and hunting licenses, we pledge continued efforts to improve all recreational areas.

ATOMIC ENERGY

In the field of atomic energy, we pledge ourselves:

(1) To maintain vigorous and non-partisan civilian administrations, with adequate security safeguards;

(2) To promote the development of nuclear energy for peaceful purposes in the interests of America and mankind;

(3) To build all the atomic and hydrogen fire-power needed to defend our country, deter aggression, and promote world peace;

(4) To exert every effort to bring about bonafide international control and inspection of all atomic weapons.

SOCIAL SECURITY

Our national system of social security, conceived and developed by the Democratic Party, needs to be extended and improved.

Old Age and Survivors Insurance. We favor further strengthening of old age and survivors insurance, through such improvements as increasing benefits, extending them to more people and lowering the retirement age for women.

We favor the complete elimination of the work clause for the reason that those contributing to the Social Security program should be permitted to draw benefits upon reaching the age of eligibility and still continue to work.

Unemployment Insurance. We favor a stronger system of unemployment insurance, with broader coverage and substantially increased benefits including an allowance for dependents.

Public Assistance. We favor further improvements in public assistance programs for the blind, the disabled, the aged and children in order to help our less fortunate citizens meet the needs of daily living.

Private Plans. We favor and encourage the private endeavors of social agencies, mutual associations, insurance companies, industry-labor groups, and cooperative societies to provide against the basic hazards of life through mutually agreed upon benefit plans designed to complement our present Social Security program.

Needs of Our Aging Citizens. Our older citizens constitute an immense reservoir of skilled, mature judgment and ripened experience. We pledge ourselves to give full recognition to the rights of our older citizens to lead a proud, productive and independent life throughout their years.

In addition to the fundamental improvements in Old Age and Survivors Insurance, which are outlined above, we pledge ourselves in cooperation with the States and private industry to encourage the employment of older workers. We commend the 82nd Congress for eliminating the age restriction on employment in the Federal Government.

Health. We will continue to work for better health for every American, especially our children. We pledge continued and wholehearted support for the campaign that modern medicine is waging against mental illness, cancer, heart disease and other diseases.

Research. We favor continued and vigorous support, from private and public sources, of research into the causes, prevention and cure of disease.

Medical Education. We advocate Federal aid for medical education to help overcome the growing shortages of doctors, nurses, and other trained health personnel.

Hospitals and Health Centers. We pledge continued support for Federal aid to hospital construction. We pledge increased Federal aid to promote public health through preventive programs and health services, especially in rural areas.

Cost of Medical Care. We also advocate a resolute attack on the heavy financial hazard of serious illness. We recognize that the costs of modern medical care have grown to be prohibitive for many millions of people. We commend President Truman for establishing the non-partisan Commission on the Health Needs of the Nation to seek an acceptable solution of this urgent problem.

Housing. We pledge ourselves to the fulfillment of the programs of private housing, public low-rent housing, slum clearance, urban redevelopment, farm housing and housing research as authorized by the Housing Act of 1949.

We deplore the efforts of special interests groups, which themselves have prospered through government guarantees of housing mortgages, to destroy these programs adopted to assist families at low income.

Additional Legislation. We pledge ourselves to enact additional legislation to promote housing required for defense workers, middle income families, aged persons and migratory farm laborers.

Veterans' Housing. We pledge ourselves to provide special housing aids to veterans and their families.

EDUCATION

Every American child, irrespective of color, national origin, economic status or place of residence, should have every educational opportunity to develop his potentialities.

Local, State and Federal Government have shared responsibility to contribute appropriately to the pressing needs of our educational system. We urge that Federal contributions be made available to state and local units which adhere to basic minimum standards.

The Federal Government should not dictate or control educational policy.

We pledge immediate consideration for those school systems which need further legislation to provide Federal aid for new school construction, teachers' salaries and school maintenance and repair.

We urge the adoption by appropriate legislative action of the proposals advocated by the President's Commission on Higher Education, including Federal scholarships.

We will continue to encourage the further development of vocational training which helps people acquire skills and technical knowledge so essential to production techniques.

Child Welfare. The future of America depends on adequate provision by Government for the needs of those of our children who cannot be cared for by their parents or private social agencies.

Maternity, Child Health and Welfare Services. The established national policy of aiding states and localities, through the Children's Bureau and other agencies, to insure needed maternity, child health and welfare services, should be maintained and extended. Especially important are the detection and treatment of physical defects and diseases which, if untreated, are reflected in adult life in draft rejections and as handicapped workers. The Nation as a whole should provide maternity and health care for the wives, babies and pre-school children of those who serve in our armed forces.

School Lunches. We will enlarge the school lunch program which has done so much for millions of American school children and charitable institutions while at the same time benefitting producers.

Day Care Facilities. Since several million mothers must now be away from their children during the day because they are engaged in defense work, facilities for adequate day care of these children should be provided and adequately financed.

Children of Migratory Workers. The Nation as a whole has a responsibility to support health, educational and welfare services for the children of agricultural migratory workers who are now almost entirely without such services while their parents are engaged in producing essential crops.

Veterans. The Democratic Party is determined to advance the welfare of all the men and women who have seen service in the armed forces. We pledge ourselves to continue and improve our national program of benefits for veterans and their families, to provide the best possible medical care and hospitalization for the disabled veteran, and to help provide every veteran an opportunity to be a productive and responsible citizen with an assured place in the civilian community.

STRENGTHENING DEMOCRATIC GOVERNMENT

Streamlining the Federal Government. The public welfare demands that our government be efficiently and economically operated and that it be reorganized to meet changing needs. During the present Democratic Administration, more reorganization has been accomplished than by all its predecessors. We pledge our support to continuing reorganization wherever improvements can be made. Only constant effort by the Executive, the Congress, and the public will enable our government to render the splendid service to which our citizens are entitled.

Improving the Postal Service. We pledge a continuing increase in the services of the United States Postal Service. Through efficient handling of mail, improved working conditions for postal employees, and more frequent services, the Democratic Party promises its efforts to provide the greatest communication system in the world for the American people.

Strengthening the Civil Service. Good government requires a Civil Service high in quality and prestige. We deplore and condemn smear attacks upon the character and reputations of our Federal workers. We will continue our fight against partisan political efforts to discredit the Federal service and undermine American principles of justice and fair play.

Under President Truman's leadership, the Federal Civil Service has been extended to include a greater proportion of positions than ever before. He has promoted a record number of career appointees to top level policy positions. We will continue to be guided by these enlightened policies, and we will continue our efforts to provide Federal service with adequate pay, sound retirement provisions, good working conditions, and an opportunity for advancement.

We will use every proper means to eliminate pressure by private interests seeking undeserved favors from the Government. We advocate the strongest penalties against those who try to exert improper influence, and against any who may yield to it.

Democracy in Federal Elections. We advocate new legislation to provide effective regulation and full disclosure of campaign expenditures in elections to Federal office, including political advertising from any source.

We recommend that Congress provide for a non-partisan study of possible improvements in the methods of nominating and electing Presidents and in the laws relating to Presidential succession. Special attention should be given to the problem of assuring the widest possible public participation in Presidential nominations.

Strengthening Basic Freedoms. We will continue to press strongly for world-wide freedom in the gathering and dissemination of news and for support to the work of the United Nations Commission on Human Rights in furthering this and other freedoms.

Equal Rights Amendment. We recommend and endorse for submission to the Congress a constitutional amendment providing equal rights for women.

Puerto Rico. Under Democratic Party leadership a new status has been developed for Puerto Rico. This new status is based on mutual consent and common devotion to the United States, formalized in a new Puerto Rican Constitution. We welcome the dignity of the new Puerto Rican Commonwealth and pledge our support of the Commonwealth, its continued development and growth.

Alaska and Hawaii. By virtue of their strategic geographical locations, Alaska and Hawaii are vital bastions in the Pacific. These two territories have contributed greatly to the welfare and economic development of our country and have become integrated into our economic and social life. We therefore urge immediate statehood for these two territories.

Other Territories and Possessions. We favor increased self-government for the Virgin Islands and other outlying territories and the Trust Territory of the Pacific.

District of Columbia. We favor immediate home rule and ultimate national representation for the District of Columbia.

American Indians. We shall continue to use the powers of the Federal Government to advance the health, education and economic well-being of our American Indian citizens, without impairing their cultural traditions. We pledge our support to the cause of fair and equitable treatment in all matters essential to and desirable for their individual and tribal welfare.

The American Indian should be completely integrated into the social, economic and political life of the Nation. To that end we shall move to secure the prompt final settlement of Indian claims and to remove restrictions on the rights of Indians individually and through their tribal councils to handle their own fiscal affairs.

We favor the repeal of all acts or regulations that deny to Indians rights or privileges held by citizens generally.

Constitutional Government. The Democratic Party has demonstrated its belief in the Constitution as a charter of individual freedom and an effective instrument for human progress. Democratic Administrations have placed upon the statute books during the last twenty years a multitude of measures which testify to our belief in the Jeffersonian principle of local control, even in general legislation involving nation-wide programs. Selective Service, Social Security, Agricultural Adjustment, Low-Rent Housing, Hospital, and many other legislative programs have placed major responsibilities in states and counties and provide fine examples of how benefits can be extended through Federal-State cooperation.

In the present world crisis with new requirements of Federal action for national security, and accompanying provision for public services and individual rights related to defense, constitutional principles must and will be closely followed. Our record and our clear commitments in this platform measure our strong faith in the ability of constitutional government to meet the needs of our times.

Improving Congressional Procedures. In order that the will of the American people may be expressed upon all legislative proposals, we urge that action be taken at the beginning of the 83rd Congress to improve Congressional procedures so that majority rule prevails and decisions can be made after reasonable debate without being blocked by a minority in either House.

Civil Rights. The Democratic Party is committed to support and advance the individual rights and liberties of all Americans.

Our country is founded on the proposition that all men are created equal. This means that all citizens are equal before the law and should enjoy equal political rights. They should have equal opportunities for education, for economic advancement, and for decent living conditions.

We will continue our efforts to eradicate discrimination based on race, religion or national origin.

We know this task requires action, not just in one section of the Nation, but in all sections. It requires the cooperative efforts of individual citizens and action by State and local governments. It also requires Federal action. The Federal Government must live up to the ideals of the Declaration of Independence and must exercise the powers vested in it by the Constitution.

We are proud of the progress that has been made in securing equality of treatment and opportunity in the Nation's armed forces and the Civil Service and all areas under Federal jurisdiction. The Department of Justice has taken an important part in successfully arguing in the courts for the elimination of many illegal discriminations, including those involving rights to own and use real property, to engage in gainful occupations and to enroll in publicly supported higher educational institutions. We are determined that the Federal Government shall continue such policies.

At the same time, we favor Federal legislation effectively to secure these rights to everyone: (1) the right to equal opportunity for employment; (2) the right to security of persons; (3) the right to full and equal participation in the Nation's political life, free from arbitrary restraints. We also favor legislation to perfect existing Federal civil rights statutes and to strengthen the administrative machinery for the protection of civil rights.

CONCLUSION

Under the guidance, protection, and help of Almighty God we shall succeed in bringing to the people of this Nation a better and more rewarding life, and to the peoples of the entire world, new hope and a lasting, honorable peace.

The 1952 Platform of the Republican Party

Adopted by the Republican National Convention
at Chicago, Illinois, July 11, 1952

PREAMBLE

We maintain that man was not born to be ruled, but that he consented to be governed; and that the reasons that moved him thereto are few and simple. He has voluntarily submitted to government because, only by the establishment of just laws, and the power to enforce those laws, can an orderly life be maintained, full and equal opportunity for all be established, and the blessings of liberty be perpetuated.

We hold that government, and those entrusted with government, should set a high example of honesty, of justice, and unselfish devotion to the public good; that they should labor to maintain tranquility at home and peace and friendship with all the nations of the earth.

We assert that during the last twenty years, leaders of the Government of the United States under successive Democrat Administrations, and especially under this present Administration, have failed to perform these several basic duties; but, on the contrary, that they have evaded them, flouted them, and by a long succession of vicious acts, so undermined the foundations of our Republic as to threaten its existence.

We charge that they have arrogantly deprived our citizens of precious liberties by seizing powers never granted.

We charge that they work unceasingly to achieve their goal of national socialism.

We charge that they have disrupted internal tranquility by fostering class strife for venal political purposes.

We charge that they have choked opportunity and hampered progress by unnecessary and crushing taxation.

They claim prosperity, but the appearance of economic health is created by war expenditures, waste and extravagance, planned emergencies, and war crises. They have debauched our money by cutting in half the purchasing power of our dollar.

We charge that they have weakened local self-government which is the cornerstone of the freedom of men.

We charge that they have shielded traitors to the Nation in high places, and that they have created enemies abroad where we should have friends.

We charge that they have violated our liberties by turning loose upon the country a swarm of arrogant bureaucrats and their agents who meddle intolerably in the lives and occupations of our citizens.

We charge that there has been corruption in high places, and that examples of dishonesty and dishonor have shamed the moral standards of the American people.

We charge that they have plunged us into war in Korea without the consent of our citizens through their authorized representatives in the Congress, and have carried on that war without will to victory.

FOREIGN POLICY

The present Administration, in seven years, has squandered the unprecedented power and prestige which were ours at the close of World War II.

In that time, more than 500 million non-Russian people of fifteen different countries have been absorbed into the power sphere of Communist Russia, which proceeds confidently with its plan for world conquest.

We charge that the leaders of the Administration in power lost the peace so dearly earned by World War II.

The moral incentives and hopes for a better world which sustained us through World War II were betrayed, and this has given Communist Russia a military and propaganda initiative which, if unstayed, will destroy us.

They abandoned friendly nations such as Latvia, Lithuania, Esthonia, Poland and Czechoslovakia to fend for themselves against the Communist aggression which soon swallowed them.

They required the National Government of China to surrender Manchuria with its strategic ports and railroads to the control of Communist Russia. They urged that Communists be taken into the Chinese Government and its military forces, and finally they denied the military aid that had been authorized by Congress and which was crucially needed if China were to be saved. Thus they substituted on our Pacific flank a murderous enemy for an ally and friend.

In all these respects they flouted our peace-assuring pledges such as the Atlantic Charter, and did so in favor of despots, who, it was well known, consider that murder, terror, slavery, concentration camps and the ruthless and brutal denial of human rights are legitimate means to their desired ends.

Tehran, Yalta and Potsdam were the scenes of those tragic blunders with others to follow. The leaders of the Administration in power acted without the knowledge or consent of Congress or of the American people. They traded our overwhelming victory for a new enemy and for new oppressions and new wars which were quick to come.

In South Korea, they withdrew our occupation troops in the face of the aggressive, poised-for-action, Communist military strength on its northern border. They publicly announced that Korea was no concern to us. Then when the Communist forces acted to take what seemed to have been invited, they committed this nation to fight back under the most unfavorable conditions. Already the tragic cost is over 110,000 American casualties.

With foresight, the Korean War would never have happened.

In going back into Korea, they evoked the patriotic and sacrificial support of the American people. But by their hampering orders they produced stalemates and ignominious bartering with our enemies, and they offer no hope of victory.

They have effectively ignored many vital areas in the face of a global threat requiring balanced handling.

The people of the other American Republics are resentful of our neglect of their legitimate aspirations and cooperative friendship.

The Middle East and much of Africa seethe with anti-American sentiment.

The peoples of the Far East who are not under Communist control find it difficult to sustain their morale as they contrast Russia's "Asia First" policy with the "Asia Last" policy of those in control of the Administration now in power.

Here at home they have exhibited corruption, incompetence, and disloyalty in public office to such an extent that the very concept of free representative government has been tarnished and has lost its idealistic appeal to those elsewhere who are confronted with the propaganda of Communism.

They profess to be following a defensive policy of "containment" of Russian Communism which has not contained it.

Those in control of the Party in power have, in reality, no foreign policy. They swing erratically from timid appeasement to reckless bluster.

The good in our foreign policies has been accomplished with Republican coopera-tion, such as the organization of the United Nations, the establishment of the trusteeship principle for dependent peoples, the making of peace with Japan and Germany, and the building of more solid security in Europe. But in the main the **Republican Party** has been ignored and its participation has not been invited.

The American people must now decide whether to continue in office the Party which has presided over this disastrous reversal of our fortunes and the loss of our hopes for a peaceful world.

The **Republican Party** offers, in contrast to the performance of those now running our foreign affairs, policies and actions based on enlightened self-interest and animated by courage, self-respect, steadfastness, vision, purpose, competence and spiritual faith.

The supreme goal of our foreign policy will be an honorable and just peace. We dedicate ourselves to wage peace and to win it.

We shall eliminate from the State Department and from every Federal office, all, wherever they may be found, who share responsibility for the needless predicaments and perils in which we find ourselves. We shall also sever from the public payroll the hordes of loafers, incompetents and unnecessary employees who clutter the admin-istration of our foreign affairs. The confusions, overlappings, and extravagance of our agencies abroad hold us up to the ridicule of peoples whose friendship we seek.

We shall substitute a compact and efficient organization where men of proven loyalty and ability shall have responsibility for reaching our objectives. They will reflect a dynamic initiative. Thus we can win the support and confidence which go only to those who demonstrate a capacity to define and get results.

We shall have positive peace-building objectives wherever this will serve the en-lightened self-interest of our Nation and help to frustrate the enemy's designs against us.

In Western Europe we shall use our friendly influence, without meddling or im-perialistic attitudes, for ending the political and economic divisions which alone prevent that vital area from being strong on its own right.

We shall encourage and aid the development of collective security forces there, as elsewhere, so as to end the Soviet power to intimidate directly or by satellites, and so that the free governments will be sturdy to resist Communist inroads.

In the balanced consideration of our problems, we shall end neglect of the Far East which Stalin has long identified as the road to victory over the West. We shall make it clear that we have no intention to sacrifice the East to gain time for the West.

The **Republican Party** has consistently advocated a national home for the Jewish people since a Republican Congress declared its support of that objective thirty years ago.

In providing a sanctuary for Jewish people rendered homeless by persecution, the State of Israel appeals to our deepest humanitarian instincts. We shall continue our friendly interest in this constructive and inspiring undertaking.

We shall put our influence at the service of peace between Israel and the Arab States, and we shall cooperate to bring economic and social stability to that area.

Our ties with the sister Republics of the Americas will be strengthened.

The Government of the United States, under Republican leadership, will repudiate all commitments contained in secret understandings such as those of Yalta which aid Communist enslavements. It will be made clear, on the highest authority of the President and the Congress, that United States policy, as one of its peaceful purposes, looks happily forward to the genuine independence of those captive peoples.

We shall again make liberty into a beacon light of hope that will penetrate the dark places. That program will give the Voice of America a real function. It will mark the end of the negative, futile and immoral policy of "containment" which abandons countless human beings to a despotism and Godless terrorism, which in turn enables the rulers to forge the captives into a weapon for our destruction.

We shall support the United Nations and loyally help it to become what it was designed to be, a place where differences would be harmonized by honest discussion and a means for collective security under agreed concepts of justice. We shall seek real meaning and value for our regional security treaties, which implies that all parties shall contribute their loyal support and fair shares.

We shall see to it that no treaty or agreement with other countries deprives our citizens of the rights guaranteed them by the Federal Constitution.

We shall always measure our foreign commitments so that they can be borne without endangering the economic health or sound finances of the United States. Stalin said that "the moment for the decisive blow" would be when the free nations were isolated and were in a state of "practical bankruptcy." We shall not allow ourselves to be isolated and economically strangled, and we shall not let ourselves go bankrupt.

Sums available by this test, if competently used, will be more effective than vastly larger sums incompetently spent for vague and endless purposes. We shall not try to buy good will. We shall earn it by sound, constructive, self-respecting policies and actions.

We favor international exchange of students and of agricultural and industrial techniques, and programs for improvement of public health.

We favor the expansion of mutually-advantageous world trade. To further this objective we shall press for the elimination of discriminatory practices against our exports, such as preferential tariffs, monetary license restrictions, and other arbitrary devices. Our reciprocal trade agreements will be entered into and maintained on a basis of true reciprocity, and to safeguard our domestic enterprises and the payrolls of our workers against unfair import competition.

The policies we espouse will revive the contagious, liberating influences which are inherent in freedom. They will inevitably set up strains and stresses within the captive world which will make the rulers impotent to continue in their monstrous ways and mark the beginning of their end.

Our Nation will become again the dynamic, moral and spiritual force which was the despair of despots and the hope of the oppressed. As we resume this historic role, we ourselves will come to enjoy again the reality of peace, security and solvency, not the shabby and fleeting counterfeit which is the gift of the Administration in power.

NATIONAL DEFENSE

On the prudent assumption that Communist Russia may not accommodate our own disgracefully-lagging program for preparedness, we should develop with utmost speed a force-in-being, as distinguished from paper plans, of such power as to deter sudden attack or promptly and decisively defeat it. This defense against sudden attack requires the quickest possible development of appropriate and completely-adequate air power and the simultaneous readiness of coordinated air, land and sea forces, with all necessary installations, bases, supplies and munitions, including atomic energy weapons in abundance.

Generally, we shall see to it that our military services are adequately supported in all ways required, including manpower, to perform their appropriate tasks in relation to the defense of this country and to meet our treaty obligations.

We shall coordinate our military policy with our foreign policy, always seeking universal limitation and control of armaments on a dependable basis.

We shall review our entire preparedness program and we shall strip it clean of waste, lack of coordination, inertia, and conflict between the services. We shall see that our fighting men in Korea, or wherever they may be, shall not lack the best of weapons or other supplies or services needed for their welfare.

COMMUNISM

By the Administration's appeasement of Communism at home and abroad it has permitted Communists and their fellow travelers to serve in many key agencies and to infiltrate our American life. When such infiltration became notorious through the revelations of Republicans in Congress, the Executive Department stubbornly refused to deal with it openly and vigorously. It raised the false cry of "red herring" and took other measures to block and discredit investigations. It denied files and information to Congress. It set up boards of its own to keep information secret and to deal lightly with security risks and persons of doubtful loyalty. It only undertook prosecution of the most notorious Communists after public opinion forced action.

The result of these policies is the needless sacrifice of American lives, a crushing cost in dollars for defense, possession by Russia of the atomic bomb, the lowering of the Iron Curtain, and the present threats to world peace. Our people have been mired in fear and distrust, and employees of integrity in the Government service have been cruelly maligned by the Administration's tolerance of people of doubtful loyalty.

There are no Communists in the **Republican Party.** We have always recognized Communism to be a world conspiracy against freedom and religion. We never compromised with Communism and we have fought to expose it and to eliminate it in government and American life.

A Republican President will appoint only persons of unquestioned loyalty. We will overhaul loyalty and security programs. In achieving these purposes a Republican President will cooperate with Congress. We pledge close coordination of our intelligence services for protecting our security. We pledge fair but vigorous enforcement of laws to safeguard our country from subversion and disloyalty. By such policies we will keep the country secure and restore the confidence of the American people in the integrity of our Government.

SMALL BUSINESS IN A FREE ECONOMY

For twenty years the Administration has praised free enterprise while actually wrecking it. Here a little, there a little, year by year, it has sought to curb, regulate, harass, restrain and punish. There is scarcely a phase of our economic and social life today in which Government does not attempt to interfere.

Such hostility deadens initiative, discourages invention and experiment, and weakens the self-reliance indispensable to the Nation's vitality. Merciless taxation, the senseless use of controls and ceaseless effort to enter business on its own account, have led the present Government to unrestrained waste and extravagance in spending, irresponsibility in decision and corruption in administration.

The anti-monopoly laws have been employed, not to preserve and foster competition, but to further the political ambitions of the men in power. Wage and price controls have been utilized, not to maintain economic stability, but to reward the friends and punish the enemies of leaders of the Party in power.

Neither small nor large business can flourish in such an atmosphere. The **Republican Party** will end this hostility to initiative and enterprise.

We will aid small business in every practicable way. We shall remove tax abuses and injurious price and wage controls. Efforts to plan and regulate every phase of small business activity will cease. We will maintain special committees in Congress whose chief function will be to study and review continuously the problems of small business and recommend legislation for their relief. We shall always be mindful of the importance of keeping open the channels of opportunity for young men and women.

We will follow principles of equal enforcement of the anti-monopoly and unfair-competition statutes and will simplify their administration to assist the businessman who, in good faith, seeks to remain in compliance. At the same time, we shall relentlessly protect our free enterprise system against monopolistic and unfair trade practices.

We will oppose Federal rent control except in those areas where the expansion of defense production has been accompanied by critical housing shortages. With local cooperation we shall aid slum clearance.

Our goal is a balanced budget, a reduced national debt, an economical administration, and a cut in taxes. We believe in combatting inflation by encouraging full production of goods and food, and not through a program of restrictions.

TAXATION AND MONETARY POLICY

Only with a sound economy can we properly carry out both the domestic and foreign policies which we advocate. The wanton extravagance and inflationary policies of the Administration in power have cut the value of the dollar in half and imposed the most confiscatory taxes in our history. These policies have made the effective control of Government expenditures impossible. If this Administration is left in power, it will further cheapen the dollar, rob the wage earner, impoverish the farmer and reduce the true value of the savings, pensions, insurance and investments of millions of our people. Further inflation must be and can be prevented. Sound tax and monetary policies are essential to this end. We advocate the following tax policies:

1. Reduction of expenditures by the elimination of waste and extravagance so that the budget will be balanced and a general tax reduction can be made.

2. An immediate study directed toward reallocation of fields of taxation between the Federal, State and municipal governments so as to allow greater fiscal freedom to the States and municipalities, thus minimizing double taxation and enabling the various divisions of government to meet their obligations more efficiently.

3. A thorough revision and codification of the present hodgepodge of internal revenue laws.

4. Administration of the tax laws free from politics, favoritism and corruption. We advocate the following monetary policies:

1. A Federal Reserve System exercising its functions in the money and credit system without pressure for political purposes from the Treasury or the White House.

2. To restore a domestic economy, and to use our influence for a world economy, of such stability as will permit the realization of our aim of a dollar on a fully-convertible gold basis.

AGRICULTURE

The good earth is the food storehouse for future generations. The tending of the soil is a sacred responsibility. Development of a sound farm program is a high national duty. Any program that will benefit farmers must serve the national welfare. A prosperous agriculture with free and independent farmers is fundamental to the national interest.

We charge the present Administration with seeking to destroy the farmers' freedom. We denounce the Administration's use of tax money and a multitude of Federal agencies to put agriculture under partisan political dictation and to make the farmer dependent upon government. We condemn the Brannan plan which aims to control the farmer and to socialize agriculture. We brand as unscrupulous the Administration's manipulation of grain markets during the 1948 election campaign to drive down farm prices, and its deliberate misrepresentation of laws passed by the Republican 80th Congress, which authorized a long-range farm price support program and provided for adequate grain storage.

We condemn as a fraud on both the farmer and the consumer the Brannan plan scheme to pay direct subsidies from the Federal Treasury in lieu of prices to producers.

We favor a farm program aimed at full parity prices for all farm products in the market place. Our program includes commodity loans on non-perishable products, "on-the-farm" storage, sufficient farm credit, and voluntary self-supporting crop insurance. Where government action on perishable commodities is desirable, we recommend locally-controlled marketing agreements and other voluntary methods.

Our program should include commodity loans on all non-perishable products supported at the level necessary to maintain a balanced production. We do not believe in restrictions on the American farmers' ability to produce.

We favor a bi-partisan Federal Agricultural Commission with power to review the policies and administration of our farm programs and to make recommendations.

We support a constructive and expanded soil conservation program administered through locally-controlled local districts, and which shall emphasize that payments shall be made for practices and improvements of a permanent nature.

Flood control programs should include the application of sound land use, reforestation and water-management practices on each water shed. These, so far as feasible, should be decentralized and locally-controlled to insure economy and effective soil conservation.

We recommend expanded agricultural research and education to promote new crops and uses, new markets, both foreign and domestic, more trustworthy crop and market estimates, a realistic trade program for agriculture aimed at restoring foreign markets and developing new outlets at home. Promotion of world trade must be on a basis of fair competition.

We support the principle of bona fide farmer-owned, farmer-operated cooperatives and urge the further development of rural electrification and communication, with federally-assisted production of power and facilities for distribution when these are not adequately available through private enterprise at fair rates.

We insist that an adequate supply of manpower on the farm is necessary to our national welfare and security and shall do those things required to assure this result.

The **Republican Party** will create conditions providing for farm prosperity and stability, safeguarding the farmers' independence, and opening opportunities for young people in rural communities. We will do those things necessary to simplify and make efficient the operation of the Department of Agriculture, prevent that Department from assuming powers neither intended nor delegated by Congress, and to place the administration of farm programs as closely as possible to State and local levels.

LABOR

The **Republican Party** believes that regular and adequate income for the employee together with uninterrupted production of goods and services, through the medium of private enterprise, are essential to a sound national economy. This can only be obtained in an era of industrial peace.

With the above in mind, we favor the retention of the Taft-Hartley Act, which guarantees:—

To the working man:

The right to quit his job at any time.

The right to take part in legal union activities.

The right to remain in his union so long as he pays his dues.

The right to protection against unfair practices by either employer or union officials.

The right to political activity of his own choice and freedom to contribute thereto.

The right to a job without first joining a union.

The right to a secret ballot in any election concerned with his livelihood.

The right to protection from personal financial responsibility in damage cases against his union.

To the labor unions:

The right to establish "union shop" contracts by agreement with management.

The right to strike.

The right to free collective bargaining.

The right to protection from rival unions during the life of union contracts.

The right to assurance from employers that they will bargain only with certified unions as a protection against unfair labor practices.

We urge the adoption of such amendments to the Taft-Hartley Act as time and experience show to be desirable, and which further protect the rights of labor, management and the public.

We condemn the President's seizure of plants and industries to force the settlement of labor disputes by claims of inherent Constitutional powers.

NATURAL RESOURCES

We vigorously advocate a full and orderly program for the development and conservation of our natural resources.

We deplore the policies of the present Administration which allow special premiums to foreign producers of minerals available in the United States. We favor reasonable depletion allowances, defense procurement policies, synthetic fuels research, and public land policies, including good-faith administration of our mining laws, which will encourage exploration and development of our mineral resources consistent with our growing industrial and defense needs.

We favor stockpiling of strategic and critical raw materials and special premium incentives for their domestic exploration and development.

We favor restoration to the States of their right to all lands and resources beneath navigable inland and offshore waters within their historic boundaries.

We favor protection of our fisheries by domestic regulation and treaties, including safeguards against unfair foreign competition.

PUBLIC WORKS AND WATER POLICY

The Federal Government and State and local governments should continuously plan programs of economically justifiable public works.

We favor continuous and comprehensive investigations of our water resources and orderly execution of programs approved by the Congress. Authorized water projects should go forward progressively with immediate priority for those with defense significance, those in critical flood and water-shortage areas, and those substantially completed.

We favor greater local participation in the operation and control, and eventual local ownership, of federally-sponsored, reimbursable water projects.

We vigorously oppose the efforts of this national Administration, in California and elsewhere, to undermine State control over water use, to acquire paramount water rights without just compensation, and to establish all-powerful Federal socialistic valley authorities.

PUBLIC LANDS

We favor restoration of the traditional Republican public land policy, which provided opportunity for ownership by citizens to promote the highest land use. We favor an impartial study of tax-free Federal lands and their uses to determine their effects on the economic and fiscal structures of our State and local communities.

In the management of public lands and forests we pledge the elimination of arbitrary bureaucratic practices. To this end we favor legislation to define the rights and privileges of grazers and other cooperators and users, to provide the protection of independent judicial review against administrative invasions of those rights and privileges, and to protect the public against corrupt or monopolistic exploitation and bureaucratic favoritism.

VETERANS

We believe that active duty in the Armed Forces of the United States of America during a state of war or national emergency constitutes a special service to our Nation, and entitles those who have so served to aid and compensation in return for this service. Consequently we propose:

That the aid and compensation given to veterans of previous wars be extended to veterans of the Korean conflict;

That compensation be fairly and adequately adjusted to meet changes in the cost of living;

That aid be given to veterans, particularly disabled veterans, to obtain suitable employment, by providing training and education, and through strict compliance with veterans' preference laws in Federal service;

That the Veterans' Administration be maintained as a single, independent agency in full charge of all veterans' affairs, and that the Veterans' Administration manage veterans' affairs in an efficient, prompt and uniform manner;

That the Veterans' Administration should be equipped to provide and maintain medical and hospital care of the highest possible standard for all eligible veterans.

SOCIAL SECURITY

Inflation has already cut in half the purchasing power of the retirement and other benefits under the Federal Old Age and Survivors Insurance system. Sixty million persons are covered under the system and four and one-half million are now receiving benefits.

The best assurance of preserving the benefits for which the worker has paid is to stop the inflation which causes the tragic loss of purchasing power, and that we propose to do.

We favor amendment of the Old Age and Survivors Insurance system to provide coverage for those justly entitled to it but who are now excluded.

We shall work to achieve a simple, more effective and more economical method of administration.

We shall make a thorough study of universal pay-as-we-go pension plans.

HEALTH

We recognize that the health of our people as well as their proper medical care cannot be maintained if subject to Federal bureaucratic dictation. There should be a just division of responsibility between government, the physician, the voluntary hospital, and voluntary health insurance. We are opposed to Federal compulsory health insurance with its crushing cost, wasteful inefficiency, bureaucratic dead weight, and debased standards of medical care. We shall support those health activities by government which stimulate the development of adequate hospital services without Federal interference in local administration. We favor support of scientific research. We pledge our continuous encouragement of improved methods of assuring health protection.

EDUCATION

The tradition of popular education, tax-supported and free to all, is strong with our people. The responsibility for sustaining this system of popular education has always rested upon the local communities and the States. We subscribe fully to this principle.

CIVIL RIGHTS

We condemn bigots who inject class, racial and religious prejudice into public and political matters. Bigotry is un-American and a danger to the Republic.

We deplore the duplicity and insincerity of the Party in power in racial and religious matters. Although they have been in office as a Majority Party for many years, they have not kept nor do they intend to keep their promises.

The **Republican Party** will not mislead, exploit or attempt to confuse minority groups for political purposes. All American citizens are entitled to full, impartial enforcement of Federal laws relating to their civil rights.

We believe that it is the primary responsibility of each State to order and control its own domestic institutions, and this power, reserved to the States, is essential to the maintenance of our Federal Republic. However, we believe that the Federal Government should take supplemental action within its constitutional jurisdiction to oppose discrimination against race, religion or national origin.

We will prove our good faith by:

Appointing qualified persons, without distinction of race, religion or national origin, to responsible positions in the Government.

Federal action toward the elimination of lynching.

Federal action toward the elimination of poll taxes as a prerequisite to voting.

Appropriate action to end segregation in the District of Columbia.

Enacting Federal legislation to further just and equitable treatment in the area of discriminatory employment practices. Federal action should not duplicate State efforts to end such practices; should not set up another huge bureaucracy.

CENSORSHIP

We pledge not to infringe by censorship or gag-order the right of a free people to know what their Government is doing.

EQUAL RIGHTS

We recommend to Congress the submission of a Constitutional Amendment providing equal rights for men and women.

We favor legislation assuring equal pay for equal work regardless of sex.

STATEHOOD

We favor immediate statehood for Hawaii.

We favor statehood for Alaska under an equitable enabling act.

We favor eventual statehood for Puerto Rico.

DISTRICT OF COLUMBIA

We favor self-government and national suffrage for the residents of the Nation's Capital.

INDIAN AFFAIRS

All Indians are citizens of the United States and no longer should be denied full enjoyment of their rights of citizenship.

We shall eliminate the existing shameful waste by the Bureau of Indian Affairs which has obstructed the accomplishment of our national responsibility for improving the condition of our Indian friends. We pledge to undertake programs to provide the Indians with equal opportunities for education, health protection and economic development.

The next Republican Administration will welcome the advice and counsel of Indian leaders in selecting the Indian Commissioner.

CIVIL SERVICE

We condemn the flagrant violations of the Civil Service merit system by the Party in power.

We favor a personnel program for the Federal career service comparable to the best practices of progressive private employers. Federal employees shall be selected under a strengthened and extended merit system. Civil servants of ability and integrity shall receive proper recognition, with merit the sole test for promotion.

DELIVERY OF MAIL

We pledge a more efficient and frequent mail delivery service.

GOVERNMENT REORGANIZATION

We pledge a thorough reorganization of the Federal Government in accordance with the principles set forth in the report of the Hoover Commission, which was established by the Republican 80th Congress.

We denounce the duplicity in submitting to Congress for approval, reorganization plans which were represented as being in accordance with the principles of the Hoover Commission recommendations, but which in fact were actually intended to further partisan political purposes of the Administration in power.

CORRUPTION

The present Administration's sordid record of corruption has shocked and sickened the American people. Its leaders have forfeited any right to public faith by the way they transact the Federal Government's business.

Fraud, bribery, graft, favoritism and influence-peddling have come to light. Immorality and unethical behavior have been found to exist among some who were entrusted with high policy-making positions, and there have been disclosures of close alliances between the present Government and underworld characters.

Republicans exposed cases of questionable and criminal conduct and relentlessly pressed for full investigations into the cancer-like spread of corruption in the Administration. These investigations uncovered a double standard in Federal tax law enforcement—lenient treatment to political favorites including even some gangsters and crooks, but harassment and threats of prosecution for many honest taxpayers over minor discrepancies.

Besides tax fixes and scandals in the Internal Revenue Bureau, investigations have disclosed links between high officials and crime, favoritism and influence in the RFC, profiteering in grain, sale of postmasterships, tanker-ship deals in the Maritime Commission, ballot-box stuffing and thievery, and bribes and payoffs in contract awards by officials in agencies exercising extraordinary powers and disbursing billions of dollars.

Under public pressure, the Administration took reluctant steps to clean house. But it was so eager to cover up and block more revelations that its clean-up drive launched with much fanfare ended in a farce.

The **Republican Party** pledges to put an end to corruption, to oust the crooks and grafters, to administer tax laws fairly and impartially, and to restore honest government to the people.

REPUBLICAN 80TH CONGRESS

The **Republican Party** does not rest its case upon promises alone. We have a record of performance which was grossly defamed by the Party in power. The Republican 80th Congress launched the program to stop Communism; unified the armed services; authorized a 70-group Air Force which the President blocked; enacted a national service law; balanced the budget; accumulated an eight-billion-dollar surplus; reduced taxes, with 70 per cent of the tax savings to those with incomes under $5,000; freed 7,400,000 wage earners in the lower brackets from having to pay any further income tax at all, allowed married couples to divide their incomes for tax purposes, and granted an additional $600 exemption to those over 65 years of age and to the blind; enacted the Taft-Hartley law for equitable labor-management relations; passed the first long-range agriculture program; increased social security benefits; and carried out every single pledge they made to the voters in the 1946 election.

CONCLUSION

Upon this statement of truths and this pledge of performance, the **Republican Party** stands confident that it expresses the hopes of the citizens of America and certain that it points out with integrity a road upon which free men may march into a new day—a new and better day—in which shall be fulfilled the decent aspirations of our people for peace, for solvency and for the fulfillment of our best welfare, under the guidance of Divine Providence.

Index

alternatives: (1) one party (2) matti (3) Realign (4) antialying

Dangers: Am. can't unified   Decentral.
         we don't have majority rule   Natl. bosses from centralized.

Pres. powers:
1. Veto + threat
2. State of union message
3. Threat of general sessions.

Liabilities:

1. adm. weakness.
2. extremism
3. Economic depression
4. assorted political mistakes.
5. liability or advantage of war.
6. maintaining adequate leadership.

Candidates:

1. Maintain popular support.
2. Be a communicator
3. Have ability to work with his own party.
4. come from the right state.
5. Belong to right church.
6. Nat'l. background.
7. military background
8. Good heatin.
9. money

Calhoun's "concurrent Majorities"